CASSELL COMPANION TO

20th-century
Music

CASSELL COMPANION TO

20th-century
Music

DAVID PICKERING

CASSELL

First published as *Brewer's Twentieth-century Music* in 1994;
this revised and updated edition 1997
by Cassell
Wellington House
125 Strand
London WC2R 0BB

This edition first published in paperback 1998

Reprinted 1999

British Library Cataloguing-in-Publication Data
A catalogue record for this book is available from the British Library

ISBN 0–304–35099–0

Typeset by York House Typographic
Printed and bound in Great Britain by
Mackays of Chatham plc, Chatham, Kent

Preface

This, as music journalists have been announcing for some time now, is the age of the 'crossover' in music, with artists and audiences alike enthusiastically exploring an unprecedented and even bewildering range of styles and traditions in the search for the ultimate musical experience. Bluesmen have formed collaborations with folk artists, jazzmen have forged relationships with classical composers and rock groups have flirted with everyone from ethnic musicians and country singers to symphony orchestras, choirs and brass bands. Their loyal devotees have similarly broken down barriers in order to sample the riches of superficially distinct musical genres and new radio stations have been established to cater for broader listener tastes. It is commonly acknowledged that the once-automatic assumption that someone who adores Pavarotti or Louis Armstrong is necessarily debarred from appreciating Van Morrison, Oasis or the Spice Girls no longer applies.

With this new diversity, evident from virtually every modern music-lover's collection of CDs, tapes, records or souvenir concert programmes and t-shirts, comes a need for a new kind of music reference book – one that will go some way towards responding to expanded interests in a wealth of musical forms and traditions. This volume, a revision and updating of *Brewer's Twentieth-century Music* (Cassell, 1994), recognizes this and attempts to bring together the many different strands of musical development in the current century, including within its scope modern classical music, film soundtracks, blues, jazz, rock and pop, and everything in between.

As well as offering the reader straightforward biographies and other factual information, the text has a strong anecdotal element and probes many of the odd nooks and crannies that have given the century's music its unique character. Thus, alongside entries giving the career details of famous composers, guitarists, songwriters and record labels will be found diverting coverage of such topics as Beatlemania, cellist's nipple, colour music, devil's music, football songs, gold discs, heavy metal, music hall, one-hit wonders, payola, serialism, Tin Pan Alley, Top of the Pops and Woodstock – among many more.

In many instances the text is punctuated with tales and quotations chosen for their pithy and often biting relevance, shedding light on the humour, tragedy and downright peculiarity of much twentieth-century musical activity. For some readers the book will prove invaluable both as a basic alphabetically-organized, fully cross-referenced, information source and also as a 'dictionary of last resort', a source of eclectic information that may not easily be found in more conventional manuals and companions. Others, hopefully, will find it a rich and thought-provoking fount of musical curiosities and legend.

My apologies go to anyone who finds a personal favourite of their own omitted due to the constraints of space, and my thanks to (among others) my family, Guy Bean, the late Alan Moyse, Andrew Pickering, Alistair Alcock and the editors and production staff at Cassell for their assistance.

David Pickering

A

A & M Records US recording company, founded in 1966 by Herb ALPERT and Jerry Moss. The company's headquarters are on the site of the Hollywood movie studios once used for the films of Charlie Chaplin. Now a multi-million dollar enterprise, the company, which was sold to PolyGram in 1989, was set up with funds of just $500.

AACM Association for the Advancement of Creative Musicians. Influential JAZZ cooperative set up in Chicago in 1965 with the specific aim of nurturing talented Black musicians. It has its own school and recording facilities, and encourages artists to experiment with new sounds, rather than concentrating on technique alone, and to explore the boundaries of FREE JAZZ. Similar co-operatives were subsequently established in many other US cities.

Aaronson, Irving (1895–1963) US bandleader, pianist and composer, whose band was immensely popular in the 1920s and 1930s. When he was 11 years old, Aaronson played piano in the cinema and later led the Versatile Sextette, the Crusaders Dance Band and, finally, Irving Aaronson and his Commanders, appearing both in the USA and throughout Europe. His hits included 'The Song Angels Sing' and 'The Loveliest Night of the Year', which were both written for films. Members of his bands included Gene KRUPA and Artie SHAW.

Abba Swedish group, which enjoyed massive commercial success in the 1970s. Founded in 1973 and winner of the EUROVISION SONG CONTEST at the second attempt in 1974 (with 'Waterloo'), the group derived its name from the first letters of its four members' names: Agnetha Fältskog (1950–), Björn Ulvaeus (1945–), Benny Andersson (1946–) and Annifrid Lyngstad (1945–). Subsequent hits included the singles 'Mamma Mia' (1975), 'Dancing Queen' (1976), 'Knowing Me Knowing You' (1977) and 'The Winner Takes It All' (1980), all of which reached Number One in the UK.

By 1978 the group had become the most successful pop enterprise since the BEATLES and was earning more foreign currency for Sweden than any other domestic concern, surpassing even the car manufacturers Volvo. Abba's success in the UK was particularly remarkable considering the stars' less than perfect grasp of the language in which they sang (they learned the words of their early hits phonetically). Only one grammatical error has been noticed in the long series of Number Ones – in the lyrics of 'Fernando' (1976):

> Since many years I haven't seen a rifle in your hand.

The group finally disbanded in 1983, by which time the marriages of the two couples had come to an end, but was revived in the shape of various TRIBUTE BANDS in the early 1990s.

Abbado, Claudio (1933–) Italian conductor, who established an international reputation in the 1960s. He made his first appearance in the UK in 1965, conducting the HALLÉ ORCHESTRA, and subsequently became director of music at LA SCALA, Milan (1968–86) and conductor of the VIENNA PHILHARMONIC (1986–91), of the LONDON SYMPHONY ORCHESTRA (1979–88) and of the BERLIN PHILHARMONIC (1989–). He is particularly acclaimed for his conducting of the works of Verdi and Rossini, among others.

Abbey Road The recording studio in St John's Wood, London NW8, which became the most famous studio in the world through its association with the BEATLES in the 1960s. Owned by EMI, 3 Abbey Road had been converted into a recording studio (by the Gramophone Company) in 1929, and even before the first Beatles session in 1962 it played host to many stars, including Sir Edward ELGAR, Gracie FIELDS and Glenn MILLER. The Beatles contributed 15 to the total of 74 Number One hits to emanate from the building (the studio had seven Number Ones in just 23 weeks in

1963). With George MARTIN producing almost all their work there, the Beatles continued to use Abbey Road for seven years, and they made the zebra crossing outside the building famous after they used a photograph of themselves on it for the SLEEVE of their *Abbey Road* album (1969). In later years PINK FLOYD and Kate BUSH also recorded there.

> Is that the Fuzzy Wuzzies? Because we'd better close the door – in case they charge.
> SIR JOHN BARBIROLLI, on seeing the Beatles at Abbey Road

ABC British NEW ROMANTIC pop group, which enjoyed major commercial success in the 1980s. Led by singer Martin Fry (1958–), guitarist Mark White (1961–) and saxophonist Stephen Singleton (1959–), ABC came together in 1981 after journalist Fry interviewed White and Singleton for a rock fanzine. The group's first hit, 'Tears are Not Enough' (1981), was followed by such best-sellers as the singles 'The Look of Love' (1982) and 'Poison Arrow' (1982) and the albums *The Lexicon of Love* (1982), *Alphabet City* (1987) and *Absolutely ABC* (1990). Lead singer Martin Fry also released a solo album after fighting a long battle against cancer.

Abercrombie, John (1944–) US JAZZ guitarist, who is considered one of the finest guitarists to emerge since the Second World War. He established his reputation with the band of Johnny 'Hammond' Smith in the 1960s and subsequently played with many other leading stars. As a member of Billy Cobham's JAZZ-ROCK band Spectrum, he reconstructed his playing style, then formed his own trios Timeless and Gateway and a quartet. Acclaimed works include his role in the recording of Charles MINGUS's *Epitaph*.

Abrahám, Paul (1892–1960) Hungarian composer, who was one of the last writers of traditional Viennese operettas. Abrahám's career blossomed in Germany in the early 1930s, and his most popular songs included the lively 'Mausi' ('Mousie'), 'Today I Feel So Happy' and 'My Golden Baby', which combined the traditions of Austro-Hungarian operetta with elements borrowed from RAGTIME and DIXIELAND JAZZ. The Nazis took exception to Abrahám's music, and he moved to Vienna and thence to France and the USA. He failed to repeat his German successes, however, and was a patient in a mental hospital until 1956, when friends traced him and brought him back to Germany, where he eventually died in an asylum.

Abrahams, Maurice (Maurie Abrams; 1883–1931) US composer, born in Russia, who wrote many popular hits for leading vaudeville artists. Married to the vaudeville star Belle Baker, he ran his own publishing company and established himself as one of the most successful TIN PAN ALLEY composers with such hits as 'Hitchy-koo' (1912), 'He'd Have to Get Under, Get Out and Get Under' (1913) and 'The Twentieth Century Rag' (1914).

Academy of St Martin-in-the-Fields British chamber orchestra, based at the church of St Martin-in-the-Fields in London's Trafalgar Square, which is renowned for its performances of a wide range of established classics and modern works. Founded in 1959 by Sir Neville MARRINER, the orchestra's achievements were recognized by the Queen's Award for Export in 1993.

AC/DC Australian HEAVY METAL band, which emerged as one of the more influential HARD ROCK groups of the mid-1970s. Led by singer Scottish-born Bon Scott (1946–80) (originally chauffeur to the band) and guitarist Angus Young (1959–), AC/DC came together in Sydney in 1974 and rapidly earned a reputation as one of the most theatrical live acts of the era. The band's stage show was enhanced by Young's adoption of a mock schoolboy costume complete with cap and short trousers (his sister's idea). Its hit albums included *Highway to Hell* (1979), the last album on which Scott appeared before his death. Englishman Brian Johnson (1947–), former lead singer of the rock band Geordie, took Scott's place as lead vocalist, and the band retained its status as one of the most successful heavy metal outfits with such albums as *The Razor's Edge* (1980), *For Those About to Rock* (1981), *Blow Up Your Video* (1988) and *Ballbreaker* (1995).

Imitators of the band included a Swedish rock band that adopted the name AB/CB; it released one strong album and then disbanded, fearing legal action from its more famous Australian counterparts. Another fan claimed the music of AC/DC had inspired him to even more dubious acts;

this was the notorious Los Angeles serial killer Richard Ramirez, who said he had been influenced by the band's 1985 album *Fly on the Wall*.

The expression AC/DC (borrowed from the terminology of electricity) is widely used of bisexuals or of those homosexuals who take both passive and active roles in a sexual encounter. *See also* MONSTERS OF ROCK.

acid house Popular music genre, which developed in the UK in the late 1980s. Acid house, or simply house, was typically loud, driving, synthesized and repetitive dance music of a type suitable for playing in clubs and at acid-house parties; enthusiasts also adopted their own distinctive styles in fashion and related paraphernalia. The style first emerged in the USA, where it was known as Chicago House, and was then married with the EURO-DISCO style by three British disc jockeys working in Ibiza – Paul Oakenfold, Danny Rampling and Nicky Holloway. The three brought the new acid-house style (so-called, it is suggested, in reference to the US slang phrase 'acid burn', meaning SAMPLING) to the UK, where it quickly caught on, musicians building new songs on out-takes from established classics.

House music soon became associated with the taking of hallucinogenic drugs (especially Ecstasy), which were frequently available at clubs and parties where the music was played. The holding of acid-house parties at unlicensed premises, such as warehouses and derelict buildings, and the involvement of drug dealers quickly led to confrontation with the police and to demands from the press for action to be taken to prevent the holding of such parties or 'raves'. In the USA the style developed into what was dubbed the TECHNO style.

acid rock ROCK genre of the late 1960s, which was associated with the taking of LSD and other hallucinogenic, 'mind-expanding' drugs. A product of the hippie movement that prospered in San Francisco and other major US cities, the genre threw up such bands as JEFFERSON AIRPLANE and the GRATEFUL DEAD, which explored the possibilities of distorted and sometimes improvised ELECTRONIC ROCK (often accompanied by weird and disorientating visual effects) in creating sounds that mirrored the 'spaced-out' experiences of their audiences.

action music Genre of modern classical music, in which physical gestures are intended to be as significant as the music itself. John CAGE was among the composers to write such pieces, which included several items composed in the 1950s for the pianist David Tudor.

Acuff, Roy (1903–93) US COUNTRY singer-songwriter, who led some of the most popular country bands over a 30-year playing career and became one of NASH-VILLE's foremost spokesmen. Having abandoned early ambitions to become a baseball player, Acuff established a reputation as a country singer and became one of the leading stars on the GRAND OLE OPRY. He stuck to an overtly emotional and relatively unsophisticated traditional country style as leader of the Smoky Mountain Boys and made many classic recordings, among them 'Wabash Cannonball', 'Tennessee Waltz', 'Mule Skinner's Blues', 'Will the Circle be Unbroken' (with the NITTY GRITTY DIRT BAND), 'Freight Train Blues' and 'Great Speckled Bird'. Odd moments in his career have included a televised lesson on playing with a yo-yo, delivered for the benefit of President Richard Nixon. His activities were reduced after a car crash in 1965; he was elected to the COUNTRY MUSIC HALL OF FAME in 1962 (the first star to be thus honoured while still alive). With songwriter Fred ROSE, Acuff founded a highly influential country music publishing company in 1943.

> To hell with Roosevelt, to hell with Babe Ruth, to hell with Roy Acuff!
>
> Taunt shouted by Japanese soldiers at their US enemies on Okinawa during the Second World War

Adam and the Ants British pop group, which enjoyed repeated chart success in the early 1980s. The band, led by singer Adam Ant (Stuart Goddard; 1954–   ), achieved stardom in 1981 with the Number One hit single 'Stand and Deliver', a raunchy, colourful song about highwaymen, which was ideally suited to the theatrical, pseudo-romantic image the group had adopted, complete with bizarre make-up and quasi-historical costumes (an image that was largely the invention of Goddard, a former art student, in collaboration with punk record producer Malcolm McLaren). The accompanying album *Kings of the Wild Frontier* was equally successful, blending elements of punk with the rolling drum rhythms (called the 'Burundi beat') of African tribal music.

Adam and the Ants rapidly acquired the status of TEENY-BOP idols, and the media began to talk of 'Antmania'. Two more UK Number Ones – 'Prince Charming' and 'Goody Two Shoes' – followed in the next 12 months or so before the group's success faltered, later singles being credited to Adam Ant alone. Goddard later concentrated on acting, although Antmania underwent a revival in the 1990s and Adam Ant's single 'Room at the Top', from *Manners and Physique*, reached the Top 20 in 1990. Another album, *Wonderful*, was released in 1995.

Adama, Salvatore (1943–) Belgian composer and singer, born in Sicily, who emerged as a popular star in the 1960s. His many hit songs have included 'Vous permettez, Monsieur?', his first great success, 'Les filles du bord de mer', 'La nuit' and 'Ah, les belles dames'.

Adams, Bryan (1959–) Canadian rock star, of British descent, who established an international following in the late 1980s. Such rock albums as *Cuts Like a Knife* (1983) and *Reckless* (1984) attracted attention and produced several hit singles, although it was the 1991 single 'Everything I Do, I Do It For You', the theme tune for the film *Robin Hood, Prince of Thieves*, that proved his biggest success. The song remained at Number One in the UK for 15 weeks, longer than any other song had managed since 1953. Earlier releases were sometimes less well received; when his first album flopped, Adams threatened to release his second LP under the title *Bryan Adams Hasn't Heard of You, Either*. Both *Waking Up the Neighbours* (1991) and *So Far So Good* (1994) topped the UK charts.

Adams, Cliff (1923–) British conductor and arranger, who became nationally known as leader of the Cliff Adams Singers, stars of the long-running BBC radio programme *Sing Something Simple*. Trained as a chorister, pianist and organist, Adams formed the Stargazers vocal group in 1949 and the Cliff Adams Singers in 1954. He also wrote the music for a number of television advertisements and the musical *Liza of Lambeth* (1976).

Adams, John (1947–) US composer, who emerged as a significant figure in the MINI-MALIST movement in the 1970s. Having studied at Harvard under Roger SESSIONS and others, he established his reputation with a series of works exploring minimalist technique, one of the most notable of which was *Shaker Loops* (1979).

Adams, Pepper (Park Adams; 1930–86) US JAZZ saxophonist, composer and arranger, nicknamed the Knife for his incisive playing, who was acknowledged as the leading baritone saxophonist of post-war BOP. After serving in the Korean War, Adams developed his jazz career, playing with such stars as Stan KENTON, Dizzy GILLESPIE and Benny GOODMAN, and he rapidly established a reputation for his passionate but disciplined style. His career was cut short by his relatively early death from cancer. He often explained that the only reason he took up the baritone saxophone in the first place was that he was offered one at a price he could afford.

Adamson, Harold (1906–80) US lyricist, who worked with many of the most celebrated JAZZ composers and contributed songs to many successful Broadway and Hollywood musicals between the 1930s and the 1950s. Collaborating with the likes of Hoagy CARMICHAEL and Duke ELLINGTON, he provided the lyrics for such standards as 'Time on my Hands', 'You're as Pretty as a Picture', 'Manhattan Serenade', 'It's a Most Unusual Day' and 'My Resistance is Low'. Films on which he worked as lyricist included *Kid Millions* (1935), *That Certain Age* (1938) and *Gentlemen Prefer Blondes* (1953).

Adderley, 'Cannonball' (Julian Edwin Adderley; 1928–75) US JAZZ alto saxophonist, who was considered one of the most distinguished of Charlie PARKER's successors. A pioneer of the genre known as soul jazz, Adderley established his reputation after moving to New York in the late 1950s. Among his collaborators were such distinguished names as Miles DAVIS, Art BLAKEY and John COLTRANE. Such hits as 'This Here' (1958), 'Mercy, Mercy, Mercy' (1967) and 'Country Preacher' (1970) were major chart successes, reflecting the strong influence of BLUES and GOSPEL singing. He also recorded the SOUNDTRACK for the Clint Eastwood thriller *Play Misty for Me* (1971). Friends at school originally dubbed him Cannibal in reference to his huge appetite.

Addinsell, Richard (1904–77) British composer, who was particularly celebrated for his film SOUNDTRACKS. Having written music for the theatre, he wrote his first soundtracks in the mid–1930s and also provided music for such classics as *Fire Over England* (1937), *Goodbye, Mr Chips* (1939), *Gaslight* (1939), *Blithe Spirit* (1945) and *The Prince and the Showgirl* (1957). His most famous single work, however, remains the so-called *Warsaw Concerto* featured in the 1941 film *Dangerous Moonlight*. His most successful contributions to the theatre included his collaborations on a series of revues starring Joyce Grenfell.

Addison, John (Mervin) (1920–   ) British composer, who is best known for his music for the theatre and the cinema. Having decided against a military career, he studied several instruments and in 1950 was appointed professor of composition at the Royal College of Music in London. He was appointed musical director for the Boulting Brothers in 1949 and rapidly established himself as one of the most accomplished writers of film music, his SOUNDTRACKS including those for *The Guinea Pig* (1948), *Private's Progress* (1956), *Reach for the Sky* (1956), *Lucky Jim* (1957), *Look Back in Anger* (1959), *The Entertainer* (1960), *A Taste of Honey* (1961), *The Loneliness of the Long Distance Runner* (1962), *Tom Jones* (1963), *The Charge of the Light Brigade* (1968), *Sleuth* (1972) and *A Bridge Too Far* (1977). He also wrote the acclaimed revue *Cranks* (1955) and scores for MUSICALS.

Ade, King Sunny (Sunday Adeniyi; 1946–   ) Nigerian singer-songwriter and guitarist, nicknamed the Minister of Enjoyment, who emerged as one of the foremost exponents of JUJU music in the 1960s and became the first African star to be signed to a major UK label (ISLAND). His football song 'Challenge Cup' (1967) was a huge hit, and he consolidated his reputation with many more, modernizing the sound of his band and becoming one of the first African musicians to take up the steel guitar. He has toured widely, singing songs relevant to Nigeria's social problems and releasing numerous albums. He formed a new band, Golden Mercury, in the mid-1980s.

Adler, Larry (Lawrence Cecil Adler; 1914–   ) US harmonica player and composer, who earned an international reputation as the master of the harmonica. Until Adler adopted it the harmonica was regarded as little more than a toy, but when he won a talent competition at the age of 13 playing a Beethoven minuet on the instrument he was serving notice of his intention to elevate the humble harmonica's status. As well as playing much 'light' popular music by his own hand, he also performed works written especially for him by such composers as Malcolm ARNOLD, Darius MILHAUD and Ralph VAUGHAN WILLIAMS. Perhaps his best-known piece is the theme and incidental music of the 1953 film *Genevieve*. Adler experienced problems in the late 1940s when he was one of the stars accused by the US authorities of communist sympathies, as a result of which he moved to the UK.

Adler, Lou (1935–   ) US pop impresario and songwriter, who was among the most successful managers of the 1960s and early 1970s. Having written 'Wonderful World' with Sam COOKE and Herb ALPERT among other hits in the 1950s, Adler exercised considerable influence over US BUBBLEGUM MUSIC and pop as manager for such stars as Carole KING and the MAMAS AND THE PAPAS and as founder of his own successful labels. He was one of the organizers of the 1967 MONTEREY POP FESTIVAL.

Adler, Richard (1923–   ) US composer and lyricist, whose most successful songs were written in collaboration with the singer Jerry Ross (1926–55). Adler and Ross met in 1950, and together they wrote for both the theatre and for radio, their most successful songs including 'Rags to Riches', which sold a million copies in 1953. They also enjoyed huge success with the scores they wrote for the MUSICALS *The Pajama Game* (1954), which spawned such hits as 'Steam Hit', and *Damn Yankees* (1955). Ross died in 1955, and Adler's solo effort, the musical *Kwamina* (1961), was a failure, persuading him to concentrate henceforth on music for commercials and his work as an arts administrator.

adult-oriented rock ROCK music genre of the 1970s and 1980s, which catered for the changing tastes of the youth of the 1960s. Adult-oriented rock (or AOR) was harmonious, technically proficient but unchallenging as a force for social change in comparison with the socially committed music of such predecessors as the ROLLING STONES and Bob DYLAN. Typical purveyors of the genre, which had enormous appeal to record companies nervous of controversy and anxious to appeal to a more mature, more affluent audience, included FLEET-WOOD MAC, Mike OLDFIELD, JOURNEY and FOR-EIGNER.

> They are extremely successful – but a single record like 'Louie Louie' by the Kingsmen probably had more influence on the development of rock than Journey's entire output.
> PETE FRAME

Aeolian Quartet British string quartet, which is renowned for its performances of the music of Haydn. The quartet was founded in 1927 and was originally named the Stratton String Quartet after its first leader, George Stratton (1897–1954). Emanuel Hurwitz (1919–) became leader after Stratton.

Aerosmith US rock band, which earned an international reputation for fusing RHYTHM-AND-BLUES and ROCK'N'ROLL with a basic HEAVY METAL style. Founded in Boston, Massachusetts, in 1970, the band was led by vocalist Steven Tyler (1948–) and guitarist Joe Perry (1950–), who were dubbed the Toxic Twins because of their notorious indulgence in drink and drugs. A number of critics compared them with the ROLLING STONES, who enjoyed a not dissimilar reputation for energetic music and controversial off-stage lives. The band's most successful albums included *Toys in the Attic* (1975) and *Rocks* (1976). The album track 'Dream On' (1973) became a best-seller when released as a single in 1976. The band went into decline after Perry temporarily left (1979–85) but revived with a hit single, 'Walk This Way' (1986), and the albums *Permanent Vacation* (1987), *Pump* (1989) and *Get a Grip* (1993).

Afro-Cuban JAZZ style of the 1940s and 1950s in which various Latin-American elements were incorporated. Exponents of the style included Dizzy GILLESPIE and Stan KENTON as well as a number of leading Cuban musicians and others who had developed parallel forms of Afro-Cuban music as far back as the nineteenth century.

Afro-rock Genre of ROCK music from Africa, which exerted a profound influence on western rock in the 1980s, when interest was being shown in the music traditions of the Third World. Afro-rock emerged as a distinct style in the 1960s, when several states won independence and indigenous cultural traditions enjoyed a revival. Mixing the instruments of western JAZZ and rock with African drums and other percussion instruments, musicians from several African countries established their own unique styles, which blended such influences as the Cuban SALSA and CALYPSO with rock, jazz and traditional FOLK MUSIC. Among the most important pioneers were Fela KUTI in Nigeria, saxophonist Manu Dibango in Cameroon and Alpha Blondy and the Bambeya Jazz National Band in Guinea, where the government offered official support. Other stars to emerge have included Mory Kanté, Salif Keita, Touré Kunda, Youssou n'Dour, Mamadou Konte, King Sunny ADE and South Africa's Johnny Clegg. Leading African artists were invited to tour western countries and won recording contracts that brought them an international audience as well as finding new enthusiasts among such established western artists as Paul SIMON and the POLICE, who were quick to absorb their influence. Important sub-genres of Afro-rock include HIGH LIFE and JUJU, both of which enjoyed something of a vogue beyond Africa in the 1970s, although the dominant African pop style remains 'soukous'.

> Afro-rock is a term frequently used in contemporary African music. Manu Dibango, Osibisa, Fela Anikulapo-Kuti and Victor Uwaifor are internationally famous in this new brand of African soul music.
> LAZ NNANYELU EKWUEME, *The Times*, 1977

Ager, Milton (1893–1979) US composer, who wrote many hit songs both on his own and in partnership with Jack Yellen (1892–1958). Early successes included the Al JOLSON song 'Everything is Peaches down in Georgia' (1918); among other hits were 'I'm the Last of the Red-hot Mommas' (1929), 'Ain't She Sweet?' (1927) and 'Happy Days are Here Again' (1930), which was adopted as a campaign song for Franklin D. Roosevelt's New Deal.

aggregate A group of notes that are played together (though not as part of a conventional chord). John CAGE used the term while composing for the PREPARED PIANO, which is, for example, capable of playing more than one note when a key is pressed, and went on to write pieces incorporating such aggregates.

agitpop POP music that is recognized as being a vehicle for the propounding of some highly political message. Notable exponents of such music (named after the Russian *agitprop* – agitation propaganda) have included the Jamaican REGGAE artist Bob MARLEY, and Billy BRAGG, who was a champion of the political left in Thatcherite Britain in the 1980s.

A-Ha Norwegian pop group, which achieved TEENY-BOP idol status in the mid-1980s. Reversing the almost legendary failure of Norwegian groups to have any impact on European pop music (notably in the EURO-VISION SONG CONTEST), A-Ha became the first Scandinavian band since ABBA to reach the top of the charts in both the UK and the USA. Pal Waaktar (1961–), Magne 'Mags' Foruholmen (1962–) and Morten Harket (1959–) became popular icons with such hits as 'Take on Me' (1985), which got to Number One in the USA and to Number Two in the UK, and prospered on their photogenic good looks. 'Take on Me' had actually been released once before but had sold only 300 copies; the addition of a 100,000 partly animated video to go with it ensured its success. 'The Sun Always Shines on TV' reached Number One in the UK in 1986, while such albums as *Scoundrel Days* (1986), *Stay on These Roads* (1988), *East of the Sun* (1990) and *Memorial Beach* (1993) also sold well. A-Ha contributed the theme to the James Bond movie *The Living Daylights* (1987).

Ahlert, Fred E. (1892–1953) US composer, who wrote a series of hits for such singers as Bing CROSBY and Fats WALLER in the 1920s and 1930s. His first song was published in 1914, and he composed such TIN PAN ALLEY standards as 'I'd Love to Fall Asleep and Wake up in My Mammy's Arms' (1920), his first big hit, 'I'll Get By' (1928) and 'I'm Gonna Sit Right Down and Write Myself a Letter' (1935).

air force songs Although the air force was essentially a twentieth-century development, a strong tradition of airmen's songs, parallelling those of the army and the navy, has already arisen. As in the other wings of

the forces, the songs are generally adaptations of popular hits given relevant, often bawdy, lyrics. The first air force song is thought to have been 'The Bold Aviator' (or 'The Dying Airman') by C.H. Ward-Jackson, which began life as 'The Tarpaulin Jacket':

> Take the cylinders out of my kidneys,
> The connecting rod out of my brain,
> From the small of my back take the
>   crankshaft
> And assemble the engine again.

Other RAF hits included 'We Are Fred Karno's Air Corps' (from the hymn 'The Church's One Foundation'), while the Royal Naval Air Service adopted 'Bless 'em All', which, with somewhat more suitable words, became a popular hit during the First World War. Subsequent hits included 'He Had to Go and Prang 'er in the Hangar' (based on 'She Had to Go and Lose it at the Astor'), which was devised by 609 Squadron in the Second World War, and 'We are McIndoe's Army, We are his Guinea Pigs' (a reference to the celebrated plastic surgeon who treated many badly burned RAF personnel). A remark by a US pilot as he struggled to land his damaged aircraft 'on a wing and a prayer' inspired the song 'Comin' in on a Wing and a Prayer' in 1943, the success of which turned the remark into a catchphrase common to all the Allied air forces.

A number of composers have dedicated music to the air forces of their countries, among them Kenneth J. ALFORD, who dedicated his march 'Cavalry of the Clouds' to the Royal Flying Corps.

> We're making a beeline for Berlin,
> Blindfolded, we'll soon find the way.
> We're making a beeline for Berlin,
> Though no one will ask us to stay.
> It's true that we've not been invited –
> We just want to spring a surprise.
> We bet poor old Fritz
> Will have forty-nine fits
> When we start laying eggs in the sky,
> When we start laying eggs in the sky.
> Second World War RAF bomber crews' song,
> to the tune of 'My Bonnie Lies Over the
> Ocean'

air guitar The wholly imaginary guitar wielded by legions of HEAVY METAL fans as they rock with their favourite bands during a concert. Imitating the movements and playing style of their 'AXE heroes', some exponents of the air guitar go so far as to bring along their own cardboard cut-out guitars. *See also* HEADBANGER.

Air Supply Australian SOFT ROCK group, which enjoyed major international success as Australia's top band in the late 1970s and 1980s. Singer Russell Hitchcock (1949–), guitarist Graham Russell (1950–), keyboards player Frank Elser-Smith (1948–91), guitarist David Moyse (1957–), bassist David Green (1949–), drummer Ralph Cooper (1951–) and, later, guitarist Rex Goh (1951–) established their reputation with such hits as 'Love and Other Bruises' (1976) and 'All Out of Love' (1980). Other hit singles have included 'The One That You Love' (1981), 'Making Love Out of Nothing At All' (1983) and 'Just As I Am' (1986). Recent albums include *News from Nowhere* (1993).

AIRO Acoustical Investigation and Research Organization. A system of electrical amplification that is deployed in sophisticated modern auditoria with the purpose of achieving a more 'authentic' sound (in other words, making an orchestra sound more like an orchestra). The need for such systems has become greater since home audiences have become accustomed to the 'perfect' sound delivered by advanced COMPACT DISC systems. For some, the GRAMOPHONE record and the CD have profoundly upset listening habits, since cognoscenti at a concert now automatically seek the same detailed, clinical playing they hear at home. This induces artists to play in a concert as though for a record; AIRO enhances this effect.

> The gramophone record sets standards of perfection, mechanical not musical, which the concert hall seldom confirms. ... Those who consider undisturbed technical neatness the prerequisite of a moving musical experience no longer know how to listen to music.
> ALFRED BRENDEL

Aitken, Laurel (1928–) Cuban-born singer, who first established an international reputation as an exponent of SKA in Jamaica in the 1950s. Aitken became a star in Jamaica with such hits as 'Boogie Rock' and 'Little Sheila' but eventually moved to the UK, where he experimented in a variety of styles. His numerous ska and REGGAE hits, many with his band the Full

Circle, have included 'Deliverance Will Come', 'Skinhead Train', the bawdy 'Pussy Price' and 'Rudy Got Married', which was a hit during the TWO-TONE craze of the early 1980s.

Akst, Harry (1894–1963) US composer, who wrote several hit songs for Broadway and Hollywood between the wars. Trained to play the piano by his father, a professional musician, Akst was performing in public by the time he was 10 years old, and he planned a career in serious music. To raise the money to study classical music in Germany he worked as a song-plugger in a music shop, but became interested in popular music and changed his plans. He served as a soldier in the First World War and later collaborated with such leading figures as Irving BERLIN, his own hits including 'Laddie Boy' (1918), 'Baby Face' (1926), 'Am I Blue?' (1929) and 'Stand Up and Cheer' (1934).

Alabama US COUNTRY-ROCK band, which enjoyed huge commercial success with both country and pop fans in the 1970s and 1980s. The band – the cousins, guitar-playing Jeffrey Alan Cook (1949–) and Randy Yeull Owen (1949–) and bassist Teddy Wayne Gentry (1952–), together with drummer Mark Joel Herndon (1955–) – had no fewer than 18 Number Ones in a row in the early 1980s. Its most successful releases have included 'I Want to be With You' (1977), 'Why Lady Why' (1981), 'Love in the First Degree' (1982), 'The Closer You Get' (1983) and 'She and I' (1986). Albums include *Mountain Music* (1982), *The Touch* (1986) and *Cheap Seats* (1993).

Albany, Joe (Joseph Albani; 1924–88) US JAZZ pianist, who was much admired for his collaborations with some of the most respected jazz musicians of his era and was one of the pioneers of BOP. Influenced by Art TATUM and Teddy WILSON, he worked with Charlie PARKER – with whom he eventually quarrelled – and subsequently teamed up with Lester YOUNG, Stan GETZ and Charles MINGUS. Addiction to drugs disrupted his progress in the 1950s and 1960s, although he made something of a come-back in the 1970s.

Albert the Great *See* Albert CHEVALIER.

Albion Band, the British FOLK-ROCK band,

which became one of the most enduring and popular of all folk-rock outfits formed in the early 1970s. The band was founded in 1971 and has gone through a long series of line-ups, key members including mentor and bassist Ashley Hutchings (1945–), guitarists Martin CARTHY (1940–) and Richard THOMPSON and drummer Dave Mattocks (1948–). The band established its reputation building on traditional songs of English rather than Celtic origins and had major commercial success with such albums as *No Roses* (1971), *Morris On* (1972), *The Battle of the Field* (1976), *The Prospect Before Us* (1977), *Rise Up Like the Sun* (1978), *Under the Rose* (1986), *Stella Maria* (1987) and *Give Me a Saddle, I'll Trade You a Car* (1989).

album titles Titles for rock, pop and jazz albums have ranged from the pedestrian to the pretentious, enigmatic, absurd and downright bizarre. Among the more unusual have been:

> *Surrealistic Pillow* (Jefferson Airplane; 1967)
> *Ogden's Nut Gone Flake* (Small Faces; 1968)
> *The Doughnut in Granny's Greenhouse* (Bonzo Dog Doo Dah Band; 1968)
> *Golden Bisquits* (Three Dog Night; 1971)
> *Catch Bull At Four* (Cat Stevens; 1972)
> *Thick as a Brick* (Jethro Tull; 1972)
> *Goat's Head Soup* (Rolling Stones; 1973)
> *We All Had Doctors' Papers* (Max Boyce; 1975)
> *Never Mind the Bollocks* (Sex Pistols; 1977)
> *New Boots and Panties!!* (Ian Dury; 1977)
> *Scary Monsters and Super Creeps* (David Bowie; 1980)
> *No Sleep Til Hammersmith* (Motörhead; 1981)
> *Dirty Deeds Done Dirt Cheap* (AC/DC; 1981)
> *Learning to Crawl* (Pretenders; 1984)
> *Slippery When Wet* (Bon Jovi; 1985)
> *Look What the Cat Dragged In* (Poison; 1986)
> *Open Up and Say Ahh* (Poison; 1988)
> *Shooting Rubberbands at the Stars* (Brickell; 1988)
> *Hormonally Yours* (Shakespear's Sister; 1992)

The US rock band AMERICA named six albums with words beginning with the letter H – *Homecoming* (1972), *Hat Trick* (1973), *Hearts* (1975), *Hits* (1975), *Hideaway* (1976) and *Harbour* (1977) – while

STYX named an album *7-7-77* because it was due to be released on 7 July 1977. On somewhat similar lines, presumably lacking inspiration at the time, the KINKS guitarist Dave Davies released a solo album in 1980 under the title *AFL 3603* (its record company catalogue number).

Many albums are named after the strongest track on them – but this has led to the odd anomaly. The DOORS album *Waiting for the Sun* (1968) is just one example of an LP that, when finally released, lacked the song after which it had been named, the track in question having been deleted at the last moment.

When a record company planned to sell a Tom PETTY and the Heartbreakers album at $9.98 against Petty's wishes, Petty threatened to call the album *The $8.98 Album*, quoting the price he thought was justified; the company quickly changed its mind and the album finally appeared as *Hard Promises* at the price Petty favoured.

Aldeburgh Festival Annual music festival held at the coastal town of Aldeburgh in Suffolk, UK. The festival was founded in 1948 by the composer Benjamin BRITTEN (a resident of the town) and various friends (including the tenor Peter PEARS) associated with the English Opera Group, for whom Britten wrote many works to be performed at Aldeburgh itself. Many of Britten's most important operas and other works were premiered at Aldeburgh, among them *A Midsummer Night's Dream* (1960) and *Death in Venice* (1973). Performances are also given at the Maltings at Snape nearby and at the church in Orford. A major setback in the history of the festival was the destruction by fire of the Maltings on the first night of the 1969 festival, although it was restored in time for the festival one year later.

Aldrich, Ronnie (1916–93) British conductor, arranger, saxophonist and pianist, who was leader of the popular SWING band the Squadronaires in the 1940s and 1950s. A serving member of the RAF, he guided the Squadronaires with great success. After leaving them, he worked with various radio orchestras and with his own band.

aleatorism The practice of employing an element of chance in the performance of a piece of music. The idea was raised to new heights by such avant-garde composers as Charles IVES, Karlheinz STOCKHAUSEN and John CAGE, who preferred the term INDE-TERMINANCY. Extreme examples of aleatory music include Stockhausen's *Klavierstück XI* (1956), which invited performers to assemble fragments of music in any order; other composers allowed musicians to make their own decisions about how to approach certain passages and sometimes presented them with deliberately unplayable instructions in the hope that they would then be obliged to find their own solutions. In some cases no notation was supplied to the musicians at all. Cage himself used the *I Ching* – the ancient Chinese system of divination by numbers – as a guide for his *Music of Changes* (1951). Interest in the genre faded somewhat after the 1960s.

> Composing ... is simply a series of musical decisions, the most basic being the decision to make decisions.
> LARRY AUSTIN, in *American Composers*, 1982

Alexander, Arthur (1940–93) US RHYTHM-AND-BLUES singer-songwriter, who in the early 1960s released a number of classic hits that were later covered by many other top bands. Having started out as a gospel singer, Alexander had success on both sides of the Atlantic with such hits as 'You Better Move On', 'Anna' and 'Go Home, Girl'.

Alf *See* Alison MOYET.

Alford, Harry (1883–1939) US composer, who wrote many popular marches, including several for the bands associated with leading American football clubs. His best-known tunes included 'Purple Carnival' and 'Glory of the Gridiron'.

Alford, Kenneth J. (Major Frederick Joseph Ricketts; 1881–1945) British composer and bandmaster, who wrote some of the best-known military marches of modern times. He joined the band of the Royal Irish Regiment as a boy and rose to be bandmaster of the 2nd Battalion, the Argyll and Sutherland Highlanders, for which he wrote the classic march 'The Thin Red Line' (1909). He wrote his most celebrated march, 'Colonel Bogey', in 1913 and later such similar pieces as 'Cavalry of the Clouds' (dedicated to the Royal Flying Corps), 'The Great Little Army' (of the British Expeditionary Force in the First World War) and 'H.M. Jollies', which was written for the band of the Royal Marines, which he took over in 1928. Further marches followed in the Second World War before his death.

'Colonel Bogey' became one of the most widely heard anthems of both world wars, often with the addition of bawdy lyrics. Alford supposedly had the idea for the tune while walking across a golf course. When he did not respond to cries of 'Fore!' a player (alleged to have been a colonel) tried to attract his attention by whistling two loud notes at him, and these two notes (C and A) became the starting point for the classic march, which was named in honour of the whistling colonel (a 'bogey' in golf being a hole scored in par – that is, with the number of shots stipulated for a 'scratch' player). The tune was memorably employed in the SOUNDTRACK of the classic movie *Bridge Over the River Kwai* (1957).

Of the many versions of the march that were sung by the forces, the best known traded under the title 'Hitler has Only Got One Ball':

> Hitler has only got one ball,
> Goering has two but very small,
> Himmler has something similar,
> But poor old Goebbels
> Has no balls at all.

This ribald version was lastingly popular and is still heard on the lips of British rugby players and others.

Allegri Quartet British string quartet, which is famous for its impassioned performances of many new British works, as well as many established classics. The quartet, all respected soloists, premiered two new works by Benjamin BRITTEN among others.

Allen, Henry 'Red' (1908–67) US JAZZ trumpeter, singer and composer, who was considered by some the equal of Louis ARMSTRONG. The son of a celebrated brass band trumpeter, Allen joined his father's band and played with, among others, King OLIVER, Fate Marable (1890–1947), Luis RUSSELL, Fletcher HENDERSON and Armstrong himself. He also led his own bands and toured widely until shortly before his death from cancer. His style ranged widely from the traditional BLUES roots of jazz as it was played in New Orleans to BOP, MAINSTREAM and even AVANT-GARDE jazz.

Allen, Thomas (1944–   ) British baritone, who has won recognition as one of the leading singers of his generation. Having made his first appearance in 1969 in the part of Figaro in Mozart's *The Marriage of Figaro*, he has since consolidated his reputation in a wide range of opera roles, being especially famed for his performances as the Don in *Don Giovanni*, as well as winning acclaim for his interpretations of songs by Ralph VAUGHAN WILLIAMS and others.

Allison, Mose (1927–   ) US pianist, trumpeter and singer, who, although White, emerged as a popular jazz-blues star in the late 1950s. He first attracted attention playing with the band of Stan GETZ (1956–57) and with Gerry MULLIGAN. He went on to form his own trio and to exert a strong influence on the development of RHYTHM-AND-BLUES in the 1960s (his admirers including Georgie FAME, Pete Townshend (*see* the WHO) and John MAYALL). His hits included 'Back Country Suite' (1957) and 'Parchman Farm' (1958).

Allman Brothers US rock group of the early 1970s. Led by Duane Allman (1946–71) on guitar and Gregg Allman (1947–   ), nicknamed Skydog, on keyboards, vocals and guitar, the band came together in 1969 and toured extensively, building up a massive following as purveyors of SOUTHERN ROCK. The double album *At Fillmore East* (1971) was a big hit, but the group's future was put in doubt when first Duane Allman and then bassist Berry Oakley (1948–72) were killed in separate motorcycle accidents. The band continued in business, however, with guitarist Richard 'Dickie' Betts (1943–   ) playing a bigger role until 1976 and saw their album *Brothers and Sisters* (1972) spend five weeks at Number One in the USA – although critics agreed that their early work was the most important. Eric CLAPTON, who was deeply moved by Duane Allman's death (Allman had played lead guitar on 'Layla' for him), gave a classic version of the Allman Brothers' hit 'Statesboro Blues' at his funeral. There were occasional reunions of the remaining members of the group throughout the 1980s. Recent recordings include *Where It All Begins* (1994). Greg Allman was twice married to singer CHER, divorcing her in 1977 and again in 1978.

Almanac Singers Celebrated FOLK group, which was formed in 1940 by Pete SEEGER, Lee Hays and Millard Lampell (with Woody GUTHRIE joining a year later). The group did much to revive the US folk tradition, while addressing their songs, which included such numbers as 'The Ballad of Harry Bridges' and 'Reuben James', to current social and political issues (such as the question of US involvement in the Second World War and the duties of the unions). They broke up in 1942 as the various members concentrated on their solo careers.

Almeida, Laurindo (1917–   ) Brazilian guitarist, who played a crucial role in popularizing the BOSSA NOVA in the USA in the 1950s. The son of a concert pianist, Almeida played for Stan KENTON and others before embarking on a successful solo career in which he attempted to fuse classical and Latin elements with JAZZ. Among his most influential releases were the albums *Viva Bossa Nova* (1962) and *Guitar from Ipanema* (1964). He also contributed music to such films as *A Song Is Born* (1948) and *The Old Man and the Sea* (1958).

Almond, (Peter) Marc (1956–   ) British pop singer-songwriter, who established himself as a prominent NEW WAVE artist as leader of SOFT CELL, alongside SYNTHESIZER player Dave Ball (1959–   ). Almond made an entertainingly camp frontman, and such singles as the chart-topping 'Tainted Love' (1981) and 'Torch' (1982) put Soft Cell among the leading bands of the day. Splitting from Ball in 1984, Almond worked with several other bands and released such solo albums as *Vermin in Ermine* (1984), *Stories of Johnny* (1985), *Mother Fist and Her Five Daughters* (1987), *Jacques* (1990) and *Fantastic Star* (1996). His single 'The Lover Spurned' was reputed to have cost as much as the average album.

Alpert, Herb (1937–   ) US bandleader, trumpeter, singer and composer, who achieved fame with the 'Tijuana brass' sound. Prior to establishing his reputation, Alpert worked in a variety of musical capacities, appearing as an extra in such films as Cecil B. de Mille's 1956 epic *The Ten Commandments* (in which he beat a drum as Moses descended from the mountain) and in the 1959 Bing CROSBY vehicle

Say One For Me (in which he played the trumpet in a night club band). In 1960 he won fame as one of the writers of Sam COOKE's hit 'Wonderful World', following which he conceived the idea of the Tijuana sound while watching a bullfight in Tijuana, Mexico. In Alpert's hands the traditional Tijuana style was combined with elements taken from ROCK and JAZZ and backed by the noise of the crowd. His single 'The Lonely Bull' was a major hit in 1962; subsequent successes included 'Spanish Flea' (1965), 'Zorba the Greek' (1966), 'This Guy's in Love with You' (1968) and the disco-influenced 'Rise' (1979). Most of his records were released on the A & M record label of which he was a co-founder in 1962.

Altamont *See* the ROLLING STONES.

Alter, Louis (1902–80) US composer, who wrote many hit songs for the cinema. Having worked as a cinema pianist and as accompanist to Beatrice Lillie (1898–1989) and other stage stars, he started writing for a series of Broadway revues before returning to the cinema in 1929. His hits included the film songs 'Love Ain't Nothin' but the Blues', 'Isn't Love the Grandest Thing', 'Twilight on the Trail' and 'Rainbow on the River' and such instrumentals as 'Manhattan Serenade'.

Alwyn, William (1905–85) British composer, who is remembered chiefly for his music for many famous films. A student of, and later a teacher at, London's Royal Academy of Music, he contributed soundtracks for such films as *Fires Were Started* (1942), *The True Glory* (1945), *The Fallen Idol* (1948), *Carve Her Name With Pride* (1958) and *The Running Man* (1963). His other compositions included concertos for the harp, symphonies, string quartets and piano music.

Amadeus Quartet British string quartet, which was considered one of the finest quartets anywhere in the world for many years. It members were Norbert Brainin and Sigmund Nissel (violins), Peter Schidlof (viola) and Martin Lovett (cello), and the quartet was renowned above all for its performances of Mozart and Schubert. It also excelled in the performance of modern British works, which included Benjamin BRITTEN's third string quartet (written especially for them). The

quartet, which gave its first public performance in 1948, was disbanded on the death of Peter Schidlof in 1987.

Ambrose (Albert Ambrose; 1897–1971) British bandleader and violinist, who led a highly acclaimed dance band at London's Mayfair Hotel for many years. Ambrose divided his early career between the UK and the USA, finally settling at the Mayfair Hotel in 1927 and making his band one of the most admired in the country. Stars associated with his band included Ted HEATH, George SHEARING and singer Vera LYNN. Among his hits were 'Love Locked Out' (1934), 'I'm on a See-saw' (1935) and 'I'm in a Dancing Mood' (1936); his signature tune was 'When Day is Done'. He switched his attention to theatre management in the mid–1950s.

ambulatory music A genre of contemporary classical music, understandably rare, which calls upon one or more of the players to walk across the platform during the piece in order to play with different players, sharing their desk. The idea is to create different perspectives of sound and, at the very least, to add extra interest by turning a mere performance into a 'happening'.

In Thea MUSGRAVE's clarinet concerto, for example, the soloist has just such an ambulatory part. Gervase de PEYER played it at the first performance in 1969 at the ROYAL FESTIVAL HALL, managing to walk from section to section without knocking over any music stands or being injured by the bows of the violinists. When he finally returned to the other clarinettists, however, he was chastened to find, instead of his music waiting for him, a succinct note telling him precisely what he could do with himself.

Amen Corner British pop group (from Wales) of the late 1960s, which enjoyed considerable chart success. Led by vocalist Andy Fairweather Low (1948–), the group was formed in 1966 and established its reputation with such singles as 'Gin House Blues' (1967), 'Bend Me Shape Me' (1968) and '(If Paradise Is) Half As Nice' (1969), which reached Number One in the UK. The band broke up but re-formed under the title Fairweather and enjoyed a further hit with 'Natural Sinner' before breaking up once more as the various members concentrated on solo careers or SESSION work.

America US pop group, which was formed in

1969 by three dependants of US servicemen based in the UK, Dewey Bunnell (1952–), Gerry Beckley (1952–) and Dan Peek (1950–). The group established its reputation with the single 'A Horse With No Name' (1972), which reached Number One in the USA, and a further 10 songs get into the US Top 40. George MARTIN became the trio's producer in 1974, but it went into something of a decline, despite a minor come-back in the 1980s. Beckley went on to sing on the soundtracks of the Simpsons cartoons. A new album, *Hourglass*, was released in 1994.

American Bandstand US pop music television programme, which became one of the most celebrated and longest-lived programmes of its kind. Hosted by Dick CLARK, the programme was launched (with a live audience) in 1957 as a daily afternoon show on the national ABC network. It stuck closely to records that were making an impression in the charts and helped to promote many artists as nationally known stars, as well as making stars of regular members of the invited audience, who delivered their verdict on new releases and received piles of fan mail. David Seville's NOVELTY single 'The Chipmunk Song' (1958) achieved transient fame when it was given the lowest rating in the programme's history.

America's Tuning-fork *See* Pete SEEGER.

Ames Brothers, the US male vocal group, which had some success in the 1950s before the advent of ROCK 'N' ROLL. The group, whose members were the brothers Joe Ames (Joseph Urick Ames; 1924–), Gene Ames (1925–), Vic Ames (1926–) and Ed Ames (1927–), was regularly in the charts with such hits as 'Undecided' (1951), 'You, You, You' (1953), 'The Naughty Lady of Shady Lane' (1954), 'Melodie d'Amour' (1957) and 'Tammy' (1957). After the group broke up in 1960, Ed Ames had a brief career as a solo star.

Amfitheatrof, Daniele (1901–83) US composer and conductor, of Russo-Italian parentage, who is usually remembered for the SOUNDTRACKS he wrote to many Hollywood movies of the 1940s and 1950s. Having studied music in St Petersburg and Prague and in Rome under Ottorino RESPIGHI, he worked as a conductor with Radio Turin before emigrating to the USA in

1937. He wrote music for more than 80 films, among them *Lassie Come Home* (1943), *The Naked Jungle* (1954) and *Heller in Pink Tights* (1960).

Ammons, Albert C. (1907–49) US pianist, who was one of the most popular of all BOOGIE-WOOGIE performers. Based in Chicago, he recorded a number of hits with his Rhythm Kings in the 1930s and 1940s as well as others with fellow-pianist Pete JOHNSON, his most successful numbers including 'Cuttin' the Boogie' and 'Barrelhouse Boogie'. His son, Gene 'Jug' Ammons (1925–74), proved a fine tenor saxophonist, although his career was somewhat disrupted by drug addiction and consequent prison sentences.

amp An amplifier, as used to magnify the sound of guitars and other instruments or voices in the course of a POP, ROCK or other kind of concert. An essential piece of equipment for every modern guitarist, the amp was unknown in the UK until the 1950s. One of the first UK bands to use amplifiers was that of Tommy STEELE, one of the first British ROCK 'N' ROLL stars:

> We'd bring the amps in – and they'd never seen amps. They'd *never* seen amps! And you'd start setting this stuff up and the Fire Department would come round and say 'What is that?' and you'd say 'It's an electric amplifier. ...' 'Electric? D'you mean you're bringing live stuff on apart from the microphone belonging to the theatre?' And so we used to end up in every city having to pay for a fireman to stand on each side of the theatre, by the stage; and we had to put, at the side of each amp, a big red bucket with FIRE written on it, full of sand.

Amy, Gilbert (1936–) French composer and conductor, who was greatly influenced by Pierre BOULEZ. Amy was a co-founder and later director of the Domaine Musical, which was dedicated to the promotion of new music. His works have included such orchestral pieces as *Antiphonies* (1963), *Trajectories* (1966) and pieces for wind sextet and piano.

Ancliffe, Charles (1880–1952) Irish composer and conductor, who wrote a number of popular marches, waltzes and songs. A bandmaster with the Somerset Light Infantry and the South Wales Borderers, he directed the Scarborough Military Band and various orchestras after leaving the army in

1918. His most popular pieces include the waltz 'Nights of Gladness' (1912) and the intermezzo 'Secrets' as well as the marches 'Castles in Spain' and 'The Liberator'.

Andersen, Lale (1910–72) Danish CABARET singer, who is chiefly remembered for her husky-voiced classic recording of 'Lili Marlene' (1939), which was the biggest hit of the Second World War. The song made Andersen famous and remained her greatest success, although she had another hit with 'Never on Sunday' in 1960 and also won the EUROVISION SONG CONTEST in 1961.

Her wartime career, which was traumatized by considerable harassment from the Nazis, was dramatized for the screen in Rainer Werner Fassbinder's *Lili Marleen* (1980). The lyrics of 'Lili Marlene' were originally written in 1917 by the German soldier Hans Liep (1894–1983), reminiscing about two girls – Lili and Marleen – who used to meet him each evening (as the song describes) while he was on leave in Berlin. With music added by Norbert Schultze (1911–   ) in 1938, the song was rejected by 30 German publishers before Andersen took it up in 1939 (when it sold just 700 copies). The song's eventual success was assured when it was broadcast at regular intervals by German wartime radio. Troops from both sides in the conflict (especially those in North Africa) adopted the tune as their own and on more than one occasion troops from opposing armies were heard singing it as they moved into battle against each other. Rumour had it that the 51st Highland Division even launched an attack against German positions in the hope of capturing a copy. Hitler himself was said to be furious when he learnt that Allied troops had appropriated the tune and set their own words to it and he went so far as to report it as a breach of the Geneva Convention. This did not stop French and Italian soldiers adding their own versions of the classic song, which was recorded with renewed success by Marlene DIETRICH and Ann SHELTON among others.

> Get the right deflection,
> Check reflector sight,
> Give your speed correction,
> And see your range is right.
> Then you press the tit, old son,
> And blow the Hun to kingdom come,
> Poor Marlene's boyfriend will
> Never see Marlene.
> Version of 'Lili Marlene' sung by Allied dive-bomber crews

Anderson, Bill (1937–   ) US singer-songwriter, businessman and media personality, nicknamed Whispering Bill, who wrote numerous COUNTRY hits – many of them duets – in the late 1950s and early 1960s. The best of Anderson's songs, which included the million-selling 'City Lights' (1958) and 'Mama Sang a Sad Song' (1962), dealt expressively with urban isolation and other contemporary social problems facing the southern USA. His nickname referred to the soft, half-spoken delivery of such classics as 'Still' (1963), although he experimented with several styles and even moved into disco in the 1970s. Hits provided for other artists have included Ken Dodd's 'Happiness'. He went on to host his own television shows and also made several film appearances.

Anderson, Cat (William Alonzo Anderson; 1916–81) US JAZZ trumpeter, who remained one of the leading stars of Duke ELLINGTON's band on and off for some 30 years (1944–71). Having learned to play the trumpet while at an orphanage (where he was dubbed Cat after beating up a bully), he played with the bands of Lionel HAMPTON and others and eventually proved a valuable addition to the Ellington set-up. Many of the band's most celebrated hits of the 1950s and 1960s were written round his impassioned upper register playing (he boasted a remarkable five-octave range).

Anderson, Ivie (Marie) (1905–49) US JAZZ singer, who won acclaim as the ideal vocalist with the band of Duke ELLINGTON. She established her reputation while appearing at the COTTON CLUB in the early 1920s and made her début with Ellington in 1931. She went on to sing on many of the Duke's greatest hits, including 'Stormy Weather' (1933), 'It Don't Mean a Thing' (1932) and 'I Don't Mind' (1942). She retired to open a restaurant in Los Angeles in 1942.

Anderson, John Murray (1886–1954) US producer and lyricist, who presented many of the most successful Broadway REVUES of the 1920s and 1930s. His hits included the *Greenwich Village Follies* (1919–24), *Dearest Enemy* (1925), *Ziegfeld Follies* (1934, 1936 and 1943) and *Life Begins at 8.40* (1934).

Anderson, Laurie (1947–   ) US multimedia performer, who attracted a cult audience in the 1970s and 1980s as one of a group of controversial AVANT-GARDE artists based in New York. Her radical extended single 'O Superman' proved a big hit with rock fans in 1982 and promoted media interest in her theatre works, in which she explored the boundaries of music and speech through the use of synthesizers and complex technical effects. Her albums have included *Big Science* (1982), *Mister Heartbreak* (1986), *Strange Angels* (1989) and *Bright Red* (1994), with Lou Reed. Her extraordinary live act provided the basis for the five-album set *United States* (1984).

Anderson, Leroy (1908–75) US composer and conductor, of Swedish descent, who is remembered for the host of light and frequently humorous compositions he wrote for the Boston Pops and other leading orchestras in the 1940s and 1950s. Trained as an organist and choirmaster, he numbered among his most successful creations 'Sleigh Ride' (1950), 'Blue Tango' (1951), which reached the top of the pop charts, 'The Typewriter' (1953), which incorporated the sound of a typewriter working furiously away and was featured in the film *But Not For Me* (1959), and his theme tune 'Forgotten Dreams' (1955). He also contributed the score for the Broadway MUSICAL *Goldilocks* (1958).

Anderson, Lynn (1947–) US COUNTRY singer, who released a series of hit singles that appealed to both country and pop audiences in the late 1960s and 1970s. Among her most popular recordings were the GRAMMY-winning '(I Never Promised You a) Rose Garden' (1971), 'How Can I Unlove You?' (1971) and 'Last Love of My Life' (1978).

Anderson, Marian (1902–93) US contralto, who became the first Black singer to appear at the New York METROPOLITAN OPERA HOUSE (1955). Equally admired for her interpretation of classical and Black FOLK music, she was particularly admired for her singing of songs by Jean SIBELIUS as well as for her delivery of spirituals, which she helped to popularize throughout the West. She used her high public profile to argue for racial equality in the USA and was rewarded with many honours for her work both on and off the stage. She was also briefly a delegate to the United Nations in the late 1950s.

The voice that comes once in a hundred years.
ARTURO TOSCANINI, of Marian Anderson

Anderson, Moira (1938–) Scottish singer, who became widely known for her delivery on television of many well-known traditional Scottish airs. A student of the Royal Academy of Music, she made her début for the BBC in 1959 and achieved fame through her appearances on the *White Heather Club* music programme, through her own series and as presenter of *Stars on Sunday* in the 1970s.

Andrews, Julie (Julia Elizabeth Wells; 1935–) British actress and singer, sometimes known as the Iron Butterfly, who became one of the best-loved stars of the film MUSICAL in the 1950s and 1960s. She made her stage début as a child and went on to feature in the popular radio series *Educating Archie* in the 1950s before emerging as a major star through her roles in the stage musicals *The Boy Friend* (1954), *My Fair Lady* (1956) and *Camelot* (1960) and in such films as *Mary Poppins* (1964), in which she won an OSCAR, *The Sound of Music* (1965), *Thoroughly Modern Millie* (1967) and *Star!* (1968). Attempts to ditch the saccharin-sweet image acquired playing Mary Poppins by appearing naked in *SOB* (1981), directed by her film director husband Blake Edwards, and by wearing a badge declaring 'Mary Poppins is a junkie' were only partially successful. Enduring standards uniquely associated with her name include 'Supercalifragilisticexpialidocious' from *Mary Poppins* and 'My Favourite Things' from *The Sound of Music*.

She has that wonderful British strength that makes you wonder why they lost India.
MOSS HART

Working with her is like being hit over the head with a Valentine's card.
CHRISTOPHER PLUMMER, after working with Julie Andrews in *The Sound of Music*

Andrews Sisters, the US all-female close-harmony vocal group, which had considerable success in the late 1930s and 1940s. Laverne Andrews (1915–67), Maxine Andrews (1918–) and Patti Andrews (1920–) first attracted public attention in 1937 with the song 'Bei mir bist du schön', which became their theme tune, and consolidated their reputation with such hits as 'Boogie Woogie Bugle Boy', 'Pennsylvania Polka' and 'Don't Fence Me In', all of which also featured in the many light musical films they made. With some 60 million record sales, the Andrews Sisters remain the most successful commercial all-girl group in the history of twentieth-century music.

Animals, the British RHYTHM-AND-BLUES band, formed in Newcastle in 1962 as the Alan Price Combo, which became one of the top groups of the decade. Singer Eric Burdon (1941–   ), guitarist Hilton Valentine (1943–   ), singer and keyboard player Alan PRICE (1942–   ), bassist Bryan 'Chas' Chandler (1938–   ) and drummer John Steel (1941–   ) were spotted by record producer Mickie MOST, who steered them to chart success with such singles as 'House of the Rising Sun', which reached Number One on both sides of the Atlantic in 1964, and 'Please Don't Let Me be Misunderstood' (1965). The group broke up in 1967 not long after Price and then Most embarked on new projects. The Animals re-formed for reunions in 1976 and 1983, releasing the albums *Before We Were So Rudely Interrupted* (1976) and *Ark* (1983).

The band's greatest hit, 'The House of the Rising Sun', was borrowed from Bob DYLAN, who in turn had taken it from Woody GUTHRIE, in the process transposing it into a more menacing minor key (it was in fact a much older song, about a brothel, which dated from the turn of the century). Mickie Most recalled that it was recorded in an astonishingly quick time:

> They had been on tour with Chuck Berry, and they took an all-night train, and we picked them up at seven-fifteen in the morning. Took their equipment and them in a truck around to the recording studio. We started recording at eight o'clock in the morning, and by eight-fifteen 'The House of the Rising Sun' was finished.

Not content with having completed one of the greatest pop recordings of the decade before most people had finished their breakfast, the band went on to lay down the substantial part of a whole album before lunch.

Anka, Paul (1941–   ) Canadian singer-songwriter, of Syrian descent, who became a pop teen-idol of the mid-1950s. Anka's single 'Diana', allegedly written for the family's babysitter and recorded in 1957 when he was just 16 years old, became Number One on both sides of the Atlantic and was followed by such hits as 'You are My Destiny', 'Lonely Boy' and 'Put your Head on My Shoulder'. As a songwriter, he was also responsible for the Buddy HOLLY hit 'It Doesn't Matter Any More', Frank SINATRA's 'My Way', Tom JONES's 'She's a Lady' and Donny OSMOND's 'Puppy Love', as well as the theme song for the movie *The Longest Day* (1962), in which he also appeared. He continued to record through the 1960s and returned to the US Top 10 with a series of singles in the mid-1970s. He has also written several songs for Michael JACKSON.

Ansell, John (1874–1948) British composer and conductor, who wrote much music for the theatre both before and after the First World War. He was musical director of the Playhouse (1907–13) and the Alhambra (1913–20) and was also connected with the Shaftesbury Theatre, the Adelphi and the Winter Garden Theatre. As well as incidental music for plays, he also produced such musical scores as *Rip Van Winkle* (1911) and *Eastward Ho!* (1919) and such independent pieces as 'Aubade', 'A Children's Suite' and the ballet *The Shoe*.

Antheil, George (1900–59) US composer, pianist and journalist, who enjoyed a reputation as one of the most controversial composers of his generation. Most notorious of the pieces by Antheil's hand was the *Ballet mécanique* (1926), which incorporated the sounds of eight pianos, two electric doorbells, a pianola, four xylophones, a tam-tam, four bass drums, a siren and two aircraft propellers. When the *Ballet mécanique* was given its premiere the audience was stunned, one concertgoer hoisting a white handkerchief on his cane to indicate surrender.

Antheil gave as his reasons for such unconventionality the desire to 'warn the age in which I am living of the simultaneous beauty and danger of its mechanistic philosophy'. His other activities included writing books on 'glandular criminology' and military prophecy and also running a newspaper agony column.

> Art cannot hold its breath too long without dying.
> GEORGE ANTHEIL, *Bad Boy of Music*, 1945

Anthony, Ray (Raymond Antonini; 1922–) US JAZZ trumpeter, bandleader and composer, who enjoyed many hits with his own band in the 1950s and 1960s. Influenced by the smooth sound of Glenn MILLER, in whose band he played before the Second World War, he ensured the popularity of his own band after the war with such numbers as 'Trumpet Boogie', 'Cook's Tour' and 'Rollin' Home', as well as appearing in a number of films.

AOR *See* ADULT-ORIENTED ROCK.

Apollo Theatre The theatre in Harlem, New York, which acquired semi-legendary status as a launchpad for many celebrated careers in RHYTHM-AND-BLUES and other genres of Black music. Originally called Hurtig and Seamon's Music Hall, the theatre was renamed the Apollo in 1934 and prospered with a mixed programme of Black jazz artists and other entertainers. The Apollo's amateur night, held every Wednesday, was especially popular; among the celebrated guests were such performers as Duke ELLINGTON, Billie HOLLI-DAY, Count BASIE and Ella FITZGERALD.

Between the 1950s and 1970s the theatre, variously nicknamed Mother Church and the Uptown Palace, played host to many rhythm-and-blues stars, including Dionne WARWICK and Smokey ROBINSON. Acts that failed were cruelly treated; those that succeeded were wildly acclaimed, some members of the audience in the Second Balcony – nicknamed the Buzzard's Roost – even vaulting into the pit to show their approval. The theatre closed in 1976 after a shooting, was reopened and then closed once more in 1983, after it which it was taken over by a cable television company, which restored it as a leading venue for top stars.

> The Apollo was like my home after school and I would study backstage between shows.
> STEVIE WONDER

> I miss the card games between shows and the way people used to sell hot furs and jewellery backstage. And we used to have hot dogs for dinner there. We put them on light bulbs to heat them up and ate them after the show.
> PATTI LABELLE

Apple The recording label on which several BEATLES albums were released in the late 1960s. Apple Records, a subsidiary of EMI's Parlophone label, became uniquely identified with the Beatles, although the Black Dyke Mills Band and Mary HOPKIN were among other artists to record on it. After the Beatles disbanded the label was quietly dropped in the mid-1970s.

Apple Corps The BEATLES-owned company that was founded in 1968 to oversee the group's business interests and to breathe some fresh air into conventional marketing practices. The Beatles took a keen interest in the setting up of the company and planned several unconventional projects under its aegis. The company, based in London's Savile Row, attempted to fuse the ideals of love, peace and commerce and to put into practice a system that would, in John LENNON's words 'wrest control from the men in suits'. One project envisaged for the future (though never realized) was an Apple School, which would cater for the children of the four stars and for those of other company employees.

The enterprise was blighted from the start by the incompetence of its appointed managers and was soon in dire financial straits. Among the bosses was a tarot card reader, who was empowered to veto any decisions made on the basis of his readings. It was on the roof of the Apple Building that the Beatles gave their last performance, on 30 January 1969.

> It's a pun – apple core – see?
> PAUL McCARTNEY

Archer, Harry (Harry Auracher; 1888–1960) US composer, who wrote and directed a series of successful MUSICALS in the 1920s. Having led his own orchestra and played in the band of Paul WHITEMAN, he wrote the scores of such hit musicals as *Love for Sale* (1915), *Peek-a-boo* (1922), *Little Jesse James* (1923), from which came the song 'I Love You', *My Girl* (1924) and *Twinkle, Twinkle* (1926).

Archer Street A small street, off Windmill Street in London's West End, where freelance musicians (mainly those involved in non-classical music) used to congregate in the hope of meeting a FIXER able to offer them a booking. It was, in effect, a sort of musicians' mop fair, with much of the bartering taking place outside (the players being too poor to afford a drink under cover). *See also* TIN PAN ALLEY.

Archies, the US cartoon characters, whose BUBBLEGUM song 'Sugar Sugar' was a huge hit on both sides of the Atlantic in 1969. The Archies – Archie, Betty, Veronica, Jughead and Moose – were originally launched in 1942 as a comic strip but were adopted by Don Kirshner, the record producer who created the MONKEES, as a vehicle for music written by the songwriters associated with the BRILL BUILDING. 'Sugar Sugar' was not the only hit: 'Bam Shang-A-Lang' (1968) and 'Jingle Jangle' (1969) made the Top 10, and the success of the enterprise spawned a whole generation of cartoons based on famous pop groups such as the OSMONDS.

aristo-pop POP music associated with the 'aristocracy of pop' – that is, those few artists who earn the most and have remained at the top of their profession for a number of years. Members of the pop aristocracy in recent decades may safely be assumed to include Mick JAGGER, David BOWIE and Elton JOHN.

Arlen, Harold (Hyman Arluck; 1905–86) US composer, who wrote scores of hit songs for a host of leading singers between the 1930s and the 1950s. Arlen began his music career by playing the piano on lake steamers and in various clubs in his home town of Buffalo, for a time with his own band, the Buffalodians. In the mid-1920s he moved to New York, where he led his own JAZZ band, often assuming the role of singer. His song 'Get Happy', written in collaboration with Ted KOEHLER, attracted attention and provided a hit for Ruth ETTING in 1930, after which Arlen wrote many more for revues at the COTTON CLUB.

Such classics as 'Between the Devil and the Deep Blue Sea' (1931), 'It's Only a Paper Moon' (1932), 'Stormy Weather' (1932) and 'April in Paris' (1932) provided Duke ELLINGTON and others with some of their most popular hits and marked Arlen out as one of the leading song composers of the era. He later contributed to numerous stage shows and to many celebrated films, of which the most successful was *The Wizard of Oz* (1939). The talent of Judy GARLAND raised such standards as 'Somewhere Over the Rainbow' to become classics of the time, although other songs written by Arlen for the cinema showed that he had a wide range and could tackle comic material

equally well. Among his other well-known songs were 'That Old Black Magic' (1942), 'One for My Baby' (1943), 'Ac-centtchuate the Positive' (1944), 'Any Place I Hang My Hat is Home' (1946) and 'The Man That Got Away' (1954).

Armatrading, Joan (1950–) West Indian-born British singer-songwriter, who emerged as a popular solo artist in the mid-1970s. Having moved with her family to the UK in 1958, she achieved fame in 1976 with the hit single and album entitled *Love and Affection*, which established her credentials as an introspective 'bedsit balladeer' with feminist sympathies. Subsequent hits included the singles 'Show Some Emotion' (1977), 'To the Limit' (1978) and 'Me, Myself, I' (1980). After some years of relatively little success, she returned to the charts with *Hearts and Flowers* (1990), *Very Best of Joan Armatrading* (1991), *Square the Circle* (1992) and *What's Inside* (1995).

Armstrong, Lil (Lillian Hardin; 1898–1971) Black US JAZZ pianist, bandleader and composer, who was married (1924–38) to Louis ARMSTRONG. Lil Armstrong was an important jazz pioneer in her own right, playing with King OLIVER in Chicago before meeting Armstrong. She played a leading role in the famous Hot Five and Hot Seven recordings of the mid-1920s and wrote such classic numbers as 'Jazz Lips', 'Just for a Thrill' and 'Skit-dat-de-dat'. She remained a respected jazz pianist until she died while appearing at a memorial concert for her ex-husband.

Armstrong, Louis (1901–71) Black US JAZZ trumpeter, variously nicknamed Satchmo (an abbreviated form of 'Satchelmouth', Black slang for anyone with a wide mouth), Dippermouth and Pops, who became of all giants of twentieth-century popular music perhaps the most celebrated. Born in the New Orleans district of STORYVILLE, the birthplace of jazz itself, Armstrong learned to play the cornet while at the Colored Waifs' Home, to which he was sent at the age of 13 after he fired a gun belonging to his mother. Supporting himself by delivering coal with a horse and cart, he continued to perfect his playing technique whenever he could, appearing with a host of local bands. He emerged as a startling and unconventional talent in Chicago in the 1920s and made many classic recordings with Fletcher HENDERSON's orchestra in New York and with his own bands the Hot Five and the Hot Seven, often in collaboration with his second wife, pianist Lillian Hardin (*see* Lil ARMSTRONG). He eventually exchanged his cornet for the trumpet and also developed his unique singing style, which ensured the worldwide success of such recordings as 'Hello Dolly' (1964) and 'What a Wonderful World' (1968) and many classic blues songs (*see also* SCAT).

Armstrong's easy, humorous style and inspired playing made him an international favourite and the most famous jazzman of them all, although critics felt his music was sacrificed to some extent to the projection of his endearing personality in his later years, particularly his showy performances with the small All-Stars band he led from the late 1940s. Accusations that he compromised too often on the issue of Black civil rights in the 1950s were laid largely to rest when he took exception to the treatment of Black children attending segregated schools in Alabama and added his influential voice to those demanding change. Musically, his success paved the way for a whole generation of Black jazz musicians, who were unanimous in acknowledging their debt to him:

> If it hadn't been for him, there wouldn't have been none of us. I want to thank Mr Louis Armstrong for my livelihood.
> DIZZY GILLESPIE, on the occasion of Armstrong's 70th birthday

> A lotta cats copy the Mona Lisa, but people still line up to see the original.
> LOUIS ARMSTRONG, when asked his views of his many imitators

Armstrong, Sheila (1942–) British soprano, who has won equal acclaim on the concert platform and on the opera stage since winning the Kathleen Ferrier Prize in 1965. A student of the Royal Academy, she has attracted praise in a wide range of works, from Mozart's *Così fan tutte* and Sir Edward ELGAR's oratorio *The Apostles* to Northumbrian folk-songs.

army songs The twentieth century has seen numerous additions to the already huge international repertory of military-oriented songs. The First World War, with its static trench warfare and vast armies, gave birth to a legion of more or less disreputable classics, the best of which were based on the tunes and lyrics of contemporary hits (as preserved in the theatre in the classic war documentary musical *Oh! What a Lovely War*). The most famous included 'Goodbye-ee', 'Tipperary', 'Pack up Your Troubles', 'Keep the Home Fires Burning' and – from the much earlier song 'Three Prussian Officers Crossed the Line' – another still-rendered anthem, 'Mademoiselle from Armenteers'.

'There's a Long, Long Trail a-Winding', another famous song from the 1914–18 conflict, was written by Alonzo Elliott, a young US student at Yale University, in 1913. In fact, Elliott was not thinking of the contemporary political situation at the time that he wrote his masterpiece, but of the burning of Moscow as Napoleon retreated in 1812. The song failed to find a publisher in the USA, but it was an immediate hit in the UK in 1914 and was adopted by both UK and US troops on their way to the trenches in France. Elliott grew rich on the royalties and used the money to study how to write operas, producing his first – *What Price Glory?* – 19 years later.

'It's a Long Way to Tipperary', another wartime standard, was written as the result of a bet in a pub in Stalybridge, Cheshire, in 1912, when a party of actors wagered that Jack Judge and Harry J. Williams could not write and perform a new song in the space of a single day. Judge and Williams premiered their song at the Stalybridge Grand Theatre 24 hours later and won their bet. The first line of the song was engraved on Williams's tombstone, and the song itself was widely revived in the Second World War:

> It's a long time since I saw Blighty,
> It's a long time ago,
> It's a long time since I saw Blighty,
> To fight to Tokyo.

> Goodbye, Jungle Burma,
> Malay, Singapore,
> It's a long, long time since I saw Blighty,
> But I'll soon be there.
> Variant sung by troops returning from the Far East

Songs from the Second World War were, if anything, even more ribald, but also included a number of cherished classics, of which the most popular with both sides was 'Lili Marlene', as immortalized in the recording made by Lale ANDERSEN. Among others were Kenneth ALFORD's classic march 'Colonel Bogey' and 'Kiss Me Good-night, Sergeant Major'. *See also* FORCES' SWEETHEART.

> Oh, the colonel kicks the major,
> And the major has a go.
> He kicks the poor old captain,
> Who then kicks the NCO.
> And as the kicks get harder,
> They are passed on down to me.
> And I am kicked to bleeding hell
> To save democracy.
> 'The Colonel Kicks the Major', to the tune of 'Macnamara's Band', 1940s

One army song from a previous century that provided a popular modern hit was 'Aura Lea' by William Whiteman Fosdick (1825–62), which was taken up by both sides in the US Civil War (1861–65). The song was revived in 1956 by Elvis PRESLEY, under the new title 'Love Me Tender'.

Arndt, Felix (1889–1918) US composer, bandleader and pianist, who wrote a number of hits during the First World War era. Far and away his most successful composition was 'Nola' (1915), which was dedicated to his wife Nola Arndt (1889–1977).

Arnheim, Gus (1897–1955) US bandleader and composer, who led a popular band in the 1930s and 1940s and supported many of the best-known singers of the era. Having begun his musical career as a pianist in Chicago, he went on to form the Syncopated Five and provided backing for Sophie TUCKER. He toured Europe and the USA with his next band, formed in 1928, and eventually settled at the Coconut Grove in Los Angeles. His band, whose members included Bud JOHNSON, Woody HERMAN and Stan KENTON, enjoyed a close association with Bing CROSBY and other stars and also appeared in several films. Among Arnheim's own hit compositions were 'I Cried for You', 'Sweet and Lovely' and 'I'm Gonna Get You'.

Arnold, Eddy (1918–) US COUNTRY-AND-WESTERN star, nicknamed the Tennessee Plowboy, who had many hits in a long career that began in the 1940s. He first attracted attention in collaboration with Pee Wee King in the early 1940s and rose to national prominence as a star of the GRAND OLE OPRY. His hits included, from the 1940s, 'That's How Much I Love You', 'Bouquet of Roses' and 'Anytime' and, from the 1960s, 'What's He Doing with

My World', 'Misty Blue' and 'Turn the World Around'. By the end of the 1970s he had sold some 70 million records. He was the first country-and-western performer to appear at Carnegie Hall (1966) and that same year was elected to the COUNTRY MUSIC HALL OF FAME.

Arnold, Sir Malcolm Henry (1921–) British composer, who earned a wide reputation with his tuneful and accessible compositions from the late 1940s onwards. Having begun his career as a professional trumpet player, playing chiefly for the LONDON PHILHARMONIC ORCHESTRA and the BBC SYMPHONY ORCHESTRA, he concentrated on writing music from 1948. His best-known works include the ballet *Homage to the Queen* (1953), the *Tam O'Shanter Overture* (1955) and the soundtrack for the film *Bridge Over the River Kwai* (1958). He has also written a number of compositions for brass bands, the most popular of them including 'Fantasy for Brass Band' and 'The Padstow Lifeboat'. His most unusual composition remains 'A Grand, Grand Overture', which he wrote for Gerard HOFF-NUNG's Music Festival of 1956: it was scored for three vacuum cleaners, a floor polisher, four rifles and an orchestra.

Arrau, Claudio (1903–91) Chilean pianist, who emerged as one of the great modern interpreters of the music of Beethoven, Schumann and Liszt among other composers. Arrau was a child prodigy, giving his first recital when he was five years old. Subsequently he appeared all over the world and even had a street in Santiago (where he opened a piano school) named in his honour. In 1935 he embarked on a series of concerts in which he played the entire keyboard works of J.S. Bach; on concluding the series he vowed never to play Bach again in public, explaining that his work was not suited to the modern piano.

Art Ensemble of Chicago US JAZZ band that has established a strong international reputation since its foundation as an off-shoot of the AACM in 1968. The original members of the Ensemble were saxophonists Roscoe Mitchell (1940–) and Joseph Jarman (1937–), trumpeter Lester Bowie (1941–) and bassist Malachi Favors (1937–), who were subsequently joined by drummer Famoudou

Don Moye (1946–). The band, which was based in Paris from 1969 to 1971, attracted attention with their highly theatrical live act and avant-garde, free-form style, which took in the influences of many other genres, from traditional NEW ORLEANS JAZZ to the rhythms of African music and ROCK 'N' ROLL. Sensational public appearances have included one in which Jarman emerged on stage wearing only the sling for his saxophone.

art rock ROCK music in which elements of classical or other traditional music are incorporated, mainly in terms of instrumentation. The phrase was applied initially to such artists as the BEATLES and Bob DYLAN, whose work progressed beyond the superficial and commercially minded, but it was later used of a wide range of groups of debatable merit whose work had some pretensions to be 'artistic' (one extreme being represented by such HEAVY METAL bands as CAN and Deaf School).

> Ever since that group recorded *Sergeant Pepper* in 1967, there have been many excursions into art-rock, the fusion of conservatoire style in instrumentation with the electronics and idioms of pop.
> ROBERT SHELTON, *The Times*, 1972

ASCAP American Society of Composers, Authors, and Publishers. The Society, which seeks to protect musical copyrights in the USA, was established in 1914 and fought its first test case over the song 'Sweethearts' by Victor HERBERT, which had been played without permission in a New York restaurant. Royalties collected by the Society, now the predominant songwriters' trade union, are shared among its members.

Asche, Oscar (John Strange Heiss; 1871–1936) Australian-born actor, singer, director and producer, who also wrote the librettos for a number of popular MUSICALS. Initially an acclaimed Shakespearian actor, he enjoyed huge success with the oriental spectacular *Chu Chin Chow* (1916); his other librettos included those for *Eastward Ho!* (1919), *The Good Old Days* (1925) and *El Dorado* (1930).

Ascher, Leo (1880–1942) Austrian composer, resident in the USA from 1938, who wrote a number of popular operettas and much music for films and the theatre. He established his reputation with the operetta *Vergeltsgott* (1905) and enjoyed his finest hour in 1912 with *Hoheit tanzt Walzer*; other works included *Die arme Lori* (1909), *Der Soldat der Marie* (1917) and *Sonja* (1925).

Ashford and Simpson US vocal duo and songwriting team, which first emerged as a top SOUL attraction in the late 1960s. Nickolas Ashford (1942–) and Valerie Simpson (1946–), first met in 1964 and married in 1974, by which time they had established their reputation as songwriters with such hits as 'Let's Get Stoned' (1966), recorded by Ray CHARLES, the duets 'Ain't Nothing Like the Real Thing' (1968) and 'Ain't No Mountain High Enough' (1968) for Marvin GAYE and Tammi Terrell, and other numbers for Diana ROSS, Gladys KNIGHT and other MOTOWN stars. Subsequently they emerged as recording artists in their own right, their most popular singles including 'Send It' (1977), 'I Found a Cure' (1979) and 'Solid' (1985).

Ashkenazy, Vladimir (Davidovich) (1937–) Russian-born pianist and conductor, who was recognized as one of the leading pianists of his generation when he shared victory in the 1962 Tchaikovsky Competition with John OGDON. Ashkenazy left for the West a year later and eventually settled in Iceland, the homeland of his wife, and took out Icelandic nationality. He is particularly admired for his playing of Mozart, Beethoven and Chopin as well as for his interpretation of the works of leading Russian composers such as Sergei PROKOFIEV and Sergei RACHMANINOV. He was appointed music director of the ROYAL PHILHARMONIC ORCHESTRA in 1987 and chief conductor of the Berlin Radio Symphony Orchestra in 1989.

Asmussen, Svend (1916–) Danish violinist and singer, who was unrivalled as a master of the JAZZ violin. Asmussen formed his own quartet in 1933 and became widely known through regular broadcasts and recordings, collaborating with a number of celebrated artists, including Fats WALLER and Stéphane GRAPPELLI. He has appeared at many major international festivals, at which he has often indulged his talent for comedy.

associate artist US euphemism for an accompanist. *See also* COLLABORATIVE PIANIST.

Association, the US pop group of the late 1960s, which had a string of close harmony SOFT ROCK hits. Formed in 1965, the Association was led by guitarist Russ Giguere (1943–) and bassist Brian Cole (1944–72), and it hit the headlines when it was banned from singing at Disneyland after its hit single 'Along Comes Mary' was alleged to be about marijuana. Subsequently the group dominated the charts with such songs as 'Cherish', 'Windy' and 'Never My Love' and starred at the MONTEREY POP FESTIVAL in 1967. It broke up in 1972 on the death of Cole from a drug overdose but reunited 1981–4 and in 1995 released the album *A Little Bit More*, as well as touring.

Association for Contemporary Music State organization that was founded in Soviet Russia in the 1920s with the express aim of encouraging new music. The Association was formed in response to the idea that the country was embarking on a new beginning and a new music would be appropriate in such a context. Such experimental composers as Alexander Mossolov (1900–73), Popov, Protopopov and Dmitri SHOSTAKOVICH were officially sanctioned by the new regime and given the chance to prove themselves 'worthy citizens' by creating such music. By 1931, however, the organization had been eclipsed by the RUSSIAN ASSOCIATION FOR PROLETARIAN MUSIC and such composers were now called to account for their 'formalist' tendencies. *See also* PORNOPHONY; SOCIALIST REALISM.

Astaire, Fred (Frederick Austerlitz; 1899–1987) US film star, dancer and singer, who was one of the most successful popular singers of the 1930s. Astaire's proverbial dancing ability as displayed (often in partnership with Ginger Rogers) in numerous Hollywood MUSICALS from the early 1930s onwards tended to mask his not inconsiderable talent as a singer. His precise and unhurried delivery of the songs of Jerome KERN, Cole PORTER, Irving BERLIN and George GERSHWIN marked him out as one of the finest interpreters of such music, and he was their first choice on many occasions. Among the classics most closely associated with his name were 'Lady be Good', 'Night and Day', 'The Way You Look Tonight', 'I Guess I'll Have to Change My Plan' and 'A Fine Romance', to name but a few.

As a songwriter himself – he admitted that he had always hoped to work primarily in this field – he penned such popular songs as 'Blue Without You' (1930), 'Rise and Shine' (1936) and 'Lovely Melody' (1956).

Can't act. Slightly bald. Can dance a little.
Conclusion of early Astaire screen test

Atkins, Chet (Chester Burton Atkins; 1924–) US COUNTRY-AND-WESTERN guitarist, nicknamed the Country Gentleman, who had a profound influence upon the development of country music in the 1940s and 1950s. Acclaimed as a performer himself, reaching a wide audience through appearances on the GRAND OLE OPRY, he took an executive role at a NASHVILLE recording studio and there pioneered the 'Nashville sound' in which increasing use was made of electronic instruments. He also promoted the early careers of a host of up-and-coming performers, among them Elvis PRESLEY, Jim REEVES and the EVERLY BROTHERS, and eventually became vice-president of RCA (1968). He was elected to the COUNTRY MUSIC HALL OF FAME in 1973.

Atlanta Pop Festival US rock festival, held in Atlanta in July 1969, which was the first major festival devoted to HARD ROCK. Some 14,000 people turned up to see, among others, CANNED HEAT, LED ZEPPELIN and Johnny WINTER.

Atlanta Rhythm Section US rock group, which established a strong following in the 1970s. The group – guitarists J.R. Cobb (1944–) and Barry Bailey (1948–), keyboard player Dean Daughtry (1946–), bassist Paul Goddard (1945–) and drummer Robert Nix – came together as backing musicians for Roy ORBISON and emerged as leading exponents of SOUTHERN ROCK, although gradually extending its repertoire to include a number of more thoughtful ballads. Hit singles included 'Doraville' (1974), 'So in to You' (1977) and 'Imaginary Lover' (1978); among the albums were *Atlanta Rhythm Section* (1972), *Dog Days* (1975) and *Champagne Jam* (1978).

Atlantic Records US record company, which was founded by Herb Abramson and Ahmet Ertegun in New York in 1947 and went on to sign up many hugely successful JAZZ, ROCK and POP acts. Initial releases included numerous jazz classics, but the label later diversified into RHYTHM-AND-BLUES and signed such stars as Ray CHARLES, Ruth BROWN, LaVern BAKER and the DRIFTERS. A new jazz division was established in 1956, and John COLTRANE, Charles MINGUS and Ornette COLEMAN were among those to record on Atlantic. An alliance was formed with STAX RECORDS in 1960, making Atlantic the leading SOUL label and distributor of hits by singers such as Otis REDDING. Success with a wider rock and pop audience in the 1960s was assured with the signing of such artists as CROSBY, STILLS, NASH AND YOUNG, LED ZEPPELIN, Eric CLAPTON and the BEE GEES. Atlantic became part of the Warner Communications empire in 1968.

atonality Umbrella term for various forms of modern classical music in which the emphasis is placed on atonal rather than diatonic principles (in other words, no key is used). The term has been used of such musical systems as SERIALISM and 12-NOTE MUSIC, although some composers preferred other titles to describe their work – Arnold SCHOENBERG, for instance, used the word pantonality, to avoid the implication that such compositions were simply deviant forms of tonal music.

> Atonality is against nature. There is a centre to everything that exists. The planets have the sun, the moon, the earth ... all music with a centre is tonal. Music without a centre is fine for a moment or two, but it soon sounds all the same.
> ALAN HOVHANNES

> We can no longer tolerate this fetishism of tonality, which has been a burden on entire generations of musicians.
> ARTHUR HONEGGER, I am a Composer, 1951

> Nowadays harmony comes almost as a shock.
> KATHLEEN RAINE, in letter to Arthur Bliss

Atwell, Winifred (Winifred Levishohn; 1914–83) Trinidadian pianist, resident in Australia from the 1960s, who enjoyed considerable fame as a novelty act of the mid-1950s. Playing a rickety piano (her 'other' piano) that had cost £2.50 in a Battersea junk shop, the generously built native of Port-of-Spain had two UK Number Ones, with 'Let's Have Another Party' (1954) and 'Poor People of Paris' (1956), making her the first Black musician to top the charts in the UK. Other hits included 'Black and

White Rag' (1952), 'Britannia Rag' (1953) and 'Coronation Rag' (1953). Her career effectively ended with the advent of ROCK 'N' ROLL. Before achieving fame playing boogie on her 'other' piano, she had trained as a qualified chemist in Trinidad and had also studied to become a classical pianist.

Aufderheide, May (Francis) (1888–1972) US composer and pianist, who was one of the most influential early pioneers of RAGTIME piano music. Her compositions, which were published with financial assistance from her businessman-father, included 'Dusty Rag' (1908), 'Buzzer Rag' (1909) and 'Novelty Rag' (1911).

Auger, Arleen (1939–93) US soprano, who established a reputation as one of the world's leading dramatic sopranos of her generation. Her greatest successes have included Mozart's *Exultate, Jubilate*, which she sang at the wedding of Prince Andrew in 1986.

Auger, Brian (1939–) British RHYTHM-AND-BLUES keyboard player, who played with many leading stars of the 1960s and 1970s. Having begun as a jazzman, Auger switched to R 'N' B in 1964 and went on to work with, among others, Rod STEWART, Alexis KORNER, Julie Driscoll and the YARDBIRDS (for whom he played harpsichord on 'For Your Love'). He later ventured into JAZZ-ROCK and continued to win acclaim for his occasional collaborations with Driscoll and other stars in the 1980s.

Auric, Georges (1899–1983) French composer, who was a member of Les SIX. Auric was something of a child prodigy, meeting Erik SATIE at the age of 14 and being hailed as one of the leading composers in Paris while still a young man. His works, which bore the influence of Igor STRAVINSKY, Maurice RAVEL, Arnold SCHOENBERG and popular music, included ballets for Serge Diaghilev's Ballets Russes and SOUNDTRACKS for the films of Jean Cocteau, with whom he enjoyed a long and fruitful association. His best-known work is probably the ballet *Les Matelots* (1925), though British film audiences would be more likely to recognize his soundtrack for the 1951 comedy thriller *The Lavender Hill Mob*.

Austin, Gene (Eugene Lucas; 1900–72) US singer, pianist, composer and lyricist, who enjoyed considerable success in the 1920s and 1930s as the Voice of the Southland. Austin ran away to the circus at the age of 15 before serving as a soldier in Mexico and in the First World War. He formed his first band in 1919 and became one of the first of the CROONERS, recording such hits as 'How Come You Do Me Like You Do?' (1924), 'My Blue Heaven' (1927), 'Ramona' (1928) and 'Carolina Moon' (1929). The extraordinary success of 'My Blue Heaven', which sold 5 million copies, remained unsurpassed until the release of Bing CROSBY's 'White Christmas'. He continued to record and write songs and to appear in films well into the 1930s; it is estimated that in all he sold some 86 million records between 1924 and 1942.

Australian Marie Lloyd, the *See* Florrie FORDE.

authentic music *See* EARLY MUSIC MOVEMENT.

Autry, Gene (1907–) US film actor and singer, nicknamed the Singing Cowboy, who became one of the most famous stars of the Hollywood western in the 1930s and 1940s. The son of a Baptist minister and quite unfamiliar with the world of the cowboy as a child, Autry (and his faithful horse Champion) sang his way through around 100 westerns and had a hand in writing many of the songs he sang himself, including 'That Silver-haired Daddy of Mine' (1931), 'Ridin' down the Canyon' (1931), 'Tumbling Tumbleweeds' (1936), 'South of the Border' (1939) and his theme song 'Back in the Saddle Again' (1940). His music had a marked influence on the development of COUNTRY-AND-WESTERN, although he also sang several songs on other subjects than the Wild West (among them 'Rudolph the Red-nosed Reindeer' and 'Frosty the Snowman'). It was largely through Autry's success – built on by his successor Roy ROGERS and others after the war – that a stylized Western costume became the accepted dress for virtually all country performers.

> Them bandits have beat up mah mother, ravished mah girl, burned down mah house, killed mah best friend and stolen mah prize cattle. Ah'm gonna git 'em if'n it's the last thing ah do – but first, folks, ah'm gonna sing ya a little song.
> Parody of Gene Autry in *Country Music Story*, 1966

Avalon, Frankie (Francis Thomas Avallone; 1940–) US pop singer, nicknamed the Golden Boy in reference to his teen-idol status in the mid-1950s; the huge sums Avalon earned from his hit singles were held in trust for him until 1961, when he reached the age of 21 and was able for the first time to taste the fruits of his success. Originally a trumpeter, Avalon switched to vocals in 1956, even though his voice was relatively weak, and he reached a national audience through the television programme *American Bandstand*. His hits included 'DeDe Dinah' (1958), 'Ginger Bread' (1958), 'Venus' (1959), 'From Bobby Sox to Stockings' (1959) and 'Why' (1960), which got to Number One. He also starred in several films, still preserving his cleancut, wholesome image, as well as playing a teen-idol in the film of the musical *Grease* (1978). The success of his first hit, 'DeDe Dinah', depended heavily upon the novelty of Avalon's singing voice, the potential of which was only realized after he recorded the song holding his nose as a joke.

avant-garde Term used to describe the people and works that represent the most progressive elements in one of the arts. First heard in the early 1900s, the term was commonly applied to certain groups of writers, artists, film-makers and musicians after the Second World War. The classical musical avant-garde has at various times included such names as Pierre BOULEZ, Karlheinz STOCKHAUSEN and Luciano BERIO (*see also* MODERNISM), although the term is not confined to the classics alone. Even HEAVY METAL claims its avant-garde, represented by such as Celtic Frost, Gong and Henry Cow.

> When a work of art appears to be in advance of its period, it is really the period that has lagged behind the work of art.
> JEAN COCTEAU, *Le Coq et l'arlequin*, 1918

Average White Band Scottish SOUL group of the 1970s, which enjoyed particular success in the USA. Formed in 1972, the Average White Band rapidly established its reputation as a leading white FUNK band, supporting Eric CLAPTON on tour in 1973 and reaching Number One in the USA with the album *AWB* (1974). The line-up included guitarists Onnie McIntyre (1945–) and Hamish Stuart (1949–), singer and bassist Alan Gorrie (1946–), saxophonist and keyboard player Roger Ball (1944–), Malcolm 'Molly' Duncan (1945–) and drummer Robbie McIntosh

(1950–74). The death of McIntosh from a heroin overdose in 1974 was a blow, but the band continued to consolidate its US standing, where it was by then based, producing a series of albums and hit singles until 1982, when it broke up, although the remaining members came briefly together once more in 1989 and for a 1994 tour.

axe Slang for the ELECTRIC GUITAR, as wielded in an axe-like manner by numerous frenzied players ('axe-heroes') over the years. In fact, back in the 1930s Black JAZZ musicians often called their instruments axes, especially when talking of the saxophone or the trumpet.

Axton, Hoyt (1938–) US singer-songwriter and actor, who wrote many classic COUNTRY and pop songs. He made his recording début in 1957 and penned hits for such singers as THREE DOG NIGHT (notably 'Joy to the World' in 1971), Waylon JENNINGS, Glen CAMPBELL, John DENVER and Ringo STARR. His own hits included 'When the Morning Comes' (1974), 'Flash of Fire' (1976), 'Della and the Dealer' (1979) and 'Rusty Old Halo' (1979). Songwriting evidently ran in the family: Axton's mother, Mae Boren Axton, composed Elvis PRESLEY's 'Heartbreak Hotel'. As an actor, Axton appeared in the films *ET* (1983) and *Gremlins* (1984).

Ayer, Nat D. (1887–1952) US composer and pianist, resident in the UK from 1911, who wrote many highly successful musicals for the London stage. His hit shows included *The Bing Boys are Here* (1916), *Look Who's Here* (1916), *The Bing Boys on Broadway* (1918), *Baby Bunting* (1919) and *Somewhere in England* (1939). Among his hit songs were 'Oh, You Beautiful Doll' (1911) and 'If You Were the Only Girl in the World' (1916).

Ayers, Roy (1940–) US vibraphonist and singer, who emerged as a leading JAZZ FUNK star of the 1970s and 1980s. Given his first instrument as a child by Lionel HAMPTON, Ayers led a variety of notable bands before acquiring a reputation as one of the most talented explorers of various FUSION styles, mixing the BLUES, jazz, SOUL, RHYTHM-AND-BLUES and ROCK elements. His group Ubiquity, formed in 1970, released several influential albums and enjoyed a major disco hit with 'Running Away' (1977). His collaborators have included George BENSON and Fela KUTI. More recent albums have included *In* the Dark (1984) and *You Might be Surprised* (1985).

Ayler, Albert (1936–70) US JAZZ saxophonist, who was considered one of the most talented players of his generation before his death in mysterious circumstances in 1970. Having begun as alto saxophonist with his father's band, Ayler emerged as a leading AVANT-GARDE musician in the mid-1960s but provoked much controversy with his unconventional playing. He rejected the label 'jazz' and sought a fresh, emotionally charged form in which melody played a dominant role and rhythm was often ignored (against the current trend away from melody and towards rhythmic complexity). His most remarkable compositions included 'Mothers' and 'Ghosts'.

He went missing; his body was found in New York's East River and rumours that he had been shot in the neck on police orders were rife (though a verdict of accidental death was eventually decided and friends revealed he had talked of committing suicide not long before). One rumour had it that his corpse was discovered tied to a juke box. In the UK, the BBC quietly erased tapes they held of his music for fear of the furore his innovative music might cause.

> I like to play something that people can hum ... songs like I used to sing when I was real small.
> ALBERT AYLER

Aznavour, Charles (Shanaur Varenagh Aznavourian; 1924–) French-born Armenian singer, actor and composer, who first became a huge popular star in the 1950s. Having written the hit song 'J'ai bu', he was taken up by the great Edith PIAF, for whom he wrote such classics as 'Il pleut' (1949) and 'Il y avait' (1950) and ventured his first appearances as a singer in his own right. These were not initially well received, one critic rounding savagely on him with the now-infamous review:

> To put oneself before the public with such a voice and such a physique is pure folly!

Hordes of female admirers vehemently disagreed, however, and responded with enthusiasm to his blend of appealing if not exactly classically handsome looks and often melancholy songs. He soon had a worldwide reputation and consolidated his success by appearing in a host of successful films. His most successful songs include 'Il faut savoir' (1949), 'Je t'attends' (1961), 'La mamma' (1964), 'She', which enjoyed four weeks at the top of the UK chart in 1974 and 'The Old-fashioned Way' (1974).

Happy people have nothing to tell.

CHARLES AZNAVOUR, of his often sombre songs, quoting a traditional French saying

B

B–52s US NEW WAVE band, which created a considerable stir with its eccentric ways in the late 1970s. Formed in Georgia in 1976 by brother and sister Ricky Wilson (1953–85) and Cindy Wilson (1957–), the B–52s borrowed the nickname of the bouffant hairstyles that were popular in the 1950s (named in turn after the US military aircraft). Other members of the band were singer Fred Schneider (1954–), drummer Keith Strickland (1953–) and singer and keyboard player Kate Pierson (1948–). Mixing elements of POP, ROCKABILLY and FUNK, it established a niche on both sides of the Atlantic with hits including 'Rock Lobster' (1979) and the albums *The B–52s* and *Wild Planet*. Its progress was interrupted in 1985 by the death of Ricky Wilson but recovered with *Cosmic Thing* (1989) and *Good Stuff* (1992).

Babbitt, Milton (Byron) (1916–) US composer, who became one of the leading proponents of SERIALISM. Having studied mathematics, he collaborated with Roger SESSIONS and produced some radical and very strict serial music in which he made extensive use of electronic instruments. His other works included string quartets, *Philomel* (1964), for soprano and tape, and *Melismata* (1982).

> The 12-tone set must absolutely determine every aspect of the piece ... I believe in cerebral music and I never choose a note unless I know why I want it there.
> MILTON BABBITT

Bacharach, Burt (1928–) US songwriter and conductor, who produced much popular light music in collaboration with Hal David (1921–). He aimed originally at a career as a footballer but became interested in BEBOP and formed his own band, appearing alongside such jazz legends as Dizzy GILLESPIE and Charlie PARKER. He worked as arranger and accompanist for Marlene DIETRICH among other stars before establishing a reputation as a songwriter. His most successful songs, written for such singers as

Gene PITNEY, Perry COMO, Tom JONES and Dionne WARWICK and often composed in collaboration with lyricist Hal David, have included 'Magic Moments', 'Walk on By', 'What the World Needs Now is Love', 'I'll Never Fall in Love Again', 'Do You Know the Way to San José', 'Alfie' and 'This Guy's in Love with You'. He has also written much film music, winning an OSCAR for 'Raindrops Keep Falling on My Head' from *Butch Cassidy and the Sundance Kid* (1969), and enjoyed success with the stage MUSICAL *Promises, Promises* (1968). He split with David after a quarrel in 1973. He won another Oscar for 'Arthur's Theme' (1981) before teaming up with (and marrying) singer-songwriter Carol Bayer Sager (1946–).

Bachman-Turner Overdrive Canadian rock group, which enjoyed commercial success on both sides of the Atlantic in the 1970s. Singer and guitarist Randy Bachman (1943–), bassist Fred Turner (1943–), drummer Robbie Bachman (1953–) and (from 1974) guitarist Blair Thornton (1950–) emerged from Randy Bachman's previous group, Guess Who, in 1972 and enjoyed their biggest hit with the raunchy single 'You Ain't Seen Nothing Yet' (1974), which reached Number One in the USA and number two in the UK. Other hits before the band petered out in the mid-1980s included the albums *Not Fragile* (1974) and *Four Wheel Drive* (1975). The tag Overdrive was borrowed from the title of a US truckers' magazine.

backbeat Style of JAZZ drumming, in which the offbeat is stressed, as also in many RHYTHM-AND-BLUES and ROCK 'N' ROLL pieces.

Bad Company British rock band, which was formed in 1973 by former members of FREE, MOTT THE HOOPLE and KING CRIMSON. The band – singer Paul Rodgers (1949–), drummer Simon Kirke (1949–), guitarist Mick Ralphs (1944–) and bassist

Boz Burrell (1946–) – enjoyed commercial success throughout the 1970s and early 1980s with such albums as *Bad Company* (1974), *Straight Shooter* (1975) and *Rough Diamonds* (1984), which included such straightforward rock classics as 'Can't Get Enough'. The band split in 1983 but was re-formed without vocalist Rodgers in 1986 and continued in a more melodic soft-rock vein.

Bad Manners British pop group of the late 1970s, which enjoyed commercial success with its brand of lighthearted SKA music. Led by the somewhat overweight, shavenheaded and manic Buster Bloodvessel (Douglas Trendle; 1958–), the band attracted media interest with its extravagant costumes and anarchic humour. Hit singles included 'Lip Up Fatty', 'Special Brew' (written in praise of Carlsberg lager), 'Lorraine' (which was addressed to an inflatable doll) and 'Can Can', while the album *Gosh It's Bad Manners* (1981) also did well in the charts. Ska went out of fashion in 1982 but the band continued to tour and release further albums in the same style.

Badfinger British pop group of the late 1960s and early 1970s, which prospered through its association with the BEATLES. Settling down with a line-up of guitarists Pete Ham (1947–75) and Joey Molland (1948–), bassist Tom Evans (1947–83) and drummer Mike Gibbins (1949–), Badfinger was signed by the APPLE label. Paul MCCARTNEY recorded 'Day after Day' with the group, while Ringo STARR's film *The Magic Christian* featured a SOUNDTRACK by Badfinger. Todd RUNDGREN produced the albums *No Dice* (1970) and *Straight Up* (1971), and members of the band also played on solo albums by George HARRISON, John LENNON and Ringo Starr. Hit singles included 'Maybe Tomorrow', 'No Matter What' and 'Baby Blue'. It all petered out, however, in the mid-1970s and Ham hanged himself in 1975, blaming the music business and the group's US manager in his suicide note. The band was re-formed in 1978 and enjoyed some minor success before Evans also hanged himself after a bitter argument over the royalties due on the Ham/Evans hit 'Without You' (recorded by Harry NILSSON in 1972), following which the group relocated to the USA.

Baez, Joan (1941–) US FOLK-singer, who was famous as one of the leading PROTEST SONG performers of the 1960s. Having sprung to fame after appearing at the NEWPORT FOLK FESTIVAL in 1963, Baez formed a temporary partnership with Bob DYLAN and became a figurehead for social protest in the 1960s. Dylan accompanied her on long anti-racist and anti-war tours, but the collaboration eventually broke down as Dylan tired of being considered a political leader and Baez grew frustrated at his indulgence in a rock star life-style (Dylan retaliated by nicknaming her 'the most beautiful nun'). Her most celebrated recording was of Pete SEEGER's classic 'We Shall Overcome', which was adopted as an anthem by the civil rights movement. In 1965 Baez founded an Institute for the Study of Non-violence and for a time sacrificed her music to her pursuit of various political ideals. (She was imprisoned in 1967 for civil disobedience after an anti-Vietnam demonstration, and her husband David Harris went to gaol in 1969 after refusing to be drafted.) She returned to music in 1975 with the deliberately commercial *Diamonds and Rust*, excusing herself on the grounds that she needed the money (the title song of the album referred to her affair with Dylan); other releases explored new musical directions with COVER versions of songs by such artists as U2 and PINK FLOYD. For her continuing championship of humanitarian causes in many parts of the world she received the accolade of Chevalier de la Légion d'honneur.

Bailey, De Ford (1899–1982) Black US harmonica-player, nicknamed the Harmonica Wizard, who was the first Black artist to appear regularly on the GRAND OLE OPRY. Playing BLUES numbers and traditional dance music, he starred with the show through the late 1920s and 1930s at a rate of just $5 a time. By 1941, when he was dropped from the programme, he was reduced to running a shoeshine stand – although he was invited back on the *Opry* in the 1970s. He is also thought to have been the first performer to make records in NASHVILLE.

Bailey, Mildred (Mildred Rinker; 1907–51) US BLUES and JAZZ singer, nicknamed the Rockin' Chair Lady after one of her hits, who was one of the first White vocalists to establish a reputation singing in a jazz style. In the 1930s and 1940s she performed and recorded with many famous figures, including Benny GOODMAN, her husband the xylophonist Red NORVO, Paul WHITEMAN and Teddy WILSON, as well as appearing as a solo artist with considerable success and entertaining on her own radio show. A large woman, she died penniless of heart-related problems at the age of 44.

Bailey, Norman (1933–   ) British baritone, who has established a reputation as a leading Wagnerian. Having trained in South Africa and at the Vienna Music Academy, he won praise in major roles in several Austrian and German companies in the 1960s before joining the Sadler's Wells company (1967–71).

Bailey, Pearl (1918–90) Black US JAZZ singer, who enjoyed a long and varied career both as a vocalist with leading bands and as a soloist on the Broadway stage. Having established herself singing at various New York clubs and at the APOLLO THEATRE in Harlem, she consolidated her reputation appearing with the bands of such respected jazzmen as Cab CALLOWAY before embarking on a career on Broadway, as well as appearing in a number of films. Her many hits included 'Tired' (1947), 'Saturday Night Fish Fry' (1949) and 'Takes Two to Tango' (1952). Of her MUSICALS, the most successful was her starring role in an all-Black *Hello, Dolly!* (1967); others included *St Louis Woman* (1946) and *Bless You All* (1950).

Baillie, Dame Isobel (1895–1983) Scottish soprano, nicknamed Bella Baillie, who was highly acclaimed for her performances of the works of Handel and Brahms among other classical composers. She made her début in London in 1923 and established herself as one of the most popular sopranos of her generation. It is estimated that she sang Handel's oratorio *Messiah* over 1,000 times.

> I have never found her anything but noteperfect.
> SIR HENRY WOOD

Baker, Chet (Chesney H. Baker; 1929–88) US JAZZ trumpeter and singer, who was considered one of the foremost exponents of 'cool' jazz. After his discharge from the army, he played with Charlie PARKER and other greats of the 1950s but fell prey to the pressures of leading his own band, finding solace in drugs, to which he became addicted. Other setbacks included losing many of his teeth after being mugged in San Francisco in 1968. He continued to appear in public, however, into the 1980s, when he guested with such pop artists as Elvis COSTELLO. He died after falling, or jumping, from a hotel window in Amsterdam. His life was chronicled in the film *Let's Get Lost* (1989).

> Nothing's that funny.
> CHET BAKER, after a colleague dismissed Baker's many wrinkles as laughlines

Baker, George (1885–1976) British baritone, who was particularly popular in roles from the operettas of Gilbert and Sullivan. One of the first artists to establish a reputation in the recording studio, he sang mainly light opera and was still performing into his eighties.

Baker, Dame Janet (1933–   ) British mezzo-soprano, who was widely recognized as one of the leading singers of the postwar era. She sang a wide range of roles but was particularly admired for her interpretations of the romantic song-cycles of Gustav MAHLER and Richard STRAUSS and for her long association with the works of Benjamin BRITTEN (the part of Kate in his 1971 television opera *Owen Wingrave* was written for her). She made both her COVENT GARDEN and New York débuts to great acclaim in 1966 and eventually retired from opera while still at her best in 1982, her last part being Orfeo in Gluck's eponymous opera.

> I'm a performer by birth, but not by nature. I go into the music of an opera naked and raw and defenceless, because no other way can I perform.
> JANET BAKER, 1971

Baker, Josephine (1906–75) Black US singer and dancer, who first emerged as a star of revue in Paris in the 1920s. She diversified into variety, operetta and films, acquiring a somewhat scandalous reputation built on her extravagant stage appearances. Celebrated highlights of her early career included the revue *Un Vent du folie* (1927), in which she appeared with two cheetahs and was decorated only with a string of fake bananas, and appearances alongside Maurice CHEVALIER. She often sang without a microphone; hit songs included her signature tune 'J'ai deux amours'. She was honoured by the award of the Croix de Guerre for her work with the French Resistance in the Second World War, and after the war she opened an orphanage in the Dordogne, which she funded with further stage appearances. She continued to top bills in musical productions and revues in Paris, New York and London into her old age, appearing for the last time just five days before her death.

Baker, Kenny (1921–   ) British trumpeter, bandleader and composer, who first emerged as one of the most capable JAZZ musicians in the UK in the 1940s. Having begun his career playing in brass bands, he went on to play for such respected bandleaders as Jack HYLTON and Ted HEATH before leading his own Baker's Dozen in the 1950s, since when he has continued to make regular recordings and appearances with prominent contemporaries. His music was heard by a wide audience in the late 1980s when he recorded the soundtrack for the popular television series *The Beiderbecke Affair* and *The Beiderbecke Tapes*. He also won acclaim in 1989 for recordings recreating the Louis ARMSTRONG sound.

Baker, LaVern (1928–97) Black US RHYTHM-AND-BLUES singer, nicknamed Little Miss Sharecropper (in reference to her rural origins, a sharecropper being a tenant farmer), who was one of the top r 'n' b artists of the late 1950s. With a background as a gospel singer, she moved into r 'n' b as a teenager and shared top billing with Ruth BROWN with such hits as 'Jim Dandy' (1956), 'That's All I Need' (1955), 'Tweedle Dee' (1955) and 'I Cried a Tear' (1959). She continued to record into the 1960s, her best albums including *LaVern Baker Sings Bessie Smith*. Her music had a profound influence upon the early development of pop and she was also credited with having taught Johnnie RAY how to sing the blues.

Balearic Genre of DISCO music of the 1980s. The name reflects the popularity of such music – generally cheerful if brainless uptempo chart successes – which was played at the various holiday destinations in the Balearic islands (including Majorca and Minorca) that were popular with British tourists.

Ball, Eric (Walter John) (1903–89) British composer, arranger and conductor, who became one of the most respected composers for the brass band and choir. Many of his works were written for use by Salvation Army bands, several of which he conducted himself, and for other top brass ensembles with which he was connected, including the Brighouse & Rastrick Band. Among his best-known compositions are 'The Conquerors', 'Akhnaton', 'Rosslyn' and 'Torch of Freedom'.

Ball, Ernest R. (1878–1927) US composer, who had a huge commercial impact with a series of classics written in a broad 'Irish' style. Such songs as 'Mother Macree' (1910), 'When Irish Eyes are Smiling' (1913) and 'A Little Bit of Heaven' (1915) quickly attained the status of standards and provided stars such as John McCORMACK with some of their greatest hits; others included 'Will You Love Me in December as You Do in May?' (1905), 'Till the Sands of the Desert Grow Cold' (1911) and 'Let the Rest of the World Go By' (1919).

Ball, Kenny (1930–   ) British JAZZ trumpeter and bandleader, who became one of the most widely known exponents of TRAD jazz in the 1960s. Kenny Ball and his Jazzmen enjoyed such hits as 'Samantha', 'Midnight in Moscow' and 'March of the Siamese Children' and have continued to tour widely through the UK, Europe and the USA. He was made an honorary citizen of New Orleans in 1963. In 1981 he was invited to play at the wedding reception of Prince Charles and the Princess of Wales.

Ballard, Hank (1936–   ) US RHYTHM-AND-BLUES singer-songwriter, who had numerous hits in the 1950s. He is usually remembered for his song 'The Twist', which became a huge international hit when it was covered by Chubby CHECKER in 1960. Other notable songs included the daring 'Work With Me Annie' (1954) and its sequels 'Annie Had a Baby' and 'Annie's Aunt Fanny', 'Teardrops on Your Letter' (1958) and 'Finger Poppin' Time' (1960). Later releases failed to make much impact. 'The Twist' was given to Chubby Checker after Ballard failed to turn up to perform it on *American Bandstand*, and Checker was recruited at the last minute to fill in for him.

Bananarama British pop trio, whose series of hit singles in the 1980s made them the most successful UK all-female group in pop history. Sarah Dallin, Keren Woodward and Siobhan Fahey came together in 1981 and enjoyed their first hits in collaboration with the Funboy Three (notably with 'It Ain't What You Do'). Other hits included 'Na Na Hey Hey, Kiss Him Goodbye', 'Robert De Niro's Waiting', 'Venus', 'I Heard a Rumour' and 'I Want You Back'. Fahey left in 1988 and went on to form the successful duo Shakespear's Sister with Marcella Detroit. She was replaced by Jacquie Sullivan. The band was among the stars recruited for the BAND AID effort of 1984. Sullivan left in 1992 and the group continued as a duo.

Band, the US-Canadian rock band of the 1960s and 1970s, which sprang to fame through their association with Bob DYLAN. Guitarist Jaime 'Robbie' Robertson (1943–), organist Garth Hudson (1937–), singer and pianist Richard Manuel (1943–86), bassist Rick Danko (1942–) and drummer and singer Levon Helm (1943–) teamed up with Dylan in 1965, enjoying a dual career as his backing group and as a band in their own right. The group's albums included *Music from Big Pink* (1968), *The Band* (1969) and *Rock of Ages* (1971). An emotional last concert, at Winterland in San Francisco in 1976, was filmed by Martin Scorsese as *The Last Waltz*. The individual members then went their separate ways: Robertson went into films, but the others experienced something of a decline, and Manuel eventually hanged himself. The remaining members of the group reunited for further live performances in the late 1980s.

Band Aid The all-star SUPERGROUP assembled in 1984 by Bob GELDOF to raise money for the starving in Africa. Geldof managed to galvanize the British pop establishment with his demands for action to help those threatened by famine in Ethiopia and elsewhere, and he teamed up with Midge Ure (see ULTRAVOX) to write the moving single 'Do They Know It's Christmas?' for performance by some of the best-known names in contemporary pop. Sales of the single exceeded all expectations, and it went straight in at Number One in the charts, remaining there for five weeks and becoming the best-selling single of all time in the UK. The single returned to the top three the following Christmas, by which time Geldof had been persuaded into organizing the almost legendary LIVE AID concert.

As well as Geldof and Ure, Band Aid included Adam Clayton and Bono from U2; Phil COLLINS; Johnny Fingers, Simon Crowe and Peter Briquette from the BOOMTOWN RATS; David BOWIE; Paul MCCARTNEY; Holly Johnson from FRANKIE GOES TO HOLLYWOOD; Chriss Cross from ULTRAVOX; Simon Le Bon, Nick Rhodes, Andy Taylor, John Taylor and Roger Taylor from DURAN DURAN; Paul YOUNG; Tony Hadley, Martin Kemp, John Keeble, Gary Kemp and Steve Norman from SPANDAU BALLET; Glenn Gregory and Martyn Ware from Heaven 17; Francis Rossi and Rick Parfitt from STATUS QUO; Sting (see the POLICE); Jon Moss and BOY GEORGE from Culture Club; Keren Woodward, Sarah Dallin and Siobhan Fahey from BANANARAMA; Marilyn; Jody Watley from Shalamar; Paul Weller (see the JAM) from the Style Council; Robert Bell, James Taylor and Dennis Thomas from Kool and the Gang; and George MICHAEL.

band names From the earliest days of ROCK 'N' ROLL, pop and rock musicians have prided themselves on thinking up novel and arresting names for their bands in the hope that they will stick in the minds of the buying public and convey the kind of image they seek to establish. Names were relatively conventional in the 1950s, with most bands being named after their leader – as in Bill HALEY and the Comets or Johnny KIDD and the Pirates – or else being a little more adventurous and opting for such relatively straightforward tags as the SHADOWS, the PLATTERS and the DRIFTERS. Perhaps the most popular category of name of the late 1950s and 1960s was animals, as evidenced by such bands as the Crickets, the BEATLES, the ANIMALS, the BYRDS, the MONKEES and even the long-extinct Tyrannosaurus Rex. Later bands preferred references to parts of the body, as in Little Feat, Stiff Little Fingers, TALKING HEADS and the Butts Band. Still more were happy with anything as long as it was zanier or more obscure than anything else around at the time – as the following list of more unusual band names testifies:

Anthrax
Atomic Rooster
Bedbugs
Blue Oyster Cult
Bow Wow Wow
Brewer's Droop (led by Mark Knopfler)
Chord-A-Roys
Crypt-Kickers Five

Dead Kennedys
Disco Turkeys
Disposable Heroes of Hip Hoprisy
Echo and the Bunnymen
The Forever Ancients Liberation
  Loophole
Hedgehoppers Anonymous
Inspiral Carpets
Main Ingredient
Manic Street Preachers
Mark Skid and the Y-Fronts (later the
  Boomtown Rats)
Marmalade
Meatloaf
Mott the Hoople
Mumps
Orchestral Manoeuvres in the Dark
Prefab Sprout
Procul Harum
Rigamorticians
Sigue Sigue Sputnik
Snake Stretchers
Spooky Tooth
Teardrop Explodes
Three Dog Night
Two Puerto Ricans, a Black Man and a
  Dominican
Two Tons of Fun
Vanilla Fudge
Venereal and the Diseases (later
  James)
Weather Report
ZZ Top

band rat A female who follows a group around, often offering sex in exchange for a share of its celebrity status. *See also* GROUPIE.

Bandy, Moe (1944–   ) US COUNTRY singer, who emerged as a top country star in the 1970s. Having switched to music after failing to succeed as a rodeo rider, Bandy attracted a loyal following with such perky honky-tonk style numbers as 'I Just Started Hatin' Cheatin' Songs Today' (1974), 'Honky-tonk Amnesia' (1974), 'Hank Williams, You Wrote My Life' (1975), 'Just Good Ol' Boys' (1979), 'Holding the Bag' (1979), 'Yesterday Once More' (1980) and 'Where's the Dress?' (1984), which lampooned the drag acts of BOY GEORGE and other contemporary pop stars. Many of his later hits were recorded as duets with Joe Stampley (1943–   ).

Bang Gang Derogatory twentieth-century nickname for the percussion section of an orchestra, otherwise known as the kitchen department. *See also* TIMPS.

The percussion and the bass . . . function as a central heating system.
IGOR STRAVINSKY

Then there was a terrible moment when Muir Matheson once asked one of the percussion players to 'give that thing a good bang three bars before C'. It was a cymbal, I think, and Jimmy didn't like it being insulted. 'Mister Matheson,' he said. 'It isn't a thingg – it's a cymball; and he dusn't bangg it – he *draws* the *toan* out of it!'
JACK BRYMER, *From Where I Sit*, 1979

Banjo Eyes *See* Eddie CANTOR.

Bantock, Sir Granville (1868–1946) British composer and conductor, who was greatly respected for his many works written in a conservative, early romantic style. His best-known works include his setting for the *Omar Kháyyám* (1906–9) and the *Hebridean Symphony* (1916), and he also wrote ballets, several operas and much instrumental music.

Barber, Chris (1930–   ) British trombonist, bandleader and composer, whose long-lived band became one of the best known in traditional British JAZZ. Barber became leader of his band in the mid-1950s, when Lonnie DONEGAN was one of the players, and he created his own distinct trombone-led style. His adoption of a ROCK-influenced sound on such traditional classics as 'Rock Island Line' did much to promote the development of SKIFFLE and British RHYTHM-AND-BLUES, bringing jazz and early rock audiences together. The band enjoyed a string of chart hits (including 'Whistling Rufus', 'Bobby Shafto' and 'Petite Fleur') in the 1950s, and it was the first British band to appear on the Ed Sullivan show in the USA.

Barber, Samuel (1910–81) US composer, who won many major awards for compositions written over a career of some 50 years. His best-known works, which hark back to the nineteenth century, include such early romantic pieces as the *Adagio for Strings* (1938) and the more dissonant violin concerto (1941) as well as symphonies, chamber music, choral music and three operas.

I have always believed that I need a circumference of silence. As to what happens when I compose, I really haven't the faintest idea.
SAMUEL BARBER

Barbican Arts complex on the South Bank of

the Thames in London, which is home to the LONDON SYMPHONY ORCHESTRA. The complex, which also houses the Guildhall School of Music and Drama, was opened in 1982, although it had been conceived as early as 1955 as part of the plans to redevelop the sites damaged by bombs in the Second World War.

Barbirolli, Sir John (Giovanni Battista Barbirolli; 1899–1970) British conductor, of French-Italian parentage, who was particularly admired as a conductor of romantic music, especially that of Sir Edward ELGAR, Frederick DELIUS and Ralph VAUGHAN WILLIAMS – who dubbed him Glorious John. Barbirolli began his career as a cellist but worked as conductor with such important orchestras as the NEW YORK PHILHARMONIC (1937–43) and the HALLÉ ORCHESTRA (1943–68), earning the sobriquet the Last Romantic.

Like other leading conductors of his day, he was renowned for his energy and often scathing wit:

> You're singing about Angels and Archangels, not Gold Flake and Players.
> SIR JOHN BARBIROLLI, to a chorus under his baton

and on another occasion, to another chorus:

> I want you to sound like 22 women having babies *without* chloroform.

> Barbirolli has worked wonders with the Hallé. He has transformed it into the finest chamber orchestra in the country.
> SIR THOMAS BEECHAM

Barclay James Harvest British rock band, which enjoyed some success as a leading PROGRESSIVE ROCK outfit in the late 1960s and early 1970s. Guitarist John Lees (1948–), drummer Melvyn Pritchard (1948–), bassist Les Holroyd (1948–) and keyboard player Stuart 'Woolley' Wolstenholme (1947–) came together in 1966 and went on to release a series of hit albums, the best including *Time Honoured Ghosts* (1975) and *Gone to Earth* (1977). Personnel changes disrupted further progress, despite an acclaimed free concert given on the steps of the Reichstag in Berlin in 1980, which spawned a successful live album. Later releases throughout the 1980s sold particularly well in Europe.

Bard of Barking, the *See* Billy BRAGG.

Bard of the Bedsits, the *See* Leonard COHEN.

Barenboim, Daniel (1942–) Israeli pianist and conductor, born in Buenos Aires, who has held a number of prestigious conducting posts with such orchestras as the ENGLISH CHAMBER ORCHESTRA and the Orchestre de Paris. He was taught the piano by his parents and has played with and conducted many of the best orchestras in both Europe and the USA. As a pianist, his recordings include complete sets of Mozart's piano concertos and of the piano sonatas and concertos of Beethoven. His career has not been without its moments of controversy – his departure from the Orchestre de Paris in 1988 being a particularly bitter incident for all concerned (he then accepted the baton of the CHICAGO SYMPHONY ORCHESTRA). He was married to the cellist Jacqueline DU PRÉ.

Barnet, Charlie (1913–91) US bandleader, saxophonist and composer, who was one of the most popular exponents of SWING in the 1930s and 1940s. Having joined his first JAZZ band at the age of 16, he confirmed his popular standing in 1939 with his recording of 'Cherokee', which was followed by such hits as 'Things Ain't What They Used To Be', 'That Old Black Magic', 'Where was I?' and 'Skyliner'. Another hit, 'We're All Burnt Up', was his laconic response to the loss of his band's instruments in a fire. Born into a wealthy New York family, Barnet enjoyed a life-style denied to many less prosperous jazzmen, but he improved the lot of many less fortunate Black players by including both Black and White musicians in his own band as early as 1935. He broke up his famous big band in 1949 and worked mostly with smaller ensembles. He was reputed to have been married 11 times.

barrelhouse A rowdy piano-playing style, which was adopted by the resident pianists who entertained drinkers in US drinking dens where liquor (usually bootleg) was served from makeshift bars of planks and barrels. Such music was loud and rough, with elements of BOOGIE-WOOGIE. The pianists themselves adopted the style out of necessity, playing on inadequate instruments that had to be treated with some vigour if anything was to be heard above the general din (which was often intensified by the presence of a JUKE BOX). *See also* HONKY-TONK.

Barry, John (John Barry Prendergast;

1933–   ) British composer and arranger,
who is well known for his numerous compositions for the cinema. As a teenager he
worked in his father's cinemas but formed
the John Barry Seven in the late 1950s,
eventually rising to the post of musical
director for EMI. His many SOUNDTRACKS
have included those for *From Russia with
Love* (1963) and several subsequent James
Bond movies, the two OSCAR-winning
scores for *Born Free* (1966) and *The Lion in
Winter* (1968), *Superman 2* (1980), *Body
Heat* (1981) and *Out of Africa*, which
brought him a third Oscar in 1985.

Bart, Lionel (Lionel Begleiter; 1930–   )
British composer and lyricist, who is best
known for the hit MUSICAL *Oliver!* (1960).
Bart (who began as a member of the
SKIFFLE group the Cavemen, alongside
Tommy STEELE) first emerged as a composer and lyricist of promise while with Joan
Littlewood's Theatre Workshop in the
1950s, his contributions to that enterprise
including the music and lyrics of *Fings
Ain't Wot They Used T'Be* (1959) and then
Oliver! itself. *Blitz* (1962) and *Maggie May*
(1964) were moderately well received but
confirmed Bart as the decade's leading
composer of musicals. Somewhat against
expectations, however, his career then
took a permanent nosedive with *Twang!!*
(1965), a musical version of the adventures of Robin Hood, which failed to please
the critics and resulted in Bart himself
being declared bankrupt (Noël COWARD
was among those who advised Bart against
putting the show on). Hit songs for the POP
market included Cliff RICHARD's 'Living
Doll'.

Bartók, Béla (1881–1945) Hungarian
pianist and composer, who is often
described as the most important of all
Hungarian musicians. Acclaimed for his
research into, and use of, traditional FOLK
MUSIC in his compositions, he produced a
body of work that included six string quartets, three piano concertos, the opera *Duke
Bluebeard's Castle* (1911) and much
orchestral writing, of which the most
popular remains the *Concerto for Orchestra*
(1943). He described the process of composition as similar to a wrestling bout (he
actually entitled one piano piece *Wrestling*)
and also explored so-called 'night music',
which was inspired by his fascination with
birds and insects. Bartók's admirers hailed
his incorporation and redefinition of traditional themes in his work, although some
critics found him cold and unappealing:

> He not only never wears his heart on his
> sleeve; he seems to have deposited it in
> some bank vault.
> COLIN WILSON, *Brandy of the Damned*, 1964

> Bartók ... was completely inhuman. He
> hardly existed as a personality, but his
> impersonality was tremendous – he was
> the living incarnation and embodiment of
> the spirit of music. He was pure spirit, in
> fact, and his frail, intense and delicate
> physique gave the impression of some-
> thing ethereal and disembodied, like a
> flame burning in oxygen.
> CECIL GRAY, *Musical Chairs*, 1948

Bartók emigrated to the USA in 1940 and
died there in conditions of poverty from
leukaemia, his health destroyed by the
arduous tours he was obliged to
undertake:

> The trouble is that I have to go with so
> much still to say.
> BÉLA BARTÓK, on his deathbed

Bartolozzi, Bruno (1911–   ) Italian composer, who was a leading proponent of
SERIALISM in the postwar years. His best-
known works include the *Concerto for
Orchestra* (1952) and *Collage* (1967). His
distinctive chord formations, described in
his book *New Sounds for Woodwind* (1967),
came to be called 'Bartolozzi sounds'.

Basie, Count (William Basie; 1904–84) US
Black JAZZ pianist, composer and bandleader, who was one of the giants of
twentieth-century SWING. Hailing from
Red Bank, New Jersey, Basie was a pianist
in the dance halls of Harlem and had
lessons from Fats WALLER before embarking
on tours with a number of leading bands.
A radio announcer in Kansas City, where
he was appearing in 1936, dubbed him
'Count' and the tag stuck.
    By the end of the 1930s his band
(formed in 1935) was recognized as the
finest of all the swing outfits, and it
remained in demand with a succession of
great soloists until the 1960s. Among the
musicians appearing with the Count were
the near-legendary rhythm section including guitarist Freddie Green, bassist Walter
Page and drummer Jo Jones, and the brilliant tenor saxophonist Lester YOUNG.
Singers with the Basie outfit included
Frank SINATRA, Ella FITZGERALD and Tony

BENNETT, while Quincy JONES ranked among his arrangers. In all, Basie led a big band virtually without a break for some 50 years (1935–84), although many critics traced his finest period back to the 1930s, finding fault with his pop-influenced recordings of later decades. His theme tune was his first hit, 'One o'Clock Jump' (1935); other classic recordings included 'Jumpin' at the Woodside' (1938) and the 1957 album *The Atomic Mr Basie*.

Basin Street The street in New Orleans in which JAZZ first developed. Basin Street, in the Black quarter, was the location of the city's red light district, and various pioneering musicians used to meet to entertain the clients of the brothels and in so doing created their own unique sound. Composer Spencer Williams (1889–1965) wrote the number 'Basin Street Blues' in 1928.

bass-slapping Bass guitar technique, in which the instrument is slapped between notes for rhythmic effect. The technique, much used in FUNK, is usually credited to bassist Stanley Clarke.

Bassey, Shirley (1937–) British singer, born in Wales of West Indian parentage, who enjoyed a series of pop hits in the early 1960s and remained one of the most popular stars in CABARET and light entertainment for many years, winning recognition as the most successful solo female artist in British chart history. Discovered by Jack HYLTON, she recorded her first hit – a version of the 'Banana Boat Song' – in 1957 and consolidated her reputation with such chart successes as 'As I Love You' (1959), 'As Long as He Needs Me' (1960), 'Reach for the Stars' (1961), 'Goldfinger' (1964), 'Big Spender' (1967), 'Something' (1970) and 'Diamonds are Forever' (1972). She went into retirement in Switzerland in 1980.

Bath Festival Famous British annual music festival, held in the historic city of Bath. Founded in 1948, the festival concentrated on music of the eighteenth century (in keeping with the age of many of the city's most famous buildings). It lapsed in 1955 but was revived in 1958 by Yehudi MENU-HIN. The Bath Festival Orchestra was renamed the Menuhin Festival Orchestra in 1968, and the range of the festival has been extended to include drama, painting and other artistic activities.

Bath, Hubert (1883–1945) British composer and conductor, who is usually remembered for his SOUNDTRACKS for a series of movies from the 1930s. A student of the Royal Academy of Music, he collaborated on the light opera *Young England* (1916) and on other work for the theatre before turning to the cinema. He contributed the soundtrack for the first full-length British talkie, *Blackmail* (1929), and also wrote the music for such films as *Chu Chin Chow* (1932) and *The Thirty-Nine Steps* (1935); he was working on the soundtrack of *The Wicked Lady* when he died.

bathroom record A longer than average record, or two shorter ones played without a break, broadcast by a DISC JOCKEY during the course of a programme to allow him time to make a visit to the bathroom.

Batt, Mike (1950–) British songwriter, producer and arranger, who created a number of hits for himself and other artists in the 1970s and 1980s and had particular success with his compositions for children. As well as various JINGLES, he wrote such popular hits as 'The Wombling Song' (1974) and 'Summertime City' (1975). 'Bright Eyes', from the cartoon version of *Watership Down* (1978), reached Number One in a recording by Art Garfunkel (*see* SIMON AND GARFUNKEL). More ambitious concept albums, such as *Schizophrenia* (1977) and *The Hunting of the Snark* (1986), were less well received.

Bax, Sir Arnold (Edward Trevor) (1883–1953) British composer, who was renowned for his romantic programmatic music, which bore the influence of Celtic folklore and scenery (inspiration that had its roots in his reading of the poetry of W.B. Yeats) and, after a visit to Russia in 1910, of Russian music. His best-known works include the ballet *The Truth about the Russian Dancers* (1920), symphonic poems, seven symphonies and chamber music. He also wrote novels under the pseudonym Dermot O'Byrne.

> One should try everything once, except incest and folk-dancing.
> ARNOLD BAX, *Farewell, My Youth*, 1943

Bay City Rollers, the British pop group of the 1970s, hailing from Edinburgh, which dominated the UK charts as TEENY-BOP idols in a manner reminiscent of the BEATLES in their heyday. Group members Leslie McKeown (1955–), Stuart 'Woody' Wood (1957–), Eric Faulkner (1955–), Alan Longmuir (1953–) and Derek Longmuir (1955–) had their first hit, 'Keep on Dancing', in 1971, following it with such numbers as 'Remember (Sha-la-la)', 'Bye Bye Baby', 'Give a Little Love' and 'Saturday Night'.

'Rollermania' thrived on the mock 'bovver-boy' image of the band, with fans adopting their tartan uniforms, which included trouser legs that ended somewhere just below the knee and massively heeled boots. Critics of the group's superficial music were, however, many, and there were accusations – finally admitted to be accurate – that the band did not actually play on its own records. The group's popularity suffered further when Alan Longmuir left after a rumoured suicide attempt (Faulkner also tried to kill himself) and McKeown got into trouble with the law: in 1975 he collided with and killed an elderly woman while driving in Edinburgh (just three weeks earlier his brother also killed a woman while driving down the same street). Attempts to change the band's image failed, and by the 1980s the group had been consigned to oblivion.

Bayes, Nora (Dora Goldberg; 1880–1928) US singer, who became a huge star of vaudeville and Broadway. In collaboration with the second of her five husbands, Jack NORWORTH, she wrote the classic 'Shine on Harvest Moon' (1908) and went on to star in the *Ziegfeld Follies* and many other shows in which she made effective use of her unusually low voice. Another of her songs, 'Down Where the Warzburger flows', was turned into a standard in the UK as 'Down at the Old Bull and Bush'. Other hits with which she was associated were 'Anybody Here Seen Kelly?', 'Over There' and 'Japanese Sandman'. 'The Man who put the Germ in Germany' (1918) was also calculated to appeal to wartime audiences. Her life was filmed in 1944 as *Shine on Harvest Moon*.

BBC British Broadcasting Corporation. The national broadcasting service of the UK, which was founded in 1922 and which has greatly promoted the popularity of music of all kinds over the course of its history. The Third Programme (launched in 1946) was the home of classical music on the radio for many years, being retitled the Music Programme in 1964 and, subsequently, Radio Three in 1970 when Radio One (pop music) and Radio Two (light music) were established. Other facets of the BBC's musical activities have included the foundation of the BBC SYMPHONY ORCHESTRA and other orchestras serving Wales, Scotland and the north of England and various smaller ensembles and choirs. The BBC also undertakes the organization of the annual PROMS.

In terms of television, the BBC has provided a national showplace for leading talents in every musical sphere, its most celebrated music programmes including TOP OF THE POPS and the now-defunct OLD GREY WHISTLE TEST.

BBC Symphony Orchestra Symphony orchestra, which was established by the BBC in 1930 as its chief orchestra. The ensemble rapidly built up a reputation as one of the best in the world and has over the years been conducted by such prestigious names as Arturo TOSCANINI, Sir Adrian BOULT, Sir Malcolm SARGENT and Pierre BOULEZ.

Beach Boys, the US pop group, which enjoyed huge commercial success with its brand of BEACH MUSIC in the 1960s. The brothers Brian Wilson (1942–), Dennis Wilson (1944–83) and Carl Wilson (1946–), their cousin Mike Love (1941–) and a friend, Al Jardine (1942–), came together in south California in 1961 through their love of both music and surfing. Their first song, 'Surfin'', was composed actually on the beach, and Brian Wilson later had his piano placed in a sandpit so that he could recreate the 'beach' atmosphere in the privacy of his own home.

Brian Wilson quickly proved to be a capable songwriter, his output being compared with that of the LENNON–MCCARTNEY partnership and effectively creating the surfing beat genre. 'Surfin' USA' (a reworking of Chuck BERRY's 'Sweet Little Sixteen') was the biggest of their early hits, and the group strengthened its challenge to the Beatles with such classics as 'I Get Around' (1964), 'Help Me Rhonda' (1965), 'California Girls' (1965), 'Good Vibrations' (1966) and the celebrated album *Pet Sounds*. Paul MCCARTNEY himself called 'God Only Knows' the 'best song that had ever been recorded'.

The carefree atmosphere of many of the group's early hits masked a sadder reality, however, Brian Wilson was haunted by childhood beatings from his father, while Dennis Wilson sought solace in drugs and alcohol. The strain of constant touring, drug abuse and internal divisions came to a head in 1967, when the group prepared to release what they considered their best album to date under the title *Smile*. Unfortunately, the BEATLES LP *Sergeant Pepper's Lonely Hearts Club Band* came out just before this album and stole the limelight. The album was eventually released as *Smiley Smile*. Further troubled by controversy over his links with murderer Charles Manson, Brian Wilson suffered a mental breakdown (he did not step outside his house once between 1974 and 1976) and was replaced by Glen CAMPBELL and later by Bruce Johnson.

Dennis Wilson's death by drowning in 1983 effectively brought the group to an end, although Brian Wilson, having fallen out with the rest of the band, re-emerged in 1988 with a distinctive solo album. They re-formed for touring in 1993.

It is estimated that the Beach Boys sold some 80 million copies of their records over a period of 15 years.

beach music POP music genre that emerged from South Carolina and other coastal states of the southeast USA, combining elements of SOUL and RHYTHM-AND-BLUES. Popular with the large Black population of the area, beach music has had a number of revivals, most recently in the late 1980s, when it re-appeared as accompaniment to a new dance craze called the shag. The same term has also been applied to the music of the BEACH BOYS and other artists who were identified with the world of surfing and beach culture in the 1960s.

Bean *See* Coleman HAWKINS.

Beastie Boys, the US RAP group of the late 1980s, which caused a media sensation by its outrageous behaviour. Led by Adam Horowitz (son of the playwright Israel Horowitz), the Beastie Boys thrived on public outrage at their live performances (which featured near-naked go-go dancers) and at alleged verbal cruelties to terminally ill children (denied by the band themselves). Fans of the band were also the target of criticism when they took to stealing the grille badges of Volkswagen cars (which, tilted sideways, resembled the group's 'BB' logo).

The band's hits included the album *Licensed to Kill* (1987) and the single 'You Gotta Fight For Your Right to Party'.

Beat, the British pop group of the late 1970s, which was one of the leading bands in the so-called TWO-TONE anti-racist movement. The band, which was from Birmingham, came together in 1978 and included both black and white players; the original line-up was Dave Wakeling (1956–), Andy Cox (1956–), David Steele (1960–) and Everett Morton (1951–). The single 'Tears of a Clown' was the first of a series of hit singles and albums that tackled such issues as racism and unemployment. The group broke up in the early 1980s.

beat music POP music genre of the 1960s, which was identified with the beat movement. It rejected conventional moral, political and artistic values in favour of more liberal, permissive thinking. The term was somewhat loose, being also applied to virtually any energetic, up-tempo number with a strong rhythmic beat and particularly to bands that were similar in style to the BEATLES.

Beatlemania The mass hysteria and obsessive media interest, which was inspired by the enormous success of the BEATLES throughout the 1960s. The word was first heard in 1963 in the wake of the group's appearance on *Sunday Night at the London Palladium*, which had a television audience of some 15 million viewers. At the close of the show the Beatles found themselves besieged by ecstatic fans as they attempted to leave the theatre – scenes that were splashed across the pages of the nation's newspapers the following morning. (The *Daily Mirror* was, in fact, the first newspaper to use the word 'Beatlemania'.)

Such was the rapidity with which the word came to be repeated by the media and fans alike that the group considered calling its first film 'Beatlemania'. (The word was ultimately used for the title of a Broadway show about the group's career in 1977, although the Beatles themselves threatened legal action to prevent the show going ahead.)

The cult following that the group gave rise to was deplored by the older generation, who confessed themselves bewildered and outraged at such un-British enthusiasm. They were not the only ones to take exception: towards the end of the last Beatles tour of the USA, the pilot of the group's chartered aircraft noticed that his plane had been peppered by bullets, which were believed to have been fired by jealous boyfriends of the girls who flocked to the concerts.

The Beatles were not, in fact, the first artists to receive such adulation. As far back as the 1940s Frank SINATRA had been greeted with screaming teenaged girls at his every public appearance (although some of them were apparently paid to behave in such a way), and in the early 1950s 'Cry Baby' Johnnie RAY was regularly drowned out by the hysterical screams of his fans as he collapsed in tears on stage.

> We are more popular than Jesus Christ now. I don't know which will go first. Rock and roll or Christianity.
>
> JOHN LENNON, interview in the *Evening Standard*, 1966

> These Beatles are completely anti-Christ. They are preparing our teenagers for riot and ultimate revolution against our Christian republic.
>
> REV DAVID NOEBEL, Claremont, California

Beatles, the The British pop group from Liverpool, which dominated the charts worldwide throughout the 1960s and is universally recognized as the most popular and influential pop group of all time. The most frequently used of the various nicknames that were applied to the group was the Fab Four, which caught on after the release of the 1963 album *With the Beatles*, the sleeve notes of which (written by music journalist Tony Barrow) described the group as the 'Fabulous Foursome'. Disc jockeys quickly took up the phrase, reducing it to the more succinct version known to all Beatles fans.

They were also known as the Moptops, a nickname particularly heard in the USA, in reference to the neat, rounded, hairstyle that they sported in the early 1960s. Frowned upon as effeminate and daring, mop top cuts were quickly adopted by countless fans and other prominent pop musicians, including members of the ROLLING STONES. Inspired entrepreneurs jumped onto the bandwagon by producing mop top wigs, which enabled young fans to emulate their heroes without entirely flouting the conventions of their parents. Scandinavians dubbed the style 'Hamlet', while Germans talked of the 'mushroom'.

The band had its origins in the Quarrymen, a SKIFFLE group first formed in 1957 by John LENNON – a pupil at the Quarry Bank School – whose members included the 15-year-old Paul McCARTNEY and, later, George HARRISON. Over the next three years the future stars appeared under such names as Johnny and the Moondogs, the Beatals and the Silver Beetles (according to Harrison in imitation of the Beetles motorbike gang in the 1954 film *The Wild One*). Lennon and McCartney first appeared – with George Harrison, bassist Stuart Sutcliffe (1942–62) and drummer Pete Best (1941–) – under the Beatles tag in 1960, playing at venues in Hamburg and Liverpool. Early recordings made in Germany with Tony Sheridan (1940–), however, credited the backing band as the Beat Brothers (the name Beatles being considered unfortunately close to the German *peedles*, slang for the male genitalia). The Fab Four were complete when Ringo STARR replaced Best in 1962.

Between 1962 and the split-up in 1970, the group recorded a classic series of singles and albums. Early hits, such as 'She Loves You' and 'Love Me Do', were followed by increasingly sophisticated pieces that reflected not only the development of the individual members of the band but also the aspirations and preoccupations of the age, with references to eastern mysticism, the drug culture of psychedelia and the pacifism of the anti-war movement. They established a record of 11 consecutive Number One singles, beginning with 'From Me to You' (1963), and notched up an incredible total of 18 Number Ones by the time of their last, 'The Ballad of John and Yoko' in 1969. Their most important albums included *Revolver* (1966), *Sergeant Pepper's Lonely Hearts Club Band* (1967), which is considered the first CONCEPT ALBUM, *The White Album* (1968), *Abbey Road* (1969) and *Let It Be* (1970). The last song they ever recorded together was 'I Me Mine' (3 January 1970).

The Beatles's unique contribution to pop music was officially recognized in 1965 when they were awarded MBEs, although Lennon later returned his in protest at UK involvement in the Biafran war of independence.

Rumours of a full Beatles reunion were finally laid to rest with the murder of John Lennon in 1980, although great excitement surrounded the appearance of a mysterious band called Klaatu (erroneously thought to be the Fab Four) in 1973. A three-volume anthology of Beatles songs sold over 20 million copies on release in 1995–6 and spawned the hit single 'Free as a Bird'. *See also* ABBEY ROAD; APPLE; APPLE CORPS; BEATLEMANIA; CAVERN, THE; EPSTEIN, Brian; FIFTH BEATLE; LENNON AND MCCARTNEY; MARTIN, George; MERSEY BEAT.

> Having played with other musicians, I don't even think the Beatles were that good.
> GEORGE HARRISON

> Nothing happened in the Sixties except that we all dressed up.
> JOHN LENNON

> A Beatles record is shorter and cleverer than a Henze opera.
> PIERRE BOULEZ

> The voice of 80,000 crumbling houses and 30,000 people on the dole.
> *The Daily Worker*, 1964

> The Beatles are turning awfully funny, aren't they?
> H.R.H. QUEEN ELIZABETH II, 1967

> I think the main point of the situation is that those pieces of plastic we did are still some of the finest pieces of plastic around.
> RINGO STARR

Beaux Arts Trio Celebrated US classical trio. Founded in 1955, the Beaux Arts Trio won acclaim from 1968 with a line-up of pianist Menahem Pressler, violinist Isidore Cohen (replacing Daniel Guilet) and cellist Bernard Greenhouse.

bebop Syncopated JAZZ style of the early 1940s, which represented a new, more sophisticated music that was quite distinct from the relatively simple harmonies of early jazz and was a reaction to the regimented orchestration of SWING. Championed by such performers as Lionel HAMPTON, Charlie PARKER, Thelonius MONK and Dizzy GILLESPIE, bebop – or simply bop – presented a new challenge to the best jazz players, most of whom were Black, and thus undermined the influence of the White musicians who had inherited all the best jobs.

Characteristics of bebop as it was first developed included the use of innovative broken rhythms, complex harmonies, improvisation and SCAT vocals. It was, in fact, the scat singing of Dizzy Gillespie that gave rise to the term bebop (although

Gillespie himself denied coining the word deliberately, using it simply as a convenient nonsense lyric). Subsequently the term 'bebop' fell into disuse as new genres appeared in succeeding years.

One theory has it that the word may have been modelled on the cry 'arriba!', which was often heard in Latin-American music at much the same time.

Bécaud, Gilbert (François Silly; 1927–) French composer and singer, nicknamed Monsieur 100,000 Volts, who ranked with Edith PIAF and Charles Trenet (1913–) as one of the most popular singers of the 1950s. Modelling himself on Frankie LAINE and Johnny RAY, he enjoyed huge commercial success with such songs as 'Et maintenant' (translated as 'What Now My Love'), 'Quand tu danses', 'Couventine', 'L'important, c'est la rose', 'Plein soleil', 'A Little Love and Understanding' and 'Tu le regretteras'.

Bechet, Sidney (1897–1959) Black US JAZZ clarinettist and saxophonist, who was virtually unique among his generation in mastering the soprano saxophone for jazz purposes. A native of New Orleans, he spent much of his career playing in Paris, where he was admired for his passionate style by classical composers as well as by committed jazz fans. He never learned to read music and retained the unconventional fingering he had taught himself while still a child. His on-stage tricks included taking his instrument to pieces while still playing it.

Bechet acquired his first soprano saxophone in London on his first European tour in 1919, and he was also briefly thrown into gaol there after an argument with an alleged prostitute. He visited Paris (where he was also imprisoned for a short time after a shooting incident involving pianist Mike McKendrick), returned to the USA (where he played alongside such greats as Louis ARMSTRONG) and then announced his retirement from music in 1938 to run a tailoring business in New York. A year later he was back, this time with his own band, the Feetwarmers, and he eventually settled permanently in France in 1949.

His most popular recordings included 'Summertime' (1939), 'Les Oignons' (1949) and 'Petite Fleur' (1952). This last hit he wrote while sitting on the lavatory (in French the phrase *poser les fleurs* – to plant flowers – is a slang idiom for the act of defecation). He also collaborated with James Toliver on a jazz ballet, *La Nuit est une sorcière* (1956). After his death a statue of him was erected in Antibes, where he lived, and a square was named in his honour.

Beck, Jeff (1944–) British ROCK guitarist, who emerged as one of the most respected guitarists of his generation in the late 1960s and 1970s. Beck established his reputation as Eric CLAPTON's successor in the YARDBIRDS and launched his own solo career with the single 'Hi-Ho Silver Lining' in 1967. He then formed a band, with Rod STEWART performing vocals, and enjoyed further success until an accident while racing hot-rods put him out of music for several months. He formed further bands and continued to develop his style in a series of albums during the 1970s and 1980s, the best of which included the JAZZ-influenced *Blow by Blow* (1975) and its follow-up *Wired* (1976).

Beck's legacy to other rock guitarists included his pioneering incorporation of complex harmonies derived from jazz and eastern music and his experimentation with a range of effects boxes (in parallel with similar explorations by fellowguitarist Jimi HENDRIX). *See also* TALKING BOX.

> The secret of longevity is staying out of the business for long periods of time . . . they'll eat you alive and spit the bones out. If you hang around long enough, they'll get you. But if you're not there they can't get you.
> JEFF BECK

> I never thought Jeff Beck and myself would ever play together, but I was there the night it happened.
> JIMMY PAGE

Bee Gees, the British pop group, which had several hits in the late 1960s and later reemerged as a top DISCO act of the 1970s and 1980s. The group, whose members were Barry Gibb (1946–) and his twin brothers Robin and Maurice Gibb (1949–), was named from the initials BG (Brothers Gibb). They began their music careers in Manchester in the 1950s and continued to develop after the family moved to Australia in 1958. They returned to the UK in 1967 (where they added guitarist Vince Melouney and drummer Colin Petersen) and enjoyed their first chart hit with 'New York Mining Disaster 1941'. 'Massa-

chusetts' (about a state none of the brothers had actually ever visited) reached Number One that same year, as did 'I've Gotta Get a Message to You' a year later.

After a temporary split in 1969–70, the band returned to the US charts with 'Lonely Days' and 'How Can You Mend a Broken Heart' but then adopted a lively disco sound, which led to such hits as 'Jive Talkin'' (1975), 'You Should be Dancing' (1976), 'Too Much Heaven' (1978), 'Tragedy' (1979) and 'Love You Inside and Out' (1979). Three tracks from the brothers' SOUNDTRACK for the John Travolta disco movie *Saturday Night Fever* (1976) – 'How Deep is Your Love', 'Stayin' Alive' and 'Night Fever' – reached Number One, while the album of the film became the biggest-selling LP of all time (surpassed only by Michael JACKSON's *Thriller*). The driving rhythm of 'Jive Talkin'', incidentally, was said to have been inspired by the noise of tyres on a metal bridge.

The band continued to produce hits in the 1980s as well as writing for other stars, who included their younger brother Andy Gibb (1958–88). Under their own name they reached Number One in the UK for the seventh time in 1987 with 'You Win Again'. Rare failures included the CONCEPT ALBUM *Odessa* (1969) and a disco version of *Sergeant Pepper's Lonely Hearts Club Band*.

Beecham, Sir Thomas (1879–1961) Celebrated British conductor, nicknamed TB, who was one of the legendary figures of twentieth-century classical music. Extrovert and bullish when it was in his interests to be so, he was widely respected for his conducting of such composers as Haydn, Mozart, Richard STRAUSS, Jean SIBELIUS and Frederick DELIUS. Self-taught, he founded the Beecham Orchestra in 1909, the LONDON PHILHARMONIC ORCHESTRA in 1932 and the ROYAL PHILHARMONIC ORCHESTRA in 1946. The RPO was established at the invitation of the Royal Philharmonic Society, and Beecham insisted that the orchestra, too, should enjoy the 'Royal' prefix, although no official permission for this was granted until 1966.

Beecham liked to exercise absolute control over his orchestras and would storm out if he thought his influence was being undermined. He would then simply found a new orchestra and lure to it his choice of musicians from elsewhere, using the family fortune acquired through the Beecham pharmaceutical company, an enterprise TB himself once immortalized in song:

Hark! the herald angels sing!
Beecham's pills are just the thing.
Two for a woman, one for a child ...
Peace on earth and mercy mild ...

Stories about Beecham and his waspish sense of humour are legion, as are his *bon mots*. The most famous include:

Good music is that which penetrates the ear with facility and quits the memory with difficulty.

Of music experts: A musicologist is a man who can read music but can't hear it.

Of the British as a musical race: The British may not like music, but they absolutely love the noise it makes.

and: British music is in a state of perpetual promise. It might almost be said to be one long promissory note.

Of audiences in general: There are two golden rules for an orchestra: start together and finish together. The public doesn't give a damn what goes on in between.

Of the harpsichord: Sounds like two skeletons copulating on a corrugated tin roof.

Of the upright piano: A musical growth found adhering to the walls of most semidetached houses in the provinces.

Of Elgar's First Symphony: The musical equivalent of St Pancras Station.

and, of Bach: Too much counterpoint – and what is worse, Protestant counterpoint.

Best of all perhaps was his complaint to a woman cellist under his baton:

You have between your legs the most sensitive instrument known to man, and all you can do is scratch it.

To another player, who was having trouble keeping up with the rest of the orchestra:

We cannot expect you to be with us the whole time, but maybe you would be kind enough to keep in touch now and again?

He was also renowned for his pride, rather like his rival Sir Henry WOOD:

I have the finest players in England. They are so good that they refuse to play under anybody except me.

When a colleague told him how much he had enjoyed his evening with Mozart and Beecham, the conductor growled 'Why drag in Mozart?'

Beecham was like a man who drinks and swears for six days of the week, then goes to church and prays with genuine devotion on Sunday.
COLIN WILSON, *Brandy of the Damned*, 1964

A complex character – Falstaff, Puck and Malvolio all mixed up, each likely to overwhelm the others. Witty, then waggish, supercilious, then genial, kindly and sometimes cruel; an artist in affectation, yet somehow always himself. Lancashire in his bones, yet a man of the world.
NEVILLE CARDUS

beguine Latin-American dance rhythm, which became a staple of many JAZZ bands in the 1930s and 1940s. The *biguine*, danced to a slow but sensuous rhythm, was a traditional dance from the West Indian island of Martinique, in which partners danced on the spot without their bodies touching. Attempts were made to popularize the dance in Europe in the early 1930s, but it was not until Cole PORTER wrote the hugely successful song 'Begin the Beguine' after meeting Xavier CUGAT in 1935 that the dance and its accompanying music became familiar throughout the West.

She refused to begin the 'Beguine'
Tho' they besought her to
And with language profane and obscene
She curs'd the man who taught her to
She curs'd Cole Porter too!
NOËL COWARD, 'Nina', 1945

Beiderbecke, Bix (Leon Bismark Beiderbecke; 1903–31) US JAZZ cornettist, who was a pioneer of Chicago style jazz in the 1920s and the first great White jazzman of all. Thrown out of a military academy in 1922, he impressed many contemporaries with his superb tone and strong sense of melody, characteristics that established him as one of the first White jazzmen of note. A star with the Wolverines and the bands of Frankie Trumbauer (1901–56) and Paul WHITEMAN as well as with his own Rhythm Jugglers, he played on a number of classic recordings, among them 'Dardanella', 'Singin' the Blues', 'I'm Coming, Virginia' and his own compositions 'Davenport Blues' and (for the piano)

'In a Mist'. Those influenced by him included Louis ARMSTRONG, Roy ELDRIDGE and Miles DAVIS. This was all despite the fact that he never learned to read music and used his desk to prop up thrillers.

Admiration for his technical prowess and skill at improvisation was universal within the world of jazz, but Beiderbecke suffered greatly when his own family refused to sanction his choice of a musical career (it was said that they stored all his records in a cupboard and never played them) and his health declined as he sought refuge in drink. His early death at the age of 28 – the result of the combined effects of alcohol and pneumonia – provided the basis of the legend that grew around his name over the ensuing decades. His life was retold in the novel *Young Man with a Horn* (1938) by Dorothy Baker.

Belafonte, Harry (1927–) US popular singer, nicknamed the King of Calypso, who enjoyed commercial success in the 1950s and 1960s singing traditional West Indian and CALYPSO music. A former resident of the West Indies, he sang in his own restaurant in Greenwich Village and subsequently reached the charts with such recordings as 'Jamaica Farewell' (1956), 'Banana Boat Song' (1957) and 'Mary's Boy Child' (1957), which was the first single to sell over a million copies in the UK alone and spent seven weeks at Number One (unsurpassed by any other CHRISTMAS RECORD). His hit 'Island in the Sun' inspired the name of ISLAND RECORDS. More recent releases include the African-influenced album *Paradise In Gazankulu* (1988). His admirers included Bob DYLAN.

Belfast Cowboy, the *See* Van MORRISON.

Bella Bailie *See* Dame Isobel BAILLIE.

Bellson, Louie (Louis Balassoni; 1924–) US JAZZ drummer and bandleader, who played with many prominent bands from the 1940s onwards. Having won a prestigious drumming contest in 1940, he joined the bands of such respected jazzmen as Ted FIORITO, Benny GOODMAN, Tommy DORSEY and Duke ELLINGTON and also ran his own bands with success. He married the singer Pearl BAILEY and wrote a number of jazz standards, among them 'The Hawk Talks', 'Skin Deep', in which Bellson's drums played the leading role,

and 'Ting-a-ling'. His other compositions include ballets and orchestral works.

Benatar, Pat (Patricia Andrzejewski; 1953–) US rock singer, who established a strong ADULT-ORIENTED ROCK following in the early 1980s. Having studied opera and then switching to CABARET, she attracted numerous admirers in the rock world with her impressive vocal range and enjoyed transatlantic success with such singles as 'Hit Me with Your Best Shot' (1978), 'Love is a Battlefield' (1983), 'Invincible' (1985) and 'All Fired Up' (1988). Her albums have included *In the Heat of the Night* (1978), *Crimes of Passion* (1980), the US chart-topping *Precious Time* (1981), on which she toned down her initial HEAVY METAL sound, *Get Nervous* (1982), *Tropico* (1984), *Seven the Hard Way* (1986) and *Wide Awake in Dreamland* (1988). She is married to guitarist Neil Geraldo.

Benatzky, Ralph (Rudolf Josef František; 1884–1957) Czech composer and author, who wrote many highly successful operettas, musical comedies, film scores and songs. Having studied music in Prague and Munich, he qualified as a doctor of philosophy but continued to develop a career in music, directing in CABARET and composing his first operettas. Of his many compositions the most successful was the epic operetta *White Horse Inn* (1931), which was first staged in Berlin and, later, in Austria, the UK and the USA. Benatzky emigrated to the USA in 1938 but eventually settled in Switzerland.

Beneke, Tex (1914–) US saxophonist, singer and bandleader, who became famous as one of the leading members of the celebrated Glenn MILLER band in the early 1940s. Beneke joined Miller in 1942 and remained with him until Miller's death, after which he founded his own bands to keep the Miller sound alive.

Benjamin, Bennie (1907–) West Indian composer, who wrote many hit songs and music for the cinema in the 1940s and 1950s. He moved to New York in 1927 and composed such hits as 'I Don't Want to Set the World on Fire', 'When the Lights Go on Again All Over the World' and 'I'll Keep the Lovelight Burning'.

Bennett, Richard Rodney (1936–) British composer and pianist, who reached a wide audience through his music for the cinema. A graduate of the Royal Academy of Music, he became interested in SERIALISM and studied under Pierre BOULEZ in Paris but returned to London and established a reputation for witty music with a strong JAZZ influence. His works include the ballet *Jazz Calendar* (1963–64), five operas, two symphonies, concertos and children's music as well as the SOUNDTRACKS for such films as *Far From the Madding Crowd* (1967), *Murder on the Orient Express* (1974) and *Yanks* (1981). He has also arranged music for Eartha KITT among others.

Bennett, Robert Russell (1894–1981) US composer, arranger and orchestrator, who worked on many of the most celebrated musicals of the twentieth century. He produced the orchestration for such shows as *Oklahoma, South Pacific, My Fair Lady* and *The Sound of Music* in addition to writing an opera, *Maria Malibran* (1935), and a wide range of works combining elements of JAZZ, POP and classical music. His symphonies include *Symphony in D for the Dodgers* (dedicated to the Brooklyn baseball team).

Bennett, Tony (Anthony Dominick Benedetto; 1926–) US singer and artist, who achieved commercial success in the 1960s with a string of JAZZ-influenced hits. The son of a grocer, he was promoted as a singer by Pearl BAILEY and Bob HOPE. His hits included 'Because of You', which was Number One for 31 weeks in 1951, 'Cold, Cold Heart', which also reached Number One that year, 'Rags to Riches' (1953), which gave him his third chart-topper, 'Stranger in Paradise' (1953), which was based on a theme from Borodin's opera *Prince Igor* (1888), and the classic 'I Left My Heart in San Francisco' (1962). Subsequent recordings included albums made with, among others, Count BASIE, Bill EVANS, Ray CHARLES and Stan GETZ.

Benson, George (1943–) US SOUL singer and guitarist, who enjoyed wide commercial success as a solo artist in the 1970s and 1980s. He started as a guitarist, appearing with a number of celebrated JAZZ acts, including groups led by Herbie HANCOCK, but achieved stardom on his own with such singles as 'Super Ship', 'Give Me the Night' and 'In your Eyes', and with

such FUNK-based albums as *Breezin'* (1976) and *Love Songs* (1985). More unusual recordings by Benson include *The Other Side of Abbey Road*, a track-for-track version of the celebrated BEATLES album. Benson's switch to a more accessible funky style in the 1970s alienated some of his former jazz fans, but he remained unrepentant: 'If kids can't hear it, I don't care how good it is, you can't sell it to them.' He returned to soul for *Love Remembers* (1993).

Berg, Alban (1885–1935) Austrian composer, who was described as the 'Puccini of 12-note music'. A pupil of Arnold SCHOENBERG's, he moved gradually away from the tonality of such pieces as his piano sonata of 1908 to the atonality of such works as his *Chamber Concerto* (1923–5). He adapted himself to the 12-NOTE system, producing a 12-note violin concerto in 1935. His best-known works include the operas *Wozzeck* (1914–20) and *Lulu*, which was begun in 1928 but unfinished at his death, which was the result of complications following an insect bite. His widow kept back the unfinished part of *Lulu* for many years, claiming that her husband had himself been the last victim of the destructive femme fatale he had borrowed from the plays of Frank Wedekind (and finally sentenced to death at the hands of Jack the Ripper); it was finally performed for the first time in 1979, completed by Friedrich Cerha (1926–).

Berg's last work was his admired violin concerto, which was dedicated 'to the memory of an angel', the angel in question being the recently deceased 19-year-old Manon Gropius (daughter of Mahler's widow); the composer died, however, before he could hear the finished piece.

> When I compose I always feel I am like Beethoven; only afterwards do I become aware that at best I am only Bizet.
> ALBAN BERG

Berigan, Bunny (1908–42) US trumpeter and bandleader, who won acclaim with many of the most celebrated BIG BANDS of the 1930s and came to be ranked second only to Louis ARMSTRONG himself. In the early 1930s he played with the bands of such prominent jazzmen as Paul WHITEMAN, Benny GOODMAN and Tommy DORSEY, following which he formed his own band (1937–40). The success he enjoyed with his recording of such classics as 'Marie',

'West End Blues' and 'I Can't Get Started' confirmed his popular standing, but the combination of overwork and over-indulgence in alcohol led to the band's dissolution and to his early death.

Berio, Luciano (1925–   ) Italian composer, who became one of the leading proponents of SERIALISM. He pioneered the use of tape recordings in composition and live performance and in the 1960s produced a number of collage-type pieces, as well as purely instrumental works, some using electronic instruments, and pieces for his former wife, the soprano Cathy Berberian (1925–83). His best-known pieces include the *Sequenza* series for solo instruments (1958–75), *Circles* (1960) and *Points on a Curve to Find* (1974). His work *Amores* required the building of a special theatre for its performance.

Berkeley, Sir Lennox (Randal Francis) (1903–89) British composer, who was a proponent of SERIALISM in the tradition of Arnold SCHOENBERG. Influenced by Nadia BOULANGER and a friend of Benjamin BRITTEN's (with whom he collaborated on the 1937 orchestral suite *Mont Juic*), he wrote melodic tonal music until the 1960s, when he began to explore atonality. His best-known pieces include the *Four Poems of St Teresa of Avila* (1947), written for Kathleen FERRIER, *Five Songs* (1946) and *Songs of the Half-Light* (1964), which was dedicated to Peter PEARS as well as four operas, four symphonies, ballet, theatre, film and religious music.

Berkshire Festival Important US music festival, which takes place at Tanglewood, Massachusetts. It was founded in 1937 by Serge KOUSSEVITSKY, and the Boston Symphony is the resident festival orchestra.

Berlin, Irving (Israel Baline; 1888–1989) Russian-born US composer, who became one of the most celebrated of all the TIN PAN ALLEY and Hollywood songwriters. Baline came to the USA with his family when he was four years old, and he spent his childhood in conditions of extreme poverty, being obliged to find work at the age of eight when his father died. He sold newspapers and then guided a blind busker called 'Old Sol' through the streets before taking up the business of busking for a living himself. He found work as a singing waiter and learned to play the piano (although he played in an unorthodox fashion – always in the key of F sharp – and never learned to read music properly). When his first songs were published his name appeared as 'Irving Berlin' as the result of a printer's error and he decided to keep it as his own.

As Irving Berlin, he was taken on as a lyric-writer and enjoyed his first major successes with humorous songs and such rag numbers as 'Alexander's Ragtime Band' in the years immediately preceding the First World War. He became one of the most popular of all Broadway songwriters and contributed many hits for Florenz ZIEGFELD's *Follies* and various revues as well as for the newly developing film industry.

Among the most famous of the 1,500 or more songs he created during the course of his immensely long career were 'Oh, How I Hate to Get Up in the Morning' (1918), 'A Pretty Girl is Like a Melody' (1919), 'Always' (1925), which was a wedding present for his wife, 'Marie' (1929), 'Putting on the Ritz' (1929), 'Let's Have Another Cup of Coffee' (1932), 'Easter Parade' (1933), 'Top Hat, White Tie and Tails' (1935), 'Let's Face the Music and Dance' (1936), 'God Bless America' (1938), which became the USA's unofficial national anthem, 'White Christmas' (1942), which became the best-selling record in the history of the music business, 'There's no Business Like Show Business' (1946), 'A Couple of Swells' (1948) and 'It's a Lovely Day Today' (1950).

Berlin spent the last decades of his long life in seclusion. He was always frank about his motives; when asked by a colleague if he wrote for posterity, he replied 'No, for prosperity'.

> Irving just loves hits. He has no sophistication about it – he just loves hits.
> OSCAR HAMMERSTEIN II

Berlin Philharmonic Orchestra German orchestra, founded in 1888, which has long been regarded as one of the finest in the world. Famous conductors associated with the orchestra have included Artur NIKISCH (1895–1922), Wilhelm FURTWÄNGLER (1922–45 and 1952–54), Herbert von KARAJAN (1954–89), whose departure in controversial circumstances shortly before his death caused the greatest trauma in the ensemble's history, and Claudio ABBADO (1989–   ). Its home, the

Philharmonie (Philharmonic Hall), was rebuilt in 1963 after the destruction of the original building during the Second World War.

Bernard, Felix (1897–1944) US songwriter and pianist, who enjoyed huge success with 'Dardanella', one of the best-selling songs of the 1920s. 'Dardanella' (1919) was the first dance record to sell more than a million copies, and it remained Bernard's biggest hit, although 'Winter Wonderland' (1934) also sold well.

Bernie, Ben (Benjamin Woodruff Anzelovitz; 1891–1943) US bandleader, nicknamed the Old Maestro, who led a popular dance band in the 1920s and 1930s. After establishing a reputation in vaudeville, he formed his first band in 1922 and went on to popularize such hits as 'It's a Lonesome Old Town' and 'Au Revoir, Pleasant Dreams'; other songs written by Bernie included 'Sweet Georgia Brown' and 'Strange Interlude'. He made several film appearances, and through his regular radio broadcasts his catchphrase 'Yowsah!' became nationally known.

Bernstein, Elmer (1922–) US composer and conductor, who is best known for his many JAZZ-influenced SOUNDTRACKS. They include those for *The Ten Commandments* (1956), *The Magnificent Seven* (1960), *Thoroughly Modern Millie* (1967), for which he won an Oscar, *Airplane* (1980) and *Trading Places* (1983).

Bernstein, Leonard (1918–90) US composer, pianist and conductor, who enjoyed equal success working in classical and more popular modes but is best known for such ground-breaking musicals as *Candide* (1956) and *West Side Story* (1957). Bernstein first attracted attention in the early 1940s and became an established star in the role of sole conductor of the NEW YORK PHILHARMONIC (1958–69) as well as working with many other leading orchestras around the world. *On The Town* (1944) was his first major Broadway success, and although *Candide* picked up several awards it did not achieve huge box office success. It was *West Side Story* – written in collaboration with Stephen SONDHEIM – that triumphed in all departments and ensured Bernstein's niche in the history of popular music (he made a hit recording of the score in 1984). His other

compositions, which ranged from JAZZ to classical works, included three symphonies, ballets, the opera *A Quiet Place* (1987), the *Mass* (1971) and *The Chichester Psalms* (1965). His film scores included *On the Waterfront* (1954). As a conductor he won particular acclaim for his versions of works by Beethoven, Brahms and MAHLER as well as of his own compositions.

> The Peter Pan of music.
> *New York Times*, 1960

> The epitome of glamour combined with quality, and thank heaven for him – the heaven of the golden gods of yore.
> NED ROREM, on Bernstein's 70th birthday, 1988

> His conducting had a masturbatory, oppressive and febrile zeal, even for the most tranquil passages. Today he uses music as an accompaniment to his conducting.
> OSCAR LEVANT, *Memoirs of an Amnesiac*, 1965

> It would be nice to hear someone accidentally whistle something of mine, somewhere, just once.
> LEONARD BERNSTEIN, *The Joy of Music*, 1960

Berry, Chuck (Charles Edward Anderson Berry; 1926–) US RHYTHM-AND-BLUES star of the 1950s, nicknamed Crazy Legs because of the famous 'duck walk' he always performs during live appearances, whose distinctive guitar sound had a profound influence on the development of early ROCK 'N' ROLL. Jerry Lee LEWIS, among others, called him the King of Rock 'n' Roll. Born in St Louis, Missouri, he had an eventful youth, spending a period in reform school for stealing cars, getting married, finding employment with General Motors, being imprisoned for armed robbery and working as a hairdresser before he first entered a studio and set about redefining the 12-bar boogie at the ripe old age of 29. His most successful recordings included the classic numbers 'Maybelline' (1955), one of a series of songs celebrating the cult of the car (he first sang it in a mock country style as a NOVELTY number in his live act), 'Rock 'n' Roll Music' (1957), 'Sweet Little Sixteen' (1958), 'Johnny B. Goode' (1958) and 'Roll Over Beethoven', which have since been covered by innumerable artists.

Berry's career faltered somewhat at the end of the decade when he got into trouble with the law for transporting an under-age girl (a white female fan) over a State line and was sentenced to two years in gaol. While inside, he wrote such further classics as 'Promised Land', 'You Never Can Tell' and the aptly titled 'No Particular Place to Go'. Even when his own recordings failed to keep pace with changing tastes in the 1960s and 1970s, tributes from some of the leading performers of later decades kept his name from being forgotten, and he toured regularly with his old hits. There was further embarrassment, however, in 1979, when he was charged with tax evasion shortly before appearing in front of President Carter at the White House; this time he served 120 days in prison. In 1990 he was given another suspended sentence for possession of a small amount of marijuana, and the previous year he was alleged to have videotaped women in the lavatories of his restaurant.

Surprisingly, it was not until 1972, when the NOVELTY RECORD 'My Ding-a-ling' topped the charts, that he had a Number One in the UK. *See also* CRAZY LEGS.

> Names of it can vary, but music that is inspiring to the head and heart, to dance by and cause you to pat your foot, it's there. Call it rock, call it jazz, call it what you may. If it makes you move, or moves you or grooves you, it'll be here.
> CHUCK BERRY

> If you tried to give rock 'n' roll another name, you might call it 'Chuck Berry'.
> JOHN LENNON

Berté, Heinrich (1858–1924) Hungarian composer, who achieved lasting fame with his score for the operetta *Das Dreimäderlhaus* (*Lilac Time*, US title *Blossom Time*; 1916), which was an adaptation of music by Franz Schubert. His other works included further operettas and a series of ballets.

bhangra Indian-influenced POP music, which first established a vogue in the British Indian community in the 1980s. It combines elements of western ROCK with traditional Punjabi folk music.

big band The SWING band of the 1930s and 1940s, usually with more than 15 members, which was the mainstay of the so-called 'Big Band Era'. These popular JAZZ combos specialized in dance music and were often more than a little theatrical, with the musicians wearing dazzling sequined jackets and making choreographed moves. The emphasis was very much on section work, with few solo breaks. Leading bands of the big band era included those of Charlie BARNET, Duke ELLINGTON, Benny GOODMAN, Fletcher HENDERSON, Woody HERMAN, Stan KENTON, Glenn MILLER and Artie SHAW. Their counterparts in the UK included AMBROSE and Jack HYLTON.

The phrase 'big band' was first heard in the mid-1930s, when it was sometimes used in a derogatory sense to compare such outfits with the much smaller groups playing 'pure' NEW ORLEANS JAZZ. It was heard less often in later decades when the cost of having so many musicians playing together made such outfits too expensive, although rare examples did survive many more years under the leadership of such jazz greats as Lionel HAMPTON.

Big Bopper (J(iles) P(erry) Richardson; 1930–59) US ROCK 'N' ROLL singer, who was a star on both sides of the Atlantic in the 1950s. Having started out as a disc jockey and consolidating his fame by establishing a record of non-stop broadcasting for over 122 hours, he branched out as a star in his own right with such hits as 'Chantilly Lace' and 'Big Bopper's Wedding' (both 1958). The Big Bopper died at the peak of his success in the disastrous air crash in which Buddy HOLLY and Ritchie VALENS were also killed.

Big Country Scottish rock band of the 1980s, which enjoyed a series of hit singles on both sides of the Atlantic. Singer and guitarist Stuart Adamson (1958–), guitarist Bruce Watson (1961–), bassist Tony Butler (1957–) and drummer Mark Brzezicki (1957–) established a reputation with such singles as 'Fields of Fire' (1983), 'In a Big Country' (1983) and 'East of Eden' (1984), combining elements of ROCK, FOLK, POP and HEAVY METAL. Big Country have not achieved the consistency of former years recently but they still tour regularly.

Big Joe *See* Joe TURNER.

Big Mama *See* Big Mama THORNTON.

Big Maybelle (Mabel Louise Smith; 1924–72) US RHYTHM-AND-BLUES singer, nicknamed the Mother of Soul, whose recordings of the 1940s and 1950s paved the way for the development of SOUL in the 1960s. She toured with the Sweethearts of Rhythm before going solo in 1947. Best known for her live act, which made her a regular star at the APOLLO THEATRE in Harlem, she released such hits as 'Grabbin' Blues', 'Way Back Home', 'My Country Man', 'Candy' and the original version of 'Whole Lotta Shakin' Going On' (1955). A come-back in the mid-1960s saw 'Don't Pass Me By' and 'Ninety-six Tears' reach the charts. A big woman, she suffered increasingly from diabetes in her last years.

Big O, the See Roy ORBISON.

Bigard, Barney (1906–80) US JAZZ clarinettist, saxophonist and composer, who won recognition as the leading clarinettist of his time in 1928–42 when he was with the band of Duke ELLINGTON. He helped to write many of the band's most popular hits but left to lead his own band in California. He subsequently also played with the bands of Louis ARMSTRONG and others.

biker rock See GREBO ROCK.

Bilk, Acker (Bernard Stanley Bilk; 1929–) British JAZZ clarinettist, singer and bandleader, who first emerged as one of the best-known figures in traditional British jazz in the 1950s. Bilk's greatest hit – 'Stranger on the Shore' (1962) – made him the first British artist to reach Number One in the US charts; among his other hits with the bowler-hatted and striped-waistcoated Paramount Jazz Band (founded in 1958) were 'Summer Set' (1960), 'Buona Sera' (1960) and 'That's My Home' (1961). His albums have included *Sheer Magic* (1967). 'Acker' is an old slang term, meaning 'mate'.

> Do you know the difference between a banjo and a trampoline? You take your shoes off before you jump on a trampoline.
> ACKER BILK, on BBC radio's *Jazz Score*

Billboard The US weekly music magazine, which is famous for its CHARTS giving details of current best-selling songs and albums. Founded in 1894, *Billboard* also carries advertisements and articles on all types of music.

Binge, Ronald (1910–79) British composer, arranger, pianist and conductor, whose many hit tunes included a series written for the MANTOVANI orchestra. He was first recruited by Mantovani in 1934 and provided him with such hits as 'Spitfire' and 'Charmaine' as well as masterminding the 'cascading strings' sound for which the outfit became renowned. His other compositions included the worldwide success 'Elizabethan Serenade' (1952), a symphony, songs, a 'Festival Te Deum' and music for brass and military bands (notably the 'Cornet Carillon' of 1961).

Bird See Charlie PARKER.

Birmingham Symphony Orchestra, City of Symphony orchestra that was founded in Birmingham in 1920. ELGAR himself conducted the orchestra's first concert; conductors have included Sir Adrian BOULT and (since 1980) Simon RATTLE.

Birtwistle, Sir Harrison (Paul) (1934–) British AVANT-GARDE composer and clarinettist, who first emerged as a leading figure in contemporary classical music in the 1960s. He was one of the co-founders (with Alexander GOEHR, Peter MAXWELL DAVIES and John OGDON) of the New Music Manchester Group, and accepted the post of musical director at the South Bank National Theatre. He wrote a number of influential theatrical works in the late 1960s, among them *Punch and Judy* (1967) – described on its release as the only truly modern opera – and the dramatic cantata *Down by the Greenwood Side* (1969). He explored such themes as man's place in the natural order in the instrumental pieces *Medusa* (1970) and *The Triumph of Time* (1972), and more recent works have included the fragmentary ... *agm* ... (1979), the opera *Orpheus* (1973–84), *Earth Dances* (1986) and the operas *Gawain* (1991) and *The Second Mrs Kong* (1994).

Björk (Björk Gudmundsdóttir; 1965–) Icelandic rock singer, who established an international following in the early 1990s. Born in Reykjavik, she signed her first record deal at 11 and fronted Exodus, Jam 80, Tappi Tikarrass, Kukl, and the Sugarcubes before achieving solo stardom with the albums *Debut* (1993) and *Post* (1995), from which came the hit single 'It's Oh So Quiet'.

Black, Bill (William Patton Black, 1926–65) US bass player, who began his career backing Elvis PRESLEY and later led a successful group of his own. He deserted

Presley in 1957 because of the low salary he was getting and went on to forge his own blend of COUNTRY and RHYTHM-AND-BLUES music, having hits with, among others, 'White Silver Sands' (1960), 'Josephine' (1961) and 'Don't Be Cruel' (1961). His band continued in business long after his death from a brain tumour and became one of the most respected country outfits.

Black, Cilla (Priscilla Maria Veronica White; 1943–) British singer and entertainer, born in Liverpool, who was a pop star of the 1960s before developing her career as a television presenter. Capitalizing on her cheeky Liverpudlian humour and benefiting from the success of fellow-Liverpudlians the BEATLES (she was briefly a cloakroom attendant at the CAVERN club before being taken up by Brian EPSTEIN), she enjoyed chart success with such strident love songs as 'Anyone Who Had a Heart' (1964) and 'You're My World' (1964), which both reached Number One in the UK, and such hits as 'Alfie' and 'Step Inside Love'. She acquired the name Cilla Black early in her career when an enthusiastic journalist got her name wrong in his review.

Black, Stanley (1913–) British composer, arranger, pianist and conductor, who is best known for his radio, television and film music. Having worked for a number of dance bands in the 1930s and for the BBC Dance Orchestra in the 1940s, he contributed the music for such popular radio series as *The Goons* and *Much Binding in the Marsh*. His film scores have included *Laughter in Paradise* (1950), *The Young Ones* (1961) and *Summer Holiday* (1963), for which he shared an IVOR NOVELLO AWARD.

Black Beatles, the *See* the COMMODORES.

Black Elvis, the *See* Jimi HENDRIX.

black metal Sub-genre of HEAVY METAL, which is characterized by an interest in satanism and black magic. The first black metal bands emerged in the early 1970s and became associated with SPEED METAL through their frenzied, up-tempo music. Typical black metal bands included Angelwitch, Satan and Venom, who developed the SATANIC METAL style of such predecessors as BLACK SABBATH and BLUE OYSTER CULT.

Black Moses *See* Isaac HAYES.

Black Sabbath British rock band, which established a big following in the 1970s with its brand of SATANIC METAL. Group members vocalist 'Ozzy' Osbourne (1948–), bassist Terry 'Geezer' Butler (1949–), guitarist Tony Iommi (1948–) and drummer Bill Ward (1948–) started out under the name Earth, but in 1969 they changed this to Black Sabbath, a named derived from the title of a novel by Dennis Wheatley. Such early albums as *Black Sabbath* (1970) and *Paranoid* (1970) established the band's credentials for heavy, pessimistic rock with occult overtones. Keyboard player RICK WAKEMAN guested in 1977 for the album *Sabbath Bloody Sabbath*, but the band went into decline a year later with the departure of Osbourne, the charismatic lead singer (he formed a new band and caused a furore when he bit the head off a dead bat during his live act). Attempts to replace Osbourne with Ian Gillan were not well received, and a new version of the group formed for LIVE AID in 1985 retained only Iommi from the original line-up. Recent albums include *Headless Cross* (1989), *Dehumanizer* (1992) and *Forbidden* (1995).

Osbourne's solo hit 'Suicide Solution' (1985) was the subject of a court case in the USA after it was cited as having contributed to the suicide of a young US fan.

Blackmore, Ritchie (1945–) British rock guitarist, who was acknowledged as one of the leading guitar heroes in heavy rock after joining DEEP PURPLE on its formation in 1967. Blackmore was largely responsible for the band's distinctive and highly successful sound but finally left the group in 1975 when the other members turned away from their HEAVY METAL roots. He formed his own band, Rainbow, which also became a respected HARD ROCK act.

Blackwell, Otis (1931–) US songwriter, singer and pianist, who wrote hits for such stars as Elvis PRESLEY and Jerry Lee LEWIS. His compositions included Presley's 'Don't be Cruel', 'Return to Sender' and 'All Shook Up'; Lewis's 'Great Balls of Fire' and 'Breathless'; and Peggy LEE's 'Fever'.

Blades, James (1901–) British percussionist, who became famous for his work with the LONDON SYMPHONY ORCHESTRA and as a teacher and lecturer on music. His greatest claim to fame remains his striking of the gong that was the trademark of Rank

Films (the gong actually seen being struck – by Bombardier Billy Wells – was made of cardboard, while the gong heard measured something like 12 inches (30cm) across). He was also instrumental in winning recognition for the skills of percussionist Evelyn GLENNIE.

Blake, Eubie (James Hubert Blake; 1883–1983) Black US JAZZ pianist, who was one of the pioneers of early jazz. The son of slaves, he began his career in jazz like many of his contemporaries, playing for the clients of a brothel. He suffered the same prejudices as so many of his fellows and once commented, in reply to the question why he used so many black notes in his songs: 'Down South where I come from, you don't go round hittin' too many white keys.' He rapidly established a reputation as a RAGTIME pianist, his classic hits including 'Charleston Rag' (1899) and 'I'm Just Wild about Harry' (1921), which came from the all-Black musical *Shuffle Along* and was adopted by Harry S. Truman as his election song in 1948. He wrote many more songs, including 'Memories of You' (1930), for various REVUES and enjoyed a come-back during the ragtime revival of the 1970s, being invited to play at the White House and receiving several honours.

> If I'd known I was going to live this long, I'd have taken better care of myself.
> EUBIE BLAKE, remark made on his 100th birthday about his weakness for tobacco, women and alcohol

Blakey, Art (1919–90) US JAZZ drummer and bandleader, who played beside many of the great names in jazz from the 1940s to the 1980s. In fact, Blakey trained first as a pianist but changed to the drums (legend has it) on the instructions of a gangster (another version has it that he made the switch when the regular drummer was taken ill). He appeared alongside such jazz greats as Thelonius MONK, Charlie PARKER, Dizzy GILLESPIE and Miles DAVIS and became the leading figure in what became known as 'hard bop'. Many celebrated jazz musicians issued from the ranks of his band, the Jazz Messengers, which was formed in 1955.

Blakey proved endlessly innovative, and Miles Davis himself once remarked: 'If Art Blakey's old-fashioned, I'm white.' His technical tricks included resting his elbow on the drumskin to change the sound produced. He changed his name to Adbullah Ibn Buhaina after his conversion to Islam, his friends nicknaming him 'Bu'.

> The message my men have tried to deliver, no matter what personnel we had, was always jazz. When you get away from swinging, get away from the lines that were started by Dizzie Gillespie and Charlie Parker, then you are in danger of losing the essence of jazz.
> ART BLAKEY

Bland, Bobby (Robert Calvin Bland; 1930–) US BLUES singer, nicknamed Blue, who had a series of 36 Top Thirty R 'N' B hits between 1952 and 1972. His most successful recordings included 'It's My Life', 'I'm Sorry', 'That's the Way Love Is', 'Little Boy Blue' and 'Cry, Cry, Cry'. He switched to a SOUL style in the 1970s and collaborated with B.B. KING on the albums *Together for the First Time* (1974) and *Together Again . . . Live* (1976).

Blane, Ralph (Ralph Uriah Hunsecker; 1914–) US composer, singer and actor, who wrote a series of successful Broadway and Hollywood MUSICALS in the 1940s. Having established his reputation as a singer and arranger in such Broadway hits as *DuBarry was a Lady* (1939) and *Louisiana Purchase* (1940), he teamed up with Hugh Martin (1914–) to write such successes as the stage musical *Best Foot Forward* (1941) and the Judy GARLAND movie *Meet Me in St Louis* (1941), the highlights of which included 'Have Yourself a Merry Little Christmas'.

Blanton, Jimmy (1918–42) US JAZZ bassist, who recreated the role of the bass in the jazz line-up and made it one of the principal instruments. He was given wide scope for such development when he was bass player with Duke ELLINGTON's band, and he made a number of recordings in which the piano and bass took the limelight before his premature death from tuberculosis at the age of 23.

bleeding chunks Excerpts of larger works (particularly those of Wagner), which are served up in concert and out of context. The term was first used by the musicologist Sir Donald Francis Tovey (1875–1940), who referred to the 'bleeding chunks of butcher's meat chopped from Wagner's operas and served up on Wagner nights'.

Bliss, Sir Arthur (1891–1975) British composer, who won acclaim both for his AVANT-GARDE works and for pieces written for the cinema and for major ceremonial events. Early works included the oratorio *Morning Heroes* (1930), which was dedicated to the memory of his brother, who was killed in the First World War. Among the most celebrated works that followed were three ballets, the theme for the film *Things to Come* (1936), a piano concerto (1938) and fanfares for the Investiture of the Prince of Wales in 1969. He was appointed Master of the Queen's Music in 1953. *See also* COLOUR MUSIC.

> There is only a little of the spider about me, spinning his own web from his inner being. I am more of a magpie type.
> ARTHUR BLISS, *As I Remember*, 1970

Blitzstein, Marc (1905–64) US composer, who acquired a controversial reputation for his committed left-wing musical shows. Trained by Nadia BOULANGER and Arnold SCHOENBERG, he was influenced by Brecht's music theatre and dedicated himself to conveying left-wing messages in his compositions. His musical drama *The Cradle Will Rock* (1937) proved influential, although the first performance took place only after a hasty relocation to another theatre, when the original venue was prohibited from staging it (the actors, led by Orson Welles, overcame an order preventing them from appearing on stage by performing in the auditorium). His other compositions included the revue *Regina* (1949) and a version of Kurt WEILL's *The Threepenny Opera* (1954).

Bloch, Ernest (1880–1959) Swiss-born US composer, who achieved a reputation with highly romantic works, a number of which were influenced by his Jewish heritage. His works included the opera *Macbeth* (1910), *Three Jewish Poems* (1913), *Schelomo* (1916), *Suite for Viola and Orchestra* (1919), a violin concerto (1937–38), *String Quartet Number Two* (1945) and *Sinfonia Breve* (1952).

> I aspire to write Jewish music not for the sake of self-advertisement, but because it is the only way in which I can produce music of vitality ... it is the Jewish soul that interests me, the complex, glowing, agitated soul that I feel vibrating through the Bible.
> ERNEST BLOCH

Blondie US pop group of the late 1970s and 1980s, that prospered on the visual and musical appeal of lead singer Debbie Harry (1945–). Before achieving stardom as a singer Debbie Harry had a varied career in and around the fringes of music and at one time worked as a bunnygirl at the New York Playboy Club. On one occasion she may have come close to a premature and grisly end when she was offered a lift from a man who later turned out to be the serial killer Ted Bundy.

Having appeared with the FOLK-ROCK group the Wind in the Willows and then with the Stilettoes, Harry founded Blondie (named after a popular US comic strip) in 1975 with guitarist Chris Stein (1950–). The band emerged as one of the most commercially viable expressions of the NEW WAVE and enjoyed chart success with such singles as 'Denis, Denis', 'Sunday Girl', 'Heart of Glass' and 'Call Me'. The group broke up in 1981 after internal arguments and Debbie Harry carried on both as a solo artist and as an actress.

Blood, Sweat and Tears US JAZZ-ROCK group, which enjoyed a series of hits in the late 1960s and early 1970s. Led by keyboard player and vocalist Al Kooper (1944–) and guitarist and singer Steve Katz (1945–), the band came together in 1967 and recorded *Child is Father to the Man* (1968) and the million seller, *Blood Sweat and Tears* (1969), in which it gave BLUES-ROCK versions of a number of established classics. Its most successful singles included 'You've Made Me So Very Happy', 'Spinning Wheel' and 'And When I Die' (all 1969).

Blood and Honour British extreme right-wing political movement (and magazine), which incorporates around 30 associated rock groups. Most BH events feature performances by bands linked to the movement, concerts attracting up to 2,000 fans (mostly young skinheads). The movement is overtly racist, as reflected by lyrics from the leading BH group, Skrewdriver:

> Europe awake, for the white man's sake,
> Europe awake, before it is too late,
> Europe awake, Europe awake now.

Concerts include short political speeches and heavy rock performances against a backdrop of Hitler posters, swastikas and the flags of South Africa's pro-apartheid

Afrikaaner Resistance Movement. Fans give Nazi salutes and yell 'Sieg Heil' in imitation of their Nazi German role-models. *See also* OI MUSIC.

> It's great when the whole crowd is doing it, united as one. It gives you a good feeling.
>
> IAN DONALDSON, of Skrewdriver

blow In JAZZ slang, to participate in a JAM session or simply to play an instrument (originally from blowing a wind instrument). Similarly, a musician who excels in performance may be said to be 'blowing fire'.

Blue *See* Bobby BLAND.

blue blowing The playing of such home-made instruments as the kazoo, comb and paper, and jug. Several bands made a good living with such music from the 1920s onwards, the best known being William 'Red' McKenzie's Mound City Blue Blowers, which introduced the term 'blue blowing' *c*.1924.

blue collar Name applied to ROCK music that reflects the lives of ordinary working people. The term is often linked with the music of US rock star Bruce SPRINGSTEEN, whose songs frequently evoke the experiences of the average US manual worker through the machismo of such numbers as 'Working on the Highway' and 'Tougher Than the Rest'. Many of Springsteen's hits (for instance, 'Drive All Night' and 'Wreck on the Highway') employ the imagery of the US car industry, and it is no accident that some of his most fervent fans are to be found in such 'car cities' as Detroit.

The lineage of blue collar rock includes the folk music of Woody GUTHRIE and LEAD-BELLY, who were similarly concerned with the challenges that faced working people in a developing industrial society. Springsteen's version of blue collar is, however, noticeably less optimistic than their work, and much of his music takes the form of an explanation for the apathy, and even an apology for the crimes, of the urban deprived.

> Now I been lookin' for a job but it's hard to find
> Down here it's just winners and losers
> And don't get caught on the wrong side of the line

> Well, I'm tired of comin' out on the losin' end
> So honey, last night I met this guy
> And I'm gonna do a little favour for him.
>
> BRUCE SPRINGSTEEN, 'Atlantic City', 1982

Blue-eyed Soul Brothers, the *See* the RIGHTEOUS BROTHERS.

blue note JAZZ term for a slighty 'depressed' (in other words, flattened) note. The term derives from the BLUES, in which the third or seventh notes of the scale are characteristically flattened.

Blue Oyster Cult US rock group, which was at the forefront of HARD ROCK in the 1970s. Variously known as Soft White Underbelly, Oaxaca and Stalk Forest, the band – the brainchild of rock writers Sandy Pearlman and Richard Meltzer – adopted its final name around 1970 and, with a constantly changing line-up, rapidly established a reputation as the only acclaimed heavy rock band to venture into ART ROCK, although the members' adoption of Nazi insignia and other emblems qualified them as exponents of SATANIC ROCK. Live appearances were spectacular, with extravagant use of lasers and other special effects. The band's most successful releases included the single '(Don't Fear) The Reaper' and the albums *Blue Oyster Cult* (1972) and *Agents of Fortune* (1976). Although it went into decline in the 1980s, the band continued to tour and issue occasional albums.

bluebeat *See* REGGAE.

bluegrass A style of traditional HILLBILLY music, which is particularly associated with the state of Kentucky, the Bluegrass State, where the grass is said to be so lush it is almost blue. Bluegrass is traditionally played chiefly on acoustic stringed instruments, with prominence being given to the guitar and the banjo, although postwar bands often added a range of amplified instruments. Leading exponents in the mid-1940s, when the term bluegrass was coined, included Bill MONROE's Bluegrass Boys, among whose hits was 'Blue Moon of Kentucky' (subsequently recorded by Elvis PRESLEY). A revival of interest in the form, promoted by the success of the bluegrass soundtrack of the film *Deliverance* in the 1970s, saw contemporary exponents identified as 'newgrass'.

blues Genre of twentieth-century Black music, which originated in the impoverished former plantation areas of the southern USA. The blues were the FOLK-songs of the oppressed Black poor and reflect the Black experience both in their languid African rhythms and in their pessimistic, resigned tone. Typical subjects of traditional blues songs included poverty and disease, unemployment, the harshness of life in the prisons of the USA, sex, alcohol and mob-lynching. Early exponents of the style ranged from poor sharecroppers to prison inmates, whose lives were all too often brutish, tragic and short – at least 10 notable blues artists were murdered by rivals or mistresses (many more died from alcohol and drug abuse).

Traditional blues songs are based on a five-note harmonic scale and are played in 12 bars in 4/4 time and make extensive use of so-called BLUE NOTES and improvisation. The usual instruments are guitars and mouth organs, although blues songs of one sort or another have since been written for every kind of instrument used in JAZZ, ROCK 'N' ROLL and POP. At least until the 1920s, much of the rhythm was pounded out by the guitar rather than on the drums, reflecting the fact that when they were working on the plantations Black slaves were forbidden to use drums (the plantation owners fearing that drums might be used to communicate plans of revolt).

Jazz and several other varieties of modern music (including rock 'n' roll) stemmed ultimately from the blues, which may be counted as perhaps the most influential of all twentieth-century musical genres. Even classical composers absorbed its influence: Maurice RAVEL called the slow movement of his violin sonata (1923–27) 'Blues', and both Aaron COPLAND and Sir Michael TIPPETT incorporated features of the style. Antonín Dvořák (1841–1904) for one insisted that: 'The future music of this country [America] must be founded on what are called the Negro melodies.'

Famous exponents of traditional blues included the singers Ma RAINEY, Bessie SMITH and Willie Mae Big Mama THORNTON, although by no means all singers of the blues were Black. LEADBELLY may have protested that 'No white man ever had the blues', but others saw its

appeal and relevance as universal.

W.C. HANDY played a key role in the formalization of the blues by having many blues songs written down for the first time, though it was not until the 1950s, when RHYTHM-AND-BLUES enjoyed widespread popularity, that the blues had their full impact on the course of modern music. Giants in blues-oriented music since the 1950s have included John Lee HOOKER, Muddy WATERS, Eric CLAPTON, John MAYALL, B.B. KING and Jeff BECK.

Blues, First Lady of the See Billie HOLIDAY.

Blues, Queen of the See Dinah WASHINGTON.

Blues Incorporated British SKIFFLE and BLUES group, which was formed by Alexis KORNER in the 1950s. Among the many musicians who appeared with the group before rising to stardom were Mick JAGGER, Jack Bruce (see CREAM), Ginger Baker (see CREAM) and Paul Jones (see MANFRED MANN).

blues-rock A genre of ROCK music that has a strong BLUES content. Various blues-rockers in the late 1960s and 1970s include BAD COMPANY, FREE and LED ZEPPELIN.

blues shouting Genre of BLUES music in which the singer literally shouts out the lyrics. Blues shouting was adopted by many blues vocalists in the 1940s, partly as a means of making themselves heard above the sound of the backing band.

Blur British rock group, which rivalled OASIS in the early 1990s. Comprising singer Damon Albarn, guitarist Graham Coxon, bassist Alex James and drummer Dave Rowntree, Blur formed in 1988 (as Seymour). Attracting attention for their unruly behaviour, Blur won a huge following with such albums as *Leisure* (1991), *Modern Life Is Rubbish* (1993), *Parklife* (1994), *The Great Escape* (1995) and *Blur* (1997). Singles include 'Country House' (1995).

> The only thing we have in common with Oasis is the fact that we're both doing shit in America.
> DAMON ALBARN, in Q magazine, 1996

Bock, Jerry (1928–) US composer and successful writer of Broadway musicals in the 1950s. Having begun with songs written for a number of revues, he enjoyed success with his score for the musical *Mr Wonderful* (1956), which provided Sammy DAVIS Jr with some strong songs. Other hit shows, some written in collaboration with Sheldon Harnick (1924–), included the Pulitzer prize-winning *Fiorello!* (1959), *She Loves Me* (1963) and *Fiddler on the Roof* (1964).

Böhm, Karl (1894–1981) Austrian conductor, who established an international reputation for his celebrated work with the Dresden State Opera (1934–42) and with the Vienna State Opera (1942–44 and 1954–56). He was particularly admired for his interpretations of the music of Beethoven, Mozart, Richard STRAUSS and Wagner and made many classic recordings, including all of Mozart's symphonies. It was to his friend Böhm that Strauss dedicated his opera *Daphne* (1938).

Bolan, Marc (Mark Feld; 1947–77) British pop star of the 1970s, who was one of the leading figures in the GLAM ROCK movement as frontman of the pop group T. Rex. Bolan recorded his first single, 'The Wizard', in 1966 and then turned down an invitation to join the YARDBIRDS. He joined John's Children before teaming up with Steve Peregrine-Took (1949–80) as Tyrannosaurus Rex to play their own distinctive version of FOLK-ROCK. The album *Unicorn* (1970) mixed ethereal acoustic folk with ROCK 'N' ROLL and, after Mickey Finn (1947–) took Peregrine-Took's place in 1970, Bolan adopted a more commercial electric sound.

Now known as T. Rex and backed by bassist Steve Currie (1947–81) and drummer Bill Legend (1944–), Bolan and Finn stormed the charts with such energetic and straightforward pop classics as 'Hot Love' (1971), 'Get It On' (1971), 'Telegram Sam' (1972) and 'Metal Guru' (1972), all of which reached Number One in the UK. The albums *Electric Warrior* and *The Slider* also topped the charts. Bolan himself cultivated an image as a flamboyant pop star, appearing in films and wearing outrageous sequined clothes (he was reported to be furious when his friend David BOWIE had the idea of exploiting a sexually androgynous image before he did).

The run of successes came to an end in the mid-1970s, but Bolan was making something of a come-back as a NEW WAVE star in 1977 when he tragically lost his life

in a car crash on Barnes Common (news of his death being eclipsed somewhat by the death of Maria CALLAS at almost the same time).

> You sure got a funny little voice.
> JIMI HENDRIX, on meeting Bolan in the late 1960s

> I was the best wiggler in the world.
> MARC BOLAN

> Marc Bolan and T. Rex there – sounding as good as the day he recorded it.
> TOMMY VANCE

Bolden, Charles 'Buddy' (1877–1931) US JAZZ trumpeter, who is often described as the first of the great jazz legends. Bolden was hugely popular in New Orleans at the turn of the century and was renowned for his appealing personality, which endeared him to ever-growing audiences. His career disintegrated, however, in the first decade of the twentieth century as – like many of those who were to follow – he fell prey to alcoholism, finally ending up in Jackson Mental Institution, where he died 24 years later. Speculation that he may have made some cylinder recordings in the 1890s continues, although no trace of these has yet been discovered. Legends surrounding his name include the apparently unfounded claims that he was a barber by trade, that he ran a newspaper and that his trumpet could be heard 14 miles away.

Bolshoi Theatre Theatre in Moscow, which is renowned as perhaps the foremost venue for both ballet and opera in the whole of Russia. Opened in 1825, the original theatre was destroyed by fire in 1853 but rebuilt three years later, and it has since witnessed numerous historic ballet and opera productions by its resident companies, although the conservatism of its management meant that the reputation of the Bolshoi artists was in decline in the early 1990s.

Bolton, Guy (1884–1979) British-born librettist of US parentage, who was responsible for many of the most celebrated MUSICALS of the twentieth century. A collaborator with such figures as Jerome KERN and P.G. Wodehouse (1881–1975), he wrote the libretti for such shows as *Sally* (1920), *Lady Be Good* (1924), *Rosalie* (1928), *Girl Crazy* (1930) and *Anything Goes* (1934).

Bon Jovi US HARD ROCK band, which had huge commercial success in the 1980s. Led by vocalist Jon Bon Jovi (John Francis Bongiovi; 1962–), who attracted attention after working as a menial at a record company for two years, the band came together in 1982, when it was launched in a wave of media hype. Other members were David Bryan (David Rashbaum; 1962–), Richie Sambora (1959–), Alec John Such (1956–) and Tico Torres (1953–). The first album was coolly received but the second, *Slippery When Wet* (1987), justified the record company's interest and became the top-selling rock album of the year. After extensive tours (in the course of which the band became the first HEAVY METAL outfit to play in Moscow), Jon Bon Jovi turned his attentions to developing a solo career and acting. Recent albums include *New Jersey* (1989), *Blaze of Glory* (1990), *Keep the Faith* (1992) and *These Days* (1995).

> I'll never be satisfied. I'm not happy that we have the Number One album, single, CD, video, that I sold out every show … and that I can buy a huge mansion if I want to. Next year I plan to do better. I want a bigger record, more shows. I want to be able to buy two houses instead of one.
> JON BON JOVI

Bonds, Gary 'US' (Gary Anderson; 1939–) US SOUL singer, who had several hits in the early 1960s and returned to the limelight 20 years later when Bruce SPRINGSTEEN COVERed several of his songs. Bonds' gravelly voice ensured the success of 'Quarter to Three' (1961) among other singles, and it was this number that Springsteen revived as an encore for live appearances in the early 1980s. Other hits included the extraordinary 'High School USA' (1959), which was recorded in 28 versions giving the names of schools in 28 different US cities. 'School is Out' (1961), 'Twist Twist Senora' (1962) and, more recently, 'This Little Girl' (1981) and 'Out of Work' (1982).

Bones *See* Frank SINATRA.

Boney M. German-based group, which enjoyed massive international success as a top DISCO band in the late 1970s. Singers Marcia Barrett (1948–) and Liz Mitchell (1952–), both from Jamaica, West Indian Bobby Farrell (1949–) and Monserrat-born Maizie Williams (1951–) released a series of nine Top 10 hits,

beginning with 'Daddy Cool' (1976). The group's biggest hit was 'Brown Girl in the Ring', which was derived from a traditional Jamaican nursery rhyme. The hits stopped after 1981, but the group re-formed in 1989.

Bonynge, Richard (1930–) Australian conductor, who has won particular acclaim for his presentations of neglected nineteenth-century operas. Many of his most celebrated operas have featured performances by his wife, the soprano Joan SUTHERLAND. He served as director of the Australian Opera (1976–84).

Bonzo Dog Doo Dah Band British pop group of the late 1960s, which almost uniquely, mined a seam of satirical pop. The Bonzos, led by vocalist and trumpeter Vivian Stanshall (1943–95) and pianist, guitarist and vocalist Neil Innes (1944–), began as a popular pub band, which quickly earned a reputation for eccentricity and fun. Other members included drummer 'Legs' Larry Smith (1944–) and saxophonists Roger Ruskin Spear (1943–) and Rodney Slater (1944–). The début album *Gorilla* (1967) lampooned a range of targets and made use of a parodic 1920s style of instrumentation. Further albums, including *The Doughnut in Granny's Greenhouse* (1968) and *Tadpoles* (1969), were hits and repeated the same formula, with the music, allied to a Monty Pythonesque humour, being aimed at all manner of bourgeois institutions. The band's most memorable hit was the single 'I'm the Urban Spaceman' (1969).

boogie To dance to pop music at a disco, party or concert. In musical terms, the word 'boogie' may be taken to refer to any form of song based on a three-chord structure, be it ROCK 'N' ROLL, BLUES, or HEAVY METAL. The word was also often applied to DISCO music of the 1970s. The form is descended from the simplified structures used in traditional BOOGIE-WOOGIE.

boogie-woogie A loud and lively style of JAZZ piano playing derived from guitar BLUES, which was first heard in the lower Mississippi area in the early twentieth century, when it was pioneered by such Black musicians as Clarence 'Pinetop' SMITH. The essence of boogie-woogie is a bouncing beat and a rolling rhythm provided by the left hand playing the bass notes at a brisk eight beats to the bar (leaving the right hand conveniently free for drinking purposes). As well as Smith, whose record *Pinetop's Boogie-Woogie* (1928) popularized the name, 'CowCow' DAVENPORT, 'Blind' Leroy Garnett, 'Tennessee' Ernie FORD and Merrill E. Moore were among those to enjoy huge success with such music both in the 1930s and in the years prior to the development of ROCK 'N' ROLL, of which it was in many ways a predecessor.

The word 'boogie' in US slang signifies a Black performer, while 'woogie' is simply a rhyming additive. In some areas examples of the style were known as BARRELHOUSE or stomps. *See also* BLUES; HONKY-TONK; RAGTIME.

Booker T. and the M.G.s US mixed-race SOUL band, which recorded several acclaimed instrumental hits in the 1960s. Led by multi-instrumentalist Booker T. Jones (1944–) and guitarist Steve Cropper (1941–), the group established its place in rock history with the 1962 single 'Green Onions' and consolidated its reputation with such later releases as 'Hang 'em High' (1968) and 'Time is Tight' (1969) before breaking up in 1971 (a brief reunion without Jones and Cropper in 1973 did not meet with success). Drummer Al Jackson (1935–75) was murdered by an intruder at his home in Memphis.

Boom-boom *See* Freddy CANNON.

Boomtown Rats Irish rock band, led by Bob GELDOF, which emerged as one of the most commercially successful bands of the NEW WAVE movement in the late 1970s. Founded by Geldof in 1975, the band (whose name derived from a phrase in a book by Woody GUTHRIE) shot to fame with the single 'Rat Trap', which reached Number One in 1976. The potential of the single was realized, legend has it, only when Geldof remarked on fans calling for the song at the end of a video of one of their concerts some months after the tape had been made.

The follow-up, 'I Don't Like Mondays' proved an even bigger hit, and the relatively articulate Geldof became a media star. The song was inspired by a tragic incident involving a young girl called Brenda Spencer, who shot several children playing in the street outside her home in San Diego;

when a journalist asked her why she had done it, her reply was simply 'I don't like Mondays'. The single was widely banned in the USA.

Further singles and albums followed, but the group fell from favour in the early 1980s, leaving Geldof to pursue his career through the BAND AID enterprise and other undertakings.

Boone, Pat (Charles Eugene Boone; 1934–) US pop singer, who ranked second only to Elvis PRESLEY as the most popular US balladeer of the late 1950s. Prospering on his clean-cut, all-American image, which appealed to a mass audience wary of the more extrovert Presley image, he began as a COUNTRY-AND-WESTERN singer and went on to enjoy chart success with such singles as 'Two Hearts', 'Ain't That a Shame', 'I'll be Home', 'Love Letters in the Sand', 'Moody River' and 'Speedy Gonzales'. In all he saw 56 of his recordings reach the charts in the USA and 27 in the UK; he collected 13 gold discs between 1956 and 1962. He also starred on television and in films, and when the commercial success came to an end he returned to country and religious music. His daughter, Debbie Boone (1956–), enjoyed one of the biggest chart hits of the 1970s with her song 'You Light Up My Life'. Both father and daughter could claim descent from the American pioneer Daniel Boone.

bootleg An unauthorized recording of a pop artist or group, which is then distributed in defiance of the copyright held by the artist and his record company. Such bootlegs have long been a problem for legitimate record companies, and some, usually made by illegal recording during concerts, have sold many thousands of copies, even though the sound quality may be less than perfect.

The original bootleggers were the smugglers of alcohol whose tricks included concealing bottles of contraband liquor in the legs of their boots. Bootlegging was a major industry in the USA during the Prohibition, when more than one contemporary band lampooned the government's liquor laws in their music.

The FOUR SEASONS planned a somewhat tardy celebration of the end of Prohibition in 1975 when they recorded a single under the title 'December 1933'; the song eventually came out as 'December, 1963

(Oh, What a Night)' and proved to be one of the group's biggest hits.

bop Synonym for BEBOP.

> Bop is the shorthand of jazz, an epigram made by defying the platitude of conventional harmony; it performs a post-mortem on the dissected melody. The chastity of this music is significant. It shuns climaxes of feeling and affirms nothing but disintegration.
> KENNETH TYNAN, the *Observer*, 1955

> Bop is mad, wild, frantic, crazy – and not to be dug unless you've seen dark days, too.
> LANGSTON HUGHES, *Simple Takes a Wife*, 1953

> Playing bop is like playing Scrabble with all the vowels missing.
> DUKE ELLINGTON, *Look*, 1954

Borel-Clerc, Charles (1879–1959) French composer, who wrote many hit songs for the likes of Maurice CHEVALIER and MISTINGUETT. An oboist with several Parisian orchestras, he established his reputation as a composer with the dance tune 'La Matchiche' (1903), which was hugely popular; later hits included 'Amour de Trottin', 'Madelon de la Victoire', which was taken up by Chevalier, and 'Le petit vin blanc'.

Boskovsky, Willi (1909–91) Austrian conductor, who enjoyed a long association with the VIENNA PHILHARMONIC ORCHESTRA as conductor (1954–79) of the celebrated New Year concerts. He joined the VPO as a violinist in 1932 and subsequently made many appearances as a conductor with violin in hand. He also made many recordings and was the founder of the Vienna Octet (1947), as well as leader of his own Boskovsky Ensemble.

Boss, the *See* Bruce SPRINGSTEEN.

bossa nova Genre of dance music that became widely popular in the West after it was imported from Brazil in the late 1950s. Portuguese for 'new bump', the bossa nova was fast and cheerful and based on the samba. Popular hits in the bossa nova style included 'Desafinado' and 'The Girl from Ipenema' (Ipenema is a district of Rio). Exponents of the style ranged from Frank SINATRA to Miles DAVIS.

Bostic, Earl (1913–65) US JAZZ alto saxophonist, singer, arranger and composer, who collaborated with many of the most popular jazz bands of the 1940s. He led his own band from 1938 to 1942 and again from 1945, but also played for Paul WHITEMAN and Lionel HAMPTON among others, and recordings featuring his skills included 'Flamingo', 'Cherokee' and 'Moonglow'. Among his own compositions were 'The Major and the Minor' and 'Brooklyn Boogie'. Heart problems led to a temporary retirement from music in the 1950s and his eventual death.

> Nobody knew more about the saxophone than Bostic, I mean technically, and that includes Bird.
> ART BLAKEY

Boston US rock band, which was among the top HEAVY METAL groups of the late 1970s and early 1980s. Singer and guitarist Tom Scholz (1947–), singer Bradley Delp (1951–), drummer Sib Hashian (1947–), guitarist Barry Goudreau (1951–) and bassist Fran Sheehan (1949–) all hailed from Boston, and the band enjoyed instant acclaim with its first album, *Boston* (1976), from which came such hit singles as 'More Than a Feeling'. The band did not return to the limelight until 1986, when the album *Third Stage* was well received, with the single 'Amanda' reaching Number One. *Walk On* (1994) also sold well.

Boston Symphony Orchestra US orchestra, founded in 1881, which established a worldwide reputation in the 1920s under its conductor Serge KOUSSEVITSKY, who remained with them until 1949. The orchestra is particularly celebrated for the so-called 'Boston Pops' concerts of more accessible works, which were launched in 1885 and have since become a regular feature (notably under Arthur FIEDLER, who presented them from 1930).

Boswell Sisters, the US all-female vocal group, which enjoyed considerable success with a close-harmony JAZZ style in the 1930s. The trio, which was formed by sisters Martha Boswell (1908–58), Vet Boswell (Helvetia Boswell; 1909–88) and Connee Boswell (Connie Boswell; 1907–76), hailed originally from New Orleans, where they first became interested in jazz. They became stars of radio, the cinema and the recording studio with their innovative close-harmony style, and they collaborated with such jazz greats as the DORSEY brothers and Benny GOODMAN and appeared with Bing CROSBY among others. Connee Boswell (who was confined to a wheelchair as a result of childhood polio complicated by a fall) pursued a highly successful solo career after the trio broke up in 1935 and numbered among her hits 'Stormy Weather' and 'Sand in my Shoes'. Among those who admitted to being strongly influenced by the sisters were Ella FITZGERALD and the ANDREWS SISTERS.

Botsford, George (1874–1949) US composer, who wrote many classic RAGTIME numbers at the turn of the century. His hits included 'Black and White Rag' (1908), which Winifred ATWELL adopted, 'Klondike Rag' (1908), 'Grizzly Bear Rag' (1910), which was re-written by Irving BERLIN, 'Honeysuckle Rag' (1911) and 'When Big Profundo Sang Low C' (1921).

bottleneck Guitar-playing technique in which a metal or glass tube is worn on the finger that presses against the strings to produce a smooth glissando effect. Also known as 'slide guitar', bottleneck playing was first perfected by BLUES guitarists in the early years of the century, when players used the broken necks of glass bottles to obtain the effect.

Boulanger, Nadia (Juliette) (1887–1979) French music teacher, conductor and composer, who instructed many of the leading figures in twentieth-century classical music. Her students included BERKELEY and COPLAND among many others, and she had a profound influence of their work, which reflected her championship of STRAVINSKY and FAURÉ. Among her own works were the cantata *La Sirène* (1908) and music for d'Annunzio's *Città Morte* (1911) and Verhaeren's *Les Heures claires* (1909–12). She was the first woman to conduct a complete symphony concert in London (1937). Of her own compositions she observed that they were 'not bad, but useless'.

> Legend credits every US town with two things – a five-and-dime and a Boulanger pupil.
> VIRGIL THOMSON

> Nadia Boulanger told me this way she has of deciding who to accept for students. Those who have no talent, and those who have no money; these are not acceptable. There are those who have talent but no money. These she accepts. Those who have little talent but much money she also accepts. But those who have much talent and much money she says she never gets.
> ROY HARRIS

> Do not take up music unless you would rather die than not do so.
> NADIA BOULANGER, advice to her pupils

Boulez, Pierre (1925–   ) French composer and conductor, who is often described as one of the most important classical composers of the century. He rejected a career in engineering, which would have capitalized on his talent as a mathematician, and studied under Olivier MESSIAEN, going on to adopt a radical AVANT-GARDE style based on his own mathematical formulae, which required extensive improvisation from players and the use of electronic instruments. His works include *Le Marteau sans maître* (1957), *Le visage nuptial* (1957), *Pli selon pli* (1960) and, more recently, such pieces as *Notations* (1980) and *Dialogue de l'Ombre Double* (1986). He was chief conductor of the BBC SYMPHONY ORCHESTRA (1971–75) and of the NEW YORK PHILHARMONIC (1971–77). In 1976 he was appointed director of IRCAM, the French institution researching the techniques of modern composition.

> Just listen with the vastness of the world in mind. You can't fail to get the message.
> PIERRE BOULEZ, of his music

> Boulez is a great composer. He is also a very intelligent man. He understands all the changes and they make him suffer ... he thinks that advancing the language is all. He feels he must be in the advance guard and he doesn't like what is happening there.
> OLIVIER MESSIAEN

> Pierre is a hen that hatches slowly.
> VIRGIL THOMSON

Boult, Sir Adrian (1889–1983) British conductor, who became one of the most famous conductors of the modern era. A champion of such English composers as Sir Edward ELGAR, he was also admired for his conducting of Wagner. He was the first conductor of the BBC SYMPHONY ORCHESTRA (1930–50) and principal conductor of the LONDON PHILHARMONIC (1950–57) and of the City of BIRMINGHAM SYMPHONY ORCHESTRA (1924–30; 1959–60). Notable productions under his baton included the first performance of *The Planets* by Gustav HOLST (1918) and the UK premiere of Alban BERG's *Wozzeck* (1934).

Bowie, David (David Robert Jones; 1947–) British pop star, nicknamed the Thin White Duke, who has maintained his position as one of the UK's biggest rock artists over a period of some 30 years through frequent changes in style. As David Bowie (a name he adopted to avoid confusion with Davy Jones of the MONKEES), he sprang to fame in 1969 with the single 'Space Oddity', even though US record companies were at first nervous of accepting such a doom-laden tale of space travel at a time when the Apollo series was under way. On its re-release in 1975 the record completed the journey it had begun in 1969 and became the UK Number One. The story of Major Tom, the luckless space traveller in Bowie's song, was continued in the sequel 'Ashes to Ashes', which reached Number One in 1980.

Bowie went on to cultivate a highly individual public persona, which combined the controversial, the bizarre and the musically adventurous. The hit album *Hunky Dory* (1971) was followed by the CONCEPT ALBUM *The Rise and Fall of Ziggy Stardust* (1972), which was based around the extravagant image of a fictitious rock star and his band the Spiders from Mars and explored new ground both musically and in terms of live performance, with Bowie impersonating his creation in striking make-up and transsexual costumes. His appearance in this and later roles was enhanced not only by his imaginative clothes but by the fact that his eyes are different colours (the result of a stabbing incident in his youth).

Bowie continued to indulge his taste for the dramatic in a series of albums that ranged in style from GLAM ROCK to FUNK and NEW WAVE, the best of them including *Aladdin Sane* (1973), *Diamond Dogs* (1974), which was inspired by the George Orwell novel *1984*, *Young Americans* (1975), *Station to Station* (1976), *Heroes* (1977), *Scary Monsters (And Super Creeps)* (1980) and *Let's Dance* (1983), and in the process stamped his influence on a whole generation of rock musicians. In 1988 he formed his own HARD ROCK band, Tin Machine, with whom he made three albums. More recent recordings include *Black Tie White Noise* (1993), *Outside* (1995) and *Earthling* (1997). He has also enjoyed a lengthy alternate career as an actor appearing in a number of film and stage roles.

> I don't think there's any point in doing anything artistically unless it astounds. The mums and dads thought I was weird, but I'm not an innovator. I'm really just a photostat machine.
> DAVID BOWIE, 1975

Bowlly, Al (Albert Alick; 1899–1941) South African singer, born in Mozambique of Greek-Lebanese descent, who was a hugely popular star in the UK in the 1930s. Dark and handsome, he began his musical career singing to the customers in his father's barber shop in Johannesburg but travelled to the UK (via Berlin), where he made many successful recordings alongside celebrated bandleaders. His biggest hits included 'The Very Thought of You' (1934). He was killed in 1941 when a German land mine exploded outside his London flat.

box Slang name for a guitar. It was first use by Black musicians in the USA in the 1950s but was taken up by White guitarists on both sides of the Atlantic in the 1960s. By extension, the word is also now sometimes used of a tape-recorder or related equipment. *See also* AXE.

Boy George Stagename of singer-songwriter George Alan O'Dowd (1961–), the British pop star who enjoyed huge commercial success in the UK in the 1980s. Boy George established his reputation as front man for the group Culture Club and reached Number One with the single 'Karma Chameleon' (1983). Much of his success depended on his deliberately flamboyant image, which incorporated the use of heavy make-up and pretty dresses. His career faltered somewhat towards the end of the decade when his addiction to drugs was publicly revealed. In 1987, however, he triumphed over the setbacks to reach Number One with the David Gates (*see* BREAD) song 'Everything I Own' (originally intended as an epitaph to one of Gates's own family). Recent albums include *Cheapness and Beauty* (1995).

Boyer, Lucienne (1903–83) French singer, known for her seductive style, who became a huge star of cabaret in Paris in the 1930s. Hits such as 'Parlez-moi d'amour', 'Un amour comme le nôtre' and 'Mon p'tit

Kaki' brought her a worldwide reputation, and she appeared in New York and in a number of films.

boystown sound Slang for the type of music that is played in gay DISCOS (derived from 'Boystown', the nickname for West Hollywood, a well-known gay community in the USA).

Bradford, Perry 'Mule' (1893–1970) US composer and pianist, who was one of the most important early JAZZ pioneers. One of the first jazzmen to settle in New York, he secured a recording contract for his protégée Mamie SMITH, making her the first notable Black recording star, and he had a huge hit himself with 'Crazy Blues' (1920), thus sparking off a vogue for RACE records. He led his own band, Perry Bradford's Jazz Phools, through the 1920s, when members of his troupe included, among other significant figures, the young Louis ARMSTRONG. He also spent a period in gaol after being found guilty of breaking copyright regulations.

Bragg, Billy (1958–) British singer-songwriter, nicknamed the Bard of Barking, who emerged as one of the most politically aware singers of the 1980s. Before he achieved fame as a musician Bragg experienced life in a number of different occupations: at various times he was a goatherd, painter and decorator, bank messenger, record shop sales assistant and a tank driver in the army. Legend has it that when he won his first record contract he asked only for the first six volumes of MOTOWN Chartbusters and a tin of BEATLES talcum powder.

His first solo albums in the early 1980s established his credentials as a committed left-wing activist, whose music reflected the influence of both FOLK and PUNK ROCK. In 1986 he helped to found Red Wedge, a group of performers allied to the socialist cause, and many of his songs had things to say about the Conservative government and the Establishment on which it thrived. He was once asked to give a talk to the pupils of Eton College and obliged with the promise that when the Labour Party came into office all public schoolboys would be hanged – then he relented and said their parents would be hanged instead.

His albums include *Talking With the Taxman About Poetry* (1986); among the most highly acclaimed of his singles are the EP 'Between the Wars', 'Levi Stubbs' Tears', which dealt with inner-city decay, and a COVER version of the Beatles' song 'She's Leaving Home'.

Brain, Dennis (1921–57) British horn player, who was considered one of the foremost musicians of his generation. Brain's mastery of the horn was displayed on numerous occasions with the ROYAL PHILHARMONIC ORCHESTRA and with the PHILHARMONIA ORCHESTRA; Benjamin BRITTEN had him and Peter PEARS in mind when he wrote his *Serenade* for tenor, horn, and strings, and he also inspired works by Paul HINDEMITH and Malcolm ARNOLD. Brain's career was cut short when he died in a car crash on his way back from the Edinburgh Festival.

Brassens, Georges (1921–81) French singer-songwriter, who was a popular star of the 1950s and 1960s. He began in cabaret and enjoyed huge success singing clever songs that mocked such targets as the Church and the political Establishment. Having sold some 20 million records, he eventually succumbed on the eve of a come-back to the kidney complaint from which he had suffered for many years.

Bratton, John W. (1867–1947) US composer and producer, who wrote a number of successful musicals and popular songs. A co-founder of the music firm Leffler & Bratton, he created such stage shows as *The Liberty Belles* (1901) and *The Pearl and the Pumpkin* (1905). His hit songs included 'You Never Can Tell What a Kiss Will Do' (1900), 'Make Believe' (1904) and 'The Teddy Bears' Picnic' (1907).

Braxton, Anthony (1945–) US JAZZ saxophonist and clarinettist, who first emerged as one of the most dynamic figures in contemporary jazz in the late 1960s. Braxton joined the AACM in Chicago in 1966 and formed his first group, the Creative Construction Company, whose début album appeared in 1968. That same year also saw the release of his *For Alto* (1968), the first album ever released of solo saxophone music. Braxton collaborated with Chick COREA in the band Circle and with other leading jazz contemporaries, further establishing himself as one of the more daring members of the jazz intelligentsia with compositions that reflected the influence of such modernists as Arnold SCHOENBERG and John CAGE (though he also recorded albums in a more traditional style).

Highlights of his recent career have included the album *Creative Orchestra Music 1976*, a compilation of big band pieces in an AVANT-GARDE style, and a sequence of works deriving inspiration from various aspects of ritual and ceremony. He has also written extensively for his own quartet, exploring such concepts as pulse-track structures and multiple logics music, which involves the four musicians playing separate pieces simultaneously. His ambition is to write for 100 orchestras connected by satellite.

Brazilian Bombshell, the *See* Carmen MIRANDA.

Bread US pop group of the late 1960s and early 1970s, which enjoyed commercial success with a series of SOFT ROCK hits. Led by vocalist, guitarist and keyboard player David Gates (1940–   ), Bread was formed in 1969 and later recorded such hits as the singles 'Make It with You' (1970), 'If' (1971), and 'Everything I Own' (1972) and the albums *On the Waters* (1970), *Manna* (1971), *Baby I'm-A Want You* (1972) and *Guitar Man* (1972). By the time the band split up in 1973 (largely as a result of clashes between Gates and songwriter James Griffin) it had achieved 11 Top 40 hits in the USA. The group re-formed briefly in 1977.

break In JAZZ and ROCK, a few bars that provide a musician with an opportunity for solo improvisation (usually a linking phrase between sections of a composition).

breaker Slang term used in the music business for a popular new single release 'breaking' into the record charts for the first time.

Bream, Julian (Alexander) (1933–   ) British classical guitarist, who did much to promote the popularity of his instrument in the UK from the 1950s onwards. He also proved a master of the lute, playing Elizabethan songs in company with Peter PEARS, and he inspired works by such leading composers as Benjamin BRITTEN and Sir William WALTON. Some of his most popular recordings were duets with fellow guitarist John WILLIAMS.

Never having thought of writing for the guitar, I asked Julian for a chart which would explain what the guitar could do. I managed to write some rather pretty pieces for him, except that the first six notes of the first piece all need to be played on open strings. So when he begins to play, the audience will probably think he's tuning the bloody thing up.
WILLIAM WALTON

Brel, Jacques (1929–78) Belgian singer-songwriter and author, who became a cult figure with a uniquely satirical, bleak and bitter-sweet style. He emerged as an international star singing such memorable songs as 'La Parlotte', 'Les Biches', 'Next', 'Marieke', 'My Death', 'Jackie', 'Les Bourgeois', 'Amsterdam' and 'If You Go Away', many of which were translated and RECORDED by other leading artists. The CABARET-REVUE *Jacques Brel is Alive and Well and Living in Paris* (1968) featured many of his best-known songs and was a major hit in New York. His performing career was cut short by cancer in the late 1960s, and he became a recluse in Polynesia although he recorded a last melancholy album, *Brel*, just a year before he died.

Brendel, Alfred (1931–   ) Czech-born pianist, resident in the UK, who emerged as one of the leading international pianists of his generation. He was winner of the prestigious Busoni Competition in 1949 and has since won acclaim for his performances of Mozart, Beethoven, Schubert, Liszt and many other important composers.

Brewer, Teresa (1931–   ) US singer, who recorded numerous hits in the 1950s in a range of styles. Her first hit came in 1950 with 'Music! Music! Music!', which was followed by such similar COUNTRY-influenced singles as 'Bell Bottom Blues' (1954), 'Silver Dollar' (1955) and 'A Tear Fell' (1956). Other hits reflected the influence of RHYTHM-AND-BLUES, among them 'Bo Weevil' (1956) and 'You Send Me' (1957), although she experimented with a variety of styles and in the 1980s made several jazz recordings with, among others, Duke ELLINGTON, Count BASIE and Stéphane GRAPPELLI.

Brian, (William) Havergal (1877–1972) British composer, whose prolific output included some of the most ambitious large-scale symphonies and other compositions ever devised. Largely self-taught, he created huge, extravagant works, of which the most significant include the oratorio *The Vision of*

Cleopatra (1908), the choral *Gothic Symphony* (1919–22) and the opera *The Tigers* (1918), which called for the appearance of an elephant on stage. In all he wrote no fewer than 32 symphonies (one of them the longest symphony ever composed) and five operas in addition to piano music and songs.

Brice, Fanny (Fannie Borach; 1891–1951) US comedienne and singer, who became a popular star when Florenz ZIEGFELD put her in the *Ziegfeld Follies* between 1910 and the mid-1930s. She sang a range of comic and novelty numbers, but was best known for her torch songs, her biggest hits including 'When a Woman Loves a Man' and 'Secondhand Rose'. Her life was the basis for the film *Rose of Washington Square* (1939) and for the Broadway stage show (and film) *Funny Girl* (1964). She was married to Broadway producer Billy Rose (1899–1966).

Bricusse, Leslie (1931–) British composer and librettist, who established his reputation in the 1950s writing hit songs for both the stage and the screen. He collaborated with Anthony NEWLEY on such major hit theatre shows as *Stop the World – I Want to Get Off* (1961) and *The Roar of the Greasepaint – the Smell of the Crowd* (1965), and also wrote *The Good Old Bad Old Days* (1972), *Pickwick* (1963), for which he wrote 'If I Ruled the World', and the ill-fated *Kings and Clowns* (1978). Highlights of his career in the cinema have included the songs 'Talk to the Animals', the Oscar-winning number from *Doctor Doolittle* (1967), 'I Hate People' from *Scrooge* (1970), 'Candy Man' from *Willie Wonka and the Chocolate Factory* (1970) and music for several James Bond films. He also wrote 'My Kind of Girl' for Max BYGRAVES to sing at the 1960 EUROVISION SONG CONTEST.

Bridge, Frank (1879–1941) British composer, conductor and viola player, who was particularly admired for his chamber music. His compositions, which influenced his pupil Benjamin BRITTEN, included orchestral tone poems, piano music, an opera and much chamber music. Broadly speaking, his early works followed in the romantic tradition, while his later pieces were less accessible and less tonal.

Brill Building US songwriting 'factory' where pre-packaged pop music was turned out in a constant stream in the 1970s. Founded by impresario Don Kirshner in the 1950s, Kirshner's Aldon Music songwriting company was actually based originally in premises opposite the Brill Building on Broadway. Writers who contributed much to the company's success included Neil SEDAKA, Burt BACHARACH, Carole KING, Neil DIAMOND and LEIBER AND STOLLER. Artists who benefited from their efforts ranged from Dusty SPRINGFIELD and the BYRDS to Aretha FRANKLIN, the ANIMALS and the MONKEES.

British Dylan, the *See* DONOVAN.

British Elvis Presley, the *See* Tommy STEELE.

British invasion Media term for the success enjoyed by British ROCK and POP performers in the USA, the traditional home of ROCK 'N' ROLL, in the mid-1960s. Inspired by the RHYTHM-AND-BLUES music of such Black American artists as Chuck BERRY, Muddy WATERS and LITTLE RICHARD, groups from the UK made significant inroads into the US market from 1964 on and, rather against the odds, won the approval of the US press. Chief among the 'invaders' were such groups as the BEATLES, the DAVE CLARK FIVE, the ROLLING STONES, the KINKS, the ANIMALS and the WHO.

Some US bands naturally resented the presence of British groups in their home territory. The Manchesters, led by David Gates (*see* BREAD), even released a single called 'I Don't Come from England' by way of a protest.

A second 'British invasion' in the late 1970s, powered by PUNK ROCK, startled the US musical establishment, which had settled into a comfortable but unadventurous rut based on straight rock and COUNTRY-oriented music.

Britt, Elton (1917–72) US COUNTRY singer-songwriter and yodeller, who recorded a number of major hits in the 1940s. A star of the GRAND OLE OPRY and of his own radio show, he had huge success with 'There's a Star-spangled Banner Waving Somewhere' (1942), which became one of the top-selling singles of the Second World War and was the first country song to sell over a million copies. Other hits included 'Chime Bells' (1948) and 'Candy Kisses' (1949). He was the first country star invited to perform at the White House.

Britten, Benjamin (1913–76) British composer and pianist, who was widely considered the most significant classical composer in British music of the postwar period. Britten wrote his first pieces at the age of just five and by the time he left preparatory school had produced 10 piano sonatas, six string quartets, three suites for piano, an oratorio and numerous songs. After further studies at the Royal College of Music and elsewhere (he was a pupil of Frank BRIDGE) he teamed up with the poet W.H. Auden and the GPO documentary unit in 1935, writing the music for such memorable short films as *Night Mail* (1936). *Variations on a Theme of Frank Bridge* (1937) caused a sensation at the Salzburg Festival, and he consolidated his international reputation with the brilliant use of traditional English folk-songs in his compositions, many of which were written specifically for his friend the tenor Peter PEARS.

Britten moved to the USA with Pears when war threatened and continued to develop throughout the war years, producing such important works as *Ceremony of Carols* (1942), *Serenade* for tenor, horn and strings (1943) and the celebrated opera *Peter Grimes* (1945), which won him recognition as the country's foremost composer. His sojourn in the USA came to an end in 1942 when he and Pears became homesick while reading an account of the poet George Crabbe by E.M. Forster and, after completing a dangerous Atlantic crossing on board a small Swedish cargo ship, the pair settled at Snape and then at Aldeburgh, helping to found the English Opera Group, which dedicated itself to performances of Britten's works. Together they made the ALDEBURGH FESTIVAL (inaugurated in 1948) one of the most prestigious musical gatherings in the world and began a tradition that long outlasted Britten's death.

Britten's other works included *The Young Person's Guide to the Opera* (1946), *Billy Budd* (1951), *Gloriana* (1953), which was composed for the coronation of Elizabeth II, *Noye's Fludde* (1958), *A Midsummer Night's Dream* (1960), *Curlew River* (1964), *The Burning Fiery Furnace* (1966) and his masterpiece, the *War Requiem* (1961), which was created for the rededication of bomb-damaged Coventry Cathedral and which sold more copies than any other contemporary classical work. Britten, a convinced pacifist from an early age, constructed this last great work for performance by a Russian (the soprano Galina VISHNEVSKAYA), a Briton (Pears) and a German (Dietrich FISCHER-DIESKAU) to illustrate his hopes for international harmony; the work did not please everyone, however, and Igor STRAVINSKY for one jibed at its emotional intensity, dismissing it as 'Kleenex music'.

The life peerage bestowed on Britten in the year of his death made him the first musician to be so honoured.

> I remember the first time I tried the result looked rather like the Forth Bridge.
> BENJAMIN BRITTEN, recollecting his beginnings as a composer, the *Sunday Telegraph*, 1964

Brooks, Elkie (Elaine Bookbinder; 1945–   ) British pop singer, nicknamed Manchester's Brenda LEE at the start of her career, who enjoyed success as a solo star in the 1970s and 1980s. She sang in cabaret and with RHYTHM-AND-BLUES and JAZZ-ROCK bands in the 1960s and in the rock group Vinegar Joe before establishing her solo career with such hit songs as 'Pearl's a Singer' and 'Lilac Wine' and with the albums *Pearls* (1981) and *Pearls II* (1982). After a lull, she returned to the top of the charts with the album *No More the Fool* (1986). *Bookbinder's Kid* eand *Nothin' But the Blues* followed in 1994.

Brooks, Garth (Troyal Garth Brooks, 1962–   ) US COUNTRY singer, who emerged as a top star in the 1990s. The son of a country singer, he burst on the scene in 1990 with *Garth Brooks*, which appealed to both country and pop audiences. Subsequent releases have included *No Fences* (1990), *Ropin' the Wind* (1991), *In Pieces* (1995) and *Fresh Horses* (1995). His phenomenal success in the USA has not been matched in Europe.

Brooks, Shelton (1886–1975) US composer, lyricist and entertainer, who wrote a series of hit songs during the First World War era. A RAGTIME pianist and vaudeville star, he established his reputation as a songwriter with 'Some of These Days' (1910), which was taken up with great success by Sophie TUCKER. He also wrote for such singers as Al JOLSON and Nora BAYES, his hits including 'You Ain't Talking to Me' (1910), 'Walkin' the Dog' (1916) and the best-selling 'The Darktown Strutters' Ball' (1917).

Broonzy, 'Big Bill' (William Lee Conley Broonzy; 1893–1958) US Black BLUES singer and guitarist, who was hailed as one of the most accomplished of the original bluesmen to issue from Chicago in the 1930s. He constructed his first guitar from an old cigar box at the age of 11 and formed a series of duos and trios in his home town, winning fame for his rapid fingerwork and rough blues voice, which also caused a sensation when he became the first leading blues musician to tour Europe in the early 1950s. Memorable recordings of his songs include one in which he is so intense that he breaks down in tears and another that ends in a fit of coughing (a precursor of the illness that eventually killed him). His best-known hits included 'Trucking Little Woman', 'When I been Drinking', 'Trouble in Mind', 'See See Rider' and 'Bossie Woman'.

> I guess all songs is folk-songs. I never heard no horse sing 'em.
> BIG BILL BROONZY

Bros British pop group of the late 1980s, which enjoyed huge commercial success as teen-idols, acquiring their own army of devoted fans, dubbed 'Brosettes'. Vocalist Matt Goss, drummer Luke Goss and bassist Craig Logan first came together as Caviar, then adopted the name Gloss before finally settling on Bros. The group's hit singles, which depended largely on the clean-cut image of its members, included 'When will I be Famous?' (1988) and – without Logan – 'Too Much' (1989). The duo broke up Bros rather bitterly in 1990 in the wake of financial problems and the rise of rivals NEW KIDS ON THE BLOCK.

> Of course, Bros have always been popular; it's just taken people a long time to realize it.
> ADRIAN JOHN

Brown, Arthur (1944–) British PSYCHE-DELIC rock singer, who had a brief career at the top of the charts in the late 1960s. As front man for the Crazy World of Arthur Brown, he got to Number One in the UK and Number Two in the USA with the raucous single 'Fire' (1968) and established himself as an eccentric but exciting live performer in distinctive cape and helmet, which spouted flames. His band

split shortly after its first album was released, and he enjoyed only limited success with new bands in ensuing years.

Brown, Clarence 'Gatemouth' (1924–) US BLUES and COUNTRY singer, guitarist and fiddler, who established himself as a popular star with a wide range of blues, country and JAZZ audiences. He began as a drummer but then concentrated on developing his talent as a blues guitarist, releasing such hits as 'Okie Dokie Stomp' (1955). He switched to country music in the 1960s and toured widely, and in the 1970s he started to incorporate jazz elements with such albums as *Blackjack* (1976) and *Makin' Music* (1979). Subsequent albums included the blues-oriented *Alright Again!* (1982) and *Standing My Ground* (1989).

Brown, James (1928–) Black US RHYTHM-AND-BLUES and SOUL singer, variously nick-named Mister Dynamite, Soul Brother Number One, Godfather of Soul and King of Soul, who, in the 1960s, was acknowledged to be the most important soul singer of all. The young James Brown worked as a pimp and shoe-polisher and tried his luck at base-ball and then boxing before settling on a musical career after winning a talent competition (he was also imprisoned for four years in 1949 for petty theft). He quickly established a reputation as an energetic and unconventional stage performer, his fast footwork dating from his days as a boxer. His first major hit was 'Please, Please, Please' (1956), which was quickly followed by the Number One single 'Try Me' (1958). Many hits – mostly with the backing of his band the Famous Flames – followed, among them 'Night Train', 'Prisoner of Love', 'Out of Sight', 'Poppa's Got a Brand New Bag' and 'I Got You (I Feel Good)', and he was soon being hailed the master of r 'n' b and soul. The album *Live at the Apollo* (1962) was the first live album by an r 'n' b artist to sell over a million copies, and Brown's live act became one of the most popular in contemporary music. More recent hits have included the sensual and provocative 'Get Up I Feel like being a Sex Machine' (1970), a string of funky DISCO and RAP numbers and 'Living in America' (1986), which was used as the theme tune for the film *Rocky IV*.

During the 1960s he allied himself with the cause of Black civil rights, which was reflected in the hit 'Say it Loud – I'm Black and I'm Proud', and he helped to prevent riots following the assassination of Martin Luther King in 1968. He also had a number of brushes with the law; he was gaoled for drug offences in 1988 and received a further sentence a year later for assault, to the outrage of his many fans. Michael JACKSON and PRINCE are among the many leading Black performers who have acknowledged their debt to Brown.

> Let's not forget James Brown picked cotton. James Brown shined shoes. And yet James Brown is still active. Because James Brown worked all the way to the top. . . . I first started tryin' to get a decent meal, a decent pair of shoes, so when I got to where I could do that, I thought I was on the top anyway.
> JAMES BROWN, *Los Angeles Weekly*, 1984

Brown, Les (1912–) US bandleader, arranger, saxophonist and clarinettist, who led one of the most popular big bands of the 1930s and 1940s. After varied experience alongside such jazz greats as Jimmy DORSEY, he founded his own band in 1938 and established himself as a recording and broadcasting star with such hits as 'Joltin' Joe DiMaggio' (1941), 'I've Got My love to Keep Me Warm' (1948) and his theme tune 'Leap Frog'. He also wrote such hits as 'Sentimental Journey' (1944), recorded with Doris DAY, and worked closely with Bob HOPE over the course of some 30 years.

Brown, Lew (Louis Brownstein; 1893–1958) US lyricist and producer, who collaborated on a long series of hit songs of the 1920s and 1930s. He wrote many of his best-known lyrics in partnership with composer Ray HENDERSON, his most celebrated songs including 'Give Me the Moonlight, Give Me the Girl', 'Life is Just a Bowl of Cherries' and 'Sonny Boy' as well as contributions to such hit shows as *Greenwich Village Follies* (1922), *George White's Sandals* (1928 and 1931) and *Stand Up and Cheer* (1934).

Brown, Nacio Herb (1896–1964) US composer, who wrote numerous hit songs for Hollywood movies and revues. He worked as a vaudeville pianist, as a tailor and as an estate agent before concentrating on songwriting and penning the hits 'The Wedding of the Painted Doll' and 'You were Meant for Me' for the first MGM MUSICAL, *The Broadway Melody* (1929). He wrote such classic songs as 'Singin' in the Rain', originally for *Hollywood Revue* (1929) but later performed by Gene KELLY in the film of the same name, 'You are My Lucky Star', for *The Broadway Melody of 1936* (1935), 'Good Morning', from *Babes in Arms* (1939), and 'Make 'em Laugh', from *Singin' in the Rain* (1952).

Brown, Rosemary British psychic, who in the 1960s claimed to be communicating new works from a number of long-dead composers. Rosemary Brown, from Balham in south London, was the most extraordinary of several mediums who claimed to have such contact with famous musicians from another time, and her claims have never been convincingly disproved.

She had her first visitation, from a figure she later realized was Franz Liszt, when she was seven years old, but it was not until 1964 that Liszt reappeared and the flow of music from beyond the grave began in earnest. At the apparent dictation of unseen and unheard commands she took down complete new works by Bach, Beethoven, Chopin, Liszt and Igor STRAVINSKY, despite admitting to next to no musical knowledge herself (Brahms and Sergei RACHMANINOV stepped in here to help her improve her piano technique). Schubert allegedly attempted to sing the notes to her, but this was not a great success – Mrs Brown complained that he did not have a very good voice.

The scores of these works, which included Beethoven's 10th and 11th Symphonies (both unfinished) and a sonata by Schubert, were shown to many experts, who admitted they were confounded by them, although they remained unwilling to accept them as genuine. Among those who were impressed by Brown's claims was Richard Rodney BENNETT, who observed:

> A lot of people can improvise, but you couldn't fake music like this without years of training. I couldn't have faked some of the Beethoven myself.

Brown, Ruth (1928–) Black US RHYTHM-AND-BLUES singer, nicknamed Miss Rhythm, who ranked among the most popular r 'n' b performers of the 1950s. The daughter of a Methodist preacher, she defied her parents' wishes by interesting herself in the BLUES and in JAZZ and left home to pursue her career. She married trumpeter Jimmy Brown and toured widely, eventually switching to rhythm-and-blues, and she enjoyed considerable chart success with such hits as 'Teardrops from My Eyes' (1950), 'Daddy Daddy' (1952), 'Mambo Baby' (1955) and 'What a Dream' (1955).

Browne, Jackson (1948–) US singer-songwriter, born in Germany, who established a strong cult following in the 1970s. While still a child he sang in HOOTE-NANNIES in California and then graduated as a singer-songwriter, pianist and guitarist with songs for such artists as Nico and the EAGLES (notably 'Take it Easy'). His own hits during the 1970s included 'Doctor my Eyes', 'Jamaica Say you Will' and 'Stay'. His albums also sold well, the most notable including *For Everyman* (1973), *Late for the Sky* (1974), *The Pretender*, which concerned the suicide of his wife, *Running on Empty* (1978) and *Hold Out* (1980). He was closely associated with the Campaign for Nuclear Disarmament in the late 1970s, a link that culminated in a short gaol sentence in 1981, and with Third World issues. More recent releases include the albums *Lives in the Balance* (1986), *World in Motion* (1989) and *Looking East* (1996).

Browns, the US vocal COUNTRY trio, who were among the top country stars of the late 1950s. James Edward Brown (1934–) and his sisters Bonnie Brown (1937–) and Ella Maxine Brown (1932–) became popular broadcasting stars in the mid-1950s and had their biggest hit in 1959, with 'The Three Bells', which was derived from the original Edith PIAF hit 'Les trois cloches'. Other singles included 'Scarlet Ribbons' (1959) and 'The Old Lamplighter' (1960). 'Jim Ed' Brown carried on as a solo performer after 1967 and eventually teamed up with Helen Cornelius, with whom he recorded such hits as 'I Don't Want to Have to Marry You' (1976) and 'You Don't Bring Me Flowers' (1979), before resuming a solo career in 1981.

Brubeck, Dave (1920–) US JAZZ pianist and composer, who emerged as one of the most popular of contemporary jazz figures since the Second World War. Given early piano lessons by his mother, he joined his first jazz band at the age of 13 and under Arnold SCHOENBERG and Darius MILHAUD. He formed a series of groups after the war and achieved stardom leading a brilliantly talented quartet performing 'cool' jazz in the 1950s and 1960s. In more recent years he has explored a rock-influenced style in

company with his sons Darius, Chris and Danny. His most celebrated recording remains the jazz classic 'Take Five' (1959), on which he collaborated closely with his saxophonist Paul DESMOND; others have included ballets, piano concertos, a musical, a mass, an oratorio, two cantatas and film music. He has performed at many major festivals and on two occasions (1964 and 1981) at the White House.

> Jazz is about the only form of art existing today in which there is freedom of the individual without the loss of group contact.
> DAVE BRUBECK

bruitism The use of sheer noise in a composition, as employed by various composers of works associated with FUTURISM and other radical musical genres (from the French *bruit*, noise).

Brymer, Jack (1915–) British clarinettist, who established a reputation as one of the leading clarinettists of his generation. He enjoyed a long and fruitful association with the ROYAL PHILHARMONIC ORCHESTRA, being recruited by Sir Thomas BEECHAM in 1947 and remaining its principal clarinettist for another 16 years.

bubblegum Genre of catchy and simplistic, uncontroversial US POP music of the 1960s that was specifically aimed at the pre-teenage market (teenagers and their younger siblings having been identified as the major consumers of bubblegum sweets). The earliest examples of the genre were in fact ROCK-based advertising jingles designed to sell brands of chewing-gum. Bubblegum hits included 'Yummy Yummy Yummy' by the Ohio Express, 'Sugar Sugar' by the ARCHIES and many others released under the influence of US pop producer Neil Bogart, the manager of the Buddah record label who was nicknamed the Bubblegum King. *See also* TEENY-BOP.

> Older rock fans dismiss the stuff as 'bubblegum music', but Micky Dolenz, one of the Monkees, the pre-packaged group which capitalized on subteens in the 1960s, defends the genre as 'first-grade music for kids in first grade'.
> SARA DAVIDSON, *The Atlantic*, 1973

Bubbles *See* Beverly SILLS.

Buchanan, Jack (1891–1957) Scottish singer, dancer, actor and director, who was often described as a British version of Fred ASTAIRE. A star of the London musical stage during the First World War and through to the 1950s, he appeared in many hit shows and films on both sides of the Atlantic, his hit songs including 'And Her Mother Came Too', from *A to Z* (1921), 'Fancy Our Meeting', from *That's a Good Girl* (1928), 'I'm in a Dancing Mood', from *This'll Make You Whistle* (1936), 'By Myself', from *Between the Devil* (1937) and 'I Guess I'll Have to Change My Plan', from *The Band Wagon* (1953).

Buck, Gene (1885–1957) US lyricist, writer and director, who is remembered for his long association with Florenz ZIEGFELD's *Follies*. Buck began as a designer of covers for sheet music but ventured into songwriting after his sight deteriorated, and he quickly attracted interest with such songs as 'Daddy has a Sweetheart and Mother is her Name' and 'Some Boy', both of which became million-sellers. Ziegfeld used some of Buck's material in the *Follies* of 1912, and Buck contributed to some 20 editions of the show. His hits included 'Tulip Time' (1919), ''Neath the Southern Moon' (1924) and 'Lovely Little Melody' (1924).

Bucks Fizz British pop group that sprang to fame with victory in the 1981 EUROVISION SONG CONTEST. The group was formed after hundreds of applicants were auditioned for the UK entry for the contest, in which they sang 'Making your Mind Up'. Modelled on ABBA, the group – Mike Nolan (1954–), Bobby G. (Robert Gubby; 1953–), Jay Aston (1961–) and Cheryl Baker (1954–) – won a large middle-of-the-road following with such singles as 'Land of Make Believe' (1981) and 'My Camera Never Lies' (1982), both of which reached Number One in the British charts. Nolan was seriously injured in a coach crash involving the group in 1984, and there were further personnel changes before the band finally disappeared from view as the members pursued other careers in show business.

Buffalo Springfield US FOLK-ROCK group of the mid-1960s, which brought together some emerging major new talents at the start of their careers. Named after an item of farm machinery, Buffalo Springfield comprised singer Richie Furay (1944–), drummer Dewey Martin (1942–) and singer-songwriters and guitarists Stephen Stills

(1945–) and Neil YOUNG. Such releases as the albums *Buffalo Springfield* (1966) and *Again* (1967) and the single 'For What It's Worth' (1967) attracted much attention and anticipated the success of CROSBY, STILLS, NASH AND YOUNG. Internal divisions disrupted further progress, however, and the album *Last Time Around* (1968) was recorded with various members being dubbed so as to avoid their having to come face to face at the studio. The band finally broke up that same year.

Buffet, Jimmy (1946–) US COUNTRY-ROCK singer-songwriter, who established himself as a top star in the 1970s. The album *A White Sport Coat and a Pink Crustacean* (1973) was his first significant hit, mixing elements of semi-autobiographical material with social satire and humour. *Changes in Attitude* (1977) brought him his first major commercial success and included the hit singles 'Margaritaville' and 'Changes in Attitude'. Since then, popular releases have included the comedy single 'Cheeseburger in Paradise' (1978) and such albums as *Son of a Son of a Sailor* (1978), *Last Mango in Paris* (1985), *Fruitcakes* (1994) and *Barometer Soup* (1995).

Bunn, Teddy (1909–78) US JAZZ and BLUES guitarist and singer, who won acclaim playing with many of the jazz greats of his time, as well as with the Spirits of Rhythm group of the 1930s and 1940s. Having switched to an electric guitar around 1940, he won many admirers playing jazz with the bands of Duke ELLINGTON and Lionel HAMPTON among others and ultimately switched to RHYTHM-AND-BLUES in the 1950s.

Burke, Joe (1884–1950) US composer, who wrote many hits for Hollywood movies of the 1920s and 1930s. His best-known compositions included 'Down Honolulu Way' (1916), 'Carolina Moon' (1928), 'Tip-toe Through the Tulips' and 'Painting the Clouds with Sunshine', from *Gold Diggers of Broadway* (1929) and 'Dancing with Tears in My Eyes' (1930).

Burke, Johnny (1908–64) US lyricist, who wrote many hit songs for the stage and for Hollywood movies. His best-remembered compositions include 'Pennies from Heaven' (1936), 'Moonlight Becomes You' (1942) and the Oscar-winning 'Swinging on a Star' (1944).

Burke, Solomon (1936–) US SOUL singer and minister, nicknamed the King of Rock 'n' Soul, who ranked among the biggest soul artists of the 1960s. Having sung in gospel choirs as a child, Burke made his recording début in the mid-1950s and achieved stardom with such hits as 'Cry to Me', 'The Price', 'Can't Nobody Love You', 'Goodbye Baby (Baby Goodbye)', 'Got to Get You Off My Mind' and 'Tonight's the Night'. He returned to the charts spasmodically through the 1970s and has since concentrated on gospel music.

Burnette, Johnny (1934–64) US COUNTRY and ROCK 'N' ROLL singer-songwriter and guitarist, who enjoyed a series of hits in the early 1960s. Having failed to make an impact as a straight rock 'n' roller, he adopted a countrified sound and had major commercial success as a teen-idol with such songs as 'Dreamin'' (1960), 'You're Sixteen' (1960) and 'Little Boy Sad' (1961). His career, which suffered somewhat through constant comparison with Elvis PRESLEY, ended prematurely with his death in a boating accident on Clear Lake in California.

His brother, Dorsey Burnette (1932–79), had hits with such numbers as 'Tall Oak Tree' and 'Hey Little One' in the early 1960s.

Burrows, Stuart (1933–) Welsh tenor, who has established an international reputation appearing at virtually all the major opera venues around the world. Having won a singing prize at the Royal National Eisteddfod in 1959, Burrows went on to win particular acclaim in the operas of Mozart, although he has also won praise as a singer of ballads. His most popular roles have included Don Ottavio in *Don Giovanni*.

Burton, James (1939–) US guitarist, who has won wide recognition for his work with a range of leading stars since the late 1950s. Having backed a series of COUNTRY artists, Burton went on to work with singers such as Ricky NELSON, Elvis PRESLEY, Hoyt AXTON, Randy NEWMAN, Judy COLLINS, Emmylou HARRIS and John DENVER, and he was acknowledged as one of the leading COUNTRY-ROCK stylists. He has also recorded two solo albums.

Bush, Alan Dudley (1900–) British classical composer, whose works were strongly influenced by his communist sympathies.

Founder of the Workers' Music Association in 1936, he admired such contemporaries as Arnold SCHOENBERG, Béla BARTÓK and Paul HINDEMITH; his works include *Dialectic* (1929) for string quartet, three symphonies, and the operas *Wat Tyler* (1953), *Men of Blackmoor* (1960) and *Joe Hill* (1970).

> Is there a high social role of music here in our decadent bourgeois society? Yes, there is, if we embrace partisanship in our art, and place it at the service of those who are partisans in the glorious struggle of mankind for the new world of true freedom, which socialism and communism will secure for all.
> ALAN BUSH, *The Modern Quarterly*, 1945

Bush, Kate (1958–) British singer-songwriter, who leapt to fame in the late 1970s and has maintained her status as one of the more original pop stars of the 1980s. Bush first indulged her taste for music by knocking out tunes on an ancient harmonium in the family barn – but she had to find another instrument after its inner workings fell victim to the teeth of resident mice. Dave Gilmour of PINK FLOYD 'discovered' the teenaged Bush and prepared her for stardom (she signed her first contract for EMI when she was 13 years old). 'Wuthering Heights' spent four weeks as UK Number One in 1978, and Bush enjoyed equal success with her début album *The Kick Inside*. Always performing her own material, she enjoyed particular success in the LP market, three of her records – *Never for Ever* (1980), *Hounds of Love* (1984) and *The Whole Story* (1986) – reaching Number One in the UK. She returned to literature as a source of inspiration in 1989, this time drawing on James Joyce's *Ulysses* for *The Sensual World*. *Red Shoes* followed in 1993.

She has only toured once, in 1979; the demands of 17 costume changes and intensive rehearsal of dance and mime routines proved too much and she vowed never to tour again.

One of the most unusual Bush releases was her 12-inch single 'Sensual World', which had two sets of grooves: according to which groove the needle landed in the listener would hear either the instrumental or the vocal line.

busk To play music in the street in the hope of receiving money from passers-by. The word probably comes from nautical slang, in which it means 'to cruise about' (from the French *busquer sa fortune*, to seek one's fortune, or from the Italian *boscare*, to prowl or to filch). From the turn of the century 'busking' has had primarily musical connotations, although it formerly also encompassed the activities of such street entertainers as jugglers and magicians.

Busoni, Ferruccio Benvenuto (1866–1924) German-Italian composer and pianist, based for most of his life in Berlin and Switzerland, who is usually remembered for the operas *Turandot* (1917) and *Doktor Faust* (unfinished at his death). Having established an international reputation as a virtuoso pianist, being particularly admired for his performances of Bach, he concentrated on writing operas in the last years of his life.

A kind of musical Leonardo.
WILHELM KEMPFF

If one only knows Busoni as a musician, one does not know him. (And who knows him as a musician?)
ALFRED EINSTEIN

He could conceive wonderful things in music; unfortunately he could not consistently turn them into music.
NEVILLE CARDUS, the *Manchester Guardian*, 1937

Butler, Jerry (1939–   ) US SOUL singer, nicknamed the Ice Man because of his 'cool' style, who established a reputation as one of the best soul artists while with the IMPRESSIONS in the 1950s and 1960s. Among his hits, both with the Impressions and, later, as a solo artist, were 'For Your Precious Love' (1958), 'I'm a Telling You' (1961), 'Moon River' (1961), 'Make it Easy on Yourself' (1962), 'Let It be Me' (1964), 'Never Gonna Give You Up' (1968), 'Ain't Understanding Mellow' (1972) and 'I Wanna Do It to You' (1975). Notable albums included *Ice on Ice* (1968) and *Suite for the Single Girl* (1977).

Butt, Dame Clara (1872–1936) British contralto, who became one of the most celebrated classical singers of the early twentieth century. An imposing figure at over 6 feet tall, she enjoyed huge fame for her delivery of 'Land of Hope and Glory', which she sang at venues throughout the Empire. Other memorable performances during her successful career included the première performance of Sir Edward ELGAR's *Sea Pictures* (1899) and her interpretation of Gluck's *Orfeo* (1920).

Legend has it that it was Clara Butt who, on the eve of a tour of Australia, received the immortal tip from Dame Nellie MELBA to the effect 'Sing 'em muck – it's all they can understand'. Questioned about this years later, Melba denied it entirely, adding: 'In Clara's case, it wasn't necessary.'

What we need are more songs like 'The Lost Chord'. There is something of the stature and grandeur of Beethoven about it.
CLARA BUTT

Butterfield, Billy (1917–88) US JAZZ trumpeter, who was among the leading exponents of jazz trumpet in the 1940s and 1950s. He played with many bands, including those of Bob CROSBY, Artie SHAW, Benny GOODMAN and Louis ARMSTRONG, with whom he recorded such standards as 'Blueberry Hill'. An attempt to form his own big band ended in financial disaster, but he did lead a number of smaller groups with success.

Butterfield, Paul (1942–87) US BLUES-ROCK singer and harmonica player, who led the most influential White blues band of the 1960s. The son of a Chicago lawyer, he formed his Blues Band in 1963 and gradually perfected his electric blues style, which caused a sensation at the NEWPORT FOLK FESTIVAL in 1965, when his band (without Butterfield himself) backed Bob DYLAN using an ELECTRIC GUITAR for the first time. Among his most influential albums were *Paul Butterfield Blues Band* (1966) and *East-West* (1966); later releases – mostly with his new Better Days band – explored RHYTHM-AND-BLUES and SOUL with mixed success. He also made guest appearances with the likes of John MAYALL and the BAND among others. His last releases included *North-South* (1981) and *The Legendary Paul Butterfield Rides Again* (1986).

Butterworth, George (Sainton Kaye) (1885–1916) British composer, who was one of the small group of English composers who found inspiration in traditional folk music in the early years of the century. Like his contemporaries Ralph VAUGHAN WILLIAMS and Cecil SHARP, who befriended him at Oxford, Butterworth compiled his own collection of folk tunes and used many of them in his own works. Among his most popular compositions were the song-cycle *The Banks of Green Willow* (1914) and the rhapsody and song-cycle *A Shropshire Lad*

(1913), which was based on the poems of A.E. Housman. He died in action on the Somme during the First World War.

Buzzard's Roost, the *See* APOLLO THEATRE.

Bygraves, Max (Walter Bygraves; 1922–   ) British singer and comedian, who first became a popular MIDDLE-OF-THE-ROAD entertainer in the 1950s. Having appeared on radio's *Educating Archie*, he enjoyed a series of hits with such 'family' numbers as 'Cow-puncher's Cantata', 'You Need Hands', 'Out of Town' and 'Deck of Cards'. Several compilations of his hits and other well-known songs have been released as 'Singalong' albums over the years. He acquired the name Max by virtue of his imitations of comedian Max Miller during RAF service in the Second World War.

Byrds, the US pop rock group of the 1960s, which pioneered FOLK-ROCK and psychedelia with huge commercial success. Guitarist and singer Roger McGuinn (1942–   ), guitarist David Crosby (1941–   ), singer-songwriter Gene Clark (1942–91), bassist Chris Hillman (1942–   ) and drummer Michael Clarke (1943–93) came together in Los Angeles in 1964 and quickly attracted interest with their fusion of the vocal harmonies of traditional folk with contemporary guitar lines. The group's COVER version of Bob DYLAN's 'Mr Tambourine Man' in 1965 sold over a million copies (although, in fact, McGuinn actually played on the recorded version, with session men doing the rest of the work). Other hits included Pete SEEGER's 'Turn, Turn, Turn' and other Dylan tracks.

The band experimented with so-called space rock, in which it employed early versions of the SYNTHESIZER, and also ventured into COUNTRY music with the album *Sweetheart of the Rodeo* (1968), which was effectively the first COUNTRY-ROCK LP ever released. Another departure was marked by the album *Eight Miles High*, in which the group incorporated a range of oriental sounds. Clark left in 1966, and Crosby dropped out a year later. When replacements Gram Parsons and Clarence White also died (Parsons of drug abuse and White in an accident with a drunk driver), the band finally broke up in 1973. Over the years, McGuinn has re-formed the group for the occasional album or concert.

The American Beatles.
GEORGE HARRISON

C

Caballé, Montserrat (1933–) Spanish soprano, who first established an international reputation in 1965 in Donizetti's *Lucretia Borgia*. She is particularly admired for her powerful voice, at its best in performances of works by Verdi, Donizetti, Wagner, Mozart, Puccini and Strauss. She also ventured into rock in 1988 when she recorded with Freddie Mercury (*see* QUEEN).

cabaret Form of night club entertainment with a strong musical element that thrived in various major European cities between the 1880s and the 1930s. The pace was set in the early years by the night clubs of Paris, where the 'Chat Noir' was especially popular with the AVANT-GARDE (Erik SATIE was one of the pianists who appeared there on a regular basis). The night clubs of Berlin offered some of the best cabaret shows (Arnold SCHOENBERG writing a number of pieces for such performances in the first decade of the century). In the interwar period cabaret bills were dominated by JAZZ music and retained their reputation for daring, sophisticated entertainment. German night clubs in particular adopted an increasingly strident political tone, with contributions from Bertolt Brecht and Kurt WEILL among others during the 1920s and the 1930s (a period covered by the classic musical *Cabaret*). After the war cabaret at most venues degenerated into a somewhat disreputable and unambitious form of variety entertainment.

cadence Dance rhythm from Martinique and Guadeloupe, which caught on in many other countries in the 1970s. It is strongly influenced by CALYPSO and the BEGUINE among other rhythms as well as reflecting elements borrowed from REGGAE.

Caesar, Irving (1895–) US lyricist and librettist, who wrote the words for many famous songs by George GERSHWIN and other leading composers. His best-known lyrics included those for 'Swanee' (1919), which he and Gershwin put together in just 10 minutes, 'Tea for Two' (1924) and 'Just a Gigolo' (1930). He also worked as librettist on a number of shows, among them the *Greenwich Village Follies* (1922–25), *No, No, Nanette* (1925), several editions of the *Ziegfeld Follies* and *George White's Scandals*, and *White Horse Inn* (1936).

Cage, John (1912–92) US AVANT-GARDE composer, who became one of the best-known proponents of what he dubbed INDETERMINACY and in the process one of the most influential and controversial of all twentieth-century composers. A pupil of Arnold SCHOENBERG's, he explored new sounds and wrote some of his most controversial pieces for the PREPARED PIANO and for percussion orchestras, which used such 'instruments' as tin cans. He worked in radio, was recruited to compose and play for the Merce Cunningham Dance Company and went on to absorb the influence of Dadaism and Zen Buddhism. He challenged audiences to respond to a redefined music that incorporated all manner of random novel effects, electronic instruments and even SILENCE itself. Other works had a multi-media aspect and were close to theatre (*HPSCHD*, for instance, included instructions for seven amplified harpsichords, tape players and lighting).

Cage's works include *Sonatas and Interludes* (1948), *Imaginary Landscape No. 4* (1951), which was written for 24 randomly tuned radio sets, the notorious *4' 33"* (1952), which was entirely silent, and *Apartment Building 1776* (1976); *Inlets* was scored for water-filled conch shells. He also experimented with music notation, an exhibition of such pieces actually winning an art award.

Although none of his works is likely to remain in the standard repertory (he actually admitted several of his creations were boring to listen to), Cage's output had a profound influence on modern music and has proved to be a stimulus to further experimentation and unconventionality.

Which is more musical, a truck passing by a factory or a truck passing by a music school?

JOHN CAGE, *Silence*, 1961

Schoenberg said I would never be able to compose, because I had no ear for music; and it's true I don't hear the relationships of tonality and harmony. He said: 'You will always come to a wall and you won't be able to go through'. I said, well then, I'll beat my head against that wall; and I quite literally began hitting things, and developed a music of percussion that involved noises.

JOHN CAGE, the *Observer*, 1982

Everything we do is music.

JOHN CAGE

Cahn, Sammy (Samuel Cohen; 1913–93) US lyricist and librettist, who wrote many of Broadway's most celebrated hit songs. After his first hits, Cahn arrived in Hollywood in 1942 and, in collaboration with Jule STYNE, enjoyed his first Broadway success in 1947 with *High Button Shoes*. Subsequent musicals that benefited from his contributions included the Oscar-winning *Three Coins in the Fountain* (1954). Cahn also established a reputation as a radio and television personality and recorded many of his own songs himself. Among his most famous songs are 'Shoe Shine Boy' (1936), 'Bei mir bist du schön' (1937), 'I'll Walk Alone' (1944), 'All the Way' (1957), 'High Hopes' (1959), 'Call Me Irresponsible' (1963) and 'Thoroughly Modern Millie' (1965). His compositions for Frank SINATRA included 'Love and Marriage', 'My Kind of Town' and 'September of My Years'.

Cale, J.J. (John Cale; 1939–   ) US rock singer and guitarist, who achieved belated stardom in the early 1970s after Eric CLAPTON recorded Cale's 'After Midnight' (1965). His albums since his 'discovery' in the wake of Clapton's success have included *Naturally* (1972), *Troubador* (1976), *Travel-Log* (1989) and *Number 10* (1992). His sensitive playing technique influenced many other musicians: Carlos SANTANA and LYNYRD SKYNYRD were among those to COVER his songs, and Clapton himself had an even bigger success with Cale's 'Cocaine'. Cale rarely leaves his ranch in the midwest, and his wife maintains that he plays his best as he watches the sun set each evening.

Callas, Maria (Maria Anna Kalogeropoulos; 1923–77) US soprano, of Greek descent, who enjoyed superstar status as one of the most admired coloratura singers of the postwar era. A graduate of the Athens conservatory, she established an international reputation after appearing in Ponchielli's *La Gioconda* at Verona in 1947 and went on to appear at major venues throughout the world to universal acclaim, her acting prowess making up for any deficiencies in her singing voice. Having established her abilities in a range of both light and heavy roles, she was persuaded to concentrate on the lighter parts in which she was unsurpassed; her finest roles included Tosca, Violetta in *La Traviata*, and parts in the operas of Bellini, Donizetti and Cherubini. Her voice was past its best by the late 1960s, but she continued to give recitals until the early 1970s. Throughout her life she was plagued by intense media interest in her private romances, which were generally unhappy (the most tempestuous and long-lived of them all being that with the Greek shipping magnate Aristotle Onassis).

Calloway, Cab (1907–94) US bandleader, singer and composer, nicknamed the King of Hi-de-ho, who became one of the great characters of BIG BAND JAZZ from the 1940s onwards. Calloway worked with a number of bands in the late 1920s and 1930s, developing a unique, eccentric style that incorporated the use of SCAT singing. Flamboyantly dressed in a 'zoot suit' and wide-brimmed hat, with a watch-chain that reached the floor, he delighted audiences with his hip patter, and his 'hi-de-hi' catchphrase was soon widely known.

Calloway's band succeeded that of Duke ELLINGTON at the COTTON CLUB in 1931 and then went on tour with such hits as their signature tune 'Minnie the Moocher' (1931) – one of several songs to include references to drugs and sex – 'Kicking the Gong Around' (1931), 'Reefer Man' (1932), 'Jumpin' Jive' (1939) and 'Blues in the Night' (1942). Stars under his control included Dizzy GILLESPIE and drummer Cozy COLE. Calloway retired from the big band business in 1948, although he oversaw occasional reunions. Subsequently he toured in GERSHWIN's *Porgy and Bess* and also appeared in such shows as *Hello, Dolly!* and *Bubbling Brown Sugar* as well as featuring in the films *The Blues Brothers* (1980) and *The Cotton Club* (1985).

calypso The Carribean art of improvising words and music on a topical subject, usually to the accompaniment of a steel band. Calypso first developed in the cotton plantations, where the slaves got round bans on idle conversation by chanting their news to tom-tom rhythms. The rhythms themselves are similar to those of the South American SAMBA; the influence of African music is also detectable. The calypso is particularly associated with Trinidad, where calypso competitions are held along the lines of the Welsh eisteddfods. The first calypso recordings were made in 1914. In time calypso was absorbed by ROCK to produce REGGAE.

The origin of the word calypso is obscure: Calypso was the name of a Greek goddess – but of silence. Most likely it relates to the word *kaiso*, which is shouted out by excited listeners to express their enjoyment. John DENVER's 'Calypso' (1975), incidentally, was dedicated to Jean-Jacques Cousteau's ocean research vessel of the same name (all proceeds going to the Cousteau Society).

Calypso, King of *See* Harry BELAFONTE.

Campbell, Barbara Pseudonym adopted by Sam COOKE when writing such hits as 'Everybody Likes to Cha Cha' and 'Wonderful World' (with Lou ADLER and Herb ALPERT). In reality, Barbara Campbell was Cooke's wife (later married to singer Bobby Womack).

Campbell, Glen (Travis) (1936–) US COUNTRY singer and guitarist, who was associated with some of the most celebrated pop groups of the 1960s and 1970s. Before establishing himself as a star in his own right, Campbell played guitar for a wide range of leading artists, including Nat King COLE, Frank SINATRA, Dean MARTIN, the MONKEES, the MAMAS AND THE PAPAS and the BEACH BOYS (replacing Brian Wilson). His solo hits included 'Turn Around and Look at Me' (1961), 'Gentle on My Mind' (1967) and 'By the Time I Get to Phoenix' (1967). The single 'Rhinestone Cowboy' provided him with another hit in 1975. Among his many best-selling albums are *Gentle On My Mind* (1967), *I Remember Hank Williams* (1974) and *Still Within the Sound Of My Voice* (1988). His film appearances have included *True Grit* (1969).

Can German AVANT-GARDE rock band, which established an international reputation for its brand of ELECTRONIC rock in the 1970s. Keyboard player Irwin Schmidt (1937–),

bassist Holgar Czukay (1938–), who had both studied under STOCKHAUSEN, guitarist and violinist Michael Karoli (1948–), drummer Jaki Leibezeit (1938–) and singer Kenji 'Damo' Suzuki (1950–) came together in 1968 and built up a cult audience with such albums as *Tago Mago* (1971) and *Future Days* (1973). After its most challenging album, *Landed* (1975), the band adopted a more accessible style and had chart success with such singles as 'I Want More' and 'Silent Night'. The group broke up at the end of the 1970s but reformed for the album *Incandescence* (1986).

canary In JAZZ slang, a female singer (likening her to the songbird).

Canned Heat US BLUES band, which attracted a cult following in the late 1960s. Formed by musicologists Bob Hite (1945–81), who was called the Bear because of his large frame and beard, and Al Wilson (1943–70), dubbed Blind Owl because of his glasses and university education, Canned Heat was completed by various highly experienced blues musicians and quickly attracted attention with its brand of rock-based blues. The name Canned Heat, incidentally, was taken from the title of a blues number by Tommy Johnson.

The group won praise at the MONTEREY POP FESTIVAL in 1967, and the 1968 single 'On the Road Again' became the first White blues recording to sell over a million copies. Canned Heat appeared at WOODSTOCK in 1969 and continued to appear at major festivals, also recording albums in collaboration with John Lee HOOKER and LITTLE RICHARD before going into decline. Wilson died in an accident (from hypothermia in Canada as the result of a foolish bet) and Hite succumbed to a heart attack, although even after that the band remained in business on the strength of various former members returning to the fold.

Musicians influenced by the band ranged from John MAYALL to Eric CLAPTON and the ROLLING STONES. Among the best albums were *Canned Heat* (1967), *Boogie with Canned Heat* (1968) and *Future Blues* (1970). Bob Hite's own record collection ran to over 60,000 titles.

canned music The anodyne and bland background music, which is played in public places, including shopping centres and waiting rooms, with the intention of soothing emotions and creating a relaxing atmosphere. The use of such music, which is sometimes known by the tradename MUZAK, has always provoked mixed feelings. Many find it intensely irritating, especially when played over the telephone while a connection is made, but the manufacturers argue that it promotes a general sense of well-being in potential customers and thus aids business transactions.

> Canned music is like audible wallpaper.
> ALISTAIR COOKE, broadcaster

Cannon, Freddy (Frederick Anthony Picariello; 1940–) US ROCK 'N' ROLL singer, nicknamed Boom-boom or the Last Rock 'n' Roll Star, who had a brief career at the top of the charts in the early 1960s. His song 'Tallahassee Lassie', a big hit in 1959, was followed by the singles 'Okefenoke' and 'Way Down Yonder in New Orleans' and by the hit album *The Explosive Freddy Cannon*, which got to Number One in the UK in 1960. Other hits included 'Chattanooga Shoeshine Boy', 'Palisades Park' and 'Action' before he faded from view in the mid–1960s. He enjoyed a minor come-back in 1981 with 'Let's Put the Fun Back in Rock 'n' Roll'.

Cantor, Eddie (Isidore Israel Itzkowitz; 1892–1964) US comedian, singer and dancer, nicknamed Banjo Eyes because of his wide-eyed looks, who was a popular star of vaudeville, revue and cinema. Cantor's many hit songs included 'Yes Sir, That's My Baby', 'Dinah', 'Makin' Whoopee', 'Ma! He's Makin' Eyes at Me' and 'If You Knew Susie'; among his films were *Whoopee* (1930), *Kid Millions* (1934) and *Thank Your Lucky Stars* (1943). He was one of the victims of the 1929 Wall Street Crash in which he lost his fortune, but he built up a second fortune with his many show business successes. His denunciation of alleged Fascists within the US Establishment in the 1930s made him controversial at the time but in the long run only added to his popularity.

Capitol US record label, which was founded in Hollywood in 1942 by Glenn Wallichs, Johnny MERCER and Buddy DESYLVA and went on to sell recordings by many of the great names of twentieth-century music. Among the legends signed to Capitol have been Nat King COLE, Stan KENTON, Miles DAVIS, Peggy LEE, Frank SINATRA, Benny GOODMAN, Art TATUM, Gene VINCENT, the BEACH BOYS, the BEATLES, the BAND, PINK FLOYD and numerous classical and COUNTRY stars.

Captain Beefheart Stagename of Don Van Vliet (1941–), the eccentric US rock star, poet and painter, who emerged as a star attraction of PSYCHEDELIA in the late 1960s. After a childhood spent with his family in the Mojave desert, Van Vliet joined forces with schoolfriend Frank ZAPPA (who named him Captain Beefheart) and later worked alongside such stars as Ry COODER and with his own Magic Band. His highly eclectic albums included *Safe as Milk* (1967), *Trout Mask Replica* (1969), *Mirror Man* (1970) and *Lick My Decals Off, Baby* (1970). He released further less interesting albums through the 1970s but eventually returned to the desert to pursue his painting career.

Cardus, Sir Neville (1889–1975) British music critic and writer on cricket, who was considered one of the finest critics of his generation. He was music critic for the *Daily Citizen* and subsequently for the *Manchester Guardian* (1917–39), to which he contributed many trenchant reviews of celebrated works and performers.

> Most quartets have a basement and an attic, and the lift is not working.
> NEVILLE CARDUS, *The Delights of Music*, 1966

> The opera ... is the only one in existence that might conceivably have been composed by God.
> Of Mozart's *The Magic Flute*, 1961

> If any of us were to die and then wake hearing it we should know at once that (after all) we had got to the right place.
> Of Mozart's A major Piano Concerto (K.488), 1938

> Sawdust and spangles.
> Of Liszt's Second Piano Concerto, 1938

> Pussycats.
> Of Bruch's violin concertos, 1938

Carmichael, Hoagy (Howard Hoagland; 1899–1981) US composer, pianist, singer and actor, who deserted law studies for a life in JAZZ music in the late 1920s. Taught to play the piano by his mother, who worked in the local cinema, he sold his first song in 1926 and went on to write many jazz classics over the next 30 years or more. His best-known numbers, many of which were recorded by fellow-musicians as well as by Carmichael himself, included his greatest hit 'Stardust' (1927), which was made famous in a version recorded by Artie SHAW, 'Georgia on My Mind' (1930), 'Rockin' Chair' (1930), 'Lazybones' (1933), 'Two Sleepy People' (1938), 'Ole Buttermilk Sky' (1946) and 'My Resistance is Low' (1951). He also wrote the musical comedy *Walk with Music* (1940).

Carney, Harry (1910–74) US JAZZ saxophonist and bass clarinettist, who was Duke ELLINGTON's right-hand man for nigh on 50 years. He joined Ellington's band in 1926 and emerged as the first great master of the baritone saxophone. He also served as Ellington's chauffeur, driving him from one engagement to the next, and contributed as a co-author of such hits as 'Rockin' in Rhythm'. Among his most celebrated solos were those on such recordings as 'Slap Happy' (1938) and 'Dancing in the Dark' (1960). He remained with the band until Ellington's death, dying himself just four months later.

> Without Duke I have nothing to live for.
> HARRY CARNEY, 1974

Carpenters, the The US brother-and-sister pop duo Karen Carpenter (1950–83) and Richard Carpenter (1946–), who enjoyed huge commercial success in the 1970s. Having begun in a JAZZ-oriented style, the duo won fame in the early 1970s with a string of hits that included Burt BACHARACH's 'Close to You', which had been turned down by Herb ALPERT because he objected to the sentimental lyrics (particularly the word 'moonglow'), 'Goodbye to Love', 'Yesterday Once More' and 'Please, Mr Postman', all of which made the most of Karen's warm, distinctive voice (although she had begun as a drummer). The duo remained at the top of the charts on both sides of the Atlantic for some years but experienced a drastic decline in fortune when the NEW WAVE signalled a change in taste away from such bland MIDDLE-OF-THE-ROAD pop. Karen Carpenter eventually succumbed to a heart attack brought on by anorexia nervosa in 1983, not long after making a come-back with the album *Made in America* (1981).

The Carpenters were the only group ever to be asked to leave Disneyland, where they were due to play, the reason given being that they looked like hippies.

Carr, Michael (Maurice Cohen; 1904–68) British-born songwriter, who wrote many light popular songs in the 1930s and 1940s. After an adventurous youth – he ran away to sea while still a teenager and then found employment as a journalist in Hollywood – he established a reputation as a songwriter, often in collaboration with Jimmy KENNEDY. His hits included 'Orchids to My Lady' (1935), 'Why Did She Fall for the Leader of the Band?' (1935), 'Merrily We Roll Along' (1938), 'South of the Border' (1939) and 'We're Gonna Hang Out the Washing on the Siegfried Line' (1939).

Carreras, José (1946–) Spanish tenor, who won recognition as one of the three most celebrated tenors of his generation. He made his début in Verdi's *Nabucco* and has appeared at major venues throughout the world opposite such stars as Montserrat CABALLÉ and Agnes Baltsa. His career was threatened in the late 1980s when he contracted leukaemia, but he survived and established the José Carreras International Leukaemia Foundation to help other sufferers of the disease. In 1990 he teamed up with Placido DOMINGO and Luciano PAVAROTTI to record *In Concert* at the World Cup Finals in Rome; the resulting album became the best-selling classical album of all time with sales of 5 million.

Carroll, Earl (1893–1948) US producer, director, composer and lyricist, who staged the immensely successful series of revues known as *Earl Carroll's Vanities* among other shows. Having travelled the world as a youth, he established himself as a composer for the stage, and after serving as a pilot in the First World War he ventured into theatre management. The *Vanities* were first staged in 1923 at his own Earl Carroll Theatre in New York, and they continued to run until 1932, by which time they were second only to the *Ziegfeld Follies*. Stars of these musical extravaganzas included Jessie MATTHEWS and Sophie TUCKER. Carroll himself died in an aircrash.

Carson, Fiddlin' John (1868–1949) US singer and fiddler, who was one of the first musicians to record a substantial body of HILLBILLY music and one of the first COUNTRY artists to win a major following. Variously employed as a jockey, a worker in a cotton mill, a decorator and an elevator operator, he was famous for his fiddle playing, which he pursued in his spare time. He won many competitions and in 1922 became one of the first hillbilly artists to broadcast on the radio. His hits included 'The Little Old Log Cabin in the Lane', 'Boston Burglar', 'Old Joe Clark' and 'You Will Never Miss Your Mother Until She's Gone'.

Carter, Benny (Bennett Lester Carter; 1907–) US JAZZ saxophonist, trumpeter, composer and bandleader, nicknamed the King, who has enjoyed a long career as one of the most acclaimed saxophonists of them all. Born into poor circumstances in New York, he went on to play with many of the great bands, including those of Earl HINES and Fletcher HENDERSON, and wrote and arranged for many more (among them the bands of Duke ELLINGTON, Benny GOODMAN and Count BASIE). His hits have included 'Blues in My Heart' (1931), 'Lonesome Nights' (1934), 'I Gotta Go' (1936), 'When Lights are Low' (1936) and 'Cow Cow Boogie' (1941). He has also written music for a number of Hollywood movies.

Carter, Elliott (Cook) (1908–) US composer, who was recognized as one of the most important heirs of Igor STRAVINSKY. A pupil of Nadia BOULANGER in Paris and a friend of Charles IVES, he wrote early works in a NEO-CLASSICAL style but explored the possibilities of ATONALITY in such pieces as his first quartet (1951), the double concerto (1961) and the piano concerto (1965). Other works, which are noted for their rhythmical complexity and mathematical nature, include ballets, symphonies, choral works and chamber music, of which he is considered a master.

> I am a radical, having a nature that leads me to perpetual revolt.
> ELLIOTT CARTER, c.1939

Carter Family, the Celebrated US FOLK group, based on the Carter and Addington families of Virginia, which made many important recordings and did much to promote interest in native American folk music in the 1920s and 1930s. Led by Maybelle Addington Carter (1909–78), often dubbed the Queen of Country Music, the Carter family – a trio completed by Alvin Pleasant Carter (1891–1960) and Maybelle's cousin Sara Dougherty (1889–1979) – achieved national fame in 1928 with a million-selling

recording of 'Wildwood Flower'. The Carter Family broadcast and recorded regularly until 1942, after which the tradition was continued both by the original members of the trio and their various offspring. Maybelle's daughter June was particularly successful and eventually married singer Johnny CASH; she was also mother of yet another country singer, Carlene Carter (1955–). Songs preserved by the Carters through their early recordings included 'Will the Circle be Unbroken', 'This Land is Your Land' and 'Amazing Grace'.

Carthy, Martin (Martin Dominic Forbes Carthy; 1941–) British singer, guitarist and mandolin player, who emerged as one of the most influential figures in the FOLK-ROCK movement of the 1960s and 1970s. His recordings of such folk-songs as 'Scarborough Fair' inspired songs by such prominent singer-songwriters as SIMON AND GARFUNKEL and Bob DYLAN, and he attracted a strong cult following with a series of folk-based albums through the 1960s. He made several albums in partnership with Dave Swarbrick (*see* FAIRPORT CONVENTION) and played on the first two STEELEYE SPAN albums as well as with the ALBION BAND; he alternated between pursuing a solo career and joining various other admired bands (among them the Watersons and Brass Monkey). Recent solo releases have included the album *Right of Passage* (1989).

Caruso, Enrico (1873–1921) Italian tenor, nicknamed the Man with the Orchid-lined Voice, who was the most celebrated tenor of his – and arguably any other – age. Caruso's legendary musical career began in 1894 in Naples, when he played the role of Loris in the premiere of Umberto Giordano's 1898 opera *Fedora*. It was some time before he perfected his vocal technique, however, and a poor reception in Naples in 1901 made him vow never to sing there again. He was received with acclaim at both COVENT GARDEN in London and at the METROPOLITAN (where he made over 600 appearances) in New York, his roles including Canio in Leoncavallo's *I Pagliacci* and Dick Johnson in the premiere of Puccini's *The Girl of the Golden West* (1910). He made many recordings, his fame surpassing that of any contemporary performer, and he could claim the status of most commercially successful singer of all time; his estate at the time of his early death from pleurisy was worth $9 million. Among his most influential records was 'Vesti la giubba' (1903) from *I Pagliacci*, which in time became the first disc to sell more than a million copies.

Outside music, Caruso was renowned for both his practical joking and his prodigious appetite (it was said he could eat an entire dish of spaghetti in one mouthful). During one dramatic love scene opposite Nellie MELBA he bent low over her and squeaked a rubber toy in her ear, reducing her to a state of helpless giggling. He was also an admired cartoonist.

> Who sent you to me – God?
>
> GIACOMO PUCCINI, on hearing Caruso for the first time

> You know whatta you do when you shit? Singing, it's the same thing, only up!
>
> ENRICO CARUSO

carving contest *See* CUTTING CONTEST.

Casals, Pablo (1876–1973) Spanish cellist, conductor and composer, who was acknowledged as one of the leading performers of his generation. Casals excelled both as a solo artist and in ensemble, winning particular acclaim for his interpretation of Bach. He founded his own orchestra in Barcelona in 1919 and inspired new works by such prominent composers as Gabriel FAURÉ, Sir Donald Tovey (1875–1940) and Arnold SCHOENBERG. He moved to France in 1940 in protest at the Franco government and finally settled in Puerto Rico in 1956. His unsurpassed mastery of the cello, for which he devised new fingering and bowing techniques, was preserved on the many recordings he made with violinist Jacques THIBAUD and pianist Alfred CORTOT. His unswerving defence of democracy won him many admirers, and honours heaped upon him included the United Nations Peace Prize.

> I need Bach at the beginning of the day almost more than I need food and water.
>
> PABLO CASALS

Cash, Johnny (1932–) US ROCKABILLY and COUNTRY-AND-WESTERN singer, nicknamed the Man in Black, who became one of the legendary figures of country music in the 1950s and 1960s. Cash's beginnings were humble in the extreme; he was born in a railroad shack to an impoverished cotton farmer and could claim part-Indian ancestry. He served in the US air force in Korea

and then, backed by the Tennessee Three (Luther Perkins, Marshall Grant and W.S. Holland), he established a big following both within country music and in popular music generally with such hits as 'I Walk the Line', 'Ballad of a Teenage Queen', 'Ring of Fire' and 'A Boy Named Sue'. He recorded many more classics, including duets with Bob DYLAN and with his second wife June Carter (who also helped to wean him off alcohol and drugs and inspired him to commit himself to Christianity).

The best of his 50 or so albums include *At San Quentin* (1969), which was recorded in the prison (he was briefly imprisoned himself for smuggling). His daughter Rosanne Cash (1955–) also found fame as a country singer in the early 1980s. *See also* CARTER FAMILY; MILLION-DOLLAR SESSION.

> God's got his hand on you, son. Keep singing.
>
> JOHNNY CASH, quoting his mother

cassette Word used for audio-cassette, a compact and highly popular recording medium that emerged as a serious rival to the conventional plastic disc in the late 1960s. The first 'musicasettes' were shown to the public by Philips Records at the Berlin Radio Show in 1965 and quickly proved to combine the advantages of older reel-to-reel tape recorders with far greater convenience of use. The fact that enthusiasts could use them to make their own recordings and that the size of cassette-players made them ideal for in-car entertainment did much to promote their success, and the cassette soon overtook the LP in terms of sales and continued to dominate the music market until the 1980s, when the advent of digital recording and the COMPACT DISC ushered in a new age.

Cassidy, David (1950–) US TEENY-BOP idol, son of actors Jack Cassidy and Evelyn Ward, who enjoyed considerable pop stardom in the 1970s. Cassidy first established a popular following as an actor in the television pop show series *The Partridge Family* and went on to musical success with such singles as 'I Think I Love You', 'Breaking Up is Hard to Do' and 'How Can I be Sure'. Revelations in a *Rolling Stone* interview that he liked to indulge in sex and drugs and that he heartily disliked the television series that had made him famous threatened to disrupt the success in 1972, and he further challenged his 'nice guy' image by sanctioning the publication of semi-nude photographs of himself. In 1974 he gave up live performing after a young fan died at a concert.

In 1983 he succeeded Andy Gibb in the lead role of the musical *Joseph and the Amazing Technicolour Dreamcoat* on Broadway and enjoyed a brief come-back in 1985 when his single 'The Last Kiss' reached the Top 10. Two years later he replaced Cliff RICHARD in the musical *Time*. He returned to the upper reaches of the charts in 1990, with *David Cassidy*.

cat music Nickname for RHYTHM-AND-BLUES, which was widely heard in Texas in the 1950s. Elvis PRESLEY himself was sometimes called the Hillbilly Cat.

Cavern, the Club in Liverpool, which became internationally known through its association with the BEATLES at the time that they rose to stardom in the early 1960s. Known as the Home of the Beatles, the Cavern was opened in cellars (previously used as air-raid shelters) beneath some warehouses in Mathew Street, Liverpool, in 1957. The Beatles made their first appearance on 21 March 1961 and became established as regular guests, making a total of 292 appearances before their last gig in August 1963. Other stars to play at the Cavern included Gene VINCENT, GERRY AND THE PACEMAKERS, FREDDIE AND THE DREAMERS, LITTLE RICHARD and the HOLLIES.

The management went bankrupt in 1966, and the club closed, despite protests by dedicated fans. Prime minister Harold Wilson performed a reopening ceremony, but the club was shut for good in 1973, when the premises were demolished.

A New Cavern Club opened across the street, complete with a statue honouring the Beatles and, renamed Eric's, helped to foster such emerging talents as Elvis COSTELLO, FRANKIE GOES TO HOLLYWOOD, ECHO AND THE BUNNYMEN and ORCHESTRAL MANOEUVRES IN THE DARK. A Cavern Walks complex was later constructed on the site of the original club, incorporating bricks taken from the first Cavern Club itself. The Cavern name has also been honoured with a number of albums featuring bands that played there, in the names of local streets and in a musical entitled *Cavern of Dreams* (1984).

> Dark, damp and smelly. I regretted my decision immediately, the noise was deafening.
> BRIAN EPSTEIN, on his first visit to the Cavern, diary, 1961

CBS International record label, part of the Columbia Broadcasting System organization, which ranks among the oldest and biggest of all recording giants. Countless stars have been signed by CBS over the years, among them Igor STRAVINSKY, Aaron COPLAND, Louis ARMSTRONG, Duke ELLINGTON, Benny GOODMAN, Count BASIE, Miles DAVIS, Thelonious MONK, Bob DYLAN, Janis JOPLIN, Bruce SPRINGSTEEN and Michael JACKSON. Landmarks in the label's history have included the introduction of the LP, replacing the old 78, in 1948. The CBS label was finally acquired by Sony in 1987 for $2 billion.

CD *See* COMPACT DISC.

cellist's nipple Medical ailment, identified in the twentieth century, which is unique to female players of the cello. Brought to public notice by the *British Medical Journal*, the discomfort caused in the region where the cello rests against the body can fortunately be relieved by the wearing of a padded bra.

censorship The banning of a particular work or body of works on religious, political, moral or other grounds, as sanctioned in one form or another by governments and radio stations in virtually every country of the world. In the West attitudes towards daring and provocative works of all kinds have become more liberal than ever before during the course of the twentieth century, but many famous works have still suffered from the censor's blue pencil.

In the UK the reasons for a record being banned have varied considerably. In addition to objections to sexual, political or moral content and so forth, records have been banned in the past from being played on the air simply because they were judged to be 'too morbid' – as was the case with the Mark Dinning hit 'Teen Angel', which was refused airplay in 1959, and with the Ray Peterson classic 'Tell Laura I Love Her', which the BBC also rejected (thus obliging Decca to destroy the 25,000 copies of the record that had been prepared).

The BBC refuses to play records that mention commercial products. Notable victims of this policy have included Chuck BERRY's 'Maybellene', which lists well-known US car models (Cadillac Coupe

DeVille, etc), and the KINKS, who were obliged to sing about cherry cola instead of Coca-Cola in the 1970 hit 'Lola'. Even the BEATLES fell foul of the censors: 'A Day in the Life' was banned by the BBC because of its supposed links with drugs, while the cover of the 1968 double album was left blank after plans to have semi-nude shots of the Beatles on it were blocked (hence its nickname, 'The White Album').

Sex has often been the cause of difficulty between record companies and the censors. Olivia NEWTON-JOHN's 'Physical' (1981) was banned in Boston for being too sexually explicit (the Bostonians objected to the invitation 'Let's get animal'), while the words 'make some girl' were bleeped out of the ROLLING STONES classic 'Satisfaction' on US television in 1965. Banning 'Relax' by FRANKIE GOES TO HOLLYWOOD in the early 1980s served only to boost sales and help it get to Number One, to the embarrassment of the DISC JOCKEYS who had refused to play it (as had happened many years previously in the case of the steamy 'Je t'aime', recorded by Jane Birkin and Serge Gainsbourg in 1969).

Celebrated victims of the censor on the grounds that they backed the use of drugs included the ASSOCIATION's 'Along Comes Mary' (though the Beatles classic 'Lucy in the Sky with Diamonds', loosely about LSD, escaped the net).

Bad language is another risky area, and in the 1980s it was suggested that albums containing possibly offensive words should carry a warning sticker. The idea was not well received within the music establishment, as evidenced by the satirical label heavy metal band Metallica planned for the album *Master of Puppets*:

> The only track you probably won't want to play is 'Damage Inc' due to the multiple use of the infamous 'f' word. Otherwise there aren't any 'sh–ts', 'f–cks', 'p–ss–s', 'c–nts', 'm–th–rf–ck–rs', or 'c–cks–ck–ers' anywhere on this record.

British and US attitudes to censorship are, however, mild in the extreme compared to those in some more restrictive regimes. Few, though, have gone as far as the Iranians:

> Music is no different than opium. Music affects the human mind in a way that makes people think of nothing but music and sensual matters. . . . Music is a treason to the country, a treason to our youth, and we should cut out all this music and

replace it with something instructive.
AYATOLLAH KHOMEINI, 1979

See also SOCIALIST REALISM.

cha-cha-cha Dance rhythm, on which numerous hits were based during the 1950s and 1960s. Of Cuban origins, the cha-cha-cha caught on in the West after it was taken up by many popular dance bands. Most famous of all the hits associated with the rhythm was 'Tea for Two', which was recorded initially by Tommy DORSEY in 1958. Other cha-cha-cha classics included 'La Engañadora' (1953) and 'Cherry Pink and Apple Blossom White' (1955).

Chairman of the Board, the *See* Frank SINATRA.

Chaliapin, Feodor Ivanovich (1873–1938) Russian operatic bass, who was considered one of the finest musical actors. Born into a peasant family in Kazan, he was largely self-taught and gradually won recognition in opera in the 1890s after making his début in Moscow. He won acclaim in such roles as Boris in Mussorgsky's *Boris Godunov*, Ivan the Terrible in Rimsky-Korsakov's *The Maid of Pskov*, Melnik in Dargomyzhsky's *Rusalka* and Onegin in Tchaikovsky's *Eugene Onegin* and, having left Russia after the Revolution, he went on to establish an international reputation with appearances at LA SCALA, Milan, the METROPOLITAN in New York, the Paris Opéra and COVENT GARDEN, London.

True to his peasant origins, Chaliapin retained his taste for vodka and women throughout his life. On one occasion, after spending the night with a compliant young woman, he offered her two opera tickets in payment for her services; when the woman objected, saying it was bread she wanted, not opera tickets, he retorted: 'If it was bread you wanted, why didn't you spend last night with a baker?'

Chandler, Gene (1940–   ) US SOUL singer, who had numerous hits in the 1960s and 1970s. The million-selling 'Duke of Earl' (1961) brought Chandler widespread fame and was reflected in his stage act, in which he appeared complete with ducal robes, top hat, cane and monocle. After further lesser hits in the 1960s, he reappeared in the guise of a top DISCO star in the late 1970s, despite having served a prison sentence for drug offences in 1976, with such hits as 'Get Down', 'When You're Number One' and 'Does She Have a Friend'. More recent releases have included the album *Your Love Looks Good To Me* (1985).

Chapin, Harry (1942–81) US singer-songwriter, who established his reputation as a FOLK-ROCK artist in the early 1970s. Such singles as 'Taxi' (1972), 'WOLD' (1973) and 'Cat's in the Cradle' (1974) were considerable commercial successes, though subsequent releases tackled various social and political issues and had less mass appeal (the title of a posthumously released album dubbed him the Last Protest Singer). In 1979 he was appointed to the Presidential Council on World Hunger by President Carter. He died of a heart attack while driving near New York on his way to a benefit concert.

Chaplin, Saul (Saul Kaplan; 1912–) US composer and pianist, who wrote a number of hit songs for various orchestras and for several Hollywood movies. His best-known compositions include 'Until the Real Thing Comes Along' (1936) and 'Shoeshine Boy' (1936), and music for such films as *On the Town* (1949), *An American in Paris* (1951), *Kiss Me Kate* (1953), *Seven Brides for Seven Brothers* (1954), *High Society* (1956) and *West Side Story* (1961).

Charles, Ray (Ray Charles Robinson; 1930–) US pianist and singer, nicknamed the Genius, who became a giant of RHYTHM-AND-BLUES, SOUL music and JAZZ in the 1950s and 1960s. Blind since the age of six as the result of glaucoma, Charles learned to compose using braille and went on to write numerous soul classics. He formed his first group in the late 1940s and in the early 1950s established himself as a promising performer with a series of hits, combining GOSPEL and the BLUES. His most successful recordings, which include 'It Should Have Been Me' (1954), 'What'd I Say' (1959), 'Georgia on My Mind' (1960), 'Hit the Road, Jack' (1961) and 'I Can't Stop Loving You' (1962), have been COVERED many times by other leading artists, and Charles has become one of the most admired stars of his generation. One joke has it that Columbus sailed to America in order to discover Charles. 'Georgia on My Mind', incidentally, was

adopted as the State's official anthem after Charles performed it in front of the legislature in 1981.

The album *Modern Sounds In Country and Western Music* (1962) proved particularly influential as it was the first time rhythm-and-blues and COUNTRY-AND-WESTERN and, indeed, pop had been combined in such a complete manner. Later releases were disrupted somewhat over the next two decades as Charles wrestled with drug addiction, but he continued to consolidate his reputation as one of the legends of contemporary soul music.

The Genius changed his name to Ray Charles in order to avoid confusion with the boxer Sugar Ray Robinson. Ironically, another boxer, Sugar Ray (Charles) Leonard, was named in the musician's honour.

Charlot, André (1882–1956) French producer and director, who staged a hugely successful series of intimate musical revues in the 1920s and 1930s. Featuring such stars as Jack BUCHANAN, Beatrice Lillie (1898–1989) and Gertrude LAWRENCE, the Charlot revues were equally successful on both sides of the Atlantic. His other hit shows included *Very Good, Eddie* (1918), *Buzz-Buzz* (1918) and *London Calling!* (1923) among many more. He moved to Hollywood to work in films in 1937.

Charpentier, Gustave (1860–1956) French composer, who is usually remembered for the opera *Louise* (1900). Charpentier was working in a mill when his employer recognized his talents and sponsored his entry into the Paris Conservatoire. Despite the attractions of a Bohemian life-style, he won the Prix de Rome in 1887 with the cantata *Didon* and followed it up with various symphonic dramas and other pieces. *Louise* was given its première at the Opéra-Comique and brought Charpentier immediate fame and wealth. He established his own conservatoire and won many honours, though he wrote little more of interest other than the opera *Julien* (1913).

charts The weekly listings giving the details of top-selling recordings based on their relative sales, which have been issued in various forms by a number of companies since the 1950s. *Billboard* magazine in the USA had released lists of new songs as far back as 1913, while *Variety* joined in with its own list in 1938. In fact, the first competitive listing based on sales was compiled for the radio programme *Your Lucky Strike Hit Parade* (1935–59), the first 'Number One' being 'Lovely to Look At' by Jerome KERN. *Billboard* published its first competitive chart in 1940, and subsequently separate listings were drawn up to give the top 100 recordings in three categories – COUNTRY, RACE (later RHYTHM-AND-BLUES) and POP. The first record to make an impact in all three US charts was Bill HALEY's 'Rock Around the Clock' (1954). Haley, now remembered as one of the first rock 'n' rollers, was even acclaimed 'Number One Rhythm-and-Blues Personality of the Year' by one magazine.

The first British chart was the *New Musical Express*'s Hit Parade, which began in 1952, although *Melody Maker* had begun to publish lists of new songs in 1946. For many years 'Rock Around the Clock' held the record for the number of consecutive weeks (43) that it spent in the British Top 100; it was eventually overtaken by SOFT CELL's 'Tainted Love', which spent 45 weeks in the charts in 1982.

The charts were once considered the essential barometer of a song's success, but the PAYOLA SCANDAL and other similar revelations about how the charts were 'fixed' by the record companies and crooked DISC JOCKEYS brought them into some disrepute. In recent years similar charts have been introduced for videos and computer games. *See also* GOLD DISC; PLATINUM DISC.

chatter box US Black slang for a record-player.

Cheap Trick US rock band, which established itself as a leading attraction as support to such groups as QUEEN and KISS in the 1970s. Formed in 1972 by vocalist Tom Petersson (1950–) and Rick Neilsen (1946–), later joined by Robin Zander (1952–), the band enjoyed hits with such albums as *In Color* (1977), *Heaven Tonight* (1978) and *At Budokan* (1979), went into decline without Petersson (1982–86), and revived with the use of a new recording for the film *Top Gun* and had its greatest success to date with the 1988 album *Lap of Luxury*.

Checker, Chubby (Ernest Evans; 1941–) US RHYTHM-AND-BLUES star, who enjoyed a series of classic hits in the early 1960s. Checker's career in music was the result of the proverbial lucky break, which came after he was heard singing over the PA system of the store where he plucked chickens. Given the stagename Chubby Checker in deliberate imitation of that of Fats DOMINO, he went on to record such hits as 'The Class' (1959), 'The Twist' (1960) and 'Let's Twist Again' (1962). At one point he had no fewer than five albums in the US Top 15 at the same time. Later hits included a number of singles that were, like 'The Twist', associated with a current dance craze. His career fizzled out with the advent of the BRITISH INVASION and he switched to SOUL and ultimately to DISCO music. He married former Miss World 1962 Catherine Lodders.

Cheltenham Festival Derogatory term that is often applied to music that is unadventurously conservative in character. The expression refers to the Cheltenham International Festival, the annual music festival that has been staged at Cheltenham since 1945. The festival covers both orchestral and chamber music as well as stage productions, but it has laboured for a number of years under a reputation for lack of imagination. Since the 1960s, however, it has been revived with a new policy that ensures that important modern works are played.

Cher (Cherilyn La Pierre Sarkisian; 1946–) US pop singer and actress, who first achieved fame in the 1960s in partnership with her then husband Sonny Bono (Salvatore Bono; 1935–). Her first release, a duet with Sonny Bono on which she was credited as 'Bonnie Jo Mason', was the single 'Ringo I Love You' (1964), an attempt by Phil SPECTOR to cash in on BEATLEMANIA; fans hearing her low-pitched voice assumed it was a boy singing and most decided against buying it.

As Sonny and Cher, the two singers established a reputation as major stars with such hits as 'I Got You Babe' (1965), which was inspired by DONOVAN's 'Catch the Wind', but they eventually broke up to pursue separate careers (divorcing in 1974). Glamorous and strong-minded, Cher enjoyed three solo Number One singles in the USA in the early 1970s and made a come-back in the late 1980s with the album *Heart of Stone*. She also enjoyed great success in her second career as an OSCAR-winning film actress; her films have included *Silkwood* (1983), with Meryl Streep, and *Moonstruck* (1987).

Cher has suffered more than her fair share of harassment from deranged fans. She was one of the targets of a madman who had already murdered his own brother and on another occasion was posted a fan's own ear, cut off with a butcher's knife.

Chess Records US record company, based in Chicago, which played a crucial role in the development of electric BLUES in the 1950s. Founded in 1947 by club owners Leonard and Phil Chess, the company identified and signed up many Chicago artists destined for fame, among them Muddy WATERS, Bo DIDDLEY, John Lee HOOKER and Chuck BERRY. In the early days, the Chess recording studio technicians achieved echo effects by suspending a microphone in a toilet.

Chevalier, Albert (Onesime Britannicus Gwatheveoyd Louis) (1861–1923) British comedian and singer, who was one of the most popular stars of the late Victorian and Edwardian music hall. He began as a straight actor and was a reluctant recruit to the music hall. However, he soon attracted a big following with his comic songs and sketches. Variously nicknamed Albert the Great, the Coster's Laureate, Old Dutch and the Kipling of the Music Hall, he wrote much of his own material (or collaborated with his brother, Auguste). His most popular numbers included such cockney-style hits as 'Knock'd 'em in the Old Kent Road' and 'My Old Dutch'.

Chevalier, Maurice (1888–1972) French actor, singer and entertainer, who was equally successful in the cinema and in stage MUSICALS and REVUES. Born into impoverished circumstances in Paris, where he spent much of his childhood in children's homes, he made his first stage appearance in 1906 and achieved fame as dancing partner to MISTINGUETT at the *Folies Bergère*. Wounded and captured by the Germans in the First World War, he made his London début in 1919 and continued to consolidate his reputation in both the straight theatre and in revue, making trademarks of his straw hat and untamed French accent.

Towards the end of the 1920s he launched a film career and became a star of Broadway and Hollywood, appearing in such movies as *Innocents of Paris* (1929), *The Love Parade* (1930) and *Love Me Tonight* (1932), often opposite Jeanette MACDONALD. He performed in Paris and in prisoner-of-war camps during the Second World War and had to face charges of collaboration with the Nazis (of which he was acquitted). Postwar films included *Gigi* (1958). Among the celebrated songs particularly associated with his name were 'Louise', 'Mimi', 'Thank Heaven for Little Girls' and 'I Remember It Well'.

> You're not going to believe this, but it's for a very good reason. When I get up in the morning, I like to have the choice of getting out of bed from either side.
> MAURICE CHEVALIER, explaining why he never married

Chic US pop group, which was among the top bands of the DISCO era of the 1970s and became the biggest-selling act ever signed by ATLANTIC RECORDS. The brainchild of bassist Nile Rodgers (1952–) and guitarist Bernard Edwards (1952–96), the group manufactured a stream of slick, uptempo and almost characterless disco dance records, which became huge hits in both the British and US charts and spawned numerous imitators. Two female singers – Norma Jean Wright (later replaced by Luci Martin) and Alfa Anderson – were recruited as figureheads for the group, which also worked with Diana ROSS among other stars. Among Chic's many chart-toppers were 'Dance Dance Dance' (1977), 'Le Freak' (1978) and 'Good Times' (1979). Rodgers and Edwards split up in 1983, although they reunited in 1992.

Chicago US JAZZ-ROCK group, which had huge commercial success on both sides of the Atlantic in the late 1960s and 1970s. Guitarist Terry Kath (1946–78), bassist Peter Cetera (1944–), keyboard player Robert Lamm (1944–), drummer Danny Seraphine (1948–), brass players Lee Loughnane (1946–) and James Pankow (1947–), and reed player Walt Parazaider (1945–) were among the foremost jazz-rock pioneers, though in time they adopted a more conventional MIDDLE-OF-THE-ROAD, soft rock style. Such singles as 'Does Anybody Really Know

What Time It Is?' and 'If You Leave Me Now' became million-sellers in the 1970s, and the band enjoyed a revival in the 1980s with the Number One hit 'Hard to Say I'm Sorry' among other releases.

Chicago blues Genre of the BLUES, which flourished in Chicago in the 1940s and early 1950s and which marked the first development of the modern amplified RHYTHM-AND-BLUES style. Such legendary bluesmen as Sonny Boy WILLIAMSON, Jimmy REED, Willie DIXON, HOWLIN' WOLF and Muddy WATERS were attracted to Chicago – already the heartland of JAZZ after the clean-up of New Orleans – after the early 1940s and went on to adopt ELECTRIC GUITARS and microphones and to forge an aggressive new style that incorporated jazz elements. Their work laid the foundation of much ROCK music of the 1960s, when such stars as the ROLLING STONES reworked many r 'n' b classics; their heirs in Chicago itself have included such singers as Jimmy Dawkins, Buddy Guy, Hound Dog Taylor and Junior Wells. *See also* CHESS RECORDS.

Chicago jazz Genre of early JAZZ that was particularly associated with the jazz pioneers of Chicago in the 1920s and 1930s. The style represented a development from that heard in the birthplace of jazz, New Orleans, in that individual musicians were encouraged to take centre-stage while the rest of the band provided the backing, rather than always playing as an ensemble. Leading bands linked to the genre included the McKenzie and Condon Chicagoans.

Chicago Symphony Orchestra US orchestra, founded in 1891, which is ranked among the most distinguished anywhere in the world. The orchestra entered a golden period in 1969, when Sir Georg SOLTI was appointed conductor, and has since continued to prosper under Daniel BARENBOIM, appointed in 1991.

Chieftains, the Irish FOLK band, which established an enduring reputation as one of the leading forces in traditional Irish music in the 1960s. Numerous respected folk musicians have played in the ranks of the Chieftains since the band's formation in the early 1960s, among them harp player Derek Bell and Paddy Moloney on uillean pipes (bagpipes) and tin whistle. Notable

albums have included *Chieftains* (1964), *Bonaparte's Retreat* (1976), *Celtic Wedding* (1987) and *The Long Black Veil* (1995). Among the Chieftains' best-known songs are 'Morgan Magan' and 'Women of Ireland', which won an Oscar as part of the SOUNDTRACK of the film *Barry Lyndon* (1975). The band has appeared with, among others, VAN MORRISON and Art Garfunkel (*see* SIMON AND GARFUNKEL), and in 1979 it played before the largest audience in rock history, some 1.3 million people, during a visit by the Pope to Phoenix Park.

Chiffons, the US pop group, which was among the most successful all-girl vocal groups of the 1960s. Singers Barbara Lee (1947–92), Patricia Bennett (1947–), Syvia Peterson (1946–) and Judy Craig (1946–), who had met at school, prospered on the strength of such hits as 'He's So Fine' (1963), 'One Fine Day' (1963), 'I Have a Boyfriend' (1964) and 'Sweet Talkin' Guy' (1966). 'He's So Fine' returned to the charts in 1972 after a court found that George HARRISON's hit 'My Sweet Lord' had been based on it.

Chinn and Chapman Highly successful British TEENY-BOP songwriting team, which was responsible for many of the chart-toppers of the 1970s. Australian-born Nicky Chinn (1945–) and Briton Mike Chapman (1947–), initially in collaboration with producer Mickie MOST, created such hits as 'Blockbuster' for the SWEET, 'Tiger Feet' and 'Oh Boy' for MUD, and 'Can the Can' and '48 Crash' for Suzi QUATRO – among many others.

Chisholm, George (1915–) British JAZZ trombonist and comedian, born in Glasgow, who is recognized as the finest trombonist to issue from the UK. Also proficient on the piano and a number of other instruments, Chisholm, who was largely self-taught, played with various dance bands in Glasgow before coming to London in 1936. He played alongside many of the best British and US jazzmen as well as serving as a long-time member of the RAF's Squadronaires (1939–50), of the BBC Show Band (1950–55), and with his own Gentlemen of Jazz, making many television appearances in the course of which he demonstrated his taste for comedy and flamboyant dress.

Chocolate Coloured Coon, the *See* G.H. ELLIOTT.

Christian, Charlie (1916–42) US JAZZ guitarist, who did much to promote the role of
the amplified guitar as a solo instrument in
the jazz ensemble. Born into poverty, the son
of a blind itinerant guitarist, Christian made
his first guitar out of cigar boxes. He played
with a number of bands in the Oklahoma
area in the 1930s before attracting the
admiration of John HAMMOND, who tried to
get Benny GOODMAN to sign him up. Goodman, however, who disliked the electric
guitar, was reluctant and refused. Hammond then smuggled Christian on to the
stage in the interval of one of Goodman's
shows, to the latter's annoyance. Goodman
launched into 'Rose Room', which he
assumed Christian would not know – and
was then astounded, like the audience and
the rest of the band, when Christian improvised brilliantly in the course of a version of
the number that lasted an incredible 45
minutes; Christian remained a member of
Goodman's band for the next two years and
lasting fame was assured. As a regular star
at MINTON'S PLAYHOUSE, Christian was also
enormously influential in paving the way –
with Dizzie GILLESPIE and Charlie PARKER –
for the development of BEBOP.

Weakened by his indulgence in drugs,
alcohol and women, Christian was diagnosed as having tuberculosis in 1940 and
died of pneumonia after friends smuggled
him out of his sanatorium in order to get him
to a party.

Christian metal Sub-genre of HEAVY METAL in
which the lyrics convey some Christian
message. Christian metal developed largely
in reaction to the popularity of satanic BLACK
METAL. Exponents of the style include
Barren Cross, Blood Good and Stryper.

Christiné, Henri Marius (1867–1941)
Swiss-French composer, who wrote many
hit songs for leading CABARET artists and
popular singers of the 1920s and 1930s.
Although he also composed a number of
popular light operettas, he is usually
remembered for such classic songs as
'Valentine', which became one of Maurice
CHEVALIER's biggest hits, and 'La petite Ton-
kinoise', which was sung with great success
by Josephine BAKER.

Christmas records The issue of special festive
records to coincide with the annual spending spree leading up to Christmas is a time-
honoured tradition in the music industry.

The best-selling Christmas record of all
remains the Bing CROSBY classic 'White
Christmas' (1942), second place going to
Bobby Helms with 'Jingle Bell Rock' (1957).
Other notable Christmas hits have included
'Rudolph the Red-nosed Reindeer' (1950)
by Gene AUTRY, 'Rockin' Around the Christ-
mas Tree' (1960) by Brenda LEE, and innu-
merable hits released by artists as varied as
SLADE, Cliff RICHARD and BAND AID.

The BEATLES were among those who regularly issued novelty Christmas records for
the benefit of their fan clubs. These jokey
items incorporated spoken messages from
the group members, versions of Christmas
carols and even a recording of them singing
'Yesterday' out of tune.

Christoff, Boris (1918–93) Bulgarian bass
singer, who first established an international reputation for his performances in
Russian opera in the late 1940s. With the
help of King Boris of Bulgaria, Christoff
emerged as a leading singer after his London
début at COVENT GARDEN in 1949, taking
Boris in Mussorgsky's *Boris Godunov*. He
appeared at all the major international
venues and won particular acclaim for his
interpretations of Verdi and Wagner.

Chung, Kyung-Wha (1948–   ) Korean
violinist, who established a worldwide reputation after sharing victory in the 1967
Leventritt Award with Pinchas ZUKERMAN.
Other members of her family who have also
won international acclaim are her sister,
cellist Myung-Wha Chung (1944–   ), and
her brother, pianist and conductor Myung-
Whun Chung (1953–   ), who succeeded
Daniel BARENBOIM as conductor at the Bastille Opéra in Paris (1989).

Churchill, Frank (1901–42) US composer,
who is best remembered for the music he
wrote for a series of classic Disney cartoons.
He won OSCARS for the music he composed
for *Dumbo* (1941) and *Bambi* (1942), while
his score for *Snow White* (1937) yielded such
hits as 'Someday My Prince Will Come',
'Heigh-ho' and 'Whistle While You Work',
and *The Three Little Pigs* (1933) inspired
'Who's Afraid of the Big Bad Wolf?'

Cilèa, Francesco (1866–1950) Italian composer, who is usually remembered for the
opera *Adriana Lecouvreur* (1902). A respected teacher in Naples and Palermo, he also
wrote the opera *L'Arlesiana* (1897), which

incorporated the celebrated aria 'Lamento di Federico', as well as further choral and orchestral music and songs.

clap track Pre-recorded applause, which is added to a piece of music at a late stage in the recording process.

clap trap In classical music, the term used of the deceptive point in some pieces of music where the end appears to have been reached, so triggering applause before the piece has actually ended. Twentieth-century pieces notorious for clap traps include SIBELIUS's Fifth Symphony, which contains several such moments.

Clapton, Eric (1945–   ) British rock guitarist, nicknamed Slowhand, in reference to his apparently effortless but much-admired technique, or simply 'God', who emerged as one of the leading White RHYTHM-AND-BLUES guitarists of his generation. A relatively late convert to the guitar (he began to play when he was 17 years old), Clapton joined the YARDBIRDS in 1963 and consolidated his reputation with John MAYALL's Bluesbreakers and with the SUPERGROUP CREAM, as well as working with George HARRISON on a number of BEATLES classics (notably 'While My Guitar Gently Weeps' in 1968).

After Cream broke up, Clapton played with Blind Faith (which he formed with Steve Winwood (see TRAFFIC), Ric (see FAMILY) Grech and Ginger Baker) and the Plastic Ono Band (see John LENNON), and then formed Derek and the Dominoes, whose greatest hit was the single 'Layla' (1970). 'Layla' (derived from the ancient Persian book *Layla and Majnun*) was inspired by Clapton's feelings for Harrison's wife Patti Boyd – an obsession that led to Clapton becoming a heroin addict (at one point he had to sell his guitars to pay for further supplies).

The album *461 Ocean Boulevard* – the address of the studio in Miami where the recording was made in 1974 – restored Clapton to chart success, and the single 'I Shot the Sheriff' (by Bob MARLEY) reached Number One. Clapton was present at the farewell concert of the BAND in 1976 and enjoyed further solo success with such albums as *Slowhand* (1977) and *Backless* (1978) before his career was disrupted by alcoholism. He returned to form in 1986 with the album *August*. Since then he has

had further chart success with such albums as *Journeyman* (1989), *Unplugged* (1993) and *From the Cradle* (1994) and in 1990 inaugurated a series of annual concerts at London's Royal Albert Hall.

Clapton's private life has been blighted by tragedy. Patti Harrison married Clapton in 1979 (Harrison conceding 'I'd rather she was with him than some dope'), but they split up in 1986; the son he then had by actress Lori Del Santo died in a fall from their 53rd-floor apartment in Manhattan in 1991 (it was for him that Clapton wrote the hit single 'Tears in Heaven'). He was also deeply affected by the death of the guitarist Duane ALLMAN and years later by the tragic deaths of three members of his touring group when their helicopter crashed in Wisconsin in 1990.

> Clapton is God.
> Graffito seen in London in the 1960s

Clark, Buddy (Samuel Goldberg; 1912–49) US singer, who was one of the most popular recording and broadcasting stars of the 1930s and 1940s. He made his name singing with the Benny GOODMAN band in the mid-1930s and appeared with other leading bands, presented his own radio show and acted in such films as *I Wonder Who's Kissing Her Now* (1947). His hits included 'Linda' (1947), 'Peg o' My Heart' (1947) and (with Doris DAY) 'Love Somebody' (1948). Just as he was consolidating his reputation as a nationally known entertainer he was killed in a plane crash in Los Angeles.

Clark, Dick (1929–   ) US DISC JOCKEY and television star, nicknamed the World's Oldest Teenager, who did much to promote ROCK 'N' ROLL in the mid-1950s. As presenter of AMERICAN BANDSTAND, he became as big a star as many of the performers he introduced, although his reputation was threatened by revelations during the PAYOLA SCANDAL investigations of 1960.

Clark, Petula (Sally Owen; 1932–   ) British singer and actress, who enjoyed a series of hits in the 1950s and 1960s. Petula Clark began as an actress, playing Jack Warner's daughter in the radio series *Meet the Huggetts* in the postwar years. She established herself as a lively singer and was regularly in the Top 10 in the late 1950s and 1960s, reaching Number One in the UK with 'Sailor' (1961) and 'This is

My Song' (1967), which was written by Charlie Chaplin, who was by then in his seventies.

She has rendered more than one of her hits in a number of languages to promote overseas sales: 'Downtown' (1964), for example, was released in English, French, German and Italian, while 'This is My Song', also recorded in four languages, topped the charts across Europe. Petula Clark, who has also starred in several film and stage MUSICALS, now lives in Switzerland.

Clarke, Grant (1891–1931) US lyricist, who provided the words for many hit songs between the First World War and his death. Writing for such singers as Al JOLSON, Nora BAYES and Fanny BRICE as well as for Hollywood movies from 1924, he contributed the lyrics for such standards as 'Ragtime Cowboy Joe' (1912), 'He'd Have to Get Under' (1913), 'Second-hand Rose' (1921) and 'Am I Blue?' (1929).

Clarke, Kenny (1914–85) US JAZZ drummer, nicknamed Klook in reference to his 'klook-mop' drumming sound, who was the most influential BEBOP drummer of the 1940s. As drummer with Charlie PARKER, Dizzy GILLESPIE, Thelonious MONK and other stars at MINTON'S PLAYHOUSE club and other venues, he re-created jazz drumming, experimenting with broken rhythms and developing a more fluid, exciting style that elevated the drums above their previous role of mere beat-keeping. A favourite trick that he developed was 'dropping bombs' – sudden explosions of sound from the bass and snare drums. He led several groups of his own and toured widely, especially in France from the mid-1950s, where he teamed up with pianist Francy Boland (1929–).

Clash, the British PUNK ROCK band, which emerged as one of the most influential groups in the UK in the late 1970s. Guitarists Joe Strummer (John Mellors; 1952–) and Mick Jones (1955–), bassist Paul Simenon (1956–) and drummer Nicky 'Topper' Headon (1956–) made considerable impact with their overtly political, uncompromising musical style, and the Clash was quickly recognized as one of the most original and musically competent punk bands. The group absorbed the influ-

ence of REGGAE and moved into more mainline rock with such albums as *London Calling* (1979) and *Sandinista!* (1980). Later releases were disappointing, and the band broke up in 1983 (Headon was gaoled for drug offences in 1987). Bizarre incidents in the band's history included the levying of a court fine on Headon in 1982 after he was found guilty of stealing a bus stop.

The Clash's success was not limited to the UK – on its delayed US release in 1979, the band's début album sold 100,000 copies, a record for an import.

> We're nothing like the Sex Pistols. We don't set out to shock people through being sick on stage or through self-mutilation. I was never one for sticking a pin in me nose.
>
> MICK JONES, *Time*, 1979

Clayderman, Richard (Phillipe Pages; 1954–) French pianist, who became an internationally known star through his many recordings in the EASY LISTENING style. Reputedly brought up in the modest surroundings of a one-roomed flat, he trained as a classical pianist before working as accompanist to various pop stars and embarking on a highly successful solo career in the 1970s after 'Ballade pour Adeline' became a massive hit around the world. The scale of Clayderman's success must be attributed as much to his photogenic looks as to his slick but often bland music, which ranges from tunes by Chopin to versions of contemporary pop standards.

Clayton, Buck (Wilbur Dorsey Clayton; 1911–91) US JAZZ trumpeter and arranger, who achieved stardom as a leading member of the band led by Count BASIE in the 1930s and 1940s. One of Basie's most admired players, Clayton collaborated with other prominent jazzmen, including Benny GOODMAN and Sidney BECHET, but concentrated on his work as an arranger after surgery failed to repair damage done to his lips during his long playing career, becoming one of the most influential figures in MAINSTREAM jazz.

> There's a very famous album called 'The Buck Clayton Jam Session'. Bruce Turner always refers to it as 'The Jack Clayton Bum Session'.
>
> DIGBY FAIRWEATHER, on BBC Radio's *Jazz Score*

Clef Club US music organization, which was founded in 1910 to protect the interests of

Black US musicians. The Club ran its own Clef Club Orchestra, which staged some remarkable concerts over the years; one of the most unusual, at Carnegie Hall in 1914, featured 30 pianists playing on 10 pianos.

Cleveland Orchestra Respected US symphony orchestra, which was founded in Cleveland, Ohio, in 1918. Conductors of the orchestra have included George SZELL and Lorin MAAZEL.

Cliburn, Van (Harvey Lavan) (1934–) US pianist, who established an international reputation after winning the prestigious Tchaikovsky Piano Competition in Moscow in 1958. He has made many recordings, including highly successful interpretations of works by Tchaikovsky.

Cliff, Jimmy (James Chambers; 1948–) Jamaican-born REGGAE singer-songwriter, who was the first reggae singer to enjoy superstar status. Cliff recorded a number of SKA numbers in the 1960s before finally establishing himself on an international basis in 1969 with such reggae numbers as 'Wonderful World, Beautiful People'. Among the many hits that followed were 'Wild World', 'You Can Get It If You Really Want' and 'Many Rivers to Cross' (written for the 1972 film *The Harder They Come*, in which he starred). Later in the 1970s he was somewhat eclipsed by Bob MARLEY, but reclaimed his role as leading reggae performer after Marley's death. His duet, 'Hakuna Matata', written with Lebo M, featured in Disney's *The Lion King* (1995).

Cline, Patsy (Virginia Petterson Hensley; 1932–63) US COUNTRY singer, who was one of the most popular country stars of her generation until her career was cut short by her early death. Cline's reputation was sealed in 1957, when she won a prestigious television talent contest, singing her first hit 'Walkin' After Midnight'. Cline herself disliked the song and resisted several attempts to persuade her to record it before she finally gave in (the same was also true of several of her subsequent hits, among them her 1961 single 'I Fall to Pieces').

Just when she had established herself as a nationwide star and the first female country singer to appeal to a pop audience, Cline died when the private aircraft in which she was travelling crashed on 5 March 1963 (the first member of the search party to reach the scene was singer Roger MILLER). Among the others who died in the tragedy were country stars Lloyd 'Cowboy' Copas and Harold 'Hawkshaw' Hawkins, with whom Cline had just appeared in a memorial concert in Kansas City for the disc jockey Cactus Jack Call, who had recently died in a car crash. The train of tragedies did not come to an end until the day of Cline's funeral, when yet another country singer, Jack Anglin, perished in a car accident on his way to the ceremony.

In 1981, in somewhat dubious taste, recordings made by Cline were dubbed with others made by the late Jim REEVES to create new duets with the two deceased stars apparently singing together.

Clooney, Rosemary (1928–) US singer, who enjoyed a series of popular hits in the 1950s. She made her recording breakthrough with the Number One single 'Come On-a My House' (1951); other hits included 'Tenderly' (1952), 'Botch-a-me' (1952), 'This Ole House' (1954) and 'Hey There' (1954). At the peak of her fame, she also worked with, among other stars, Duke ELLINGTON, Benny GOODMAN, Marlene DIETRICH and Bing CROSBY. Her career went into decline with the advent of ROCK 'N' ROLL.

cluster A group of adjacent notes (usually on a keyboard instrument) that are sounded together. The concept of note clusters is thought to have been introduced by Henry COWELL in his *The Tides of Manaunaun* (c.1912) and was developed by such AVANT-GARDE composers as Béla BARTÓK and Karlheinz STOCKHAUSEN, who gave instructions for whole blocks of notes to be played using the forearm, the elbow or the fist. Stockhausen and György LIGETI even extended the idea to the orchestra as a whole in the 1950s.

Clutsam, George H. (1866–1951) Australian composer, arranger and pianist, who enjoyed success with various operettas, songs and other compositions during and after the First World War. Having worked as accompanist to Dame Nellie MELBA, he established himself as a popular composer for the musical stage, collaborating on such hit shows as *Young England* (1916) and the enduring *Das Dreimäderlhaus* (*Lilac*

Time; 1922), which was adapted from the Viennese original using the tunes of Schubert. His hit songs included 'Ma Curly Headed Babby' (1926).

Coasters, the Black US pop group, which enjoyed massive commercial success in the late 1950s as kings of the DOO-WOP style; there was no point between 1956 and 1961 when the group did not have at least one single in the charts. The band came together as a breakaway outfit from the Robins (first formed in 1949) and subsequently underwent many changes in personnel. Among the leading members were Bobby Nunn (1925–86) and Carl Gardner (1928–   ), with saxophonist King Curtis (1934–71) playing on many of the group's hits. Coasters hits, mostly written by the songwriting team of LEIBER AND STOLLER, included 'Riot in Cell Block Number Nine', 'Yakety Yak', 'Poison Ivy' and 'Charlie Brown'; the group's hits 'Little Egypt' and 'Girls! Girls! Girls!' were covered by Elvis PRESLEY. The band made come-backs in 1964 with 'Tain't Nothin' to Me' and again in 1971 with the hit 'Love Potion Number Nine', although they had to fight a number of legal battles to prevent various versions of the Coasters formed by previous members using the same name.

Coates, Eric (1886–1957) British composer and viola player, nicknamed the Uncrowned King of Light Music, who won a large audience with his light classical music in the 1930s and 1940s. His best-known works included 'The Three Bears' (1926), 'London Bridge' (1934), 'Calling All Workers' (1940) and the suite *The Three Elizabeths* (1944). The march 'Knightsbridge', from the suite *London* (1932), was adopted as the theme tune of the popular radio programme *In Town Tonight* and helped to confirm Coates's reputation as the leading British composer of light classical music of his generation. 'By a Sleepy Lagoon' has been immortalized as the signature tune of BBC radio's long-running *Desert Island Discs*, and 'Calling All Workers' was used for *Music While You Work*. His other works included songs and a number of movie SOUNDTRACKS, of which the most celebrated remains the march for *The Dambusters* (1954).

Cochran, C(harles) B(lake) (1872–1951) British impresario and producer, who

staged many lavish musical spectaculars and REVUES in the 1920s and 1930s. His hugely popular shows, a kind of British equivalent of the *Ziegfeld Follies*, included five musicals by Noël COWARD and such entertainments as *Music Box Revue* (1923), *Cochran's Revue of 1926*, *Blackbirds* (1926), *Wake Up and Dream* (1929) and *Anything Goes* (1935). His revues were especially famous for their choruses of beautiful girls, who were popularly known as Mr Cochran's Young Ladies.

Cochran, Eddie (1938–60) US ROCK 'N' ROLL singer-songwriter and guitarist, who was Elvis PRESLEY's leading rival until his untimely death in a car accident. Cochran began his career as half of a HILLBILLY duo in 1954, but his solo career took off in 1956 when 'Sitting in the Balcony' reached the Top 20; subsequently he confirmed his status as one of the giants of the rock 'n' roll era with the classics 'Summertime Blues', 'C'mon Everybody', on both of which he played all the instruments, and 'Somethin' Else'. His film appearances included roles in *The Girl Can't Help It* and *Untamed Youth*.

Cochran's career ended tragically on 17 April 1960, when the taxi in which he, his fiancée and Gene VINCENT were travelling from Bristol to London Airport for a brief trip home to the USA during a British tour crashed into a lamp-post on the A4 near Chippenham, Wiltshire, after a tyre burst. Both Cochran and Vincent suffered severe injuries; Vincent recovered but Cochran died later that morning. Tradition has it that the first man on the scene of the fatal crash was police officer David Harman, who was later to enjoy fame as Dave Dee of DAVE DEE, DOZY, BEAKY, MICK AND TICH.

Cochran's premature death at the age of 21 confirmed his status as a rock legend and ensured the success of a string of posthumous hits (notably 'Three Steps to Heaven').

cock rock Slang for HEAVY METAL in which the artist or artists concerned reveal a weakness for strutting about the stage in the manner of a cockerel showing off his feathers.

Cocker, Joe (John Robert Cocker; 1944–   ) British RHYTHM-AND-BLUES and SOUL singer, influenced by Ray CHARLES, whose distinctive, gravelly voice won him a huge following on both sides of the Atlantic in the late 1960s. Born in Sheffield, where he worked as a gas-fitter before taking up music, he was lead singer with Vance Arnold and the Avengers before finding fame as a solo artist with his own song 'Marjorine' (1968) and then with his acclaimed COVER of the BEATLES hit 'With a Little Help from My Friends' (1968). Follow-up hits included 'Delta Lady' and 'The Letter'.

Cocker was hailed for his appearance at WOODSTOCK in 1969, but lost money in business and alienated his audience through bizarre on-stage behaviour while under the influence of drugs and alcohol and suffered a breakdown. He made a come-back in 1983 singing 'Up Where We Belong' with Jennifer Warnes and with the albums *Sheffield Steel* (1983), *Unchain My Heart* (1986) and *Have A Little Faith* (1994).

> I've always done me little theatricality bit of throwing me arms about with the music. Some people think it's a bit too much. Like when I was on Ed Sullivan, they surrounded me with thousands of dancers to keep me hidden.
> JOE COCKER

Cogan, Alma (1934–66) British pop singer, remembered for her infectious chuckle and flamboyant costumes, who outsold all her rivals in the UK in the 1950s, when no fewer than 20 of her records reached the charts. Her most successful releases included 'Little Things Mean a Lot', 'Why Do Fools Fall in Love', 'The Story of My Life', 'I Can't Tell a Waltz from a Tango', 'Never Do a Tango with an Eskimo' and 'Dreamboat', which reached Number One in the UK in 1955. A close friend of BEATLES manager Brian EPSTEIN, 'the girl with the laugh in her voice' hosted her own television show and continued to record into the 1960s, when she released COVER versions of 'Yesterday' and other Beatles classics, before her premature death from cancer.

Cohan, George M(ichael) (1878–1942) US producer, composer, actor, writer and director, whose many hit shows made him one of the legends of Broadway. Having worked in vaudeville, he exercised his talents as a producer, composer and writer in such successful shows as *Little Johnny Jones* (1904), *Forty-Five Minutes from Broadway* (1906), *The Yankee Prince* (1908), *The Cohan Revue of 1918* and *Little Nellie Kelly* (1922). His hit songs included 'The Yankee Doodle Boy', 'Give My Regards to Broadway' and 'Over

There' (1917). His colourful life provided the storyline for the film *Yankee Doodle Dandy* (1942), in which James Cagney played Cohan, and for the MUSICAL *George M!* (1968).

Cohen, Leonard (1934–) Canadian singer-songwriter, poet and novelist, often known as the Bard of the Bedsits, whose highly literary songs and often awkward guitar accompaniment made him a unique figure in the history of postwar popular music. Cohen began as a poet but ventured on a career as a singer-songwriter with his début album *Songs of Leonard Cohen* (1968), a melancholy but deeply melodic collection of songs that spawned such classic singles as 'Suzanne' and 'So Long Marianne'. Later albums, such as *Songs from a Room* (1969), which raked over the embers of a former love affair, *Songs of Love and Hate* (1971) and *New Skin for the Old Ceremony* (1974), continued in the same vein, but the 1970s and 1980s saw new departures, with Phil SPECTOR producing the 1977 album *Death of a Lady's Man* and the introduction of more sophisticated orchestration and effects.

The Jennifer Warnes album *Famous Blue Raincoat* (1986), a collection of covers of Cohen classics, helped to revitalize his career and a new generation of fans joined his established audience in buying such releases as *I'm Your Man* (1988) and *The Future* (1992).

Cole, Cozy (William Randolph Cole; 1909–81) US JAZZ drummer, who was universally recognized as one of the most influential drummers in the SWING tradition. He played for many notable jazzmen, including Jelly Roll MORTON, Cab CALLOWAY and Benny GOODMAN, before joining Louis ARMSTRONG's All Stars and working on various film SOUNDTRACKS. He led his own band in the 1950s, recording such hits as 'Topsy' (1958), and toured widely as well as being active as a teacher of drumming technique.

Cole, Nat 'King' (1917–65) Black US JAZZ singer and pianist, who achieved almost legendary status as a singer of sentimental ballads in the 1940s and 1950s. Cole led his first band in Chicago in 1934 and later won acclaim as a gifted and innovative pianist with the King Cole Trio (finally disbanded in 1951). Having distinguished himself as a singer with such recordings as 'Fly Right'

(1944), 'It's Only a Paper Moon' (1945), 'Nature Boy' (1948) and 'Mona Lisa' (1950), he concentrated on developing his fame as a singer with such classic hit songs as 'Too Young' (1951), 'Pretend' (1953) and 'Ramblin' Rose' (1962). His version of 'Stardust', on the album *Love Is the Thing* (1957), was considered by many critics one of the best ever recorded. Among the respected stars with whom he collaborated were Count BASIE and Lester YOUNG. He also appeared in numerous films – notably *St Louis Blues* (1958) – and was the first Black television presenter.

Cole's enormous success as a CROONER did much to open doors for other Black performers, although he himself was the object of considerable racial harassment during his career, not least from civil rights activists who accused him of making too many compromises in pursuing fame. On one occasion, in 1956, he was actually beaten up by Whites at a concert in Birmingham, Alabama. His career ended early with his death from cancer.

> If I had only one artist to listen to through eternity, it would be Nat Cole.
> CHUCK BERRY

Cole, Natalie (1950–) Black US SOUL singer, daughter of Nat King COLE, who inherited her father's reputation as a leading vocalist. Such releases as 'This Will Be' and the album *Inseparable* (1975) sold well and were followed by such hit albums as *Unpredictable* (1977), *Thankful* (1977) and (with Peabo Bryson) *We're the Best of Friends* (1979). Trouble in her private life and addiction to drugs led to a decline in the early 1980s, but she bounced back with the album *Everlasting* (1986) and an appearance at the Nelson Mandela Concert in 1988. In 1991 she enjoyed a huge hit with the 'duet' (and album) 'Unforgettable', in which she sang along with the image of her long-deceased father.

Coleman, Cy (Seymour Kaufman; 1929–) US singer, composer and pianist, who wrote numerous hit songs for such artists as Frank SINATRA and Carolyn LEIGH. His best-known compositions include 'Witchcraft', which provided Sinatra with one of his biggest hits in 1957, 'Firefly' (1958), 'You Fascinate Me So' (1958), 'The Best is Yet to Come' (1959) and 'Pass Me By' (1965). He also wrote the scores for

such acclaimed Broadway MUSICALS as *Sweet Charity* (1966) and *Barnum* (1980).

Coleman, Ornette (1930–) US JAZZ saxophonist, trumpeter, violinist and composer, who emerged as one of the controversial figures of postwar jazz with his innovative, free-flowing style. Dismissed by some critics and hailed by others, Coleman formed his own quartet in the late 1950s and effectively created the genre of FREE JAZZ, in which the restraints of harmony and chordal structure were abandoned – a development that was to have profound implications for succeeding generations of jazz musicians. His most important albums included the aptly named *Free Jazz* (1961), although he also composed a number of film SOUNDTRACKS and other works combining elements of jazz and classical music, notably the suite *Skies of America* (1972), which was made in collaboration with the LONDON SYMPHONY ORCHESTRA. The triple album *The Empty Foxhole* (1966) was unusual in that it featured Coleman's nine-year-old son on drums. From the mid-1970s he started to incorporate ROCK rhythms and electronic instruments and continued to stir up very mixed feelings: Miles DAVIS called him psychotic and another fellow-musician assaulted him physically, while his admirers included Leonard BERNSTEIN.

Legend has it that Coleman's interest in innovative techniques dates back to an error he made when first learning the saxophone at the age of 14, thinking the low C on his instrument was the A indicated in his tutor manual.

> Trouble is, he can't play it straight.
> CHARLES MINGUS

Coleridge-Taylor, Samuel (1875–1912) British composer, who is usually remembered for the phenomenally successful oratorio trilogy *Hiawatha* (1898–1900), which was regularly staged at the Royal Albert Hall between the wars. A student of the Royal College of Music, Coleridge-Taylor was also the author of the enduring *Petite Suite de Concert* (1910) and a violin concerto (1911) among other works.

collaborative pianist US euphemism for an accompanist. Unlike the similar term associate artist, this tag has a slightly insulting ring to it, as it suggests that such a pianist never plays on his own but is obliged to collaborate with another musician.

collage In music, the grouping of a number of musical fragments in the construction of a finished work. Named after the French word meaning 'necklace', the collage was first explored by such AVANT-GARDE composers as Charles IVES but was taken up in a serious way only after the Second World War, when numerous composers attempted to assemble works using snippets of tape-recorded material; Edgar VARÈSE's *Poème électronique* is a celebrated example of the technique.

Collins, Albert (1932–93) Black US BLUES guitarist and singer-songwriter, nicknamed the King of the Telecaster (after his guitar), who emerged as the leading exponenet of so-called 'Texas blues' in the 1960s. Having worked as a SESSION musician for such singers as LITTLE RICHARD and Big Mama THORNTON in the 1950s, Collins established a strong reputation with his lively and accomplished blues guitar technique, and he appeared to acclaim at several major festivals. His albums include *Love Can be Found Anywhere Even in a Guitar* (1968), *Ice Pickin'* (1978), on which he led his own band, *Frostbite* (1980), *Don't Lose Your Cool* (1983) and *Showdown!* (1985). Robert CRAY, who has often worked as backing musician for Collins, is just one of many blues guitarists to admit to having been profoundly influenced by his style. Collins was the only bluesman invited to participate in the LIVE AID events in 1985.

Collins, Judy (1939–   ) US FOLK-singer and actress, who became an international star in the 1960s and early 1970s. Ranging from political protest songs to traditional folk tunes, her music found a wide audience and helped to promote the careers of other singer-songwriters such as Bob DYLAN and Leonard COHEN. Her most successful hits included a COVER of Joni MITCHELL's 'Both Sides Now' (1967), the album *Wildflowers* (1967), 'Amazing Grace' (1970) and 'Send in the Clowns' (1975).

Collins, Phil (1951–   ) British singer and drummer, who emerged as a leading commercial solo pop star after succeeding Peter GABRIEL as frontman with the rock group GENESIS. A child actor in his youth, with appearances as the Artful Dodger in the stage version of *Oliver!* (1964) and in the BEATLES film *A Hard Day's Night* to his credit, Collins joined Genesis as drummer (on a salary of £10 a week) in 1970 and played an

increasing role in providing the vocals on a series of CONCEPT ALBUMS before Gabriel finally left in 1975. With Collins at the helm, the band adopted a more commercial style, while Collins also established a separate solo career. The breakup of his marriage prompted him to venture into songwriting and his first album, *Face Value* (1981), was an immediate success.

While keeping up his contacts with Genesis, Collins continued to issue further commercial solo albums and singles through the 1980s, the most notable albums including *Hello, I Must Be Going* (1982), *No Jacket Required* (1985), *But Seriously ...* (1989) and *Both Sides* (1993). Among his hit singles were 'You Can't Hurry Love' (1982), 'Against All Odds' (1984), 'One More Night' (1985) and 'Separate Lives' (1985), all of which reached Number One on both sides of the Atlantic. Collins was the only artist to appear in both the UK and US LIVE AID concerts in 1985 and also busied himself with film roles, including the lead in *Buster* (1988). He finally quit Genesis in 1996.

colour music The concept of music as colour, which exercised some influence over such AVANT-GARDE composers as Arnold SCHOENBERG and Olivier MESSIAEN. Originally a nineteenth-century idea, the association of music with colour was made explicit in the invention (1895) of such remarkable 'instruments' as A. Wallace Rimington's colour organ, a keyboard linked to a screen on which colours were displayed as the keys were pressed, thus expressing the 12-semitone musical scale in terms of the 12-colour spectrum. More sophisticated was the clavilux invented by Thomas Wilfrid (1888–1968) in 1922. Wilfrid's machine abandoned such a strict correlation between the two 'scales' and instead created shifting combinations of colour with their own rhythms. Ultimately the concept was perhaps most successfully realized in that section of Walt Disney's *Fantasia* (1940), which was based on Bach's Toccata and Fugue in D minor.

Arthur BLISS was one of several composers to develop the colour-and-music link in a different way, identifying sections of his *A Colour Symphony* (1922) under the names of different colours. Several of his contemporaries associated certain keys with certain colours – but could not agree which was appropriate to which (what was bright blue to Messiaen was a totally different colour to Alexander SCRIABIN).

> I found myself referring to the programme to find out whether I ought to be seeing red or looking blue at certain moments, and some of it made many of the audience feel green.
>
> The Times, review of Bliss's A Colour Symphony, 1922

Coltrane, John (1926–67) Black US JAZZ saxophonist, who established his reputation as one of the most gifted tenor saxophonists of them all, ranking alongside such innovative greats as Dizzy GILLESPIE, Miles DAVIS and Thelonious MONK. Having begun in a navy band, Coltrane emerged as an important jazz innovator in the mid–1950s, notably when playing as one of the Miles Davis sextet (1955–57), during which time he developed his 'sheets of sound' technique (in which he played arpeggios almost as chords). He overcame his addictions to heroin, alcohol and tobacco in 1957 and continued to work with Davis and Monk before ultimately forming his own highly influential quartet in 1960.

Between 1960 and his death he went on to expand the borders of contemporary jazz further than any other performer of his generation, establishing himself as the master of the AVANT-GARDE movement and inspiring a whole generation of saxophonists. His most celebrated numbers included his remarkable improvisations on the 'My Favourite Things' tune and the best-selling album A Love Supreme (1964). His premature death, the result of cancer of the liver, helped to consolidate his cult status.

Columbia US record label, which is the oldest still-running label in the world. Founded in 1889 as a franchise of the North American Phonograph Company, Columbia released its first catalogue of cylinder recordings in 1891 and quickly came to dominate the world record market, with several branches opening in Europe by the end of the century. The company went into receivership in 1923 but revived and attracted such stars as Bing CROSBY and Paul WHITEMAN, before shrinking during the Depression and ultimately merging with HIS MASTER'S VOICE to form EMI in 1931. The US version of the company prospered with sales of HILLBILLY and RACE MUSIC and eventually came under the control of CBS.

Columbo, Russ (Ruggiero de Rudolpho Columbo; 1908–34) US CROONER, actor, composer, violinist and bandleader, who was a popular heart-throb of the early 1930s. Having started as a professional JAZZ violinist, playing in the band that backed Bing CROSBY, he inherited the role of lead vocalist after Crosby left and rapidly attracted a devoted following. He formed his own band in 1931 and enjoyed huge success with regular broadcasts of such hits as 'Prisoner of Love' (1931), 'Let's Pretend There's a Moon' (1934) and 'Too Beautiful for Words' (1934), as well as starring in such films as Moulin Rouge (1934) and Wake Up and Dream (1934). He died at the peak of his career as the result of a freak shooting accident, being killed by a ricochet after a friend struck a match on a duelling pistol he had mistakenly thought was not loaded.

Colyer, Ken (1928–88) British JAZZ trumpeter, guitarist and bandleader, who was a figurehead of the British traditional jazz revival in the 1950s and 1960s. As a member of the Merchant Navy, Colyer jumped ship to play with some of the jazz bands in New Orleans as a young man and, on his enforced return to the UK, formed his own influential groups. With a band that included such burgeoning talents as Chris BARBER and Lonnie DONEGAN, he was largely responsible for fostering the birth of the SKIFFLE craze of the mid–1950s, even though the band split as the various members disagreed over playing styles, with Colyer remaining loyal to the TRAD version. He continued to champion the original New Orleans jazz style until his death, by which time he had acquired almost legendary status among other British jazzmen.

combo Abbreviation of 'combination', as used by JAZZ musicians when talking of a small band. The word first became current in the 1930s and remains restricted to the jazz context.

Comden, Betty (1917–   ) US librettist and lyricist, who collaborated with Adolph GREEN on a long list of acclaimed stage MUSICALS and Hollywood films. Among their most successful shows were Leonard BERNSTEIN's On the Town (1944), High Button Shoes (1947), Wonderful Town (1953), Do Re Mi (1960) and Applause (1970). Among the MGM musicals they worked on were *Good News* (1947), *Singin' in the Rain* (1953) and *The Band Wagon* (1953).

Comets, the *See* Bill HALEY.

Commodores, the US SOUL group, led by vocalist Lionel RICHIE, nicknamed the Black Beatles, which prospered in the 1970s. Formed in 1968 and named as the result of a trawl through an English dictionary, the Commodores joined MOTOWN in 1971 and released a series of successful soul ballads. The most popular included 'Easy', 'Three Times a Lady' and 'Still'. The group went into decline after Richie went solo in 1981, although the album *Nightshift* (1985) saw something of a return to form.

Como, Perry (1912–   ) US singer, nicknamed the Singing Barber in reference to the barber shop he originally ran, who enjoyed a succession of light, popular hits in a career that extended over some 30 years. Como first attracted attention with 'Deep in the Heart of Texas' (1942), and after the war he released a series of hits, notably 'Till the End of Time', 'Dream Along with Me', which became his signature tune, 'Don't Let the Stars Get in Your Eyes', 'Catch a Falling Star', 'Magic Moments' and 'It's Impossible'. Famed for his relaxed and charming personality (personified by his celebrated cardigans), by the mid-1950s he was the world's highest-paid television entertainer, particularly noted for his hugely popular Christmas specials.

compact disc (CD) A pre-recorded acrylic plastic disc of the type that largely displaced the vinyl LP in the 1980s. Measuring 12 centimetres (approximately $4\frac{3}{4}$in) across, the CD offers high-quality sound reproduction and greater resilience to wear than other comparable systems, the sound recorded on its surface being 'read' by a low-intensity laser rather than by a conventional needle or tapehead. The signal is transferred to one side of the disc only in the form of billions of minute pits of varying depth arranged in a spiral $2\frac{1}{2}$ miles long; the surface is then coated with reflective aluminium and plastic, which protects the disc from dust and scratching. Most discs are capable of carrying over an hour's worth of music.

The introduction of CDs by Philips and Sony in 1983 was hailed as a revolution in the music industry, but by the end of the decade questions were being asked about the relatively high price charged for them, and other technological developments suggested that the CD itself may soon be outmoded – the compact video disc, for instance, offers both sound and pictures and the record industry is now marketing the so-called mini-disc.

The first CD to sell more than a million copies was the DIRE STRAITS album *Brothers in Arms* (1986).

concept album An album that is constructed around some theme or storyline, which is designed to lend added impact to the whole enterprise. The first concept album was probably Frank SINATRA's *In the Wee Small Hours* (1955), which was unified by the theme of parted lovers, although it was the BEATLES' *Sergeant Pepper's Lonely Hearts Club Band* (1967) that really broke new ground with its enigmatic cast of characters and kaleidoscopic structure. Largely as a result of *Sergeant Pepper*, many other artists devised their own concept albums, and many bands specialized in the form in the 1970s when many striking – though all too often highly pretentious and obscure – variations on the concept album were released. Notable exponents of the concept album included GENESIS, YES and PINK FLOYD.

concert party Musical entertainment of the type that was commonly presented at seaside resorts the length and breadth of the UK every summer between 1900 and the Second World War. Typical concert party troupes – who often adopted the frilled white costumes of Pierrot – performed songs, comic sketches, dances and other miscellaneous acts to holiday-makers. Among the finest companies of such players were the Co-Optimists, who were regularly seen on the London stage.

concert pitch Standard musical pitch, which was agreed internationally in 1939 to facilitate the tuning of musical instruments. In technical terms, concert pitch is understood to be based on an A note of 440 hertz.

Concertgebouw The most prestigious venue for classical music in the Netherlands, which was opened in Amsterdam in

1888 and is now home of the celebrated Royal Concertgebouw Orchestra. Celebrated conductors at the Concertgebouw have included Wilem Mengelberg (1871–1951), Eugen JOCHUM (1961–64) and Bernard HAITINK (1964–88).

concrete music A genre of AVANT-GARDE classical music in which recordings of both natural and artificial sounds are manipulated to create exciting new musical works. Pioneered by the French composer Pierre Schaeffer (1910–) from 1948, concrete music represents an attempt to construct a more 'realistic' music compared to the 'abstract' music achieved with conventional instruments. Typical sounds employed by Schaeffer and other composers included dustbins, heartbeats and train noises.

Condon, Eddie (1905–73) US guitarist, banjoist and bandleader, who was acclaimed as a rhythm guitarist with a series of top DIXIELAND bands. Having first made a name for himself as a player in the 1920s, he recorded with many leading stars – including Louis ARMSTRONG, Gene KRUPA and Red McKenzie (1899–1948) – and ultimately moved into jazz promotion, opening his own jazz club in New York. He was famous for his bluff good humour and convivial spirit, often turning down invitations to play his guitar, which he nicknamed Porkchop, in favour of sharing a drink with his fans. He once remarked of BOP 'We don't flatten our fifths; we drink 'em'.

> In his book, Bing Crosby states that the first thing he does in the morning is to play an Eddie Condon record.
> DIGBY FAIRWEATHER, on BBC Radio's *Jazz Score*

Confrey, Zez (Edward Elzear Confrey; 1895–1971) US composer, pianist and bandleader, who wrote a number of hugely popular novelty piano pieces. An established vaudeville star, who led his own orchestra in the 1920s and played with, among others, Paul WHITEMAN, he is best remembered for such lighthearted hits as 'Dizzy Fingers' (1923) and 'Kitten on the Keys' (1924).

Connelly, Reg (1895–1963) British songwriter, who wrote many hits in collaboration with Jimmy Campbell. The success of 'Show Me the Way to Go Home' (1925) provided the finance for them to establish their own music publishing company. Subsequent hits included 'The Two of Us' (1926), 'Underneath the Arches' (1932) and 'Try a Little Tenderness' (1932).

Conniff, Ray (1916–) US trombonist, arranger and conductor, who provided the backing for many hit singers of the 1950s. He played in the bands of such notable jazzmen as Artie SHAW and Bunny BERIGAN before accepting the post of musical director for Columbia Records. He worked with many of the star names associated with the label, generally sticking to a conventional SWING style. He also issued a long series of EASY LISTENING albums, consisting of watered-down versions of tunes from the hit parade.

Conrad, Con (Conrad Dober; 1891–1938) US composer, who wrote the scores for many hit MUSICALS for the stage and Hollywood. His most successful shows included (for the stage) *Greenwich Village Follies* (1923) and *Americana* (1926) and (for the screen) *Happy Days* (1930), *The Gay Divorcée* (1934) and *The Story of Vernon and Irene Castle* (1939). Among his best-known songs were 'Singin' the Blues' (1920), 'Ma, He's Making Eyes at Me' (1921), 'Prisoner of Love' (1931) and 'The Continental' (1934).

Conway, Russ (Trevor Herbert Stanford; 1927–) British pianist and composer, who emerged as a popular light musical entertainer in the 1950s. Conway won the DSM serving in the navy during the Second World War but managed to develop a career as a club pianist after his discharge, despite having lost the tip of one of his fingers after cutting it in a breadslicer. Subsequently he released a series of top-selling hits, of which both 'Side Saddle' (1959) and 'Roulette' (1959) reached Number One.

Cooder, Ry (Ryland Peter Cooder; 1947–) US guitarist and singer, who acquired a reputation for his atmospheric BOTTLENECK playing style in the 1970s. Having played with a wide range of groups from the EVERLY BROTHERS to the ROLLING STONES and CAPTAIN BEEFHEART, Cooder enjoyed success as a solo star with such albums as *Into the Purple Valley* (1972), *Chicken Skin Music* (1976), *Bop Till You Drop* (1979), *Borderline* (1980) and *The Slide Area* (1982), but he then concentrated on writing SOUNDTRACKS, the most memorable including that for the

1984 movie *Paris, Texas*. Recent projects have included acclaimed collaborations with musicians from India and Africa, notably *Talking Timbuktu* (1994).

Cook, Will Marion (1869–1944) Black US composer, conductor and violinist, who wrote a number of hit songs for stage MUSICALS in the early years of the century. Having studied in Europe and the USA under Antonín Dvořák and others, he established his reputation with music for such shows as *Clorindy* (1898), *In Dahomey* (1903) and *Abyssinia* (1906). Among his hit songs were 'Down de Lover's Lane' (1900), 'Lovey Joe' (1910) and 'I'm Coming, Virginia' (1927). He also formed an all-Black orchestra to tour Europe and the USA in 1919 and, as a formally trained Black musician, had a profound influence on the success of such Black stars as Duke ELLINGTON.

Cooke, Sam (Sam Cook; 1935–64) Black US SOUL singer-songwriter, nicknamed the Father of Soul, who had a profound influence on the development of soul and RHYTHM-AND-BLUES in the 1950s and early 1960s. Having begun as a GOSPEL singer, he switched to pop under a pseudonym, Dale Cook, to avoid offending fans of his religious music. His hit songs included such classics as 'You Send Me' (1957), described as the first great soul record, 'Only Sixteen' (1959), 'Wonderful World' (1960), 'Chain Gang' (1960), 'Twistin' the Night Away' (1962), 'Having a Party' (1962) and 'A Change is Gonna Come' (1964), which became associated with the emerging civil rights movement.

Cooke died in very bizarre circumstances. He was apparently shot by the manageress of a Los Angeles motel – although the exact circumstances remain obscure – after he entered the wrong room by mistake.

cool In JAZZ slang, music that is cerebral and sophisticated, even elegant, in nature and thus worthy of serious attention. 'Cool jazz' was first developed by chiefly White jazzmen on the West Coast of the USA in the 1950s out of BOP, which had itself emerged largely in reaction to the uptempo rhythms and hectic optimism of other long-established jazz styles such as SWING. Championed by, for example, Miles DAVIS, Gerry MULLIGAN, Chet BAKER, John COLTRANE, Charles MINGUS, Art BLAKEY and

Dave BRUBECK, this new, laid-back, progressive style represented a step forwards in the graduation of jazz as a musical form capable of conveying a deep intellectual content that would appeal to a more refined ear – although critics all too often found it bland and deliberately focused on commercial requirements. Ultimately, 'cool jazz' gave birth to FREE JAZZ, which saw musicians pursuing a more radical, AVANT-GARDE line. Outside music, the term 'cool' came to signify anything excellent or admirable.

Cooley, Spade (Donnell Clyde Cooley; 1910–69) US violinist, singer and bandleader, of part-Cherokee Indian extraction, nicknamed the King of Western Swing, who became a popular star playing a wide range of music encompassing COUNTRY-AND-WESTERN and JAZZ in the 1940s. Called Spade in reference to love of card-playing, he formed his own band in the early 1940s and went on to host his own radio programme, enjoying success with such hits as 'Shame on You' (1944). Cooley was a heavy drinker and in 1961 his career came to a sudden halt when he was gaoled for murdering his second wife.

Coolidge, Rita (1945–) US pop singer, who emerged as a star with a series of hits in the 1970s. The daughter of a Baptist minister and a Cherokee Indian, she was employed as a backing singer and inspired Joe COCKER's 'Delta Lady' (1969) before embarking on a solo career in the early 1970s. Such releases as 'Higher and Higher' (1977), 'The Way You Do the Things You Do' (1977) and 'I'd Rather Leave While I'm in Love' (1980) appealed to both pop and COUNTRY audiences. Other hits included several duets with her husband (1973–79) Kris KRISTOFFERSON.

Cooper, Alice (Vincent Damon Furnier; 1948–) US rock star, who achieved stardom in the early 1970s with his brand of SHOCK ROCK. Furnier, the son of a minister, formed his first band in the early 1960s and adopted the name 'Alice Cooper' following a ouija board session in which a spirit identified him as the reincarnation of a seventeenth-century witch of that name.

By 1969, when Cooper came under the influence of Frank ZAPPA, the band was acquiring a reputation for outrageous live performances, which made use of such props as a guillotine, an electric chair and a live python; Zappa decided to get involved after being present at an Alice Cooper concert where the entire audience walked out. Cooper himself made a striking frontman, with his leering grimaces and smeared black eye make-up. The band finally broke through in 1972, with the chart-topping single and album *School's Out* (inspired by the line 'Wise Up, School's Out' in one of the Dead End Kid's movies). A string of hit albums, including *Billion Dollar Babies* (1973), followed before the group split up in 1975.

Attempts to restyle Cooper, without make-up, as a singer of sentimental ballads confused the old audience and the next few years were marked only by his treatment for chronic alcoholism and the occasional, coolly received album release. In 1989, however, Cooper made a come-back in his old style with *Trash* and its follow-up *Hey Stoopid* (1991). *The Last Temptation of Alice Cooper* appeared in 1995.

Cooper's famous snake finally died in 1977 after it was bitten by the rat intended for its supper; its owner was distraught at the loss.

Coots, J. Fred (1897–) US composer and pianist, who wrote a series of hit Broadway MUSICALS of the 1920s and 1930s. Successful shows included *Artists and Models* (1925), *Gay Paree* (1925) and *A Night in Paris* (1926). Among his hit songs were such standards as 'Time Will Tell' (1922), 'Santa Claus is Coming to Town' (1934) and 'You Go to My Head' (1938).

Copland, Aaron (1900–90) US composer, who is often described as the first important composer from the USA. The son of Russian immigrants, Copland was a pupil of Nadia BOULANGER in Paris before making his mark with such challenging AVANT-GARDE works as a symphony for organ and orchestra (1925), the piece that prompted conductor Walter Damrosch to observe:

> If a young man at the age of twenty-three can write a symphony like that, in five years he will be ready to commit murder.

Subsequently he produced work that had more appeal to a mass audience, although he did not compromise his musical ideals. His most popular pieces included *El salón México* (1936), which incorporated Mexican folk music, *A Lincoln Portrait* (1942), the opera *The Tender Land*, and such ballets as *Billy the Kid* (1938), *Rodeo* (1942), and

the Pulitzer Prize-winning *Appalachian Spring* (1944). Several of his most celebrated early works achieved a highly successful fusion of classical structures with JAZZ motifs, while later pieces experimented with ATONALITY and SERIALISM, and others drew on US FOLK traditions. He also contributed the SOUNDTRACKS for such films as *Of Mice and Men* (1939) and *The Heiress* (1948).

> The whole problem can be stated quite simply by asking, 'Is there a meaning to music?' My answer to that would be, 'Yes'. And 'Can you state in so many words what the meaning is?' My answer to that would be, 'No'.
> AARON COPLAND, *What to Listen for in Music*, 1939

> The best we have.
> LEONARD BERNSTEIN of Copland

Corea, Chick (Armando Anthony Corea; 1941–) US JAZZ pianist, who was one of the pioneers of jazz FUSION. He collaborated with Miles DAVIS from 1968, playing electric piano, and worked closely with Anthony BRAXTON as a member of the band Circle. After joining the Church of Scientology, he formed a series of his own bands, usually quartets, exploring Latin-American sounds and then incorporating a strong rock element. Releases with his JAZZ-ROCK band Return to Forever, which broke up in 1976, included *Hymn of the Seventh Galaxy*, *My Spanish Heart* and *Return To Forever: Live*. Among more recent albums have been *Lyric Suite for Sextet* (1983) and *Children's Songs* (1985), a collection of piano solos.

> Did you know that Chick Corea is a devout Scientologist? I know because he won't switch on the electric lights on Saturdays. He has to get a non-Scientologist to come in and do it for him.
> RONNIE SCOTT, on BBC Radio's *Jazz Score*

Cortot, Alfred (1877–1962) French pianist and conductor, born in Switzerland, who played in the celebrated trio completed by violinist Jacques THIBAUD and cellist Pablo CASALS. He was particularly admired for his distinctive, although not always strictly accurate, performances of the works of Chopin. As a conductor, he was admired for his interpretations of Wagner, although his love of Germanic music caused some friction with his French countrymen during the Occupation in the Second World War.

Coslow, Sam (1902–) US composer and

lyricist, who wrote many hit songs for Hollywood movies of the 1930s and 1940s. His best-known compositions include 'Sing You Sinners' (1930), 'Moonstruck' (1933) and 'Cocktails for Two' (1934). In 1940 he also invented (with one Colonel James Rossevelt) a sophisticated version of the JUKE BOX, which played short sequences of film with sound, called 'Soundies'.

Costello, Elvis (Declan Patrick McManus; 1955–) British singer-songwriter, who emerged from the NEW WAVE phenomenon in the late 1970s. Sharing the aggressive anti-Establishment stance of other successors of PUNK ROCK, Costello, the son of a BIG BAND singer, attracted attention with his first album *My Aim is True* (1977) and went on to release a series of musically varied albums with his band, the Attractions. The LP *Armed Forces* reached the Top 10 on both sides of the Atlantic, while such singles as 'Watching the Detectives' and 'Oliver's Army' were also huge hits. Later releases ranged even more widely, *Get Happy* (1980) bearing the influence of SOUL and *Almost Blue* (1981) venturing into COUNTRY. More recent albums have included *Mighty Like a Rose* (1991), *The Juliet Letters* (1993) and *All This Useless Beauty* (1996).

Costello is renowned for both his aggressiveness to the media and for his anarchic humour: when 'This Year's Model' came out the record company discovered he had scratched 'Ring Moira for prize' and the company's telephone number on the run-off groove, and its switchboard was besieged with telephone calls from excited fans.

Coster's Laureate, the *See* Albert CHEVALIER.

Cotrubas, Ileana (1939–) Romanian soprano, who established a reputation as one of the leading operatic sopranos of her generation. Among her greatest successes were the roles of Mélisande, Violetta and Mimi.

Cotton, Billy (1899–1969) British bandleader, who led one of the most popular DANCE BANDS of the 1930s. Having started as a drummer, he formed his first band in 1926 and soon established himself as a star bandleader. He was known to a wide audience through his regular performances on radio and television and prospered with his brand of brash humour; his catchphrase 'Wakey wakey!' was universally recognized.

Among his most lively novelty numbers was 'I've Got a Lovely Bunch of Coconuts', during performances of which large cotton-wool balls were cheerfully tossed at the audience. His chart hits included 'I Saw Mommy Kissing Santa Claus' (1953).

Cotton Club The almost legendary night club opened in Harlem, New York, in 1918, which became the leading JAZZ venue of the 1920s and 1930s. The management, who were infamous for their alleged links with the Mafia, presented many of the most celebrated names in early jazz at the club, including Duke ELLINGTON and Cab CALLOWAY. The chiefly White audiences attracted to the club and its brilliant – mostly Black – entertainers in its heyday ranged from the rich and famous to notorious gangsters and their molls. The club moved premises in 1936 and closed for good in 1940, although its memory was preserved in the show *Bubbling Brown Sugar* (1976) and in the 1985 film *Cotton Club*.

The Aristocrat of Harlem.
LADY MOUNTBATTEN

country Genre of light pop music that emerged from the southern USA in the 1930s and became established as almost a US national musical style. The music had its origins in the FOLK MUSIC sung by settlers who moved west in the nineteenth century, music that was itself descended from the songs brought over with English colonists. This music was gradually transformed until it had developed into a quite distinct form, with most of the musicians playing fiddles, banjos, mandolins and guitars. Typical songs were melodic and sentimental, and they dealt with topics relevant to the ordinary rural American, ranging from laments for lost loves to joyful, often humorous, 'hoedown' party music (*see* BLUEGRASS; HILLBILLY).

The genre did not travel out of the southern States until the 1920s, when radio stations picked it up and began to broadcast such recordings to wider areas and the first records were distributed. Radio WSM in NASHVILLE, Tennessee, launched a regular Saturday night country show, the GRAND OLE OPRY, and this became a springboard for future country stars as well as anticipating Nashville's development as a centre of US pop. The genre acquired its own musical language, with distinctive guitar-picking techniques and a range of yodelling and drawled vocal styles, and, initially at least, there were many regional differences.

The first nationally known country star, often called the Father of Country Music but otherwise known as the Singing Brakeman, was Jimmie RODGERS. Other notable pioneers included the celebrated CARTER FAMILY and fiddle player John CARSON. In the wake of the success of cinema's singing cowboys, Roy ROGERS and Gene AUTRY (see COUNTRY-AND-WESTERN), country music became increasingly commercial in outlook in the 1940s and 1950s, when the influence of Nashville created a relatively homogenous national country style, with the emphasis on slick production and songs of equal relevance to urban and rural audiences. Line-ups were also 'modernized', with amplified instruments and drums being introduced, and fans and musicians alike assumed the now-traditional ranchhand outfits that have become associated with the genre.

A new generation of country legends emerged, the most famous names including Hank WILLIAMS, whose music influenced many ROCK 'N' ROLL artists, Patsy CLINE, Jim REEVES, Roy ACUFF and Johnny CASH, and their heirs, Dolly PARTON, Roger MILLER, Emmylou HARRIS and Tammy WYNETTE – all of whom established reputations far beyond the borders of the USA. The domination of the 'Nashville sound', which eventually developed into the smooth but unadventurous 'countrypolitan' style of the early 1970s, threatened to stifle creativity, and it needed the emergence of COUNTRY-ROCK and the unconventionality of such 'outlaws' as Willie NELSON in the 1970s to breathe new life into the genre – Nelson's *Red-headed Stranger* (1975) was the first country album to go platinum. Country music's ability to renew itself by relating in new ways to such allied genres as rock ensured a further revival of interest in the 1980s and 1990s, when innovative new stars included the phenomenally successful Garth Brooks.

country-and-western Tag that was first applied in the 1960s to COUNTRY music that incorporated Western 'cowboy songs'. The dividing line between country and country-and-western is extremely vague, and the two terms are now virtually indistinguishable, although originally country-and-western was taken to denote those songs that evoked the life of the cowboy on the

range, with his homely campfire ballads and yearnings for the settled life, the perfect wife, the ranch of his own and so on. Other ballads told of the lives of Gold Rush speculators and railroad workers. Famous names linked with music descended from this cowboy tradition included the Singing Cowboy himself, Gene AUTRY and his successor Roy ROGERS.

Since the 1960s, the sub-genre has attracted devotees far beyond the borders of the USA, with many clubs and bands being formed in the UK, for instance, for enthusiasts to enjoy the music and indulge their fondness for cowboy lore (even to the extent of wearing cowboy hats, neck ties and check shirts and carrying imitation six-shooters). *See also* WESTERN SWING.

> I know all the songs that the cowboys know
> 'Bout the big corral where the dogies go
> 'Cos I learned them all from the radio
> Yippee Ki O Ki Ay.
> JOHNNY MERCER, 'I'm an old cowhand'

Country Gentleman, the *See* Chet ATKINS.

Country Music Hall of Fame Institution, which was founded in 1961 to honour the most significant names in the history of COUNTRY music. Those elected to the Hall of Fame by the 250 people entitled to vote are commemorated by bronze plaques bearing their name. Among the many recipients of the honour have been Jimmie RODGERS, Hank WILLIAMS, Jim REEVES and Patsy CLINE. It was originally intended that only deceased stars would be thus honoured, but the election of the still-living Roy ACUFF in 1962 marked a change in the rules.

country-rock Genre of COUNTRY music, first explored in the 1960s, in which basic rock elements are incorporated in the hope that the result will appeal equally to fans of both styles. Noteworthy names in the history of the genre have included Gram PARSONS, Bob DYLAN, Johnny CASH and Hank WILLIAMS as well as such bands as the EAGLES. *See also* SOUTHERN ROCK.

Covent Garden The name usually used for the Royal Opera House, Covent Garden, London, which has long been the most prestigious venue for opera in the UK. The original Covent Garden was the site of a convent before it was built over in 1732 by the actor and theatre manager John Rich (*c.*1682–*c.*1761), using the money he had earned from John Gay's *The Beggar's Opera* (which, it was said, made Gay rich and Rich gay). For many years the theatre staged a mixed bill of musical and dramatic entertainments, including opera, and continued to prosper – being rebuilt in 1809 and again in 1858 after destruction by fire. It now houses both the Royal Ballet and the Royal Opera companies. Celebrated conductors seen at Covent Garden in recent decades have included Karl Rankl (1898–1968; musical director 1946–51), Rafael KUBELIK, Sir Georg SOLTI, Sir Colin DAVIS and Bernard HAITINK.

cover To record a song (or even an entire album) that has already been recorded by someone else. The history of JAZZ, ROCK and POP would not be complete without the long list of covers that have actually proved better and often more commercially successful than the originals (although this has not always, of course, been the case).

Many songs have been covered more than once. 'Earth Angel', first recorded by the Penguins in 1955, for instance, has been returned to *Billboard*'s Hot 100 by no fewer than four other artists; the Platters hit 'Only You' got into the CHARTS six times between 1955 and 1974 (when Ringo STARR had a go at it); and 'Mack the Knife' charted in the Hot 100 a total of eight times between 1956 and 1960 (Bobby DARIN's version spending 10 weeks at Number One).

Among the most-covered of all songs is the BEATLES classic 'Yesterday', which was penned by Paul MCCARTNEY in 1965 and was reckoned by McCartney to be 'the most complete thing I've ever written'. It became one of the most popular songs of the century, and by 1972 it existed in an astonishing total of some 1,186 published versions, including ones by Cilla BLACK, Pat BOONE, Nat King COLE, Elvis PRESLEY, Ray CHARLES, Perry COMO, Marianne FAITHFULL, Tom JONES, Otis REDDING, Smokey ROBINSON and Frank SINATRA.

Coward, Sir Noël (1899–1973) British playwright, actor, singer and entertainer, nicknamed the Master, who enjoyed an unrivalled reputation as a suave and debonair star and achieved equal success in the cinema and on the stage. He had strong reservations about his nickname, largely because it had already been bestowed on William Somerset Maugham

(1874–1965) and was also shared by US film director D.W. Griffiths (1875–1948).

As a songwriter Coward developed a unique line in satirical humour, performing many of his songs himself to universal acclaim, although he could, in fact, play in only three keys. His imperishable hits included 'Poor Little Rich Girl' (1924), 'Dance, Little Lady' (1928), 'Mad About the Boy' (1932), 'Mad Dogs and Englishmen' (1932), 'Don't Put Your Daughter on the Stage, Mrs Worthington' (1935), 'I've Been to a Marvellous Party' (1939), 'The Stately Homes of England' (1939), 'London Pride' (1941) and 'There are Bad Times Just Around the Corner' (1952), as well as a host of more sentimental songs, such as 'Some Day I'll Find You' (1930), which came from the play *Private Lives*, and 'I'll See You Again' (1929), which he wrote in the course of a New York taxi ride.

Coward was also the author of a series of highly successful MUSICALS, notably *Bitter Sweet* (1929), the patriotic *Cavalcade* (1931) and *Conversation Piece* (1934). Many of his best songs were reprised in the revue *Cowardy Custard* (1972).

> Extraordinary how potent cheap music is.
> NOËL COWARD, *Private Lives*, 1930

Cowell, Henry Dixon (1897–1965) US composer and pianist, who established a reputation as an innovator in both composition and performance from the 1920s on. Having established himself as a star pianist, he explored such AVANT-GARDE ideas as note CLUSTERS (in which the forearm, fist or elbow is used to sound several notes) and interference with the sounding of the strings in the piano. He was co-inventor (with Lev Theremin) of the RHYTHMICON, an electrical instrument designed to produce several rhythms at once. His output was prodigious, including 20 symphonies, a piano concerto, much instrumental and piano music, two ballets and an opera, as well as five string quartets and other chamber music. As a teacher, his pupils included George GERSHWIN and John CAGE.

> I believe a composer must forge his own forms out of the many influences that play upon him and never close his ears to any part of the world of sound ... for myself I have always wanted to live in the whole world of music.
> HENRY DIXON COWELL

Cowpat School of English Music Derogatory description, which was applied by critics to the 'countrified' style of English classical music pioneered by Ralph VAUGHAN WILLIAMS and others. In an attempt to free English music of the heavy influence of the German tradition and in the hope of launching a distinctive new national style, Vaughan Williams and his contemporaries turned to FOLK MUSIC as a source for their works, drawing on morris dances, folksongs and similar pieces, just as Igor STRAVINSKY and Béla BARTÓK and others were doing abroad, a move partly driven by the belief that folk music everywhere was dying. Typical examples of the style included Vaughan Williams' 'Greensleeves', from the opera *Sir John in Love* (1925–29), and *On Wenlock Edge* (1909).

Cox, Ida (1896–1967) US BLUES singer-songwriter, who made many classic recordings with, among others, Fletcher HENDERSON, Hot Lips PAGE and, in her final years, Coleman HAWKINS and Roy ELDRIDGE. Her most successful songs included 'Monkey Man Blues', 'Graveyard Bound Blues' and several of her own compositions, such as 'Bone Orchard Blues' and 'Mojo Hand Blues'.

Crawford, Jesse (1895–1962) US organist, nicknamed the Poet of the Organ and the Wizard of the Wurlitzer, who recorded many hit tunes in the 1920s and 1930s. His best-known releases included 'Roses of Picardy' and 'At Dawning'. He led his own dance band for a time in the late 1930s and often performed alongside his wife, also an organist.

Crawford, Randy (Veronica Crawford; 1952–) Black US SOUL singer, who achieved an international reputation with a series of hits in the 1970s and 1980s. She first attracted attention singing JAZZ-SOUL with the Crusaders in the 1970s and also appeared with such stars as George BENSON and Quincy JONES. Subsequently she developed her solo career, enjoying chart success with such singles as 'One Day I'll Fly Away' (1980), 'You Might Need Somebody' (1981) and 'Rainy Night in Georgia' (1981).

Cray, Robert (1953–) US BLUES guitarist and singer, who emerged as a leading electric blues performer in the 1980s. Tackling such traditional blues themes as

betrayal and despair, he confirmed his reputation as a brilliantly talented innovator with the solo album *Strong Persuader* (1986), which sold over a million copies and included the hit single 'Smoking Gun'. Subsequently he collaborated with such stars as Eric CLAPTON and had further success with such albums as *Don't Be Afraid Of the Dark* (1988) and *I Was Warned* (1992).

Crazy Legs *See* Chuck BERRY.

Cream British SUPERGROUP, which was formed in 1966 around the brilliant rock guitarist Eric CLAPTON. Clapton, drummer Ginger Baker (1939–) and bassist Jack Bruce (1943–) won instant acclaim for their unrivalled BLUES-oriented rock and for their prowess as a live band that thrived on improvisation. The band released three albums, *Fresh Cream* (1966), *Disraeli Gears* (1967) and *Wheels of Fire*, as well as such singles as 'I Feel Free' and 'Sunshine of Your Love' before finally folding in 1968, Clapton and Baker reuniting briefly as Blind Faith shortly after.

Creamer, the *See* Johnny DESMOND.

Creedence Clearwater Revival US rock band, which had great success in the late 1960s playing straightforward rock music at a time when the fashion was for psychedelia. Guitarist and singer John Fogerty (1945–), guitarist Tom Fogerty (1941–90), bassist Stu Cook (1945–) and drummer Doug Clifford (1945–) began as the Golliwogs before changing their name in 1967 and turning professional. Having developed a style that harked back to the BLUES and Cajun music, as well as to the ROCK 'N' ROLL of the 1950s, the band won a huge following with such albums as *Creedence Clearwater Revival* (1968), *Bayou Country* (1969), *Green River* (1969), *Willy and the Poor Boys* (1970) and *Cosmo's Factory* (1971), and with such singles as 'Suzie Q', 'Proud Mary', 'I Heard It through the Grapevine' and 'Bad Moon Rising'. In 1970 the band enjoyed no fewer than five US Number Ones. Tom Fogerty then left, and the band, plagued by internal rifts and corrupt managers, split up for good in 1972. John Fogerty subsequently embarked on a brief solo career in the mid-1980s.

Crespin, Régine (1927–) French soprano, who established herself as one of the foremost operatic sopranos of her generation in the 1960s. Having won praise for a recording of the Berlioz song-cycle *Les Nuits d'été*, she went on to excel in a range of Wagnerian roles such as Elsa in *Lohengrin*.

Crickets, the *See* Buddy HOLLY.

Croce, Jim (1943–73) US singer-songwriter, who had a series of hit singles and albums in the early 1970s. A former truck driver, Croce established his reputation overnight with the album *You Don't Mess Around with Jim* (1972) and subsequently had success with such singles as 'Bad, Bad Leroy Brown' and – posthumously – 'Time in a Bottle' and 'I'll Have to Say I Love You in a Song'. It all came to an end just a year after his big breakthrough when he was killed in an aircraft crash in Louisiana during a tour.

Croche, Monsieur Fictional character, who was invented by Claude DEBUSSY as a means of expressing his critical opinions without revealing his true identity (*croche* is French for quaver). 'Monsieur Croche' – 'the dilettante-hater' – became one of the most entertaining and widely read critics of his time, combining wit with cheek:

> A stranger would take it for a railway station and, once inside, would mistake it for a Turkish bath ... they continue to produce curious noises which the people who pay call music, but there is no need to believe them implicitly.
> Of the Paris Opéra

> The attraction of the virtuoso for the public is very like that of the circus for the crowd. There is always the hope that something dangerous may happen: M Ysaÿe may play the violin with M Colonne on his shoulders; or M Pugno may conclude his piece by lifting the piano with his teeth.
> Of virtuosos

> Does no one care sufficiently for Saint-Saëns to tell him he has written music enough?
> Of Saint-Saëns

> A pink sweet stuffed with snow.
> Of Grieg's music

Croon Prince of Swoon *See* Frank SINATRA.

crooner A singer of sentimental love songs and ballads of the type that enjoyed a vogue in the years before the emergence of ROCK 'N' ROLL. The style was facilitated by the development of the microphone in the late 1920s, with exponents singing in a soft, sweet tone 'somewhere near the written notes, but preferably never actually on those notes' (Eric Blom). Most famous of all the crooners was Bing CROSBY; others included Perry COMO, Rudy VALLEE and 'Whispering' Jack SMITH. The word 'croon' itself is thought to have been derived from Black slang, in which it signified 'mellow' singing, although ultimately the word may be descended from the Middle Low German *Krönen*, meaning to groan or lament.

Crosby, Bing (Harry Lillis Crosby; 1904–77) US singer and light comedian, nicknamed the Old Groaner (by himself) and Der Bingle (by German soldiers during the Second World War), who was the first and most popular of the CROONERS of the 1930s and 1940s. Bing Crosby began as a member of a close-harmony trio, but by 1931 he was already establishing himself as a solo star. Subsequently he enjoyed worldwide success as a recording artist, a live performer and as a filmstar in a long series of comedies, many of them also starring the comedian Bob HOPE, with whom he traded innumerable amiable insults. In such films as *Road to Singapore* (1940) and *Road to Morocco* (1942) Hope got the laughs while Bing got the girl and invariably got to sing.

In 1960 Crosby was awarded with a PLATINUM DISC to mark his achievement in selling some 200 million copies of the 2,600 singles and 125 albums he had recorded; in 1970 he was presented with another platinum disc as his sales allegedly passed 300 million. His 1942 recording of Irving BERLIN's 'White Christmas' was, for many years, the best-selling song ever made. Other chart-toppers included 'Silent Night', 'San Antonio Rose', 'Jingle Bells', 'Don't Fence Me In', 'Now is the Hour', 'Swinging on a Star', 'Pennies from Heaven' and 'Moonlight becomes You'; his theme song, though, was 'Where the Blue of the Night'. He died from a heart attack after finishing a round of golf.

> He was an average guy who could carry a tune.
> BING CROSBY's epitaph for himself

> I think that every man who ... listens to my records, or who hears me on the radio, believes firmly that he sings as well as I

do, especially when he's in the bathroom.
BING CROSBY

Crosby, Bob (1913–) US bandleader, singer and composer, brother of Bing CROSBY, who established his reputation singing with SWING bands in the 1930s. He consolidated his success with the Bobcats, assembled from members of the BIG BAND with which he appeared and, as a solo singer, became a regular performer on radio and television and appeared in a number of movies. His band's signature tune was GERSHWIN's 'Summertime'.

Crosby, Stills, Nash and Young US SUPER-GROUP, which brought together four of the most admired singer-songwriters of the late 1960s. The group – David Crosby (1941–), Stephen Stills (1945–), Graham Nash (1942–) and Neil YOUNG – was unveiled in 1969, although Young did not join until 1970. Such COUNTRY-ROCK albums as *Crosby Stills and Nash* (1969), *Déjà Vu* (1970) and *Four Way Street* (1971) were hugely successful, as were such singles as 'Ohio' and 'Woodstock'. The band rapidly disintegrated as the four members sought to develop their solo careers, although various reunions have been staged since.

Cross, Joan (1900–93) British soprano, who helped to promote the performance of operas in English during her highly successful career. A pupil of Gustav HOLST, she was a co-founder of the National School of Opera in 1948 and played an important role with the English Opera Group, Benjamin BRITTEN writing such parts as Ellen Orford in *Peter Grimes* and Elizabeth I in *Gloriana* for her.

crossover In the parlance of ROCK and POP, a style of music in which the features of any two distinct genres are mixed. In cold terms, if successful, such recordings may double sales by appealing to followers of both types, although, of course, they may appeal to neither. Examples include such phenomena as FOLK-ROCK and FUNK-METAL.
The term is also used of works that attempt to fuse classical music with pop, jazz and other modern forms (as in the highly successful career of 'pop' violinist Nigel KENNEDY in the early 1990s). Many ostensibly classical composers and performers have been keen to demonstrate

their skills in jazz and pop, from Igor STRA-VINSKY, who wrote his *Ebony Concerto* expressly for Woody HERMAN, Leonard BERNSTEIN and André PREVIN to Kiri TE KANAWA and Placido DOMINGO. Others have become pop 'stars' long after their own deaths; Beethoven himself contributed the oldest tune ever to reach Number One in BILLBOARD's Hot 100 in the form of his Fifth Symphony. His *Moonlight Sonata*, meanwhile, provided the basis for the BEATLES track 'Because' through the simple device of reversing the chords. Other notable adaptations have included 'I'm Always Chasing Rainbows', from Chopin's *Fantaisie Impromptu*, 'Avalon', from Puccini's *Tosca*, 'Till the End of Time', from Chopin's Polonaise in A flat, 'Red Wings', from Schumann's 'The Merry Peasant', 'The Story of a Starry Night', from Tchaikovsky's Sixth Symphony and 'Blues on Parade', from Rossini's *Stabat Mater*.
One popular composer, Alec Templeton (1919–63), made something of a career out of writing contemporary pieces evoking the style of earlier composers, creating such irreverent works as 'Mozart Matriculates', 'Mendelssohn Mows 'em Down' and 'Beethoven in Tin Pan Alley'.

> You know my temperature's risin',
> The juke box's blowin' a fuse,
> My heart's beatin' rhythm,
> My soul keeps a singin' the blues –
> Roll over Beethoven,
> Tell Tchaikovsky the news.
> CHUCK BERRY, 'Roll over Beethoven'

Crouse, Russel (1893–1966) US humorist, who collaborated on a number of hit Broadway MUSICALS, often in partnership with Howard LINDSAY. Libretti on which he worked included those for *Anything Goes* (1934), *Call Me Madam* (1950) and *The Sound of Music* (1959).

Crown Prince of Soul, the See Otis REDDING.

Crudup, Arthur 'Big Boy' (1905–74) Black US BLUES guitarist and singer, who was one of the first bluesmen to use an ELECTRIC GUITAR, thus paving the way for ROCK 'N' ROLL. After leaving Mississippi for Chicago in 1941, Crudup went on to record many classic songs, of which the most important were 'Mean Old Frisco' and 'That's All Right Mama' (later to be immortalized by Elvis PRESLEY). Sadly,

Crudup was unable to profit from such hits, having sold the rights to them for a relatively small sum during a particularly bleak period – in fact, he even had to change the words of his old songs so that he could still perform them without fear of litigation. A veteran who recorded some 30 albums, he died in poverty.

Crumit, Frank (1889–1943) US entertainer and composer, who enjoyed great popularity as a singer and radio star in the 1920s and 1930s. Presenter (with his wife) of the hit radio quiz *Battle of the Sexes*, he recorded such cheery numbers as 'Ukelele Lady', 'The Prune Song', 'Abdul Abulbul Amir', 'Granny's Old Armchair', 'My Grandfather's Clock' and 'The Pig Got Up and Slowly Walked Away'.

Cry Guy, the *See* Johnnie RAY.

Crystals, the US all-girl vocal group, which recorded a number of imperishable hits in the early 1960s. Produced by Phil SPECTOR and named after the daughter of their manager, the Crystals emerged as one of the most successful groups of the period with such hits as 'Da Doo Ron Ron' and 'Then He Kissed Me'. More controversial was 'He Hit Me (and It Felt Like A Kiss)', which provoked numerous protests (it was recorded to fulfil a contractual obligation). Leading members of the line-up included Dee Dee Kennibrew (Delores Henry; 1945–), Dolores 'LaLa' Brooks (1946–), Mary Thomas (1946–), Barbara Alston (1945–) and Pat Wright (1945–). A version of the band continued to tour into the 1990s.

Cugat, Xavier (Francisco de Asis Javier Cugat de Bru y Deulofeo; 1900–90) Spanish-American composer, violinist and bandleader, who did much to popularize Latin-American music in the USA in the 1930s and 1940s. After working as a professional violinist with orchestras in Havana, Cuba, he moved to the USA, where he helped to provide the backing at concerts by Enrico CARUSO and subsequently formed his own orchestra. His adaptations of Latin-American music were hugely influential and reached a wide audience as SOUNDTRACKS for a number of MGM movies.

Cult, the British HARD ROCK band, which built up a large following in the 1980s. Formed by vocalist Ian Astbury (1962–)

in 1981, the band – originally called Southern Death Cult – modelled itself on such bands as LED ZEPPELIN and AC/DC and became established with such hit albums as *Love* (1985), *Electric* (1987), *Sonic Temple* (1989) and *Ceremony* (1991). The lineup of the original Southern Death Cult was completed by bassist Barry, drummer Aky and guitarist Buzz – whose real identities were apparently unknown even to their record company.

Culture Club *See* BOY GEORGE.

Cure, the British pop group, which emerged from the NEW WAVE in the late 1970s. Led by singer and guitarist Robert Smith (1957–), the band first came together in 1977 and gradually earned a dedicated following with such pessimistic but atmospheric albums as *Boys Don't Cry* (1979), *Faith* (1981) and *Pornography* (1982). After a brief split, the Cure re-formed in 1983 and went on to release a further series of albums and singles, the most successful of which – the album *Kiss Me Kiss Me Kiss Me* (1987) – won international recognition. Such was the excitement when the Cure played in South America in 1987 that a riot broke out and a hot dog salesman and several police dogs were killed.

The group's singles were released as highly imaginative videos and regularly reached the Top 30, but another split was announced in 1989. The band was back in action by 1990, however; recent albums have included *Mixed Up* (1990), *Wish* (1992) and *Paris* (1993).

The Cure has always avoided identification with any particular political stance, unlike other bands that emerged at the same time: at one point the members even considered buying an entire Cornish village where they might create their own self-enclosed community.

Curzon, Sir Clifford Michael (1907–82) British pianist, who was particularly admired for his performances of Mozart, Beethoven and Schubert. A graduate of the Royal Academy of Music, he was a protégé of Sir Henry WOOD and also studied under Artur SCHNABEL, Wanda LANDOWSKA and Nadia BOULANGER.

cut To record a track or indeed an entire

103

CUTTING CONTEST

album in the studio. The tracks themselves are also occasionally referred to as cuts.

cutting contest A more or less friendly musical duel, in which two JAZZ musicians pit their musical skills against each other, taking turns to demonstrate their skill at improvisation in solo breaks. Also called carving contests (as though the musicians were fighting with knives), they were usually decided by the applause of any listeners present.

A jam session is a polite endeavour – an exchange of compliments. In the old days, they had cutting contests where you defended your honour with your instrument.

DUKE ELLINGTON, 1968

D

Dago, the *See* Frank SINATRA.

Dallapiccola, Luigi (1904–75) Italian composer and pianist, who became the leading Italian exponent of SERIALISM. Dallapiccola decided on a musical career after hearing a performance of Richard Wagner's *The Flying Dutchman* in 1917 and wrote his first works under the influence of Claude DEBUSSY and Italian madrigals. His friend Alban BERG converted him to the cause of serialism, and his compositions in this vein included such choral works as *Coro degli Zitti*. He was particularly noted for his sympathy for political prisoners everywhere, a concern that surfaced in a number of works ranging from the anti-fascist *Canti di prigionia* (1938–41) to the opera *Il prigioniero* (1944–48); he had himself been interned with his family in Graz during the First World War. Later compositions, which were admired for their lyricism, included the instrumental work *Three Questions with Two Answers* (1962) and the opera *Ulisse* (1968).

Daltry, Roger *See* the WHO.

Dameron, Tadd (Tadley Ewing Peake; 1917–65) US JAZZ pianist and arranger, who collaborated with many leading jazz bands on both sides of the Atlantic. As an arranger whose music appealed to both SWING and BEBOP fans, he worked with such distinguished musicians as Count BASIE, Dizzy GILLESPIE, Charlie PARKER, Miles DAVIS, Ted HEATH and Artie SHAW. Among his biggest hits were 'Hot House', 'Lady Bird' and 'If You Could See Me Now'. His drug habit caused some disruption to his career, and he served three years in prison in the late 1950s.

Damned, the British PUNK ROCK band, which emerged as one of the most influential outfits of the late 1970s. Vocalist (and former grave-digger) Dave Vanian (David Letts), guitarist Brian James (Brian Robertson), bassist Captain Sensible (Ray Burns; 1955–) and drummer Rat Scabies (Chris Miller; 1957–) formed the Damned in 1976 and released 'New Rose', acknowledged to be the first punk single, in the same year. The album *Damned, Damned, Damned* (1977) managed to reach the charts and helped trigger the punk explosion. A second, less influential album, *Music for Pleasure*, followed but the band then split. It re-formed a number of times with changing personnel and continued to attract a cult following with such albums as *Machine Gun Etiquette* (1979), *Black Album* (1980), so called in ironic reference to the Beatles' *White Album*, *Strawberries* (1982), the pop-oriented *Phantasmogoria* (1985), *Anything* (1986) and the compilation *Light at the End of the Tunnel*. The band's best-selling single was 'Eloise' (1986).

Damone, Vic (Vito Rocco Farinola; 1928–) US singer, who was a top balladeer of the late 1940s and 1950s. Among his hits were 'I Have But One Heart' (1947), 'Again' (1949), 'You're Breaking My Heart' (1949), 'Sometimes I'm Happy' (1955) and 'On the Street Where You Live' (1956).

> The best set of pipes in the business.
> FRANK SINATRA

dance band An instrumental group of brass, reed (including saxophones) and rhythm instruments (including guitars, drums and double bass), which plays popular dance music. The heyday of the dance band, which encompassed all styles from DIXIELAND to SWING, was from the 1920s to the 1940s, after which the advent of electrified instruments heralded a decline. Among the most popular of all dance bands were those of Duke ELLINGTON, Count BASIE, Benny GOODMAN, Glenn MILLER, Artie SHAW and, in the UK, Jack HYLTON, Jack PAYNE and Joe LOSS. *See also* JAZZ.

> Accompanying tap-dancers is like trying to play with someone bombarding you with Smarties.
> HUMPHREY LYTTELTON

Daniels, Charles Neil (1878–1943) US composer, who wrote numerous bestselling songs under the pseudonym Neil Moret. His first big hit came with 'Margery', which he wrote at the tender age of 18; later hits included the hugely successful 'Hiawatha' (1901), 'Moonlight' (1905), 'That Banjo Rag' (1912), 'Moonlight and Roses' (1925), 'Chloe' (1927) and 'She's Funny That Way' (1928).

Dankworth, Johnny (1927–) British JAZZ clarinettist, saxophonist, composer, arranger and bandleader, who is best known for his long collaboration with his wife, the jazz singer Cleo LAINE. A disciple of Charlie PARKER and other BEBOP stars, he has led his own band since 1953. His compositions, which have frequently explored musical forms other than jazz, include 'Improvisations' (1959), 'Tom Sawyer's Saturday' (1967), 'Piano Concerto' (1972) and the ambitious nine-movement *Fair Oak Fusions* (1982), as well as numerous film scores, such as those for *Saturday Night and Sunday Morning* (1960) and *The Servant* (1964). He also composed the theme tune for the television series *The Avengers*.

Darewski, Herman (1883–1947) British composer, conductor and publisher, born in Russia, who wrote the scores for many popular REVUES seen on the London stage. Founder of his own publishing company and orchestra, he created the scores for such shows as *Happy Days* (1914), *The Better 'Ole* (1917), *As You Were* (1918) and *The Shop Girl* (1920). His other works included numerous marches and songs, among the most popular of which were 'I Used to Sigh for the Silvery Moon' (1909), 'Sister Susie's Sewing Shirts for Soldiers' (1914) and 'If You Could Only Care' (1918).

Darin, Bobby (Walden Robert Cassotto; 1936–73) US pop singer, who was promoted as the successor to Frank SINATRA in the late 1950s. Darin (who chose his stage-name after thumbing through a telephone book) overcame perpetual ill-health – he suffered heart problems after attacks of rheumatic fever as a child – to enjoy such hits as 'Splish Splash', 'Queen of the Hop', 'Dream Lover' and 'Mack the Knife'. He was equally successful with his own compositions (ranging from 'Multipli-cation' to 'Be Mad Little Girl') and even ventured into FOLK-ROCK with a cover version of 'If I Were a Carpenter'.

Darin was moderately successful in CABARET (he was the youngest singer ever to perform at the Copacabana), and he planned a career in politics until he discovered that the woman he thought was his sister Nana was really his mother (a potential scandal that precluded any chance of attaining high public office). He did, however, enjoy a successful film career, being nominated for an Oscar as Best Supporting Actor in the film *Captain Newman, MD* (1963). He died of heart failure after collapsing on stage at the Las Vegas Hilton aged 37, having defied medical advice that he would not live beyond his eighteenth birthday.

> If I'm great now, just think what I'll be like when I'm Sinatra's age.
> BOBBY DARIN, aged 25

Darling Diva, the *See* Lesley GARRETT.

Darmstadt school Influential summer school that was first hosted at Darmstadt in 1946. Intended as a primarily educational gathering based on lectures and concerts, the event became an annual fixture and brought together such emerging talents as Karlheinz STOCKHAUSEN, Luciano BERIO, Sylvano Busotti, Olivier MESSIAEN and Pierre BOULEZ, all of whom had inherited the mantle of Arnold SCHOENBERG and were developing their own versions of the 12-NOTE system under the influence of Anton WEBERN and other acknowledged leaders in contemporary music. The summer school became an international forum for the latest developments in SERIALISM and other forms of modern classical music, although there were frequent differences of opinion over the issues such music presented (rarely more intense than they were in 1958 when John CAGE was present for the first time). The summer school was organized on a biannual basis from 1970.

DAT Digital Audio Tape. An advanced recording system in which sound can be digitally recorded onto magnetic tape, thus offering better recording and reproduction quality than the standard tape CASSETTE. Although used in studios, DAT systems have yet to break into a wider market, largely because of the high cost of such systems and the popularity of oher high-tech alternatives (notably the COMPACT DISC).

Dave Clark Five, the British pop group, which was among the most serious rivals to the BEATLES in the mid-1960s with the TOTTENHAM SOUND. Drummer Dave Clark (1942–), singer and keyboard player Mike Smith (1943–), bassist Rick Huxley (1942–), saxophonist Denis Payton (1943–) and guitarist Len Davidson (1944–) enjoyed a string of hit singles including 'Glad All Over', 'Bits and Pieces', 'Can't You See that She's Mine' and the title track from the group's 1965 film *Catch Us If You Can*. The Dave Clark Five was particularly well received in the USA where the group spearheaded the so-called BRITISH INVASION, becoming in 1964 the first band from the UK to make a US tour and making more appearances on the influential *Ed Sullivan Show* than any other pop group. Mike Smith wrote most of the group's hits, but he proved to lack the versatility and imagination of LENNON AND MCCARTNEY; tastes changed and the band was finally dissolved in 1970. Many years later Dave Clark, a successful business-man, was behind the hit MUSICAL *Time* (1987).

> We were at our height with our own plane, the DC–5. I mean, we had been arriving at airports and getting a key to every city in the States. We'd have two Cadillac limos and six motorcyclists escorting us. It was like being president, or king for a day. It was wonderful.
> DAVE CLARK

Dave Dee, Dozy, Beaky, Mick and Tich British pop group of the 1960s, which had some success with a series of novelty BEAT singles. Led by former policeman Dave Dee (David Harman; 1943–) and completed by Trevor 'Dozy' Davies (1944–), guitarist John 'Beaky' Dymond (1944–), Michael 'Mick' Wilson (1944–) and Ian 'Tich' Amey (1944–), the band reached the Top 10 in several European countries with such hits as 'Hold Tight', 'Hideaway', 'Bend It', 'Save Me' and 'Legend of Xanadu' (their only Number One) before splitting up.

Davenport, 'Cow-Cow' (Charles Edward Davenport; 1894–1955) US BOOGIE-WOOGIE composer and pianist, who

recorded a number of his own hit songs in the 1920s and 1930s. Having been thrown out of theological college, he concentrated on developing a career as a RAG-TIME and vaudeville pianist and went on to create such popular hits as 'Cow-Cow Blues' (1928), which was released in 1942 as 'Cow-Cow Boogie', 'Mama Don't Allow' (1929) and 'I'll be Glad When You're Dead, You Rascal, You' (1931).

Davis, Carl (1936–) US composer, resident in the UK, who is celebrated for his many film scores and television work. As well as contributing new scores for such silent classics as *Napoleon* (1927) and *The Crowd* (1928), he has also composed music for such movies as *Up Pompeii* (1971) and *The French Lieutenant's Woman* (1981), for which he won a British Film Academy Award.

Davis, Sir Colin Rex (1927–) British conductor, who first emerged as one of the leading conductors of his generation in the 1950s. A former bandsman with the Household Cavalry, he attracted attention with his interpretations of Mozart with the Chelsea Opera Group and was invited to conduct the BBC Scottish Orchestra, the Sadler's Wells Opera, the BBC SYMPHONY ORCHESTRA, the COVENT GARDEN OPERA, the Metropolitan Opera and (since 1983) the Bavarian Radio Symphony Orchestra. Notable operas performed under his baton have included works by Benjamin BRITTEN, Sir Michael TIPPETT and Hector Berlioz.

Davis, Eddie 'Lockjaw' (1922–86) US JAZZ saxophonist, nicknamed Jaws, who was admired as one of the most able jazz musicians of his generation, playing in the bands of Louis ARMSTRONG and Count BASIE among others. He led his own band in the late 1940s and created numerous hits – among them 'Lockjaw', which gave him his nickname. He formed a trio in 1955 before reuniting with Basie and going on to assume the role of Basie's road manager. His most popular recordings with Basie included 'Hobnail Boogie', 'Paradise Squat' and 'Whirlybird'.

Davis, Jimmie (1902–) US singer-songwriter, who combined a successful career as a COUNTRY star with those of an academic historian, film actor, police commissioner and governor of Louisiana

(1944–48 and 1960–64). His numerous hit songs included 'Nobody's Darling but Mine' (1935), 'You are My Sunshine' (1940), which he used as a campaign song, and 'Worried Mind' (1942). He ventured into GOSPEL music in the 1950s and again in the 1970s, and was elected to the COUNTRY MUSIC HALL OF FAME in 1972. His extraordinary life story provided the plot for the film *Louisiana* (1947).

Davis, Mac (1942–) US singer-songwriter, nicknamed the Song Painter, who wrote many classic COUNTRY-influenced hits for a range of celebrated artists in the 1960s and 1970s. Among those to use material by Davis have been Glen CAMPBELL, Elvis PRESLEY, Kenny ROGERS and Nancy SINATRA. His best-known compositions have included 'I'm in the Ghetto' and 'Don't Cry, Daddy', both of which were successfully recorded by Presley, and 'Something Burning', which Kenny Rogers turned into a hit. In 1980 Davis had a lucky escape when he left the MGM Grand Hotel in Las Vegas shortly before a disastrous fire which claimed several lives.

Davis, Miles Dewey (1926–91) Black US trumpeter, bandleader and composer, who pioneered the development of COOL jazz and in the process became one of the most influential figures in twentieth-century music. A graduate of the Juillard School in New York, Davis (the son of a dentist) arrived on the jazz scene in the mid-1940s, playing alongside such fellow-greats as Charlie PARKER, and he went on to record a series of arrangements by Gil EVANS, which reached their climax in the recordings later gathered together as *The Birth of The Cool* (1957).

In the late 1950s (after kicking his drug habit) he led his own quintet, which included Charles MINGUS and John COLTRANE, and recorded such jazz classics as *Miles Ahead* (1957), *Milestones* (1958) and *Kind of Blue* (1959) before diversifying with the adoption of various electronic instruments in the 1960s (a stage in the development of JAZZ-ROCK). Important albums from this period, when his band was enriched by the presence of such talents as John MCLAUGHLIN (1942–) and Keith Jarrett (1945–), included *In a Silent Way* (1969) and the innovative *Bitches' Brew* (1969), which challenged accepted conventions about what 'jazz' really was. He

ventured into mainstream POP, FUNK, DISCO, the BLUES and even RAP to prove his point that he did not feel obliged to play in a recognizable 'jazz' manner.

His last years were plagued by ill-health and the legacy of pain that was a consequence of a serious car crash in 1972 in which he broke both legs. His private life was never dull, and at various points in his stormy career he was troubled with clashes with the authorities (he was arrested and beaten by the New York police in 1959), further drug problems and a shooting incident (1975). He also courted controversy by voicing his resentment of racial bias within the recording industry, threatening on one occasion to establish his own 'Mammy' awards for Black artists in competition with the White-dominated GRAMMY system. Nonetheless, his music was never less than of the highest quality. When he eventually died tributes included one by Django Bates, who said that his favourite Davis recordings were those made between 1926 and mid-1991.

Davis Jr, Sammy (1925–90) Black US singer, actor and dancer, who emerged as an enormously popular all-round entertainer, appearing with equal success in cabaret, films, television and the theatre throughout his long career. The son of vaudeville performers, he made his stage début at the age of eight and came to rank alongside such international stars as Frank SINATRA. His most successful Broadway appearances included roles in *Mr Wonderful* (1956) and *Golden Boy* (1964), both of which were written for him. Hit recordings included 'The Way You Look Tonight' (1950), 'Something's Gotta Give' (1954), 'That Old Black Magic' (1955) and 'Candy Man' (1972). Having lost an eye in a car crash in 1954, he often joked that he was the world's only 'one-eyed Jewish nigger', and in truth, he never quite escaped the attention of racist bigots. He once observed of his star status:

> Being a star has made it possible for me to get insulted in places where the average Negro could never hope to get insulted.

Davis, Skeeter (Mary Frances Penick; 1931–) US COUNTRY singer, who emerged as a popular star of the 1950s and 1960s. She began as half of a Davis Sisters duo in 1953 but gave up music for a time when her partner, Betty Jack Davis, died in a car accident. She revived her career towards the end of the decade with such hits as 'Set Him Free' (1959) and consolidated it with such best-selling recordings as 'The End of the World' (1962), 'I'm Saving My Love' (1963), 'Gonna Get Along Without You' (1964) and 'I'm a Lover – Not a Fighter' (1969). She also ventured into ROCK from time to time, appearing alongside Buddy HOLLY and with the ROLLING STONES.

Davison, 'Wild Bill' (William Edward Davison; 1906–89) US JAZZ cornettist, trombonist, singer and bandleader, who was one of the most admired DIXIELAND players. Renowned for his passionate playing style, he established his reputation with the Ohio Lucky Seven in the 1920s and went on to lead his own bands with great success as well as collaborating with Eddie CONDON among others. In 1932 he was the driver of the car in which clarinettist Frank Teschemacher (1906–32) died in an accident.

Dawson, Peter (1882–1961) Australian singer-songwriter, who became one of the most prolific and popular of all early recording artists, with some 3,000 recordings to his credit. Dawson arrived in the UK in 1902 to study with the baritone Sir Charles Santley (1834–1922) and made his début at COVENT GARDEN in 1909. He concentrated on recording and concert work, and consolidated his reputation with such hits as 'Floral Dance' and 'Boots', which was based on the poem by Rudyard Kipling and released by Dawson under the pseudonym J.P. McColl (just one of many pseudonyms he used in the course of his career). His many other records included a series of COVERS of the songs of music hall star Harry Lauder (issued under the name Hector Grant), the success of which was said to have caused Lauder considerable annoyance.

Day, Doris (Doris Mary Anne Von Kappelhoff; 1922–) US film actress and singer, who was a popular singing star of the 1940s and 1950s, capitalizing on her image of stainless cheerfulness. Day sang with DANCE BANDS in the early 1940s and included among her biggest hits 'My Dreams are Getting Better' and 'Sentimental Journey', both of which reached Number One in the USA. She appeared in numerous Hollywood movies, in the course of which she sang such hits as the OSCAR-winning 'Secret Love' (1954) and 'Que será, será' (1956), both of which reached Number One in the UK. She hosted her own television series in the late 1960s but has been in virtual retirement from show business since the mid–1970s.

'Que será, será' was inspired by the 'Che sera, sera' motto quoted in the 1954 movie *The Barefoot Contessa* – the writers of the song giving it in its Spanish version rather than the original Italian on the grounds that, because more people spoke Spanish than Italian, this would bolster its worldwide appeal (although Day herself doubted it was hit material).

> I've been around so long I can remember Doris Day before she was a virgin.
> GROUCHO MARX (also attributed to Oscar Levant)

> She thinks she doesn't get old. She told me once it was her cameraman who was getting older. She was going to fire him.
> JOE PASTERNAK

De Burgh, Chris (Christopher Davidson; 1950–) British singer-songwriter, born in Argentina and resident in Ireland, who enjoyed huge commercial success in the 1980s. After years as a support artist, he broke through to the charts in 1983 with 'Don't Pay the Ferryman' and consolidated his reputation with such follow-ups as 'Lady in Red' (1986), which he wrote for his wife, and 'Missing You' (1988), although he generally had greater success in the album market, with such LPs as *Man on the Line* (1984), *Into the Light* (1986), *Flying Colours* (1988), *Power of Ten* (1992) and *This Way Up* (1994).

De Los Angeles, Victoria (Victoria Gomez Cima; 1923–) Spanish soprano, who emerged as a leading opera star of the postwar period. A graduate of the Barcelona Conservatory, she made her professional début in 1945 in Monteverdi's *Orfeo* and excelled in performances of PUCCINI, Wagner and FALLA, her most acclaimed roles including Madam Butterfly and Mimi.

De Paul, Gene Vincent (1919–88) US composer and pianist, who wrote a number of acclaimed scores for Hollywood in the 1950s. His best-known compositions included the scores for the MUSICALS *Seven Brides for Seven Brothers* (1954), which earned him an Oscar, and *You Can't Run Away From It* (1956), as well as songs for the Disney cartoon *Alice in Wonderland* (1951) and the score for the Broadway musical *L'il Abner* (1950).

De Rose, Peter (1900–53) US songwriter, who created many hit songs for REVUES in the 1920s and 1930s. Among his best-known songs were 'Muddy Water' (1926), 'Wagon Wheels' (1931), 'Somebody Loves You' (1932) and 'Lilacs in the Rain' (1939).

Dead Kennedys US PUNK ROCK band, which was one of the few to establish a significant following in the USA. Vocalist Jello Biafra, guitarist East Bay Ray, bassist Klaus Fluoride and drummer Ted came together in 1977 in San Francisco and quickly established a reputation for relatively sophisticated punk music, which had often witty and politically relevant lyrics. The band's first album, *Fresh Fruit for Rotting Vegetables* (1980), contained such classic punk tracks as 'Kill the Poor' and 'Nazi Punks Fuck Off'. The album *Plastic Surgery* (1982) was also well received, but later releases showed less imagination, and the group ran into trouble with the authorities over *Frankenchrist* (1985), which came with an obscene poster that prompted many outlets to ban its sale. Attempts by Biafra to be elected mayor of San Francisco in 1979 came to nothing (his manifesto included a requirement that all businessmen should wear clown costumes). The group split up in 1987.

Deadhead A fan of the US rock group the GRATEFUL DEAD (known to their devotees simply as 'the Dead').

Dean, Jimmy (1928–   ) US singer-songwriter, nicknamed the Long Tall Texan, who had several COUNTRY hits in the 1950s and 1960s. Among his most successful releases was 'Big Bad John' (1961), which was inspired by tall fellow-singer Johnny Mento; others included 'Bummin' Around' (1953), 'Stand Beside Me' (1966) and 'A Thing Called Love' (1968). He retired from music in the 1970s to concentrate on his sausage business.

death metal A radical version of THRASH, in which the emphasis is placed strongly on images of death and mutilation. Songs are generally short and very noisy, and what

lyrics there are are virtually impossible to decipher. Exponents of this unlovely brand of high-speed HEAVY METAL have included Death, Carcass and Slayer.

> Intenacious, intersecting
> Reaving fats from corporal griskin …
> Skeletal groats triturated,
> Desinently exsiccated.
> Carcass lyrics

Debussy, (Achille-) Claude (1862–1918) French composer, who ranks among the most important classical composers of the century. A graduate of the Paris Conservatoire, he won the prestigious Prix de Rome in 1884 with the cantata *The Prodigal Son* and was instantly recognized as a major talent, although in 1885 he admitted: 'I don't know if I'm big enough to do what I have in mind.' He broke new ground with such works as the opera *Pelléas et Mélisande* (1892–1902) – arguably his masterpiece – and the controversial *Prélude à l'après-midi d'un faune* (1894). Reactions from the musical establishment ranged from extreme admiration and hostile dismissal to plain confusion. After attending the premiere of *Pelléas et Mélisande* Gabriel FAURÉ remarked: 'If that was music, I have never understood what music was.'

Debussy established a reputation for atmospheric, impressionist writing based on a classical structure, but he won over many listeners with his more humorous pieces, notably the jaunty 'Golliwog's Cake Walk' from the *Children's Corner* suite, written in 1906–08 and dedicated to his daughter 'Chouchou' Claud-Emma. Among his most important other works were the *Nocturnes* (1899), the symphonic sketches *La Mer* (1905), the ballet *Jeux* (1913), in which a game of tennis is treated as a metaphor for all love games, the *Danse sacrée et danse profane* and much piano music.

Debussy's private life was chaotic. He lived with a succession of women, and his first marriage, to Lilly Texier, was stormy and beset by financial difficulties (the composer gave a piano lesson on the day of his wedding in 1899 in order to pay for the reception). His second marriage was more stable, but the composer was deeply shocked by the outbreak of the First World War and eventually succumbed to cancer at a time when he was still producing compositions of the highest quality, even though he himself lamented 'Music has quite left me'.

He quarrelled with virtually every other leading composer of his day, yet remained one of the most influential figures in modern classical music. When Béla BARTÓK visited Paris and was told he could meet anyone he desired, he instantly requested that he be introduced to Debussy; warned that Debussy would almost certainly be rude to him, his hosts demanded 'Do you want to be insulted by Debussy?' Bartók's reply was firm: 'Yes.'

> Mon plaisir!
> CLAUDE DEBUSSY, when asked what rule he followed

> The colour of my soul is iron-grey and sad bats wheel about the steeple of my dreams.
> CLAUDE DEBUSSY, letter, 1894

> I would soon lose my voice if I went round roaring vacuously like a faun celebrating its afternoon.
> STEPHEN MALLARMÉ, of Prélude à l'après-midi d'un faune

> Better not listen to it; you risk getting used to it, and then you would end by liking it.
> RIMSKY-KORSAKOV, of Debussy's music

deca-rock Alternative term for GLAM ROCK (from *decad*ent *rock*).

decay The fading of a note or other sound, of particular relevance in electronic music where the speed and quality of the decay is readily controllable.

Decca International record label, which was founded in 1929 by British stockbroker Edward Lewis. Destined to become the second largest record company in the world, Decca boasted many of the most celebrated stars of twentieth-century music. Famous names signed or distributed by Decca over the years included Al JOLSON, Bing CROSBY, Louis ARMSTRONG, Gracie FIELDS, Vera LYNN, Tommy STEELE, LITTLE RICHARD, the EVERLY BROTHERS, Eddie COCHRAN, Roy ORBISON and the ROLLING STONES. Decca is also remembered by many as the record company that (in the early 1960s) turned down the BEATLES. The British branch of the company was eventually acquired by POLYGRAM in 1980.

Deep Purple British HARD ROCK band, which achieved legendary status among HEAVY METAL fans in the 1970s. Deep Purple came into being in 1968 and, after various changes in personnel, won fame with the celebrated line-up of singer Ian Gillan (1945–), guitarist Ritchie BLACKMORE, bassist Roger Glover (1945–), keyboard player Jon Lord (1941–) and drummer Ian Paice (1948–). The album *Deep Purple in Rock* (1970) was a landmark in the development of heavy metal. Other releases included such hit singles as 'Black Night' and 'Strange Kind of Woman', although the quintessential Deep Purple track remains 'Smoke on the Water', an epic inspired by an incident during a Frank ZAPPA concert in 1971, when a fire broke out in the lakeside Montreux casino.

The band was rivalled only by LED ZEPPELIN as the world's top hard rock band, and its reputation was bolstered by such releases as *Made in Japan* (1973), which was based on its live act. The group split in 1976 but reunited in 1984, recording a further three albums. Gillan eventually left and was replaced by Joe Lynn Turner. Blackmore's replacement, Tommy Bolin, survived the band's dissolution by only a few months, dying of a heroin overdose. Reunited with Gillan in 1992, the band released *The Battle Rages On* in 1993.

Def Leppard British HARD ROCK band, which built up a massive following in the 1980s. Guitarist Pete Willis, bassist Rick Savage (1960–), drummer Rick Allen (1963–), vocalist Joe Elliott (1959–) and guitarist Steve Clark (1960–91) first came together in 1978 and played early rehearsals in a small room at a spoon factory in Sheffield. Having attracted attention as a support band, Def Leppard won more fans with such early albums as *On Through the Night* (1980) and *Pyromania* (1983), bringing in Phil Collen (1957–) as replacement to the unreliable Willis. The group suffered a setback in 1984 when drummer Allen lost an arm in a car crash, but he stayed with the band after he learned how to play the drums using his remaining arm and his feet. *Hysteria* (1987) proved a huge success, and the band toured widely before the death from alcohol and drug abuse of Steve Clark in 1991. The band stayed together, however, and released a further hit album, *Adrenalize*, in 1992. *Slang* followed in 1996.

Dekker, Desmond (Desmond Dacris; 1942–) Black Jamaican-born singer, who was one of the first REGGAE stars. Among his biggest hits were 'Honour Your

Mother and Father' (1963), '007 (Shanty Town)' (1967), the Number One single 'Israelites' (1969) and 'You Can Get It If You Really Want' (1970).

Del Monaco, Mario (1915–82) Italian tenor, who established an international reputation appearing at leading opera venues around the world after the Second World War. He made his professional début in 1941 and went on to win particular acclaim in French and Italian operas of the nineteenth century.

Del Riego, Teresa (1876–1968) British songwriter, who wrote a series of hugely successful songs in the early years of the century. A trained musician, she joined the ranks of the leading songwriters of the age with such classics as 'O Dry Those Tears' (1901) and 'Homing' (1917). Widowed when her husband was killed on active service in France during the First World War, she was also the composer of 'The Unknown Warrior', which was revived every year on British Armistice Day for many years after.

Delius, Frederick (1862–1934) British composer of German descent, who is considered one of the most significant classical composers of the century. The son of a Bradford wool merchant, Delius was expected to settle on a business career, but he rebelled and toured Europe instead before moving to the USA to take over an orange plantation. It was while listening to the close-harmony singing of the Black workers on the plantation one summer night that he realized his future lay in music. He returned to Europe and took up music studies in Leipzig, where he met Edvard Grieg (1843–1907) and undertook his first compositions.

Delius moved with his wife Jelka Rosen, a painter, to Grez-sur-Loing, near Paris and developed his personal, highly coloured style, writing such works as *Nocturne, Paris: The Song of a Great City* (1899), *Sea-Drift* (1903–04) and *On Hearing the First Cuckoo in Spring* (1912), one of many classic works to draw inspiration from nature.

Delius lost his sight and became paralysed after the First World War as a result of syphilis, and in his later years he depended on the assistance of his amanuensis Eric Fenby (1906–87). His other works included a number of now largely forgotten operas, including *Over the Hills and Far Away* (1895), *A Village Romeo and Juliet*

(1900–01), *Appalachia* (c.1896–1902), *A Mass of Life* (1905), *Brigg Fair* (1907), *In a Summer Garden* (1908), *A Song of the High Hills* (1911), *Arabesk* (1911) and *Songs of Farewell* (1931). Among his greatest champions in the UK was Sir Thomas BEECHAM.

> It is only that which cannot be expressed otherwise that is worth expressing in music.
> FREDERICK DELIUS, *At the Crossroads*, 1920

> As Beethoven is the morning and Wagner the high noon, so Delius is the sunset of that great period of music which is called Romantic.
> PETER WARLOCK

> I never dreamt that anyone except myself was writing such good music.
> RICHARD STRAUSS

> Music to rock the convalescents of rich neighbourhoods.
> CLAUDE DEBUSSY, of Delius's music

> The musical equivalent of blancmange.
> BERNARD LEVIN, *Enthusiasms*, 1983

Deller, Alfred (1912–79) British countertenor, who was considered the finest counter-tenor of his generation. Blessed with a naturally high voice, he was able to perform many of the roles hitherto associated with castrati singers. His performances did much to popularize late seventeenth-century English music (notably the works of Purcell) and to promote public acceptance of the counter-tenor. Roles written specially for him included that of Oberon in Benjamin BRITTEN's *A Midsummer Night's Dream* (1960).

To pre-empt idle speculation he wore a beard, but he still did not manage to escape discussion of the origins of his high voice. He was much in demand on the Continent and was once asked by a Frenchman 'Monsieur Dellaire, are you – how do you say in England – eunuch?' to which Deller replied quite properly 'Well yes, you could say I am. Unique.'

Delta blues Traditional BLUES music from the Delta region of Mississippi, south Louisiana, where the genre originated. More accurately, the Delta covered an area stretching from Vicksburg to Memphis, where there were many cotton plantations. Most Black musicians who established a commercial reputation for themselves escaped the region for the relative luxury of Chicago.

Delysia, Alice (Alice Lapize; 1889–1979) French singer and actress, who became a huge star of revue in Paris and London in the early years of the century. One of the sex symbols of her age, she appeared in numerous revues, including those of C.B. COCHRAN. Her hit songs included 'If You Could Care' (1918), 'Dardanella' (1920), 'Poor Little Rich Girl' (1925) and 'Every Woman Thinks She Wants to Wander' (1933).

demo A recording that is prepared as a sample of the work of a particular band or artist in the hope that it will persuade a record company or theatre management into offering a recording contract or booking.

Dennis, Matt (1914–) US composer, arranger, singer and pianist, who worked with several leading DANCE BANDS and wrote a long list of hit songs. He was arranger for Tommy DORSEY and Glenn MILLER and also enjoyed success as a solo performer singing his own material; other singers who recorded his songs included Frank SINATRA and Jo STAFFORD. His best-known compositions included 'Everything Happens to Me' (1940), 'Skunk Song' (1941), 'You'd Never Know the Old Place Now' (1941), 'We Belong Together' (1952) and 'Angel Eyes' (1953).

Denver, John (John Henry Deutschendorf; 1933–) US singer-songwriter, who became one of the top US stars of the early 1970s. Naming himself after the city of Denver, Colorado, he was regularly in the upper reaches of the US charts with such hits as 'Rocky Mountain High', 'Take Me Home Country Roads' and 'Annie's Song'. He also wrote such hits as 'Leaving on a Jet Plane' for PETER, PAUL AND MARY and continued to prosper both as a pop singer and as a television presenter through the 1980s.

'Annie's Song' provided Denver with his only significant UK hit, reaching Number One in 1975; it was inspired by his wife Ann Martell and was composed while Denver was riding on a ski lift.

Denver's father, Henry Deutschendorf, won a place in the record books when he broke a world speed record in a B–58 Hustler bomber aircraft in 1961.

Depeche Mode British pop group, which pioneered SYNTHESIZER pop in the 1980s. Keyboard players Martin Gore (1961–), Vince Clarke (1961–) and Andy Fletcher (1961–) came together in 1976 and emerged as stars in the NEW ROMANTIC style. Success in the singles market with such songs as 'Just Can't Get Enough' was consolidated by such well-received albums as *Speak and Spell* (1981). Clarke was replaced by Alan Wilder (1963–) and the band adopted a sharper rock image, releasing such hits as 'Blasphemous Rumours' and 'People are People' as well as the top-selling albums *Music for the Masses* (1987) and *Songs of Faith and Devotion* (1993).

Der Bingle *See* Bing CROSBY.

Desert Island Discs Long-running BBC radio programme, in which an invited guest is asked to choose his or her eight favourite pieces of music (and a favourite book and a single luxury), with which to be marooned on a mythical desert island. The creation of Roy Plomley, who presented it from its inception in 1942 until his death in 1985, the programme is a British institution and claims the honour of being the longest-running radio programme in the world. British comedian and singer Arthur Askey (1900–82) appeared on the programme a record four times. Notable invitees who refused to take part in the prestigious programme included George Bernard Shaw, Laurence Olivier, and the BEATLES (although Brian EPSTEIN appeared in 1964, and George MARTIN did the same in 1982; in that same year Paul MCCARTNEY was the 1,629th castaway).

Desmond, Johnny (Giovanni Alfredo De Simone; 1920–85) US singer and actor, nicknamed the GI Sinatra (in reference to his army career) and the Creamer, who was one of the most popular singers of the 1940s and 1950s. He attracted attention as singer for the Bob CROSBY band and joined the Gene KRUPA Orchestra and the Glenn MILLER Army Air Force Band, thus acquiring his nickname. Like Sinatra, he also enjoyed a reputation as a screen actor, as well as appearing on Broadway. His biggest hits included 'Play Me Hearts and Flowers' and 'Yellow Rose of Texas'.

Desmond, Paul (Paul Emil Breitenfeld; 1924–77) US JAZZ saxophonist, who established his reputation as one of the leading members of the Dave BRUBECK Quartet (1951–67). He wrote much material for the quartet, including its greatest hit of all, 'Take Five'. He also played with distinction for Gerry MULLIGAN and Jim Hall among others. He once observed that his ambition was to make his alto saxophone 'sound like a dry martini'.

DeSylva, Buddy (George Gard DeSylva; 1895–1950) US lyricist and producer, who collaborated on numerous successful Broadway shows and provided the lyrics for many hit songs. He was also active as a film producer (notably of several Shirley Temple films) and ultimately the head of Paramount Pictures. Among the hits for which he wrote the lyrics were 'April Showers' (1921), 'California, Here I Come' (1924), 'If You Knew Susie' (1925), 'Button Up Your Overcoat' (1929) and 'Sonny Boy' (1929). Many of his biggest hits were written in collaboration with Lew Brown (Louis Brownstein; 1893–1958) and Ray Henderson (1896–1970).

Detroit Wildman, the *See* Ted NUGENT.

devil's music Derogatory term, which was applied to JAZZ by those who opposed it when it achieved wide popularity in the 1920s. The spread of commercial jazz dance music after the First World War was deplored by many conservative elements in society, who saw in such music a threat to civilized Christian standards and morals. Monseigneur Conefrey, writing in the *New York Times* in 1934, claimed that: 'Jazz was borrowed from Central Africa by a gang of wealthy international Bolshevists from America, their aim being to strike at Christian civilization throughout the world.' The president of the Christian Endeavour Society called jazz dancing 'an offence against womanly purity', while the medical director of a girls' high school felt strongly enough about the effects of the music to conclude that 'the consensus of opinion of leading medical and other scientific authorities is that its influence is as harmful and degrading to civilized races as it has always been among the savages from whom we borrowed it'. The *New Orleans Times*, meanwhile, hastened to disown its musical progeny: 'It has been widely suggested that this form of musical vice had its birth in this city, that it came from doubtful surroundings in our slums. We do not recognize the honour of parenthood'.

These opponents were joined by many traditional classical musicians and critics who perceived the development of jazz as an attack on their own music. Igor STRAVINSKY said of the genre: 'Jazz opposes to our classical conception of music a strange and subversive form chaos of sounds ... it is a fashion and, as such, destined some day to disappear.' Sir Thomas BEECHAM was even more dismissive, describing jazz as: 'nothing but the debasement of noble brass instruments by blowing them into mutes, hats, caps, nooks, crannies, holes, and corners.'

> The jazz band can be used for artificial excitement and aphrodisiac purposes, but not for spreading eternal truths.
> ARTHUR BLISS, 1941

Dexy's Midnight Runners British SOUL band, based in Birmingham, which made its mark in the UK charts in the early 1980s with a series of hit singles. Led by singer-songwriter Kevin Rowland (1953–), the band achieved overnight fame with its second single, 'Geno' (a tribute to soul legend Geno Washington), which reached Number One. The album *Searching for the Young Soul Rebels* (1980) was well received, and the band's second album, the Celtic-influenced *Too Rye-Ay*, produced another Number One, 'Come On Eileen', and further hit singles. Rowland, who at one point replaced every member of the band save one, dissolved the band and went bankrupt, but it re-formed in 1993.

Diamond, Neil (1941–) US singer-songwriter, who recorded many top-selling singles in the late 1960s and 1970s. After a tough Brooklyn childhood, he wrote his first songs in the late 1950s; he emerged as a CABARET star and attracted international attention in 1966 when the MONKEES made his 'I'm a Believer' a huge hit. One of the writers associated with the BRILL BUILDING songwriting company, he also wrote 'A Little Bit Me, a Little Bit You' for the Monkees, as well as hits for LULU ('The Boat That I Row') and DEEP PURPLE ('Kentucky Woman').

Diamond's recording of 'Sweet Caroline' (1969) established him as a star performer in his own right, and it was followed by such hits as 'Cracklin' Rosie' (1970), which reached Number One, 'I Am I Said' (1971), 'Song Sung Blue' (1972), the duet 'You Don't Bring Me Flowers' (1978), which he made with Barbra STREISAND, 'Forever in Blue Jeans' (1979) and 'Love on the Rocks' (1980). Among his albums were *Tap Root*

Manuscript (1970), *Beautiful Noise* (1974), *Headed for the Future* (1986), *Lovescape* (1991), and *Tennessee Moon* (1996).

In 1963 Diamond was actually dropped by COLUMBIA records after his single 'Clown Town' earned royalties of just $15; 10 years later the company signed him again, this time for $4.5 million dollars. In 1980 he was paid $5 million to star in and write the music for the film *The Jazz Singer*.

Dickenson, Vic (1906–84) US JAZZ trombonist, who was admired for his work with many of the leading jazz bands of the 1930s and 1940s. He abandoned his first career as a plasterer after an accident and excelled in the bands of Benny CARTER, Count BASIE and Sidney BECHET among others, as well as leading his own band in the late 1940s.

Diddley, Bo (Elias/Ellas McDaniel, born Elias Bates; 1928–   ) Black US singer and guitarist, nicknamed Mister Jungle Man, who was one of the most influential stars to emerge in the heyday of ROCK 'N' ROLL in the mid-1950s. Born in Mississippi and later adopted, Diddley played RHYTHM-AND-BLUES in the clubs of Chicago in the 1940s and unsuccessfully attempted to attract attention by incorporating obscene language and racist taunts in his songs. In 1955 he began to adapt the rhythms of rock 'n' roll to his music and created his own unique sound by adding the 'jungle beat' of African drumming. The nickname 'shave-and-a-haircut-six-bits' was given to the distinctive rhythm of his in the 1950s; the phrase was meant to imitate the rhythm of Diddley's pounding guitar and drum or maraccas-dominated beat.

'Hey Bo Diddley' (1955), which was based on the traditional English FOLK-song 'Hush Little Baby', was his first huge hit and was rapidly followed by such classics as 'Diddy Wah Diddy', 'I'm a Man', 'Mona', 'Road Runner' and 'Pretty Thing', which proved equally popular with both Black and White audiences.

Ranked alongside LITTLE RICHARD and Chuck BERRY, Diddley – sporting a distinctive rectangular guitar – continued to prosper, touring widely and developing his style as tastes changed into the 1960s and beyond. Several Diddley hits have since been COVERED by other leading artists, among them Buddy HOLLY, who rendered 'I'm a Man', and 'Not Fade Away', which was later covered by the ROLLING STONES.

Dietrich, Marlene (Maria Magdalene von Losch; 1902–92) US film actress and singer, born in Germany, who became one of the legends of twentieth-century show business. Dietrich (who had hoped to become a violinist) began her career singing as a member of the chorus in musical revues in Germany in the 1920s, but she became a star of stage and screen under Max Reinhardt and Josef von Sternberg, whose film *The Blue Angel* (1930) made her internationally famous. She later lived and worked in the USA, consolidating her reputation as one of the great screen goddesses but also continuing to enjoy success as a CABARET singer with a unique, husky voice.

Her most celebrated songs included 'Falling in Love Again' (from *The Blue Angel*), 'See What the Boys in the Back Room Will Have' (from *Destry Rides Again* in 1939), 'Lili Marlene', which she recorded in response to the huge success of the version by Lale ANDERSEN, and 'Where Have All the Flowers Gone'.

Inevitably, she had (and still has) many imitators. Asked whether she minded these efforts at mimicry, she replied: 'Only if they do it badly.'

She was one of the many famous figures whose images were selected for the cover of the BEATLES album *Sergeant Pepper's Lonely Hearts Club Band*.

Dietz, Howard (1896–1983) US lyricist and librettist, who collaborated with composer Arthur SCHWARTZ on many successful REVUES. He provided the lyrics for such shows as *The Little Show* (1929), *The Band Wagon* (1931), *Follow the Sun* (1936) and *Sadie Thompson* (1944), his best-known songs including 'I Guess I'll Have to Change My Plan', 'Dancing in the Dark', 'You and the Night and the Music' and 'Love is a Dancing Thing'. As an executive with MGM, he was creator of the company's famous lion trademark.

digital recording Technologically advanced recording system, in which sound is transferred to an audio tape or COMPACT DISC in the form of digits. The process involves the sampling of each music signal up to 30,000 times a second. Advantages of the system include the elimination of distortion and interference.

d'Indy, (Paul Marie Théodore) Vincent (1851–1931) French composer and music teacher, who composed many epic works reflecting both his patriotism and the influence of the Germanic musical tradition. D'Indy devoted himself to music after service with the National Guard in the Franco-Prussian War, and many of his early works, such as the *Poème des Montagnes* (1881), show the influence of Richard Wagner and his teacher César Franck. *Symphonie sur un chant montagnard français* (1886) was one of several pieces in which he demonstrated his interest in traditional French FOLK-song.

After the First World War he composed much lighter pieces, including the *Diptyque méditerranéen* (1925–26), and continued to influence a younger generation of composers through his teaching (he co-founded the Schola Cantorum in Paris and was a professor at the Paris Conservatoire).

dinosaur rock Rock music as performed by the elder statesmen of modern music. Chiefly survivors of the 1960s and 1970s, such long-established stars as the ROLLING STONES, LED ZEPPELIN and STATUS QUO remained in business long after some of their contemporaries had faded from the scene. Fans delighted in their continued careers, although critics accused them of indirectly hindering the emergence of fresh talent and, by all too often relying on old hits, giving way to commercial, rather than artistic, instincts. Many bands perfected the art of boosting interest in flagging careers by announcing series of farewell appearances and much publicized come-backs, often – as in the case of Gary GLITTER – with not inconsiderable success.

Dion and the Belmonts US male vocal group, which ranked among the top White DOO-WOP acts of the 1960s. Dion DiMucci (1939–   ), Fred Milano (1939–   ), Angelo D'Aleo (1940–   ) and Carlo Mastangelo (1938–   ) came together in New York in 1958 and named themselves after nearby Belmont Avenue. The group established a reputation with such hits as 'I Wonder Why' (1958), 'A Teenager in Love' (1959) and 'Where or When' (1960), before Dion, a drug addict, temporarily left. The band returned to the charts with a vengeance in 1960 with the Number One 'Runaround Sue'; other releases included 'The Wanderer' (1961) and the somewhat macabre 'Abraham, Martin and John' (1968), which was dedicated to the assassinated US leaders, Abraham Lincoln, Dr

Martin Luther King and John F. Kennedy. Dion continued on a solo basis through the 1970s, finally overcoming his long-standing drug problems.

Dippermouth *See* Louis ARMSTRONG.

Dire Straits British rock band, which enjoyed enormous commercial success in the late 1970s and 1980s. The band was formed in 1977 by respected guitarist Mark Knopfler (1949–   ), and it developed a COUNTRY-ROCK style that put Knopfler's cool and distinctive guitar work to the fore. The band's first album, *Dire Straits* (1978), was well received, and the track 'Sultans of Swing' became a hit single and, ultimately, the band's signature tune. Subsequently, with such albums as *Communiqué* (1979), *Making Movies* (1980), *Love Over Gold* (1983), *Brothers in Arms* (1985), which sold upwards of 15 millon copies and reached Number One on both sides of the Atlantic, and *On Every Street* (1991), the band took a firm hold on melodic MIDDLE-OF-THE-ROAD rock and toured widely with consistent success, becoming the best-selling band of the decade. Hit singles included the epic 'Private Investigation', which reached Number Two in the UK in 1983, despite lasting some seven minutes, and 'Money for Nothing', which got to Number One in the USA in 1985. Several of the group's most celebrated releases were accompanied by dazzling state-of-the-art videos, which contributed greatly to their success.

Often described as the last of the guitar heroes, Knopfler has also played with DYLAN (on *Slow Train Coming* and as producer of *Infidels*) and with other contemporary greats.

disc jockey (DJ or dee-jay) In radio jargon, the presenter of a music programme, who plays the records and provides links between them as well as undertaking such additional tasks as running phone-ins, competitions and other items. The first such presenters were heard in the 1920s, but DJs did not emerge as popular mouthpieces for the younger music fan until the 1950s, when the best of them became nationally known figures in both the USA and the UK. Seminal figures in the early development of the role included the USA's Alan Freed and Dick Clark (who were both victims of 1960's PAYOLA SCANDAL concerning bribes paid to play certain records); in the UK the first nationally known pop disc jockeys included Alan Freeman.

The phrase 'disc jockey' was coined by *Variety* magazine in 1937, although it was not until the 1950s that the best presenters acquired anything like cult status. Some disc jockeys actually crossed the divide to become established musical stars – among them, B.B. KING, Bill HALEY, James BROWN, J.P. Richardson (the BIG BOPPER) and Sly STONE. Jim Lowe and Rick Dees are, however, the only serving DJs to have enjoyed Number One hits (with 'The Green Door' (1956) and 'Disco Duck' (1976) respectively).

One disc jockey, Cleveland's Eddie O'Jay, was amply rewarded for his services in popularizing the Mascots when the group renamed itself in his honour and went on to carry his name around the world as the O'Jays.

Most 'dee-jays' or 'jocks' are required to be able to chat at any length on virtually any subject without boring the listener or causing offence, although not all are renowned for their insight into music or wider issues and most, at one time or other, have fallen prey to the odd gaff:

> This is the greatest record of all time for me at the moment.
> STEVE WRIGHT

> On Monday we'll have Jerry Lee Lewis, on Tuesday Chuck Berry and on Wednesday Elvis Presley, though not in that order.
> DAVE KID JENSEN

> Here's some Spike Milligan. Good Friday should be a bit silly.
> DAVE LEE TRAVIS

> And you can't get much further outside the Top 10 than Number 11.
> JIMMY SAVILLE

> What's your name, Kate?
> SIMON BATES

> And don't forget – on Sunday you can hear the two-minute silence on Radio One.
> STEVE WRIGHT

disco POP music genre, which enjoyed a huge vogue in the 1970s and early 1980s, when dancing in discotheques was at its most popular. The demand for up-tempo, cheerful and intellectually unchallenging pop that was easy to dance to swamped the charts with such music for several years –

partly in reaction to the excesses of PUNK ROCK – and created many stars, from ABBA to CHIC and Donna SUMMER and John Travolta (1954–   ). Many more, notably the BEE GEES, learned to adapt to the disco style and revived flagging careers with enormous commercial success, and even such respected established artists as Miles DAVIS and David BOWIE attempted to make use of disco motifs and rhythms in their compositions.

Sly STONE is sometimes credited as being the first artist to perfect the style, when he successfully married SOUL, FUNK and ROCK in a way that would have equal appeal to Black and White audiences. Other significant figures in the genre's emergence were the US songwriting partnership of Nile Rodgers and Bernard Edwards and Munich-based Giorgio Moroder, who helped trigger the European version of what had begun as a dance craze in New York's gay community.

The intellectual sterility of the style eventually left it outmoded in the 1980s, when it was largely replaced by the more 'streetwise' pop purveyed under such labels as RAP, ACID HOUSE and ELECTRO-FUNK.

Disco Queen *See* Gloria GAYNOR; Donna SUMMER.

Distel, Sacha (1933–   ) French singer-songwriter and guitarist, who became a pop idol of the 1960s and 1970s. Distel established his reputation as a guitarist, being voted France's best guitarist five years in a row and playing alongside many distinguished jazzmen visiting from the USA. In the late 1950s he concentrated on developing a career as a singer, subsequently attracting a big following with such melodic hits as 'Scoubidou', 'Oh Yeah-Yeah', 'Sacha's Theme', 'The Good Life', 'That Italian Summer', 'Baby, I Love You' and his most popular hit of all, 'Raindrops Keep Falling on My Head' (1970).

> I worked with Sacha Distel on TV recently. He played nice guitar, sang well and smelled absolutely adorable.
> RONNIE SCOTT, on BBC Radio's *Jazz Score*

District, the Nickname of STORYVILLE, the area of NEW ORLEANS where JAZZ had its birthplace in the early years of the century.

Divine Miss M., the *See* Bette MIDLER.

Divine One, the *See* Sarah VAUGHAN.

Dixie Dew-drop, the *See* Uncle Dave MACON.

Dixieland The cheerful, up-tempo JAZZ style, which originated from NEW ORLEANS around the time of the First World War. 'Dixie' is a commonly heard nickname for New Orleans, referring to the old French ten (*dix*) dollar bills issued there in the early nineteenth century. The name was popularized among music fans by the ORIGINAL DIXIELAND JAZZ BAND, a White band formed around 1912, and the style itself (based on the combination of trombone, clarinet and trumpet) came to be played by both Black and White jazz bands. In time Dixieland was largely replaced by SWING and BEBOP, and now virtually any up-tempo 'traditional' jazz risks being labelled 'Dixie'.

Dixon, Reginald (1905–85) British organist, who became famous as resident organist at Blackpool's Tower Ballroom (1930–70). He became widely known for his cheerful organ music through regular broadcasts and was uniquely associated with the tune 'I Do Like to be Beside the Seaside'.

Dixon, Willie (1915–91) US BLUES singer-songwriter and bass-player, who was one of the most important figures in the history of Chicago blues. He moved into music after a successful boxing career and went on to write such classics of the 1950s and early 1960s as 'Hoochie Coochie Man', 'Little Red Rooster' and 'Seventh Son'. Among his collaborators as a producer for CHESS RECORDS were musicians of the stature of Bo DIDDLEY and Muddy WATERS.

DJ *See* DISC JOCKEY.

dobro A variety of crude, acoustically amplified guitar, much used in COUNTRY music, in which the strings are raised and a conical aluminium resonator is incorporated in the body. The dobro was named after its inventors, the *Dopyera Brothers*, who made the first such instrument in California in 1925.

Dr Feelgood British RHYTHM-AND-BLUES band, which had considerable commercial success in the 1970s. Founded in 1971 and named after a reference in a 1962 hit by Johnny KIDD and the Pirates, the band was formed by guitarist Wilko Johnson (John Wilkinson; 1947–), singer Lee Brilleaux (1948–94), bassist John 'Sparko' Sparks (1953–) and drummer the Figure (John Martin; 1947–). Success as a live act with a strong PUB-ROCK following was consolidated by the popularity of such recordings as *Stupidity* (1976) and *Sneakin' Suspicion* (1977). A number of personnel changes accompanied a gradual decline in the 1980s.

Dr Hook and the Medicine Show US pop group, which enjoyed transatlantic success with a series of hit singles in the 1970s. Singer Ray Sawyer (1937–), who wore a distinctive black eyepatch, guitarist Dennis Locorriere (1948–), keyboard player Bill Francis (1942–), George Cummings (1938–) and drummer John David (1942–) formed the group in 1968. The group's satirical line in pop songs attracted immediate attention, and the single 'Sylvia's Mother', which was intended as a send-up of COUNTRY music in general, was a huge hit in both the UK and the USA in 1972. Subsequent releases, which trod a similarly eccentric path, included 'The Cover of Rolling Stone' (1973), before the group adopted a more straightforward pop image and returned to the charts with such hits as 'Only Sixteen' (1976), 'When You're in Love with a Beautiful Woman' (1979) and 'Sexy Eyes' (1980). The group broke up in 1985.

Dodds, Johnny (1892–1940) US JAZZ clarinettist, who worked with many of the leading figures in the early development of jazz in the 1920s and 1930s. He proved invaluable to Louis ARMSTRONG and participated in the highly influential 'Hot Five' recordings, as well as working with Jelly Roll MORTON and others. His brother Warren 'Baby' Dodds (1898–1959) was a celebrated jazz drummer.

dodecaphony *See* I2-NOTE MUSIC.

doghouse JAZZ musicians' slang, dating from the 1940s, for a double bass, which is often regarded as one of the more risible orchestral instruments.

> A dangerous rogue elephant.
> CHARLES VILLIERS STANFORD, of the double bass

Dohnányi, Ernö (1877–1960) Hungarian pianist and conductor, who was considered the foremost of Liszt's successors in his day. Although he wrote a great many more serious works, he is usually recalled today for his lighthearted *Variations on a Nursery Theme* (1913), which made use of the the the children's tune 'Twinkle, Twinkle, Little Star'.

Dolby Noise reduction system, trademarked by the US inventor R. Dolby (1933–   ), which is incorporated in cassette-recorders and video machines to enhance playback quality.

Dolmetsch, Arnold (1858–1940) Swiss violinist and instrument maker, who did much to promote the performance of early music on authentic instruments. Having moved to Haslemere in Surrey, UK, in 1917, he founded an influential annual festival of early music there in 1925. His son, Carl Dolmetsch (1911–   ), took control of the festival after his father's death and also earned a reputation as the world's leading authority on the recorder.

Dolphy, Eric (1928–64) US JAZZ saxophonist, flautist and clarinettist, who enjoyed a brief but celebrated career playing with some of the most distinguished progressive jazzmen of his generation. Dolphy played with a number of bands before joining Charles MINGUS in 1959. He subsequently collaborated with John COLTRANE and also released such influential albums as *Out To Lunch* (1964) under his own name. He did much to promote the development of FREE JAZZ before his early death as a result of diabetes.

Domingo, Placido (1941–   ) Spanish tenor, who became a cult figure in the 1980s at a time when opera was seeking an audience beyond the traditional élite. Born in Spain but resident in Mexico from 1950, Domingo studied the piano and conducting as well as singing, and he made his début as a baritone before discovering his talent as a tenor, in which role he first performed in Verdi's *La Traviata* in 1960. He sang with the Israeli National Opera (1962–65) and at all the leading international venues, winning acclaim both for his voice and for his sensitive acting. Among his most acclaimed performances have been those as Alfredo in *La Traviata*, the title part in Verdi's *Otello* and Don José in *Carmen*, although he has also taken parts in Wagner with huge success and has

delved into the world of pop with recordings made with such singers as John DENVER and Sarah Brightman.

Having starred in a number of films based on popular operas, he reached new heights of fame as one of the 'three great tenors', alongside José CARRERAS and Luciano PAVAROTTI, at the widely screened concert staged in Rome in 1990 as part of the celebrations surrounding football's World Cup. In 1983 he won wide praise for his efforts on behalf of victims of a major earthquake in Mexico.

> I think it's a duty for a singer while he is at his best to let everyone around the world hear him.
> PLACIDO DOMINGO, 1972

Domino, Fats (Antoine Domino; 1928–   ) Black US singer and pianist, who perfected the marriage of RHYTHM-AND-BLUES and ROCK 'N' ROLL in the mid-1950s. Domino began his musical career playing BOOGIE in the bars of the southern USA and New Orleans in the 1940s, and he gradually built up a loyal following with Black audiences, despite the severe injuries that he suffered to his hands at an early age.

Already established in the r 'n' b charts with such hits as 'The Fat Man' (1949), the singer's reputation as a pop star was established after Pat BOONE enjoyed a hit with a COVER version of his 'Ain't That a Shame' in 1955. Domino's own recording of the song subsequently spent 11 weeks at Number One. He had numerous other hit singles, including such classics as 'Blueberry Hill', 'Blue Monday' and 'Walking to New Orleans', and it was estimated that in all he sold some 70 million records in his heyday (rivalling the sales of Elvis PRESLEY and ranking him alongside LITTLE RICHARD and Chuck BERRY as one of the three most successful Black rock 'n' roll performers).

Called Fats in reference to his generous proportions, Domino once lived up to his name when he actually broke through the stage during a concert in Paris in 1985 on leaping up to greet his audience.

> Rock 'n' roll is nothing but rhythm-and-blues and we've been playing it for years in New Orleans.
> FATS DOMINO

Donahue, Sam (Samuel Koontz; 1918–74) US JAZZ bandleader and saxophonist, who divided his playing career between running his own bands and appearing with some of the most respected jazzmen of the day. He formed his first band in the 1930s and subsequently formed further outfits in between engagements with the bands of Gene KRUPA, Harry JAMES, Benny GOODMAN, Artie SHAW and Stan KENTON among others. Taking over Tommy DORSEY's band in 1961, he provided backing for Frank SINATRA for a time. His hits included 'My Melancholy Baby' and 'Saxaboogie'.

Donaldson, Walter (1893–1947) US composer, who wrote many hit songs for Broadway and Hollywood in the 1920s and 1930s. Having begun as a song plugger and pianist, Donaldson founded his own music publishing company and concentrated on writing for the cinema after contributing the scores for the Broadway MUSICALS *Sweetheart Time* (1926) and *Whoopee* (1928). A collaborator on such movies as *Glorifying the American Girl* (1929), *Kid Millions* (1934), *Here Comes the Band* (1935), *Panama Hattie* (1942) and *Follow the Boys* (1944), he also wrote such hits as 'How You Gonna Keep 'em Down on the Farm' (1919), 'My Mammy' (1919), 'Carolina in the Morning' (1922), 'Yes Sir, That's My Baby' (1925), 'My Blue Heaven' (1927), 'Makin' Whoopee' (1928) and 'Little White Lies' (1930).

Donegan, Lonnie (Anthony Donegan; 1931–) British singer and guitarist, born in Glasgow and nicknamed the King of Skiffle, who shot to fame in the mid–1950s as a SKIFFLE star. Adopting the name 'Lonnie' in imitation of bluesman Lonnie Johnson, Donegan played guitar and banjo with the Tony Donegan Jazz Band, Ken COLYER's Jazzmen and with Chris BARBER before establishing himself as a solo star.

In 1956 Donegan's 'Rock Island Line', which has been described as 'Britain's first home-grown pop breakthrough', became the first British pop record to reach the US Top 10 (ironically it was first released as a NOVELTY RECORD). Donegan later released a further 26 hit singles, 10 of which reached the Top 10 in just 18 months, and made skiffle the dominant musical form in the UK. His best-known songs included 'Midnight Special', 'Gamblin' Man/Putting on the Style', 'Railroad Bill', 'Cumberland Gap', 'Does your Chewing-gum Lose its

Flavour (on the Bedpost Overnight)' and 'My Old Man's a Dustman' (a bowdlerized version of the traditional pub song 'What Do You Think About That?').

In 1985 news that Donegan had undergone a heart operation caused share prices to plunge on the Japanese stock market; things returned to normal, however, when dealers realized that the patient in question was an English pop star and not, as the interpreters had mistakenly thought, US president Ronald Reagan.

> Lonnie Donegan was the first music star to make a big impression on me. Donegan and skiffle just seemed made for me.
> GEORGE HARRISON

donkey music Derogatory nickname for 12-NOTE MUSIC, which is often heard from reluctant performers of such works. Performers on the whole dislike such music, which is fragmentary and unmelodic, and often requires large leaps between notes, which makes it difficult to play.

> Here's to music, joy of Joys:
> One man's music – another man's noise.
> Anonymous

Donovan (Donovan Leitch; 1946–) Scottish-born singer-songwriter, nicknamed the British Dylan because of the extent to which he modelled himself and his music upon his celebrated US counterpart. Donovan achieved stardom in the flower power era of the mid-to late 1960s. Several of his FOLK-tinged songs bore a striking resemblance to DYLAN's originals, although critics found they lacked some of the impact of their inspiration, but they were individual enough to ensure his success with British fans. Dylan himself befriended Donovan, as did Joan BAEZ, and soon the Scot was winning fans on both sides of the Atlantic.

The best of his output included such songs as 'Catch the Wind' (1965) and – after 'turning electric', as Dylan had done, in 1966 – 'Sunshine Superman' (1966) and 'Mellow Yellow' (1967), on which Paul MCCARTNEY played (George HARRISON meanwhile gave Donovan his first lesson on the sitar). 'Mellow Yellow' was widely interpreted as a hymn in praise of soft drugs and inspired many fans to try smoking dried banana skins. Other compositions reflected the influence of PSYCHEDELIA and the drug culture of the age, as well as that of Eastern mysticism. His career faded with the decline of the hippie ethos in the early 1970s, although he continued to record a number of critically acclaimed albums and to make live appearances.

> What pop does is make me very rich.
> DONOVAN

Donovan, Dan (1901–86) Welsh singer, who enjoyed success as a CROONER in the 1920s and 1930s. He sang with many leading bands, notably with Henry HALL, and numbered among his many hits 'Red Sails in the Sunset' and his theme tune 'When Day is Done'. He was one of the first great radio stars in the UK, making more than 8,000 broadcasts.

doo-wop Vocal RHYTHM-AND-BLUES style, in which a tenor lead was supported by an all-male backing group, which sang various nonsense phrases in close harmony. 'Doo wop', or the 'street corner sound', emerged in the mid-1950s, when many youths of impoverished Italian and other immigrant communities in the big cities of the USA adopted it, often singing in the stairwells of the large tenements in which they lived in order to get a good echo effect. The best of these groups attracted the attention of the record companies, which made stars of such outfits as the PLATTERS, the COASTERS and the DRIFTERS, which enjoyed long careers at the top of the charts. Typical of others who managed only a single best-seller were Frankie Lymon and the Teenagers, which returned to obscurity after reaching Number One with 'Why Do Fools Fall in Love' (Lymon himself died a heroin addict in 1968).

The phrase 'doo wop', sung in many songs belonging to the genre, may have originated in the 'doo da' refrain of traditional Black vocal music ('wop' being, perhaps significantly, a derogatory name for an Italian).

Doobie Brothers US ROCK band, which established a strong following in the 1970s. Formed in 1970, the founder members were guitarist Tom Johnston, bassist Dave Shogren and drummer John Hartman (1950–), though various changes of personnel over the years meant that only Hartmann of the original trio remained by the 1980s. Having begun in a FOLK-ROCK vein, the band – called the Doobie Brothers in reference to slang for marijuana cigarettes – adopted a heavier

rock style with such hit albums as *Toulouse Street* (1972) and *The Captain and Me* (1973). Hit singles included 'Listen to the Music' (1972) and 'Black Water', which reached Number One in the USA in 1975. After guitarist Jeff 'Skunk' Baxter (1948–) and keyboard player and singer Michael McDonald (1952–) joined in the late 1970s, the band switched to a White SOUL style and released such hits as the album *Minute by Minute* (1978), from which came the US Number One single 'What a Fool Believes'. Dormant in the early 1980s, the band reunited in 1988 to resume its recording career with such albums as *Cycles* (1988) and *Brotherhood* (1991).

doom metal Sub-genre of HEAVY METAL, in which the emphasis is laid on long, loud chords and pessimistic lyrics of death and destruction. Doom metal evolved as a slowed-down version of THRASH metal, and exponents such as Bathory and Candlemass took their inspiration from the dark, early works of BLACK SABBATH and other seminal rock bands of the 1970s.

Doonican, Val (Michael Valentine Doonican; 1928–) Irish singer and guitarist, who enjoyed a long career both as a live and television performer in the style originally set by Perry COMO. Having worked as a guitarist and drummer, he made his television début in the early 1950s and later sang chiefly sentimental ballads on his own television shows – often seated in the rocking chair that became his trademark – as well as in variety and CABARET and on the radio. His first hit was 'Walk Tall' (1964).

Doors, the US rock group, led by charismatic vocalist Jim MORRISON, which attained near-legendary status as one of the great bands of the late 1960s. Morrison, keyboard player Ray Manzarek (1935–), bassist Robby Krieger (1946–) and drummer John Densmore (1945–) developed a musical style that perfectly expressed the schizophrenic angst of nihilistic, anti-Establishment, artificially stimulated youth (as well as betraying the influence of DYLAN and a RHYTHM-AND-BLUES background). Such tracks as 'The End', 'Light My Fire' (the band's first US Number One single), 'LA Woman' and 'Riders on the Storm', most of which were composed under the influence of hard drugs, gave voice to the protest movement of the age and were enthusiastically taken up by radical political and anti-Vietnam groups. Other hits included the single 'Hello, I Love You', which reached Number One in 1968, although its similarity to 'All Day and All of the Night' by the KINKS resulted in the band's having to pay the British group considerable damages. Among the Doors' albums were *The Doors* (1967), *Strange Days* (1967) and *Waiting for the Sun* (1968).

The album *LA Woman* (1971) represented the peak of the group's achievement but also marked the beginning of the end, coming in the same year as Morrison's departure and death, after which the band continued as a trio until finally splitting up in 1972.

The name the Doors came from the title of Aldous Huxley's *The Doors Of Perception*, about the use of drugs, which was itself derived from a quotation from the poems of the visionary William Blake, with whom Morrison felt he was cosmically linked:

If the doors of perception were cleansed everything would appear to man as it is, infinite...

Dorati, Antal (1906–88) US conductor and composer, born in Hungary, who was recognized as one of the leading conductors of his generation. A pupil of Béla BARTÓK and Zoltán KODÁLY, he recorded the complete symphonies of Haydn in collaboration with the Philharmonia Hungarica, which was formed from Hungarian refugees.

Dorsey, Jimmy (1904–57) US bandleader, saxophonist and composer, who was one of the most popular characters in the SWING era of the 1930s and 1940s. After playing with a number of other DANCE BANDS, Dorsey, and his brother Tommy DORSEY, formed the celebrated Dorsey Brothers Orchestra in 1934 and enjoyed a string of hits, including 'Contrasts', 'John Silver', 'Green Eyes', 'Maria Elena', 'Amapola', 'Embraceable You' and 'Tangerine'. The band continued to prosper – without Tommy – throughout the 1930s and early 1940s and made a number of film appearances. Tommy was reunited with Jimmy in 1953, and they formed a new band under their joint leadership, which lasted until Tommy's death three years later.

Dorsey, Lee (1924–86) Black US RHYTHM-AND-BLUES singer, who was one of the most

successful SOUL artists of the 1960s. After service in the Marines and a period as a boxer, fighting as 'Kid Chocolate', he made his first recordings in the early 1960s and went on to establish himself with such hits as 'Ya Ya', 'Do-re-mi' and 'Hoodlum Joe', before teaming up with songwriter Allen TOUSSAINT in 1965. Subsequent hits included such singles as 'Ride Your Pony', 'Working in the Coal Mine', 'My Old Car', which was made originally as the soundtrack for a Coca-Cola advertisement, and 'Everything I Do Gonna be Funky'. In the 1970s Dorsey gave up music and went back to his car-repair business in New Orleans, eventually dying of emphysema.

I never know whether I was a better body-and-fender man or vocalist.
LEE DORSEY

Dorsey, Thomas A(ndrew) (1899–1993) US singer-songwriter, pianist and guitarist, known as Georgia Tom and the Father of Gospel Music, who pioneered GOSPEL music in the 1920s and 1930s. The son of a Baptist minister and a former accompanist to Ma RAINEY, he concentrated on gospel music from the late 1920s and distributed many songs as well as forming his own vocal groups and fostering the careers of such GOSPEL stars as Mahalia JACKSON. His prolific output of gospel songs, which established the genre on a nationwide basis, included 'Peace in the Valley' and 'Sweet Bye and Bye'.

Dorsey, Tommy (1905–56) US bandleader, trombonist and composer, nicknamed the Sentimental Gentleman of Swing from his big hit 'I'm Getting Sentimental over You' (1932), who was widely admired for his skills as a trombonist with his own band. He collaborated with his brother, Jimmy DORSEY, in the Dorsey Brothers Orchestra before quarrelling with him and taking over the band of Joe Haymes in 1935. He demonstrated his talents as a trombonist on such hits as 'I'm Getting Sentimental over You' (his theme tune) and backed such stars as Frank SINATRA, who was strongly influenced by his smooth playing style. His highly influential hits, many of which were arranged by Sy OLIVER, included 'Blue Moon', 'Marie' and 'Music, Maestro, Please'. Notable players in the ranks of his band included Buddy RICH, Bunny BERIGAN and Gene KRUPA. He eventually reunited with his brother in

1953, but died three years later when he choked in his sleep after a big meal.

double album A pair of LPs, which come as a single package under a single title. The very first double album was Bob DYLAN's *Blonde on Blonde*. Notable double album sets subsequently released have included the BEATLES' *White Album*.

Drifters, the US Black vocal group, which recorded many hits over its 40-year history. The group has existed in many different forms, with over 50 musicians appearing in the line-up since its formation in 1953. The most famous version of the Drifters was that of the late 1950s and 1960s, when the group was led by singer Ben E. King (1938–   ) and recorded such songs as 'There Goes My Baby' (1959) and 'Save the Last Dance for Me' (1960), which reached Number One. Among later hits were 'Up on the Roof' (1963), 'Under the Boardwalk' (1964), 'Saturday Night at the Movies' (1964) and 'Kissing in the Back Row of the Movies' (1974).

Du Pré, Jacqueline (1945–87) British cellist, who won wide acclaim before her career was cut short by multiple sclerosis. Having studied at the London Violincello School from an early age, she swept the board for awards at the Guildhall School of Music and then went on to study with Paul TORTELIER and Mstislav ROSTROPOVICH. An unidentified donor provided her with a 1672 Stradivarius cello, and she made her professional début with huge success at the age of 16 in 1961. Six years later she married Daniel BARENBOIM and formed fruitful collaborations with Itzhak PERLMAN and Pinchas ZUKERMAN as well as touring with the BBC SYMPHONY ORCHESTRA and attracting particular praise for her inspired interpretation of works by Beethoven, Elgar and Schumann among others. Alexander GOEHR wrote his *Romance* (1968) for cello and orchestra expressly for her.

After her illness prevented her from playing in public from 1972, she pursued a career as a teacher, giving a celebrated series of televised masterclasses.

dub To add a SOUNDTRACK to a film or to add another track to a multi-track recording. The development of sophisticated dubbing techniques in recent decades has made possible all manner of effects and, in many cases, has done away with the necessity for large numbers of expensive session musicians.

Examples of extreme versions of dubbing include the single 'Let's Get Together' (1961) in which Hayley Mills sang a duet with herself (the credit on the label reading 'Hayley Mills and Hayley Mills'). The process of dubbing also created a Number One hit in the form of the Neil DIAMOND/Barbra STREISAND duet 'You Don't Bring Me Flowers', which came about after an enterprising disc jockey spliced together separate versions of the song made by the two artists – the cobbled-together result was received with such enthusiasm that it was decided to record the song properly as a duet. Another extreme example of the dubbing process was the best-selling duet 'Unforgettable' (1991), in which the voice of Natalie COLE was dubbed over that of her long-dead father Nat 'King' COLE to create the somewhat macabre effect that the living and the dead were singing together.

The word has also been applied to a style of REGGAE music, in which only the bass and drum tracks are played.

Dubin, Al (1891–1945) US lyricist, born in Switzerland, who provided the lyrics for many hit songs, including many for Hollywood movies. His best-known lyrics included those for such songs as 'Lullaby of Broadway', 'Tiptoe Through the Tulips', 'Painting the Clouds with Sunshine' and 'I Only Have Eyes for You'.

Duchin, Eddy (1910–51) US pianist, bandleader and composer, who was a popular broadcasting and recording star in the 1930s and 1940s. Leader of his own band from 1931, he perfected an easily accessible style and played with many stars as well as hosting his own radio show. His signature tune was 'My Twilight Dream'. His life, which ended early as a result of leukemia, was dramatized in the film *The Eddy Duchin Story* (1956), in which Tyrone Power played the title role.

Dukas, Paul Abraham (1865–1935) French composer, critic and music teacher, who is usually remembered for his scherzo for orchestra *The Sorcerer's Apprentice* (1897), which was used in Walt Disney's *Fantasia*. A student (and later teacher) at the Paris Conservatoire, he was befriended by Claude DEBUSSY, to whom he dedicated

La Plante, au loin, du faune ... (1920).
Debussy himself and others, including Igor
STRAVINSKY, were inspired by *The Sorcerer's
Apprentice* to write similar works of their
own. Other notable works by Dukas
included the orchestral overture *Polyeucte*
(1891), which demonstrated the influence
of Wagner, the balletic tone poem *La Péri*
(1891), a symphony in C (1897) and the
opera *Ariane et Barbe-Bleue* (1897–1907),
although he destroyed all but a dozen of his
works after finding they did not meet his
own high standards. His pupils included
Olivier MESSIAEN.

> Is it not in music, and in music alone that
> the secret of music must be sought?
> PAUL DUKAS

Duke, Vernon (Vladimir Dukelsky;
1903–69) US composer, born in Russia,
who wrote many classic songs for revues
in the 1930s and 1940s. Born at a railway
station in Russia, he moved to the USA in
1921 and turned to composing popular
music only after his more serious compositions failed to earn him enough money.
With the assistance of George GERSHWIN he
built up a reputation with music for such
best-selling stage shows as *Americana*
(1932), the *Ziegfeld Follies* of 1934 and
1936, *Cabin in the Sky* (1940) and *Two's
Company* (1952). His most successful songs
included 'April in Paris' (1932), 'I Can't
Get Started' (1936), 'Honey in the Honey-
comb' (1940) and 'We're Having a Baby'
(1944).

Dumbarton Oaks Concerto Popular name
of Igor STRAVINSKY's Concerto in E flat.
Dumbarton Oaks was the home in Washington, D.C. of Mr and Mrs Robert Woods
Bliss, who commissioned the work and
presented its première there.

Duplex-Coupler piano Variety of piano that
was invented by the Hungarian composer
and pianist Emanuel Moór (1863–1931)
in 1921. The piano had two keyboards,
which were one octave apart.

Dupré, Marcel (1886–1971) French
organist and composer, who taught Olivier
MESSIAEN. Organist at St Sulpice, Paris,
from 1934 and director of the Paris Conservatoire (1954–56), he was the first
organist to present the complete cycle of
Bach's organ music and was also widely
acclaimed for his talents as a recitalist,

when he revealed a particular skill for
improvisation. He wrote organ music,
chamber music and songs.

> The Liszt of the organ.
> OLIVIER MESSIAEN

Dupree, 'Champion' Jack (William
Thomas Dupree; 1910–92) US singer and
pianist, who established himself as an outstanding BARRELHOUSE pianist after working as a boxer (hence his nickname). He
made his first recordings, including the hit
'Junker's Blues', in 1940 and subsequently
ventured into RHYTHM-AND-BLUES, influencing such stars as Fats DOMINO and
appearing with, among others, Alexis
KORNER and Eric CLAPTON.

Duran Duran British pop group, nicknamed the Fab Five in imitation of the
BEATLES (the Fab Four), which was among
the most successful bands to emerge from
the NEW ROMANTIC movement in the early
1980s. Founded in Birmingham in 1978,
Duran Duran took its name from the villain in the sci-fi movie *Barbarella* (1967).
Lead vocalist Simon Le Bon (1958–),
keyboard player Nick Rhodes (Nicholas
Bates; 1962–), bassist John Taylor
(1960–), guitarist Andy Taylor
(1961–) and drummer Roger Taylor
(1960–) – all unrelated – had their first
chart success with 'Planet Earth' in 1981;
among the hits that followed were 'Girls on
Film' (1981), 'Save a Prayer' (1982),
'Hungry Like the Wolf' (1982), 'Is There
Something I Should Know' (1983), 'The
Reflex' (1984) and 'Wild Boys' (1984). Le
Bon and Rhodes became major media personalities, and adoring fans were dubbed
'Durannies'. Andy Taylor left in 1986, but
the band re-formed as a trio with Le Bon,
who had only narrowly survived a yacht-
ing accident in 1985, Rhodes and John
Taylor and went on to release such albums
as *Big Thing* (1988). The group's fortunes
received a setback in 1987 when producer
Alex Sadkin was killed in a car crash,
although the 1993 album *Ordinary World*
was reasonably well received.

Durante, Jimmy (1893–1980) US actor,
comedian, singer and composer, nicknamed Schnozzle or Schnozzola on
account of his large nose, who was a
popular star of films, stage MUSICALS and
CABARET. Of Italian parentage, he first
attracted attention as a RAGTIME pianist,

being described by one critic as 'the best White ragtime pianist who ever lived'. He used his distinctive gravelly voice to great comic effect in such hit songs as 'Inka Dinka Doo' and 'I'm the Guy Who Found the Lost Chord'. His mysterious signing-off catchphrase, 'Goodnight, Mrs Calabash, wherever you are', is thought to have originated as a greeting to his long-dead wife.

Durbin, Deanna (Edna Mae Durbin; 1921–) US singer and film actress, who was a huge star of film MUSICALS of the 1930s and 1940s, when she was second only to Judy GARLAND in popularity. She starred in numerous light musicals built around her, among them *Three Smart Girls* (1936) and *Can't Help Singing* (1944) but eventually realized that tastes had moved away from her clean-cut public image and retired to France when she was only 27 years old. Among her hit songs were 'More and More' and 'Spring will be a Little Late This Year'.

Durey, Louis (1888–1979) French composer, who was a member of Les SIX and who wrote much politically left-wing music. Influenced in his early career by Erik SATIE and Igor STRAVINSKY, he produced a notable setting of Cocteau's *Le printemps au fond de la mer* (1920); later works included settings of the writings of Mao and Ho Chi Minh.

Durham, Eddie (1906–87) US guitarist, trombonist and arranger, who worked with many of the most illustrious BIG BANDS of the 1930s and 1940s. Among those he collaborated with were Bennie Moten (1894–1935), Count BASIE, Glenn MILLER and Artie SHAW. His most successful arrangements included those of 'Hittin' the Bottle', 'Topsy', 'Time Out', 'In the Mood' and, legend has it, 'One o'Clock Jump'. Leader of his own all-girl band among other troupes, he was also co-writer of the classic song 'I Don't Want to Set the World on Fire' (1941).

Duruflé, Maurice (1902–86) French composer and organist, who is celebrated for his colourful organ and chamber music. A pupil of Paul DUKAS and Louis Vierne (1870–1937), Duruflé became organist at St Etienne du Mont, Paris, in 1930 and was appointed a teacher at the Paris

Conservatoire in 1943. His most admired works include a requiem (1947), a mass (1967) and a small body of pieces for organ, chamber music and orchestra.

Dury, Ian (1942–) British rock singer, born in east London, who enjoyed a series of hits in the late 1970s. Overcoming the physical disability that was the result of a childhood polio attack, Dury first attracted attention as leader of the new wave band Kilburn and the High Roads. After teaming up with Chaz Jankel, he built up a large punk following before forming Ian Dury and the Blockheads. *New Boots and Panties* (1977) reached the charts and was followed by such humorous hit singles as 'What a Waste', 'Sex and Drugs and Rock 'n' Roll', 'Hit Me with Your Rhythm Stick', which reached Number One in 1978, and 'Reasons to be Cheerful'. The albums *Do It Yourself* (1979) and *Laughter* (1980) followed, and then Dury went solo and developed an acting career (although the Blockheads re-formed for a time in 1984). His single 'Spasticus Autisticus', which referred to the issue of physical handicap, was banned by the BBC in 1981.

> Music is ... well I *know* it's better than working in Ford's.
> IAN DURY

> I don't care if my so-called work dies the minute I die. I don't want to be Shakespeare. I just want to do my gig.
> IAN DURY, *Sounds*, 1978

Dutilleux, Henri (1916–) French composer, who won acclaim for his symphonic works in the 1960s and 1970s. A student at the Paris Conservatoire, he began writing fairly conventional works in the style of Maurice RAVEL before developing a more free-flowing style; his compositions include symphonies, a ballet and much chamber and piano music.

Dutoit, Charles (1936–) Swiss conductor, who has won acclaim as music director of the Montreal Orchestra since 1978. He has made many notable recordings.

Dylan, Bob (Robert Allen Zimmerman; 1941–) US singer-songwriter who emerged as one of the most influential figures in popular music of the late twentieth century. Dylan began playing FOLK-songs while a student in Minnesota but subsequently drove along Highway 61 to visit the great

Woody GUTHRIE in hospital and established himself as a folk-singer in New York.

His first great hit was the classic PROTEST SONG 'Blowin' in the Wind' (1962), which was quickly followed by such celebrated acoustic numbers as 'The Times They are A-changin'', 'A Hard Rain's Gonna Fall' and 'Mr Tambourine Man' (1964). These songs and others that attacked a wide range of targets won him a huge audience and made him the uncrowned king of the protest movement (his name was closely linked with that of Joan BAEZ for a time). Albums like *The Freewheelin' Bob Dylan* (1963), *The Times They Are A-Changin'* (1963) and *Another Side of Bob Dylan* (1964), from which such classics came were equally rapturously received, but in 1965, in the course of *Bringing It All Back Home*, he changed direction with an ELECTRIFIED ROCK backing. Some of his fans were outraged when he toured with his new electric sound and greeted him – and the BAND – with jeers at the NEWPORT FESTIVAL. When he appeared in London at the Royal Albert Hall in 1966 a shout of 'Judas!' drew from Dylan the retort 'I don't believe you – you're a liar!'

Further success came with the highly poetic albums *Highway 61 Revisited* (1964) and *Blonde on Blonde* (1966), which are sometimes described as his masterpieces, but he went into temporary retirement after sustaining a broken neck in a motorbike accident and he gave up the life of drugs and excess that had come with his adoption of a heavier FOLK-ROCK image. *John Wesley Harding* (1968), incorrectly named after the legendary outlaw John Wesley Hardin, saw a return to a more direct and simpler style and was followed by the equally influential *Nashville Skyline* (1969), which had a COUNTRY feel.

Dylan stormed back as a live performer at the end of the decade, appearing at the ISLE OF WIGHT FESTIVAL (1970), the Concert for Bangladesh (1971) and subsequently undertaking the celebrated Rolling Thunder Revue tour. The albums also kept coming, ranging from the SOUNDTRACK for the move *Pat Garrett and Billy the Kid* (1973) to *Blood on the Tracks* (1975) and *Desire* (1976). After *Hard Rain* (1976) and *Street-Legal* (1978), he became (temporarily) a born-again Christian, as evidenced by the religious overtones of *Slow Train Coming* (1979) and *Saved* (1980). He returned to a harder rock sound in *Infidels* (1983) but otherwise released little of interest until *Oh Mercy* (1989). His latest releases include the largely acoustic *Good As I Been To You* (1992) and *World Gone Wrong* (1993).

The star's choice of the name Dylan has intrigued Dylanologists over the years. Early commentators speculated that he intended a link with the Welsh poet Dylan Thomas or else with Matt Dillon, the hero of television's *Gunsmoke*. The singer finally revealed all in 1965: 'I took the name Dylan because I have an uncle named Dillon. I changed the spelling but only because it looked better. I've read some of Dylan Thomas's stuff, and it's not the same as mine. We're different . . . I've done more for Dylan Thomas than he's ever done for me. Look how many kids are probably reading his poetry now because they heard that story.'

Dylan is so brilliant. To me, he makes William Shakespeare look like Billy Joel.

GEORGE HARRISON

E

E flat audience An audience that is disappointingly smaller than expected. The term has its origin in the E flat clarinet, which is much smaller than its cousins. A very old joke has it that throwing a piano down a coal shaft produces a flat miner.

Eagles, the US COUNTRY-ROCK band, which became one of the most successful bands of the 1970s. The name the Eagles was carefully chosen to evoke a series of images relevant to street culture, Red Indian lore and a host of other contexts. Vocalists and guitarists Glenn Frey (1946–) and Bernie Leadon (1947–), bassist Randy Meisner (1946–) and drummer Don Henley (1946–) came together in 1971 and won immediate acclaim with *The Eagles* (1972), from which came three top-selling singles, notably the group's signature tune 'Take it Easy'. The band consolidated its reputation with *Desperado* (1973), which, like the first album, was recorded in the UK, *On the Border* (1974), from which came the Number One single 'Best of My Love', and *One of these Nights* (1975), which reached Number One in the USA (as did the title track in the singles charts). Guitarist Joe WALSH (1945–) replaced Leadon in 1975. Further success came with the albums *Hotel California* (1976), which sold 11 million copies, *The Long Run* (1979) and *Eagles Live* (1980), before the band split in 1981.

Despite Henley's denials that there would ever be a complete reunion, the Eagles came together for a hugely successful comeback tour in 1995–6 and the accompanying album *Hell Freezes Over* entered the US charts at Number One.

ear music US JAZZ slang for any improvised music. Thus, a musician who cannot read music but picks up everything 'by ear' is often called an 'ear-man'.

Early Music Consort of London British ensemble that specializes in the performance of medieval and Renaissance music on authentic instruments. The ensemble, which was founded in 1967, has revived many long-forgotten works as well as performing new pieces by such composers as Peter MAXWELL DAVIES.

early music movement The revival of interest in music dating from before the conventional classical era (essentially the eighteenth and nineteenth centuries), which transfigured the development of contemporary classical music from the 1930s on. Such musicians as Wanda LANDOWSKA had anticipated the movement earlier in the century, reviving works by composers of the seventeenth and early eighteenth centuries and laying great emphasis on playing their works on the 'authentic' instruments for which they had been intended. Prominent figures in the promotion of such music included Nadia BOULANGER, Adolph Busch (1891–1952) and David MUNROW, who founded the influential EARLY MUSIC CONSORT OF LONDON in 1967. Numerous recordings of old compositions featuring 'original' instruments were made in the 1970s, and living composers have written many new pieces for such traditional instruments as the harpsichord and the recorder.

Earth, Wind and Fire US SOUL and jazz FUNK band, which enjoyed great commercial success in the 1970s. Singer Maurice White (1941–) and his brother bassist Verdine White (1951–), singer Philip Bailey (1951–), keyboard player Larry Dunn (1953–), guitarists Johnny Graham (1951–) and Al McKay (1948–), saxophonist Andrew Woolfolk (1950–) and drummer Ralph Johnson (1951–) came together in the early 1970s and were led by Maurice White; a third White brother, drummer Freddie White (1955–), joined in 1975. *Head to the Sky* (1973), which established the group as a top attraction, was followed by the even more successful albums *Open Your Eyes* (1974) and *That's the Way of the World*, which reached

Number One in the USA in 1975 and produced the Number One single 'Shining Star'. The group continued to top the charts on both sides of the Atlantic with a 'Best of . . . ' album and such singles as 'Got to Get You into My Life' (1978) and 'Boogie Wonderland' (1980) before breaking up. The band reunited in the late 1980s, releasing such albums as *Touch the World* (1987) and *Millenium* (1993).

easy listening A broad category of light music, which ranges from the blandest of ROCK and POP to songs from popular MUSICALS and the hits of the CROONERS and their successors.

Ebb, Fred (1932–   ) US lyricist and librettist. He won acclaim for his contribution to such MUSICALS as *Cabaret* (1966), *Chicago* (1975) and *Woman of the Year* (1981), on all of which he collaborated with composer John KANDER. They also worked together on the films *Funny Girl* (1975) and *New York, New York* (1977), among others.

Echo and the Bunnymen British ART ROCK band of the early 1980s, which established a loyal following with a series of original albums and singles. Based in Liverpool, charismatic vocalist Ian McCulloch (1959–   ), guitarist Will Sergeant (1958–   ) and bassist Les Pattinson (1958–   ) came together in 1978. They first played as the Bunnymen, Echo being the name they gave to the drum machine they used before recruiting drummer Pete De Freitas. The band established its reputation with such hit singles as 'Pictures on My Wall' and with the albums *Crocodiles*, *Heaven Up Here*, *Porcupine* and *Ocean Rain*, considered by many their best. McCulloch left in 1987 after *Echo and the Bunnymen* and De Freitas died in a motorcycle accident. Despite little success without him, all the band re-formed in 1997 with the single 'Nothing Lasts Forever'.

echo chamber A sealed room containing a loudspeaker and a microphone, which is used to achieve echo and reverberation effects in a recording. Alternatives to the echo chamber include the various echo pedals and other devices that have been developed to produce similar effects electronically.

Eckstine, Billy (William Clarence Eckstein;

1914–93) US singer, trumpeter and bandleader, who played a prominent role in the advent of BEBOP in the mid-1940s. Eckstine first attracted attention as a vocalist, but subsequently won respect as a trumpeter and bandleader, forming (with Budd Johnson) a highly influential band in 1944 and recruiting to its ranks players of the calibre of Dizzy GILLESPIE, Charlie PARKER, Art BLAKEY and Miles DAVIS. By the time the band broke up in 1947, it had exercised a profound effect on the development of jazz. Eckstine continued on a solo basis as well as establishing himself as a popular CABARET star.

Eddy, Duane (1938–   ) US ROCK 'N' ROLL star, nicknamed the Guitar Man, who was one of the most influential rock 'n' roll guitarists. His 'twangy' guitar sound, created by picking out tunes on the bass strings of his guitar and enriching them by the use of a primitive echo, made hits of such songs as 'Rebel Rouser' (1958), 'Deep in the Heart of Texas' (1962) and '(Dance with the) Guitar Man' (1963). His hit albums included *Have Twangy Guitar Will Travel* (1959). He also guested on recordings by many other leading contemporaries, including Nancy Sinatra (1940–   ), for whom he played guitar on 'These Boots are Made for Walking' (1966). He enjoyed a come-back in 1975 with the hit 'Play Me Like You Play Your Guitar' and again in 1985 with the Art of Noise version of his 'Peter Gunn'; a year later he released a new album, which included performances by such luminaries as Paul MCCARTNEY and Ry COODER.

Strangely, although he reached the charts on both sides of the Atlantic some 20 times, he never had a Number One hit, either in the UK or the USA.

Eddy, Nelson (1901–67) US singer and actor, nicknamed the Singing Capon, who achieved star status as a singer in early film MUSICALS. Specializing in the old-fashioned style of the Viennese operetta, he made many recordings and appeared in many successful films, often alongside Jeanette MacDonald (1901–65). Their most popular films included *Rose-Marie* (1936), *The Girl of the Golden West* (1938) and *Bitter Sweet* (1940).

Edgar Wallace of Songwriters, the *See* Horatio NICHOLLS.

Edinburgh Festival, the Prestigious international festival of music and drama that has been held in August in Edinburgh on an annual basis since 1947, when it was founded on the suggestion of Sir Rudolph Bing (1902–) as a means of reopening cultural links between European countries after the Second World War. Lasting three weeks, the Festival has witnessed many fine programmes of music, with leading composers, conductors and orchestras from all over the world. Star guests at the very first Festival included Bruno WALTER and the VIENNA PHILHARMONIC ORCHESTRA; among subsequent top-billing attractions at the event have been the GLYNDEBOURNE Opera Company and SCOTTISH OPERA. A number of important works by contemporary composers, including Sir Michael TIPPETT, have had their first performances in Edinburgh. The Festival is also famous for its thriving fringe activities.

Acknowledged to be the largest arts festival in the world, the Edinburgh Festival regularly hosts some 10,000 performances of various kinds. Professor Gerald Berkowitz holds the record for having seen the greatest number of shows in any one year (145 in 1979).

Edison, Harry 'Sweets' (1915–) Black US JAZZ trumpeter, who played with many of the great jazzmen between the 1930s and the 1970s. Among the prestigious bands with which he appeared were those of Count BASIE (1938–50 and again in the 1960s and 1970s), Jimmy RUSHING and Buddy RICH; he was also acclaimed for his performances with the band backing Frank SINATRA in the 1950s. He was credited as co-writer on a number of classic Basie recordings, including 'Jive at Five' and 'Shorty George'.

Edmunds, Dave (1944–) Welsh rock guitarist and singer, who has enjoyed a 25-year career both as a band member and as a solo star. He first attracted attention with his group Love Sculpture in the late 1960s, recording such hits as 'Sabre Dance' (1968), which reached the Top 10 in the UK, and then on a solo basis with the Number One 'I Hear You Knocking' (1970), on which he played all the instruments. Further hit singles followed in the early 1970s, and in 1975 he released his influential solo album *Subtle as a Flying Mallet*. He teamed up with Nick Lowe to

form Rockpile, releasing *Seconds of Pleasure* (1980). Other solo hits have included 'Girls Talk' (1979) and the albums *Get It* (1977), *Repeat When Necessary* (1979) and *Closer to the Flame* (1989). He was also producer of the Stray Cats, among a number of leading bands, and helped to organize the EVERLY BROTHERS' come-back in 1984.

Edwards, Cliff (1895–1972) US singer and entertainer, nicknamed Ukulele Ike, who was a popular star of Broadway MUSICALS and Hollywood movies of the 1920s and 1930s. His biggest stage hits included *Lady Be Good* (1924) and the *Ziegfeld Follies* (1927) and among his most popular recordings was 'Singin' in the Rain' (1929). He also provided the voice of Jiminy Cricket in Walt Disney's *Pinocchio* (1939).

Edwards, Gus (1879–1945) US songwriter, entertainer and producer, of German extraction, who became one of the most successful Broadway producers of the pre-First World War era. His prolific output included such shows as the *Ziegfeld Follies* of 1910, which he wrote, *Hollywood Revue of 1929*, for which he provided the music, and a long list of hit songs – among them, 'I Can't Tell Why I Love You, But I Do' (1900), 'He's My Pal' (1905), 'By the Light of the Silv'ry Moon' (1909) and 'Laddie Boy' (1918).

eel-ya-dah Nonsense phrase used to describe the various meaningless sounds uttered by JAZZ singers of the 1940s and 1950s, when BEBOP was all the rage (*see* SCAT).

eight to the bar The underlying rhythm employed in BOOGIE-WOOGIE piano playing, as first heard in the 1930s.

eighty-eight US JAZZ slang for a piano, which normally has 88 keys.

Eisler, Hanns (1898–1962) German composer, whose left-wing views brought him into conflict with the authorities in both Nazi Germany and the USA. A pupil of Arnold SCHOENBERG in Vienna, Eisler eventually left Germany after harassment from the Nazis and moved to the USA, where he consolidated his reputation with his film and theatre music. A friend of Bertolt Brecht (1898—1955), he was arraigned before the Committee for Un-American Activities and sent to prison, although intervention by such contemporaries as Charles Chaplin and Albert Einstein resulted instead in his deportation (he eventually moved to East Germany). His works included two operas, a choral symphony, the *Lenin Requiem* (1937; with words by Brecht), the quintet *14 Ways of Describing Rain*, chamber music and songs.

Eldridge, (David) Roy (1911–89) US JAZZ trumpeter, drummer and vocalist, nicknamed Little Jazz, who won equal fame as a soloist with some of the most famous names in jazz and as leader of his own SWING band. He formed his first band in 1927 and subsequently worked alongside Fletcher HENDERSON, Gene KRUPA, Billie HOLIDAY, Benny GOODMAN, Artie SHAW and Ella FITZGERALD, among others. Among his many disciples was Dizzy GILLESPIE. His playing career ended with a stroke in 1980.

electric guitar The staple instrument of the ROCK and POP band, which revolutionized popular music after its development and adoption by JAZZ and BLUES guitarists in the late 1940s and 1950s (*see* FENDER). Although most firmly identified with modern rock, the electric guitar has influenced many other music forms, even modern classical composition, with Karlheinz STOCKHAUSEN and Pierre BOULEZ being among the composers who have written parts for such instruments.

The guitars of famous stars arc often highly valued: a Fender Stratocaster belonging to Jimi HENDRIX sold for £198,000 when it was auctioned at Sotheby's in 1990. The largest working AXE ever constructed was built by students at a US high school in 1991; it was 38ft (11.5m) tall and required six players to operate it.

Many guitarists develop a close relationship with their instruments and refuse adamantly to consider swapping them. QUEEN guitarist Brian May remained faithful to his original axe throughout his highly successful career despite the fact that it was a homemade instrument he had put together with the help of his father: the body had been constructed from an old wooden fireplace, the trim from some pieces of plastic shelf edging and the tremolo arm from a piece of saddlebag holder and a knitting needle (at a total cost of £8).

Electric guitars are an abomination,

whoever heard of an electric violin? An electric cello? Or for that matter an electric singer?
ANDRÉS SEGOVIA

Electric Light Orchestra British pop group of the 1970s, which enjoyed a number of hits mixing pop with a light classical sound. Three members of the ELO were players with the LONDON SYMPHONY ORCHESTRA; founder-members – all from Birmingham – included guitarist Jeff Lynne (1947–), who was the band's leader, drummer Bev Bevan (1946–) and vocalist Roy Wood (1946–), who soon left. No fewer than 26 ELO numbers reached the UK Top 40; these included '10538 Overture', 'Mister Blue Sky', 'Roll Over Beethoven', 'Sweet Talking Woman', 'Livin' Thing', 'Telephone Line', 'Shine a Little Love' and – with Olivia NEWTON-JOHN – 'Xanadu' (1980), the only occasion on which ELO reached Number One. The group's most successful albums were *Eldorado* (1974) and *A New World Record* (1976). The band ceased operations in 1983 but was revived in 1986 and again in 1991, as ELO Part Two.

When *Out of the Blue* was released the recording company marked the event by erecting the most costly advertising billboard ever constructed on Hollywood's Sunset Boulevard.

electro-funk Genre of modern electronic POP music, which had its roots in SOUL, FUNK and RHYTHM-AND-BLUES. Using the full range of sophisticated electronic instruments employed in conventional rock, electro-funk became the dominant pop music of the 1980s, when leading exponents, most of whom were Black, built on the foundations laid by such stars as Stevie WONDER and EARTH, WIND AND FIRE in the 1970s, the most notable of them including PRINCE and Michael JACKSON. Characteristics of the style include the extensive use of drum machines, the incorporation of break dancing and other energetic dance routines and an often overtly sexual content.

electrochord Electronic musical instrument, which was invented by Peter Eötvös for use in works by Karlheinz STOCKHAUSEN. It was made from a 15-string Hungarian peasant zither linked up to a SYNTHESIZER.

electronde Electronic musical instrument, which was invented by Martin Taubmann in 1929. Similar to the THEREMIN, it offered greater control over amplification and *glissando* effects.

electronic music Any composition in which use is made of a range of electronic instruments. The TELHARMONIUM, built in 1906, is regarded as marking the beginning of electronic music, although others have pointed to an instrument called the Singing Arc, which was designed as early as 1897 on the same principle as the new carbon arc street lamps, which sometimes emitted a sharp whistle in operation. A largely postwar phenomenon, electronic music was first experimented with by such AVANT-GARDE composers as Karlheinz STOCKHAUSEN and Luciano BERIO and was subsequently developed by John CAGE and Pierre BOULEZ among others in the classical world, while numerous pop bands of the 1970s and 1980s relied almost exclusively on electronic instruments (chiefly the SYNTHESIZER).

The term 'electronic music' was originally confined to music that was produced by actual instruments, but it soon came to be applied also both to music that depended on the use of tape recordings of both conventional musical instruments and natural sounds and to computer-generated music. *See also* CONCRETE MUSIC; ELECTROCHORD; ELECTRONDE; ONDES MARTENOT; THEREMIN.

> It is by rules and compasses that the Greeks discovered geometry – musicians might do well to be inspired by their example.
> 'PIERRE SCHAEFFER, 1960

> What we want is an instrument that will give us a continuous sound at any pitch. The composer and the electrician will have to labour together to get it.
> EDGAR VARÈSE, 1922

> Electrical instruments ... will make available for musical purposes any and all sounds that can be heard.
> JOHN CAGE, *Silence*, 1961

electronic organ A keyboard instrument, which depends upon the incorporation of electronic oscillators for its sound and which is, therefore, open to wide manipulation by the player. The first electric organs were built by Laurens Hammond (*see* HAMMOND ORGAN) in 1935 but were first sold on a wide scale in the 1960s, when they were enthusiastically bought up by both professional players (who saw in them possibilities as concert or theatre organs) and by

amateurs, who rushed to buy them in much the same way that Victorians and Edwardians had furnished their homes with pianos. They were even given serious consideration by leading contemporary composers, Karlheinz STOCKHAUSEN making use of electronic organs in *Momente* (1962–64, 1972) and *Mikrophonie II* (1965).

As time passed, improved technology meant that an even wider range of sounds was possible, and attempts to imitate the various instruments of the orchestra became somewhat more successful, although few machines proved capable of producing anything like a convincing substitute for the real thing. Many models incorporate their own drum machines and tape recorders, which offer limited SAMPLING possibilities. At their most sophisticated, the dividing line between the electronic organ and the SYNTHESIZER proper disappears.

electronic rock Genre of ROCK music in which extensive use is made of SYNTHESIZERS and other electronic instruments. At its most radical, the genre, which was at its height in the early 1970s, has produced works that consist of little more than a series of electronic hums and buzzes. Leading exponents of such music have included CAN and TANGERINE DREAM.

electronium Electronic instrument that was invented by Harald Bojé for use in the works of Karlheinz STOCKHAUSEN. It consisted of a SYNTHESIZER connected to a keyboard or potentiometer.

Elf, the *See* Errol GARNER.

Elgar, Sir Edward (1857–1934) British composer, who was hailed as one of the great names in English music long before his death. Born in Broadheath, near Worcester, Elgar was one of the foremost composers of the English countryside, drawing inspiration from nature from an early age (his first compositions included an attempt to render the 'song' of the reeds by the River Teme). He lived much of his later life in Malvern, where his house is now preserved in his memory.

Elgar lacked any substantial formal training in music and this contributed to the originality of much of his work. The son of a music dealer and organist, he succeeded his father as a church organist in Worcester and led a number of local ensembles, including the Worcester County Lunatic Asylum Band. He married one of his piano pupils before establishing himself as a significant composer in his forties, notably with his *Imperial March*, composed for Queen Victoria's Diamond Jubilee in 1897, the oratorio *Caractacus* (1898) and the celebrated ENIGMA VARIATIONS (1899), which prompted Sir Hubert Parry (1848–1918) to advise: 'Look out for this man's music; he has something to say and knows how to say it.'

The oratorio *The Dream of Gerontius* (1900), which was inspired by Elgar's Catholicism, consolidated the composer's international reputation, although a poor first performance at Birmingham was a temporary setback, and such works as the *Pomp and Circumstance* marches (notably 'Land of Hope and Glory') confirmed his place as the leading writer of ceremonial 'public' music. He was knighted in 1904, when a three-day festival of his music was held at COVENT GARDEN, and he continued to write both grand patriotic pieces and more personal works up to the First World War, the most important of which included two symphonies (1908 and 1910), a violin concerto (1910) and the symphonic study *Falstaff* (1913).

The tragedy of the war made its mark on Elgar and was evident in his moving cello concerto (1919). His wife died the following year and he subsequently produced little of any significance, although he did supervise the recording of much of his work. Hailed as the first major English composer in 200 years, he was made Master of the King's Musick in 1924 and was created a baronet in 1931, in which year he composed the *Nursery Suite* for the Duchess of York and her two daughters; he was planning a third symphony when he died.

> There is music in the air, music all around us, the world is full of it, and you simply take as much as you require.
>
> EDWARD ELGAR

> Edward Elgar, the figure head of music in England, is a composer whose rank it is neither prudent nor indeed possible to determine. Either it is one so high that only time and posterity can confer it, or else he is one of the Seven Humbugs of Christendom.
>
> GEORGE BERNARD SHAW, *Music and Letters*, 1920

> Gentlemen, let us now rehearse the greatest symphony of modern times, written by the greatest modern composer.
>
> HANS RICHTER, to the Hallé Orchestra, referring to Elgar's First Symphony

> The musical equivalent of St Pancras Station.
>
> THOMAS BEECHAM, on Elgar's First Symphony

Ellington, Duke (Edward Kennedy Ellington; 1899–1974) Black US JAZZ bandleader, pianist and composer, who ranks among the most important and popular figures in the history of twentieth-century music. The nickname 'Duke' marked him out as one of the jazz 'aristocrats' of his generation, although he earned it originally while still at school in Washington, D.C., where he was noted for his sartorial elegance. The son of a butler who once worked in the White House, he was given music lessons by a Miss Clinkscales and subsequently worked as accompanist to a travelling magician and fortune teller. He then set about establishing his reputation playing the piano in night clubs every evening (working as a signwriter during the day to supplement his income). Ultimately he moved to New York with his own band (having realized that the bandleader took home more money than the other musicians) and proved himself unrivalled in his mastery of tone 'colouring', which won him comparisons with Claude DEBUSSY and Frederick DELIUS.

Taken on at the COTTON CLUB in 1927, the band became famous for its JUNGLE MUSIC, in which much use was made of mutes and rough 'growling' sounds. Regular radio broadcasts from the club assured Ellington of national fame, and soon his admirers ranged from fellow-jazzmen and live audiences to such musical legends as Leopold STOKOWSKI and Igor STRAVINSKY.

Although Ellington's own piano playing technique was considered relatively conventional by many critics, he enjoyed huge fame with his celebrated band – he claimed 'my band is my instrument' – and as writer of many of the best-known DANCE BAND tunes, his style changing constantly as the years passed. It is estimated that he wrote between 2,000 and 5,000 tunes, his many hits including 'The Mooche', 'Creole Love Call', 'Rockin' in Rhythm', 'It Don't Mean a Thing if It Ain't Got That Swing', 'Mood Indigo', 'Sophisticated Lady', 'Don't Get Around Much Anymore', 'Concerto for Cootie', 'Take the A Train' and 'In a Sentimental Mood'. He also experimented with religious music and with classical works, producing inspired jazz interpretations of such pieces as Tchaikovsky's *Nutcracker* suite. The success of such compositions enabled Ellington to hire excellent musicians and to keep his band together long after the era of the BIG BAND had ended. Notable musicians on the Ellington payroll included arranger Billy Strayhorn (1915–67), saxophonist Ben Webster (1909–73) and bassist Jimmy Blanton (whose death in 1943 at the age of 23 was greatly regretted).

A classic concert at the Newport Jazz Festival in 1956 confirmed Ellington's reputation as one of the great figures in contemporary music, and he remained in huge demand right up to his death, following which his son Mercer Ellington (1919–   ) kept the band going for a little while longer.

> There are only two kinds of music: good and bad.
> DUKE ELLINGTON

> When it sounds good, it *is* good.
> DUKE ELLINGTON

> A Harlem Dionysus drunk on bad bootleg liquor.
> ERNEST NEWMAN, of Duke Ellington

Elliott, G(eorge) H(enry) (1884–1962) British MUSIC HALL singer, nicknamed the Chocolate Coloured Coon, who enjoyed huge success as a black-face singer in the early years of the century. He made his first appearance in the London music halls in 1902 and subsequently sang many of the classic songs relating to the old black-face tradition, as well as such new ones as 'I Want to Go to Idaho', 'Rastus Brown' and 'I Used to Sigh for the Silv'ry Moon'.

Elliott, Ramblin' Jack (Elliott Charles Adnopoz; 1931–   ) US FOLK-singer and guitarist, nicknamed the Singing Cowboy from Brooklyn, who acquired cult status as one of the pioneers of folk-blues. Influenced by his close friend Woody GUTHRIE among others, he was particularly well received in the UK, where he toured in the 1950s and has since wandered much of the world with his guitar, acquiring an almost legendary reputation. He has issued many albums of Guthrie material and has also collaborated a number of times with Guthrie's successor Bob DYLAN.

> Jack sounds more like me than I do.
> WOODY GUTHRIE

Ellis, Don (1934–78) US JAZZ trumpeter and bandleader, nicknamed the Father of the Time Revolution, who was at the forefront of JAZZ-ROCK in the 1960s and emerged as one of the most innovative players of his generation. Ellis acquired his first trumpet at the age of two and formed his first quartet while still at school. Influenced by Dizzie GILLESPIE and John CAGE among others, he went on to lead a variety of bands (including a Hindustani Jazz Sextet with which he explored Indian music) and recorded many experiments with unconventional time signatures. His own highly complex compositions included 'Indian Lady', 'Turkish Bath', *Contrasts for Two Orchestras and Trumpet*, the cantata *Reach* and the GRAMMY-winning SOUNDTRACK for the film *The French Connection* (1971).

> I am not concerned whether my music is jazz, third stream, classical or anything else, or whether it is even called music. Let it be judged as Don Ellis noise.
> DON ELLIS

Ellis, Vivian (1904–   ) British composer and author, who wrote many popular musical comedies and hit songs. Trained as a concert pianist, he began writing for REVUES in the early 1920s and subsequently enjoyed success as creator of such shows as *Mercenary Mary* (1925), from which came 'Over My Shoulder', *Kid Boots* (1926), *Cochran's Revue of 1926* (1926), *The Girl Friend* (1927), *Charlot's Revue* (1928), *Mr Cinders* (1929), *The Song of the Drum* (1931), *Jill Darling* (1933), *The Fleet's Lit Up* (1938), *Bless the Bride* (1947) and *And So To Bed* (1951). His hit songs included 'Spread a Little Happiness', 'I Want to Cling to Ivy' and 'Me and My Dog'.

Elman, Mischa (1891–1967) US violinist, born in Russia, who was regarded as one of the most gifted violinists of his generation. Something of a child prodigy, he made his professional début in 1904 and founded the celebrated Elman Quartet in 1926.

> You know, the critics never change; I'm still getting the same notices I used to get as a child. They tell me I play very well for my age.
> MISCHA ELMAN

Elvira Madigan Concerto Nickname by which Mozart's Piano Concerto in C (K467) came to be known to modern audiences after it became a notorious example of a BLEEDING CHUNK (an extract of a larger work used totally out of context). In this case, the producer of the film *Elvira Madigan* (1967) took a fancy to a few bars of the slow movement of Mozart's concerto and, for no apparent reason, faded them in and out during the action of the film (about the romance and suicide of a circus tightrope walker and a soldier in nineteenth-century Sweden). This did not do much for the film, but since then the concerto has been rechristened by the same title, even on concert programmes.

> Beautifully photographed and set to a Mozart piano concerto; you may be enchanted by it if you don't laugh yourself sick.
>
> *Time Out* review of *Elvira Madigan*

> I strongly resent the use of great and familiar music in the background of films. In nine cases out of ten it reduces the music to the level of the film rather than raising the film to the level of the music, which is obviously the filmmaker's intention. There is nothing more disgusting than to find Mozart's [piano concerto] labelled as the Elvira Madigan Concerto.
>
> SATYAJIT RAY

Elvis the Pelvis *See* Elvis PRESLEY.

Emerson, Lake and Palmer British rock band, which was one of the foremost PRO-GRESSIVE ROCK outfits of the 1970s. Keyboard player Keith Emerson (1944–), bassist and singer Greg Lake (1948–) and drummer Carl Palmer (1951–) came together in 1970 and quickly established themselves as a top rock attraction with the albums *Emerson, Lake and Palmer* (1970) and *Tarkus* (1971). The band's highly theatrical (to many, pretentious) live act, highlights of which included an extravagant laser show and Emerson assaulting his organ with knives, also pleased the fans, and recording success continued with a version of Mussorgsky's *Pictures at an Exhibition* (1971) and such albums as *Brain Salad Surgery* (1973). The fashion for ELP's rather cumbersome style gradually faded, however, and attempts to revive the band in the late 1970s, in the midst of the PUNK ROCK revolution, met with little success. The individual members concentrated on solo efforts in the 1980s, though Lake and Emerson re-formed – with drummer Cozy Powell (1947–) – to make another album in 1986 and again, this time with Palmer, in 1992.

EMI Electrical and Musical Industries. The British recording company, which emerged as one of the giants of the music industry in 1931 after the merger of COL-UMBIA with the Gramophone Company. Proprietors of the ABBEY ROAD studio in London and of numerous well-known subsidiary labels, EMI enjoyed a virtual monopoly of the recording industry for many years, handling the records of most of the great stars of JAZZ, classical and popular music until the 1950s, when some of the company's old rivals grew in strength. Having acquired Capitol in 1955, EMI consolidated its reputation in the 1960s through the phenomenal success of the BEATLES, who signed to EMI's Parlophone label – run by George MARTIN – in 1962. (The group initially got just one penny in royalties on the sale of each doublesided record, although from 1967 it got 10 per cent of the retail price.) Other artists signed by EMI in the 1960s included PINK FLOYD, Cilla BLACK, the HOLLIES and GERRY AND THE PACEMAKERS. Leaner times followed in the 1970s, but business picked up considerably in the 1980s when acts signed to EMI included QUEEN, David BOWIE and the ROLL-ING STONES.

Empress of the Blues, the *See* Bessie SMITH.

Enescu, Georges (1881–1955) Romanian composer, conductor and violinist, resident in Paris for most of his life, who wrote a number of acclaimed works in a Romantic and nationalist vein and who was celebrated for his interpretations of Bach. A contemporary of Gabriel FAURÉ and Jules Massenet (1842–1912), Enescu produced the opera *Oedipus* (1931), three symphonies, two *Romanian Rhapsodies* (1901–02), and orchestral, chamber and piano music as well as a number of songs. As a teacher of the violin, he coached the young Yehudi MENUHIN.

In one famous incident, Enescu sought to aid a young violinist of his acquaintance by accompanying him at the piano at his Carnegie Hall début, while pianist Walter GIESEKING turned the pages for him; a review of the performance read: 'The man who should have been playing the piano was turning the pages, and the man who should have been turning the pages was playing the violin.'

English Chamber Orchestra Prestigious

British orchestra, which was formed in 1960 from the Goldsborough Orchestra, which specialized in baroque music, when the ensemble decided to widen the scope of its material. Conductors of the orchestra have included Daniel BARENBOIM, Pinchas ZUKERMAN and (from 1985) Jeffrey Tate.

English Folk Dance and Song Society Society, which was formed in the UK in 1932 by the amagamation of the Folksong Society and the English Folk Dance Society. The society aims to study and preserve British FOLK MUSIC; its first directors included Cecil SHARP and Ralph VAUGHAN WILLIAMS. Internal divisions threatened the organization's future during the second folk revival that took place in the 1980s.

English Music Theatre Company British opera company that was founded (as the English Opera Group) in 1947 under the aegis of Benjamin BRITTEN. The company – a small ensemble rather than a full-scale orchestra – specialized in the performance of new works and presented premieres of many of Britten's pieces as well as music by Sir William WALTON, Sir Lennox BERKELEY and Sir Harrison BIRTWISTLE. The company played a key role in the foundation of the ALDEBURGH FESTIVAL in 1948 and has toured internationally (under its present name since 1975).

English National Opera British opera company, which was originally founded by Lilian Baylis (1874–1937) in 1931 and was known as the Sadler's Wells Opera until 1974. Acclaimed for productions of Benjamin BRITTEN, Wagner and Sergei PROKOFIEV over the years, the company has also presented many new works and has attracted to its ranks many of the most distinguished figures in contemporary classical music. Musical directors of the company have included Sir Alexander GIBSON, Sir Colin DAVIS, Sir Charles MACKERRAS, Sir Charles GROVES and Mark Elder (1947–).

Enigma Variations Informal title of Sir Edward ELGAR's *Variations on an original theme for Orchestra*, which was first performed in 1899. The dedication runs 'To my friends pictured within', and the work was intended as a portrait gallery of the composer's friends, each variation representing a different character, whose initials were employed as the title. 'Nimrod' was dedicated to the publisher of Elgar's music, A.J. Jaeger (*Jäger* being the German word for a hunter and Nimrod being the name of a biblical hunter). Other dedicatees included Caroline Alice Elgar (the composer's wife) and Elgar himself (through his wife's pet name for him – 'Edu').

These allusions are relatively easy to work out, but the real enigma remains: the identity of the unplayed theme that Elgar claimed ran throughout the entire work. According to those who have speculated about the matter, the stated theme of the work was a counter-subject to a well-known tune, one that goes unheard throughout the piece but that would be recognized at once if it were played ('Auld Lang Syne' is a possibility, as are 'Pop Goes the Weasel' and a theme from the slow movement of Mozart's Prague Symphony (number 38), which, perhaps significantly, completed the bill at the first performance of Elgar's own work). Elgar himself never let on, although his wife and probably also Jaeger knew.

Elgar liked musical games. He once illustrated in a letter to the *Musical Times* how a movement from Tchaikovsky's Sixth Symphony 'went' (that is, harmonized) with 'God Save the Queen'. The Enigma Variations was not the only work into which he incorporated this taste for mystery. He played a similar trick on the public in 1910, in the dedication of his Violin Concerto in B minor (which he recorded with enormous success with the young violinist Yehudi MENUHIN). The piece was prefaced with the tantalizing inscription '*Aquí est à encerrada el alma de ...*' ('the soul of ... lies shrouded within').

Eno, Brian (Brian Peter George St John de Baptiste de la Salle Eno; 1948–) British SYNTHESIZER-player and composer, who first emerged as one of the leading figures in AVANT-GARDE rock and pop in the 1970s. Eno established his reputation while keyboardist with ROXY MUSIC in the early 1970s and went on to collaborate with other like-minded stars, including Robert FRIPP and David BOWIE, exploring such concepts as tape-delay and AMBIENT MUSIC (a sophisticated form of MUZAK)and appealing to a cult audience with such albums as *Taking Tiger Mountain (by Strategy)* (1974) and *Music for Airports* (1979). His association with the more commercially oriented TALKING HEADS resulted in the hit single 'Once in a Lifetime' (1981) and in his own album *My Life In The Bush Of Ghosts* (1981). He also helped to produce the classic U2 albums *The Unforgettable Fire* (1984) and *The Joshua Tree* (1987). Notable releases since then have included *Wah Wah* (1994).

ENSA Entertainments National Service Association. The association, formed in the Second World War, which provided morale-boosting entertainment for British troops serving all around the world. Many leading musical figures participated in ENSA tours, and by the end of the war some two and a half million performances had been given. In the USA an equivalent service was provided by the USO (United Service Organizations).

envelope The 'shape' of a sound as it changes, as controlled in ELECTRONIC MUSIC.

EP Extended Play. A single-sized vinyl record, 7in (17.5cm) across, which could play for longer than a conventional SINGLE because it had more grooves. In the pop world EPs typically had two songs on each side and were otherwise known as maxisingles. They were released by many successful artists in the 1960s and 1970s.

Epstein, Brian (1934–67) British pop group manager, who is remembered for his crucial association with the BEATLES. Having failed in his attempts to start an acting career, he worked in a record store in Liverpool and became interested in the local music scene, meeting the Beatles for the first time at the CAVERN in 1961. As manager, he cleaned up the band's image (he stopped them from smoking on stage and made them wear smart suits) and won them a recording contract. He also managed Cilla BLACK and GERRY AND THE PACEMAKERS and presented his own television shows.

A growing dependency on drugs and disillusionment with his role preceded his death at his London home, which was apparently due to an accidental overdose of Carbitol (although many observers suggested it was a suicide). After his death, the group decided to continue without a manager; many have traced the band's eventual break-up to the fact that they lacked Epstein's leadership.

Controversial incidents in Epstein's career included a holiday he took with John LENNON in 1963, which led to speculations about an affair between the two men (Epstein being a declared homosexual); the rumours were never substantiated, although Epstein was known to have propositioned Pete Best, the so-called FIFTH BEATLE.

Epstein himself is said to have been the 'rich man' referred to in the Beatles number 'Baby, You're a Rich Man', which was released as the B side to 'All You Need is Love'.

Essex, David (Albert David Cook; 1947–   ) British pop singer and actor, who was a popular teen-idol of the early 1970s. He began his musical career in the 1960s as a JAZZ drummer and finally achieved national fame after starring in the musical *Godspell* (1971) and in the ROCK 'N' ROLL film *That'll Be the Day*, from the SOUNDTRACK of which came his first hit as a solo singer, 'Rock On' (1973). Among the hits that followed were 'Lamplight' (1973), 'Gonna Make You a Star' (1974) and 'Hold Me Close' (1975). Further movie appearances and a burgeoning stage career kept Essex in the public eye through the 1980s and early 1990s (he also hosted his own television series for a time).

Etting, Ruth (c.1896–1978) US singer and actress, called the Queen of the Torch Singers, who starred in many popular stage MUSICALS and REVUES as well as in a number of Hollywood movies. She emerged as a star of revue in the mid-1920s and subsequently appeared in such popular shows as *Whoopee* (1928) and the *Ziegfeld Follies* (1931). Her hit songs included 'Love Me or Leave Me' (1928), 'Get Happy' (1930) and 'Shine on Harvest Moon' (1931). Her marriage to mobster Martin 'Moe the Gimp' Snyder was turbulent and culminated in their separation: Snyder shot Etting's pianist (who fortunately survived).

eurhythmics A health and fitness dance work-out system, which is conducted to a musical accompaniment. Eurhythmics, a word deriving from a combination of the Greek word for 'proportion' and the Latin word for 'rhythm'), enjoyed a considerable vogue in the 1980s, when numerous classes for such dance activities were set up across the USA and UK (mostly using DISCO music, which has a heavy, regular beat).

Much earlier a similar approach had been employed at the Dalcroze Institute of Eurhythmics that was founded in Dresden in 1910 by the Swiss composer Émile Jaques-Dalcroze (1865–1950) to promote the music and dance education of children, specifically by training them to respond to a rhythm by body movement.

Euro-disco The name given to the European version of DISCO music, which developed in response to the wave of US disco artists who dominated the charts in the mid-1970s. A key figure in the development of Euro-disco was producer Giorgio Moroder, who brought such stars as Donna SUMMER and the THREE DEGREES to Europe.

Euro-rock Broad descriptive term, which came to be applied to commercial ROCK music emanating from continental Europe in the 1970s and 1980s. Few foreign-language bands have broken into British and US markets with significant success, although many have grappled with English lyrics in an attempt to emulate their English-speaking heroes. Rare examples of groups that have enjoyed some popularity with their brand of Euro-rock include Golden Earring and KRAFTWERK.

Europe, James Reese (1881–1919) US pianist, violinist and conductor, who did much to improve the lot of Black musicians before his premature death. As founder of the Amsterdam Musical Association (1906) and of the CLEF CLUB orchestra, he vigorously defended the interests of Black players. Subsequently he backed the dancers Vernon and Irene Castle with his own orchestra, founded in 1910, and led a celebrated army band but died after he was stabbed in an argument with a deranged drummer.

Eurovision Song Contest Annual international television event in which selected performers from various European nations compete against each other with MIDDLE-OF-THE-ROAD songs written specially for the occasion. Modelled on the Miss World contest, the competition was launched by the BBC in 1956 (when Switzerland won) but has always laboured under the burden of derision poured on it by the more 'serious' musical establishment. Nonetheless, several major stars have made reputations for themselves after appearing in the contest, the most notable including Sandie SHAW,

who won in 1967 with 'Puppet on a String', ABBA, who were winners in 1973, and Brotherhood of Man (1976) and BUCKS FIZZ (1981). Only rarely have already proven stars deigned to participate – the most famous of them being Cliff RICHARD, who swept aside the opposition in 1968 with 'Congratulations'. Norway has a special place in the history of the contest, having notched up a total of no points whatsoever two years running.

Eurythmics British pop duo of the 1980s, which recorded a series of major hit singles ranging from TECHNO POP to RHYTHM-AND-BLUES and straight rock. Vocalist and keyboard player Annie Lennox (1954–   ) and guitarist and keyboard player Dave Stewart (1952–   ) met in a restaurant where Aberdeen-born Lennox was working as a waitress. They embarked on a romantic and professional collaboration, first as part of the Tourists and then, after their romance ended and the Tourists split up in 1981, as Eurythmics.

The duo first tasted success under the new name in 1982 with *Sweet Dreams (Are Made Of This)*, which prospered on the strength of a striking video. The single 'Love is a Stranger' also proved a big hit and was followed by such numbers as 'Who's That Girl', 'Here Comes the Rain Again' and 'There Must be an Angel', which reached Number One in the UK in 1985. The duo's top-selling albums have included *Revenge* (1986), *Savage* (1987) and *We Too Are One* (1989). Both stars also developed solo careers, Stewart frequently working as a producer. Among Lennox's solo hits have been 'Walking on Broken Glass' and 'Love Song for a Vampire', from the album *Diva* (1992).

Evans, Bill (William John Evans; 1929–80) US JAZZ pianist and composer, who was a pioneer of the COOL style. He established his reputation in 1956 with a solo album and subsequently played with Miles DAVIS (featuring on the influential *Kind of Blue* album of 1958) and Charles MINGUS among other leading contemporaries before forming his own trio in 1959 and winning a wide audience with his piano-led jazz style. He also recorded further solo albums, of which the most influential included *Undercurrent* (1959) and *Conversations with Myself* (1963). His most successful compositions included 'Blue in Green' and 'Waltz for

Debby'. His death, which came while he was still at the height of his powers, was hastened by drug addiction.

Evans, Sir Geraint (Llewellyn) (1922–92) Welsh baritone, who was widely acclaimed for his performances in such great operatic roles as Falstaff and Figaro. Born in Pontypridd, he studied at the Guildhall School of Music and in Hamburg and Geneva before making his COVENT GARDEN début in 1948 in Wagner's *Die Meistersinger von Nürnberg*. He was particularly effective in comedy parts; his other roles included Wozzeck in Alban BERG's opera and Donizetti's Don Pasquale. He made his last Covent Garden appearance in 1984.

Evans, Gil (Ian Ernest Gilmore Green; 1912–88) Canadian JAZZ pianist and composer, of Australian parents, who emerged as one of the most influential jazz musicians of the 1950s. Having taught himself to play the piano, he produced innovative arrangements for a number of leading bands, notably that of Miles DAVIS, and won acclaim for such hits as 'Moondreams' and 'Boplicity' and other pieces immortalized as *The Birth of the Cool*. His arrangements for his own 19-piece band on such classic Davis albums as *Miles Ahead* (1957) and *Sketches of Spain* (1959–60) put him among the jazz greats of the period, after which he continued to appear with many of the finest jazz musicians on both sides of the Atlantic, always keeping abreast of the latest developments in pop (he arranged and recorded several Jimi HENDRIX numbers). He was sometimes referred to as 'Svengali' (an anagram of his real name).

Evans, Tolchard (Sydney Evans; 1901–78) British songwriter, whose prolific output of over 1,000 songs established him as one of the leading songwriters of his generation. Leader of his own band between 1925 and the 1950s, he wrote such hits as 'Lady of Spain' (1931), 'Let's All Sing Like the Birdies Sing' (1932), 'Dance, Gypsy, Dance' (1937), 'Everywhere' (1955) and 'My September Love' (1956). Another of his creations, 'If', was revived with huge success by Perry COMO in the 1950s and subsequently recorded by Telly Savalas among many others.

Everly Brothers, the US COUNTRY-ROCK duo of the 1950s and 1960s, who were among the most popular acts of their generation. The brothers, Don Everly (1937–   ) and Phil Everly (1939–   ), first ventured into music when they were only young, playing on their parents' country radio show. Their first single, 'Bye Bye Love' (1957), which introduced their unique acoustic, close-harmony vocal style, was a huge hit and was quickly followed by such classics as 'Wake Up Little Susie' (1957) and 'All I Have to Do is Dream' (1957), which reached Number One on both sides of the Atlantic. Husband-and-wife team Boudleaux Bryant (1920–87) and Felice Bryant (1925–   ), who wrote many Everly Brothers classics, claimed 'All I Have to Do is Dream' took just 15 minutes to compose. 'Cathy's Clown' (1960) was another transatlantic Number One, while other Everly Brothers standards included 'Bird Dog' and 'Ebony Eyes'.

The hits came to a halt while the brothers completed military service in the early 1960s and were further disrupted in 1963 when Don suffered a nervous breakdown. They enjoyed an isolated hit, 'The Price of Love', in 1965, but in 1973 the brothers quarrelled and split up to pursue solo careers. They were reconciled in 1984 for an acclaimed concert at London's Royal Albert Hall.

Bands influenced by the distinctive Everly Brothers sound included the BEATLES, SIMON AND GARFUNKEL and the BEACH BOYS.

Excitement, Mister *See* Jackie WILSON.

Expressionism A movement in the arts, especially painting but 'borrowed' by musicians, which exercised considerable influence in the 1920s. The aim of Expressionism was to communicate the essence of an object in emotive and subjective rather than in purely observational terms. Of particular relevance to German and Austrian composers of the period, it had a strong influence on the works of Arnold SCHOENBERG and Alban BERG, who rejected conventional musical forms and notions of tonality in their search for expression of what they considered innermost realities.

F

Fab Five, the *See* DURAN DURAN.

Fab Four, the *See* the BEATLES.

Fabian (Fabiano Forte Bonaparte; 1943–)
US pop singer, who was a teen-idol in the
USA in the late 1950s. Variously dubbed
the Tiger (and, in the UK, 'the worst singer
in the world'), he was 'discovered' when he
was 17 years old by a record producer, who
saw potential in his exceptional good looks.
An extensive media campaign ensured the
success of his third single, 'I'm a Man'
(1959), and another eight Fabian singles
reached the Top 40 in the USA, although
British fans never warmed to him and
agreed with his own assessment that he
could not sing a note. Fans at his live
appearances greeted him with the kind of
hysteria that audiences a few years later
reserved for the BEATLES. He appeared in
several movies, but vanished from the
scene as the hits ran out, although he did
pose nude for photographs in *Playgirl* in
1973.

Faces, the *See* the SMALL FACES.

Fain, Sammy (Samuel Feinberg; 1902–89)
US songwriter, nicknamed the Singing
Composer, who wrote many classic numbers for a host of leading Broadway and
Hollywood stars. Having taught himself to
play the piano, he had his first song pub-
lished in 1925 and subsequently made a
name for himself writing light, JAZZ-influ-
enced songs – mostly in collaboration with
Irving Kahal (1903–42) or Sammy CAHN –
for such stars as Maurice CHEVALIER, Doris
DAY and Dean MARTIN as well as recording
some of them himself (hence his nickname).
His numerous hits included 'Let a Smile be
Your Umbrella', 'I Can Dream, Can't I',
'Was that the Human Thing to Do?', 'By a
Waterfall', 'Secret Love', 'April Love' and
'Love is a Many-splendored Thing'. As well
as contributing many songs for Hollywood
movies, among them the Disney cartoons
Alice in Wonderland and *Peter Pan* and

Calamity Jane, he also wrote for the stage,
his biggest Broadway successes including
the revue *Hellzapoppin* (1938), *Right This
Way* (1935) and *George White's Scandals*
(1939).

Fairport Convention British rock band,
which pioneered the development of FOLK-
ROCK in the late 1960s and early 1970s.
Guitarist Simon Nicol (1950–), guitarist
and vocalist Richard THOMPSON, bassist
Ashley Hutchings (1945–), vocalist Judy
Dyble (1948–) and drummer Martin
Lamble (1949–69) came together in 1967,
naming the band after Nicol's house. The
group rapidly established its reputation
after Dyble was replaced by Sandy Denny
(1947–78). The album *What we Did on Our
Holidays* (1969) was well received, as was
Unhalfbricking. Lamble died in a car accident and was replaced by Dave Mattacks
(1948–), and Dave Swarbrick (1941–)
was brought in to play fiddle on the hugely
influential *Liege and Lief* (1970). In time
Denny and Hutchings left the band's ranks,
and bassist Dave Pegg (1947–) joined
for *Full House*, while further changes
meant that eventually none of the original
members was involved (breakaway groups
included STEELEYE SPAN). Denny returned
briefly in 1975 but left to develop her solo
career, which ended with her premature
death from a brain haemorrhage after falling downstairs at a friend's house. The
group itself broke up in 1979, after 18
albums, but re-formed in the mid-1980s
and went on to release such new albums as
Expletive Deleted (1986), *Red and Gold*
(1989) and *Jewel in the Crown* (1995).
Annual Fairport Convention festivals are
held every summer at Cropredy, Oxford-
shire.

Faith, Adam (Terry Nelhams; 1940–)
British pop singer and actor, who established himself as one of the most successful
British stars of the early 1960s. Faith's vul-
nerable cockney persona greatly promoted
his career, which began with a SKIFFLE

group before he set out as a solo performer in 1959. 'What Do You Want' (1959) reached Number One, as did 'Poor Me' (1960), and a host of follow-up singles all made the Top 20, elevating Faith to the same rank as Cliff RICHARD. He later concentrated on producing and on developing an acting career, starring in the long-running television series *Budgie* and *Love Hurts*.

Faith, Percy (1908–76) Canadian composer, arranger and conductor, whose string orchestra became one of the most popular recording and broadcasting orchestras of the postwar period. Faith began his musical career as a pianist but had to switch to arranging and conducting after burning his hands in an accident. He developed his own distinctive JAZZ-influenced EASY LISTENING style and made many records as well as writing for a number of films. His recordings 'Delicado' (1952), 'Song from Moulin Rouge' (1953) and 'Theme from a Summer Place' (1960) all reached Number One.

Faithfull, Marianne (1946–) British pop singer, who sprang to fame in the mid-1960s as the girlfriend of Mick JAGGER. Educated at a convent school, she was signed up by the ROLLING STONES management and marketed as a virginal innocent in stark contrast to the Stones themselves. Her first single, 'As Tears Go By' (1964), which was written by Jagger and Richards, was an immediate success, after which she returned to the Top 10 with 'Come and Stay with Me', 'This Little Bird' and 'Summer Nights', which were all ideally suited to her fragile voice. Subsequently she made guest appearances with the BEATLES and became a darling of the press, who revelled in details of her romances and drug problems. She attempted suicide when her relationship with Jagger disintegrated and eventually left him ('Wild Horses' on the Stones album *Sticky Fingers* is supposedly about her). In 1979 she staged a comeback with the husky-voiced *Broken English* and remained in the limelight through the 1980s with further acclaimed album releases and an autobiography (1994).

Fall, the British NEW WAVE band, which was among the most admired groups to emerge from the PUNK era. Led by singer Mark E. Smith (1960–), the band quickly attracted a cult following with such hard-edged

albums as *Live at the Witch Trials* (1979) and *Dragnet* (1979). Numerous other albums followed over the course of the next 15 years, highlights including *Hip Priests and Kamerades* (1985). The line-up, however, underwent many changes.

Falla, Manuel de (1876–1946) Spanish composer, who wrote much passionate popular music loosely based on traditional Spanish musical styles. Influenced by Edvard Grieg (1843–1907), he first attracted attention with a series of *zarzuelas* (a type of opera) written for the theatre and with the prize-winning opera *La Vida Breve* (*Life is Short*, 1904–05) but left for Paris in 1907 in search of wider opportunities. There he became a friend of Claude DEBUSSY, Maurice RAVEL, Paul DUKAS and Igor STRAVINSKY (who was once heard to describe Falla as 'modest and withdrawn as an oyster').

Having consolidated his reputation with *Seven Popular Spanish Songs* (1914), he returned to Spain after the First World War broke out and established himself as the leading Spanish composer of the day with the stage work *Le Amor brujo* (*Love, the Magician*; 1915), the highlight of which was the celebrated 'Ritual Fire Dance', his masterpiece *Noches en los Jardines de España* (*Nights in the Gardens of Spain*; 1916), for piano and orchestra, and the ballet *El Sombrero de Tres Picos* (*The Three-Cornered Hat*), which was first produced by Diaghilev (with choreography by Massine and scenery by Picasso) in 1919. Later works included the *Fantasia Bética* (1919) for piano and orchestra, which was created specially for Artur RUBINSTEIN, a puppet opera based on *Don Quixote*, composed in collaboration with the poet Federico García Lorca and called *El Retablo de Maese Pedro* (*Master Peter's Puppet Show*; 1923), a harpsichord concerto (1926), which was written for Wanda LANDOWSKA, and the uncompleted oratorio *La Atlántida*.

Falla died in Argentina, where he had emigrated during the Spanish Civil War, the outbreak of which caused him much distress and triggered a decline in his health. His body was brought back to Spain and laid to rest in Cadiz cathedral.

> The Spanish Gershwin.
> GEORGE GERSHWIN

Fame, Georgie (Clive Powell; 1943–) British pop singer-songwriter, who has enjoyed a long career playing in a wide variety of styles. Fame was 'spotted' while playing at a Butlins holiday camp and subsequently worked as a keyboard player with a JAZZ band before backing Eddie COCHRAN on his ill-fated tour of the UK in 1959–60. After Cochran's death, Fame joined Billy FURY's band and then, in 1962, formed the Blue Flames, playing RHYTHM-AND-BLUES. The single 'Yeh Yeh' reached Number One in the UK in 1965, as did 'Get Away' (written for a petrol commercial) in 1966, after which Fame returned to jazz for a while (he worked briefly with Count BASIE) before reviving his chart career with another Number One single 'The Ballad of Bonnie and Clyde' (1968). In 1971 he recorded another hit, 'Rosetta', with Alan PRICE, with whom he formed a fruitful partnership. More recent ventures have included recordings of GERSHWIN songs and others made with the band of Van MORRISON.

Family British PROGRESSIVE ROCK band, which was one of the leading 'underground' bands of the late 1960s and early 1970s. Vocalist Roger Chapman (1944–), bassist Ric Grech (1946–90), guitarist John 'Charlie' Whitney (1944–), saxophonist Jim King (1945–) and drummer Rob Townsend (1947–) came together in 1966 and consolidated their growing reputation with such early albums as *Music in A Doll's House* (1968) and *Family Entertainment* (1969). The band's further progress was hindered by several changes in personnel; subsequent releases before it broke up in the mid-1970s included *A Song For Me* (1970), *Anybody* (1970) and *Fearless* (1971). Chapman went on to record as a solo artist and moved to Germany, where he made a further five albums with his band Streetwalkers and then continued as leader of another group under the name Shortlist.

Farnon, Robert (1917–) Canadian composer, arranger and conductor, who first established a reputation as one of the most able composers of light classical and film music in the 1940s. Having worked with Percy FAITH in the 1930s, he led a Canadian army band – considered the equal to that led by Glenn MILLER – during the Second World War. He later arranged for such British orchestra leaders as GERALDO and Ted HEATH before assembling his own orchestra. He also backed such artists as Frank SINATRA, Tony BENNETT and Vera

LYNN. Writing for films including *Spring in Park Lane* (1948), *Captain Horatio Hornblower* (1951) and *Shalako* (1968), he composed such popular items as 'Jumping Bean' (1948), 'Peanut Polka' (1951), 'Westminster Waltz' (1956) and (for television) 'Colditz March' (1972). Other works include symphonies and many other orchestral works.

> The greatest arranger in the world.
> ANDRÉ PREVIN

fat lady. The opera's not over till the fat lady sings Catchphrase of musical origins, which is widely heard in a variety of contexts, meaning loosely that a situation will not be resolved until a certain event has taken place. The phrase is particularly beloved of football commentators, who utter it in the closing stages of a game to indicate that there is still time for a change in fortunes before the final whistle is blown.

This colourful idiom is commonly thought to have had its roots in the popular belief that most traditional nineteenth-century operas climax with a vast prima donna in a suitable Valkyrie costume complete with horned helmet delivering some well-known aria to thunderous applause at the close of the evening. In fact, very few classic operas end like this, the one notable exception being *Tristan and Isolde* where such a piece is delivered towards the end of the performance.

This is not the only suggested explanation, however. Some have it that the saying dates back only to the 1970s and refers to a large US singer called Kate Smith, who was famous for her spirited renditions of 'God Bless America', which she gave before home games involving the Philadelphia Flyers ice hockey team. Every time she sang it the team won (the game being thus effectively 'over' before it had even begun). Various rival teams are reputed to have offered large sums to lure her favours to their own sides.

A third explanation avoids any connection with music whatsoever. According to this, stokers of steam engines and ship boilers nicknamed their charges 'fat ladies': when a sufficient head of steam had been raised a safety whistle sounded, indicating that the engine was ready for operation.

Fatha *See* Earl HINES.

Father of Bluegrass *See* Bill MONROE.

Father of British Blues, the *See* Alexis KORNER. The name has also been bestowed on Graham Bond (1937–), another pioneer of the RHYTHM-AND-BLUES style in the UK in the 1960s.

Father of Country Music, the *See* Jimmie RODGERS; Hank WILLIAMS.

Father of Gospel Music, the *See* Thomas A. DORSEY.

Father of Soul, the *See* Sam COOKE.

Father of Swing, the *See* Ben POLLACK.

Father of the Blues, the *See* W.C. HANDY.

Father of the Time Revolution, the *See* Don ELLIS.

Fauré, Gabriel Urbain (1845–1924) French composer, nicknamed Robespierre because of his reformist zeal as director of the Paris Conservatoire (1905–20), who was unrivalled as the finest composer of French songs. Having trained as an organist and choirmaster under Camille SAINT-SAËNS, he occupied various posts while trying to establish himself as a composer as well as serving in a light infantry regiment during the Franco-Prussian War.

Fauré is best known for the *Requiem* (1887), which was inspired by the death of his father. Other compositions included the song 'Après un rêve', the opera *Penelope* (1900), music for the play *Pelléas et Mélisande* (1898), *Masques et Bergamasques* (1919), as well as chamber music and nocturnes, barcarolles and other pieces for the piano, of which the most famous was perhaps the *Dolly Suite* for two pianists. Towards the end of his life he was troubled increasingly by deafness, to the point where he could no longer hear what he composed. Among his pupils were Nadia BOULANGER, George ENESCU and Maurice RAVEL.

> When I am no longer here you will hear it said of my works: 'After all, that was nothing much to write home about!' ... I did what I could ... now ... let God judge!
> GABRIEL FAURÉ, last words

> The play of the graceful, fleeting lines described by Fauré's music may be compared to the gesture of a beautiful woman without either suffering from comparison.
> CLAUDE DEBUSSY, *Gil Blas*, 1903

> I not only admire, adore and venerate your music, I have been and still am in love with it.
> MARCEL PROUST, letter to Fauré, 1897

Faye, Alice (Alice Jeanne Leppert; 1912–) US singer and film actress, who enjoyed hits with a number of songs she sang in the course of her many musical films. Starring in movies like *On the Avenue* (1937), *Rose of Washington Square* (1939) and *State Fair* (1962), she recorded such hits as 'You Say the Sweetest Things, Baby', 'Wake Up and Live' and 'You'll Never Know'.

feed In JAZZ slang, to play a backing line to a soloist.

Feldman, Victor (1934–87) British JAZZ pianist, vibraphonist and drummer, who emerged as one of the leading jazzmen in the UK in the 1950s. Hailed as a child prodigy, he made a guest appearance as a drummer with the band of Glenn MILLER when he was only 10 years old. After collaborating with Ronnie SCOTT, Johnny DANKWORTH and Ted HEATH among others, he moved to the USA in 1955 and there appeared (chiefly as a vibraphonist and pianist) with such stars as Woody HERMAN and Cannonball ADDERLEY. Towards the end of his career he also ventured into JAZZ-ROCK, playing with the likes of Miles DAVIS and STEELY DAN. His career ended prematurely with his death as the result of an asthma attack.

Feliciano, José (1945–) Puerto Rican singer-songwriter and guitarist, who established a strong international following in the late 1960s. Blind from birth, Feliciano enjoyed huge success with his first two albums, *The Voice and Guitar of José Feliciano* (1965) and *Feliciano!* (1968), which introduced his accessible, JAZZ-influenced, Latin-based style (although a version of 'Star-spangled Banner' proved controversial). As the years passed he emerged as the elder statesman of modern Latin pop. More recent releases include the albums *Escenas de Amor* (1982), *Los Excitos de* (1984) and *Street Life '92* (1992).

Fenby, Eric (1906–97) British composer and writer, who served Frederick DELIUS as his amanuensis (1928–34) after the latter became blind and paralysed. It was through Fenby's dedicated assistance that Delius was able to complete such works as

A *Song for Summer*, *Songs of Farewell* and
the third violin sonata. Fenby later wrote of
his collaboration with the great composer
and also created several of his own works,
including the mock overture *Rossini on
Ilkla Moor* as well as taking the post of
Professor of Composition at the Royal
Academy of Music.

> There was always something incredibly
> sinister about the Delius household ...
> even before the onset of the terrible illness
> from which he suffered for so many years,
> and eventually died ... I can only say that
> I am amazed at Mr Fenby's fortitude in
> enduring, for several years, experiences
> that nearly drove me insane after only a
> few days.
> CECIL GRAY, *Musical Chairs*, 1948

Fender Guitar-manufacturing company,
which marketed the first commercially available ELECTRIC GUITARS in the late
1940s. Leo Fender (1909–91), an account-
ant, lost his job in the Wall Street Crash
of 1929. Subsequently he indulged his
interest in amplifying musical instruments
electrically and opened an electrical repair
shop, where he made his first models,
among which were the Champ and the
Deluxe, which is still on sale some 40 years
later. The solid-bodied Fender Broadcaster,
later renamed the Telecaster, marked the
dawn of the ROCK era when it was introduced in 1948, and it was quickly followed
by the Fender Precision Bass (1951),
although it was some time before guitarists
began to realize the considerable potential
of these new instruments. Of their many
successors, the most popular included the
Stratocaster range, introduced in 1954,
which was favoured by Buddy HOLLY, the
BEATLES, the ROLLING STONES, Jimi HENDRIX,
Eric CLAPTON and Bryan ADAMS among
many others.

When Japanese manufacturers started
producing fake Fenders at a cheaper price,
the Fender company (acquired by CBS in
1965) imaginatively opened a factory in
Japan to produce cheap copies of its own
guitars.

Ferguson, Maynard (1928–   ) Canadian
trumpeter and bandleader, who played
with many prominent US JAZZ bands after
moving to the USA in 1949. He won
acclaim for his distinctive high register
playing in the bands of such distinguished
jazzmen as Jimmy DORSEY, Charlie BARNET

and Stan KENTON and ultimately formed his
own band (1956–67), after which he
worked in both the UK and India, venturing into the JAZZ-ROCK field.

Ferrier, Kathleen (1912–53) British contralto, who was acclaimed one of the most
gifted and beloved singers of her generation before her tragically early death from
cancer. Born in Lancashire, she trained
initially as a pianist and then worked as a
telephonist but went on to establish her
reputation in the 1940s singing works by
Handel, Bach and Sir Edward ELGAR. Benjamin BRITTEN wrote the main part in *The
Rape of Lucretia* (1946) for her, and she
subsequently starred at GLYNDEBOURNE as
Orpheus in *Orpheus and Eurydice*. Bruno
WALTER, Arthur BLISS and Sir John BARBI-
ROLLI also interested themselves in her
career, and she continued to demonstrate
her exceptional talent at the EDINBURGH
FESTIVAL and at other leading international
venues, including COVENT GARDEN, before
her death at the height of her powers.
She was particularly admired for her performances of Brahms and Gustav
MAHLER, although she also recorded such
FOLK-songs as 'Blow the Wind Southerly'
with great success.

> Now I'll have *eine kleine* pause.
> KATHLEEN FERRIER, last words

Ferry, Bryan (1945–   ) British singer-
songwriter, who has enjoyed a long career
first as singer with ROXY MUSIC and then as
a solo artist. Ferry gave up his job as a
teacher to pursue music and formed Roxy
Music in 1970, going on to establish a
reputation with such singles as 'Virginia
Plain' and with the début album *Roxy
Music* (1972). The band broke up in 1976
and Ferry concentrated on a solo career,
returning to the charts with *Let's Stick
Together* (1976), *In Your Mind* (1977) and
The Bride Stripped Bare (1978) and prospering on the strength of his suave,
lady-killing image. Roxy Music re-formed
in 1978, with Ferry continuing to attract
most of the attention as the frontman. He
resumed his solo career with such albums
as *Boys and Girls* (1985), *Bête Noire* (1987),
Taxi (1993) and *Mamouna* (1994).

festival A gathering of musicians and audiences at a particular location for the playing
and appreciation of music, sometimes the
works of a particular composer or of a

school of composers. The festival is a largely twentieth-century phenomenon, with numerous venues being added to the festival calendar alongside such older established names as Bayreuth (dedicated to Wagner) and Salzburg (which pays homage to Mozart). The festivals have served to help propagate and popularize modern classical works (especially since the Second World War), although audiences at festivals of solely new music are notoriously small and frequently consist chiefly of critics and music publishers. The most notable modern festivals include those held at ALDEBURGH (famous for its association with Benjamin BRITTEN), EDINBURGH, Huddersfield, Cheltenham, La Rochelle, Metz, Warsaw (noted for popularizing the music of Karlheinz STOCKHAUSEN, Pierre BOULEZ and others) and Zagreb.

Music lovers who attend such festivals are usually on holiday, and the relaxed atmosphere at many a festival contributes to the success of the occasion, as Bernard Levin once observed: 'With the cares of daily life left behind, the claims of eternal life can be heard; no wonder music seems more intense at a festival, where music-making, for those weeks out of time, is the whole purpose of the place.'

Standards of playing are usually high, despite the fact that there is often insufficient rehearsal time (or perhaps because of this as players are obliged to concentrate harder). The festivals do have their detractors, however. Sir Thomas BEECHAM thought: 'All festivals are bunk. They are for the purpose of attracting trade to the town. What that has to do with music, I don't know.'

In terms of ROCK and POP, the great age of the festival was the late 1960s, the age of flower power, when hundreds of thousands of fans flocked to see some of the great artists of the day on both sides of the Atlantic. In the USA, the festival became a combined musical and political expression of youth culture, with mass indulgence in drugs, free love and the voicing of a desire for a better world. The biggest events included those held at MIAMI (1968), NEWPORT (1969), ATLANTA (1969) and WOODSTOCK (1969), which represented the climax of the phenomenon with some 450,000 people attending the three-day concert. There was another large gathering at Louisville, Texas, but the movement finally fell foul of the authorities after a fan was murdered during a free ROLLING STONES concert at Altamont in 1969, and such massive festivals were banned (although a record 725,000 fans attended a rock event in San Bernardino in 1983).

In the UK similar festivals included those held on the ISLE OF WIGHT and the somewhat smaller annual gatherings that continue to be staged at Glastonbury and Donington.

fiddler's neck A medical ailment, which is unique to players of the violin. An ugly discoloration of the skin occurs under the left jaw, where the violin is gripped. The condition is especially embarrassing as it may easily be mistaken for a love-bite.

Fiedler, Arthur (1894–1979) US violinist, of Austrian parentage, who won acclaim for his long-term leadership of the Boston Pops Orchestra. Having trained as a violinist, pianist and conductor, he joined the BOSTON SYMPHONY ORCHESTRA before forming the Boston Sinfonietta in 1924 and finally taking over the Boston Pops in 1930 and remaining with them for some 40 years.

Fields, Dorothy (1904–74) US lyricist and librettist, who provided the words for a number of classic hits over her long career. Daughter of the comedian Lew Fields, she wrote for the COTTON CLUB REVUES and for many other stage shows and films, often in collaboration with Jerome KERN and Harold ARLEN. Among her best-known songs were such standards as 'The Way You Look Tonight', 'I Can't Give You Anything but Love' (which Fields claimed she based on a comment she overheard from a couple gazing at the window of Tiffany's in New York), 'I'm in the Mood for Love', 'On the Sunny Side of the Street', 'A Fine Romance', 'Lovely to Look at', 'Big Spender' and 'If My Friends Could See me Now'. Most celebrated of her many librettos were those for *Annie Get Your Gun* (1946) and *Sweet Charity* (1966).

Fields, Dame Gracie (Grace Stansfield; 1898–1979) British singer and entertainer, nicknamed Our Gracie, who became a great favourite of the 1930s. Born in Rochdale, Lancashire, she worked in a cotton mill before establishing herself as a popular MUSIC HALL performer, making the most of her natural northern high spirits and good humour. Her appearances in such movies as *Sally in Our Alley* (1931), *Sing As We Go* (1934) and *Shipyard Sally* (1939) made her a major star, reinforced by her cheerful delivery of such eternally popular songs as 'I Took My Harp to a Party', 'The Biggest Aspidistra in the World' and 'Wish me Luck as you Wave me Goodbye', which was enthusiastically adopted by British troops leaving for France at the beginning of the Second World War. Her signature tune was 'Sally', which she first sang in 1931.

It all turned sour, however, after Italy entered the war, and Fields, who was married to the Italian-born Monty Banks (in Italian, Mario Bianchi), left for the USA with her husband so that he could avoid internment as an alien – an act that many of her British supporters interpreted as a betrayal. In the USA she busied herself raising funds for the war effort, but failed to win back her old audiences on her return to Britian in 1941, and the role of FORCES' SWEETHEART, which she had considered hers by right, passed to Vera LYNN.

From 1952 she lived on the island of Capri, although she did continue to make occasional appearances in films and was a regular performer at the Royal Variety Performance, having gradually made her peace with her British fans. In 1978 she travelled back to Rochdale for a theatre to be named in her honour.

Fifth Beatle, the Nickname bestowed on various people who had close links with the BEATLES at different times in the group's history.

The first contender for the title was the charismatic if introverted bassist Stuart Sutcliffe (1940–62), who played with the band in its early years when it was, indeed, a quintet. Sutcliffe met John LENNON while they were both students at Liverpool Art College and subsequently acquired a bass guitar so he could join the group, which he suggested calling the Beetles (Lennon later changing the spelling). He accompanied the band to Hamburg but fell out with Paul MCCARTNEY, with whom he fought on stage. When the Beatles returned to the UK, Sutcliffe stayed behind to develop his artistic career, but died of a brain haemorrhage at the age of 21; his image was subsequently included on the cover of the *Sergeant Pepper's Lonely Hearts Club Band* album and the Beatles track 'Baby's in Black' is said to have been written about his girlfriend Astrid Kirchherr in mourning after his death. The story of his life was retold in the film *Backbeat* (1994).

The second contender for the title was drummer Pete Best (1941–), who joined the Beatles on the eve of their departure for Hamburg in 1960 and who stayed with them until 1962, when he was replaced by Ringo STARR. He and Paul McCartney were deported from Germany after being accused of trying to set fire to their lodgings (in fact, they had tried to provide a little illumination in their unlit rooms by burning rubber contraceptives). In the UK, Best was considered leader of the group, and his drum kit was actually placed at the front of the stage. His subsequent sacking was thus a major shock, and the reasons for it remain unclear, although it has been suggested that the other members of the band may have been jealous of his success with female fans. Local feeling about Best's dismissal surfaced when outraged members of the audience attacked the group and gave George HARRISON a black eye. Best subsequently formed his own band but left music in 1968 to work in a bakery and then in the civil service.

Others who were sometimes also described as the Fifth Beatle included road manager Neil Aspinall, manager Brian EPSTEIN, producer George MARTIN, keyboard player Billy Preston and deputy drummer Jimmy Nicol. When a US disc jockey, Murray the K, started calling himself the Fifth Beatle after meeting them in 1964, Epstein was quick to demand that he stop.

> It has often been said that George Harrison was the fifth Beatle …
>
> Capitol Radio disc jockey

Fillmore, Henry (1881–1956) US composer, conductor and trombonist, who played in and conducted many of the best-known bands of his day and contributed a host of popular marches to the repertoire. He became a regular broadcasting star and was composer of such familiar marches as 'Noble Men', 'Americans We' and 'The President's March' as well as of such RAGTIME trombone pieces as 'Hot Trombone' and, for the clarinet, 'Lightning Fingers'.

film music *See* SOUNDTRACK.

Finck, Herman (Hermann von der Finck;

1872–1939) British composer and conductor, of German descent, who wrote much music for the London stage. His best-known compositions included 'In the Shadows' (1910) and music for such shows as *The Passing Show* (1914), *Vanity Fair* (1916) and *Leap Year* (1924).

Finegan, Bill (1917–) US composer, arranger and conductor, who collaborated with some of the best-known bandleaders of his day. Working with, among others, Glenn MILLER and Tommy DORSEY, he won acclaim for his arrangements of such pieces as 'Little Brown Jug', 'Jingle Bells', 'Yankee Doodletown' and 'Doodletown Races'. Also much admired was his arrangement 'Sleigh Ride', which was based on the music of Sergei PROKOFIEV; highlights of the piece included Finegan beating his chest to produce the sound of horses' hooves on packed snow.

Finzi, Gerald (1901–56) British composer, who won acclaim for his songs and orchestral pieces, which bore the influence of Sir Edward ELGAR and Ralph VAUGHAN WILLIAMS. He devised celebrated settings of lines by William Shakespeare and Thomas Hardy and also attracted praise for his concertos for clarinet and for cello among other orchestral works – the best of which included *Dies Natalis* for voice and strings (1926–50). He was an influential teacher at the Royal Academy of Music and founded the Newbury String Players ensemble in 1939.

Fiorito, Ted (1900–71) US composer, pianist and bandleader, who recorded many hits with his own popular DANCE BANDS. Best known for his theme tune 'Rio Rita', he numbered among his other hits 'Toot Toot Tootsie, Goodbye', 'When I Dream of the Last Waltz with You' and 'Roll Along, Prairie Moon'.

Fires of London, the British ensemble, which is particularly known for its performances of the works of its co-founder Peter MAXWELL DAVIES. The ensemble was set up, as the Pierrot Players (because it frequently performed Arnold SCHOENBERG's *Pierrot Lunaire*), by Maxwell Davies and Harrison BIRTWISTLE in 1967 and renamed in 1970, since when it has performed many new works with a constantly changing personnel.

First Lady of Country Music, the *See* Tammy WYNETTE.

First Lady of Soul, the *See* Aretha FRANKLIN.

First Lady of the Blues, the *See* Billie HOLIDAY.

First Tycoon of Teen, the *See* Phil SPECTOR.

Fischer-Diskau, Dietrich (1925–) German baritone and conductor, who has been acclaimed as one of the finest singers in the world. After two years as a prisoner-of-war in Italy, he made his professional début in 1947, in Brahms's *Requiem*, and subsequently won particular praise for his interpretations of songs by such composers as Beethoven, Mendelssohn, Schubert, Schumann and Richard STRAUSS. He has appeared at all the leading international venues, proving equally skilled in opera and in the concert hall. His operatic roles have included Falstaff, Figaro, Don Giovanni and Wozzeck.

Fisher, Doris (1915–) US composer, author and singer, daughter of Fred FISHER, who wrote a number of hit songs for the cinema during the 1940s. Also active as a bandleader and night club singer, she had her first hit in 1940 with 'Whispering Grass'; later hits included 'Into Each Life a Little Rain Must Fall' (1944), 'Put the Blame on Mame' (1946) and 'You Can't See the Sun when You're Crying' (1946).

Fisher, Eddie (1928–) US singer, of Russian descent, who emerged as a huge media star of the 1950s. He ranked alongside Frank SINATRA as a show business personality and had consistent commercial success with such recordings as 'I'm Walking Behind You', 'I Need You Now', 'Wish You Were Here', 'Downhearted', 'Everybody's Got a Home but Me', 'Cindy, Oh Cindy' and 'Games that Lovers Play'. The press got great copy from his many tempestuous affairs, his desertion of Debbie Reynolds in favour of Elizabeth Taylor causing a particular sensation.

Fisher, Fred (Frederic Fischer; 1875–1942) US composer, born in Germany, who wrote numerous hit songs between his first success in 1906 and the Second World War. His first hit, 'If the Man in the Moon were a Coon', enjoyed sales of over a million and was followed by such standards as 'When I Get You Alone Tonight' (1912), 'There's a Little Bit of Bad in Every Good Little Girl' (1916) and 'Dardanella' (1919), which was one of the great hits of the era and continued to sell in large numbers into the 1960s. Fisher's life provided the basis of the film *Oh, You Beautiful Doll* in 1949.

Fitzgerald, Ella (1918–96) Black US JAZZ singer and songwriter, who was first hailed as one of the jazz greats in the 1940s. Fitzgerald's career as a singer really began when she won a talent contest in New York (although she had originally intended to compete as a dancer and only resorted to a song after her nerve failed her). She did well at further talent shows and attracted the attention of bandleader Chick Webb (who took the 16-year-old orphan on and actually adopted her legally).

She enjoyed her first big hit with 'A-tisket, A-tasket' (1938), which she helped to write, and then took over Webb's band after he died (1939). Two years later she set about establishing herself as a solo artist, recording a string of hit songs in the 1940s with backing from the INK SPOTS and earning particular praise for her mastery of SCAT singing. She went on to win further acclaim singing with the bands of such great jazzmen as Count BASIE, Duke ELLINGTON and Oscar PETERSON as well as making occasional film and television appearances.

Her most popular hits included various 'Songbook' recordings of numbers by GERSHWIN, Cole PORTER and RODGERS and HART, while others closely linked to her name included 'My Happiness' (1948), 'Mack the Knife' (1960) and some of her own compositions such as 'Once is Enough For Me' (1939) and 'Shiny Stockings' (1957). Considered by many the female equivalent of Frank SINATRA, she went into semi-retirement in the 1980s because of ill-health.

fixer Slang for a musicians' agent, who fixes up bookings for his clients.

Flack, Roberta (1939–) Black US RHYTHM-AND-BLUES singer, who recorded a number of classic singles in the 1970s and early 1980s. Trained as a pianist, she released her first album, *First Take*, in 1969 and emerged as a major international star three years later with the Number One

single taken from it, 'The First Time Ever I Saw Your Face' (popularized through its use in the Clint Eastwood film *Play Misty for Me*). More hits followed in collaboration with singer Donny Hathaway (1945–79), among them 'Killing me Softly with his Song' (1973), her second US Number One, and 'Feel Like Makin' Love' (1974), which completed a hat-trick of chart-toppers in the USA. The run of successes faltered after Hathaway committed suicide in 1979, although Flack had another hit with 'Tonight I Celebrate My Love' and the album *Born to Love* (both 1983). She has produced several of her own albums under the name Rubina Flake.

Flagstad, Kirsten (Malfrid) (1895–1962) Norwegian operatic soprano, who was unsurpassed in her interpretation of the music of Wagner. The daughter of a conductor, she was about to retire after some 17 years singing in opera and operetta throughout Scandinavia when she was invited to appear at Bayreuth for the first time in 1932. She established herself as an international star and appeared at most of the major international venues. As well as works by Wagner, she excelled as a singer of music by Grieg and as Dido in Purcell's *Dido and Aeneas*, in which part she gave her last performance (1953). She also served as director of the Norwegian National Opera (1959–60).

Flanagan and Allen British singing and comedy team, which was among the most popular of all variety acts of the 1930s and 1940s. Bud Flanagan (Reuben Weintrop; 1896–1968) and Chesney Allen (1894–1982) first met in 1924 and quickly established themselves as favourites as a double-act in which Allen played the well-dressed gentleman-about-town and Flanagan an eccentric in a tattered fur coat and battered straw boater. Music played a major role in their routines, and among the hits that came to be particularly associated with them were 'Underneath the Arches', their theme song, 'We're Going to Hang out the Washing on the Siegfried Line' and 'Run, Rabbit, Run'. They appeared in numerous revues and were an essential component of the Crazy Gang, which became a national institution in the late 1930s.

Flanders and Swann British musical duo, who enjoyed huge success with a host of eccentric self-written humorous songs in the 1950s. Michael Flanders (1922–75), who was confined to a wheelchair after contracting polio, and Donald Swann (1923–94) came together to write songs for REVUE in the early 1950s, and they performed their own material for the first time in 1956. Their hilarious satirical show *At the Drop of a Hat* (1956), which poked fun at contemporary popular music, was a big West End hit and such songs as 'Have Some Madeira, M'dear', 'A Gnu' and 'The Reluctant Cannibal' became standards. Other hit songs included a series about various odd animals, among them 'The Warthog', 'The Hippopotamus' and 'The Armadillo Idyll'.

Flash Harry *See* Sir Malcolm SARGENT.

Flatt, Lester (1914–79) US COUNTRY singer and guitarist, who was one of the most popular stars associated with BLUEGRASS music. Flatt escaped work in the textile mills when he turned professional as a musician in 1939 and went on to establish himself as a performer on the GRAND OLE OPRY. In 1945 he teamed up with banjo player Earl Scruggs (1924–   ) and formed the Foggy Mountain Boys, who enjoyed huge success and did much to make country music a nationally recognized musical form. The group's most famous bluegrass numbers included 'Foggy Mountain Breakdown', 'Pike County Breakdown' and 'Flint Hill Special', although later hits such as 'Nashville Cats' and 'California Uptight Band' had a more conventional pop sound. Flatt and Scruggs parted company in 1969, after which Flatt continued to lead the band under the title Nashville Brass.

flautist's chin Medical ailment, identified in the twentieth century, which is unique to players of the flute. The condition came to public notice after being reported in the *British Medical Journal*, which described an inflammation caused by an adverse reaction of silver on the chin.

> The sound of the flute will cure epilepsy and sciatic gout.
> THEOPHRASTUS

Fleetwood Mac British SOFT ROCK group, based on the West Coast of the USA from the mid-1970s, which enjoyed huge success with a series of polished and well-constructed albums and singles. Guitarist Peter Green (1946–   ), drummer Mick Fleetwood (1942–   ), guitarist Jeremy Spencer (1948–   ) and bassist Bob Brunning then John McVie (1945–   ), who was nicknamed Big Mac because of his height, first came together in 1967 and had some success as a White BLUES band, reaching Number One with the single 'Albatross' in 1968, by which time guitarist Danny Kirwan (1950–   ) had also joined. The name Fleetwood Mac was derived from the title of an unreleased track by John MAYALL's Bluesbreakers, which was, in turn, based on their surnames. Green left in 1970, while Spencer joined a religious cult in California, and the band moved into the limelight after recruiting photogenic female vocalists Stevie Nicks (1948–   ) and Christine McVie (Christine Perfect; 1948–   ), while other new members included guitarist Lindsey Buckingham (1949–   ). Among the many top-selling releases that followed were the albums *Fleetwood Mac* (1975), the exceptional *Rumours* (1977), which sold some 25 million copies and produced no fewer than four hit singles, and *Tusk* (1979). More recent highlights of the band's long career have included *Mirage* (1982), *Tango in the Night* (1987), following which Buckingham left, *Behind the Mask* (1989) and *Time* (1995).

Fletcher, Percy E. (1879–1932) British composer and conductor, who wrote a number of well-known light classical pieces and tunes for brass bands. His most popular compositions included the waltz 'Bal Masqué' (1914), 'Woodland Pictures', 'Vanity Fair' and the march 'The Spirit of Pageantry'.

flexatone Musical instrument, which was invented as a novelty by JAZZ musicians in the early 1920s. Related to the musical saw, it was used by a number of leading contemporary composers, including Arthur HONEGGER, Arnold SCHOENBERG, Aram KHACHATURIAN and Peter MAXWELL DAVIES, who all wrote flexatone passages into their works. It consists of a steel blade against which two knobs vibrate, the pitch being altered by pressure applied to the blade by the thumb.

flexidisc A recording issued on a cheaply produced, thin vinyl disc as a gimmick or for promotional purposes. Popular with advertising agencies in the 1960s and

1970s, the flexidisc was also used by the BEATLES for special Christmas messages to members of their fan club.

FM rock Slang alternative for ADULT-ORIENTED ROCK, which refers to the FM radio waveband on which most light ROCK and POP stations are to be found.

Foley, Red (Clyde Julian Foley; 1910–68) US COUNTRY singer-songwriter and guitarist, who was one of the pioneers of the country music revival. He hosted his own radio and television programmes and was a star performer on the GRAND OLE OPRY, singing such classics as 'Old Shep', 'Chattanooga Shoeshine Boy', which topped both the country and the pop charts in 1950, the duet 'Goodnight Irene' and 'Peace in the Valley'. He was reputed to have been the first major country star to record at NASHVILLE (1945).

folk music The traditional music of a particular people, tribe or other social entity, as continually renewed over the centuries through constant repetition and revival. Folk music has been recognized in the twentieth century as one of the fundamental musical forms, and it has provided endless inspiration for all manner of composers. Around the turn of the century the classical world turned its eyes towards the neglected and apparently threatened folk traditions with new interest, and such prominent figures as Ralph VAUGHAN WILLIAMS, Gustav HOLST, Edward ELGAR, Cecil SHARP, Percy GRAINGER, Benjamin BRITTEN, Béla BARTÓK, Antonín Dvořák (1841–1904) and Zoltán KODÁLY produced major works drawing heavily on the folk traditions of their various cultures.

In the form of the BLUES, the folk tradition of the Black community of the southern USA found a new voice and ultimately informed the development of JAZZ and ROCK music, while innumerable performers in the rock and pop world have built careers delivering familiar standards in new ways (see FOLK-ROCK). More recently the folk traditions of the Third World have exerted a strong influence on western musical culture (in the form of REGGAE and AFRO-ROCK, to take two examples), while the activities of succeeding generations of singer-songwriters, from Woody GUTHRIE and Bob DYLAN to Billy BRAGG and John MARTYN, have continued to broaden definitions of what 'folk' – an already broad

term – can encompass. *See also* BLUEGRASS; ENGLISH FOLK DANCE AND SONG SOCIETY; GOSPEL; HOOTENANNY; PROTEST SONG; ZYDECO.

> Only the music which has sprung from the ancient musical traditions of a people can reach the masses of that people.
> ZOLTÁN KODÁLY

folk-rock Musical genre, which combines elements of traditional FOLK MUSIC with contemporary ROCK music. The term became established on both sides of the Atlantic around 1970 in response to a revival of interest in traditional folk music. Typically, folk-rock consists of rock arrangements of traditional ballads or new songs with a traditional feel, although it also encompasses purely instrumental pieces.

The originators of the form included the band FAIRPORT CONVENTION (formed 1966 and still active through annual reunions into the mid-1990s) and its offshoot STEELEYE SPAN, both of which enjoyed considerable commercial success and had a lasting influence. Other names associated with the genre include the BYRDS, JETHRO TULL, LINDISFARNE, SIMON AND GARFUNKEL, the ALBION BAND and Richard THOMPSON. Among their descendants must be included such richly talented singer-songwriters as Billy BRAGG, Mary Coughlan and Suzanne Vega. *See also* HOOTENANNY; PROTEST SONG.

> Folk music is a bunch of fat people.
> BOB DYLAN

football songs In the UK the twentieth century has witnessed the great age of the football song, which has thrived even as the game itself has variously prospered and gone into decline. Football now boasts a substantial musical sub-culture, which is little documented but is nonetheless shared by countless thousands of fans. Examples of borrowings from the pop charts in relatively recent times have included:

John Denver's 'Annie's Song' (Sheffield United)
Harry Belafonte's 'Banana Boat Song' (Meadowbank Thistle)
Eric Idle's 'Bright Side of Life' (universal)
Glenn Miller's 'Chattanooga Choo Choo' (Crewe Alexandra)
Phil Spector's 'Da Doo Ron Ron' (Bradford City)
Tom Jones's 'Delilah' (Stoke City)

Manfred Mann's 'Doo Wah Diddy'
(Leeds United)
Dave Clark Five's 'Glad All Over' (Crystal
Palace)
Jeff Beck's 'Hi Ho Silver Lining' (Sheffield
Wednesday; Sheffield United)
The Scaffold's 'Lily the Pink' (Manchester
United; Halifax)
Manfred Mann's 'Mighty Quinn'
(universal)
Paul McCartney's 'Mull of Kintyre'
(Charlton Athletic)
Frank Sinatra's 'My Way' (Heart of
Midlothian)
Elvis Presley's 'Only Fools Rush In'
(Sunderland)
Rod Stewart's 'Sailing' (Millwall)
The Beatles' 'Twist and Shout' (Coventry
City)
Bing Crosby's 'White Christmas'
(Manchester City)

Examples of football songs that have reversed the process and become pop hits include Chelsea's 'Blue is the Colour', Tottenham Hotspur's 'Nice One, Cyril' (referring to their star player Cyril Knowles), Leeds United's 'Leeds, Leeds, Leeds' and various anthems trotted out by national teams on the eve of major international competitions (notably England's 'Back Home', 1970 and 'Three Lions', 1996).

Portsmouth is famous for the 'Pompey Chimes', which consists of the single line 'Play up Pompey, Pompey play up' repeated over and over to the tune of a chiming clock. West Ham United supporters have adopted 'I'm Forever Blowing Bubbles' as their anthem and Liverpool fans give spirited renditions of 'You'll Never Walk Alone', while Blackburn Rovers supporters sing 'The Wild Rover' and Newcastle United is uniquely associated with 'The Blaydon Races'. Fans at the FA Cup Final at Wembley sing the hymn 'Abide With Me'. North of the border, archrivals Celtic and Rangers exchange Irish revolutionary songs and patriotic loyalist hymns with heated fervour.

Among the oddest British football songs are Leyton Orient's couplet 'We're all mad, we're insane, we eat Mars bars on the train'; Notts County's refrain 'I had a wheelbarrow, the wheel fell off', which is repeated ad infinitum; and Hartlepool United's version of 'Just One of Those Songs':

Me brother's in borstal,
Me sister's got pox,

Me mother's a whore down Hartlepool
docks,
Me uncle's a pervert
Me aunty's gone mad
And Jack the Ripper's me dad,
La, la, la . . .

No less a figure than Sir Thomas BEECHAM served on the board of a major football club: he was chairman of Bolton Wanderers when they won the FA Cup in 1958.

Forces' Sweetheart, the *See* Dame Vera LYNN.

Ford, 'Tennessee' Ernie (Ernest Jennings Ford; 1919–91) US COUNTRY singer, nicknamed Mister Country Music, who had a series of hits in the late 1940s and 1950s. Widely known for his catchphrase 'Howdy, pea-pickers', he recorded such country numbers as 'Mule Train' (1949) and 'Smokie Mountain Boogie' (1949) as well as having success in both country and ROCK 'N' ROLL charts with the Number One 'Sixteen Tons' (1955) and 'Give Me Your Word' (1955). He also hosted his own television shows and issued several GOSPEL albums in the 1970s.

Forde, Florrie (Florence Flanagan; 1876–1940) Australian music hall singer, nicknamed the Australian Marie Lloyd, who was one of the best-loved MUSIC HALL stars of the First World War era. Having made her début in the UK in 1897, she enjoyed enormous success with such rousing songs as 'Hold Your Hand Out, Naughty Boy', 'Down at the Old Bull and Bush', 'Pack up Your Troubles in Your Old Kit Bag', 'It's a Long Way to Tipperary' and 'Has Anybody Here Seen Kelly?'. Her memory is preserved at the Old Bull and Bush public house in Hampstead, which boasts its own Florrie Forde bar, and in the many recordings she made.

Foreigner Anglo-American rock band, which emerged as one of the most popular ADULT-ORIENTED ROCK bands of the 1980s. Named Foreigner because the members hailed from both sides of the Atlantic, the band was formed by Englishman Mick Jones (1944–) in 1976, with the vocals being supplied by US singer Lou Gramm (1950–). Other members included Ian McDonald (1946–), Dennis Elliott (1950–) and Ed Gagliardi (1952–). The first album, *Foreigner* (1977), established the band's reputation, and it confirmed its popular standing with such releases as the albums *Double Vision* (1978), *Head Games* (1979), *4* (1981), *Records* (1982), *Inside Information* (1987) and *Unusual Heat* (1991) and the singles 'Feels Like the First Time' (1977), 'Cold as Ice' (1977), 'Waiting for a Girl Like You' (1981) and 'I Want to Know What Love Is' (1984), which reached Number One in both the US and the British charts.

Foresythe, Reginald (1907–58) British composer, arranger and pianist, who wrote many hit tunes in the 1930s. Foresythe divided his time between the UK and the USA, where he collaborated with the bands of Earl HINES and Paul WHITEMAN among others. His best-known compositions included 'Deep Forest', which became the theme tune of Hines' band, 'Strange Interlude', 'Southern Holiday' and 'Mississippi Basin'.

formalism Derogatory term, which was applied by the Soviet regime to works by Dmitri SHOSTAKOVICH, Sergei PROKOFIEV and other contemporaries in the 1930s and 1940s. Such pieces as the Shostakovich opera *Katerina Ismailova* (1936) – better known as *Lady Macbeth of the Mtsensk District* – were roundly condemned as subversive and lacking proper social Marxist concern. As a result of the criticism Shostakovich withdrew his Fourth Symphony later that year while it was still in rehearsal and it was not performed until 25 years later. Shostakovich described his Fifth Symphony as the 'creative reply of a Soviet artist to just criticism', although this meekness was seen as ironic by some critics, and a later symphony (the Thirteenth in 1962) was interpreted as a veiled attack on Stalin' government.

Somewhat confusingly, the criticism levelled at such works had nothing to do with their 'form' (indeed, approved music of the period was highly formal) but rather with the accusation that they were 'artificial' and indulged in intellectual preoccupations at the cost of their social relevance. *See also* PORNOPHONY; SOCIALIST REALISM.

> Formalism is music that people don't understand at first hearing.
> SERGEI PROKOFIEV

Formby, George (George Hoy Booth; 1904–61) British comedian and singer, who was the star of numerous light film comedies in the 1930s and 1940s. He was the son of George Formby (James Booth; 1877–1921), a popular comedian who had success with comic songs, such as 'John Willie, Come On', 'Playing the Game in the West' and 'All of a Sudden it Struck Me', and who called himself Formby after the town of that name. The younger Formby was a jockey until 1921, when he began a stage career on the death of his father, performing many of the latter's best-known hits. Projecting a gormless Lancashire stage persona, he became a huge star and appeared in many films, the action of which was regularly interrupted for Formby to sing a comedy number to the accompaniment of his ukulele-banjo. His most famous songs included 'When I'm Cleaning Windows' (1936), which was the subject of a BBC ban because of its mildly risqué lyrics, 'With My Little Stick of Blackpool Rock' (1937) and 'Leaning on a Lamp-post' (1937). Since his relatively early death within weeks of that of his wife, who had helped steer him to stardom, Formby has become the focus of a thriving Formby industry, with devotees meeting regularly to discuss and to imitate their idol's music.

formula Technical term employed by Karlheinz STOCKHAUSEN to describe the underlying melody or group of melodies in his compositions. Stockhausen's choice of word neatly underlines the mathematical preoccupations behind much of his music.

Four Seasons, the US male vocal group, led by Rudi Valli (Francis Castellucio; 1937–), which enjoyed a long series of hits in the 1960s. Named the Four Seasons after the cocktail lounge of a bowling alley, the band, which at its best consisted of Valli, Tommy De Vito (1936–), Bob Gaudio (1942–) and Nick Massi (1935–), came together in 1956 and were regularly in the charts with such falsetto vocal hits as 'Sherry' (1962), 'Big Girls Don't Cry' (1962), 'Rag Doll' (1963) and 'Walk Like a Man' (1963), all of which reached Number One in the USA. For a while the group was even touted as the US equivalent of the BEATLES.

Valli also established himself as a solo artist, enjoying similar success with 'Can't Take My Eyes off You' and 'My Eyes Adored You' and making a come-back in 1975 with 'December '63 (Oh, What a Night)'.

The group returned to the limelight with a new album in 1985 and has now amassed more chart hits over the years than any other US group.

'Sherry', the song that made the Four Seasons famous, was written just 15 minutes before it was recorded, and the percussion was provided by banging a piece of wood on the floor because the group could not afford to employ a drummer.

Four Tops, the US vocal group of the 1960s, originally founded in 1953 as the Four Aims, which emerged as one of the top MOTOWN soul acts of the era. Lead singer Levi Stubbs, Abdul Fakir, Renaldo Benson and Lawrence Payton joined Motown in 1963 and went on to enjoy a series of hit singles, of which 'I Can't Help Myself' reached Number One in the USA in 1965; others included 'Reach Out, I'll be There', which was a transatlantic Number One in 1966, 'Walk Away Renee' and 'If I were a Carpenter'. The group maintained its popular standing in the 1970s and 1980s with re-releases of old standards and such new hits as 'Indestructible' and 'Loco in Acapulco'. Levi Stubbs also provided the voice for the carnivorous plant of the movie *Little Shop of Horrors* (1986).

Fragson, Harry (Léon Philippe Pott; 1869– 1913) British singer, songwriter and pianist, of Anglo-Belgian extraction, who was one of the biggest stars of the MUSIC HALL at the time of his premature death. Popular in the halls of both Paris and London, Fragson established his reputation in the 1880s and 1890s singing clever comic songs tht he wrote himself. His best-known hits included, in France, 'Reviens!' and, in England, 'Hello! Hello! Who's Your Lady Friend?' (1913). His career was cut short at its peak when his father took exception to a plan to have him put in an old folk's home and shot his son dead.

Frampton, Peter (1950–) British rock guitarist, who emerged as one of the top 'AXE heroes' of the 1970s. Having gone to the same school as David BOWIE, he started by playing RHYTHM-AND-BLUES with the Herd and was tipped for TEENY-BOP stardom on the strength of his blond good looks, but he co-founded the heavy rock band Humble Pie and embarked on a solo career in straight rock in the early 1970s with his own band Frampton's Camel. His best-selling albums included the hugely successful live album *Frampton Comes Alive!* (1976), from which came the hit singles 'Show Me the Way' and 'Baby, I Love Your Way'. Despite a serious car crash, he enjoyed further successes up to the end of the decade before taking an extended rest, eventually returning to play for Bowie in the late 1980s.

Francis, Connie (Concetta Rosa Maria Franconero; 1938–) US singer, who was the most commercially successful female recording artist of the late 1950s and early 1960s. Having signed her first recording contract when she was just 16 years old, she failed to make any impression on the charts with her first few releases, but then established her reputation in 1958 with the 1923 song 'Who's Sorry Now', which reached Number One in the UK charts. She made the US Top 10 22 times and the UK Top 20 18 times and had further Number One hits with 'Carolina Moon/Stupid Cupid', 'Everybody's Somebody's Fool', 'My Heart has a Mind of its Own' and 'Don't Break the Heart That Loves You'. In all, these and such other enduring standards as 'Lipstick on your Collar' notched up some 40 million sales before her career went into decline during the BEATLES era. She gave music up in 1974 when she was robbed and raped after a concert but resumed live performances in the 1980s. A collection of her hits reached Number One in the album charts in the UK in 1977.

Frankie Boy *See* Frank SINATRA.

Frankie Goes To Hollywood British pop group, which had huge, if controversial, commercial success in the 1980s. Fronted by lead vocalist William 'Holly' Johnson (1960–), the band was founded in Liverpool in 1982 and named after an old newspaper headline about Frank SINATRA. Other members of the line-up were singer Paul Rutherford (1959–), bassist Mark O'Toole (1964–), drummer Peter Gill (1960–) and guitarist Brian Nash (1963–). The band achieved instant fame with the single 'Relax' (1984), which was banned by BBC Radio One because of its strong sexual content and which, largely as a consequence, stormed to Number One, as did the follow-ups, 'Two Tribes' (which took contemporary politics as its theme) and 'The Power of Love' (which took a poke at religion), making the group the first since GERRY AND THE PACEMAKERS to have their first three singles go all the way to the top. The accompanying album *Welcome to the Pleasuredome* reached Number One, and the band became the focus of a thriving Frankie Goes to Hollywood industry based on the sales of 'Frankie says' T-shirts and other accessories.

Further progress was disrupted by failure as a live band and pressures from the taxman. In the court cases that ensued, Johnson shocked the fans when he revealed that the band had not actually played on early versions of either 'Relax' or 'Two Tribes'. The group eventually split in 1987, with Holly Johnson starting a solo career. Its legacy included a whole series of bands with odd Frankie-inspired names, among them Frankie Goes To Cricklewood, Ronnie Goes To Liverpool, Pepe Goes To Cuba, Bonzo Goes to Washington and Cyril Trots To Bognor.

Franklin, Aretha (1942–) Black US RHYTHM-AND-BLUES singer, nicknamed the First Lady of Soul or the Queen of Soul, who emerged as a leading star in the late 1960s and eventually released more million-selling singles than any other female artist. The daughter of a celebrated Baptist preacher and GOSPEL singer, she established her reputation with such hits as 'Respect' (1967) and the album *I Never Loved a Man (The Way I Love You)* (1967). Among her prolific output of top hits were 'Chain of Fools' (1968), the album *Lady Soul* (1968), 'Think' (1968), a startling soul version of 'The Star-spangled Banner'(1968) and 'Angel' (1973). Her album *Amazing Grace* (1972) saw her return to her early experiences as a GOSPEL singer, while other releases included collaborations with Ray CHARLES and Stevie WONDER. Her music was somewhat eclipsed with the rise of FUNK in the late 1970s, although she returned to the charts in 1985 with singles from the album *Who's Zoomin' Who*. More recent releases include another gospel album, *One Lord, One Faith, One Baptism* (1987).

Freddie and the Dreamers British BEAT group, which enjoyed a series of light-hearted hits in the mid-1960s. Based in Manchester, the band consisted of vocalist and former milkman Freddie Garritty

(1940–), guitarists Derek Quinn (1942–) and Roy Crewsdon (1941–), bassist Pete Birrell (1941–) and drummer Bernie Dwyer (1940–). The group's hits between 1963 and 1965 included 'If You Gotta Make a Fool of Somebody', 'I'm Telling You Now', which reached Number One in the USA in 1965, 'You Were Made for Me' and 'Thou Shalt not Steal'.

Free British ROCK band of the late 1960s and early 1970s, which enjoyed huge commercial success playing blues-oriented rock. Formed in 1968, the band's members were vocalist Paul Rodgers (1949–), guitarist Paul Kossoff (1950–76), bassist Andy Fraser (1952–) and drummer Simon Kirke (1949–). Promoted by Alexis KORNER, the band prospered under Rodgers and Kossoff (son of the actor David Kossoff). The first album, *Tons of Sobs*, was followed by *Free* (1969) and *Fire and Water* (1970), from which came the classic hit single 'All Right Now'. Internal rifts within the group led to a split after the album *Highway* (1971) and the hit single 'My Brother Jake', but the group came back together to record *Free At Last* (1972) and *Heartbreaker* (1973). The band broke up for good in 1973, Rodgers and Kirke forming BAD COMPANY and Kossoff dying in 1976 of a heart attack, a consequence of drug addiction.

free jazz Genre in JAZZ, which emerged as a new – and controversial – force in the 1960s as musicians experimented with increasingly complex improvisations on a single theme and incorporated ATONALITY in their compositions. Leading exponents of free jazz of the period included Ornette COLEMAN, who pioneered the style in such highly influential albums as *The Shape Of Jazz To Come* and *Change the Century* (both 1959) and *Free Jazz* (1960).

> Free is not a style. It's a personal ability. Playing free is not having to have a style.
> ORNETTE COLEMAN, *Down Beat*, 1973

Freed, Alan (1922–65) US DISC JOCKEY, who played a crucial role in the early development of ROCK 'N' ROLL. Broadcasting from Cleveland and later from New York, he claimed to have coined the term 'rock 'n' roll' (although this is disputed) and promoted its popularity by playing records by Black artists to his predominantly White audience (a controversial step that led to riots on more than one occasion). Hailed for his contribution to pop and rock, everything turned sour when Freed was singled out and disgraced in the PAYOLA SCANDAL of 1959; he died in obscurity, a virtual alcoholic, while facing charges of income tax evasion.

Freed, Arthur (Arthur Grossman; 1894–1973) US film producer and lyricist, who was foremost among the producers of the early Hollywood film MUSICAL. Freed began his career as a vaudeville performer and later wrote for revues and army shows before producing his own highly influential shows. He contributed the lyrics for the first full-length film musical, *Broadway Melody* (1929), and went on to produce such classics for MGM as *Babes in Arms* (1939), *The Wizard of Oz* (1939), *Lady Be Good* (1941), *Girl Crazy* (1943), *Meet Me In St Louis* (1944), *Easter Parade* (1948), *On the Town* (1949), *Annie Get Your Gun* (1949), *Show Boat* (1951), *An American In Paris* (1951), *Singin' in the Rain* (1952) and *Gigi* (1958). Many of the songs featured in his films were by his own hand, often written in collaboration with composer Nacio Herb BROWN.

Freeman, Bud (Lawrence Freeman; 1906–91) US JAZZ saxophonist, who emerged as one of the giants of Chicago style jazz in the late 1920s. He played tenor saxophone for the bands of such distinguished jazzmen as Gene KRUPA, Bunny BERIGAN and Cozy COLE and was particularly celebrated for his performance of such numbers as 'The Eel', which he recorded with the band of Eddie CONDON in 1933. After the Second World War he divided his career between the USA and the UK.

Freni, Mirella (1935–) Italian soprano, who has established a worldwide reputation playing a range of operatic roles. She made her début in *Carmen* in 1955 and has since appeared at many leading venues in such works as Verdi's *La Traviata* and Puccini's *Madame Butterfly*, joining the Paris Opéra in 1970.

Friedhofer, Hugo Wilhelm (1901–81) US composer and cellist, who wrote much music for Hollywood movies of the 1940s and 1950s. Among his many film scores were those for successes starring Errol Flynn, *Brewster's Millions* (1945), *The Best*

Years of Our Lives (1946), for which he won an OSCAR, *Joan of Arc* (1948), *An Affair to Remember* (1957) and *Beauty and the Beast* (1962).

Friend, Cliff (1893–1974) US composer, who provided the scores for a series of hit MUSICAL shows and revues from which came a number of popular songs. Having begun in vaudeville, he wrote the scores for such shows as *The Passing Show of 1921* (1920), *George White's Scandals* (1929), *Earl Carroll's Vanities* (1931) and *Shine On, Harvest Moon* (1944). Among his best-known songs were 'Blue Hoosier Blues' (1923), 'Let me Linger Longer in Your Arms' (1924), 'My Blackbirds are Bluebirds Now' (1928) and 'When My Dreamboat Comes Home' (1936).

Friml, Rudolf (1879–1972) US composer, born in Prague, who wrote a series of highly successful stage MUSICALS reminiscent of Viennese operetta. The son of a baker, he studied music in Prague (at one point under Dvořák) and emigrated to the USA in 1906, where he established himself as a composer for the musical theatre with *The Firefly*. His most acclaimed musicals included *Rose Marie* (1924) and *The Vagabond King* (1925). He also wrote SOUNDTRACKS for a number of Hollywood movies.

Fripp, Robert (1946–) British guitarist and composer, who won admiration as a talented AVANT-GARDE rock musician. He became famous as lynchpin of the ART ROCK band KING CRIMSON in the late 1960s and early 1970s and strengthened his cult status with albums made in collaboration with Brian ENO, in which he explored the possibilities of ELECTRONIC ROCK (dubbed 'Frippertronics'). He revived King Crimson in 1981 and has since played with such stars as David BOWIE and Peter GABRIEL. Recent releases include *Robert Fripp and the League of Crafty Guitarists: Live!* (1986), which was based on his masterclasses.

Fuller, Jesse (1896–1976) US BLUES singer, guitarist and composer, nicknamed Lone Cat, who was recognized as a leading bluesman during the blues revival of the 1950s. Having led a wandering life for many years after running away from home (the origins of his nickname), he established himself as a blues performer in San Francisco in the late 1930s and made many recordings. He later toured internationally as a one-man band, his best-known songs including 'San Francisco Bay Blues' (1954).

funk Broad category of largely Black POP music, which encompasses up-tempo SOUL and DISCO as well as its more modern expression as ELECTRO-FUNK, in which guise it has dominated the charts on both sides of the Atlantic since 1980. It is descended from the BLUES and JAZZ and related to ROCK, RAP and other musical forms, although its chief purpose generally is to provide music to dance to. Various pulsing rhythms and electric guitar sounds may be identified as 'funky'. Top names associated with funk include James BROWN, Otis REDDING, Wilson PICKETT, EARTH, WIND AND FIRE and Stevie WONDER.

The word 'funk' was first heard in the early 1950s, as a back-formation of 'funky', which originally denoted anything bad smelling or earthy and was often applied to traditional blues music and some forms of modern jazz (it also had sexual connotations).

funk-metal Genre of rock music, which emerged in the late 1980s through the combination of FUNK with HEAVY METAL. Commercially successfully expressions of the genre at its outset included the 1986 hit single 'Walk This Way', which involved the funk group Run DMC and the heavy metal band AEROSMITH.

furniture music An early form of CANNED MUSIC, which was conceived by the composer Erik SATIE. Identified in French as *musique d'ameublement*, furniture music was intended to remain firmly in the background, as Satie himself explained: 'We must bring about a music which is like furniture – a music, that is, which will be part of the noises of the environment, which will take them into consideration.' Satie collaborated with Darius MILHAUD on his first venture into such music (although it was Arthur HONEGGER who wrote the first such work, in 1919). His friend Pierre Bertin introduced the 'performance':

> We earnestly beg of you not to attach any importance to it and to behave throughout as if it did not exist. This music ... claims to contribute to life in the same way as a private conversation, as a picture in the gallery, or the chair on which you may or may not be sitting.

Such pieces were enthusiastically received by a minority of contemporary composers and cognoscenti. Admirers included such controversial figures as Jean Cocteau, who was moved by Satie's work to demand in 1918: 'Enough of clouds, waves, aquariums, water-sprites and nocturnal scents; what we need is a music of the earth, everyday music ... music one can live in like a house.'

Some contemporary composers such as John CAGE developed the idea in frustration at the misuse of music as a means of distraction, entertainment or acquisition of 'culture', although risking their own works going unheard or being at best ill-appreciated. *See also* MUZAK.

> The use of music as a kind of ambrosia to titillate the aural senses while one's conscious mind is otherwise occupied is the abomination of every composer who takes his work seriously.
>
> AARON COPLAND

Furtwängler, Wilhelm (1886–1954) German conductor and composer, who enjoyed an international reputation as director (1922–45 and 1948–54) of the BERLIN PHILHARMONIC ORCHESTRA. The son of a noted archaeologist, he gave up composing to concentrate on conducting and won many admirers for his free interpretations of scores by such composers as Beethoven, Brahms, Bruckner and Wagner as well as new works by such contemporaries as Arnold SCHOENBERG and Paul HINDEMITH, although some critics were outraged at the liberties he took with time signatures. He made many guest appearances with leading orchestras around the world and was a regular conductor at the Bayreuth and Salzburg festivals, although his retention of his prominent position during the Nazi era did cause some controversy and he was not allowed to conduct in the USA as a result (although he eventually received permission to work in the UK). As a composer, he produced two symphonies, a piano concerto and religious and chamber music.

> Gentlemen, this phrase must be – it must be – it must – you know what I mean – please try it again.
>
> WILHELM FURTWÄNGLER, during a rehearsal

Fury, Billy (Ronald Wycherley; 1941–83) British ROCK 'N' ROLL star, who was one of the most successful UK rivals to Elvis PRESLEY and Jerry Lee LEWIS. Born in Liverpool, he sprang to fame overnight after slipping backstage at a Marty WILDE concert and persuading Wilde to listen to his songs. The following evening Fury was opening the show. 'Maybe Tomorrow', his first single, reached the charts in 1959 and his third single, 'Colette', was the first to break into the Top 10. A string of rock 'n' roll hits followed, and he established a reputation as a live performer, outraging many with his suggestive performances.

Fury adopted a more mellow tone in the early 1960s (partly to appease his own father), but the hits continued with such singles as 'Halfway to Paradise' (1961) and 'Jealousy' (1961). By 1965 he had reached the Top 10 no fewer than 11 times, although he never had a Number One. Towards the end of the decade he moved into cabaret and continued to make occasional film appearances, including *That'll be the Day* (1973).

Fury had suffered rheumatic fever as a child and was never in robust health; he died of a heart attack at the age of 42 while recording a comeback album (released as *The Only One* after his death).

fusion In JAZZ slang the blending of jazz with ROCK, Asian, classical or some other musical style. Leading exponents of fusion, which exists alongside such counterparts as MAIN-STREAM and AVANT-GARDE jazz, include Miles DAVIS, Stanley Clarke, John MCLAUGHLIN and the band WEATHER REPORT, which was at the forefront of the style when it was first identified in the early 1970s. The term is also occasionally applied to similar genres in which elements of two distinct traditions are merged (such as folk and rock), a more modern version of it being the slangy 'fuzak'. *See also* CROSSOVER; JAZZ ROCK; THIRD STREAM.

Future of Rock 'n' Roll, the *See* Bruce SPRINGSTEEN.

futurism Musical genre of the 1920s and 1930s, which placed great emphasis on addressing classical music to the modern, industrialized world. Originating from the literary movement founded by the Italian poet Filippo Tommaso Marinetti (1876–1944) in 1909, the first futurist works were heard in 1914, when Marinetti and the composer Luigi Rossolo (1885–1947) gave a concert of such music in Milan. The programme consisted of four pieces, variously titled 'Awakening of Capital', 'Meeting of Cars and Aeroplanes', 'Dining on the Terrace of the Casino' and 'Skirmish in the Oasis'. Much of the 'music' was played on a variety of odd instruments, ranging from whistles to assorted percussive devices, and the concert itself culminated in a battle between performers and audience. The genre went on to prosper after the war when it won the approval of Mussolini's fascist regime. Francesco Pratella (1880–1955) and others produced numerous works that typically incorporated or mimicked the sounds of factories and railways and so forth in an optimistic celebration of man's technological progress. The movement, somewhat predictably, fell into disrepute after the defeat of the Fascists in the Second World War.

> We shall amuse ourselves by orchestrating in our minds the noise of metal shutters of shop windows, the slamming of doors, the bustle and shuffle of crowds, the multitudinous uproar of railway stations, forges, mills, printing presses, power stations and underground railways.
> LUIGI RUSSOLO, 'The Art of Noises', 1913

> A roaring motor car ... is more beautiful than the Victory of Samothrace.
> FILIPPO MARINETTI

fuzz box An electronic device, usually operated as a foot pedal, which distorts the sound of an ELECTRIC GUITAR or other instruments to produce a rough, 'fuzzy' quality. Before the advent of the fuzz box, guitarists discovered that they could get much the same effect by using a pencil to pierce a hole in one of the speakers of their amplifiers. This idea was first tried by guitarist Link Wray, who reached number 16 in the US charts in 1958 with the instrumental 'Rumble', which featured such a sound. The innovation was an immediate success with some of the rougher elements in audiences of the day, as Wray himself recalled: 'Even the cops were scared of 'em. I had to play 'Rumble' five times for those guys, y'know. They'd line up against the stage and I'd have to start the number all over again!'

G

Gabriel, Peter (1950–) British ROCK singer, who achieved fame as lead singer of GENESIS and went on to establish a highly successful solo career. Gabriel's theatrical flair and taste for the unconventional were largely responsible for the emergence of Genesis as one of the most innovative progressive rock bands of the early 1970s. Having co-founded the band in 1968, he continued to serve as lead singer – often in bizarre make-up and fantastical costumes – until 1975, when Phil COLLINS took his place. His best-selling solo albums, four of which were issued under the simple title *Peter Gabriel*, reflected his interest in Third World issues and produced such hit singles as 'Solsbury Hill' (1977), which described his feelings on leaving Genesis, 'Biko' (1978), which was dedicated to the murdered South African Black activist, 'Games Without Frontiers' (1978) and 'Shock the Monkey' (1982). *So* reached Number One in the UK in 1986, while the single 'Sledgehammer' prospered partly on the strength of a striking animated video; other recent works have included the albums *Us* (1992) and *Secret World Live* (1994). In 1982 he organized the first of several WOMAD (World of Music, Arts and Dance) events to bring respected artists from all over the world to the UK.

Gaillard, Slim (Bulee Gaillard; 1916–91) Cuban-born US singer-songwriter, guitarist and pianist, resident in the UK from 1983, who was one of the most eccentric of all JAZZ performers. A natural comedian and storyteller, Gaillard gave many colourful accounts of his childhood and subsequent career. Extraordinary incidents included his being marooned in Crete while still a child after his father's ship sailed off without him and adventures in such occupations as boxer, undertaker and bootlegger. He worked as a tap dancing guitarist in vaudeville before forming a classic partnership with bassist Roy 'Slam' Stewart (1914–87) and going on to develop his own distinctive version of 'jive talk' (*see* VOUT).

Such hits as 'Flat Foot Floogie' and 'Cement Mixer (Put-ti Put-ti)' consolidated Gaillard's reputation and brought him into contact with Charlie PARKER, Dizzy GILLESPIE and other jazz greats. His children's song 'Down at the Station' was said to have inspired the Rev W. Awdry to write the now celebrated *Thomas the Tank Engine* stories.

By the 1950s Gaillard had attained cult status (his live act – during the course of which he played a piano with his hands upside down – was described in detail in Jack Kerouac's *On the Road*), and his face became familiar outside jazz through his appearances in films and television shows. His cameo performances on the screen ranged from *Absolute Beginners* to *Roots – the Next Generation* and *Charlie's Angels*. His score for 'Flat Foot Floogie' was one of the items buried in a time capsule at the New York World's Fair in 1939.

Gallagher, Rory (1949–95) Irish rock guitarist and singer, who won recognition as a prominent BLUES-ROCK musician in the early 1970s. Gallagher played guitar with the blues-rock band Taste in the late 1960s and subsequently established himself as a solo star, his hit albums including *Rory Gallagher* (1971), *Deuce* (1971), *Live in Europe* (1972), *Tattoo* (1973) and *Stage Struck* (1980) as well as the more recent *Fresh Evidence* (1990), which continued in a similar vein, Gallagher remaining obstinately impervious to all fads and fashions. To the end he played the same ageing Stratocaster (*see* FENDER) with which he began his career in the 1960s.

Galli-Curci, Amelita (1882–1963) Italian coloratura soprano, resident in the USA from 1916, who was one of the leading singers of her time. Having taught herself to sing, she became a top star with the New York METROPOLITAN, at which she appeared regularly over many years before her retirement in 1937. Her most celebrated roles included Gilda in Verdi's *Rigoletto*, in which part she made her operatic début in 1906, Elvira in *I Puritani* and Violetta in *La Traviata*.

Audiences remained loyal to her throughout her career, despite the fact that she often sang out of tune and could barely act.

Galway, James (1939–) Northern Ireland-born flautist, nicknamed the Man with the Golden Flute after his famous A.K. Cooper 14-carat gold flute. After rising to the position of principal flute with the LONDON SYMPHONY ORCHESTRA, he achieved fame when he joined the BERLIN PHILHARMONIC, then under Herbert von KARAJAN, in 1969. In 1975 he embarked on a solo career, winning a massive audience playing a range of classical, light and even popular music and making regular appearances in the media, despite a serious accident. Several works by major contemporary composers have been written for him, among them Thea MUSGRAVE's *Orpheus*.

garage band An amateur ROCK or POP group, which rehearses in a garage or in other modest surroundings. Notable works to issue from garages over the years have included the Zager and Evans single 'In the Year 2525', Herb ALPERT's first record ('The Lonely Bull') and the Chet ATKINS album *Country Gentlemen*.

Gardel, Carlos (1887–1935) French-born Argentinian-Uruguayan singer, nicknamed the Thrush and the Blue Voice, who achieved superstar status both in South America and Europe in the 1920s with songs set to the tango. He continued with the tango in several MUSICAL films, such as *Tango on Broadway* (1934), but his career was terminated by his death in an aircrash, following which he was given the biggest funeral in the history of Buenos Aires.

Gardiner, (Henry) Balfour (1877–1950) British composer, who did much to promote the performance of works by contemporary composers such as Gustav HOLST and Percy GRAINGER. Gardiner, who composed works including *Shepherd Fennel's Dance* (1911), organized concerts, often meeting the costs himself.

Gardiner, John Eliot (1943–) British conductor, who was widely recognized as one of the most influential figures in British contemporary classical music in the 1980s. Having studied music at King's College, London, and in Paris under Nadia BOULANGER, he served as principal conductor of the CBC Vancouver Orchestra

(1980–83), as musical director (1983–88) and chef fondateur (from 1991) of the Opéra de Lyon Orchestra and in 1991 was made principal conductor of the North German Radio Orchestra. Also, founding artistic director of the English Baroque Soloists, the Monteverdi Choir and Orchestra, he has won acclaim throughout Europe and the US for his work on baroque and choral music and his recordings which include Handel, Massenet, Monteverdi, Mozart, Purcell and Rameau.

Garland, Joe (Joseph Copeland; 1903–) US composer, arranger and saxophonist, who created many standard tunes for JAZZ bands in the 1930s and 1940s. A player with Jelly Roll MORTON in the 1920s and later with stars like Louis ARMSTRONG and Earl HINES, he wrote such classics as 'In the Mood'.

Garland, Judy (Frances Ethel Gumm; 1922–69) US film actress and singer, who achieved legendary status both for her performances and for her troubled and ultimately tragic private life. Born in Grand Rapids, Minnesota, she made her stage début at the age of five, performing alongside her two older sisters as the Gumm Sisters Kiddie Act. Encouraged by her mother, she won her first film contract, with MGM, at the age of 13 and went on to establish herself as a great favourite in a series of popular films, often with Mickey Rooney. Her rendition of 'You Made Me Love You', addressed to a picture of Clark Gable, in *Broadway Melody of 1938* (1937) proved her potential as a major singing star, and hits included 'Over the Rainbow' from *The Wizard of Oz* (1939), for which she received an Oscar, 'I'm Nobody's Baby' (1940) and 'The Trolley Song' (1944).

Despite winning huge acclaim for her roles in films like *Meet Me in St Louis* (1944), *Easter Parade* (1948) and *A Star is Born* (1954), partnering, among others, Fred ASTAIRE and Gene KELLY, she was always subject to psychiatric problems. She eventually succumbed to her addiction to drugs and alcohol, one of the most tragic victims of the 'star system'. It was reported that at the moment of her death a tornado hit Kansas (evoking memories of her greatest role, as Dorothy in *The Wizard of Oz*). She had five husbands, and her daughter, Liza MINNELLI, emerged as a major star in her own right in the 1970s.

Garner, Erroll (1921–77) US JAZZ pianist and

composer, nicknamed the Picasso of the Piano or the Elf on account of his diminutive size, who won a huge audience with his unusual blues-based piano style. Largely self-taught and unable to read music, he developed an appealing, relaxed stage act and was often seen on television (sometimes sitting on a telephone directory in order to reach the keys). He led his own trio from 1946 and made a number of European tours. His most popular compositions included the much covered 'Misty', 'Dreamy' and 'Solitaire'; among his albums was the best-selling *Concert by the Sea* (1958).

> ... that Errol Garner style – inimitable style – which has been imitated by more pianists than you've had hot dinners.
>
> HUMPHREY LYTTELTON

Garrett, Lesley (1955–) British opera singer, nicknamed the Darling Diva, who emerged as a popular star of the early 1990s, when she created a sensation with her unconventional and sensuous approach to her roles. The daughter of a headmaster, she studied at the Royal Academy of Music and won the prestigious Kathleen FERRIER Memorial Prize before establishing herself as one of the best-known opera singers of her generation, appearing regularly at such leading venues as GLYNDEBOURNE and COVENT GARDEN.

Garrett, Thomas 'Snuff' (1939–) US producer, who became one of the most successful figures in pop and COUNTRY music from the 1960s. He started as a disc jockey and established his reputation at Liberty Records, working with such singers as Johnny BURNETTE, Bobby VEE and Gary Lewis and the Playboys in the early 1960s, when he was closely associated with the BRILL BUILDING songwriters. He set up his own Viva label in the mid-1960s and went on to enjoy further success with CHER, Brenda LEE and Glen CAMPBELL among others, as well as recording his own solo album *Snuff Garrett's Texas Opera Co* (1977).

Gaskill, Clarence (1892–1947) US songwriter and author, who wrote a number of popular songs of the 1920s and 1930s. His most celebrated compositions included 'Sweet Adeline' (1919), 'Minnie the Moocher' (1931) and 'Prisoner of Love' (1931).

Gay, Noel (Reginald Moxon Armitage; 1898–1954) British songwriter and lyricist, who wrote many popular hits of the 1930s and 1940s. A child prodigy who had early training as an organist, he began writing songs for revues in 1925 and subsequently contributed to many successful shows. Among his most celebrated songs were 'The Sun Has Got His Hat On' (1932), 'I Took My Harp to a Party' (1933), 'There's Something about a Soldier' (1933), 'Leaning on a Lamp-post' (1937), the classic 'The Lambeth Walk', from his musical *Me and My Girl* (1937), 'Run, Rabbit, Run' (1939), 'Only a Glass of Champagne' (1940) and 'Are We Downhearted – No!' (1941).

'Run, Rabbit, Run' was one of the first songs to capture the wartime spirit and enjoyed equal popularity with military and civilian audiences. Written for the London Palladium show *The Little Dog Laughed*, it was made famous by FLANAGAN AND ALLEN. It was given extra piquancy when it was associated with a news item concerning the death of two rabbits after they were shot in the Shetlands by the Luftwaffe, presumably failing to find a better target. Various alternative versions of the lyrics (including 'Run Adolf Run') were soon forthcoming, all at the expense of the Nazi foe.

Gaye, Marvin (Marvin Pentz Gay; 1939–84) Black US RHYTHM-AND-BLUES singer, nicknamed Mister Perfectionist because he always insisted on the highest production standards, who became one of the most successful of all MOTOWN artists. Gaye began his musical career singing in a church choir before graduating to DOO-WOP groups and finally to Motown. Such hit singles as 'Pride and Joy' (1963), 'How Sweet It Is' (1964), the classic Number-One selling 'I Heard It through the Grapevine' (1968) and 'Too Busy Thinking about My Baby' (1969) established him as a major star, as well as indicating the range of styles in which he excelled.

Later in his career he enjoyed further success with the albums *What's Going On?* (1970) and the more carefree *Let's Get It On* (1973) and sang duets with Tammi Terrell, Kim Weston and Diana ROSS. Nevertheless, he got into financial difficulties later in the decade, filing for bankruptcy in 1978. When his marriage, to sister of Motown proprietor Berry GORDY, failed he was obliged to hand over to his former wife a large stake in the royalties of his next album, which he gave the somewhat bitter title *Here, My Dear*.

The erotic 'Sexual Healing' reached the British Top 10 in 1982 but Gaye's career, increasingly disrupted by his drug dependence, ended prematurely when his father (a retired minister) shot him dead the day before his 45th birthday in the course of a family quarrel.

Gayle, Crystal (Brenda Gail Webb; 1951–) US COUNTRY singer, who established a big following with both country and pop fans in the 1970s and 1980s. After touring with her sister Loretta LYNN, she topped the charts with such songs as 'Don't it Make My Brown Eyes Blue', which won a Grammy in 1977, 'Cry Me a River' and 'Talking in Your Sleep' as well as recording numerous hit albums. By the end of the 1970s she was the highest paid female country singer of her generation.

Gaynor, Gloria (1949–) Black US pop singer, who was known as the Disco Queen in the mid–1970s before her career was eclipsed by that of Donna SUMMER. Gaynor established herself as a disco favourite with such hits as 'Honey Bee' (1973), 'Never Can Say Goodbye' (1974), 'Reach Out I'll be There' (1975) and 'I Will Survive', which revived her fortunes by reaching Number One in both the USA and the UK in 1979. She returned to the charts in 1983 with 'I Am What I Am', from the musical *La Cage aux Folles*, but she remains best known for her earlier hits. More recently she has worked as a GOSPEL singer and radio presenter.

Gebrauchsmusik *See* UTILITY MUSIC.

Gedda, Nicolai (1925–) Swedish tenor, who has won acclaim both for his appearances in opera and for his performances of Lieder. The son of a Russian choirmaster, he made his operatic début in 1952 and has since played virtually all the great operatic tenor roles.

Geldof, Bob (Robert Frederick Zenon Geldof; 1954–) Irish pop singer-songwriter and guitarist, who won huge public acclaim in the 1980s for his efforts to raise funds to relieve famine in Africa. Educated at a Jesuit college, Geldof rebelled against his middle-class upbringing and spent some time touring the UK and Canada before

establishing his reputation as singer with the BOOMTOWN RATS, which he co-founded in 1975. The band had several chart-topping singles in the late 1970s but then faltered and faded from view.

In 1984 Geldof burst back into the limelight with his calls for the pop world to unite to provide assistance to the starving of Ethiopia and other stricken African nations. Moved by television pictures depicting the effects of the famine, he teamed up with Midge Ure (*see* ULTRAVOX) to organize the supergroup BAND AID, whose single 'Do They Know It's Christmas?' outstripped the sales of any other British release and raised £8 million. He also inspired the huge LIVE AID concerts of 1985, raising another £50 million, and had a hand in other linked efforts, acting as chief media spokesman and taunting politicians and other representatives of the Establishment into action.

Awarded an honorary knighthood in 1986, he was also nominated for the Nobel Peace Prize and remained a popular hero long after he had distanced himself from further famine relief work and had attempted to resurrect his career in pop music with such new releases as *Deep in the Heart of Nowhere* (1986).

> When I was eleven, I wanted to be Mick Jagger so bad; when I was twelve I wanted to be John Lennon; when I was thirteen I wanted to be Peter Townshend. Now I just wanna be me. I want to revitalize the rock dream that was so essential to me.
> BOB GELDOF, *Trouser Press*, 1977

Genesis British rock group, which emerged as one of the leading PROGRESSIVE ROCK bands of the 1970s and 1980s. Genesis was formed in 1967 while several of the founder-members were still at Charterhouse, the UK public school, and the first album, *Genesis to Revelation*, was released in 1969. After *Trespass* (1970), the line-up settled down in the form of lead vocalist Peter GABRIEL, keyboard player Tony Banks (1950–), bassist Mike Rutherford (1950–), guitarist Steve Hackett (1950–) and drummer and backing vocalist Phil COLLINS.

With Gabriel the driving force, the band established its reputation with such albums as *Nursery Cryme* (1971), *Foxtrot* (1972) and *The Lamb Lies Down On Broadway* (1975) as well as attracting a huge following with their highly theatrical live act. After Gabriel left in 1975, Collins emerged as his successor as lead vocalist and steered the group towards a more overtly commercial style with such best-selling albums as *Trick of the Tail* (1976), *And Then There Were Three* (1978), which followed the departure of Steve Hackett, and *Abacab* (1981).

Funding for the band's live extravaganzas comes partly from the massive business organization that has been constructed around the group, which has stakes in a range of lighting companies, studios and so forth. The group lay dormant for several years in the late 1980s but re-emerged in 1991 with *We Can't Dance*, which got to Number One in both the UK and the USA, and the release of two live albums. Collins left in 1996.

Genius, the *See* Ray CHARLES.

Gentleman Jim *See* Jim REEVES.

Gentry, Bobbie (Roberta Lee Streeter; 1944–) US COUNTRY singer and guitarist, who enjoyed transatlantic success in the pop charts in the late 1960s. A student of the Los Angeles Conservatory of Music, she adopted her stagename after seeing the film *Ruby Gentry* and had her first hit with her own song 'Ode to Billy Joe', which reached Number One in the USA in 1967. Subsequent hits included 'I'll Never Fall in Love Again', which got to Number One in the UK in 1969, and 'All I Have to Do is Dream' (1969).

Georgia Tom *See* Thomas A. DORSEY.

Geraldo (Gerald Bright; 1904–74) British bandleader, who was one of the most popular dance bandleaders of the 1930s. He led orchestras at the Savoy Hotel and elsewhere, attracting a wide following with his incorporation of South American rhythms and high quality dance music as well as backing such star singers as Al BOWLLY. After the Second World War he led bands on transatlantic liners, earning them the nickname Geraldo's Navy. His bands made regular radio broadcasts until the 1960s, when Geraldo took up work as an agent.

Gerhard, Roberto (1896–1970) Spanish composer, resident in the UK from 1939, who won acclaim for his AVANT-GARDE compositions reflecting his Spanish musical heritage. A pupil of Arnold SCHOENBERG among others, he left Spain after the Republican government fell but continued to write in a Spanish style, exploring 12-NOTE music and other modern techniques. His most admired works included such ballets as *Ariel* (1934), *Barcelona* (1936) and *Pandora* (1943–45), four symphonies, the opera *The Duenna* (1945–47), and two string quartets (1955–56 and 1960–62).

German, Sir Edward (Edward German Jones; 1862–1936) British composer, conductor and violinist, who became one of the most popular composers of the Edwardian period. He first attracted attention with the high-quality incidental music he wrote for the theatre and was subsequently invited to complete Sir Arthur Sullivan's unfinished operetta *The Emerald Isle* (1901). The most successful of all his compositions proved to be the lastingly popular light opera *Merrie England* (1902); others included the operettas *A Princess of Kensington* (1903), *Tom Jones* (1907) and *Fallen Fairies* (1909), on which he collaborated with W.S. Gilbert. Among his other works were many popular songs as well as settings of 12 'Just So' stories by Rudyard Kipling, two symphonies and further orchestral music.

Gerry and the Pacemakers British pop group, which was among the most popular outfits to emerge from Liverpool in the shadow of the BEATLES. Led by SKIFFLE player Gerry Marsden (1942–) and managed by Brian EPSTEIN, the group – completed by pianist Les Maguire (1941–), bassist Les Chadwick (1943–) and drummer Freddie Marsden (1940–) – switched to ROCK 'N' ROLL in 1959. In 1963 Gerry and the Pacemakers set a record as the first group to reach Number One with its first three releases – 'How Do You Do It?', which the Beatles had turned down, 'I Like It' and 'You'll Never Walk Alone', a song from the Rodgers and Hammerstein musical *Carousel*, which became the anthem of Liverpool Football Club fans and topped the charts once more in 1985 in aid of the Bradford City Disaster Fund. Among the group's later hits were 'I'm the One' (1964), 'Don't Let the Sun Catch You Crying' (1964), 'Ferry 'Cross the Mersey' (1964), also the title of a film featuring the group, and 'I'll be There' (1965). Marsden assembled new versions of the group in the 1970s and 1980s. He got to Number One again in 1989, in company with Holly Johnson (of FRANKIE GOES TO HOLLYWOOD) and Paul McCARTNEY singing 'Ferry 'Cross the Mersey' to raise more money for charity.

Gershwin, George (Jacob Gershovitz; 1898–1937) US composer and pianist, of Russian descent, who became one of the giants of twentieth-century music through his mastery of the popular song. Born into a poor Brooklyn family, Gershwin became interested in music at the relatively advanced age of 18 after hearing an automatic piano playing RUBINSTEIN's 'Melody in F'. Subsequently he proved a prolific as well as an immensely gifted composer, often working in collaboration with his brother Ira Gershwin (Israel Gershovitz; 1896–1983) as lyricist.

Having begun as a song-plugger for a music publisher – he described his own voice as 'small but disagreeable' – he enjoyed his first major success with the classic 'Swanee' (1919), which sold over 2 million copies in a recording by Al JOLSON. He went on to become one of the most successful writers for the MUSICAL stage, with credits including such shows as *Lady be Good* (1924), *Funny Face* (1927), *Girl Crazy* (1930), *Strike up the Band* (1930) and *Of Thee I Sing* (1931), which was the first musical to earn a Pulitzer Prize. His most popular songs included 'Somebody Loves Me', 'Someone to Watch Over Me', 'Oh, Lady be Good', 'Fascinating Rhythm', 'S'wonderful', 'Embraceable You', 'Let's Call the Whole Thing Off', 'They Can't Take That Away from Me' and 'I Got Rhythm', which he wrote in a number of variations. Acclaim for his compositions was universal and he was once prompted himself to remark: 'I am a better melodist than Schubert.'

Despite his immense success in the world of the popular song, Gershwin always longed to be recognized as a composer of serious classical music. He once asked Maurice RAVEL for lessons, but the latter refused, explaining that as Gershwin earned $100,000 a year from his music, it was he who should be giving the lessons. When he approached Arnold SCHOENBERG for tuition he got the reply: 'I would only make you a bad Schoenberg, and you're such a good Gershwin already.' Undeterred,

Gershwin combined JAZZ and classical elements in the hugely successful *Rhapsody in Blue* (1924), which he wrote for Paul WHITEMAN, and went on to compose a piano concerto (1925), the tone poem *An American in Paris* (1928) and the folk opera *Porgy and Bess* (1935), which – with such classic songs as 'Summertime' and 'It ain't Necessarily So' – remains the only US opera to have won a permanent place in the standard opera repertoire (although Virgil THOMSON described it as 'a libretto that should never have been accepted on a subject that should never have been chosen by a man who should never have attempted it').

Gershwin's career came to an abrupt and premature end when, at the age of 39, he died on the operating table during an operation to remove a brain tumour – an incalculable loss to the history of contemporary music.

> George Gershwin died last week. I don't have to believe it if I don't want to.
> JOHN O'HARA, 1937

> Mr Gershwin ... may yet bring jazz out of the kitchen.
> DEEMS TAYLOR, of *Rhapsody in Blue*, in *The World*, 1924

> He is the prince who has taken Cinderella by the hand and openly proclaimed her a princess to the astonished world.
> WALTER DAMROSCH, on hearing Gershwin's Piano Concerto in F

> An occasional work of his on a programme is all very well, but an entire evening is too much. It is like a meal of chocolate eclairs.
> RICHARD DRAKE SAUNDERS, in *The Musical Courier*, 1937

Getz, Stan (Stanley Gayetzsky; 1927–91) US JAZZ saxophonist, who emerged as one of the most prominent exponents of COOL jazz in the late 1940s. Having played tenor saxophone in the bands of such distinguished jazzmen as Stan KENTON, Jimmy DORSEY and Benny GOODMAN, among others, he teamed up with the likes of Gerry MULLIGAN and Dizzy GILLESPIE in pioneering the cool style. His most acclaimed recordings included 'Early Autumn' (1948), which he made while with Woody HERMAN, a series of releases in collaboration with Norman Granz (1918–) in the 1950s, and the album *Focus* (1961), which he made with his own small group. Subsequently he recorded such BOSSA NOVA classics as 'The Girl from Ipenema' (1963) and further developed his own uniquely elegant but still impassioned sound as well as branching out into electronic and soul music. His collaborators in his final years ranged from Chick COREA to Chet BAKER.

> I've often thought that if Stan Getz and Stuff Smith had ever got together, they could have called the group 'Getz-Stuffed'.
> ACKER BILK, on BBC Radio's *Jazz Score*

Ghiaurov, Nicolai (1929–) Bulgarian bass, who has earned an international reputation since making his début in 1955 as Don Basilio in Rossini's *The Barber of Seville*. His most celebrated role is the central part in Mussorgsky's *Boris Godunov*.

ghost note In JAZZ, a note that is played so softly it can barely be heard.

Gibbs, Mike (1937–) Zimbabwean composer, arranger, trombonist and pianist, who established a reputation as a prominent JAZZ composer in the late 1960s. Having trained in the USA, he played in the bands of such British jazzmen as Johnny DANKWORTH before developing his own JAZZ-ROCK style and dividing his career between the USA and the UK. He has also worked with several prominent rock and pop musicians, including Joni MITCHELL, Peter GABRIEL and Whitney HOUSTON.

Gibson Guitar-manufacturing company, which became famous for its well-constructed and highly innovatory guitars. Founded by guitar-maker Orville Gibson (1856–1918) in 1902, the company revolutionized guitar design, producing larger guitar bodies with the 'f' holes copied from conventional violins. Gibson guitars were popular with jazzmen in the 1930s, when the first amplified versions were sold – notably the Gibson L5, which was a favourite of Charlie CHRISTIAN. Cutaway bodies followed, and designer Lester Polfus took the electric guitar to new heights with a guitar named in his honour, the Gibson Les PAUL, which was first sold in 1952 and continued to sell in huge numbers over the next 40 years with little modification, inspiring many imitations. Devotees of the Les Paul have ranged from Eric CLAPTON and Duane ALLMAN to LED ZEPPELIN, while enthusiasts of the Gibson SG included Frank ZAPPA and Mick JAGGER.

Gibson, Sir Alexander (1926–95) Scottish conductor, who won recognition as one of the most influential figures in contemporary Scottish music. He served as music director of the Scottish National Orchestra (1959–84) and also of the Scottish Opera (1962–87).

Gieseking, Walter (1895–1956) German pianist, who was much admired for his interpretations of important French works. Among his most acclaimed recordings were pieces by Claude DEBUSSY, Maurice RAVEL, Arnold SCHOENBERG and Paul HINDEMITH.

Gigli, Beniamino (1890–1957) Italian singer, the son of a shoe-maker, who succeeded Enrico CARUSO as the most acclaimed tenor of his generation. Although not a great stage actor, he was hugely popular in such roles as Faust in *Mefistofele*, Rodolfo in *La Bohème*, the Duke in *Rigoletto* and Cavaradossi in *Tosca*, and he made noteworthy recordings of many Neapolitan folksongs among other pieces. He continued to appear with undiminished success into his sixties.

Gilbert, L. Wolfe (1886–1970) US songwriter and lyricist, born in Russia, who wrote over 250 popular songs, of which many became transatlantic hits. A performer in vaudeville and burlesque, he established his reputation as a songwriter with such classics as 'Waiting for the Robert E. Lee' (1912), 'Hitchy Koo' (1912), 'Take Me to That Swanee Shore' (1912), 'Lucky Lindy' (1927), which celebrated Lindbergh's Atlantic crossing, and 'Ramona' (1927).

Gilels, Emil (1916–85) Russian pianist, who earned a reputation as one of the leading pianists of his generation. He enjoyed particular acclaim playing the piano works of Beethoven and also pieces by Sergei PROKOFIEV, who dedicated his Eighth Piano Concerto to him.

Gillespie, Dizzy (John Birks Gillespie; 1917–93) Black US JAZZ trumpeter, bandleader, composer and arranger, who was one of the pioneers of BEBOP (a word he is said to have coined himself) in the 1940s.

Gillespie, who was taught to play the trumpet by his father, emerged as a uniquely talented musician in the 1930s, playing for the band of Teddy Hill as successor to his musical hero Roy ELDRIDGE. He acquired the nickname Dizzy after fellow-trumpeter Fats Palmer described him thus in reference to his lively behaviour in his youth (Gillespie repaid the compliment by saving Palmer's life after he was overcome by fumes resulting from a gas leak).

In 1939 Gillespie was recruited as composer and arranger by Cab CALLOWAY and, when not working for him or such other leading contemporaries as Lionel HAMPTON, began to experiment with the new ideas that were to crystallize as bebop alongside Thelonious MONK, Kenny CLARKE and others at MINTON'S PLAYHOUSE.

Gillespie left Calloway after a brawl on stage in 1941 and formed his own small group, playing with such jazzmen as Charlie BARNET, Earl HINES, singer Billy ECKSTINE and – most importantly – Charlie PARKER. In 1944 he teamed up with Eckstine and began to spread the bebop message, subsequently creating his own big band and also collaborating further with Parker as members of an All-Star Quintet, with whom he had his greatest impact.

Such compositions as 'Night in Tunisia' (1942), 'Woody 'n You' (1942) and 'Groovin' High' (1944) cemented his status as one of the giants of jazz history, as well as demonstrating his technical prowess; they also inspired many imitators. His trumpet style proved revolutionary, and soon his impact on jazz was being equated with that of Louis ARMSTRONG in an earlier era. He continued to lead his own bands and to tour the world with universal success, leading both quintets and BIG BANDS, even enjoying the patronage of the White House on goodwill tours of Africa and South America. He made further stylistic advances in the 1970s after teaming up with trumpeter Jon Faddis, although an attempt to break new ground in partnership with Stevie WONDER was not judged a great success.

Gillespie's visual trademark was the bent-upwards horn of his trumpet, which had certain technical advantages (not least the fact that when he leant forwards to read the music the horn remained pointing towards the audience). In fact, this innovatory design was not the result of a brainwave but of an accident after two slapstick entertainers fell on Gillespie's trumpet during a party for his wife, thus altering its shape.

> It's taken me all my life to learn what not to play.
> DIZZY GILLESPIE

> Man, I can't *listen* that fast.
> Unidentified jazz musician, after Gillespie and Parker played 'Shaw'nuff'

GI Sinatra *See* Johnny DESMOND.

Gitana, Gertie (1888–1957) British MUSIC HALL singer, of gypsy descent, who emerged as a major star in the Edwardian era. Among her most popular songs were 'Nellie Dean', 'Silver Bell' and 'Never Mind'.

Giulini, Carlo Maria (1914–) Italian conductor, who won acclaim as one of the foremost interpreters of the operas (and *Requiem*) of Verdi, among other composers. He served as director of LA SCALA (1951–56) and subsequently as conductor of the CHICAGO SYMPHONY ORCHESTRA and the VIENNA SYMPHONY ORCHESTRA as well as enjoying fruitful collaborations with the singer Maria CALLAS and with film directors Luchino Visconti (1906–76) and Franco Zeffirelli (1923–).

glam rock POP music genre, occasionally referred to alternatively as glitter rock, which came to dominate the British charts in the early 1970s and threw up a dazzling series of new stars. A lighter derivative of HARD ROCK, glam rock was lively, colourful, self-parodying and fun. Such glam rock legends as Marc BOLAN, SLADE, Gary GLITTER and David BOWIE placed great emphasis on the theatricality of their acts, wearing bizarre, sequined costumes with huge platform shoes and heavy make-up and even confusing assumptions about their sexuality. The genre enjoyed a brief flowering and was long gone by the time of the advent of PUNK ROCK towards the end of the decade, but it has since sparked back to life with such stars as Gary GLITTER continuing to tour and making repeated come-backs with virtually unchanged acts into the 1990s.

Glasgow Orpheus Choir Scottish choir, which earned a worldwide reputation over the course of its 50-year existence. Founded in 1901, the choir prospered under the leadership of Sir Hugh Roberton (1874–1952) and made many celebrated recordings before disbanding in 1951. It has now re-formed as the Glasgow Phoenix Choir.

Glass, Philip (1937–) US composer, who emerged as a leading figure of the AVANT-GARDE in the 1960s. Having studied under Nadia BOULANGER and Ravi SHANKAR among others, Glass established a controversial reputation composing works that employed the use of SERIALISM, ALEATORISM and other exploratory musical techniques, including minimalism. He formed his own ensemble to perform his works in 1967 and subsequently adopted an increasingly theatrical style, collaborating on such compositions as the epic multi-media opera *Einstein on the Beach* (1976). Other works by Glass include *Music in Fifths* (1970), *Music in Twelve Parts* (1971–74), *North Star* (1975), *Satyagraha* (1980), which was based on the life of Gandhi, *Glassworks* (1982), *Akhnaten* (1984), *The Juniper Tree* (1985), which was intended for young audiences, and *The Making of the Representative for Planet Eight* (1986). His experiments with electronic instruments have proved influential on many contemporary pop musicians.

> Philip Glass's Akhnaten
> Seems bound to dishearten
> As the Pharaoh emotes
> On very few notes.
> KATIE MALLET, in *How to be Tremendously Tuned in to Opera*, 1989

Glazunov, Alexander (1865–1936) Russian composer, nicknamed the Little Glinka and the Russian Mendelssohn, who established himself as one of the leading composers of his generation with his strongly nationalist style. A pupil of Nikolai Rimsky-Korsakov (1844–1908), he won recognition with his First Symphony at the age of 16 and went on to become director of the St Petersburg Conservatory (1905–28), after which he moved to the West, eventually settling in Paris. His most popular works included nine symphonies, the ballets *Raymonda* (1896–97) and *The Seasons* (1899), the Violin Concerto in A minor (1904), the Saxophone Concerto (1934) and much other music. He was always a conservative and actually walked out of a concert of an early work by Sergei PROKOFIEV, although he did offer the aspiring composer encouragement.

Glennie, Evelyn (1965–) Scottish percussionist, who established herself among the best-known musicians of the contemporary era despite being totally deaf. Glennie began to lose her hearing in 1973 but continued her musical training and learnt to 'hear' her music by sensing the vibrations produced. She joined the Royal Academy of Music in 1982 and became a major media star as well as consolidating her reputation as a musician by developing a 'four-mallet' marimba technique. Acclaimed both as an orchestral percussionist and as a soloist, several composers have written works for her and she also plays pieces of her own. In 1989 she gave the first-ever solo percussion recital to be presented as part of the PROMS.

Glitter, Gary (Paul Gadd; 1944–) British pop star, nicknamed the King of Glam Rock, who emerged as one of the most outrageous of the GLAM ROCK stars of the early 1970s. In fact, his recording career began as early as 1959, when – as Paul Raven – he covered Frankie VAUGHAN's 'Tower of Strength' and in the process created what many critics called one of the worst singles of all time. It was not until 1973, however, that he reached the charts with the largely instrumental single 'Rock 'n' Roll Part 2' (which made Number One in the USA and Number Two in the UK).

Glitter's lively stage presence and self-parodying visual appearance, complete with huge platform heels and sequined glitter jackets, won him a huge following and he had 11 Top 10 hits, of which his theme song 'I'm the Leader of the Gang (I am)' (1973), 'I Love You Love Me Love' (1973) and 'Always Yours' (1974) all reached Number One. Several of his hits were written around the catchphrases he hurled at the audience during live performances.

Declared bankrupt some years after the glam rock era had come to an end, Glitter continued to please his old fans with regular come-back tours, still wearing his fabulous sequined costumes (he was reputed to buy as many as 500 costumes for a single tour) but occasionally adding new songs to the old standards. 'Another Rock 'n' Roll Christmas' reached the UK Top 10 in 1984.

glitter rock *See* GLAM ROCK.

Glorious John *See* Sir John BARBIROLLI.

Glover, Jane (1949–) British conductor, who emerged as the best-known of all women conductors in Britain in the 1980s. She made her first appearance as a conductor in 1975 and was subsequently appointed chorus master at GLYNDEBOURNE (1980), director of the Glyndebourne Touring Opera (1982–85), artistic director of the London Mozart Players (1984–92) and principal conductor of the HUDDERSFIELD CHORAL SOCIETY.

Glyndebourne The country estate near the Sussex town of Lewes, which was chosen as the site of the now celebrated Glyndebourne Festival Theatre in 1934. Opened by John Christie (1882–1962) as a present for his wife, the singer Audrey Mildmay (1900–53), the theatre houses a world-famous annual festival of opera and other music and has long been considered one of the most prestigious venues in classical music, attracting many leading performers at the start of their careers. In the early years the emphasis was on the works of Mozart, but subsequently the programme has been widened to encompass many other pieces (including the operas of Richard STRAUSS and new works by Benjamin BRITTEN). The Glyndebourne Touring Opera was established in 1968 to take productions on tour throughout the UK. A new opera house was opened in 1994.

Gobbi, Tito (1913–84) Italian baritone and director, who established an international reputation as an opera star after the Second World War. As well as appearing in many films, he excelled on the stage in such roles as Scarpia in *Tosca*, Iago in *Otello*, the title part in Berg's *Wozzeck* and as Verdi's Falstaff, winning particular acclaim opposite Maria CALLAS. His success was all the more surprising in view of the fact that at the outset of his career he had to overcome the twin problems of a stammer and asthma.

> I don't know why it is, Tito. I don't particularly like your voice, but when you sing I forget to play.
> Unidentified orchestra member, in Gobbi's *My Life*, 1979

'God' *See* Eric CLAPTON.

Godfather of Soul *See* James BROWN.

Godfrey, Fred (1880–1953) British songwriter, who wrote several of the biggest hits of the post-Edwardian MUSIC HALL. Among his most enduring compositions were 'Now

I Have to Call Him Father' (1911), 'Who were You with Last Night' (1912) and 'Take Me Back to Dear Old Blighty' (1916).

Goehr, Alexander (1932–) British composer, born in Berlin, who first established a reputation as a leading contemporary composer in the late 1950s. The son of the conductor Walter Goehr (1903–60), he employed the techniques of SERIALISM in such works as *The Deluge* (1958) and subsequently explored the possibilities of repetition and variation in a violin concerto (1962) and the *Little Symphony* (1963). Later works have included the operas *Arden Must Die* (1966) and *Behold the Sun* (1985), the overtly theatrical *Triptych* (1968–70) and such traditionalist compositions as the piano concerto of 1972 and the oratorio *Babylon the Great is Fallen* (1979).

Goffin, Gerry (1939–) US lyricist and producer, who provided the lyrics for several hits by his wife Carole KING, among other stars. Having trained as a chemist, he collaborated with King on such hits as 'Will You Love Me Tomorrow' (1961), and they won wide acclaim providing material for, among others, the EVERLY BROTHERS, the HOLLIES and Aretha FRANKLIN. Following their divorce in 1968, Goffin continued to write and produce (somewhat less prolifically), his credits including the lyrics for such songs as 'Tonight I Celebrate My Love', a hit for Roberta FLACK in 1982, and 'Saving All My Love for You', which was released by Whitney HOUSTON in 1985.

Gold, Ernest (1921–) US composer, born in Vienna, who became a highly successful writer of film SOUNDTRACKS. A student of the Vienna State Academy, he arrived in the USA in 1938 and soon established a reputation with such hit songs as 'Practice Makes Perfect' (1940) and 'Accidentally on Purpose' (1940) in addition to classical works. He moved to Hollywood in 1945 and contributed to many films, highlights of his career including his music for *Exodus* (1960), which won an OSCAR, and the installation of his name as the first screen composer to be honoured in the Hollywood Walk of Fame.

gold disc Award presented to the performers of a record that has sold a million copies (or earned $1 million or £1 million). Various record companies observe different rules in awarding gold discs to their stars, some presenting them on the sale of 500,000 or even 200,000 copies and others including international sales in their assessment (although this is not usually the case in the USA).

The very first gold disc was presented to Glenn MILLER by his record company RCA Victor in 1942 for his classic recording of 'Chattanooga Choo Choo'. The very first record to sell a million copies was, however, made somewhat earlier, in the form of Enrico CARUSO's 'Vesti la giubba' (1903), while violinist Marie Hall was given a gold bracelet decorated with seven tiny gold discs back in 1905.

Since 1958 the issuing of gold discs in the USA has been undertaken by the Recording Industry Association of America, which has awarded some 1,200 gold discs. The record for any one artist or group is held by Elvis PRESLEY, who collected 65 gold discs in all. Runners-up were the BEATLES with 59.

Golden Boy, the See Frankie AVALON.

Golden Foghorn, the See Ethel MERMAN.

golden oldie In DISC JOCKEY slang, an old but cherished pop record that continues to appeal. First heard in the 1960s, the phrase is now applied in a wider range of contexts, even to elderly people (particularly those who express a liking for activities usually associated with the young).

Goldsboro, Bobby (1941–) US singer-songwriter and guitarist, who enjoyed considerable success with both pop and COUNTRY audiences in the 1960s and early 1970s. Having started out in country music, Goldsboro took up ROCK 'N' ROLL and became a backing guitarist for Roy ORBISON before embarking on a solo career. His hits included 'See the Funny Little Clown' (1964) and the Number One 'Honey' (1968).

Goldsmith, Jerry (1929–) US composer, who wrote numerous film SOUNDTRACKS and music for television. As well as the signature tunes for such television series as The Twilight Zone, The Man from U.N.C.L.E. and Dr Kildare, he contributed music for such films as Von Ryan's Express (1965), Stagecoach (1966), Planet of the Apes (1968), the entire score of which was created from novel sound effects, Klute (1971), The Omen (1976), for which he won an OSCAR, and Gremlins (1984).

Goodhart, Al (1905–55) US songwriter, who wrote a number of hit songs of the 1930s. His most celebrated compositions included 'Sooner or Later' (1931), 'She Shall Have Music' (1936) and 'I'm in a Dancing Mood' (1936).

Goodman, Al (1890–1972) US composer, conductor, pianist and arranger, born in Russia, who worked on many successful Broadway shows of the 1920s. He wrote such hit songs as 'When Hearts are Young' (1922) and conducted such Broadway productions as the Ziegfeld Follies, The Passing Show of 1922 and Artists and Models (1923) as well as the SOUNDTRACK for the film The Jazz Singer (1927).

Goodman, Benny (Benjamin David Goodman; 1909–86) US JAZZ clarinettist and bandleader, nicknamed the King of Swing, who led one of the most popular of all SWING bands in the 1930s. Born into a poor family in Chicago, Goodman appeared in his first jazz band in 1921 at the age of 12 and two years later was playing alongside Bix BEIDERBECKE. He transferred from Chicago to New York in 1929, where he was promoted by John HAMMOND and recorded with Billie HOLIDAY and Bessie SMITH.

After forming his first band in 1934 and signing up Fletcher HENDERSON as his arranger, Goodman did much to popularize swing in the late 1930s, becoming the first bandleader to attract a large teenage audience. He emerged as a cult figure, insisting on perfection from his players (who included musicians of the stature of Harry JAMES and Bunny BERIGAN) and rehearsing until he was totally satisfied with the sound. He also enjoyed success as leader of a trio (with drummer Gene KRUPA and pianist Teddy WILSON), which subsequently developed as a quartet after Lionel HAMPTON joined, making it the first really well-known jazz outfit that was fully racially integrated.

Constant changes in personnel brought to the Goodman fold such performers as trumpeter Cootie Williams (1908–85) and guitarist Charlie CHRISTIAN, a star of his sextet as his smaller group had now become, and Goodman made tentative explorations of BOP during the 1940s before winding up his big band (although he re-formed it briefly in 1953 in response to a wave of public nostalgia).

His most acclaimed compositions with his various jazz outfits included the likes of 'Clarinetitis' (1928), 'Stompin' at the

Savoy' (1936), 'Don't be That Way' (1938), 'Boy Meets Girl' (1940) and 'Air Mail Special' (1941). His band's theme tune was 'Let's Dance'. After establishing himself as one of the jazz greats, Goodman set about translating his success into the world of classical music. He commissioned works by such composers as Paul HINDEMITH and Aaron COPLAND and played for such distinguished conductors as Leonard BERNSTEIN and Arturo TOSCANINI, winning acclaim for his clarinet playing with outstanding orchestras and chamber groups as well as consolidating his standing as an international jazz soloist and appearing on a fairly regular basis at reunions of his old bands.

Goodman, who put his music before all else, was notorious for his meanness and for his rough handling of fellow-musicians, and his relations with other jazz legends were often strained. Players in his bands told stories of him stealing saxophonists' reeds, deliberately calling them by the wrong names, blowing his nose on their handkerchiefs and even dismissing them for admitting they admired his rival Duke ELLINGTON. When one of his musicians filmed him giving a few coins to a beggar other members of his band got great pleasure from playing the film backwards so it appeared that the great man was helping himself to the beggar's takings. On another occasion, when Goodman's sextet were rehearsing in the leader's apartment, the members complained that the room was too cold; Goodman responded at once and left the room – only to return wearing a thick sweater.

> When you're a bandleader you automatically become a prick. Automatically.
> BENNY GOODMAN

> Benny's always superb.
> CHARLIE PARKER

Goodtime George *See* George MELLY.

Goodwin, Ron (1925–   ) British composer, conductor, arranger and trumpeter, who collaborated with several leading big bands and also contributed SOUNDTRACKS for numerous films. As well as arranging for the bands of Ted HEATH, GERALDO and other bandleaders, he wrote music for documentaries and for such movies as *Murder She Said* (1961), *Those Magnificent Men in Their Flying Machines* (1965), *The Battle of Britain* (1969), *Frenzy* (1972) and *Force Ten From Navarone* (1978). Other works include

The Drake 400 Suite (1980), which was written to mark the 400th anniversary of Drake's voyage round the world.

goofus JAZZ instrument, similar in appearance to the saxophone. Fashionable in the 1920s and 1930s, it had two dozen finger points, each controlling its own single-beating reed, and could produce more than one note at once.

Goossens family Anglo-Belgian family, which has produced a number of distinguished classical musicians over the course of the century. Eugène Goossens (1845–1906) conducted the Carl Rosa Opera, as did his son Eugène Goossens (1867–1958), while his five grandchildren were also active as musicians and conductors. Sir (Aynsley) Eugene Goossens (1893–1962) conducted the Sydney Symphony Orchestra and also composed various symphonies, ballets, songs and other works, including an oboe concerto for his brother Léon Goossens (1897–1988). Horn player Adolphe Goossens died in action during the First World War, while Marie Goossens (1894–1991) established herself as a harpist, and Sidonie Goossens (1899–   ) played the harp for the BBC SYMPHONY ORCHESTRA for many years.

> It is the most wonderful of all sensations that any man can conceive. It really oughtn't to be allowed.
> SIR EUGENE GOOSSENS, on conducting

Gordon, Dexter (1923–90) US JAZZ saxophonist and actor, who became one of the most respected pioneers of COOL jazz in the 1940s. He began with the band of Lionel HAMPTON in 1940 and subsequently played for Fletcher HENDERSON and Louis ARMSTRONG as well as forming his own quintet, members of which included Nat 'King' COLE. Billy ECKSTINE brought him into contact with Dizzy GILLESPIE after recruiting him in 1944, and he went on to play with such jazzmen as Charlie PARKER, Miles DAVIS and Bud POWELL as one of the architects of BEBOP. Among his most acclaimed recordings of the mid-1940s were 'The Chase', 'Groovin' High' and 'Blue 'n' Boogie'.

Gordon spent much of the 1950s in prison for drug offences but continued to record in the 1960s, when he also worked as an actor, appearing in the play *The Connection* (1960) and later being nominated for an OSCAR for his lead role (as an alcoholic saxophonist) in the film *Round Midnight*

(1986). He lived in Denmark for much of the 1960s and 1970s but made many trips to the UK and continued to appear alongside the best of his contemporaries, including such stars as Charles MINGUS and Stan GETZ.

Gordon, Mack (Morris Gittler; 1904–59) US lyricist, who collaborated on numerous hit shows and films of the 1930s and 1940s. Having worked as a vaudeville comedian, he formed a successful partnership with composer Harry REVEL and wrote with him such shows as the *Ziegfeld Follies* of 1931 and scores for many MUSICAL films, among them *The Gay Divorcée* (1934), *Poor Little Rich Girl* (1936) and *Rebecca of Sunnybrook Farm* (1938). Later he teamed up with Harry WARREN, contributing the lyrics for such songs as 'Chica Chica Boom Chic', 'Chattanooga Choo Choo', 'Serenade in Blue' and 'I Got a Girl in Kalamazoo'.

Gordy, Berry (1929–) US record producer and songwriter, who, as founder of MOTOWN, exercised a profound influence on contemporary pop music. He had his first successes as a songwriter with such hits as 'Reet Petite' (1957) and 'I'll be Satisfied' (1959) and went on to set up his own Tamla Motown record label in 1960. In the years that followed he attracted a host of star names, including Stevie WONDER, Smokey ROBINSON, Diana ROSS and Marvin GAYE and established himself as the king of Black pop.

Gordy did not always enjoy the best of relations with the artists under his control, insisting on punctuality (he had punch clocks, as used in factories, installed in his studios) and demanding complete secrecy about how the Motown sound was put together. He also allowed artists only partial information about their earnings and fined anyone who broke the rules. The Motown studios were, however, famous for their high production standards, and in the main Gordy's stars respected him for the scale of his achievement in promoting Black pop. Only the very best songs were accepted under the Gordy regime (no less a star than Smokey Robinson had 100 tunes rejected when they did not come up to scratch).

Gordy eventually sold his Motown empire to a conglomerate (MCA) in 1988.

Gore, Lesley (1946–) US pop singer, nicknamed the Queen of the Teen Weepers, who had a series of hit singles in the 1960s. Among the releases that found favour with a huge teenage audience were the classic Number One 'It's My Party' (1963), 'Judy's Turn to Cry' (1963), 'Sunshine, Lollipops and Rainbows' (1965) and 'California Nights' (1967). Discovered by Quincy JONES, she attended the same school as the future Linda MCCARTNEY, Yoko ONO and Carly SIMON.

Górecki, Henryk (1933–) Polish composer, who achieved massive international fame with his Third Symphony (1976). Entitled *Symphony of Sorrowful Songs*, it was based in part on a poem written by a young Polish prisoner on a wall of the Auschwitz concentration camp, near which Górecki was educated. Melancholy and moving, the work came to symbolize the tragedy of the Second World War, and a recording of it by the LONDON SINFONIETTA climbed to the top of the UK charts in 1993.

Gorney, Jay (1896–1990) US songwriter, author and producer, born in Russia, who wrote many hit songs for both stage and film MUSICALS. Among his best-known compositions were 'Brother, Can You Spare a Dime?' (1932), which became possibly the most famous song of the Depression years, 'You're My Thrill' (1934) and 'Home is Where the Heart is' (1948). He also played a role in the emergence of Shirley TEMPLE as a major singing star in the 1930s.

gospel Genre of US religious vocal music, which gathered momentum in the 1930s as a descendant of the old negro spiritual. Although the style had its roots in the nineteenth century, it was only in the 1930s that gospel as it is now recognized came into being after incorporating the influence of JAZZ. Lively, impassioned and relevant to the Black experience, gospel quickly created its own stars, including Thomas A. DORSEY, dubbed the Father of Gospel Music or simply Georgia Tom, Clara Ward (1924–73), Mahalia JACKSON, called the Gospel Queen, and Sister Rosetta THARPE, among others. The first Black gospel record to sell a million copies was 'Oh Happy Day', sung by the Edwin Hawkins Singers.

The movement now boasts its own radio programmes and recording labels and has continued to attract some of the biggest names in conventional SOUL, RHYTHM-AND-BLUES and other forms of POP, among them Elvis PRESLEY, James BROWN, Aretha FRANKLIN and many MOTOWN stars.

Gospel Queen, the *See* Mahalia JACKSON.

gothic Genre of heavy ROCK music of the 1980s and 1990s, descended from PUNK ROCK, which is characterized by unfailing pessimism and the wearing of black clothes. Leading gothic bands include the CULT and Sisters of Mercy.

Gould, Glenn (1932–82) Canadian pianist, who was acclaimed for his often eccentric interpretations of Bach on the piano. A graduate of the Toronto Royal Conservatory at the age of just 12, Gould did much to promote the playing of Bach's music on the piano, although critics frequently questioned his use of erratic time signatures and other bizarre habits, which included singing along with the melody. He eventually gave up live appearances in 1964 in order to concentrate on recording.

Gould, Morton (1913–   ) US composer, of Austro-Russian descent, who enjoyed success with his compositions combining elements of classical music, JAZZ and POP. Having played in various jazz bands and having broadcast regularly on the radio, he appealed to a wide audience with such works as *American Symphonette No. 1* (1933), *Chorale and Fugue in Jazz* (1934), *Latin-American Symphonette* (1940), *Cowboy Rhapsody* (1943) and *American Ballads* (1976). He has also written a number of film SOUNDTRACKS.

Gov'nor, the *See* Frank SINATRA.

Graceland The mansion in Memphis, Tennessee, which became famous as the palatial home of Elvis PRESLEY. Presley acquired Graceland in March 1957 and eventually became a virtual recluse there, surrounded by an inner circle of sycophants. The two-storey house remains a shrine to his memory, and each day it receives some 2,500 visitors, who queue to see such highlights as the star's music room, jungle den and car collection. Legend has it that the young Bruce SPRINGSTEEN once broke into the grounds of Graceland in the hope of meeting the great star – only to find his hero was not at home.

Grainer, Ron (1922–81) Australian composer, who wrote the theme tunes for numerous celebrated television series as well as music for the theatre and films. His best-known signature tunes included those for the BBC television series *Maigret*, *Dr Who* and *Steptoe and Son*.

Grainger, (George) Percy (1882–1961) British composer and pianist, born in Australia and a US citizen from 1918, who was a leading figure in the study of English folk-song. Grainger first won fame as a concert pianist, touring widely to enthusiastic acclaim under the guidance of his mother, whose suicide in 1922 proved to be a major trauma. He began to make recordings of FOLK MUSIC as early as 1906 and subsequently collected many classic English folk-songs. He also collaborated with such prominent composers as Frederick DELIUS and Edvard Grieg (1843–1907), who were interested in reviving such traditions. The most popular of his own compositions included such pieces as 'Handel in the Strand', 'Shepherd's Hey', 'Irish Tune from County Derry', 'Country Gardens' and 'Mock Morris', although the composer himself resented the success of these 'fripperies' when his more serious works were ignored.

Grainger was renowned for his often bizarre behaviour. He turned his own marriage to the Swedish poet and artist Ella Viola Ström into a major theatrical event in 1928 when it was staged in the HOLLYWOOD BOWL in front of 20,000 people. He was also notorious for using English instructions of his own invention in his scores rather than the conventional Italian terminology – he preferred his own coinage 'louden' to the usual 'crescendo', for example. And he even offered his skeleton to his own Grainger Museum in Melbourne, which politely declined it. His professed ambition in music was to realize a form of composition that was entirely free of all the restraints of harmony, metre, form and instrumentation (what he called 'free music').

> What an artist, what a man! What a lofty idealist, what a child, and at the same time, what a broad and mature outlook he has on life. A future socialist of the purest water.
> EDVARD GRIEG, diary, 1907

> The object of my music is not to entertain, but to agonize – to make mankind think of the agony of young men forced to kill each other against their will and all the other thwartments and torturings of the young.
> PERCY GRAINGER, *Anecdotes*, 1949–54

Grammy Award for outstanding achievement in the music industry, which is presented annually by the US National Academy of Recording Arts and Sciences. Sir Georg SOLTI holds the record for the most Grammy awards received by any individual, with a total of 30 Grammies since 1958. Michael JACKSON, meanwhile, holds the record for Grammies received in one year, with eight in 1984.

gramophone The record-player, which has played a central role in the musical revolution that has occurred in the twentieth century. The machine itself was an invention of the late nineteenth century, having been invented in 1877 by Thomas Edison (1847–1931), who called it the phonograph (using a cylinder rather than a flat disc). The first words he recorded were 'Mary Had a Little Lamb'. The German inventor Emil Berliner (1851–1921) introduced shellac discs in 1888 and renamed the device the 'grammophone'. The instrument quickly caught on, and the first million-selling record, of Enrico CARUSO singing 'Vesti la giubba', was made in 1903.

Some composers realized that the gramophone could be put to practical use in the actual performance of their works; Ottorino RESPIGHI, for example, included the gramophone among the instruments of the orchestra, providing for a record of a nightingale singing to be played at a certain point in the symphonic poem *The Pines of Rome* (1924).

Ultimately, the gramophone was rivalled and eventually superseded as the most important machine for the relaying of popular music by more technologically advanced systems, notably the audio CASSETTE and the COMPACT DISC. *See also* EP; LP; 78; SINGLE.

> I can only say that I am astonished and somewhat terrified at the result of this evening's experiment. Astonished at the wonderful form you have developed and terrified at the thought that so much hideous and bad music will be put on record for ever.
> ARTHUR SULLIVAN, letter to Thomas Edison, 1888

> Should we not fear this domestication of sound, this magic that anyone can bring from a disc at will? Will it not bring to waste the mysterious force of an art which one might have thought indestructible?
> CLAUDE DEBUSSY, *La Revue SIM*, 1913

> Since the advent of the gramophone, and more particularly the wireless, music of a sort is everywhere and at every time; in the heavens, the lower parts of the earth, the mountains, the forest and every tree therein. It is a Psalmist's nightmare.
> CONSTANT LAMBERT, *Music Ho!*, 1934

Granados, Enrique (1867–1916) Spanish composer and pianist, who established a reputation as a writer in the romantic tradition influenced by traditional Spanish musical styles. Having studied music in Paris, he won comparatively late recognition with the piano suite *Goyescas*, inspired by the paintings of Goya, in 1911 and was subsequently invited to elaborate this into opera form. His other best-known works include the 12 Spanish dances composed between 1892 and 1900. His career ended prematurely when the SS *Sussex*, on which he and his wife were travelling across the English Channel, was torpedoed during the First World War; he was picked up by a lifeboat but jumped back into the water to rescue his wife, and both drowned.

Grand Funk Railroad US HEAVY METAL band, which was one of the first such groups to be formed in the USA and went on to become one of the most successful bands of the early 1970s (eventually appearing under the shortened name Grand Funk). Vocalist and guitarist Mark Farner (1948–), bassist Mel Schacher (1951–) and drummer Don Brewer (1948–) came together in Michigan in 1968 and adopted what amounted to a crude BLUES-ROCK style. Adding keyboard player Craig Frost (1948–) in 1973, the band triumphed over the scorn of the media and notched up a record 10 PLATINUM albums in a row as well as building a reputation as a live band. Hit singles included 'We're an American Band' (1973) and 'Locomotion' (1974), both of which reached Number One in the USA. The band's popularity waned in the mid–1970s leading to a split, although it reformed briefly in 1981–83.

Grand Ole Opry The Saturday night radio programme broadcast by WSM from NASHVILLE, Tennessee, which became the focus of COUNTRY music throughout the USA. The programme, which was launched in 1925, was named after producer George

Dewey Hay (1895–1968) – dubbed the Solemn Old Judge – took exception to taunts from the presenter of the classical music programme that preceded it and told his listeners: 'For the past hour we have been listening to music taken largely from grand opera, but from now on we will present the Grand Ole Opry.'

Syndicated to 30 million listeners, the show rapidly established itself as the showpiece of the country genre (although it resisted the development of WESTERN SWING in the 1930s) and all the great country stars appeared on it in subsequent years. It played a leading role in the BLUEGRASS revival of the 1960s and 1970s and has always defended traditional country values in the face of changing fashions. The programme relocated from the old Ryman Auditorium to a new home in Opryland, Nashville, in 1974.

Grant, Eddy (1948–) Guyana-born British pop singer-songwriter and producer, who emerged as the leading Anglo-Caribbean star of the 1970s and 1980s. Having arrived in the UK in 1960, Grant first attracted attention as the charismatic lead singer (complete with dyed white hair) of the multiracial pop group the Equals, which reached Number One with 'Baby Come Back' (1968) and had further hits with Grant's 'Viva Bobby Joe' (1969) and 'Black Skinned Blue-eyed Boy' (1970). Grant subsequently set up his own studios and recording label and embarked on a solo career. The album *Walking on Sunshine* (1979) yielded the hit single 'Living on the Front Line' (the 'front line' being a street in Brixton, London, where young Blacks congregate) and was followed by such successes as 'I Don't Wanna Dance' and 'Electric Avenue' (both 1982). He transferred operations to Barbados in 1981. His most recent hits include the album *Born Tuff* (1986) and the single 'Gimme Hope Jo'Anna' (1988).

graphic notation The writing of a musical score in which something other than conventional notation and symbols is used. Many contemporary composers have experimented with their own variants of accepted notation in an attempt to provoke performers of their works into playing with a new spontaneity and to look at music afresh. Some composers have had to devise new symbols to express sounds that were

unknown to earlier generations, while others have deliberately employed methods of notation that avoid implications of pitch and interpretation. Karlheinz STOCKHAUSEN and John CAGE were among the most influential experimenters in graphic notation, using various systems of diagrams and squares or plus and minus signs. Others have taken the idea further still, reducing their scores to patterns of black and white squares and even photographing them wrapped around musical instruments as complete works in themselves.

Grappelli, Stéphane (1908–97) French violinist, who pioneered the use of the violin in JAZZ. Grappelli first ventured into jazz in the early 1930s and in 1934 formed an enormously influential partnership with guitarist Django REINHARDT in the Quintette du Hot Club de France. Subsequently he consolidated his reputation as one of the most distinguished of all jazz performers, recording and touring widely (at his best in the 1970s) and playing with many other major figures, his collaborators including Yehudi MENUHIN, Earl HINES, Oscar PETERSON and Nigel KENNEDY.

Grateful Dead, the US psychedelic ROCK group, which attained semi-legendary status over a period of some 25 years. The band, named after a line in a song about a poor man's funeral, was formed from vocalists and guitarists Jerry Garcia (1942–95; nicknamed Captain Trips) and Bob Weir (1947–), bassist Phil Lesh (Philip Chapman; 1940–), who replaced John 'Marmaduke' Dawson (1945–), vocalist and keyboard player Ron 'Pigpen' McKernan (1945–73) and drummer Bill Kreutzmann (1946–). They came together in San Francisco in 1966 and rapidly became a musical figurehead for the hippie culture of the city, the band's fans being dubbed Deadheads. The group members lived in a commune and refused to charge fans for tickets to see their concerts, and they donated any profits to left-wing causes. The band's music espoused pacifism, conservation and related issues.

Ranging over a wide variety of musical styles, including BLUES and SOUL, the Grateful Dead won particular acclaim for their live appearances, which were preserved in such albums as *Live Dead* (1969). Notable studio releases of the early 1970s included *Workingman's Dead* (1970), *American Beauty* (1970) and, after the death of 'Pigpen' from liver disease, *Wake of the Flood* (1973).

The band continued to record occasional albums and to make live appearances, although several members subsequently concentrated on solo careers and further line-up changes were necessitated by the deaths of keyboard players Keith Godchaux (1948–80), who had taken the place of 'Pigpen' McKernan, and Brent Mydland (1953–90).

grebo rock Genre of heavy ROCK music, otherwise labelled biker rock, which found favour with the sub-culture of Hell's Angels and bikers in the 1970s and 1980s. Performers, generally dressed in black leathers decorated with chains and studs like the bikers themselves, extolled the virtues of motorbikes, sex, alcohol and other macho pursuits, the most successful exponents including such bands as MOTÖRHEAD and STEPPENWOLF.

Green, Adolph (1915–   ) US lyricist, librettist and singer, who wrote many hit songs in collaboration with Betty COMDEN. Together they contributed material to such successful shows as Leonard BERNSTEIN's *On the Town* (1944) and *Wonderful Town* (1953) as well as to *Bells Are Ringing* (1956), *Do-Re-Mi* (1960), *Applause!* (1970) and *On the 20th Century* (1978).

Green, Al (Al Greene; 1946–   ) US SOUL singer-songwriter, who won acclaim as a highly distinguished soul and GOSPEL singer. He began in gospel but established his credentials as a soul artist with such hits as 'I Can't Get Next to You' (1970), 'Tired of Being Alone' (1971), 'Let's Stay Together' (1971), 'You Ought to be with Me' (1972) and 'Sha-la-la (Make Me Happy)' (1974). Unhappiness in his private life caused Green to give up pop in 1980, and he dedicated himself to GOSPEL music and was ordained as a preacher.

Green, John (1908–89) US composer, arranger, conductor, bandleader and pianist, who won acclaim for his success in a wide range of popular music styles. He gave up a career on Wall Street to work as an arranger and composed and conducted film scores as well as accompanying such stars as Gertrude LAWRENCE and Ethel MERMAN. His compositions for the band of Paul WHITEMAN were highly successful, and he went on to form his own JAZZ band, which took his celebrated number 'Body and Soul' (1930) as its signature tune. Among his other hits were 'I Cover the Waterfront' (1933) and 'Easy Come, Easy Go' (1934).

From 1942 he worked on a series of Hollywood MUSICALS and received OSCARS for his contribution to *Easter Parade* (1948), *An American in Paris* (1951) and *West Side Story* (1961); among other musicals with which he was connected were *High Society* (1956) and *Oliver!* (1968). As a conductor of classical music, he won respect for his work with a number of celebrated US orchestras in the late 1950s and early 1960s. His extraordinary career was honoured in 1973 by the inauguration of the John Green Music Awards.

Green, Martyn (William Martyn-Green; 1899–1975) British actor and singer, who became famous as a popular interpreter of the comic roles of Gilbert and Sullivan. He joined the D'Oyly Carte Opera Company in 1922 and remained one of its leading performers until 1951, preserving many of his best-loved roles on record. Subsequently he concentrated on straight acting roles, despite losing a leg in an accident.

Greenaway, Roger (1938–   ) British singer-songwriter, who collaborated with Roger Cook (1941–   ) on a series of popular hits of the early 1970s. As David and Jonathan, they recorded the hit 'Lovers of the World Unite' (1966) but became better known as writers of such best-selling singles as 'You've Got Your Troubles' (1965), which was recorded by the Fortunes, 'Something's Gotten Hold of My Heart' (1967), recorded by Gene PITNEY, 'Banner Man' (1971), 'Kissin' in the Back Row of the Movies' (1971), 'I'd Like to Teach the World to Sing', which the NEW SEEKERS took to Number One in 1971, the HOLLIES hit 'Long Cool Woman (in a Black Dress)' (1972) and 'Jeans On' (1976). 'Save Your Kisses for Me', sung by Greenaway as one of the Brotherhood of Man, won the EUROVISION SONG CONTEST in 1976. Subsequently he became chairman of the PERFORMING RIGHTS SOCIETY.

Greenwich, Ellie (1940–   ) US singer-songwriter, who was one of the highly successful team of writers associated with the BRILL BUILDING in the early 1960s. In collaboration with her husband Jeff Barry (1939–   ), she wrote numerous hits for Phil SPECTOR and stars of the time. Among the most successful were 'Then he Kissed Me', 'Doo Wah Diddy Diddy', 'River Deep, Mountain High', 'Tell Laura I Love Her', 'Hanky Panky', 'Da Do Ron Ron', 'Leader of the Pack' and 'Chapel of Love'. After she and Barry split in 1965, Greenwich worked as a writer of advertising jingles and as a backing vocalist for various artists.

Grey, Clifford (1887–1941) British lyricist and librettist, who collaborated on many hit revues and musical comedies between the wars. Working on such shows as *The Bing Boys Are Here* (1916), *Sally* (1920), *Artists and Models* (1924 and 1925) and *Mr Cinders* (1929), he provided the lyrics for such classic songs as 'If You were the Only Girl in the World' and 'Spread a Little Happiness'.

grindcore Genre of HEAVY METAL, which combines elements of THRASH, PUNK ROCK and straight ROCK. Typical grindcore bands play brief, up-tempo songs at a high volume. The lyrics are virtually impossible to decipher, although many numbers treat the subjects of violence, death and putrefaction, as in closely related DEATH METAL. Exponents include Carcass and Electro Hippies.

Groovey Galahad *See* Frank SINATRA.

groupie A fan, usually female, who follows a rock band or individual star wherever they go, sometimes enjoying sexual relations with them in the hope of getting a share of reflected glory. Such groupies or 'band molls' were a feature of the rock scene from the 1960s onwards, and many major bands, including the BEATLES, had a cluster of virtually permanent hangers-on. Gradually the word 'groupie' came to be used in a wider sense of any fan of a particular group or star.

Groves, Sir Charles (1915–92) British conductor, who was among the most popular conductors of the postwar period. Orchestras with which he worked with much success included the BBC Northern Orchestra (1944–51), the Bournemouth Symphony Orchestra (1951–61), the ROYAL PHILHARMONIC ORCHESTRA (1963–77) and the ENGLISH NATIONAL OPERA (1978–79).

Gruenberg, Louis (1884–1964) US composer, born in Russia, who was one of the first classical composers to incorporate JAZZ elements in his compositions. A student of Ferrucio BUSONI in Berlin, he employed jazz motifs to great effect in such works as the operas *Jack and the Beanstalk* (1931) and *Emperor Jones* (1933) and the vocal composition *Daniel Jazz* (1925). His other works included five symphonies, concertos, chamber music and incidental music for films.

Grumiaux, Arthur (1921–86) Belgian violinist, who was among the most respected violinists of his generation. Among his many celebrated recordings were versions of sonatas by Beethoven and Mozart, on which he collaborated with pianist Clara Haskil (1895–1960), although other works in his repertory ranged from Bach to Alban BERG and Igor STRAVINSKY.

grunge ROCK genre of the early 1990s, in which elements of NEW WAVE were combined with the distorted guitar sounds usually associated with HEAVY METAL. The style first emerged in the city of Seattle, where it was pioneered by the group Mother Love Bone on the influential album *Temple of the Dog* (1991) and by such spin-off groups as Pearl Jam and NIRVANA. The rough, unpolished nature of the music purveyed by such bands was echoed in a deliberately untidy fashion style also labelled grunge.

The word grunge originally denoted anything bad, ugly or boring, and it was first heard in this sense in the early 1970s.

Guarnieri, Johnny (1917–85) US JAZZ pianist, composer and author, a descendant of the celebrated family of violin-manufacturers, who first established a reputation as a leading jazz performer in the late 1930s. Having trained as a classical pianist, he graduated to the band of Benny GOODMAN in 1939 and proved adept in playing in a range of styles, including that of Fats WALLER. Subsequently he collaborated with many of the most famous names in jazz, playing for the bands of Artie SHAW, Louis ARMSTRONG and Jimmy DORSEY among others.

Gui, Vittorio (1885–1975) Italian conductor and composer, who divided his career between his native Italy and the UK, where he enjoyed equal acclaim. He appeared regularly at such prestigious opera venues as GLYNDEBOURNE and COVENT GARDEN as well as at the leading Italian houses and revived many celebrated Italian operas by Rossini and other composers.

Guilbert, Yvette (1865–1944) French singer and author, who achieved almost legendary fame as a CABARET performer in the early years of the century. She established her reputation in the 1890s, appearing both in Paris and throughout Europe and the USA. At first she sang versions of folk-songs but later specialized in singing risqué songs by such songwriters as Léon Xanrof (1867–1953) and Aristide Bruant (1851–1925), delivering them in a unique, mesmeric style. Her most famous numbers included 'La soûlarde', in which she impersonated a drunkard.

Guilbert, one of the most celebrated singers of her time, included among her admirers Sigmund Freud and Edward VII; her image, complete with long yellow gloves, was preserved for future generations in paintings by Toulouse-Lautrec.

Guitar Man, the *See* Duane EDDY; Jerry REED.

guitar-oriented rock Genre of ROCK music of the late 1980s, which witnessed a revival in the use of basic ELECTRIC GUITARS rather than the synthesized instruments that had come to dominate POP and rock in recent years. The popularity of the guitar inspired the return of the purely instrumental album and a resurgence of interest in such allied fields as JAZZ and BLUES.

Guns N' Roses US heavy ROCK band, which enjoyed huge commercial success in the late 1980s while its members earned a somewhat controversial reputation for excess. Fronted by vocalist Axl Rose (William Bailey; 1962–) and British guitarist Slash (Saul Hudson; 1965–), the band – formed when the LA Guns and Hollywood Roses joined – began to attract attention after an inaugural tour of the USA in 1985, and subsequently *Appetite for Destruction* (1987) reached Number One. Further hit albums and singles followed, including *G N' R Lies* (1989), *Use Your Illusion I* (1991) and *Use Your Illusion II* (1991), and the group won acclaim for its mixing of PUNK ROCK, THRASH and other sub-genres. Guitarist Slash went solo in 1996.

Among notorious episodes in the group's history have been the death of two fans during an appearance at the MONSTERS OF ROCK concert in the UK in 1988, a riot sparked when Axl Rose attacked a fan who was taking unauthorized photographs; allegations of anti-gay sentiment in the single 'One in a Million'; and repeated problems with the authorities over drugs, alcohol and related issues. The depiction of a woman being raped by a robot on t-shirts advertising the band led to questions in the British House of Commons in 1989.

Axl Rose himself turns down invitations to play in towns whose name begins with the letter M, maintaining that the letter has a curse on it. Rose has actually been diagnosed a manic depressive, and his mercurial temper has led to the other members of the band insisting that he travel in a separate coach when they are on tour to lessen the chances of friction.

Gurney, Ivor (1890–1937) British composer and poet, whose compositions reflected his experience of the horrors of trench warfare in the First World War. He never fully recovered after being gassed and wounded and suffered a breakdown in 1922, spending the rest of his life in a mental hospital. He won acclaim as a composer for the 82 settings he wrote for his own poems and those of A.E. Housman (1859–1936).

gutbucket Genre of JAZZ and BLUES, which was characterized by its rough, earthy qualities. Heard in the BARRELHOUSES of poor regions of the USA, the gutbucket style got its name from the small buckets that caught the drips from liquor barrels.

Guthrie, Arlo (1947–) US singer-songwriter, son of the great Woody GUTHRIE, who followed in his father's footsteps as a folk-singer dedicated to pacifism and other causes. He emerged as a star in his own right with the album *Alice's Restaurant* (1967), which was inspired by his clashes with the authorities over the attempts to force him into military service in Vietnam and was later used as the basis of a film (in fact, he avoided being called up on the strength of a $50 dollar fine imposed for dropping litter, which 'proved' he was unsuitable for recruitment). His other hits included the single 'The City of New Orleans' (1972). Poor health restricted subsequent activities, but he has issued several more albums, among them *Arlo Guthrie* (1974) and *Power of Love* (1981).

Guthrie, Woody (Woodrow Wilson Guthrie;

1912–67) US folk singer-songwriter, who became a hero of the FOLK MUSIC revival of the 1940s and 1950s. A committed Communist who was brought up in straitened – and traumatic – circumstances in Oklahoma, Guthrie gave voice to the plight of the impoverished agrarian workers of America's rural mid-West during the Depression. One of the celebrated stars who grouped together as the Almanac Singers in the early 1940s, he was the author of approximately 1,000 songs expressing the realities of life as endured by the poor and oppressed.

Guthrie's best-known compositions included the 13 songs that made up the *Dustbowl Ballads*, which were inspired by John Ford's film (1940) of John Steinbeck's novel *The Grapes of Wrath*. Among his finest individual songs were 'So Long it's Been Good to Know You', 'Grand Coolie Dam', 'Gamblin' Man', 'Vigilante Man', 'This Train is Bound For Glory' and 'This Land is Your Land'. He was forced to give up live performances in the mid-1950s as a result of Huntington's chorea, which ultimately caused his death.

Guthrie's early death was just one factor that made his life story the stuff of legend. Among other extraordinary and tragic events was the death of his 12-year-old sister when a stove exploded, the committal of his mother to a mental asylum, and his experience of being twice torpedoed while serving with the merchant navy during the Second World War.

Bob DYLAN was Guthrie's most important admirer, imitating both Guthrie's guitar style and his TALKING BLUES; he modelled the record sleeve of his third album – *The Times They are a-Changin'* – on the cover of *Dustbowl Ballads* and acknowledged his debt in one of his earliest songs, 'Song to Woody'.

   This machine kills fascists.
   Sticker on Guthrie's guitar

H

Hackett, Bobby (1915–76) US JAZZ trumpeter and guitarist, who won acclaim for his elegant performances with several of the great jazz bands. Having started out as a guitarist, he switched to the trumpet and, after playing in a trio with Pee Wee RUSSELL, was described as Bix BEIDERBECKE's natural successor. He was later recruited by Benny GOODMAN; led his own band; and joined the band of Glenn MILLER, with whom he worked chiefly as a guitarist, the Casa Loma Orchestra, and the bands of Eddie CONDON, Louis ARMSTRONG and Jack TEAGARDEN among others. He also backed singer Tony BENNETT on a regular basis. Acclaimed on both sides of the Atlantic, he suffered throughout his career from diabetes and from addiction to alcohol.

Haggard, Merle (1937–) US COUNTRY singer-songwriter, fiddler and guitarist, who became a top NASHVILLE star in the 1960s. Haggard's background was tough in the extreme: he spent most of his childhood in abject poverty and subsequently had a turbulent youth in reform schools, from which he regularly escaped, eventually ending up as a convicted burglar in San Quentin prison (1958–60). After being paroled in 1960, he started to write and play country music. Inspired by Lefty Frizzell and Buck OWENS he scored with hits such as 'Okie from Muskogee', 'The Fugitive', 'Mama Tried', 'Workin' Man Blues' and 'Hungry Eyes'. He also recorded many popular duets with his two wives, Bonnie Campbell Owens (1932–) and Leona Williams (1943–), and a further two albums in collaboration with Willie NELSON. Around 30 of his singles reached Number One in the US country chart, and several were also received well by pop audiences.

Haitink, Bernard (Johann Herman) (1929–) Dutch conductor, who has won recognition as one of the most distinguished conductors of contemporary times.

His prodigious talent was acknowledged in 1961 when he was made the youngest principal conductor ever to lead Amsterdam's CONCERTGEBOUW ORCHESTRA (in partnership with Eugen JOCHUM but on his own from 1964). His other posts have included chief conductor of the LONDON PHILHARMONIC ORCHESTRA (1967–79) and music director at GLYNDEBOURNE (1977–88) and at COVENT GARDEN (1988–). He was awarded an honorary knighthood in 1977.

Haley, Bill (William John Clifton Haley; 1925–81) US singer and guitarist, who became a pop legend through his recordings of 'Rock Around the Clock' and other classics of the ROCK 'N' ROLL era. Haley, who was originally a COUNTRY-AND-WESTERN performer (billed as 'Yodelling Bill Haley'), first adopted a ROCKABILLY style in the early 1950s with a COVER of 'Rocket 88' (1951) by Jackie Brenston, perhaps the first rock 'n' roll record, and 'Rock the Joint' (1953). 'Shake, Rattle and Roll' (1954), his first GOLD DISC, was followed by 'Dim Dim the Lights' and 'Mambo Rock' before 'Rock Around the Clock' made it to Number One in 1955.

Haley used 'Rock Around the Clock' (identified on the label as a foxtrot) as part of his live act, until he was persuaded to record it with his band, the Comets, in 1954 as a favour to his manager (his previous recording company having turned it down). The incorporation of the song in the SOUNDTRACK of the Glenn Ford movie *Blackboard Jungle* (1955) brought it to the attention of a wide audience and it stormed to the top of the charts. Haley was quickly booked to star in a film under the title *Rock Around the Clock* and was confirmed as the first great rock 'n' roll star. The film itself created a storm of disquiet among the older generation. Many local authorities in the UK objected to fans ripping up cinema seats and jiving both inside and outside cinemas and banned showings in the interests of public order.

More hits – among them 'See You Later, Alligator' and 'Rudy's Rock' (both 1956) –

followed, but Haley's career, hampered by his less than devastating stage presence and appearance (he was 30 years old, while most of his fans were in their teens), tailed off as Elvis PRESLEY among others stole the limelight. Haley continued to trade on his old hits for many years but ultimately went into a gradual decline, becoming an alcoholic and suffering from paranoia (in his last months he lived entirely in his garage, the walls of which were painted black).

'Rock Around the Clock' returned to Number One in the UK in early 1956 and reappeared in the Top 20 in 1968 and 1974, making it the most successful Number One in pop history. Some 160 versions of it have been recorded over the years and with some 22 million sales it is probably the most successful single in rock history.

Extraordinarily enough, the song that came to epitomize the soul of rock 'n' roll was co-written by a man in his sixties – Max Freedman, who was born in 1893.

Hall, Adelaide (1909–93) US singer, resident in the UK from the Second World War, who became a star of musical revue and also recorded a number of JAZZ classics with such performers as Duke ELLINGTON. She appeared in several musical revues of the early 1920s, eventually taking over from Florence Mills (1895–1927) in *Blackbirds* in 1927 and enjoying success with her versions of such standards as 'I Can't Give You Anything but Love'. In the 1930s she was one of the singers to star at the COTTON CLUB, backed by Ellington's band, with which she had previously made such enduring recordings as 'Creole Love Call' (1928). Subsequently she ran her own club in Paris and appeared on the London stage and in several films as well as broadcasting regularly on the radio with Joe LOSS.

Hall, Henry (1898–1989) British bandleader, composer, arranger and trumpeter, who became famous as a radio broadcaster in the 1930s. Having played in Salvation Army bands and worked as a cinema pianist, he made his first radio broadcast as a bandleader in 1924 and eventually took over the BBC Dance Orchestra in 1932. His weekly *Guest Night* programme, launched in 1934, made him a nationally known figure, and many of the most popular hits of the show were by Hall himself. Among the favourites connected with his name were

'Underneath the Arches' (1932), 'Teddy Bears' Picnic' (1932), which Hall sang himself, and 'The Music Goes Round and Round' (1936); each broadcast ended with 'Here's to the Next Time'. He left to form his own orchestra in 1937 but was back with *Guest Night* in 1939. He began a new career as a successful impresario in 1945 but remained a familiar radio and television personality until his retirement in 1964.

Hall, Tom T. (1936–) US COUNTRY singer-songwriter, nicknamed the Poet of Nashville and the Nashville Storyteller, who won a wide following for his autobiographical stories and songs. A former DISC JOCKEY, he enjoyed success as author of such hits as 'DJ for a Day' (1963), 'What are We Fighting For' (1964), 'Back Pocket Money' (1964) and the Number One 'Harper Valley PTA' (1968). He also recorded many of his songs himself and had huge successes with 'I Washed My Face in the Morning Dew' (1967), 'Trip to Hyden' (1971), 'The Year that Clayton Delaney Died' (1971) and 'Old Dogs, Children and Watermelon Wine' (1973). Among more recent hits are 'Everything from Jesus to Jack Daniels' (1983) and 'PS I Love You' (1985). His publications include *The Storyteller's Nashville* (1979).

Hall, Wendell Woods (1896–1969) US singer-songwriter, nicknamed the Redheaded Music Maker, who had success with several best-selling hit songs in the 1920s. Woods, who started out as a singing xylophonist, established himself as one of the top recording artists of his day with his vaudeville ukulele song 'It ain't Gonna Rain No Mo'' (1923), which sold some 5 million copies in all, and subsequently with such compositions as 'Mellow Moon' among many others. He retired from music in 1933.

Hall and Oates US SOUL duo of singer and keyboard player Daryl Hall (Daryl Hohl; 1948–) and singer and guitarist John Oates (1949–). Hall and Oates teamed up in 1969 and attracted attention from the mid-1970s as purveyors of White, so-called 'blue-eyed', soul. Among the duo's hits were the singles 'Sara Smile' (1974), 'Rich Girl' (1977), 'Private Eyes' (1981), 'Kiss on My List' (1981), 'Maneater' (1982) and 'Out of Touch' (1984), several of which reached Number One in the USA, and such albums as *Bigger than Both of Us* (1976), *Private Eyes* (1980) and *Bigbamboom* (1985). Popular with Black and White audiences alike, the duo continued into the 1990s with such albums as *So Close* (1990), although also pursuing solo careers.

Hallé Orchestra British orchestra, founded in Manchester in 1858 by Sir Charles Hallé (1819–95), which is considered to be one of the finest in Europe. Celebrated conductors of the Hallé have included Sir John BARBIROLLI.

Halliday, Johnny (Jean-Philippe Smet; 1943–) French pop singer, who virtually created ROCK 'N' ROLL in France (while never establishing a following with foreign audiences). Modelling himself on his idol Elvis PRESLEY, Halliday concentrated on establishing himself as France's leading MIDDLE-OF-THE-ROAD pop star and built up a huge collection of some 60 gold discs in a range of styles. He began as a straight rock 'n' roller with a conventional rebellious image, his performances provoking riots in the late 1950s, but subsequently tried everything, from COVERS of celebrated US hits to soft ballads and COUNTRY music. Oddities among his catalogue of hits include the album *Hamlet – Halliday* (1976), on which he attempted a pop interpretation of Shakespeare. He was married until 1974 to another French pop star, Sylvie Vartan.

Hamilton IV, George (1937–) US COUNTRY singer, nicknamed the International Ambassador of Country Music, who had widespread success with both country and pop audiences from the early 1960s on. Recruited to the GRAND OLE OPRY in 1959, he established his reputation with such hits as 'A Rose and a Baby Ruth' (1956), 'Why Don't They Understand' (1958), 'I know Where I'm Going' (1958), 'Before This Day Ends' (1960) and 'Abilene' (1963), which got to Number One in the pop charts; others included classics by such folk-oriented singer-songwriters as Bob DYLAN and Joni MITCHELL. He has toured widely over the years with consistent success, enjoying particular acclaim in the UK, and has made television appearances all over the world.

Hamlisch, Marvin (1944–) US composer, pianist and conductor, who won acclaim as a writer of both hit songs and of a series of top Broadway MUSICALS and films.

When he was only 16 years old he had his first hit single with 'Sunshine, Lollipops and Rainbows' (1965), recorded by Lesley GORE, and he was soon mixing with such prominent stars as Liza MINNELLI, for whom he wrote numerous CABARET numbers, and Groucho Marx, for whom he worked as a pianist. He established himself as a leading screen composer in 1974 with his scores for *The Way We Were* and *The Sting*, both of which won OSCARS. Other film scores have included those for *The Swimmer* (1968) and the James Bond movie *The Spy Who Loved Me* (1977).

As a writer for the musical stage, Hamlisch joined the ranks of the very best with his score for *A Chorus Line* (1975), which earned him a Tony Award; subsequent hits have included *They're Playing Our Song* (1979).

Hamlisch is, at time of writing, the only person to have won a Pulitzer Prize, an Oscar and a GRAMMY.

Hammer, M.C. (Stanley Kirk Burrell) US pop singer, who emerged as a leading RAP recording artist and live performer in the late 1980s. Called Little Hammer because he resembled baseball legend Hank 'the Hammer' Aaron, M.C. Hammer set up his own record company and established an international reputation with the million-selling album *Let's Get It Started* (1988). His second LP, *Please Hammer Don't Hurt 'Em* (1990), was Number One in the USA for 21 weeks and produced several hit singles – although subsequent releases failed to match earlier successes.

Hammerstein II, Oscar (1895–1960) US librettist, lyricist and producer, descended from a noted theatrical family, who collaborated on several of the most successful stage MUSICALS of the century. Hammerstein made his début as a librettist in the early 1920s and numbered among his first successes his contribution to such musicals as *Rose-Marie* (1924) and *The Desert Song* (1926). Most popular of all, though, were the librettos he wrote for Jerome KERN, which included the highly acclaimed musical *Show Boat* (1925) and *Music in the Air* (1932). Even greater things were to follow, however, after he formed a new partnership, this time with composer Richard RODGERS.

Oklahoma! (1943), the result of their first collaboration, ushered in a new era in the development of the stage musical and smashed all previous Broadway records, as well as earning Hammerstein a Pulitzer Prize. Similar success came with several more collaborations with Rodgers, notably *Carousel* (1945), *Allegro* (1947), *South Pacific* (1949), *The King and I* (1951), *Flower Drum Song* (1958) and *The Sound of Music* (1959). Most successful among his collaborations with other composers was the award-winning *Carmen Jones* (1943), which framed the music of Bizet. He also won Oscars for the songs 'The Last Time I Saw Paris', from *Lady Be Good* (1941), and for 'It Might as Well be Spring', from *State Fair* (1945).

Not everyone was confident that *Oklahoma!*, originally titled *Away We Go!*, would be a success. One early review of the show is now a Broadway legend: 'No girls, no legs, no jokes, no chance.'

Hammond, Dame Joan (1912–96) New Zealand-born soprano, who became a prominent opera star after beginning her career as a professional violinist. She made her operatic début in 1929 in Sydney, studied in London and Vienna and subsequently won acclaim for her expressive but powerful voice at many leading international opera venues. Among her celebrated roles were Mimi, Violetta, Dido, Tosca and Tatyana in Tchaikovsky's *Eugene Onegin*, which she sang in the Soviet Union in Russian. She also performed choral works and oratorios. Her most successful recording was Puccini's 'O mio babbino caro', which sold over a million copies and earned her a GOLD DISC in 1969, the year before she retired.

Hammond, John Henry (1910–87) US record producer, who brought to light some of the great names of twentieth-century music. Having started out as a DISC JOCKEY, he joined the staff of COLUMBIA Records and went on to 'discover' or promote such talents as Count BASIE, Billie HOLIDAY, Bessie SMITH, Charlie CHRISTIAN, Benny GOODMAN (who married Hammond's sister), Pete SEEGER, Bob DYLAN, who was dubbed 'Hammond's Folly', Aretha FRANKLIN and Bruce SPRINGSTEEN.

His son, John Paul Hammond (1943–), established a reputation as an outstanding BLUES singer and slide guitarist, making such albums as *I Can Tell* (1968), *Southern Fried* (1970), *Triumvirate* (1973),

on which he collaborated with Dr John and Mike Bloomfield, *Factwork and Hot Tricks* (1978), *Frogs for Snakes* (1982) and *Nobody But You* (1987).

Hammond organ Tradename for a brand of ELECTRONIC ORGAN invented by Laurens Hammond (1895–1973) and first manufactured by the US Hammond Company in 1935. With two keyboards and no pipes, it operated by means of an arrangement of rotating discs and electromagnetic pickups. The instrument proved especially popular with DANCE BANDS, although many performers built careers as soloists on it.

Hampton, Lionel (1908–) Black US JAZZ vibraphonist, bandleader, pianist, drummer and singer, who emerged as one of the leading jazz performers of his time. Hampton took his first steps in music while he was a student in Wisconsin, where he was taught the basic techniques by a Dominican nun. His professional début came when he was a teenager, and he went on to work as a drummer with the bands of Les Hite and Louis ARMSTRONG. Although he had started by playing the xylophone, he took up the vibraphone in 1930 and proved its potential as a jazz instrument while playing with the Benny GOODMAN quartet (1936–40) and also occasionally appearing with Goodman's BIG BAND. From the mid-1930s he also led his own small groups, making admired recordings and recruiting many of the finest musicians then active.

Hampton formed his first big band in 1941 and made it one of the most popular of the 1940s and 1950s, incorporating elements of RHYTHM-AND-BLUES and winning equal acclaim for exciting up-tempo numbers and for atmospheric ballads. His big bands were hugely successful and appeared on tour all over the world even after most other similar outfits had been obliged to cease operations, consolidating Hampton's status as a jazz legend. Among his most celebrated compositions are 'Vibraphone Blues' (1936), 'Blues in My Flat' (1938), 'Flyin' Home' (1939), and 'Hamp's Boogie-woogie' (1945). He finally broke up his big band in 1965 and worked instead with a sextet, although he continued to lead an all-star orchestra at festivals through the 1970s and 1980s. He has also acted in a number of films.

Outside music, Hampton and his wife are noted for their support for urban-renewal projects in Harlem and for their efforts to found a Harlem University.

Hancock, Herbie (Herbert Jeffrey Hancock; 1940–   ) US JAZZ pianist, who emerged as a leading figure in a range of CROSSOVER styles in the 1960s. A child prodigy, who played Mozart with the CHICAGO SYMPHONY ORCHESTRA at the age of 12, he issued a well-received début solo album and then served as pianist in the band of Miles DAVIS (1963–68). He founded his own influential sextet (1968), which recorded such hit albums as *Headhunters* (1973). Adopting electronic instruments, he furthered the development of JAZZ-ROCK alongside such stars as Don ELLIS and went on to demonstrate his versatility by venturing into FUNK and PROGRESSIVE ROCK, as well as incorporating the influence of the BLUES, SWING and REGGAE into his music. In the late 1970s, by which time he had released a number of popular hits in the DISCO style, he switched direction once more, recording piano duets with Chick COREA and making his mark on the development of RAP through his experiments with voice synthesizers.

Hancock's most successful releases have ranged from the jazz-rock album *Maiden Voyage* (1964) to the electronic *Future Shock* (1983) and the hit single 'Gimme the Night' (1980), recorded with George BENSON. His SOUNDTRACK for the film *Round Midnight* won him an OSCAR in 1986.

Handy, W(illiam) C(hristopher) (1873–1958) US composer and conductor, nicknamed the Father of the Blues, who played a crucial role in communicating the BLUES tradition to the emerging world of JAZZ in the early years of the century. The son of a strict pastor, who forbade him to pursue his interest in music, Handy dabbled with brass band music and trumpet playing and ultimately led his own jazz and RAGTIME bands. In close contact with bluesmen while touring the southern USA, he attempted to re-create what he heard in his own compositions, which included such hugely influential songs as 'Memphis Blues' (1912), 'St Louis Blues' (1914), which was his most important single work, 'Yellow Dog Blues' (1914), 'Beal Street Blues' (1916), 'John Henry Blues' (1922), 'Harlem Blues' (1923) and 'Atlanta Blues' (1924) among many more. Publishing his own music himself, he did much to spread the blues gospel, and it was largely through his own compositions and transcriptions of traditional blues songs that the 12-bar structure became universally recognized.

Handy went blind in the early 1940s and his life story was told in the film *St Louis Blues* (1958), which starred Nat 'King' COLE.

Hanley, James F(rederick) (1892–1942) US composer and author, who established his reputation with the hit songs he wrote for Broadway during and after the First World War. He began to write for the musical stage while still in the army and subsequently won acclaim for his music for such shows as *Robinson Crusoe* (1916) and *Honeymoon Lane* (1926) and for such series as the *Ziegfeld Follies* and *George White's Scandals*. Among his best-known songs were 'Rose of Washington Square' (1920), 'Second-hand Rose' (1921) and 'Zing Went the Strings of My Heart' (1934).

Hanshaw, Annette (1910–   ) US singer, nicknamed the Personality Girl, who made many successful recordings with some of the great names in JAZZ in the 1920s and 1930s. Encouraged to sing by her future husband, she made her first record in 1926 and subsequently excelled as a singer, backed by impromptu bands that included such greats as Benny GOODMAN, Tommy DORSEY and Joe VENUTI. She retired in 1936.

Hanson, John (John Stanley Watts; 1921–   ) British singer and actor, who emerged as a popular stage and broadcasting star in the 1940s. Having made his professional début in 1946, he sang on various radio and television programmes, eventually hosting his own shows. He was particularly acclaimed in the role of the Red Shadow in *The Desert Song* and appeared in many other MUSICALS of the 1950s and 1960s. The song most closely linked to his name was his own 'A Song of Romance'.

Harbach, Otto (Otto Abels Hauerbach; 1873–1963) US librettist and lyricist, of Danish descent, who collaborated with some of Broadway's most celebrated composers in the 1920s. He established his reputation as a librettist in partnership with Karl HOSCHNA and subsequently teamed up with Rudolf FRIML, contributing to *The Firefly* (1912) and *Rose-Marie* (1924); with Louis HIRSCH; with Vincent YOUMANS, working on *Wildflower* (1923) and *No, No, Nanette* (1925); with George GERSHWIN, on *A Song of the Flame* (1925); with Jerome KERN, on such shows as *Sunny* (1925) and *The Cat and the Fiddle* (1931); and with Sigmund ROMBERG on *The Desert Song* (1926). At one point, at the height of his career in 1925, he was involved in five shows running simultaneously on Broadway.

Harburg, Yip (Isidore Hochberg; 1896–1981) US lyricist, producer and director, who wrote numerous hit songs for MUSICAL shows and films of the 1930s and 1940s. He turned to songwriting after his electrical business collapsed following the Wall Street Crash of 1929, providing lyrics for songs delivered in the course of such shows as *Earl Carroll's Vanities* (1930), the *Ziegfeld Follies* (1934), *Life begins at 8.40* (1934) and *Finiun's Rainbow* (1947) and numbering among his greatest successes 'Brother, Can You Spare a Dime?', 'April in Paris' and 'How are Things in Glocca Morra?'.

As a writer for the cinema, Harburg joined the ranks of the very best lyricists, contributing to such films as *Rio Rita* (1929), *Applause* (1929), *Take a Chance* (1933), from which came 'It's Only a Paper Moon', *The Wizard of Oz* (1939), which produced such classics as 'Over the Rainbow', *Babes on Broadway* (1941), *Cabin in the Sky* (1943), *Can't Help Singing* (1944) and *Kismet* (1944). He died in a car crash.

hard rock A style of ROCK music, in contrast to commercial and easily accessible SOFT ROCK, which is more uncompromising and demanding in terms of content and style. The term was first heard in the late 1960s with the emergence of such bands as CREAM and others, which derived their inspiration from a range of BLUES, POP and ROCK 'N' ROLL.

hardcore Alternative US name for the PUNK ROCK movement of the late 1970s. In the 1980s the term was specially reserved for the most radical forms of post-punk rock, as purveyed by such bands as the DEAD KENNEDYS.

Harline, Leigh (1907–69) US composer and conductor, who is best known for his contribution to various Walt Disney cartoons. Although he also contributed music to other Hollywood movies, his most enduring compositions were written while he was composer and arranger for the Disney Studios (1932–42), his most familiar songs including the likes of 'When you Wish on a Star', which like his score for *Pinocchio* won an OSCAR.

Harmonica Wizard, the *See* Deford BAILEY.

Harnick, Sheldon (1924–   ) US composer and librettist, who emerged as a leading figure on Broadway in the 1950s. Writing in collaboration with composer Jerry BOCK among others, he had a part in such hits as *New Faces* (1952), to which he contributed 'Boston Beguine', *Fiorello!* (1959) and *Fiddler on the Roof* (1964).

Harnoncourt, Nikolaus (1929–   ) Austrian conductor, cellist and musicologist, who has played a key role in the development of the early music movement. Performances by the Concentus Musicus of Vienna, which Harnoncourt founded in 1954, have included works dating from the twelfth century. Among Harnoncourt's many recordings are pieces by Bach, Monteverdi, Handel and Vivaldi.

Harper, Heather (1930–   ) British soprano, born in Northern Ireland, who has won particular acclaim over the years for her performances in the works of Benjamin BRITTEN – she sang in the first performance of his *War Requiem* (1962). She made her operatic début in 1954 and has since appeared at COVENT GARDEN and numerous other leading venues as well as earning a reputation as a concert performer.

Harris, Emmylou (1949–   ) US COUNTRY-ROCK singer, who emerged as a leading star in the 1970s. Early releases as a FOLK-singer failed to prosper, but she established her reputation in 1973 with the album *Pieces of the Sky* and with the Number One single 'If I Could Only Win Your Love' (1975), both of which reflected the influence of the recently deceased Gram Parsons (*see* the BYRDS). She went on to form her own group, the Hot Band, and to record as a backing vocalist with the likes of Bob DYLAN. Dubbed the Queen of Country Music, she continued to appeal to both pop and country audiences throughout the 1970s and 1980s with such best-selling albums as *Luxury Liner* (1977), *Evangeline* (1981), *The Ballad of Sally Rose* (1985), the acclaimed *Trio* (1987), on which she collaborated with Linda RONSTADT and Dolly PARTON, *Brand New Dance* (1990) and *Wrecking Ball* (1995).

Harris, Phil (1904–   ) US singer and bandleader, who emerged as a popular star in the 1930s. He sprang to fame as a star of *George White's Scandals* in the 1930s and subsequently established himself as a prominent star of radio, cinema and television. He led a popular SWING BAND, whose signature tune was 'Rose Room', but was best known for his many novelty songs. Among his most popular songs were 'Woodman, Spare That Tree', 'That's What I Like About the South', 'The Preacher and the Bear' and 'The Thing'. He also recorded COUNTRY material in the 1960s.

Harrison, George (1943–   ) British guitarist, singer and songwriter, who became internationally famous in the 1960s as one of the BEATLES. Harrison, who played in SKIFFLE groups from the mid-1950s, first teamed up with LENNON and MCCARTNEY in the Quarrymen. He proved a highly competent lead guitarist, although the group made relatively little use of his songwriting abilities, a factor in the group's eventual disintegration. Songs by Harrison that the group did use included 'Within You, Without You', which was influenced by Indian music, 'While My Guitar Gently Weeps', 'Something', which Frank SINATRA called the best love song in 30 years, and 'Here Comes the Sun'.

After the break-up of the Beatles, Harrison won acclaim for *All Things Must Pass* (1970) and topped the singles charts with 'My Sweet Lord' (1970), but he was obliged to pay compensation when it was decided he had unconsciously plagiarized the 1963 CHIFFONS hit 'He's So Fine'. Harrison was the guiding force behind the charity concerts and record in aid of the stricken in Bangladesh in 1971, although tax wrangles meant that little was paid out until 1981.

Dark Horse (1974) was reasonably well received, but subsequent releases were less successful, and Harrison spent much of his time producing other artists and developing his own Handmade Films company. He announced his retirement as a musician in 1984 but subsequently teamed up with

Bob DYLAN, Tom PETTY, Jeff Lynne and Roy ORBISON as the Traveling Wilburys. In 1987 'Got My Mind Set on You', from the hit album *Cloud Nine*, reached Number Two in the charts.

Hart, Lorenz Milton (1895–1943) US lyricist and librettist, who won fame for his lengthy collaboration with the composer Richard RODGERS on a series of hit stage MUSICALS and film scores. Having met Rodgers while still a student at Columbia University, he provided witty lyrics for numerous songs and some 30 stage shows and films, of which the most successful included *The Girl Friend* (1926), *Ever Green* (1930), *On Your Toes* (1936), *Babes in Arms* (1937), *The Boys from Syracuse* (1938) and *Pal Joey* (1940). Towards the end of his career his relations with Rodgers and others became increasingly strained as a result of his mercurial temperament and growing alcoholism. Rodgers eventually teamed up with a new partner, Oscar HAMMERSTEIN, and Hart felt the success of their show *Oklahoma!* especially keenly. Not long after, he died of pneumonia after being found insensible with drink in a rainfilled gutter outside a New York bar.

> A partner, a best friend, and a source of permanent irritation.
> RICHARD RODGERS

Hatch, Tony (1939–   ) British composer, pianist, singer and arranger, who wrote a string of hit singles in the 1960s. After early training as a chorister, he enjoyed his first hits in 1960, with 'Look for a Star' and 'Messing About on the River'; four years later Petula CLARK recorded his 'Downtown' with huge success. Subsequently he married singer Jackie Trent and wrote with her such songs as 'Where are You Now?', which Trent took to Number One in 1965, 'Don't Sleep in the Subway' and 'Joanna', as well as the musicals *The Card* (1973) and *Rock Nativity* (1975). 'Sad Sweet Dreamer', written for Sweet Sensation, reached Number One in 1974. His theme tunes for television have included those for *Crossroads* and *Emmerdale Farm*.

Hawaiian guitar Type of guitar on which the strings are stopped not by the fingers but by a steel bar, thus allowing a smooth transition from one note to another (akin to BOTTLENECK).

Hawk *See* Coleman HAWKINS.

Hawkins, Coleman (1901–69) Black US JAZZ saxophonist, nicknamed Hawk or Bean, who emerged as one of the most influential jazz musicians of his generation. In the 1920s Hawkins revolutionized the role of the tenor saxophone (until then of limited potential) by using a stiff reed that increased the volume that he could produce. This innovation meant that the saxophone could now be treated as a solo instrument above the backing of even a large jazz band, while the rich tone of Hawkins's playing alerted many others to new musical possibilities.

Hawkins consolidated his reputation with acclaimed appearances with mostly small groups – notably that of Fletcher HENDERSON (1923–34) – in both the USA and in Europe and made many important recordings, his most celebrated numbers including 'St Louis Shuffle' (1927), 'Sugar Foot Stomp' (1931), 'Hocus Pocus' (1934), the classic 'Body and Soul' (1939), which he made with his own band, 'I Surrender Dear' (1940), 'I Only Have Eyes for You' (1944) and 'Picasso' (1948). He was a pioneer of BEBOP in the mid-1940s and collaborated with many leading jazzmen of the day, including Dizzy GILLESPIE, Thelonious MONK and Django REINHARDT. A giant in MAINSTREAM jazz in the 1960s and 1970s with such albums as *The Hawk Flies High* (1957), he continued to lead his own groups until his death from pneumonia.

I like most music unless it's wrong.
COLEMAN HAWKINS

Hawkins, Erskine (1913–   ) US JAZZ trumpeter and bandleader, nicknamed the Twentieth-century Gabriel, who led one of the most popular big bands of the 1940s. Influenced by the trumpet playing of Louis ARMSTRONG, he formed his band in 1934 and established it as one of the top acts with such hits as 'Tuxedo Junction' (1939), which he helped to write, 'Dolomite' (1940), 'Someone's Rockin' My Dreamboat' (1941) and 'Tippin' In' (1945). He worked with a quartet from 1960.

Hawkwind British HARD ROCK group, which emerged as one of the most dynamic and imaginative rock outfits of the early 1970s. Inspired by science-fiction and influenced by psychedelia and the hippie culture of the late 1960s, the band earned a reputation as a major live act and first reached the Top 20 in 1971 with the album *In Search of Space*.

The live *Space Ritual* (1973) was equally successful, and the single 'Silver Machine' proved a huge hit, although subsequent releases had mixed receptions. 'Urban Guerrilla' had to be withdrawn when its release coincided with terrorist bombings in London. The band's personnel has changed over its long history; the most influential members have included singer and saxophonist Nik Turner, bassist Lemmy (Ian Kilminster), both of whom left in the 1970s (Lemmy being expelled after being charged with drug offences), singer and guitarist Dave Brock and drummer Ginger Baker (*see* CREAM). Science-fiction novelist Michael Moorcock was also a member of the group for a time. Recent releases include *Electric Teepee* (1992).

Hayes, Isaac (1942–   ) US SOUL singer-songwriter and producer, nicknamed Black Moses, who built up a massive following in the early 1970s. A giant in the world of soul music, Hayes began to attract attention while working as a songwriter for STAX RECORDS. He made his first recordings as a solo artist in 1967 and had his first hit two years later with the album *Hot Buttered Soul*. He had further hits with the albums *Movement* (1970), *To Be Continued* (1970) and *Black Moses* (1971) as well as co-writing and producing 'Soul Man' for SAM AND DAVE. In 1971 he won an Oscar with the chart-topping SOUNDTRACK for the film *Shaft* and went on to write more music for the movies before splitting from Stax in 1975 and being obliged to file for bankruptcy with debts of $6 million in 1976. He stayed in music as a producer and was in the charts once more in 1986 with the single 'Ike's Rap'. In 1995 he released the albums *Raw and Refined* and *Branded*.

Haymes, Dick (1916–80) US singer, of mixed Anglo-Irish descent, who ranked alongside Bing CROSBY and Frank SINATRA as one of the most popular singers of the 1940s. He achieved fame singing with the bands of Benny GOODMAN and Tommy DORSEY in the early 1940s and numbered among his greatest hits 'I'll Get By', 'The More I See You', 'Till the End of Time' and 'It's a Grand Night for Singing'. He starred in several movies but had less success in the 1950s, with mounting debts, a string of failed marriages and the threat of deportation, although he enjoyed a minor comeback shortly before his death.

headbanger A HEAVY METAL fan, who typically shakes his head rhythmically in response to the beat. Headbangers became an increasingly common sight at rock concerts in the 1970s, many playing imaginary AIR GUITARS, although medical experts warned that such violent head movements might cause serious injury.

Heath, Ted (1900–69) British bandleader and trombonist, who led one of the most popular SWING bands of the 1940s and 1950s. Having served as a member of a series of notable bands, including those of Jack HYLTON and GERALDO, he formed his own band in 1944 and set about creating a British equivalent of the swing style of Glenn MILLER and other US stars, his signature tune being his own 'Listen to My Music' (1944). The band remained in operation until his death and recorded many hits, including 'Swinging Shepherd Blues' and 'Hot Toddy' (both 1953). It was one of the few British BIG BANDS to win acclaim on tours of the USA.

heavy metal Loosely speaking, a genre of HARD ROCK music, in which all other considerations are secondary to a driving, repetitive beat and deafening volume. Heavy metal is now taken to cover a wide range of styles, such as THRASH, DEATH METAL and SHOCK ROCK, though to many devoted HEADBANGERS the term itself evokes the relatively basic style promulgated by such bands as DEEP PURPLE and AC/DC in the early 1970s, when similar outfits proliferated on both sides of the Atlantic. Among their successors, which rose to fame as part of the so-called New Wave of British Heavy Metal in the early 1980s, may be included MOTÖRHEAD and IRON MAIDEN.

Characteristics of most heavy metal styles include screaming, uptempo ELECTRIC GUITAR breaks and much macho posturing by performers. Lyrics are sometimes ambitious, but are more often unintelligible or simple expressions of aggression or elation.

The term heavy metal appears, in fact, to pre-date the development of the musical genre, being used – possibly for the first time – by William Burroughs in the phrase 'heavy metal thunder' in the novel *The Naked Lunch* (1959) and subsequently being employed in descriptions of powerful motorbikes before being quoted in a musical context by STEPPENWOLF in the course of 'Born to be Wild' (1968).

Hefti, Neal (1922–) US JAZZ composer, conductor and trumpeter, who collaborated with several leading jazzmen of the 1940s and 1950s. Working with such jazzmen as Earl HINES, Charlie BARNET, Woody HERMAN, Benny CARTER, Harry JAMES and Count BASIE, he wrote such hits as 'Whirlybird', 'Woodchopper's Ball' and 'Lil' Darlin'' and led his own band for a brief period in the early 1950s. Among his most frequently heard compositions is the theme tune of the US television series *Batman*.

Heifetz, Jascha (1901–87) US violinist, born in Lithuania, who proved to be one of the great violinists of the century. Heifetz, the son of a famous violinist, was a child prodigy, mastering Mendelssohn's violin concerto when he was six years old and making his first public appearances at the age of just eight. He was one of the youngest students to attend the Imperial Conservatory in St Petersburg and was launched on a long and immensely successful international career in 1912 when he was 12 years old.

Heifetz left Russia for good after the 1917 Revolution and eventually settled in the USA, although he continued to tour widely to unflagging acclaim. His brilliant and impassioned playing was preserved on numerous recordings and many composers wrote works for him – among them William WALTON, who composed his violin concerto (1939) at Heifetz's request, and Louis GRUENBERG. After his retirement as a performer, he worked as a teacher.

Henderson, (James) Fletcher (1897–1952) Black US JAZZ pianist, bandleader, composer and arranger, nicknamed Smack, who was one of the leading figures in the BIG BAND era of the 1930s. Having trained as a chemist, Henderson won acclaim with his arrangements for such singers as Bessie SMITH before forming his first big band in 1924 when, billed as the Coloured Paul Whiteman, he attracted to his banner such prodigious talents as Louis ARMSTRONG, Coleman HAWKINS, Fats WALLER and Don REDMAN, his arranger until 1927.

Narrowly surviving a car accident in 1928, which appeared to rob him of what little business acumen he had previously had, Henderson played a crucial role in creating the SWING style by organizing the brass and reed sections of his band as two distinct groups and giving a prominent role to soloists. Henderson wrote the arrangements himself, both for his own orchestra (which broke up for good in the mid-1930s) and for other bands, of which the most successful proved to be that of Benny GOODMAN, who eventually took Henderson on as his staff arranger and readily acknowledged his debt. Goodman also employed Henderson as pianist with his celebrated sextet in the late 1930s. Henderson's arrangements dominated the swing era; among his most popular hits were 'Henderson Stomp', 'Stampede', 'Hot 'n' Anxious', 'Sometimes I'm Happy', 'Stomping at the Savoy', 'King Porter Stomp' and 'Down South Camp Meeting'.

Henderson, Ray (1896–1970) US composer, who wrote numerous hit songs of the 1920s and 1930s, many in collaboration with lyricists Lew BROWN and Buddy DESYLVA. Having started out as a pianist, he concentrated on songwriting from 1922, when he teamed up with Lew Brown. Writing for popular revues and other MUSICAL shows, he numbered among his early successes such classics as 'Don't Bring Lulu' (1925), 'Bye Bye, Blackbird' (1926) and 'Alabamy Bound' (1927). After DeSylva joined forces with Henderson and Brown in 1925 the hits came thick and fast, the most popular including 'Lucky Day' (1926), 'Birth of the Blues' (1926), 'Black Bottom' (1926), 'I'm on the Crest of a Wave' (1928), 'Sonny Boy' (1928), 'My Lucky Star' (1928) and 'Button up Your Overcoat' (1929).

DeSylva left in 1935 but Henderson continued, in partnership with both Brown and others, and added to his repertoire of hits such classics as 'Life is Just a Bowl of Cherries' (1931), 'Nasty Man' (1934) and 'Animal Crackers in My Soup', which Shirley TEMPLE sang in the film *Curly Top* (1935). The history of the Henderson–Brown–DeSylva collaboration was traced in the film *The Best Things In Life Are Free* (1956).

Hendrix, Jimi (James Marshall Hendrix; 1942–70) Black US rock guitarist, at one time nicknamed, somewhat curiously, the Black Elvis, who was hailed as the most gifted rock guitarist of his generation. Of mixed Cherokee Indian and Mexican descent, Hendrix, the son of a gardener, served in a parachute regiment (leaving after an injury on his 26th parachute jump) before beginning a career in RHYTHM-AND-BLUES in 1963 and backing such stars as B.B.

KING and LITTLE RICHARD. He formed his own band, Jimmy James and his Blue Flames, and began to consolidate his growing reputation, which culminated in an invitation from Bryan 'Chas' Chandler (who promised Hendrix a meeting with Eric CLAPTON) to come to London. There he formed the celebrated Jimi Hendrix Experience trio, which rapidly made its mark playing high-volume, largely improvised rock that had at its core the screaming, unrestrained and unbelievably rapid electric guitar-work of Hendrix himself.

The single 'Hey Joe' was a hit in the UK in 1967 and was followed by 'Purple Haze' and other classic releases, including the albums *Are You Experienced?* (1967) and *Electric Ladyland* (1968), from which came such hits as 'All Along the Watchtower'. Hendrix was one of the star performers at the MONTEREY POP FESTIVAL in 1967 and two years later at WOODSTOCK, although a US tour was abandoned after opposition from the Daughters of the American Revolution, who objected to the sexual overtones of his live act.

After the trio split up, Hendrix formed a new group called the Band of Gypsies, which appeared at the ISLE OF WIGHT Festival in 1970, but further progress came to an abrupt end when Hendrix was found dead after mixing drink and drugs. Claims that a suicide note had been found were never verified. 'Voodoo Child' reached Number One in the UK on a wave of mourning in the rock community.

Playing his FENDER Stratocaster on occasion with his teeth (or else behind his back, between his legs, or on the floor) and even setting light to it – gimmicks of which he quickly tired – Hendrix explored the possibilities of electronic feedback and other effects and stretched the boundaries of accepted guitar technique (all this despite the fact that he was left-handed and played a right-handed instrument). His many admirers included Jeff BECK, Bob DYLAN, Miles DAVIS and Pete Townshend (*see* the WHO).

> Music is a safe kind of high.
> JIMI HENDRIX

> I've just got to get out. Maybe to Venus or somewhere. Some place *you* won't be able to find me.
> JIMI HENDRIX

Henecker, David (1906–) British composer, who wrote a number of highly successful stage MUSICALS. After military training, he established his reputation in the musical theatre with such shows as *Expresso Bongo* (1958), *Irma la Douce* (1958), *Half a Sixpence* (1963) and *Charlie Girl* (1965).

Henry, Pierre (1927–   ) French composer, who pioneered CONCRETE MUSIC in the 1950s. A pupil of Olivier MESSIAEN and Nadia BOULANGER, he broke new ground with his *Symphonie pour un homme seul* (1950); subsequent works included *Le Voyage* (1962), ballets, film music and various mixed-media pieces, including *Kyldex* (1973).

Henze, Hans Werner (1926–   ) German composer, who emerged as a leading figure in modern classical music after the Second World War. A former soldier, who deserted to Denmark at the end of the war, Henze was a pupil of Wolfgang Fortner (1907–87) and wrote his first compositions in a neoclassical style. He subsequently became interested in SERIALISM, which influenced such successful pieces as the opera *Boulevard Solitude* (1952). His piano concerto won the Schumann Prize in 1951, and two years later he moved to Italy, where he rejected serialist techniques in favour of a more lyrical style.

Composing such operas as *Elegy for Young Lovers* (1961) and *The Bassarids* (1966) as well as symphonies and choral and chamber works, Henze won acclaim for his integration of classical structures and romantic melody but then set off in a new direction as his music began to incorporate AVANT-GARDE concepts and to reflect Marxist ideology. His Sixth Symphony was inspired by the problems faced by Marxist Cuba, while the admired song-cycle *El Cimarrón* (1970) took as its subject the experiences of an escaped Cuban slave. *The Raft of the Medusa* – dedicated to Ché Guevara – proved so contentious it provoked a riot on its first performance in 1968 – the chorus refused to sing unless a red flag hoisted in the concert hall was taken down. Other pieces from this phase in Henze's career included the oratorios *Voices* (1973) and *Tristan* (1973).

In 1977 he inaugurated the annual music festival at Montepulciano and latterly has adopted a more temperate, story-based style.

My profession ... consists of bringing truths nearer to the point where they explode.
HANS WERNER HENZE, *Music and Politics*, 1982

Herbert, Victor (August) (1859–1924) US composer, conductor and cellist, born in Ireland, who is remembered for the many popular operettas he created in the early years of the century. Principal cellist with the Metropolitan Orchestra in New York and also active as a conductor and teacher, he enjoyed his greatest success with the operettas *Babes in Toyland* (1903), *Naughty Marietta* (1910) and *Sweethearts* (1913). His shows marked the development of the modern musical comedy, as distinct from the more old-fashioned Viennese style. Herbert also contributed what is often described as the first specially commissioned SOUNDTRACK – for *The Birth of a Nation* (1916).

Herman, Jerry (1933–   ) US composer, who first established his reputation as a writer for the musical stage in the 1950s. Having written for various revues and for CABARET, he enjoyed moderate successes with such MUSICALS as *I Feel Wonderful* (1954), *Nightcap* (1958) and *Milk and Honey* (1961) and then conquered all with the hit show *Hello, Dolly!* (1964), which became the longest-running show in the history of Broadway. Subsequent musicals by his hand have included *Mame* (1966), *Mack and Mabel* (1974) and the hugely acclaimed *La Cage aux Folles* (1983).

Herman, Woody (Woodrow Charles Herman; 1913–87) US bandleader, clarinettist, saxophonist and composer, who was one of the leading figures of the BIG BAND era. Born into a musical family, he made his stage début at the age of nine, as the Boy Wonder of the Clarinet, and subsequently worked with several bands as clarinettist and singer. He led his first band – billed the Band that Plays the Blues – in 1936 and rapidly made it one of the most popular of the day with such hits as 'At the Woodchoppers' Ball', which sold over a million copies, 'Blue Flame', which became the band's signature tune, and 'Blues in the Night'. Under Herman's direction the band, often nicknamed the Herd, was renewed several times with fresh personnel in the war years and consolidated its reputation as the best White big band with such classics as 'Apple Honey', 'Northwest

Passage', 'Do Nothing Till You Hear from Me', 'Caldonia', 'Goosey Gander' and 'Ebony Concerto', which was composed specifically for them by Igor STRAVINSKY in 1946.

A second version of the band – called the Second Herd or the Four Brothers' Band and including players of the stature of Stan GETZ and Zoot SIMS – was equally adventurous and adopted a BOP style, having hits with such tunes as 'Four Brothers', 'Keen and Peachy', and 'Early Autumn', but crippled Herman financially, obliging him to form further reincarnations of the group through the 1950s and 1960s. He continued to explore new musical possibilities and in the 1960s even experimented with JAZZ-ROCK. Thoughts of retirement in his final years were banished by the realization that he owed millions of dollars of tax because of the fraudulent activities of the band's manager.

> We never feel we're actually working *for* the man. It's more like working *with* him.
> NAT PIERCE

Herman's Hermits British pop group, which enjoyed huge success in the singles charts in the 1960s. The Hermits sprang to fame after being taken up by the producer Mickie MOST, who reshaped the group around singer and former *Coronation Street* actor Peter Noone (1947–) in 1964. The other members were guitarists Derek 'Lek' Leckenby (1946–94) and Keith Hopwood (1946–), bassist Karl Green (1946–) and drummer Barry Whitwam (1946–). The group topped the British charts with Barl Jean's 'I'm into Something Good' (1964) and consolidated its popularity – notably in the USA – with such lively hits as 'Mrs Brown You've Got a Lovely Daughter', 'I'm Henry VIII I am' and 'My Sentimental Friend' before breaking up in 1971 (Noone going on to a spasmodic solo career).

Herrmann, Bernard (1911–75) US composer, who provided the SOUNDTRACKS for numerous celebrated movies. He began as a collaborator of Orson Welles, composing the music for *Citizen Kane* (1940), and subsequently won acclaim for his highly effective partnership with director Alfred Hitchcock. He contributed symphonic scores to such films as *The Devil and Daniel Webster* (1941), for which he won an OSCAR, *The Magnificent Ambersons* (1942),

Jane Eyre (1942), *The Snows of Kilimanjaro* (1952), *The Man Who Knew Too Much* (1956), *Vertigo* (1958), *North by Northwest* (1959), *Psycho* (1960), famous for the piercing soundtrack accompanying the terrifying 'shower scene', *The Birds* (1963) and *Taxi Driver* (1975). Other compositions included the cantata *Moby Dick* (1938) and the opera *Wuthering Heights* (1950). He was also conductor of the Columbia Broadcast Symphony Orchestra for many years and did much to promote the work of Charles IVES and many unrecognized composers.

Hess, Dame Myra (1890–1965) British pianist, who was acknowledged as one of the great concert pianists of the wartime and postwar period. A scholar of the Royal Academy of Music, she established her reputation with her début playing Beethoven's Fourth Piano Concerto under Sir Thomas BEECHAM in 1907. She won international acclaim playing the works of Bach, Brahms, Mozart, Scarlatti and Schumann among others. During the Second World War she was famous for the lunchtime concerts she organized at the National Gallery as part of the effort to maintain morale in the capital. She also adapted many baroque works for the piano, her greatest successes in this field including Bach's 'Jesu, Joy of Man's Desiring'.

Heywood, Eddie (1915–89) US pianist, bandleader, composer and arranger, who worked with many of the great singers in JAZZ history. Having played in a number of bands, he served as accompanist to the likes of Billie HOLIDAY, Ella FITZGERALD and Bing CROSBY. His most successful recordings included 'Begin the Beguine' (1943) and 'Near You' (1944). He concentrated on composition after arthritis ended his playing career, composing such hits as 'Canadian Sunset', 'Land of Dreams' and 'I'm Saving Myself for You'.

hi-fi High fidelity. The reproduction of music using technologically advanced systems in which distortion is kept to a minimum and the original sound is faithfully recreated. The term was first used in the 1960s.

High-hat Tragedian of Song, the *See* Ted LEWIS.

high life Genre of African POP music, which

first caught on in Ghana and Sierra Leone in the 1920s and subsequently became established as the most influential pop style to originate in Africa in the twentieth century. High life incorporates the complex rhythms of traditional African music and applies them to the tunes and instrumentation of western pop, sub-genres taking in brass bands, religious music, BIG BAND jazz and, in the 1970s, even DISCO. Since the 1970s JUJU has largely replaced high life as the dominant musical style of Nigeria and several other states. *See also* AFRO-ROCK.

Hill, Billy (1899–1940) US songwriter and lyricist, who emerged as one of the most successful TIN PAN ALLEY composers of the 1930s. His experiences as an adventurer among the cowboys and goldminers of the West were reflected in his many hit songs, which included 'The Last Roundup' (1933), 'Wagon Wheels' (1934), 'Empty Saddles' (1936) and 'Call of the Canyon' (1940).

hillbilly Style of traditional COUNTRY music that enjoyed a revival in the 1920s and 1930s. The music of the rural southern USA, hillbilly music is generally played on string instruments and has its origins ultimately in the FOLK-songs that came to the country with the English colonists. Popular performers of hillbilly songs in the 1920s included 'Fiddlin'' John CARSON and Vernon Dalhart (best known for his 1924 hit 'The Prisoner's Song'). The unsophisticated hillbilly style was eventually eclipsed to some extent in the 1930s when other influences such as those of JAZZ, BLUES and cajun music made themselves felt in the style labelled WESTERN SWING and in the 1940s the style became virtually synonymous with COUNTRY.

Hillbilly Cat, the *See* Elvis PRESLEY.

Hindemith, Paul (1895–1963) German composer, viola and violin player and conductor, a US citizen from 1946, who first emerged as one of the most important and prolific composers of contemporary music in the 1920s. Hindemith embarked on a career as a professional musician when he was only 11 years old, playing in cafés and theatres, and by the age of 20 was leader of the Frankfurt Opera Orchestra. Subsequently he co-founded the celebrated Amar Quartet with Turkish violinist Licco Amar

and concentrated on performing modern works as well as working as a soloist. He became a leading figure in the foundation of several major music festivals in Germany and was given a music professorship in Berlin, but then fell foul of the Nazi authorities and emigrated to Turkey, eventually settling in 1939 in the USA, where he accepted a post at Yale. He moved to Zurich in 1953 and was busy in his remaining years as a conductor and soloist.

Believing that his music should expound a moral purpose, Hindemith was one of the principal writers of UTILITY MUSIC, writing many pieces specifically for amateurs and, in the process, developing a fresh set of contrapuntal techniques that were popularly dubbed 'Back-to-Bach'. He also experimented with JAZZ elements in some of his daring early compositions, although much of his most highly respected later work was written in a broadly neoclassical style incorporating compound rhythms and polyphony. Rejecting the 12-NOTE system devised by Arnold SCHOENBERG he assembled his own 12-note technique, based on natural harmonies.

Hindemith's most successful works included such operas as *Cardillac* (1926) and his masterpiece *Mathis der Maler* (1934), which was set against the background of the Peasants' Revolt of 1524 and was also adapted by the composer in symphonic form, the ballets *Nobilissima visione* (1936) and *The Four Temperaments* (1940), and much orchestral and chamber music.

Hindemith's proud boast was that he could play every instrument in the orchestra, and as if to prove it he wrote at least one sonata for virtually all the standard instruments.

> There are only two things worth aiming for: good music and a clean conscience.
> PAUL HINDEMITH, letter, 1938

> He doesn't compose, he makes music.
> PAUL DEKKER, of Hindemith (attributed)

Hines, Earl (Kenneth) (1903–83) Black US JAZZ pianist, bandleader and composer, nicknamed Fatha, who was among the most celebrated jazzmen of his generation. His professional career took off after he moved to Chicago in 1922, and he was soon making numerous recordings with such emerging talents as Louis ARMSTRONG, joining his Hot Five in 1928 and making such hits as the duet 'Weather Bird'. His full, complex and endlessly innovative playing style was enormously influential and inspired many imitators. In 1928 he graduated as a bandleader himself – for many years at the Grand Terrace in Chicago – and remained in this role until 1947, musicians under his control including such developing stars as Charlie PARKER and Dizzy GILLESPIE.

He reunited with Armstrong in 1948 but disappeared from view in the 1950s before returning to the limelight on a wave of public nostalgia in 1964. He continued to tour widely to consistent acclaim and made many more recordings in his final years, eventually dying after a heart attack. Among his most popular compositions were 'Rosetta' (1928), 'Deep Forest' (1933), which was his band's signature tune, and 'Piano Man' (1942).

hip-hop Broad term describing a range of Black POP music of the 1980s. Hip-hop originated as part of New York's street culture in the early 1980s and came to include RAP and SCRATCHING. On the dance floor it was coupled with break-dancing, robotics and other dance crazes; devotees were also linked with the contemporary fad for spray-painted graffiti. Leading acts include Africa Bambaata and Grandmaster Flash.

Hirsch, Louis A(chille) (1887–1924) US composer, who was among the most successful writers for the musical stage before and during the First World War. Having abandoned plans to become a concert pianist, Hirsch contributed to numerous Broadway shows from 1907 on. His first MUSICAL, *He Came from Milwaukee*, was staged in 1910, and he went on to consolidate his reputation with such hits as *Vera Violetta* (1911), *The Whirl of Society* (1912) and *The Passing Show* (1912), which starred Al JOLSON. Among the most popular of his later shows were *Hullo, Ragtime!* (1912) and several editions of both the *Ziegfeld Follies* and the *Greenwich Village Follies*.

His Master's Voice Tradename of record label belonging to the British Gramophone Company, which is now part of the EMI organization. The name originated in a painting of a dog staring into the trumpet of a wax cylinder phonograph player, the work of the artist Francis Barraud (1856–1924). The dog used as a model for the painting was the artist's own terrier cross, called Nipper, though the machine depicted was altered to a more up-to-date version with a brass horn at the request of the company, when they purchased the right to use the painting in publicity and on record labels in 1899 (in fact the outlines of the original machine are still discernible). The picture (kept at EMI headquarters in London) has continued to be used ever since, still with Nipper in his place of honour, although the dog himself died in 1897. Difficulties over the cultural status of the dog led to some countries being slow to accept the label – in India, for example, Nipper's place was taken by a cobra. Various parodies of the painting have been executed over the years, including one commissioned by a brewing company in which Nipper sniffs quizzically at a glass of his master's stout.

Artists recorded on HMV have included Enrico CARUSO, Harry LAUDER, Louis ARMSTRONG, MANFRED MANN and Andrew LLOYD WEBBER. Since 1968 it has been confined to classical recordings alone.

Hodges, Johnny (1907–70) US JAZZ saxophonist, variously nicknamed Jeep and Squatty Roo, who won wide acclaim as one of the pillars of the Duke ELLINGTON band. Another of his nicknames, Rabbit, was popularly supposed to be a reference to his liking for salad sandwiches but is believed by others to date from his schooldays, when he was renowned for his speed in out-running truancy officers. Hodges studied the saxophone with Sidney BECHET before establishing himself as a leading talent on the alto saxophone. He joined Ellington in 1928 and remained with him for much of the rest of his career (with a break to run his own bands in the early 1950s). His most successful recordings included 'Daydream', 'I Let a Song Go out of My Heart', 'Sunny Side of the Street', 'Things Ain't What They Used To Be', 'Passion', 'Black Butterfly', 'Junior Hop' and 'Castle Rock'.

> The band will never sound the same.
> DUKE ELLINGTON, on Hodges's death

Hoffman, Al (1902–60) US composer, born in Russia, who wrote numerous hit songs for the stage and the cinema in the 1930s and 1940s. He led his own DANCE BAND in the 1920s before concentrating on writing and subsequently provided the scores for several films starring Jack BUCHANAN, among others. His songs included 'She

Shall Have Music' (1935), 'Everything Stops for Tea' (1935), 'I'm in a Dancing Mood' (1936) and 'Mairzy Doats' (1944).

Hoffnung, Gerard (1925–59) British tuba player, cartoonist and raconteur, of German extraction, who was hugely popular for his witty send-ups of classical musicians and music. Hoffnung's cartoons were widely appreciated both inside and outside the music profession, and in the 1950s audiences flocked to special Hoffnung Music Festivals, in which he mixed comical musical passages with hilarious monologues. A number of distinguished composers collaborated with these entertainments, Sir Malcolm ARNOLD writing for Hoffnung a 'Grand, Grand Overture for Three Vacuum Cleaners, Floor Polisher, Rifles and Orchestra' and Austrian composer Joseph Horovitz (1926–) contributing *Horrortorio*.

Hogwood, Christopher (1941–) British harpsichordist, conductor and musicologist, who emerged as one of the foremost figures in the authentic music revival that gathered pace in the 1960s. Recruited as a founder member of the influential EARLY MUSIC CONSORT in 1967, he went on to establish the Academy of Ancient Music in 1973 and has since made many acclaimed recordings of eighteenth-century music using authentic instruments. He was also appointed artistic director of the Handel and Haydn Society of Boston (1986) and was director (1988–92) of the St Paul Chamber Orchestra, Minneapolis.

Holiday, Billie (Eleonora Fagan Holiday; 1915–59) Black US JAZZ singer, nicknamed the First Lady of the Blues and Lady Day (the latter name was first bestowed on her by her saxophonist Lester YOUNG, because of her regal dignity in the face of her tragic private life), who achieved legendary status as one of the great jazz singers of all time. The daughter of a jazz guitarist, she was raped as a child and washed floors in a brothel but became interested in jazz after hearing recordings by Bessie SMITH and Louis ARMSTRONG. Soon she was singing in unfashionable Harlem night clubs, where she was eventually 'discovered' by John HAMMOND (she adopted the name Billie in homage to the film actress Billie Dove, who was one of her idols as a child). She made her first

record with the band of Benny GOODMAN in 1933 and subsequently made numerous classic records with a host of small groups as well as appearing at prestigious venues, including Carnegie Hall, with such stars as Count BASIE and Artie SHAW. Her most regular accompanists included pianist Teddy WILSON and Lester Young. Eventually tiring of playing with bands, she opted for a solo career from 1939.

Holiday's lack of any formal training allowed her natural musicality full expression, and audiences were universally overwhelmed by her uniquely atmospheric, bitter-sweet style of delivery. Among her most acclaimed recordings were 'If Dreams Come True', 'Lover Man', 'A Fine Romance', 'What Shall I Say?', 'Now or Never', 'Nice Work if You Can Get It', 'Gloomy Sunday', 'Fine and Mellow' and 'Strange Fruit', a protest song concerning lynching.

The hardships of Holiday's early life had, however, left their mark, and even after she became famous she was haunted by a deep sense of insecurity, finding solace in drink and drugs and becoming a heroin addict (she was sentenced to a term in a reformatory for drug offences in 1947). Her health declined steadily from the mid-1940s, although she continued to perform with great dignity and courage throughout the 1950s – notably on European tours in 1954 and 1958 – and she remained arguably the finest jazz singer of them all until her early death from heart and liver disease. As a bitter footnote to her life, the authorities arrested her for possession of drugs even as she lay on her deathbed. Her autobiography, *Lady Sings the Blues*, was published in 1956 and filmed, with mixed results, in 1972 with Diana ROSS in the lead role.

> That girl's got it.
> MILDRED BAILEY, singer, on first hearing Holiday, c.1933

> I can't stand to sing the same song the same way two nights in succession. If you can, then it ain't music, it's close order drill or exercise or yodelling or something, not music.
> BILLIE HOLIDAY

> Lady Day is unquestionably the most important influence on American popular singing in the last 20 years.
> FRANK SINATRA, 1958

Holland, Dozier and Holland US songwriting partnership, which created numerous hits for MOTOWN in the 1960s. Lamont Dozier (1941–) and brothers Eddie Holland (1939–) and Brian Holland (1941–) came together in 1962 and created numerous hits over the next six years. Their greatest successes included several songs written for the SUPREMES, seven of which reached Number One, as well as hits for the TEMPTATIONS, the FOUR TOPS and Marvin GAYE among others. Their best-known compositions, before they finally split up in 1968, included 'Baby Love' (1964), 'Where Did Our Love Go?' (1964), 'Stop! In the Name of Love' (1965), 'I Can't Help Myself' (1965), 'You Can't Hurry Love' (1965) and 'Reach Out, I'll be There' (1966).

Hollander, Frederick (1896–1976) German composer, resident in the USA for many years, whose career was closely associated with that of Marlene DIETRICH. The son of a composer for the theatre, Hollander collaborated with Max Reinhardt in REVUE before concentrating on writing for the cinema. He carved a niche for himself in the history of film music with his score for *The Blue Angel* (1930), in which Dietrich sang the classic 'Falling in Love Again'. Subsequent scores included those for the films *Anything Goes* (1936), *Destry Rides Again* (1939), the highlight of which came with Dietrich singing 'See What the Boys in the Back Room Will Have', and *The Man Who Came To Dinner* (1942).

Hollies, the British pop group, which enjoyed more hits than almost any other British band of the same era. Based originally in Manchester, the Hollies – formed in 1962 and named in tribute to Buddy HOLLY – consisted of singer Allan Clarke (1942–), singer and guitarist Graham Nash (1942–), lead guitarist Tony Hicks (1943–), bassist Eric Haydock (1943–) and drummer Bobby Elliott (1942–). The group attracted attention playing at the CAVERN, where it was dubbed Manchester's BEATLES, and enjoyed chart success with such singles as '(Ain't it) Just Like Me' (1963), 'Searchin'', 'Stay', 'Just One Look', 'Here I Go Again', 'Yes I Will', the 1965 Number One 'I'm Alive', 'Look Through Any Window', 'I Can't Let Go', 'He Ain't Heavy, He's My Brother', which was made in 1969 and reached Number One on being re-released in the

late 1980s, 'Long Cool Woman (in a Black Dress)' and 'The Air that I Breathe'. Haydock left in 1966, being replaced by Bernie Calvert, and Nash departed for the USA in 1968 (*see* CROSBY, STILLS, NASH AND YOUNG), his place being taken by Terry Sylvester, and the band continued to win acclaim on regular tours with changing personnel (Nash returning briefly in 1981).

Holliger, Heinz (1939–) Swiss oboist and composer, who established himself as one of the most admired players of the oboe. He began playing professionally with the Basle Symphony Orchestra but then pursued a career as a soloist and founded the celebrated Holliger Ensemble. As well as playing conventional classical pieces, he has also explored new possibilities by adapting the sound of his oboe electronically and writing for the instrument such adventurous pieces as *Siebengesang* (1967), for oboe, voice and amplifiers. His mastery of the oboe has inspired many composers – including Luciano BERIO, Hans Werner HENZE and Karlheinz STOCKHAUSEN – to write works expressly for him. His wife, Ursula Holliger, is a famous harp player.

Holly, Buddy (Charles Hardin Holley; 1936–59) US singer-songwriter and guitarist, who became one of the legends of ROCK 'N' ROLL before his premature death in an air crash just 18 months after his first hit. Brought up in west Texas, Holly developed a unique ROCKABILLY style, achieving fame as lead guitarist and singer with his own band, the Crickets. 'That'll be the Day' reached Number One on both sides of the Atlantic in 1957 and made Holly (and his FENDER Stratocaster) a huge overnight star.

The stream of hits that followed confirmed his status as one of the greats of rock 'n' roll, and he quickly became a dominant figure in the charts with such classics as 'Oh Boy', 'Maybe Baby', which was co-written with Holly's mother, 'Think it Over', 'Peggy Sue', 'Listen to Me', 'Well All Right', 'Slippin' and Slidin'', 'Not Fade Away' and 'Rave On'.

'Peggy Sue' (1957) was originally given the title 'Cindy Lou' in honour of Holly's five-year-old niece, but this was changed at the request of Crickets drummer Jerry Allison (1939–), who hoped to impress one Peggy Sue Garrow, with whom he had been at school. The ploy worked, and a year later they were married, an event commemorated in the Holly follow-up 'Peggy Sue Got Married'. (Unfortunately, the marriage was not a success and lasted only eight years. Peggy Sue remarried and went on to run a drain-cleaning company in Sacramento.)

It all came to a sudden end on 3 February 1959 when, with 'It Doesn't Matter Any More' climbing the charts and a brilliant solo career beckoning, Holly died – with Ritchie VALENS and J.P. Richardson (the BIG BOPPER) – when their chartered aircraft crashed in a snowstorm near Clear Lake, Iowa, during a US tour.

The loss of Holly at the age of just 22 was immeasurable. Many subsequent performers COVERED his songs and even tried to recreate his style, complete with vocal 'hiccough', and nine of his compositions have reached Number One in one form or another since his demise. 'That'll be the Day' was the first song John LENNON learned to play, and years after Holly's death the cufflinks he was wearing on the day of the fatal crash were presented to his admirer Paul MCCARTNEY. His famous dark-rimmed glasses were relocated by local police in 1980, a full 21 years after the disaster.

> I have thought about making a career out of western music if I am good enough but I will just have to wait to see how that turns out.
> BUDDY HOLLY, English essay at the age of 16

> The day the music died.
> DON MACLEAN, of Holly's death, 'America Pie', 1971

Hollywood Bowl Huge, open-air auditorium in Hollywood, Los Angeles, which is one of the most famous venues for music anywhere in the world. Designed by the architect Frank Lloyd Wright (1869–1959), the Bowl was opened in 1921 and has a capacity of some 17,500. It plays host to a wide range of musical events, including an annual summer season of concerts by the LOS ANGELES PHILHARMONIC ORCHESTRA. The first rock concert given there took place in 1964, when the BEATLES performed before a capacity audience (one fan giving birth to a son in the car park).

Holst, Gustav Theodore (1874–1934) British composer and teacher, of Swedish descent, who won wide acclaim as composer of such enduring works as the orchestral suite *The Planets* (1914–16). Holst was a

scholar of the Royal College of Music and began his career as a professional musician playing the trombone (having given up playing the piano and the organ because of neuritis in his hand). He became a close friend of fellow-student Ralph VAUGHAN WILLIAMS and in 1903 decided to switch to teaching and composition. He accepted teaching posts at Morley College and at St Paul's Girls' School, for which he wrote the *St Paul's Suite* (1913), and continued to indulge his interest in English FOLK MUSIC, which exerted a profound influence on such compositions as *Somerset Rhapsody* (1907).

The *Rig-Veda Hymns* (1908–12) and the chamber opera *Savitri* (1908) bore witness to his study of Sanskrit, but it was *The Planets* – inspired by his interest in astrology – that made him (to his own dismay) a nationally known figure after it was performed under Sir Adrian BOULT in 1919. Subsequent works that were also well received included the *Ode to Death* (1919), using the poetry of Walt Whitman, *The Hymn of Jesus* (1920), the operas *The Perfect Fool* (1921) and *At the Boar's Head* (1924), which took up Shakespearean themes, a Choral Symphony (1924), the orchestral tone poem *Egdon Heath* (1927), which Holst considered his best work, children's songs and pieces for military bands. Holst's concert appearances became fewer after he sustained head injuries in a fall from a platform in 1923.

> Always ask for advice but never take it.
> GUSTAV HOLST

> Never compose anything unless the not composing of it becomes a positive nuisance to you.
> GUSTAV HOLST, letter, 1921

Honegger, Arthur (1892–1955) French composer, also holding Swiss nationality, who established himself as one of the most distinguished composers of the century with his intellectually demanding and innovative music. Born in Le Havre, Honegger studied the German musical tradition while in Zurich but subsequently became conversant with the contrasting lively and colourful French style while a student at the Paris Conservatoire. He combined features of both traditions in his own work and became one of the small group of young composers known as Les SIX, although his deeply serious music had little in common with that of the other members.

Honegger developed a highly complicated polyphonic style of composition, pro-
claiming J.S. Bach to be his musical ideal,
and went on to create a large body of
works, which included five symphonies,
several ballets, operas, such oratorios as
King David (1921), *Joan of Arc at the Stake*
(1935) and *The Dance of Death* (1939),
choral and orchestral works, and music for
the theatre, the radio and the cinema.
Among his more unconventional pieces
were the ballets *Skating Rink* (1921) and
Rugby (1928), which reflected the composer's passion for sport, *Pacific 231* (1924),
which was inspired by his love of trains
and mechanical machines in general
(expressed in relentless motor rhythms),
and the ballet *Semiramis* (1934), which,
like *Joan of Arc at the Stake*, incorporated
the use of the ONDES MARTENOT.

> Composing is not a profession. It is a
> mania – a harmless madness.
> ARTHUR HONEGGER, *I am a Composer*, 1951

> To write music is to raise a ladder without
> a wall to lean it against. There is no
> scaffolding; the building under construc-
> tion is held in balance only by the miracle
> of a kind of internal logic, an innate sense
> of proportion.
> ARTHUR HONEGGER, *I am a Composer*, 1951

> The public doesn't want new music; the
> main thing that it demands of a composer
> is that he be dead.
> ARTHUR HONEGGER, *I am a Composer*, 1951

honky-tonk Rough and ready style of
piano-playing, which was first played in
disreputable and down-at-heel night clubs
and BARRELHOUSES – often themselves
called honky-tonks – in the American
southwest. Patronized by impoverished
Blacks, the honky-tonks often had their
own resident pianist or small jazz group,
who entertained drinkers with the lively
tunes otherwise labelled BOOGIE-WOOGIE. A
honky-tonk piano is one which has been
deliberately detuned and usually lacks any
felt on the hammers, which gives the
instrument a distinctive percussive sound.
Sometimes wire is fitted over the hammer
felts to create the same effect.

> First when they started fighting we'd play
> extra loud, then we'd start running out
> through the windows. Rough, man,
> rough. I saw a lot of blood in those days.
> CARL PERKINS, on the joys of playing in the
> honky-tonks

Hooker, John Lee (1917–) Black US electric BLUES singer-songwriter and guitarist,
who emerged as one of the great blues
performers of the postwar era. Taught to
play the guitar by his stepfather at home in
Mississippi, Hooker learned to apply the
crude techniques of acoustic blues to the
ELECTRIC GUITAR after moving to Chicago,
and he made his first recordings in the early
1940s. 'Boogie Chillen' (1948) won him
immediate recognition as a unique talent
and influenced many other guitarists. He
enjoyed something of a revival in the
1960s, when he returned to the acoustic
guitar, with such hits as 'Dimples', which
he had recorded 1956, and 'Boom Boom'
(1962) and consolidated his reputation as
a blues legend with hugely successful tours
of the UK and Europe, thus influencing
such emerging stars as the ROLLING STONES
and the ANIMALS. He also collaborated with
such contemporary bands as CANNED HEAT
and saw his classic blues song 'Shake it
Baby' cross racial barriers by becoming a
hit with White audiences worldwide in
1968.

After recording relatively little in the
1970s and 1980s, though appearing in the
films *The Blues Brothers* and *The Color Purple*, Hooker returned to the limelight with
Jealous (1986), *The Healer* (1989), his biggest commercial success to date, *The Hot
Spot* (1990), on which he worked with
Miles DAVIS, *Mr Lucky* (1991), *Boom Boom*
(1992) and *Don't Look Back* (1997), a collaboration with Van MORRISON.

hootenanny US slang for a gathering of
folk-song enthusiasts and performers.
'Hoots' were popularized in the late 1940s
and 1950s by such programmes as the
CBS *Forecast* radio series and the American
Broadcasting Company's popular *Hootenanny* television show.

Launched in 1958, *Hootenanny* played a
major role in the US FOLK MUSIC revival and
witnessed the blending of traditional folk
music with contemporary pop. The ensuing commercialization of traditional music,
the spawning of folk music 'fanzines' and a
flood of 'new' folk recordings together with
the marketing of 'Hootenanny Boots' (*see*
BOOTLEG) provoked deep resentment among
the purists. The *Hootenanny* show itself
descended into mediocrity and became
increasingly reactionary, culminating in
singer Pete SEEGER – the leading figure in
the popularization of hootenanny – being

banned from the programme because of his leftist leanings. In consequence, the programme was boycotted by other leading folk music performers, and by the end of 1963 the hootenanny craze was over.

The word 'hootenanny' itself has long been used as a US equivalent of the UK 'thingumajig'.

Hope, Bob (Leslie Townes; 1903–   ) US comedian and singer, who has sung many hit songs in the course of his long film and stage career. Best known for his long collaboration with Bing CROSBY in the 'Road' movies of the 1940s, he numbers among his most popular songs 'It's De-lovely' (1936), 'Thanks for the Memory' (1938), which became his signature tune, 'Two Sleepy People' (1938) and 'Buttons and Bows' (1948).

Hopkin, Mary (1950–   ) Welsh pop singer and guitarist, who achieved overnight fame in 1968 with her Number One début single 'Those were the Days'. She came to public notice after Paul MCCARTNEY, alerted to her by model Twiggy, got her a contract with Apple; subsequent hits included 'Goodbye', 'Temma Harbour', 'Knock, Knock, Who's There' and two albums before she married and retired to raise a family. She made minor come-backs with 'If You Love Me' (1976) and with the albums *The Welsh World of Mary Hopkin* (1979), *Oasis* (1984) and *Spirit* (1989).

Hopkins, Sam 'Lightnin'' (1912–82) US BLUES singer and guitarist, considered by some to have been the last of the great blues vocalists. Brought up in Texas, Hopkins learned to play the guitar with the help of 'Blind Lemon' JEFFERSON, and he won a following as an electric blues player in the 1940s before switching to acoustic guitar in the early 1950s. He vanished from the scene with the development of electric blues in Chicago and the advent of ROCK 'N' ROLL, but he was eventually traced in the early 1960s after lengthy inquiries by blues enthusiast Sam Charters and persuaded to record again. Proving he was as good as his now legendary reputation and that he had lost none of his famed dexterity, he made nine albums in just a year and enjoyed huge acclaim for the rest of his life, touring throughout Europe and the USA.

Horne, Lena (1917–   ) Black US singer and actress, who was the first Black performer to be honoured with a contract with one of the major Hollywood studios. Having recorded with Charlie BARNET and Teddy WILSON, among others, and having excelled in such hit shows as *Blackbirds of 1939*, she was recruited by MGM and went on to consolidate her reputation in such MUSICALS as *Cabin in the Sky* (1942). Among her most popular songs were 'Stormy Weather', 'One for My Baby (and One More for the Road)' and "Deed I Do'. Racial prejudice hampered her career in the 1950s, but she still managed to enjoy success with 'Love Me or Leave Me' (1955), as one of the stars of the Broadway musical *Jamaica* (1957) and in her own show, *Lena Horne: The Lady and Her Music* (1981).

Horowitz, Vladimir (1904–89) Russian pianist, a US resident from the late 1920s, who is regarded as one of the most distinguished of all pianists of the twentieth century. A student of the Kiev Conservatory, Horowitz stunned critics with his musical powers after embarking on a professional career when he was 20 years old. He made his British début in 1928 and two years later won recognition as one of the great pianists with a performance of Sergei RACHMANINOV's D minor Piano Concerto. After emigrating to the USA, he consolidated his reputation, despite the bouts of ill-health that threatened to force his retirement and obliged him to rest for long periods. He finally gave up concert appearances in 1950 but continued to make greatly admired records. As well as Rachmaninov, he was particularly esteemed for his performances of works by Liszt, Prokofiev and Scriabin. He was married to Arturo TOSCANINI's daughter Wanda.

> He is so rare an aromatist of the piano . . . that to hear him with an orchestra is like trying to get the best out of champagne while eating roast beef.
>
> NEVILLE CARDUS, the *Manchester Guardian* (1936)

Hoschna, Karl (1877–1911) US composer, born in Bohemia, who enjoyed success with a series of popular operettas before the First World War. He moved to the USA in 1896 and eventually teamed up with Otto HARBACH, with whom he created the hit show *The Three Twins* (1908). Subsequent successes before his premature death included

Madame Sherry (1910), *Katy Did* (1910), *Dr De Luxe* (1911) and *The Fascinating Widow* (1911).

hot JAZZ music that is lively, rhythmic and passionate (often improvised), as opposed to the more purist and intellectual style dubbed COOL. The term was first heard in the 1920s, when bands led by jazzmen such as Louis ARMSTRONG and Jelly Roll MORTON introduced an exciting – even feverish – jazz sound. The emergence of the cool style in the late 1940s meant that 'hot jazz' came to refer to virtually any jazz dating from previous decades.

Hot Chocolate Multi-racial British POP group, which enjoyed numerous hits in the 1970s. Led by Jamaican-born singer Errol Brown (1948–) and (until 1976) Trinidadian bassist Tony Wilson (1947–), the band came together in 1970 and was encouraged in the early days by John LENNON, who also approved the group's choice of name and allowed it to perform a REGGAE version of 'Give Peace a Chance' as a début recording. Hot Chocolate reached the charts on some 26 occasions with such hits as 'Brother Louie' (1973), 'You Sexy Thing' (1975), 'So You Win Again' (1977), which was the group's only UK Number One, 'Every One's a Winner' (1978) and 'It Started with a Kiss' (1982). Brown left to pursue a solo career in 1987.

Hotter, Hans (1909–) Austrian bass-baritone, born in Germany, who established a reputation as one of the great performers in Wagnerian operas of the twentieth century. Acclaimed at COVENT GARDEN, London, at the METROPOLITAN OPERA HOUSE, New York, and at a host of other leading opera houses, Hotter was unsurpassed in such parts as Wotan in *The Ring*. His career was not without its moments of crisis, however: in 1961 he managed to fall off the mountain-top at the climax of *Die Walküre* at Covent Garden and had to haul himself ignominiously out of the 'deep chasm' into which he had plummeted, while in 1956, again at Covent Garden, he strode on as Wotan oblivious of the fact that a fluffy pink coat-hanger was still attached to his voluminous cloak.

> The only man in the world who can actually step on stage and persuade you that he is God.
> ERNEST NEWMAN

house music Genre of electronic dance music of the late 1980s, which incorporated elements of RAP and ELECTRO-FUNK. The style acquired its name from the Warehouse Club in Chicago where it first caught on, although there are also links with ACID HOUSE and with the sub-culture associated with the drug Ecstasy. Electronic effects play a key role in house music, with extensive use being made of SAMPLING, SYNTHESIZERS and drum machines. Popular exponents of the style have included the Beat Masters and Marrs.

Houston, Whitney (1963–) Black US SOUL singer and actress, daughter of the gospel star Cissy Houston (1932–) and cousin of Dionne WARWICK, who emerged as one of the top-selling artists of the 1980s and 1990s. Having started out as a model, Houston became a backing vocalist and had her first hit singing the duet 'Hold Me' (1984) with Teddy PENDERGRASS. Her first album proved the most successful début album ever released and produced a string of hit singles, of which 'Saving All My Love for You', 'How Will I Know' and 'The Greatest Love of All' reached Number One.

Whitney Houston outsold all other albums released by a female artist, with sales of over 13 million, while *Whitney* (1987) became the first album to enter both the British and the US charts at Number One. *Waiting to Exhale* topped the US charts in 1996. In the singles charts, 'I Wanna Dance with Somebody (Who Loves Me)', 'Didn't We Almost Have It All', 'So Emotional' and 'Where Do Broken Hearts Go' all reached Number One, establishing an extraordinary record of seven consecutive chart-toppers in the USA.

In the 1990s Houston's hits have included the Dolly PARTON song 'I Will Always Love You', which became one of the best-selling singles in pop history (1992). As a film actress, she starred opposite Kevin Costner in the thriller *Bodyguard* (1992), to which she also contributed the SOUNDTRACK. She is married to soul star Bobby Brown.

Howard, Joe (1878–1961) US composer and singer, who wrote numerous hit shows and songs for the stage in the years leading up to the First World War. Having run away from home to appear in vaudeville, he emerged as a star of musical comedy and as a popular songwriter, often working in collaboration with his wife Ida Emerson. Among his many compositions were the songs 'I'm Lonesome Tonight', from the MUSICAL *The Time, the Place, and the Girl* (1907), 'I Wonder Who's Kissing Her Now', from *The Prince of Tonight* (1909) and 'When the Girl You Love Loves You', from *A Broadway Honeymoon* (1911).

Howells, Herbert (1892–1983) British composer, who won acclaim for his many works written in the mainstream of the English tradition. A teacher of music, who was also professor of composition at the Royal College of Music, London, he is usually remembered for the *Hymnus Paradisi* (1938), which he composed in memory of his nine-year-old son, who had died from meningitis. His other works included much church music, two piano concertos and songs, as well as orchestral and chamber music.

Howlin' Wolf (Chester Arthur Burnett; 1910–76) US BLUES singer-songwriter and guitarist, who emerged as one of the most popular bluesmen of the postwar era. Called Howlin' Wolf in reference to his high-pitched voice, he was a farmer before taking up the life of an itinerant musician and ultimately recording his first hit, 'How Many More Years', In 1952. Many of his songs, which included such classics as 'Smokestack Lightning', 'Evil', 'Little Red Rooster' and 'Killin' Floor', were subsequently COVERED by other leading artists, and he also made recordings with, among other stars, Eric CLAPTON and Ringo STARR towards the end of his career. His death was hastened by injuries suffered in a car crash in 1973.

Hubbell, Raymond (1879–1954) US composer, who created numerous lavish revues and other musical entertainments for the stage in the first three decades of the century. Among his shows were *The Jolly Bachelors* (1910), several editions of the *Ziegfeld Follies*, *The Big Show* (1916), from which came the hit song 'Poor Butterfly', and *Sonny* (1921).

Huddersfield Choral Society British choir, which has long been one of the most celebrated choral societies in the UK. Founded in 1836, the choir drew on the singing tradition of Yorkshire's Nonconformist churches and eventually established an international reputation under such notable conductors as Sir Malcolm SARGENT and, more recently, Jane GLOVER.

Human League, the British pop group, which played a pioneering role in promoting SYNTHESIZER pop in the early 1980s. At its peak, the group consisted of singers and synthesizer players Phil Oakey (1955–), Ian Burden (1957–), Jo Callis (1951–) and Adrian Wright (1956–) – and subsequently Susanne Sulley (1963–) and Joanne Catherall (1962–). The band came together in Sheffield in 1977 and, rejecting conventional instruments, emerged as one of the leading groups of the post-PUNK era with the Number One single 'Don't You Want Me' (1981) and such follow-ups as 'Mirror Man' and 'Fascination'. Acclaimed albums included *Reproduction* (1979), *Travelogue* (1980), the best-selling *Dare* (1981), *Love and Dancing* (1982), which was a collection of remixes of previous songs, *Hysteria* (1984), *Crash* (1986) and *Romantic?* (1990). The Human League returned to the single charts in 1986 with the single 'Human', which reached Number One in the USA. Former members Ian Craig Marsh and Martyn Ware left in 1980 to enjoy similar success with their own band, Heaven 17.

Humes, Helen (1913–81) US JAZZ and BLUES singer, who became famous singing with the band of Count BASIE (1938–42) as successor to Billie HOLIDAY. Having recorded such hits as 'Sing for Your Supper' and 'Between the Devil and the Deep Blue Sea' with Basie, she went solo and had another big hit in 1945 with 'Be-baba-leba' as well as dabbling in RHYTHM-AND-BLUES. She worked for a time with Red NORVO and retired in 1967, although she made several tours in the 1970s.

Humperdinck, Engelbert (Arnold George Dorsey; 1936–) British CABARET singer, born in India, who established a popular following in the 1960s, when his hits included the Number One single 'Release Me' (1967), which remained in the charts for over a year (a record for any British hit), 'There Goes My Everything', and 'The Last Waltz', which also reached Number One in 1967. He selected his stage-name at random from a music dictionary; the real

Engelbert Humperdinck (1854–1921) was a German composer and teacher who collaborated with Wagner and composed such children's operas as *Hänsel und Gretel* (1893).

Humph *See* Humphrey LYTTLETON.

Hupfeld, Herman (1894–1951) US composer, conductor and pianist, who is usually remembered for his classic song 'As Time Goes By', as featured in the Humphrey Bogart movie *Casablanca* (1943); the song was written originally for the 1931 film *Everybody's Welcome*. He wrote for and appeared in a number of REVUES in the 1920s and included among his other hits 'Sing Something Simple' (1930), 'When Yuba Plays the Rumba on the Tuba' (1931) and 'Let's Put Out the Lights and Go to Sleep' (1932).

Hutchinson, Leslie 'Hutch' (1900–69) US singer and pianist, born in the West Indies, who became a popular revue and recording star on both sides of the Atlantic. Beginning as a café entertainer, he won the support of Cole PORTER and subsequently established a following both in Paris and London, where he triumphed in the REVUES of C.B. COCHRAN. His hit records included versions of 'Begin the Beguine' and 'A Nightingale Sang in Berkeley Square'. Revelations in the early 1980s suggested that he may have been one of the lovers of Lady Mountbatten.

Hylton, Jack (1892–1965) British bandleader, who led one of the most popular of all British DANCE BANDS of the 1920s and 1930s. Having started out as a cinema pianist, he formed his first band after the First World War and made his recording début in 1921. Subsequently he toured throughout Europe to great acclaim and recruited such talents as Ted HEATH and Coleman HAWKINS to his ranks. He even led a band in the USA, becoming the first British bandleader to make an impression in the birthplace of JAZZ. His band broadcast frequently on the BBC and was a regular feature of the celebrated *ITMA* (*It's That Man Again*) radio shows, but it eventually broke up in 1940 when the loss of many of the musicians to conscription following the outbreak of the Second World War persuaded Hylton to concentrate instead on theatrical promotion. His signature tune was 'She Shall Have Music'.

Hyman, Dick (1927–   ) US pianist, organist, clarinettist and composer, who first emerged as a leading figure in contemporary JAZZ in the 1950s. Trained as a classical musician, he defected to jazz in the late 1940s and worked with Charlie PARKER and Dizzy GILLESPIE, among others. He established a reputation as a jazz historian in the 1950s and won acclaim for his 'History of Jazz' concerts, in which he roamed from one jazz style to another with complete assurance. During the 1960s he adopted a JAZZ-ROCK style and experimented with electronic instruments, but in the 1970s he reverted to a more traditional approach, collaborating on recordings of standards by jazzmen such as Louis ARMSTRONG and Jelly Roll MORTON as well as continuing to lead his own Perfect Jazz Repertory Quintet.

His more unusual recordings include settings of works by Shakespeare and *A Pipe Organ Recital Plus One* (1982), in which he demonstrated the potential of the Wurlitzer organ as a jazz instrument.

I

Ibert, Jacques François Antoine (1890–1962) French composer and administrator, who enjoyed considerable success between the wars with a range of works written in an impressionistic, neoclassical style. Director of the French Academy in Rome (1937–60) and administrator of the Réunion des Théâtres Lyriques Nationaux (1955–56), he first indicated his potential as a musician while a student at the Paris Conservatoire, where he won several prizes. Following service in the First World War, he received the Prix de Rome in 1919 for the cantata *Le Poète et la fée* and went on to consolidate his reputation with such works as the ballet *Ballad of Reading Gaol* (1920), based on the writings of Oscar Wilde, and the symphonic suite *Escales* (*Ports of Call*; 1922).

Subsequent compositions included six operas, of which the most successful was *Angélique* (1927), the comic *Divertissement* (1930) for chamber orchestra, the *Concertino da camera* (1934) for alto saxophone and orchestra, a string quartet (1937–42), such piano pieces as *The Little White Donkey*, and further ballets, songs and chamber works, as well as music for the cinema and the theatre.

Ice Kings of Rock, the *See* TELEVISION.

Ice Man, the *See* Jerry BUTLER.

Idol, Billy (William Broad; 1955–) British rock singer, resident in the USA since the early 1980s, who emerged as one of the leading lights to come out of the PUNK ROCK movement of the late 1970s. Having co-founded the glam-punk band Generation X in 1977, Idol was frontman on a series of hits before the group broke up in 1981 and he relocated to the USA. There he experimented with a RHYTHM-AND-BLUES style and eventually had a huge hit with 'Rebel Yell' (1983), which harked back to his punk origins. Hit singles since then have included 'White Wedding', 'Catch My Fall' and 'Eyes Without a Face'. He survived a

motorbike accident in 1990 and had another huge hit with the single 'Cradle of Love'. Subsequent releases have included the album *Cyberpunk* (1993).

Ifield, Frank (1937–) British pop singer, who enjoyed a series of hit singles in the early 1960s. A total of 15 Ifield releases reached the British charts between 1960 and 1966, the most successful of them including 'I Remember You', which featured his distinctive yodel, and 'Lovesick Blues' (both of which reached Number One in 1962), and 'Wayward Wind' and 'Confessin'', which both subsequently topped the charts in 1963. With the exception of 'Nobody's Darlin' But Mine' (1963) and 'Don't Blame Me' (1964) he never reached the Top 20 again.

Iggy Pop (James Newell Osterburg; 1947–) US rock singer, who was hailed as one of the elder statesmen of PUNK ROCK in the late 1970s and early 1980s. Iggy formed the Psychedelic Stooges back in 1967 and established a notorious reputation for his gross live act, which included throwing up on stage and acts of self-mutilation, as well as indulging heavily in drugs. He re-formed the Stooges from time to time throughout the 1970s with the support of David BOWIE and saw many of his early nihilist recordings taken up by countless punk outfits. His most notable albums include *The Stooges* (1969), *Raw Power* (1973), *The Idiot* (1976), *Lust for Life* (1977), *Kill City* (1978) and *Blah Blah Blah* (1986).

Iglesias, Julio (1943–) Spanish singer, nicknamed the Spanish Sinatra, who enjoyed huge commercial success as a latter-day CROONER in the 1970s and 1980s. A former professional footballer with Real Madrid, he established himself as a pop star in the 1970s and went on to sell some 100 million records around the world. His most successful releases have included a version of 'Begin the Beguine'

(1981), 'Julio' (1983) and the album *1100 Bel Air Place* (1984), which included duets with Diana ROSS and Willie NELSON.

Impressions, the US vocal group, which had a string of hits in the 1960s. Formed in 1957 as a backing group for Jerry BUTLER, the band emerged in its own right under the leadership of Butler and Curtis Mayfield (1942–   ) and went to enjoy chart success with such hits as 'For You Precious Love' (1958), 'Gypsy Woman' (1961), 'It's All Right' (1963), 'Keep on Pushing' (1964), 'People Get Ready' (1965) and 'Choice of Colors' (1969), several of which gave tacit support for Black civil rights. Butler was replaced by Fred Cash (1940–   ), and Mayfield eventually left in 1970, but the group continued to record, later hits including 'Finally Got Myself Together' (1974).

incidental music *See* SOUNDTRACK.

Incredible String Band, the British FOLK-ROCK group of the late 1960s, which attracted a cult following as one of the foremost psychedelic bands. As a duo, Scottish guitarists and singers Robin Williamson (1943–   ) and Mike Heron (1942–   ) built up a huge audience with such eccentric albums as *The 5000 Spirits or the Layers of the Onion* (1967), *The Hangman's Beautiful Daughter* (1968) and *Wee Tam and the Big Huge* (1968) and were described as an 'underground' equivalent of the BEATLES (Williamson and Heron themselves were dubbed Scotland's LENNON AND MCCARTNEY). Further albums followed with violinist Licorice McKechnie and bassist Rosie Simpson – and subsequently singer Malcolm Le Maistre and keyboards player Gerard Dodd – joining the line-up before the group was eventually dissolved in 1974. Both Williamson and Heron then embarked on successful solo careers, in which they continue to treat Celtic themes with their distinctive eccentric humour.

indeterminacy Concept introduced by the AVANT-GARDE composer John CAGE in preference to the term ALEATORISM. The pioneer of music created 'by chance', Cage distinguished between works that are 'indeterminate of their composition' (in other words, presented as a conventional score but with notes decided, within certain limits, by the flick of a coin or some

other chance mechanism) and works that are 'indeterminate of their performance' (that is, with many decisions left to the performers, or 'realizers', of them). No two renditions of such works will be the same: the composer simply presents fragments of music, which somehow have to be juggled into place.

Cage's piece *Music of Changes* (1951) is an example of the former type, while *Inlets* (with its verbal instructions to the performers) is an example of the latter. In the Fourth Quartet (1963) by Franco Donatoni (1927–   ), the musicians are instructed to respond musically to what they read in newspapers.

> By temperament I cannot toss a coin ... chance must be very well controlled.
> PIERRE BOULEZ, letter to John Cage

indie An independent record company, as opposed to the huge commercial organizations to which the majority of famous artists are signed. A wave of 'indie' companies swept British POP music in the 1970s, catering for such 'minority' interests as PUNK ROCK and Black ethnic music, and commentators began to talk of 'indie music' as a distinct genre of its own, threatening the conventional domination of the industry by the conservative recording giants. Among the most successful of the new labels were Stiff and Factory. In the 1980s various sub-genres developed, with thriving indie rock companies specializing in such styles as HEAVY METAL and GARAGE ROCK.

industrial rock Musical genre of the 1980s in which elements of NEW WAVE and HEAVY METAL were mixed to create a highly experimental and cerebral new AVANT-GARDE style.

Ink Spots, the US vocal harmony group of the late 1930s and 1940s, which enjoyed lasting fame as one of the most polished vocal groups of the era. The original members of the group were singers Jerry Daniels, who was replaced by lead singer Bill Kenny (1915–78) in the late 1930s, Orville 'Hoppy' Jones (1905–44), Ivory 'Deek' Watson and singer-guitarist Charlie Fuqua, who came together while working as porters at the Paramount Theatre in New York. Having begun in a JAZZ style, the Ink Spots adopted a more soulful ballad approach in the late 1930s and enjoyed huge success with such recordings as 'If I Didn't Care' (1939), 'We Three (My Echo, My Shadow and Me)' (1940), 'Whispering Grass' (1940), 'Java Jive' (1940), 'Don't Get Around Much Anymore' (1943), 'The Gypsy' (1946) and 'To Each His Own' (1946). The original members were all replaced in time and the band continues to the present day in much the same old style (there was even a confused period in the 1950s when two separate versions of the band were performing under the same name).

International Ambassador of Country Music, the *See* George HAMILTON IV.

intonarumori Range of novel percussion instruments, which were devised by Italian painter and composer Luigi Russolo (1885–1946) around 1913 and which were to have considerable influence on a number of contemporary composers. Russolo demonstrated his *intonarumori* ('noisemakers') throughout Europe and attracted the attention of such composers as George ANTHEIL, Arthur HONEGGER, Igor STRAVINSKY and Edgard VARÈSE. Unfortunately little is now known of the instruments themselves as they were all destroyed in Paris during the Second World War and only a single recording survives.

intuitive music Term that was coined by Karlheinz STOCKHAUSEN in preference to 'improvisation' to describe music that is spontaneously created in response to interaction with written texts, suggestive notation and various electronic devices, such as radios and tape recorders.

INXS Australian rock band, which established an international reputation in the 1980s. Playing in a soul-influenced rock CROSSOVER style that appealed to dance fans, the band first came together in the late 1970s and consisted of singer Michael Hutchence (1960–97), guitarists Tim Farriss and Kirk Pengilly, keyboard player Andrew Farriss, bassist Garry Beers and drummer Jon Farriss. After a number of moderate successes, the band built up an international following with such albums as *The Swing* (1984), *Listen like Thieves* (1985), *Kick* (1987), from which came the single 'Need You Tonight', *X* (1990), *Welcome to Wherever You Are* (1992) and *Full Moon, Dirty Hearts* (1993).

Ireland, John (Nicholson) (1879–1962) British composer, who wrote a number of highly melodic and influential works drawing on pagan mysticism for inspiration and contributed to freeing English classical music from the domination of the Germanic tradition. A student of the Royal College of Music from the age of 14, Ireland divided his career between composing and teaching, his pupils including such distinguished names as Alan BUSH and Benjamin BRITTEN. As a composer, he was influenced both by the mystical writings of Arthur Machen (1863–1947) and by his own troubled childhood, which had left him haunted by a deep sense of insecurity. In terms of technique he was indebted to the music of Brahms and to the teaching of Charles Villiers Stanford (1852–1924), as well as by Igor STRAVINSKY and Claude DEBUSSY.

Having destroyed all the music he wrote before 1908, Ireland established his reputation with such works as the orchestral tone poem *The Forgotten Rite* (1913) and his second violin sonata (1915–17) and went on to consolidate it with a cello sonata (1923), a piano sonata (1918–20) and a piano concerto (1930) among other pieces. Other acclaimed compositions included his setting of John Masefield's *Sea Fever* (1913), the song-cycle *Land of Lost Content* (1920–21), the symphonic rhapsody *Mai Dun* (1921), which was inspired by the ruined Maiden Castle in Dorset, such piano pieces as *Island Spell* and *Amberley Wild Brooks* and *A London Overture* (1936). *Legend* (1933), for piano and orchestra, took as its starting point Ireland's discovery of an ancient track that allowed lepers access to a ruined chapel.

Rather more subversive was his setting of 'These Things Shall Be' by John Addington Symonds (1840–93), which was commissioned for the coronation of George VI; unnoticed by most listeners, it included a diguised quotation from the 'Internationale'. Among his last works were the melodic *Fantasy Sonata* (1943), for clarinet and piano and the humorous overture *Satyricon* (1946). He also wrote the music for the film *The Overlanders* (1946–47).

Iron Butterfly US ROCK band, which established a huge following in the late 1960s. Keyboard player Doug Ingle (1947–), singer Darryl DeLoach, guitarist Danny Weiss, bassist Jerry Penrod and drummer

Ron Bushy (1941–) came together in 1966, and Iron Butterfly was among the pioneers of HEAVY METAL, making a commercial breakthrough in 1968 with *In-A-Gadda-Da-Vida*, which remained in the US charts for two years. The group went through various changes of line-up, touring with bands such as the DOORS and JEFFERSON AIRPLANE and releasing another four albums, before splitting up. An attempted reunion in 1975 was not a success but the band re-formed once more in 1994.

Iron Butterfly, the *See* Julie ANDREWS; Jeanette MACDONALD.

Iron Maiden British HEAVY METAL band, which enjoyed huge commercial success in the 1980s and early 1990s. Formed in 1976 by bassist Steve Harris (1957–) and named after the medieval instrument of torture (which appears on all the band's lurid album sleeves), Iron Maiden emerged as one of the leaders of the NEW WAVE OF BRITISH HEAVY METAL, and the first album, *Iron Maiden* (1980), was enthusiastically received. The line-up settled down as Harris, guitarists Adrian Smith (1957–) and Dave Murray (1955–), lead singer Paul Dianno (1959–) and drummer Clive Burr (1957–); after *Killers* (1981) Dianno was replaced by Bruce Dickinson (1958–), and *Number of the Beast* (1982) established the group as the foremost heavy metal band of the day, with a particularly strong live act. Among its hit singles were 'Run to the Hills', 'Stranger in a Strange Land', 'Can I Play with Madness' and 'Bring Your Daughter to the Slaughter', which went straight in at Number One in 1990. The album *Fear of the Dark* topped the charts in 1992. In 1994 Blaze Bayley succeeded Dickinson as frontman when the latter went solo. Live performances are dominated by the image of 'Eddie the Head', the monstrous figure that appears on all the band's album sleeves.

Island Records Leading British record company, which was founded in Jamaica in 1959 by producer Chris Blackwell (1937–). Acts signed by Island Records, based in London since 1962, have included numerous PROGRESSIVE ROCK bands, Bob MARLEY and U2. POLYGRAM acquired the company in 1989.

Isle of Wight festival The pop festival that was staged at East Afton Farm, Freshwater, Isle of Wight, on 30 August 1970. Billed as the Third Pop Festival, it attracted perhaps as many as 400,000 fans and represented the peak of the pop festival phenomenon in the UK.

Isley Brothers, the US vocal harmony RHYTHM-AND-BLUES trio, who were regularly in the charts for many years after their début in the 1950s. Brothers O'Kelly Isley (1937–86), Rudolph Isley (1939–) and Ronald Isley (1941–) had early hits with such songs as 'Shout' (1959) and 'Twist and Shout' (1962), and the trio returned to the charts in subsequent years with such releases as 'This Old Heart of Mine', 'I Guess I'll Always Love You', and, after the trio had become a sextet by the addition of two more Isley brothers and a cousin, 'It's Your Thing' and 'Harvest for the World', which became their most enduring hit in 1975. Attempts to switch from SOUL to a DISCO style in the late 1970s met with mixed results. Among the backing musicians for the brothers in the early years was Jimi HENDRIX.

isomoodic Music, as used in music therapy, which is designed to mirror a person's prevailing mental state of mind. The theory underlying isomoodic music is that playing such 'sympathetic' sounds can actually benefit the listener's mental condition and help to correct any imbalances.

Israel Philharmonic Orchestra Israel's most respected orchestra, based in Tel Aviv, which was founded in 1936 (as the Palestine Symphony Orchestra) by Polish violinist Bronislaw Huberman (1882–1947). Its music directors have included Jean Martinon (1910–76) and Zubin MEHTA, although it is run on a co-operative basis. Arturo TOSCANINI conducted the first performances by the orchestra, which was originally formed from refugees from a range of leading European orchestras.

Istomin, Eugene (1925–) US pianist, of Russian descent, who first established an international reputation as a pianist in the 1950s. He won particular acclaim playing with Pablo CASALS (he eventually married his widow) and as part of a trio with violinist Isaac STERN and cellist Leonard Rose (1918–84).

Technique is to be able to lay open the

basic sense of a great work of art, to make it clear.

EUGENE ISTOMIN

Ives, Burl (Charles Icle Ivanhoe Ives; 1909–95) US FOLK-singer and actor, who combined success as a recording artist with a career as a star of numerous film and stage MUSICALS. He first made his name singing folk-songs in the clubs of Greenwich Village and went on to appear in such musicals as *The Boys from Syracuse* (1938) and *Show Boat* (1954). His recorded hits included versions of such folk standards as 'The Foggy, Foggy Dew' and 'Blue Tail Fly' as well as new songs in a similar vein, among them 'Big Rock Candy Mountain' and 'Hallelujah, I'm a Bum'.

Ives, Charles Edward (1874–1954) US composer, who won belated recognition as one of the most important and innovative composers of his generation and in the process did much to 'legitimize' US classical composition. He was the son of a former bandmaster who encouraged an unconventional approach to music – he liked his audiences to 'stretch their ears' and warned his son 'If you listen to the sound, you may miss the music' – and it came to be said that Charles Ives was simply composing his father's unwritten music. The younger Ives studied at Yale and subsequently enjoyed a highly successful career in insurance, pursuing composition as a private hobby of which his colleagues at work knew nothing.

Ives's radical experiments anticipated the technical breakthroughs later made by such composers as Béla BARTÓK, Arnold SCHOENBERG and Igor STRAVINSKY, and he made significant steps forwards in embracing polytonality and ATONALITY – but most of his works remained unperformed for many years because of their revolutionary nature (Ives himself rarely attended performances). Sources for his inspiration were wide ranging, and he built collages of sound on recollections of childhood songs, old hymn tunes, and memories of games, places and people. One specific inspiration was the experience of hearing four separate bands playing different tunes simultaneously in a town square at carnival time.

The composer's reputation was eventually established in 1931 when his *Orchestra Set No. 1 (Three Places in New England;* 1911–14) was given its premiere under the conductor Nicolas Slonimsky. This was quickly followed by performances of *The Fourth of July* (1911–13) and the *Concord Sonata* (1911–15), which was extravagantly praised as 'the greatest music composed by an American'. By then, diabetes and heart disease had long since substantially curtailed Ives's career as a composer, although he occupied his last years polishing and perfecting his prolific output, which included four symphonies among a wide range of other works. His Third Symphony (1904–13) won a Pulitzer Prize in 1947, while his Fourth Symphony (1906), which is subtitled *The Unanswered Question*, invites the conductor to cue instruments at his leisure and was not actually performed until 1965 (its complexity can require as many as four conductors working together to keep it on track).

Please don't try to make things nice! All the wrong notes are *right*. Just copy as I have – I want it that way.

CHARLES IVES, note to the copyist of *The Fourth of July*

Not sung by Caruso, Jenny Lind, John McCormack, Harry Lauder or the Village Nightingale.

CHARLES IVES, inscription on one of his songs

I'm the only one, with the exception of Mrs Ives and one or two others perhaps ... who likes any of my music. ... Why do I like these things? ... Are my ears on wrong?

CHARLES IVES

Ivor Novello Awards British music awards, which have been presented to outstanding POP and light music artists on an annual basis since their inception in 1955. They are awarded for distinguished achievement under such categories as best-selling song, best orchestral or instrumental work and best SOUNDTRACK.

J

Jacko *See* Michael JACKSON.

Jackson, Joe (1955–) British singer-songwriter and pianist, who won recognition as one of the leading rock musicians of the 1970s and 1980s despite failing to make a huge commercial impact. A graduate of the Royal Academy of Music, London, he formed his first bands in the mid-1970s and gained a loyal following with such albums as *Look Sharp* (1979), *I'm the Man* (1979) and *Beat Crazy* (1980), from which came the hit singles 'Is She Really Going out With Him' and 'It's Different for Girls'. He then switched direction completely on *Jumpin' Jive* (1981) to indulge his love of bop and jive, before returning to something like his earlier style with such albums as *Night and Day* (1982). More recent releases include much film music and the albums *Body and Soul* (1984), *Big World* (1986), *Laughter and Lust* (1991) and *Night Music* (1994).

Jackson, Mahalia (1911–72) US GOSPEL singer, known as the Gospel Queen, who was among the most popular gospel stars of the 1940s and 1950s. Proprietor of a beauty salon and florists, she regarded her music as something that should not be commercially exploited, but still made a number of classic recordings and toured internationally. Her most famous song of all was 'We Shall Overcome', which became the anthem of the civil rights movement of the 1960s. Among other classics associated with her name were 'You'll Never Walk Alone', 'Move on up a Little Higher' and 'God's Gonna Separate the Wheat from the Tares'.

Jackson, Michael (Joseph) (1958–) US pop superstar, variously nicknamed Jacko and the King of Pop (in reference to his standing as the most successful pop artist of recent times; although rejected by Jackson himself, the nickname is regularly chanted by his fans at his concerts), who emerged as the biggest-selling solo artist in pop history in the 1980s. Hailing from Gary, Indiana, Jackson was groomed for stardom at an early age as youngest member of the JACKSON FIVE and eventually embarked on a solo career in 1971.

Off the Wall (1979) sold more copies than any other album previously released by a Black artist but marked only the beginning of a phenomenally successful series of hits. Establishing himself as the most popular of all ELECTRO-FUNK performers, he topped the charts worldwide with such albums as *Thriller* (1982), which sold 37 million copies, *Bad* (1987), *Dangerous* (1991) and *HIStory* (1996). He also won a reputation as a talented live performer who executed well-drilled and innovative dance routines both on stage and in accompanying videos. During an international tour in 1988 he was being paid at the rate of £200 a second; in 1991 it was reported that he had signed a contract earning him £500 million over 15 years – the most costly deal in the history of pop.

Such success, coupled with Jackson's reserved attitude to the media, inevitably fuelled intense interest in his private life, and he became the most talked-about star since Elvis PRESLEY. His installation of a zoo and a full-scale railway costing $7 million at his palatial home, called Neverland after the magical kingdom of Peter Pan – the boy who never grows up – prompted commentators to suggest that he was trying to compensate for a lost childhood. The star's close relationship with a chimpanzee called Bubbles provided more material for Jacksonologists.

Other much-reported eccentricities have included extreme vegetarianism, attempts to buy the remains of John Merrick (the 'Elephant Man') and plastic surgery, allegedly intended to mask his Black identity. The progressive lightening of his skin colour seemed to confirm speculation that Jackson was attempting to 'become White', although the star himself protested that he suffered a skin pigment disorder. Another story had it that he slept in an oxygen chamber in an attempt to delay the ageing process (a rumour apparently derived from his donation of such a chamber to a burns unit after he had been badly burned himself in an accident filming a Pepsi commercial).

In 1987 he caused a sensation when he proposed marriage to Elizabeth Taylor, who turned him down but rushed to his aid when allegations of child abuse were levelled at him in 1993. A cloud hung over Jackson's future despite his support for the underprivileged and for AIDS research after the courts took up the child abuse charges in 1993, when it was also revealed that the star was addicted to pain-killing drugs and had lost his lucrative Pepsi contract. In summer 1994 he married the daughter of Elvis PRESLEY. They divorced in 1996 and Jackson married Debbie Rowe.

Jackson, Millie (1944–) Black US singer, who was among the top-selling SOUL artists of the 1970s, despite the notoriety that attached to her name because of her frankly sexual live act. Having run away from the home of her preacher grandfather, Jackson worked as a model in New York when she was a teenager before establishing a reputation as a singer and making her recording début in 1969. She became a soul and DISCO favourite with such singles as 'Ask Me What You Want' (1972) and 'It Hurts So Good' (1973), and she was regularly in the album charts with such titles as *Caught Up* (1974), *Free and in Love* (1976), *Royal Rappin's'* (1979), *Live and Uncensored* (1979), *For Men Only* (1980) and *ESP (Extra Sexual Persuasion)* (1984). 'Act of War', a duet with Elton JOHN, entered the British Top 40 in 1985. As well as arousing the wrath of Max BYGRAVES and others by her explicit performances on television, she incurred further protests from anti-apartheid groups when she appeared in South Africa (she subsequently declared herself an opponent of apartheid).

Jackson, Milt 'Bags' (1923–) US JAZZ vibraphonist, pianist and guitarist, who was a pioneer of THIRD STREAM jazz. He played the vibraphone for Dizzy GILLESPIE from 1945 and subsequently with a number of major groups, including those of Thelonious MONK and Woody HERMAN, before founding his own quartet (called the MODERN JAZZ QUARTET from 1954) in 1951, which enjoyed a long and successful career until it was finally disbanded in 1974; it was re-formed in the 1980s to play at numerous festivals.

Jackson Five, the Black US pop group of five brothers, which had a stream of transatlantic hits in the early 1970s. Jackie (Sigmund Esco Jackson; 1951–), Tito (Toriano Adryll Jackson; 1953–), Jermaine (1954–), Marlon (1957–) and Michael JACKSON, joined forces as the Jackson Five around 1965 under the somewhat heavy-handed guidance of their musical parents. Success in talent shows and as a supporting group led to a MOTOWN contract, and all the group's first four singles – 'I Want You Back', 'ABC', 'The Love You Save' and 'I'll be There' – reached Number One in 1969–70. After many more hits, Michael launched his hugely successful solo career in 1971, but the sequence of hits went on (although with Randy Jackson (1961–) replacing Jermaine and the group playing under the title the Jacksons after changing labels). Michael finally left for good in 1986. The youngest of the Jackson family, Janet (1966–), also enjoyed a highly successful solo career, her hits including 'Control' (1986) and 'When I Think of You' (1986).

Jacob, Gordon (Percival Septimus) (1895–1984) British composer and conductor, who was also one of the most influential teachers of the century. As a professor at the Royal College of Music (1926–66), he helped to shape the early careers of such prominent young composers as Malcolm ARNOLD. His own compositions included scores for ballets and films, symphonies, studies, concertos for a range of instruments, a three-handed piano concerto and chamber music. Among his most famous pieces was *Passacaglia on a Well-known Theme*, which was derived from 'Oranges and Lemons'.

Jacquet, (Battiste) Illinois (1922–) US JAZZ saxophonist and bandleader, who first emerged as one of the most influential MAINSTREAM tenor saxophone stylists in the 1940s. He played with the bands of Lionel HAMPTON – with whom he won acclaim for his blues-influenced solos on 'Flying Home' and other recordings – Cab CALLOWAY and Count BASIE among others before founding his first band in 1945. He won renewed praise in the late 1980s on both sides of the Atlantic leading his own BIG BAND.

Jaffa, Max (1912–91) British bandleader, who was lastingly popular for his romantic but refined 'tea dance' music. He led bands at various famous hotels, and after the

Second World War he also won acclaim with his Scarborough-based Max Jaffa Trio, together with Reginald Kilbey and Jack Byfield. He broadcast regularly on such BBC programmes as *Music for your Pleasure* and *Grand Hotel*.

Jagger, Mick (Michael Phillip Jagger; 1943–) British rock singer and actor, who acheived superstar status as lead singer with the ROLLING STONES. Jagger became a fan of RHYTHM-AND-BLUES while a student at the London School of Economics in the early 1960s and was subsequently a founder-member of the Rolling Stones, who made their recording début in 1963. Jagger was in his element as frontman for the group, and he delighted in living up to his image as one of the wild men of rock, being arrested for various drug offences and scandalizing many observers with the undisguised sexual innuendo of his pouting and irreverent live act. He was given a suspended prison sentence for drug offences in 1967, when he was the subject of an editorial in *The Times*, which described his punishment as 'breaking a butterfly on a wheel'.

Towards the end of the decade Jagger launched himself on a second career as a film actor, appearing in such films as *Performance* and *Ned Kelly* (both 1970), but he continued to lead the Stones with undiminished energy throughout the 1970s and 1980s, becoming one of the legends of modern pop music. In 1985 he was back at Number One in company with David BOWIE with the single 'Dancing in the Street', which raised more funds for the LIVE AID effort.

Relationships with model Chrissy Shrimpton and Marianne FAITHFULL provided much material for the media in the 1960s, as did his subsequent marriages to Nicaraguan model Bianca Perez Morena de Macias and US model Jerry Hall.

> Mick Jagger is the perfect pop star. There's nobody more perfect than Jagger. He's rude, he's ugly-attractive, he's brilliant. The Rolling Stones are the perfect pop group – they don't give a shit.
> ELTON JOHN

> The singer'll have to go, the BBC won't like him.
> ERIC EASTON

jam An improvised performance or practice session in which the musicians respond spontaneously to any inspiration that strikes them. The jam is a central element in the JAZZ tradition and has also found a revered place in the history of BLUES and ROCK music, many bands incorporating lengthy improvised passages as a matter of course in their live performances.

Jam, the British rock band of the late 1970s and early 1980s, which enjoyed critical and commercial acclaim during its brief existence. Founded in 1975, the Jam, which consisted of singer and guitarist Paul Weller (1958–), singer and bassist Bruce Foxton (1955–) and drummer Rick Butler (1955–), rapidly built up a reputation as a leading NEW WAVE group with a revived 'mod' image. The début album *In The City* (1977) was an immediate success, while subsequent hits included the LPs *Setting Sons* (1979), *Sound Affects* (1980) and *The Gift* (1982) as well as the Number One singles 'Start' (1980), 'Going Underground' (1980), 'A Town called Malice' (1982) and 'Beat Surrender' (1982).

Weller caused a sensation when he broke the band up at its peak in 1982, expressing a wish to explore new territory. He went on to lead the SOUL-influenced band Style Council, which recorded several hit singles but also split up in 1990, after which Weller launched a solo career.

The Jam's motto, written on their bass amplifier, was 'Fire and Skill'.

James, Elmore (1918–63) Black US BLUES guitarist and singer, who was effectively the originator of the Chicago SLIDE GUITAR blues style in the 1950s. James, who was born on a Mississippi plantation and constructed his first instrument from a lard can, created a whole new guitar sound, playing in a BOTTLENECK style on a heavily distorted ELECTRIC GUITAR. His version of 'Dust My Broom' (1951) was hugely influential and anticipated the birth of true ROCK a decade later; other recordings included 'The Sky is Crying' (1960) and 'It Hurts Me Too' (1965).

James, Etta (1938–) US RHYTHM-AND-BLUES singer, who had numerous influential hits in the 1960s and early 1970s. Among her most acclaimed recordings were 'Wallflower' (1955), 'Good Rockin' Daddy' (1955), 'If I Can't Have You' (1960), 'Tell Me Mama' (1967) and 'I've Found a Love' (1972). Her career was disrupted in the mid-1960s due to her drug addiction.

James, Harry (1916–83) US JAZZ trumpeter and bandleader, who emerged as a major figure in the late 1930s. James, the son of a circus bandmaster, developed a hard-hitting trumpet style, which won him a place in a series of celebrated bands, including those of Teddy WILSON and Benny GOODMAN. He established his own DANCE BAND in 1939 and attracted to it singers of the calibre of Frank SINATRA and Dick HAYMES. Among the band's most popular hits were 'Flight of the Bumble-bee', 'One o'Clock Jump' and 'You Made Me Love You'. In 1951 he suffered a temporary setback when several of his best performers defected to the ranks of Duke ELLINGTON's band in what became known in jazz circles as the Great James Raid. He continued to lead both small groups and BIG BANDS over the ensuing decades and made a number of film appearances. He was married to the film star Betty Grable between 1943 and 1965.

Janáček, Leoš (1854–1928) Czech composer, who won belated recognition as the most important Czech composer of the twentieth century. Janáček, one of the 14 children of a village schoolmaster in Silesia, received his first musical training as a chorister while a pupil at an Augustine monastery, and he subsequently braved conditions of extreme poverty to carry on his studies at the Prague Organ School. He was appointed to a post as conductor in Brno in 1876 and, after further study, rose to the office of director of the music school there.

Janáček married one of his students and concentrated on composition at about the same time as the death of his daughter Olga (his second child to die). He completed his first opera, *Šárka*, in 1887 and gave up teaching for good in 1904. His reputation was established in 1916 on the first performance of the opera *Jenůfa* (1904) – a work 'tied with the black ribbon of the long illness, pains and cries of my daughter Olga' according to the composer – at the National Theatre in Prague. Subsequently he added the operas *The Excursions of Mr Brouček* (1917), *Katya Kabanová* (1922), *The Cunning Little Vixen* (1926), *The Makropoulos Affair* (1926) and *From the House of the Dead* (1928), which was based on the novel (1861) by Fyodor Dostoevsky (1821–81). Other compositions to emerge during this remarkable late flowering of the composer's inspiration – fuelled both by his love of the countryside and by his unrequited love for

Kamila Stosslová, the young wife of one of his friends – included the choral *Glagolitic Mass* (1926), the rhapsody *Taras Bulba* (1918) and *Sinfonietta* (1926) as well as the song-cycle *Diary of a Man Who Disappeared*, such chamber pieces as the two string quartets (1923 and 1927–28) and piano music, notably the suite *Along Overgrown Paths*.

Many of Janáček's works benefited from his interest in the 'natural' music of human speech: it was said that he even jotted down for future use the 'notes' sounded by a hotel pageboy as he called out room numbers.

Janáček's death from pneumonia at the age of 74 was the result of a cold contracted during a lengthy search in his beloved woods for Stosslová's 11-year-old son, who had got himself lost.

> I do not play about with empty melodies. I dip them in life and nature. I find work very difficult and serious – perhaps for this reason.
> LEOŠ JANÁČEK, letter, 1925

Japan British NEW ROMANTIC band, which enjoyed international success in the late 1970s and 1980s. David Sylvian (David Batt; 1958–), Steve Jansen (Steve Batt; 1959–), Mick Karn (Antony Michaelides; 1958–) and Richard Barbieri (1957–) came together in 1974 and developed a distinctive GLAM ROCK style modelled on that of the NEW YORK DOLLS. Such early releases as the album *Obscure Alternatives* (1980) sold well in Japan, and British fans followed later. Among the band's most acclaimed releases were the singles 'Quiet Life' (1980) and 'Ghosts' (1982) and the album *Tin Drum* (1982). The band split up in 1982, with Sylvian going on to a successful solo career. In 1991 the original four re-formed, as Rain Tree Crow, for an album of the same name.

Jarre, Jean-Michel (1948–) French keyboard player, son of the composer Maurice JARRE, who established himself as one of the superstars of European pop in the late 1970s. Having started training as a classical musician, he switched to rock and was soon recording such well-received albums of synthesized keyboard music as *Oxygène* (1977) and *Equinoxe* (1978). He won particular acclaim for his spectacular live shows staged all over the world (including the USA and Communist China), which employed a battery of lasers, fireworks, and other theatrical devices. His *son et lumière* concerts in London's docklands in 1988 and in Paris on Bastille Day in 1990 were among his most extravagant appearances (the Paris event attracted two million people). He has continued to prosper with such hit albums as *Magnetic Fields* (1981), *Rendez-Vous* (1986), *Revolutions* (1988) and *Chronologie* (1995). He has also composed film music, ballets and even JINGLES for advertisements.

Music for Supermarkets was unusual in that just one copy of the album was pressed (subsequently acquired by a Paris art gallery).

> Music is the human treatment of sounds.
> JEAN-MICHEL JARRE

Jarre, Maurice (1924–) French composer, father of pop star Jean-Michel JARRE, who wrote much admired theatre and film music. Musical director of the Théâtre National Populaire, he was recruited by the film industry in 1951 and subsequently provided memorable SOUNDTRACKS for such movies as *The Longest Day* (1962), *Lawrence of Arabia* (1962), for which he won an OSCAR, *Dr Zhivago* (1965), which brought him a second Academy Award and *Ryan's Daughter* (1970).

Jaws *See* Eddie 'Lockjaw' DAVIS.

jazz Genre of popular music, which first swept the western world in the 1920s and 1930s and has subsequently become entrenched as one of the characterizing movements in twentieth-century culture.

In the words of Paul Whiteman, 'Jazz came to America 300 years ago in chains' – that is, from West Africa via the Black slaves who were imported to the states of the southern USA to work for White masters in the cotton plantations. The slaves built up a rich hoard of work songs and ballads lamenting their condition, and in time these settled into distinct genres, spawning the BLUES and ultimately jazz itself. It was never, however, the sole property of the Black community, other influences including the minstrel shows put on by White performers as well as RAGTIME, DIXIELAND and the predominantly White TIN PAN ALLEY tradition. George GERSHWIN for one preferred a totally non-racial definition: 'Jazz is the result of the energy stored up in America.'

Broadly speaking, the central elements of the various forms of jazz include strong syncopated rhythms, reliance on improvisation on set themes and a shared heritage – but many leading performers have rebelled over the years against the idea that their music can be contained by any single definition. To some, even the word 'jazz' is something with which they do not feel comfortable. Miles DAVIS condemned it as a word 'that White folks dropped on us', while Duke ELLINGTON claimed the word had no meaning and was condescending. No less an authority than *The Melody Maker* rejected its use, noting in 1931: 'It is a word of sarcasm. It signifies everything that is old-fashioned.'

Apparently, the word 'jazz' originated in New Orleans 'jass', which was slang for sexual intercourse, but it gradually came to be applied to anything exciting. The story goes that a band led by Johnny Stein in Chicago in 1916 was greeted with a shout of 'Jass it up, boys!' from an enthusiastic and somewhat drunk 'retired vaudeville entertainer' in the audience, who was subsequently paid to repeat the line at future gigs; the band itself was eventually renamed Stein's Dixie Jass Band (and ultimately the ORIGINAL DIXIELAND JAZZ BAND). Other commentators have traced the use of the word in a musical context even further back, the first instance in writing dating to 1909.

Briefly, jazz emerged as a thriving form of popular music after it caught on among the musicians who were paid to entertain clients in the brothels of New Orleans at the turn of the century (*see* STORYVILLE). Among the most important pioneers were cornet player Buddy BOLDEN and Jelly Roll MORTON, who often claimed he had 'invented' jazz. Subsequently the form developed under the influence of ragtime and the blues and found a new home in Chicago. It entered a golden age in the 1920s, when up-and-coming stars of the calibre of Louis ARMSTRONG and Bix BEIDERBECKE perfected the HOT style now often labelled TRAD. Such was the impact of jazz and its associated implications of liberated thought and behaviour that the carefree decade of the 1920s was itself dubbed the 'jazz age'.

The SWING era of the 1930s brought a host of legendary BIG BANDS, including those of Duke ELLINGTON, Paul WHITEMAN, Benny GOODMAN, Count BASIE and Glenn MILLER, into the limelight, while Bessie SMITH, Billie HOLIDAY and Ella FITZGERALD won huge acclaim as jazz singers. Swing was in turn outmoded by the development of BEBOP (or 'bop') and the COOL styles explored by such masters as Charlie PARKER and Dizzy GILLESPIE, which did much to 'legitimize' jazz as a musical form worthy of serious intellectual consideration. FREE JAZZ became a new force in the 1950s and 1960s under the influence of such AVANT-GARDE musicians as Miles DAVIS, Ornette COLEMAN and John COLTRANE, while more recent sub-genres have included a range of CROSSOVER or FUSION styles. *See also* BOOGIE-WOOGIE; DEVIL'S MUSIC; JAZZ-ROCK; THIRD STREAM; TRUTH.

If you have to ask what jazz is, you'll never know.
LOUIS ARMSTRONG

I don't think any music should be called jazz ... if it sounds good, that's all you need.
DUKE ELLINGTON

A jazz musician is a juggler who uses harmonies instead of oranges.
BENNY GREEN, *The Reluctant Art*, 1962

Somehow I suspect that if Shakespeare were alive today, he might be a jazz fan himself.
DUKE ELLINGTON

The most degraded form of human aberration.
SIR THOMAS BEECHAM

The public will not continue indefinitely its admiration of the hectic, unsatisfying fare known popularly as jazz ... the plague will inevitably die out, and its victims return to sanity.
GEORGE CLUTSAM, in *Melody Maker*, 1925

Jazz at the Philharmonic Celebrated series of JAZZ concerts, which was inaugurated at the Philharmonic Auditorium in Los Angeles in 1944 by US impresario Norman Granz (1918–   ). The JATP concerts, all recorded, were a highlight of US jazz in the 1940s and 1950s and did much to promote mixed race jazz. They were subsequently staged in Europe, until petering out in the late 1960s. Among the many stars who took part in the concerts were such great figures as Dizzy GILLESPIE, Roy ELDRIDGE, Charlie PARKER, Lester YOUNG, Coleman HAWKINS, Nat 'King' COLE, Gene KRUPA, Count BASIE, Duke ELLINGTON and Ella FITZGERALD.

jazz-rock Distinct CROSSOVER style, in which elements of JAZZ and ROCK are combined, as first attempted in the mid-1960s by such artists as Miles DAVIS, Herbie HANCOCK and Jimi HENDRIX. Jazz-rock represented a major development in the history of jazz, with links being made between more AVANT-GARDE jazzmen and various radical rock musicians in the expectation that the resulting music would excite fans of both genres. Jazz composers learnt to incorporate rock instruments and sounds, while rock musicians moved away from the straitjacket of heavy, regular rhythms and experimented with brass and woodwind instruments as well as making increased use of improvisation.

The genre enjoyed some popularity in the 1960s and 1970s, in particular through the efforts of such exponents as Chick COREA, Keith Jarrett (1945–   ) and WEATHER REPORT, but it became increasingly elitist and has remained at best a rarified sub-genre that has never won acceptance with the mass of followers of either TRAD jazz or conventional rock.

Jeep *See* Johnny HODGES.

Jefferson, (Clarence) 'Blind Lemon' (1897–1929) Black US singer-songwriter and guitarist, of legendary reputation, who was among the hugely influential pioneers of twentieth-century BLUES. Blind since birth, he had a tough life, working as a wrestler and entertainer and often reduced to begging. Having died in the course of a snowstorm, he won posthumous fame in the 1950s when he was recognized as one of the great bluesmen through his 1920s recordings (sometimes made in partnership with LEADBELLY) of such self-written songs as 'Cannon Ball Moan', 'Prison Cell Blues', 'Pneumonia Blues' and 'See that My Grave is Kept Clean'.

Jefferson Airplane US FOLK-ROCK band, which established a huge following in the late 1960s. Founded in San Francisco in 1965, the group originally consisted of singer-songwriters Marty Balin (Martyn Buchwald; 1943–   ) and Signe Anderson, guitarists Paul Kantner (1942–   ) and Jorma Kaukonen (1940–   ), bassist Bob Harvey and drummer Jerry Pelonquin, although there have since been many changes in personnel, with such players as Jack Casady (1944–   ), Grace Slick (1939–   ) and Spencer Dryden (1943–   ) also joining the line-up. The band's psychedelic second album, *Surrealistic Pillow*

(1967), brought stardom, and it was followed by such hit LPs as *Crown of Creation* (1968) and *Volunteers* (1970) before a decline in fortunes led to a temporary split in 1974. Among the hit singles were 'Somebody to Love' and 'White Rabbit' (both 1967).

Reunited as Jefferson Starship, led by Slick and Kantner, the band returned to the limelight with *Dragonfly* (1974) and such singles as 'With Your Love' (1976) and 'Runaway' (1978) but eventually broke up again (amid considerable acrimony) in 1985. Slick subsequently relaunched the band as Starship and had a US Number One with the single 'We Built This City' (1985); 'Nothing's Gonna Stop Us Now' reached Number One in the UK in 1987. Jefferson Airplane – with a line-up of Slick, Kantner, Balin and Kaukonen – was revived in 1989.

Jena Symphony Informal title that was bestowed on what purported to be Beethoven's Tenth Symphony, which first came to light in the German city of Jena in 1910. The discovery of the musicologist Fritz Stein, the attribution was quickly brought into question by other leading experts and soon only Stein and his publishers (who had a vested financial interest) still believed the piece to be by Beethoven's hand. Sure enough, the symphony eventually turned out to be the work of one Friedrich Witt (1771–1837), a young contemporary and imitator of Josef Haydn.

Jennings, Waylon (1937–) US COUNTRY singer-songwriter and guitarist, whose success in treading his own path between traditional country and rock in the 1970s proved hugely influential. A former member of Buddy HOLLY's band the Crickets, who only escaped sharing Holly's death on the toss of a coin for one of the last seats in the doomed aircraft, Jennings reverted to country for a time before rebelling against the accepted NASHVILLE style. Such albums as *Honky Tonk Heroes* (1973) and *Wanted! The Outlaws* (1976) attracted a new rock audience and inspired many imitators. Other recordings include collaborations with fellow-rebel Willie NELSON, among them *Waylon and Willie* (1978) and *The Highwayman* (1985), on which Johnny CASH and Kris KRISTOFFERSON also participated. He reached an even wider audience as singer of the signature tune of the popular television series *The Dukes of Hazzard*.

Jethro Tull British FOLK-ROCK band, which has enjoyed a highly successful history over a period of some 25 years. The group came together in 1967 around individualist singer and flautist Ian Anderson (1947–), who has re-formed the band several times with different personnel. Called Jethro Tull after the English inventor of the seed drill during the Agricultural Revolution, the band quickly established a reputation among BLUES-ROCK fans with such albums as *This Was* (1968), *Stand Up* (1969), which reached Number One, and *Benefit* (1970). In 1970 Jethro Tull became the first rock group to appear at the prestigious Carnegie Hall. Subsequently Anderson switched direction with the hard rock CONCEPT ALBUM *Aqualung* (1971) and the US chart-topping *Thick as a Brick* (1972) before contemplating retirement when the over-ambitious *A Passion Play* (1973) was poorly received. Further hit albums included *Minstrel in the Gallery* (1975), *Songs from the Wood* (1978), *A* (1980), *Catfish Rising* (1991) and *Roots to Branches* (1995).

Anderson himself is also known in his self-styled role as a Scottish laird and proprietor of a successful salmon farming business. In 1979 he had cause to regret his rock stardom when he suffered an accident during a concert at Madison Square Garden: he had to be taken to hospital after his eye was pierced by the thorn of a rose thrown by an adoring fan.

Jeune France, La *See* YOUNG FRANCE.

jingle Short snatch of vocal or instrumental music, which is written in order to help advertise a particular commercial product on the radio or television or in the cinema. Many notable composers from a wide range of musical backgrounds have been persuaded to offer their services in this way, while others have specialized in composing such music.

Among the most celebrated of all advertising jingles must be included 'We are the Ovaltinies, Little Girls and Boys' and the Coca-Cola advertisement of the early 1970s, which yielded an international Number One in the form of the NEW SEEKERS' 'I'd Like to Teach the World to Sing'. Others have employed excerpts of famous classical and rock works, usually totally out of context, and have inadvertently served to revive interest in the work in question.

Bach's *Air on the G-String* is a leading example, having been adapted for use in a famous cigar advertisement, which ran in various forms for many years.

> To know whether you are enjoying a piece of music or not you must see whether you find yourself looking at the advertisements of Pears' soap at the end of the programme.
> SAMUEL BUTLER, *Note-Books*, 1912

jive Up-tempo style of JAZZ music of the 1940s, otherwise labelled SWING. The same word was used of the energetic jitterbug dance steps that accompanied such music, and fans spoke their own 'jive talk', the slang that was later to provide the basis of beatnik and hippie slang.

Jobim, Antonio Carlos (1927–) Brazilian composer, guitarist and singer, who established an international reputation in the early 1960s as one of the leading writers of the BOSSA NOVA. His contributions to the SOUNDTRACK of the film *Black Orpheus* (1959) greatly promoted the bossa nova craze outside South America. Among his most popular tunes, which were much covered by such singers as Ella FITZGERALD and Frank SINATRA, were 'Desafinado' (1959) and the classic 'The Girl from Ipanema' (1963–64).

Jochum, Eugen (1902–) German conductor, who won recognition as one of the foremost conductors of the romantic repertoire. He established his reputation working with the Berlin Radio Orchestra (1932–34) and the Hamburg State Opera, where he was musical director (1934–49). He was founder and chief conductor of the Bavarian Radio Symphony Orchestra (1949–59), and was joint chief conductor of the CONCERTGEBOUW Orchestra (1961–64) in Amsterdam. He has also conducted both the LONDON PHILHARMONIC ORCHESTRA and the LONDON SYMPHONY ORCHESTRA.

Joel, Billy (William Martin Joel; 1949–) US singer-songwriter, nicknamed the Piano Man, who enjoyed massive commercial success in the 1970s and 1980s. The son of an internee at the Dachau concentration camp, Joel studied classical music and showed promise as an amateur boxer, fighting 28 bouts before turning to a musical career. He played for a number of obscure bands, calling himself Bill Martin,

but had little initial success: in 1970 he even attempted suicide by drinking furniture polish – 'but all I ended up doing was farting … I polished all my mother's chairs just sitting there!' He eventually decided on a solo career, writing about suicide in his later track 'You're Only Human (Second Wind)'.

Piano Man (1973) reached Number One, sold two million copies and brought Joel international fame. Numerous hit singles followed as well as further successful albums, among them *The Stranger* (1977), which spawned such singles as 'Just the Way You Are', *Glass Houses* (1980), *Innocent Man* (1983), which produced the UK Number One single 'Uptown Girl', *The Bridge* (1986), *Storm Front* (1989) and *River of Dreams* (1993). His music became more serious in tone in the 1980s after a serious motorcycle crash in 1982.

> The thing that impresses me most about Beethoven's Fifth is – *da da da daaa* – it's fate knocking at the door. That's one of the biggest hits in history. There's no video to it, he didn't *need* one.
> BILLY JOEL, the *Independent*, 1990

John, Elton (Hercules) (Reginald Kenneth Dwight; 1947–) British singer-songwriter and pianist, calling himself Elton John in reference to fellow-musicians Elton Dean and Long John Baldry, who became a pop superstar of the 1970s and 1980s. A piano scholarship to London's Royal Academy of Music failed to persuade John to take up a classical career, and he joined his first band, Bluesology, in 1961. In 1967, after teaming up with lyricist Bernie Taupin (1950–), he wrote copiously for other artists (one of their songs was a contender for entry in the 1968 EUROVISION SONG CONTEST), first venturing into the studios himself two years later. He joined the ranks of pop's superstars as a GLAM ROCKER in the early 1970s on the strength of such albums as *Tumbleweed Connection* (1970), *Honky Chateau* (1972), *Don't Shoot Me, I'm Only the Piano Player* (1973) and *Goodbye Yellow Brick Road* (1973) and such hit singles as 'Your Song' (1970), 'Rocket Man' (1972), 'Crocodile Rock' (1973) and 'Daniel' (1973).

Apart from his overwhelming collection of hit singles and albums, John – a flamboyant live performer, favouring exotic stage costumes – became well known for his vast collection of exotic spectacles and for his interest in Watford Football Club (of which he became Life President in 1990). Landmarks in his musical career since the early 1970s have included his unique achievement in having two albums, *Captain Fantastic and the Brown Dirt Cowboy* (1975) and *Rock of the Westies* go straight into the US charts at Number One. More recent releases include the albums *Leather Jackets* (1986), *Sleeping with the Past* (1989) and *Made in England* (1995).

Long before he became an established star, the young Reginald Dwight nearly threw it all away when he tried to gas himself; he made the mistake, however, of opening all the windows and was 'rescued' by Taupin, for whom 'Someone Saved My Life Tonight' was subsequently written. In 1976 his status as one of the biggest pop stars of his generation was acknowledged when he became the first pop artist since the BEATLES to be honoured with a wax figure in Madame Tussaud's.

Johnson, Bunk (William Geary Johnson; 1889–1949) US JAZZ trumpeter, who became one of the most revered elder statesmen of jazz of the 1930s and 1940s. Johnson was one of the pioneers of NEW ORLEANS jazz, playing (he claimed) in the band of the legendary Buddy BOLDEN in the early 1900s. He went on to play with numerous other outfits – teaching the young Louis ARMSTRONG according to his own version of events – before going into retirement in 1934 after losing his front teeth. He returned to jazz, with false teeth, in 1942 and made many recordings reviving the original TRAD sound heard in the early history of the genre.

> There's a familiar story about Bunk Johnson losing his front teeth, having to give up playing and retiring to the ricefields of New Iberia – until the day, of course, when he was rediscovered, given new teeth and so on. In reality, eyewitnesses say that he was playing local gigs all the time. He got over the shortage of teeth by winding twine around his surviving canine teeth and playing with the mouthpiece against that.
> HUMPHREY LYTTELTON, on BBC radio's *Jazz Score*

Johnson, Charles L(eslie) (1876–1950) US pianist and songwriter, who composed numerous hit songs and classic RAGTIME tunes. Having worked for many years as a pianist in bands, hotels and theatres, he established himself as a popular composer with such hits as 'It Takes a Coon to Do the Ragtime Dance' (1899) and 'Sweet and Low' (1919); his many rags included 'Doc Brown's Cakewalk' (1899), 'Porcupine Rag' (1909) and 'Snookums' (1918).

Johnson, J(ames) C. (1896–1981) US songwriter, pianist and bandleader, who wrote many hits between the wars. As well as writing for the musical stage, he penned such hits as 'Louisiana' (1928), 'Rhythm and Romance' (1935) and, in collaboration with Fats WALLER, 'The Joint is Jumpin'' (1937).

Johnson, J(ames) J. (James Louis Johnson; 1924–) US JAZZ trombonist and composer, who emerged as a leading jazzman in the 1950s and revolutionized the role of the trombone as a jazz instrument. Influenced by Jack TEAGARDEN and Tommy DORSEY, he played in the bands of Benny CARTER, Count BASIE, Dizzy GILLESPIE and Miles DAVIS among others as well as making a number of celebrated recordings, as Jay and Kai, with Danish trombonist Kai Winding (1922–83).

Johnson, James P(rice) (1894–1955) US JAZZ pianist and composer, who was one of the most influential pioneers of jazz piano playing. Taught the piano by his mother, he was accompanist to singers such as Bessie SMITH, Mamie SMITH and Ethel WATERS and had a fundamental effect on the STRIDE PIANO styles of Duke ELLINGTON, Count BASIE and Fats WALLER, his pupil. As a composer, he enjoyed success with the hit REVUE *Runnin' Wild* (1923), which popularized his classic 'The Charleston', and subsequently wrote such shows as *Messin' 'Round* (1929) and *Sugar Hill* (1931) as well as the songs 'Carolina Shout', (1925), 'If I could be with You One Hour Tonight' (1926) and 'Keep off the Grass' (1926) among many others. A competent classical pianist, he also wrote a number of classically oriented jazz works, including a piano rhapsody, a piano concerto and a blues opera, *De Organizer*.

Johnson, James Weldon (1871–1938) US author, educationalist and administrator, who did much to promote the Black musical tradition in the USA in collaboration with his composer brother J(ohn) Rosamond Johnson (1873–1954). A teacher, US consul in several countries and writer on, and collector of, Black music,

James Weldon Johnson provided the lyrics for songs written with both his brother and fellow-composer Bob Cole (1863–1911), including 'Under the Bamboo Tree' (1902), put together during a walk through the streets of New York, 'Congo Love Song' (1903) and 'Oh, Didn't He Ramble' (1902), which earned them the informal title the Ebony Offenbachs. The Johnson brothers provided numerous hits for the musical stage and also wrote the school song 'Lift Every Voice and Sing' (1900), which came to be known as the 'Negro national anthem'.

Johnson, Laurie (1927–) British composer, who has written numerous signature tunes for television as well as scores for the cinema. Among his best-known compositions are the signature tunes for television's *The Avengers* and *The Professionals*. His work for the theatre includes the score of *Lock Up Your Daughters* (1962).

Johnson, Robert (1911–38) Black US BLUES singer and guitarist, nicknamed the King of the Delta Blues Singers, who was one of the most celebrated bluesmen of the 1930s. Born into conditions of great poverty, Johnson epitomized the blues tradition of the oppressed rural Blacks of the southern States. A master of the acoustic guitar, often using a BOTTLENECK, he wrote such songs as 'Terraplane', 'Sweet Home Chicago', 'Dust My Broom', 'Crossroads' and 'Love in Vain', which were to be COVERED many times by BLUES-ROCK musicians of the 1960s. Reputedly so shy that he sometimes played with his back to his audience, he died young, supposedly poisoned by a jealous husband – or possibly by his own lover – or else as a result of his interest in black magic. The whereabouts of his grave are uncertain, and no photographs exist of this elusive genius, whose life story was loosely re-created in the film *Crossroads* (1986).

Johnston, Arthur James (1898–1954) US composer, pianist, organist and arranger, who wrote much music for both the stage and the screen in the 1930s. Among his film scores were those for *City Lights* (1931), *Thanks a Million* (1935), *The Girl Friend* (1935), *Pennies from Heaven* (1936) and *Song of the South* (1947). Hits from these and other shows included 'Moonstruck', 'Twenty Million People' and 'Cocktails for Two'.

Jolivet, André (1905–74) French composer, who emerged as a leading AVANT-GARDE composer after the Second World War. Influenced by Edgar VARÈSE and a member of the YOUNG FRANCE group of composers, he explored the possibilities of dissonance and broken rhythms in such works as the comic opera *Dolores* (1942), the oratorio *La Verité de Jeanne*, as well as in three symphonies, two ballets and numerous concertos for a range of instruments, including the ONDES MARTENOT. He also served as musical director (1943–59) of the Comédie Française.

Jolson, Al (Asa Yoelson; 1886–1950) US singer, nicknamed the World's Greatest Entertainer, who enjoyed huge acclaim as a black-face star of stage and film over the course of some four decades. Born in Lithuania but taken to the USA as a child, Jolson began his career in the circus and in vaudeville before reaching Broadway in 1899 and finally cutting his first record in 1911. By then he had adopted the blackface style of the minstrel shows and went on to win a huge audience singing such emotional, mock-negro songs as 'Mammy', 'Swanee', 'California, Here I Come', 'Toot, Toot, Tootsie, Goo'bye' and 'Sonny Boy'. Intensely egotistical, it was greatly to his satisfaction when he became one of the legends of the cinema in 1927, starring in *The Jazz Singer*, the first full-length 'talkie'. He was greatly affected by the breakdown of his marriage to actress Ruby Keeler (1909–93) in 1939, but he continued to perform, both live and in films, to huge acclaim until his death.

> Wait a minute! Wait a minute! You ain't heard nothin' yet.
> AL JOLSON, unscripted line left uncut in *The Jazz Singer*

> Al Jolson: he wasn't a singer, he was a stylist, a great salesman.
> MICKEY ADDY

Jones, George (1931–) US COUNTRY singer, who became one of the legends of country music over the course of a highly prolific career. He made his first recordings in the early 1950s, establishing his reputation with such hits as 'Why Baby Why' (1955), 'Treasure of Love' (1958), 'White Lightning' (1959) and 'Tender Years' (1961). Among his many hits since then have been 'She Thinks I Still Care' (1962), 'Walk Through This World with Me' (1967), 'Loving You Could Never be Better' (1972) and a series of duets with his wife (1969–75) Tammy WYNETTE. His private life was much disrupted by alcoholism and financial problems, but his fortunes improved in the early 1980s, when *I Am What I Am* (1980) proved to be his bestselling album so far. More recent releases include *Too Wild Too Long* (1988).

Jones, Grace (1952–) West Indian SOUL singer and model, who first emerged as a top DISCO star in the late 1970s. Capitalizing on her lithe, striking looks, she triumphed with a distinctive half-spoken vocal style on such albums as *Warm Leatherette* (1980), *Nightclubbing* (1981) and *Living My Life* (1982).

Jones, Dame Gwyneth (1936–) Welsh soprano, who has established an international reputation, notably in a range of Wagnerian roles. She began her career with the Welsh National Opera and has subsequently appeared at leading venues throughout the world, her greatest successes including the part of Brünnhilde in *The Ring* at Bayreuth in 1976.

Jones, Jo (1911–85) US JAZZ drummer, who won renown as an innovative drummer with the Count BASIE orchestra. Jones first joined Basie in 1935 and remained with him almost without a break until 1948, inspiring many imitators. After leaving Basie he played with Lester YOUNG, Ella FITZGERALD and Oscar PETERSON among others and also led his own groups.

Jones, Philly Joe (1923–85) US JAZZ drummer, who played with many leading BEBOP groups of the 1950s. He was at his best with such progressive talents as John COLTRANE, Miles DAVIS and Gil EVANS, although he also led his own bands and made appearances on both sides of the Atlantic through the 1960s and 1970s, when he switched to a JAZZ-ROCK style.

Jones, Quincy (Delight) (1933–) Black US JAZZ trumpeter, pianist, producer and composer, who has been one of the most influential figures in jazz and pop since the 1950s. Jones began as a trumpeter with Lionel HAMPTON and also studied with Nadia BOULANGER before working his way up to the post of vice-president of Mercury records, in which position he was well placed to steer the careers of numerous major stars. As a producer, he played a crucial role in promoting such singers as Tony BENNETT, George

BENSON, Ray CHARLES, Johnny MATHIS and Frank SINATRA, although nothing was to surpass the success he had producing Michael JACKSON's *Thriller*, which became the biggest-selling album ever released. He also developed his own solo career, recording such jazz-funk albums as *Walking in Space* (1969), *Smackwater Jack* (1971) and *Body Heat* (1973), and emerged as one of the most respected composers of film scores, providing music for such movies as *The Pawnbroker* (1965), *The Italian Job* (1969) and *The Wiz* (1978) as well as for television's *Roots* (1977).

Jones, Spike (1911–65) US bandleader, nicknamed the King of Corn, who earned a unique reputation for his eccentric approach to popular music-making. Having worked as a backing musician for singers including Al JOLSON and Bing CROSBY, he lighted on the idea of making eccentric recordings featuring such gimmicks as cowbells, saws, whistles, breaking glass and so forth. His City Slickers band had huge success employing such noises, and among the hits they recorded in the 1940s were 'Cocktails for Two', 'Holiday for Strings' and 'That Old Black Magic'.

Jones, Thad (Thaddeus Joseph Jones; 1923–86) US JAZZ trumpeter, bandleader, composer and arranger, who won acclaim playing in the bands of such jazz legends as Charles MINGUS, Thelonious MONK and Count BASIE. Self-taught, Jones first played for Mingus in 1954 and that same year joined the ranks of Basie's orchestra, with which he remained until 1963. He later worked on a freelance basis, leading his own band in collaboration with Mel Lewis (1929–90), and he founded his own jazz orchestra in Denmark, where he lived from 1978. He briefly returned to the Basie orchestra as its leader in 1985.

Jones, Tom (Thomas Jones Woodward; 1940–) Welsh singer and sex symbol, born in Pontypridd, who emerged as a top transatlantic MIDDLE-OF-THE-ROAD star in the late 1960s. Jones became a top attraction in 1965 with his Number One hit 'It's Not Unusual' and subsequently attracted a huge, loyal (and largely female) audience, singing such reliable ballads as 'The Green, Green Grass of Home' (1966), 'I'll Never Fall in Love Again' (1967) and, somewhat more raunchily, 'Delilah' (1968). His success in the US market led to him moving to the USA in the 1970s, when he become the highest-paid television entertainer of the day. In the 1980s, however, he staged a significant come-back in the UK under the management of his son, winning over many young fans through self-parodying appearances with contemporary bands and with unlikely COVERS of hits by PRINCE among others.

Joplin, Janis (1943–70) US rock singer, nicknamed Pearl, who acquired an almost legendary reputation as one of the most gifted and uncomprising BLUES singers of her generation before her premature death. Joplin abandoned an initial career as a teacher to sing in the clubs and bars of Austin and Los Angeles and went on to make her first recordings in the mid-1960s, when her harsh vocal style made an immediate impression. She quickly established a cult following as a live performer and, backed by the band Big Brother and the Holding Company, won acclaim for the album *Cheap Thrills*, from which came the hit single 'Ball and Chain'.

Joplin embarked on a solo career in 1968, releasing *I Got Dem Ol' Kozmic Blues Again, Mama* a year later and consolidating her notoriety as one of the wild women of rock by drinking heavily and being arrested for abusing the police. The pressures of fame, however, finally overcame her and she died of a heroin overdose in the same year as Jimi HENDRIX. Her single 'Me and Bobby McGee' reached Number One in the USA in March 1971, a full five months after her death, ranking her alongside Otis REDDING, Jim CROCE and John LENNON as the only artists to have posthumous chart-toppers. The album *Pearl* was released in 1971.

Bette MIDLER starred as a Joplin-inspired character in the film *Rose* (1979).

> She showed me the air and taught me how to fill it.
>
> JANIS JOPLIN, of blues singer Bessie Smith

Joplin, Scott (1868–1917) Black US pianist and composer, nicknamed the King of Ragtime, who became the most famous name in the RAGTIME tradition. Joplin first addressed himself to the ragtime style in the 1890s and was soon penning such hits as 'Original Rags' and 'Maple Leaf Rag' (both 1899), the second of which (named after the Maple Leaf Club in Sedalia, Missouri, where Joplin played) sold over a million copies as sheet music and did much to promote the ragtime craze, making Joplin himself a nationally known star.

The first ragtime composer to write down his songs, Joplin attempted to write longer, more serious works in the style but met with little success. He wrote two operas, *A Guest of Honour* (1903), which is now lost, and *Treemonisha* (1911), as well as a ragtime symphony but in the process only demonstrated the unsuitability of ragtime for such ambitious enterprises. Disillusioned by these failures and ravaged by the effects of syphilis, his health collapsed and he eventually died insane in a mental home.

Joplin's music found an enthusiastic new audience in the early 1970s, when his compositions were used for the soundtrack of the film *The Sting* (1973) and such pieces as 'The Entertainer' featured high in the singles charts. *Treemonisha*, derided in Joplin's lifetime, was revived in 1976.

> Syncopations are no indication of light or trashy music, and to shy bricks at 'hateful ragtime' no longer passes for musical culture.
>
> SCOTT JOPLIN, *The School of Ragtime*, 1908

Jordan, Joe (1882–1971) US songwriter, arranger, pianist and teacher, who wrote numerous hit songs in the early years of the century. Among his most popular compositions were 'Rise and Shine' (1908), 'Oh, Liza Lady' (1908) and 'Lovie Joe' (1910).

Journey US rock band, which enjoyed massive commercial success catering for an ADULT-ORIENTED ROCK audience in the 1970s and early 1980s. The group, formed from guitarist Neal Schon (1955–), bassist Ross Valory (1950–), singer Steve Perry (1949–), drummer Aynsley Dunbar (1948–), who was soon replaced by Steve Smith, and keyboard player Gregg Rolie (1948–), released its first record in 1975. It only emerged as a top attraction after Perry joined in 1977 and it switched from progressive rock to a more commercial sound. Among the hits that followed were *Infinity* (1978), *Evolution* (1979), *Departure* (1980), *Escape* (1981) and *Frontiers* (1983). Journey's output declined in the late 1980s as the various members concentrated on solo projects.

Judas Priest British HEAVY METAL band, which emerged as one of the most popular HARD ROCK groups of the 1970s and 1980s. Formed in Birmingham in 1970, the band settled down in the mid-1970s with a leather-clad line-up of guitarists K.K. Downing and Glenn Tipton (1948–), bassist Ian Hill, lead singer Rob Halford (1951–) and a succession of drummers. The group established itself as one of the most uncompromisingly heavy bands with such albums as *Sin After Sin* (1977), *Stained Class* (1978), *Killing Machine* (1978), *British Steel* (1980), *Point of Entry* (1981), *Screaming for Vengeance* (1982), *Defenders of the Faith* (1984) and *Painkiller* (1990). Halford left in 1991, after *A Touch of Evil*.

jug Improvised wind instrument, which was adopted by the so-called SPASM BANDS that played for rent money in the major cities of the USA from the early years of the century through to the 1930s. The jug (usually an empty beer or wine jug) produced a rich bass note, which combined well with the sound of the kazoos, washboards and other homemade instruments used by such bands; it continued to be used by a number of groups, including Gus Cannon's Jug Stompers, in recordings made as late as the early 1930s.

Juillard Quartet US quartet, which has established a worldwide reputation as one of the finest contemporary string quartets in existence. The quartet, founded in 1946, is part of the celebrated Juillard School based at the Lincoln Center, New York.

juju Genre of West African dance music, which first emerged in the 1930s and exercised a strong influence on African pop in the 1970s. The adoption of electric instruments in the early 1960s signalled a major new development in the history of the guitar-based genre, which was rooted in traditional African music. The style puts great emphasis on improvisation and most groups feature 'talking drums'. Leading exponents include Ebenezer Obey, King Sunny Ade and Dele Abiodun. *See also* HIGH LIFE.

juke box Electrically powered, automatic record-player, of the type that was installed in roadhouses and cafés throughout the UK and the USA from the 1930s. These icons of the ROCK 'N' ROLL era of the 1950s epito-

mized the spirit of brash, convention-smashing exuberance that was implicit in the music of Bill HALEY, LITTLE RICHARD, Elvis PRESLEY and a host of other stars, whose records were prominent among the discs from which fans could make their choice for the price of a few pennies or dimes. The most elaborate versions, which were made in the 1950s and incorporated batteries of flashing lights and illuminated logos, now fetch high prices among keen collectors.

Juke Box Jury Influential British television programme screened by the BBC in the 1960s, in which four celebrities were asked to predict which of 10 new releases would be hits. Hosted by DISC JOCKEY David Jacobs, the programme became one of the most popular television shows of the decade. Guests included John LENNON, who caused controversy when he described Elvis PRESLEY as 'today's Bing Crosby', among many contemporary music stars, actors and other well-known faces.

juke-joint US slang for a BARRELHOUSE where a JUKE BOX was installed. Musicians of the early 1950s often had to compete with the sound of the juke box and thus came to adopt amplified instruments as well as a heavier beat in an effort to make themselves heard.

jungle Type of electronic music which developed from house in the early 1990s. Often combining its structure of very fast snare drums and resonating bass (drum 'n' bass) with influences from jazz or hip-hop, this freedom of style is making jungle a popular alternative to house or techno. Mainstream DJs have included Goldie and L. T. J. Bukem.

jungle music Informal title, which was bestowed on the brand of JAZZ played by such eminent bandleaders as Duke ELLINGTON at the COTTON CLUB and various other venues from the 1920s. The title usefully evoked the steamy and somehow 'dangerous' music generated by such bands, and several outfits, including Ellington's, took to calling themselves the Jungle Band.

K

Kabalevsky, Dmitri (Borisovich) (1904–87) Russian composer, pianist and writer, who earned an international reputation for his orchestral music. A student of the Moscow Conservatory, he wrote a wide range of compositions, from operas to chamber and piano music. Among his best-known works are the overture from the opera *Colas Breugnon* (1938) and the suite *The Comedians* (1940); he also wrote four symphonies, three piano concertos, ballet scores and songs.

Kaempfert, Bert(hold) (1923–80) German bandleader and composer, who had a number of popular hits in a light, EASY LISTENING vein in the early 1960s. A former prisoner-of-war, Kaempfert set up his own orchestra in 1947 and recorded such hits as 'Spanish Eyes' (1959), 'Wooden Heart' (1960), 'Wonderland by Night' (1960), 'Swinging Safari' (1962) and 'Strangers in the Night' (1966), which provided Frank SINATRA with one of his greatest successes. Kaempfert was also an administrator with Polydor Records and served as producer to Tony Sheridan and the BEATLES for a time in the early 1960s, recording their versions of 'My Bonnie Lies Over the Ocean' and 'When the Saints Go Marching In'.

Kagel, Mauricio (1931–) Argentinian composer, resident in Germany since 1957, who emerged as one of the leading AVANT-GARDE composers of his generation. His early works were written in a strongly SERIALIST style, while later compositions made use of eccentric sounds and unusual instruments as well as unconventional means of notation. His works include *Der Schall* (1968), which was written for five musicians and 54 instruments.

Kahn, Gus (1886–1941) US lyricist and author, who provided the words for numerous popular songs of the 1920s and 1930s. Among his most celebrated creations were the lyrics for 'Toot, Toot, Tootsie' (1922), 'Carolina in the Morning' (1922),

'Yes Sir, That's My Baby' (1925), 'It Had to be You' (1925), 'Makin' Whoopee' (1928), 'One Night of Love' (1934) and 'All God's Chillun Got Rhythm' (1937).

Kalmar, Bert (1884–1947) US lyricist and librettist, who contributed the lyrics of many hit musical shows of the 1920s. Collaborating first with Harry Ruby (1895–1974) and later with Jerome KERN and Herbert Stothart (1885–1949), he worked on many songs made popular by the Marx Brothers. His most enduring hit was 'I Wanna be Loved by You', which was originally written for the Stothart MUSICAL *Good Boy* (1928). Other numbers by Kalmar and Ruby included 'Who's Sorry Now' (1923), 'Three Little Words' (1930) and 'Hooray for Captain Spaulding' (1928).

Kaminsky, Max (1908–) US JAZZ trumpeter and bandleader, who played and recorded with many of the most famous names in jazz. Kaminsky was recruited by several popular DIXIELAND bands in the 1920s and was a regular star with such bands as those of Benny GOODMAN and Eddie CONDON in the 1930s and 1940s. During the Second World War he toured widely with the band of Artie SHAW. He later played with Jack TEAGARDEN and other notable bandleaders as well as with his own group.

Kander, John (Harold) (1927–) US composer, who collaborated on several of the most acclaimed stage musicals of the 1960s and 1970s. Having worked as arranger on such MUSICALS as *Gypsy* and *Irma la Douce*, Kander emerged as a leading figure in the musical theatre after forming a lasting partnership with Fred EBB. Among the most celebrated stage musicals that followed were *Cabaret* (1966), *Chicago* (1975) and *Woman of the Year* (1981); successful film musicals included *Funny Lady* (1975) and *New York, New York* (1977).

Kansas City jazz Traditional JAZZ style that first developed in Kansas City in the 1920s and 1930s, when the city boasted a thriving night-life because of the authorities' lax attitude towards the enforcement of Prohibition. The 'Kansas City' style, which has a strong BLUES element, quickly came to encompass a wide range of big band jazz and SWING, as played at countless night clubs by, among others, Count BASIE, and it ultimately influenced the development of BEBOP. Among the pioneers of the style were the bands of Bennie Moten (1894–1935) and Jay McShann (1909–   ). Others to graduate from the city included Charlie CHRISTIAN and Jimmy BLANTON.

Kaper, Bronislaw (1902–83) US composer, born in Poland, who won fame for his many outstanding film scores. Kaper studied music in Berlin before becoming associated with the film world in Warsaw and working at studios throughout Europe and, eventually, in Hollywood. Among his most acclaimed scores were those for *Gaslight* (1944), *The Red Badge of Courage* (1951), *Lili* (1953), for which he was awarded an Oscar, *Them* (1954), *Mutiny on the Bounty* (1962) and *Lord Jim* (1964).

Karajan, Herbert von (1908–89) Austrian conductor, nicknamed the Music Director of Europe, who was considered among the finest conductors of his generation. Born in Salzburg, Karajan was a child prodigy, and he was accepted as a pupil at the Salzburg Mozarteum while he was still a schoolboy. He studied conducting at the Vienna Academy and was appointed to a series of high posts, although his membership of the Nazi party prejudiced his later career to some extent.

Karajan established his international reputation in 1937, when he conducted Wagner's *Tristan und Isolde* at the Berlin State Opera to acclaim. After a temporary ban imposed as a result of his Nazi links, he reclaimed his status as a leading conductor in 1947, when he was both appointed conductor of the VIENNA SYMPHONY ORCHESTRA and also invited to conduct in London with the LONDON PHILHARMONIC ORCHESTRA. In 1955 he became principal conductor of the BERLIN PHILHARMONIC, a post he retained until just before his death. He was also artistic director of the Salzburg Festival (1956–60 and in 1964) and founded the Salzburg Easter Festival. More controversial was the duration of his work with the Vienna State Opera (1957–64), which

ended in considerable acrimony but was eventually resolved in 1977, when he was reappointed.

Karajan was particularly admired for his conducting of the works of Beethoven, Brahms, Bruckner, Schumann, Richard STRAUSS, Verdi and Wagner.

A kind of musical Malcolm Sargent.
SIR THOMAS BEECHAM

karaoke Musical leisure activity, in which an amateur singer is able to sing along with a previously recorded backing track. The karaoke – in Japanese 'empty orchestra' – craze took off in the late 1980s, when karaoke competitions became a regular attraction in bars throughout the world (particularly in Japan, where most karaoke machines were made). Although such evenings were hugely popular for a year or two, they quickly attracted derision and by the mid-1990s were considered one of the hallmarks of a 'naff' social life.

Karas, Anton (1906–85) Austrian zither player and composer, who achieved overnight fame with the celebrated theme tune for the Carol Reed thriller *The Third Man* (1949). Karas took up zither playing after finding one in his attic, and he was 'discovered' by Reed himself while entertaining in a Viennese café. The immense success of the 'Harry Lime Theme' and the accompanying 'Café Mozart Waltz' made Karas rich and enabled him to buy a café of his own.

Kaufman, George S(imon) (1889–1961) US playwright, librettist, director and newspaper columnist, whose many highly successful works for the theatre included a series of enormously popular MUSICALS and revues. Remembered in the straight theatre for such classic plays as *The Man Who Came to Dinner*, he also collaborated with Moss Hart (1904–61), Harry Ruby (1895–1974) and George GERSHWIN, with whom he won a Pulitzer Prize for *Of Thee I Sing* (1931). It was during a performance of *Of Thee I Sing* that Kaufman – whose caustic wit made him one of the legends of Broadway – took exception to what the lead actor was doing to his script and in the interval sent a telegram to him that read: 'Am sitting in the last row. Wish you were here.' Among his most popular shows were *The Cocoanuts* (1925), *Animal Crackers* (1928), *Strike Up the Band* (1930), *The Band Wagon* (1931) and *Silk Stockings* (1955).

He shies at the slightest display of emotion, as most men flee from smallpox. At our first meeting I was wide-eyed with hero worship; Kaufman recoiled in horror. Later, however, everything turned out fine; we married and had several beautiful children.

MOSS HART, on his collaboration with Kaufman

Over my dead body!

GEORGE S. KAUFMAN's suggestion for his own epitaph

Kaye, Danny (David Daniel Kominsky; 1913–87) US actor, singer and dancer, who became one of the great stars of the Hollywood MUSICAL. Kaye began his career as a vaudeville comedy singer and emerged as a major star only in the early 1940s, when he appeared in such hit stage musicals as *Lady in the Dark* (1941) and *Let's Face It* (1941). He starred in a long series of film musicals of the 1940s and 1950s, his most successful including *The Secret Life of Walter Mitty* (1947), *Hans Christian Andersen* (1952) and *Knock on Wood* (1954). His hit songs included 'Anatole of Paris' (1939), 'I've Got a Lovely Bunch of Coconuts' (1950), 'Ballin' the Jack' (1951), 'Ugly Duckling' (1952) and 'All About You' (1954).

K.C. and the Sunshine Band US pop group, which enjoyed huge international success in the DISCO era of the 1970s. Led by singer-songwriter Harry Wayne 'K.C.' Casey (1951–) and bassist and songwriter Rick Finch (1954–), both White, and completed by guitarist Jerome Smith (1953–), drummer Robert Johnson (1953–), trumpet players Ronnie Smith (1952–) and James Weaver, conga player Fermin Goytisolo (1951–), trombonist Charles Williams (1954–) and saxophonist Denvil Liptrot, all Black, the group had transatlantic hits with such songs as 'Get Down Tonight' (1975), 'That's the Way (I Like It)' (1975) and '(Shake, Shake, Shake) Shake Your Booty' (1976), all of which reached Number One. Numerous lesser hits followed before the disco craze faded in the early 1980s.

Kelly, Gene (Eugene Curran Kelly; 1912–96) US actor, dancer, singer, director and choreographer, who became a top star of the Hollywood musical in the 1940s. Having started out as a stage performer and choreographer, Kelly became

one of the most famous film stars of his generation, starring in such lavish musicals as *DuBarry Was a Lady* (1943), *Ziegfeld Follies* (1946), *On the Town* (1949), *An American in Paris* (1951), *Singin' in the Rain* (1952), *Brigadoon* (1954) and *Invitation to the Dance* (1956) among many others. As a film director, his credits include *Hello Dolly!* (1969). Among his biggest hits were 'I Could Write a Book', 'For Me and My Gal' and 'Singin' in the Rain'.

Kempe, Rudolf (1910–76) German conductor, who was acclaimed one of the foremost twentieth-century conductors of the works of Wagner. A student of the Dresden Music High School, Kempe was first employed as an oboist but eventually made his début as a conductor in 1935 at the Leipzig Opera. After the Second World War he accepted the post of conductor at the Chemnitz opera house and then became director of music at the Dresden State Orchestra (1949–52) and general music director of the Munich State Opera (1952–54). He built up a considerable international reputation, making his first appearance at COVENT GARDEN, London, in 1953 and winning particular acclaim for his conducting of the music of Richard STRAUSS. Posts in later life included those of principal director of the ROYAL PHILHARMONIC ORCHESTRA (1961–75) – in succession to Sir Thomas BEECHAM – and of the BBC SYMPHONY ORCHESTRA (1975–76). He was also a regular guest at such prestigious events as the Bayreuth Festival, where he conducted in 1960.

Kempff, Wilhelm (1895–1991) German pianist and composer, who established an international reputation in the 1950s. Twice winner of the prestigious Mendelssohn Prize, he was particularly admired for his performances of works by Beethoven, Schubert and Schumann. His own compositions included two operas, ballets, symphonies and concertos for piano and violin.

Kennedy, Jimmy (1902–84) British songwriter, born in Northern Ireland, who first emerged as one of the most popular songwriters of his generation in the 1930s. He collaborated on such hits as 'The Teddy Bears' Picnic' (1933), 'Isle of Capri' (1934), 'Red Sails in the Sunset' (1935), 'Harbour Lights' (1937), 'South of the

Border' (1939) and the classic Second World War song 'We're Gonna Hang Out the Washing on the Siegfried Line' (1939), which was one of many successes created with composer Michael CARR. As well as serving as a captain in the army, Kennedy continued to write during the war years, his most enduring creations including 'The Hokey-cokey' (1945) and the English version of 'Lili Marlene'. Among his hits were 'Apple Blossom Wedding' (1947) and 'Love is Like a Violin' (1960). He also helped to write the award-winning musical play *Spokesong* (1977).

'We're Gonna Hang Out the Washing on the Siegfried Line', which epitomized Britain's cocky defiance of the Nazis after Dunkirk, was inspired by a *Daily Express* cartoon, which had a young soldier called Bert sending a piece of the Siegfried Line home for his mother to hang her washing on.

> South of Meiktila, down Pyawbe way,
> That's where the Jap thought that they had come to stay.
> The Borders surprised them one sunny day.
> South of Meiktila, down Pyawbe way ...
> ... Then the Japs started shouting and screaming,
> When the mortar platoon got weaving.
> But the boys didn't need any screening.
> Oh! for the Japs, they were on the run.
> Verses from 'South of Meiktila', to the tune of 'South of the Border', as sung by Allied troops in the Far East

Kennedy, Nigel (1956–) British violinist, who captured the public imagination with his unconventional approach to classical music in the 1980s. A highly talented violinist, he emerged as a star after studying at the Yehudi MENUHIN School and in New York. He shocked the music establishment with his casual clothing and deliberately non-élitist, downmarket image (he preferred to discuss the fortunes of his favourite football club, Aston Villa, rather than the intellectual content of his music).

Having turned professional in 1977, Kennedy became one of the most popular musicians in the world with his best-selling recording of Vivaldi's *The Four Seasons* (1989), which topped the classical charts for over a year. He won acclaim for his performances of Sir Edward ELGAR's violin concerto and also had considerable impact as a JAZZ violinist in the company of Stéphane GRAPPELLI. Irreverent towards the classical musical hierarchy and too self-effacing to assume the trappings of star status, he eventually announced his retirement from classical music in the 1990s and expressed his intention to develop a new career in rock music.

Kent, Walter (1911–) US songwriter, who was responsible for several popular hits of the Second World War era. Having abandoned a career as an architect, Kent wrote such enduring hits as 'The White Cliffs of Dover' (1941) and 'I'll be Home for Christmas' (1943) as well as music for a number of films and the stage show *Seventeen* (1951). In fact, he saw the white cliffs of Dover, which he had made so famous, for the first time in 1989.

Kenton, Stan (1912–79) US bandleader, arranger and composer, who led one of the most popular and progressive of all the SWING bands of the 1940s. Taught to play the piano by his mother, Kenton played with a number of bands before forming his own in 1941. Appearances on Bob HOPE's radio show made the band – dubbed by Kenton Artistry in Rhythm – famous and numerous hits followed, among them 'Eager Beaver', 'Tampico', 'And her Tears Flowed like Wine' and 'Peanut Vendor'. In the 1950s Kenton adopted a more progressive style and worked with another BIG BAND, called Innovations in Modern Music, as well as with the smaller New Concepts in Artistry in Rhythm outfit. In the 1960s his New Era in Modern Music Orchestra consolidated his reputation for continually experimenting with new ideas and instruments, and he went on to embrace both neoclassical and JAZZ-ROCK elements in his final years. Often controversial, Kenton toured widely and numbered many distinguished stars among his musicians.

Kern, Jerome (David) (1885–1945) US songwriter and composer, who effectively created the twentieth-century MUSICAL. Kern, the son of a piano salesman, studied music in New York and Heidelberg and worked as a songplugger and rehearsal pianist before establishing his reputation as a writer for the musical stage. Initially he was employed to ginger up British musicals for the US stage and spent some time in the UK. Among the hits he contributed to a long series of such shows were 'How'd You Like to Spoon with Me' (1905) and 'They Didn't Believe Me' (1914).

He composed his first complete score in 1911 and four years later signalled a sea change in the development of the twentieth-century musical with *Very Good, Eddie*, in which, for virtually the first time, the songs were made thoroughly relevant to the action taking place.

Among the most acclaimed Kern musicals that followed were *Sally* (1920), his masterpiece *Showboat* (1927), which produced such classic hit songs as 'Ol' Man River' and 'Can't Help Lovin' Dat Man', *The Cat and the Fiddle* (1931), *Music in the Air* (1932), *Roberta* (1933), from which came 'Smoke Gets in Your Eyes', and *Very Warm for May* (1939).

Kern was recruited by Hollywood in 1934 and went on to write music for such films as *Swing Time* (1936), which produced 'The Way You Look Tonight' and 'A Fine Romance', *Lady Be Good* (1941), which included his hit 'The Last Time I Saw Paris', and *Cover Girl* (1944), for which he wrote 'Long Ago and Far Away'. He was about to begin work on *Annie Get Your Gun* when he died of a heart attack (his place was taken by Irving BERLIN). Guy BOLTON, P.G. Wodehouse and Oscar HAMMERSTEIN II were among the celebrated lyricists who collaborated with Kern on some of his most famous songs.

In 1958, 13 years after Kern's death, his classic song 'Smoke Gets in Your Eyes' provided the US pop group the PLATTERS with a Number One hit.

> I am trying to do something for the future of American music, which today has no class whatsoever and is mere barbaric mouthing.
>
> JEROME KERN, in the *New York Times*, 1920

Ketèlbey, Albert (William) (1875–1959) British composer and conductor, who wrote many popular light classical hits of the 1920s and 1930s. Although he nursed ambitions as a composer of more serious works (an early piano sonata won the praise of Sir Edward ELGAR), Ketèlbey became known for such relatively lightweight, atmospheric compositions as 'Phantom Melody' (1912), 'In a Monastery Garden' (1915), 'In a Persian Market' (1920), 'Cockney Suite' (1924), 'In a Chinese Temple Garden' (1925), 'A Birthday Greeting' (1932) and 'From a Japanese Screen' (1934) among many others.

Khachaturian, Aram (Ilich) (1903–78)

Soviet composer, of Armenian descent, whose celebrated works reflected the influence of Armenian folk music. Born in Tbilisi, Georgia, Khachaturian – the son of a book-binder – was relatively late in showing any enthusiasm for music, being 19 years old when he began to interest himself in composition. A self-taught pianist, he quickly developed a fascination for the FOLK MUSIC traditions of his homeland. He enrolled as a student at the Gnesin Music Academy in Moscow and rapidly gained a reputation as a composer with such early works as *Tants* (1925) for violin and piano and *Poema* (1926) for piano.

He was accepted at the Moscow Conservatory in 1929 and went on to earn an international following with his First Symphony (1935) and D flat Piano Concerto (1936) among other works. He emerged as a prominent figure in the Union of Soviet Composers but was still criticized for FORMALIST tendencies. Nonetheless, he rose to the post of professor at the Moscow Conservatory and attracted admiration as a conductor, while continuing to create new works.

His most popular compositions include the D minor Violin Concerto (1940), which won a powerful champion in the violinist David OISTRAKH and earned the Stalin Prize, and the ballets *Gayaneh* (1942) – especially notable for its 'Sabre Dance' – and *Spartacus* (1954), which became familiar to many British listeners in the 1970s when the 'Adagio of Spartacus and Phrygia' from it was used as the theme of the BBC television series *The Onedin Line*. Married to fellow-composer Nina Makarova (1908–   ), he was awarded the title People's Artist of the USSR in 1954.

Kidd, Johnny (Frederick Heath; 1939–66) British ROCK 'N' ROLL star, who enjoyed huge – if short-lived – fame in the early 1960s as one of the most popular homegrown British pop stars. Johnny Kidd and the Pirates, who made live appearances in full pirate costume, while Kidd himself wore leathers and an eye-patch (owing to an accident with a broken guitar string), had their first hit in 1959 with 'Please Don't Touch', although the big breakthrough came a year later with the raunchy 'Shakin' All Over', which reached Number One and has been described as the only really convincing rock 'n' roll song to emanate from the British side of the Atlantic. The band had a string of successes in a RHYTHM-AND-BLUES style through the early 1960s, but it all came to an end in 1966 with the death of Kidd himself when the band's van crashed near Bury, Lancashire. Ex-Pirates guitarist Mick Green re-formed the band in 1977 and recorded another three albums.

Killer, the *See* Jerry Lee LEWIS.

King, the *See* Benny CARTER; Elvis PRESLEY; Tito PUENTE.

King, B.B. (Riley King; 1925–) Black US RHYTHM-AND-BLUES singer and guitarist, nicknamed the King of the Blues, who is considered by many to be the finest BLUES guitarist of all time. King, a former worker on a cotton plantation, began his musical career as a Memphis radio DISC JOCKEY, when he was known as the Beale Street Blues Boy (later abbreviated to B.B.), but at the same time he was acquiring his reputation as a live performer influenced by the best JAZZ guitarists in the 1950s. To the traditional blues he had learnt as a child he added elements of jazz and rock, switching to an electric guitar (a GIBSON he called Lucille) in the early 1960s.

Such hits as 'She's Dynamite', 'Please Love Me', 'When My Heart Beats Like a Hammer', 'Sweet Little Angel', 'Sweet Sixteen' and 'The Thrill is Gone' – several of which were included on the classic album *Live at the Regal* (1971) – placed him among the leading rock stars of the 1960s and made him one of the USA's musical ambassadors; in 1979 he became the first r 'n' b star to tour the USSR. Subsequent releases, on which he experimented with DISCO and FUNK styles with mixed results, have included collaborations with Bobby BLAND (1974) and the Crusaders (1979). King has also written numerous advertising JINGLES, including ditties for Pepsi-Cola and Colgate-Palmolive.

King, Carole (Carole Klein; 1942–) US singer-songwriter, who collaborated on many celebrated hits of the 1960s before emerging as a star performer in her own right. For many years she formed a highly successful songwriting partnership with her husband Gerry GOFFIN, with whom she wrote such hits as 'Will You Love Me Tomorrow?', taken to Number One in 1961 by the Shirelles, 'Up on the Roof',

which was a hit for the DRIFTERS in 1962, 'The Locomotion', which was turned into a hit by the couple's babysitter Little Eva in 1962, 'I'm into Something Good', recorded by HERMAN'S HERMITS in 1964, and 'A Natural Woman', which Aretha FRANKLIN made a hit in 1967.

'It Might as Well Rain Until September' proved a big hit when recorded by King herself in 1962, and, after separating from Goffin, she consolidated her reputation with the best-selling *Tapestry* (1972). Other releases included the albums *Jazzman* (1974), *Pearls* (1980), *Speeding Time* (1984) and *Color of Your Dreams* (1993).

It was for Carole King that Neil SEDAKA wrote 'Oh Carol'.

King, Jonathan (Kenneth King; 1944–) British songwriter, producer and broadcaster, who has masterminded numerous pop successes since the 1960s. King established his name with the 1965 hit 'Everyone's Gone to the Moon' and went on to form the novelty band Hedgehoppers Anonymous, all members of the RAF, which reached the charts with 'It's Good News Week'. He developed a career in the media, produced the very first GENESIS album, worked as producer with the BAY CITY ROLLERS, founded his own record company, signed up 10cc and had another hit himself with the somewhat frivolous 'Una Paloma Blanca' (1975). He has since concentrated on his role as a low-brow media figure.

King Crimson British rock band, which emerged as one of the most challenging PROGRESSIVE ROCK outfits of the early 1970s. Guitarist Robert FRIPP, singer and bassist Greg Lake (1948–), drummer Mike Giles (1942–), saxophonist and keyboard player Ian McDonald and synthesizer player Pete Sinfield first attracted attention supporting the ROLLING STONES in 1969. The début album *In the Court of the Crimson King* (1969), with its innovative blend of rock, JAZZ and electronics, proved a best-seller and brought fame, after which the experiments continued on such LPs as *In the Wake of Poseidon* (1970) and *Lizard* (1971). Further progress was disrupted by personnel changes, culminating in Fripp's re-forming the band from scratch with singer and bassist John Wetton (1950–), violinist David Cross (1948–) and drummers Bill

Bruford (1950–) and Jamie Muir, who triumphed with the albums *Lark's Tongue in Aspic* (1973) and *Red* (1974). The band was revived once more in 1981, folding in 1984, and again in 1993, releasing *Thrak* in 1995.

King of Calypso, the *See* Harry BELAFONTE.

King of Corn, the *See* Spike JONES.

King of Glam Rock, the *See* Gary GLITTER.

King of Hi-de-ho *See* Cab CALLOWAY.

King of Jazz, the *See* Paul WHITEMAN.

King of Pop, the *See* Michael JACKSON.

King of Ragtime, the *See* Scott JOPLIN.

King of Rock 'n' Roll, the *See* Chuck BERRY; LITTLE RICHARD; Elvis PRESLEY.

King of Rock 'n' Soul, the *See* Solomon BURKE.

King of Skiffle, the *See* Lonnie DONEGAN.

King of Soul *See* James BROWN.

King of Swing, the *See* Benny GOODMAN.

King of the Blues, the *See* B.B. KING.

King of the Chicago Blues, the *See* Muddy WATERS.

King of the Cowboys, the *See* Roy ROGERS.

King of the Delta Blues Singers, the *See* Robert JOHNSON.

King of the Hot-cha, the *See* Harry ROY.

King of the Ratpack, the *See* Frank SINATRA.

King of the Telecaster, the *see* Albert COLLINS.

King of Western Swing, the *See* Spade COOLEY.

King's College, Cambridge The home of a British choir, which has long been recognized as one of the most distinguished choirs anywhere in the world. Founded in 1441, the choir is especially renowned for its Christmas carol festival.

King's Singers, the British choral group, which enjoyed huge popular success in the 1970s and 1980s. Founded in 1968 with five choral scholars from KING'S COLLEGE, CAMBRIDGE, and one from Oxford, the group won wide television and radio coverage and has released many bestselling albums, ranging over the whole history of English choral music.

Kinks, the British pop group, which was among the most popular bands to epitomize the quirky and anarchic spirit of the 1960s. Singer and guitarist Ray Davies (1944–), whose nickname was Dippity Doo, his brother guitarist Dave Davies (1947–), bassist Pete Quaife (1943–) and drummer Mick Avory (1945–) had their first hit in 1964 with 'You Really Got Me', which stormed to Number One in the UK. Similarly rock-oriented was the follow-up 'All Day and All of the Night' on which Jimmy Page of LED ZEPPELIN fame was reputed to have played lead guitar. Ray Davies, who wrote most of the band's material, later adopted a more eccentric tone that echoed the changing philosophy of the decade.

Such hit singles as 'Tired of Waiting for You', which got to Number One in 1965, 'Dedicated Follower of Fashion', 'Sunny Afternoon', which in 1966 became the band's third Number One, 'Waterloo Sunset', 'Lola' and 'Apeman' joined the pantheon of the greatest products of 1960s pop music, although things fell apart somewhat at the end of the decade as Davies attempted far more ambitious results, as evidenced by the bizarre *Arthur or the Decline and Fall of the British Empire* album of 1969. For several years the group was banned from appearing in the USA after trouble during a tour in 1965. Faint echoes of the group's glory days were sounded in 1979 with the hits 'Low Budget' and again in 1982 with 'Come Dancing'.

Kipling of the Music Hall, the *See* Albert CHEVALIER.

Kirby, John (1908–52) US JAZZ bassist, arranger and bandleader, who led an acclaimed sextet in the 1940s and 1950s. Kirby began as a trombonist, but switched to the tuba when his trombone was stolen, and he was recruited by Fletcher HENDERSON in 1930. He transferred to the bass and played for other bands before forming his own group in 1937. Dubbed the Biggest Little Band in the Land, the sextet became one of the most admired small jazz groups of the period. It was re-formed after the Second World War but with noticeably less success, and Kirby died in obscurity.

Kirk, Rahsaan Roland (Ronald T. Kirk; 1936–77) US JAZZ multi-instrumentalist, who won widespread fame for his mastery of a range of unusual instruments. Having adopted the names Rahsaan Roland as a result of a dream in which spirits instructed him to do so, Kirk, who had been blinded while a baby, proved equally adept on such instruments as the saxophone, the clarinet, the whistle, the manzello (a type of alto sax), the strich (a form of soprano sax), the flute, the siren and the clavietta – often playing several instruments at the same time. He played in a variety of styles, from BOP to RHYTHM-AND-BLUES, and proved that his talent surpassed his gimmickry. He collaborated with Charles MINGUS and appeared with his own Vibration Society group around the world. Partial paralysis from a stroke in 1975 obliged him to learn to play with just his left hand until his death two years later. Among his most popular hits were 'Bright Moments', 'Let Me Shake Your Tree' and 'No Tonic Pres'.

Kiss US HEAVY METAL band, which enjoyed huge success in the 1970s and 1980s with its own radical brand of theatrical heavy metal GLAM ROCK. Founded in 1972 by singer and guitarist Paul Stanley (1950–), singer and bassist Gene Simmons (1949–), drummer Peter Criss (1945–) and singer and guitarist Ace Frehley (Paul Frehley; 1950–), the band built its reputation on the strength of its live act, which featured elaborate special effects and members of the group appearing in bizarre costumes and grotesque black and white make-up. Such albums as *Alive* (1975), *Destroyer* (1976) and *Love Gun* (1977) became best-sellers and their fans, known as the Kiss Army, turned such tracks as 'Rock 'n' Roll All Nite' and 'Hotter than Hell' into teen anthems.

The make-up was abandoned in 1984, but the group, with various changes in personnel, had further hits with such singles as 'Crazy, Crazy Nights' (1987) and 'Forever' (1990). Eric Carr, who replaced Criss in 1981, died of cancer in 1991. The make-up went back on in 1996.

In 1978 the four members of the band established a notable first in rock history when each released a solo album on the same day.

Kitt, Eartha (1928–) Black US singer and actress, who emerged as a top variety star in the 1950s. Her smouldering delivery of such songs as 'Monotonous', 'C'est si bon' and 'An Old-fashioned Girl' scandalized conservative audiences but assured her lasting success on the international CABARET circuit. More recent releases include the albums *I Love Men* (1984) and *My Way* (1987).

Klangfarbenmelodie A composition in which varying tone colours are employed, either at a single pitch or at a range of pitches. The term was invented by Arnold SCHOENBERG, who relied on such a technique in his *Five Orchestral Pieces* (1909), and was borrowed by composers such as Alban BERG and Anton WEBERN.

Kleiber, Erich (1890–1956) Argentinian but Austrian-born conductor, who won acclaim for his work with the Berlin State Opera (1923–35 and again in the 1950s), with which he presented the first performance of Alban BERG's *Wozzeck* (1925) among other compositions. He also held important posts in Darmstadt, Düsseldorf and Mannheim as well as in South America, Cuba and the USA (after being expelled from Germany by the Nazis). Particularly admired were his interpretations of the operas of Mozart and Richard STRAUSS.

His son, Carlos Kleiber (1930–) has also established a reputation as one of the world's leading conductors, winning respect for his exhaustive preparations for the works he undertakes.

> When there is no trouble in a theatre, I make it!
>
> ERICH KLEIBER

Klein, Manuel (1876–1919) US composer, conductor and lyricist, born in the UK, who wrote many successful musical shows in the first two decades of the century. He worked on both sides of the Atlantic and had hits with such lavish entertainments as *Mr Pickwick* (1903), *Sporting Days* (1908), *The Pied Piper* (1908), *Under Many Flags* (1912) and *Hop o' my Thumb* (1913).

Klemperer, Otto (1885–1973) German-born conductor, later a US and then an

Israeli citizen, who won wide fame for his faithful interpretations of the great works that he conducted. Brought up in Hamburg, Klemperer studied at the Hoch Conservatory, Frankfurt, and in Berlin before falling under the influence of Gustav MAHLER; it was largely through Mahler's influence that Klemperer was awarded the post of conductor of the German Opera in Prague in 1907. Later appointments included prestigious posts at the Municipal Theatre in Hamburg (1910–14), the Strasbourg Opera (1914–17), the Cologne Opera (1917–24), the State Opera, Wiesbaden (1924–27) and at the Kroll Theatre in Berlin (1927–31).

Klemperer's championship of works by such contemporary composers as Paul HINDEMITH, Leoš JANÁČEK, Arnold SCHOENBERG and Igor STRAVINSKY coupled with his Jewish ancestry incurred the wrath of the authorities and the Kroll Theatre was closed, while his appointment at the Berlin State Opera was also terminated. He moved to the USA in 1933 and took over the Los Angeles Symphony Orchestra. He returned to Europe in 1947 as conductor of the Budapest Opera. After leaving this latter post in 1950, he continued to appear with leading orchestras around the world despite the partial paralysis he suffered after a brain operation; he was made principal conductor of the Philharmonia Orchestra in London in 1955. He was particularly admired for his performances of Beethoven, Brahms and Mahler, although musicians under his baton found him less than frivolous and one claimed 'two hours with Klemperer is like two hours in church'. He wrote a number of works himself, including six symphonies and nine quartets.

> Thank God somebody understands it!
> OTTO KLEMPERER, when someone walked out while he was conducting a modern work he disliked

Klenovsky, Paul Pseudonym, which was used by Sir Henry WOOD when he was working as arranger of Bach's D minor Toccata and Fugue. The name translates roughly from the Russian as 'a member of the maple tree family' – a joke on his real name and his nickname Timber and a dig at those critics who refused to take any musician without a foreign-sounding name seriously.

Klook See Kenny CLARKE.

Knife, the See Pepper ADAMS.

Knight, Gladys (1944–   ) Black US SOUL singer, who had many hits during the 1960s and 1970s. Knight was a child prodigy, carrying off the honours in a televised talent contest when she was seven years old. A year later she made her first appearance with her long-term backing group, the Pips – her brother and two cousins.

A tour with Sam COOKE in 1956 was followed by such hits as 'Every Beat of My Heart' (1961), 'I Heard it Through the Grapevine' (1966), 'It Should Have been Me' (1968), 'Friendship Train' (1969) and, after leaving MOTOWN in 1973, 'Help Me Make it through the Night' (1972) and 'The Best Thing that Ever Happened to Me' (1974). Knight struck out on a solo career in 1988.

The GRAMMY Award-winning hit 'Midnight Train to Georgia' (1973) was actually first titled 'Midnight Plane to Houston' when it was originally being rehearsed, until it was agreed that it did not sound quite right.

knitting-pattern music Derogatory term that was applied to SERIALISM by its critics, who took exception to the mathematical nature of such music.

> It's an artificial process without strength, though it may sound busy and noisy. This wallpaper design music is not as big as a natural slushy ballad.
> CHARLES IVES, 1915

Knopfler, Mark See DIRE STRAITS.

Kodály, Zoltán (1882–1967) Hungarian composer and teacher, whose influential works reflected his keen interest in the Hungarian language and FOLK-song tradition. Kodály received early musical training from his father, a railway official and amateur violinist, and won a scholarship to study in Budapest. As a student at the Budapest Academy of Music, he indulged his fascination in Hungarian music and from 1905 collaborated with Béla BARTÓK in collecting examples of folk-songs from around the country in the belief that they would soon be lost forever. Other influences on his own compositions included church music and the ideas of such impressionists as Claude DEBUSSY, with which he became acquainted when visiting Paris in 1907 (when he also joined the staff of the Budapest Academy of Music).

Kodály's music began to be heard outside Hungary after 1910, and he gradually won recognition as one of Europe's leading composers. Among his most admired works were the *Psalmus Hungaricus* (1923), written to commemorate the amalgamation of Buda and Pest, the operas *Háry János* (1925–27) and *The Spinning Room* (1924–32) and – most popular of all his compositions – the dance sequences *Marosek Dances* (1930) and *Galánta Dances* (1933). Landmarks of his later career included the *Peacock Variations*, written for the Amsterdam CONCERTGEBOUW Orchestra in 1938, and the Concerto for Orchestra, which was composed for the Chicago Philharmonic Orchestra in 1939. He remained in Hungary during the Second World War, true to his standing as a national hero, but had little to do with the Nazi-controlled government of the day. After the war he was undisputed as the leading figure in Hungarian music and directed the musical education of the country's children under an effective system of his own devising. The most important of his postwar compositions was his Symphony in C (1961).

His collections of folk-songs, many of them specifically arranged for children to play, were mixed with new compositions in the four-volume *Bicinia Hungarica*, published 1937–42.

> Some day the ringing tower of Hungarian music is going to stand. And if in its pedestal some of these stones will be lying intact and the rest destroyed I shall ... regard without concern the night of my deep grave.
> ZOLTÁN KODÁLY, of his works, lecture, 1932

Koehler, Ted (1894–1973) US lyricist, who provided the words for many classic vaudeville and JAZZ songs of the 1920s and 1930s. Having worked as a cinema pianist, he collaborated on such celebrated hits as 'When Lights are Low', 'I Gotta Right to Sing the Blues', 'Get Happy', 'Between the Devil and the Deep Blue Sea', 'Minnie the Moocher', 'Stormy Weather' and 'Ev'ry Night About This Time'. For the movies he provided the lyrics for 'Let's Fall in Love' (from *Let's Fall in Love*; 1934) and 'Animal Crackers' (from *Curly Top*; 1935) among many other famous numbers.

Korner, Alexis (1928–84) British guitarist,

singer, bandleader, broadcaster and writer, born in France of Greek-Austrian and Turkish parentage, whose pioneering work in the developing RHYTHM-AND-BLUES scene in the UK in the 1950s and 1960s earned him the nickname the Father of British Blues. Korner arrived in London in 1940 and opened a club at the Roundhouse in Brewer Street; there he presented such major talents as Big Bill BROONZY and Muddy WATERS as well as fostering the careers of British artists such as Mick JAGGER, Chris BARBER, Eric CLAPTON and Ginger Baker. In 1962 he founded the influential band BLUES INCORPORATED, the world's first White blues band, which lasted until 1967, after which he involved himself in a number of different groups, including a rock-based big band called CCS, and continued to promote emerging new stars until his untimely death.

Korngold, Erich (Wolfgang) (1897–1957) Czech composer, a naturalized American from 1943, who won acclaim for a wide range of compositions, including film scores for Hollywood. Korngold, the son of a music critic, was a child prodigy who was described as a genius by Gustav MAHLER. He composed a highly popular ballet, *Der Schneemann* (*The Snowman*), at the age of 11 and was in his early twenties when the opera *Die tote Stadt* (1920) was hailed as one of the great works of the time. Other compositions included three more operas and much chamber and orchestral music as well as a violin concerto and a symphony.

Korngold was recruited by Hollywood in 1934 and wrote stirring romantic music for many movies, among them *Anthony Adverse* (1936), for which he won an OSCAR, *A Midsummer Night's Dream* (1936), *The Adventures of Robin Hood* (1938), which earned him a second Academy Award, *The Sea Hawk* (1940) and *King's Row* (1941).

> If Master Korngold could make such a noise at 14, what will he not do when he is 28? The thought is appalling.
> US critic, reviewing *Schauspiel-Overtüre*, 1911

Kosma, Joseph (1905–69) French-Hungarian composer, who wrote many popular songs in collaboration with Jacques Prévert. A student of the Budapest Conservatory, he joined Bertolt Brecht's theatre company in Berlin and wrote music for the cinema before moving to Paris in 1933, where he formed his partnership with Prévert. Among their most acclaimed collaborations were the songs of *Encore une fois sur le fleuve* (1946), 'Les feuilles mortes', 'Barbara', 'Je suis comme je suis' and others taken up by such popular singers as Yves MONTAND. On his own, Kosma also composed an operetta and several comic operas. He also provided the scores for such films as *La Grande Illusion* (1937), *Les Enfants du Paradis* (1945) and *Déjeuner sur l'Herbe* (1959).

Kostelanetz, André (1901–80) US conductor, pianist, composer and arranger, born in Russia, who did much to popularize light classical music and to marry classical orchestration with popular music of the day. A child prodigy, who went on to train at the St Petersburg Academy of Music, Kostelanetz arrived in the USA in 1922 and worked with the METROPOLITAN OPERA and as musical adviser to CBS. His orchestra, which included many leading jazzmen, built up a popular following recording and broadcasting light classical music and classical arrangements of familiar songs, from nursery rhymes to JAZZ standards. His biggest hits including the Perry COMO version of 'Prisoner of Love' (1946) and arrangements of songs by Cole PORTER, George GERSHWIN and Jerome KERN. Guest conductor with the NEW YORK PHILHARMONIC, he also commissioned Aaron COPLAND's *Lincoln Portrait*.

> The conductor has the advantage of not seeing the audience.
> ANDRÉ KOSTELANETZ

Koussevitsky, Serge (Sergei) Alexandrovich (1874–1951) Russian conductor and double bass player, a US citizen from 1941, who did much to promote the interests of contemporary classical music. A graduate of the Philharmonic School in Moscow, Koussevitsky became famous in international music circles in the 1890s as a virtuoso of the double bass. He went on to conduct works by Beethoven with the LONDON SYMPHONY ORCHESTRA and then undertook intensive studies in conducting in Berlin. Subsequently he established a second reputation as a conductor both of Beethoven and of various Russian and Finnish works in particular as well as founding his own orchestra.

Acclaimed as one of the leading musical figures of his generation, Koussevitsky commissioned many works by challenging new composers, among them Alexander SCRIABIN and Igor STRAVINSKY and – after emigrating to the USA after the Russian Revolution in 1917 – by a number of US composers. Important landmarks in his career included the première of Maurice RAVEL's orchestrated version of Mussorgsky's *Pictures at an Exhibition*.

He was appointed conductor of the Boston Symphony Orchestra in 1924 and remained in the post for 25 years, making the orchestra one of the most respected in the world. He also established and directed the Berkshire Music Center in Tanglewood, Massachusetts, and set up a foundation to assist promising composers (works commissioned by the foundation included Benjamin BRITTEN's *Peter Grimes*).

> Ven my stick touches the air, you play.
> SERGE KOUSSEVITSKY, to his orchestra

> Kill me; it will make me more pleasure than listen to you!
> SERGE KOUSSEVITSKY, to a clarinettist who had taken exception to his criticisms

> That Russian boor.
> ARTURO TOSCANINI, of Koussevitsky (attributed)

Kraftwerk German PROGRESSIVE ROCK group of the 1970s, which enjoyed international success with its experiments with electronic pop. Influenced by equivalent groups in the UK, Kraftwerk established its reputation in 1975 with the hit instrumental 'Autobahn'. Other releases included the CONCEPT ALBUM *Radioactivity* (1975), *Trans Europe Express* (1977), *Man Machine* (1978) and *Electric Café* (1986) and the UK Number One single 'The Model' (1981). An as yet unrealized dream of the band's members was to replace themselves with robots, which tour for them.

Kreisler, Fritz (1875–1962) Austrian violinist, a French citizen from 1938 and a US citizen from 1943, who was acclaimed one of the finest violinists in the history of music. Born in Vienna, Kreisler was a child prodigy and, encouraged by his musical father, won a place at the Vienna Conservatory when only seven years old (the youngest student ever to be accepted at the Conservatory). There he won a gold medal when he was only 10 years old, before continuing his studies at the Paris Conservatoire, where he won a second gold medal. He made his first professional appearances in 1889, on tour in the USA, but did not yet devote his time entirely to music, studying medicine and art and ultimately serving as an officer in the Austrian army.

In 1899 Kreisler made the decision to concentrate on his musical career and quickly consolidated his international reputation with appearances in Berlin and London, winning special praise for his performances of works by Beethoven and Brahms. He was awarded a gold medal by the Royal Philharmonic Society and Sir Edward ELGAR wrote a violin concerto (1910) for him before his career was further disrupted by war service with the Austrian army (in the course of which he was wounded). After the war he emigrated to the USA and went on to confirm his standing as one of the great violinists of the century. He also worked privately as a composer, although only revealing many of the apparently eighteenth-century pieces he played as his own inventions years after they were first heard (to the outrage of several leading critics). He also composed the operettas *Apple Blossoms* (1919) and *Sissy* (1923) as well as other works for the violin.

Admired for his perfect tone, the great Kreisler – whose career was nearly ended in a car crash in 1941 – never had a music lesson after the age of 12 and rarely practised before performances.

> Kreisler plays as the thrush sings in Thomas Hardy's poem, hardly conscious of his own lovely significance.
> NEVILLE CARDUS, *The Delights of Music*, 1966

Křenek, Ernst (1900–91) Austrian composer, resident in the USA from 1938, who first emerged as a leading contemporary composer in the 1920s. Born in Vienna, Křenek studied under Franz Schreker (1878–1934) at the Academy of Music there and in Berlin, where he came under the influence of Ferruccio BUSONI, Artur SCHNABEL and Arnold SCHOENBERG. Having written his first compositions in a late Romantic style, he began to experiment with ATONALITY and polyphony but otherwise proved himself to be true to the Austrian symphonic tradition (he married Mahler's daughter Anna in 1922).

Křenek composed his first operas in the 1920s, when he worked at several leading opera houses. His innovative JAZZ opera

Jonny Spielt Auf (Johnny Strikes Up; 1927), concerning the affairs a Black jazz violinist has with a series of White women, was a huge success and established his international reputation, although it was less well received by German Nazis. Later operas and other works enjoyed moderate success through the 1930s, the best of them including the song-cycle *Reisebuch aus den österreichischen Alpen (Travel Book from the Austrian Alps*; 1929) and Křenek turned increasingly to the more challenging musical theories being propounded in the serialist works of Alban BERG and Anton WEBERN.

Křenek left Austria after the *Anschluss* of 1938 and went on to write chamber operas, choral works and symphonies in a SERIALIST mode. Among the most ambitious of these later works were the musical play *Karl V* (1938) and the operas, *Tarquin* (1941), *Der Goldene Bock* (1964) and *Sardakai* (1969).

> To my knowledge I am the only composer of my generation who has thoroughly and consistently practised what is called 'serialism', and I have been blamed (a) for doing it at all, (b) for doing it too late, and (c) for still being at it.
> ERNST KŘENEK, *Horizons Circled*, 1974

Kristofferson, Kris (1936–   ) US pop and COUNTRY singer-songwriter and actor, who had a number of hits in the 1970s. A graduate of Oxford University, Kristofferson built his reputation in country music writing such hits as 'Me and Bobby McGee', 'Help Me Make It Through the Night' and 'For the Good Times', and he became a recording star himself in the early 1970s when he released *Silver Tongued Devil and I* (1971) and other albums. His film credits include *A Star is Born* (1976) and the ill-fated *Heaven's Gate* (1980). He was married to Rita COOLIDGE from 1973 to 1979.

Krupa, Gene (1909–73) US JAZZ drummer, bandleader and composer, who ranked among the most celebrated drummers of his generation and was the first man to demonstrate the potential of the drums as a solo instrument. Brought up in Chicago, Krupa rejected plans for him to become a Catholic priest and played with numerous local bands before making his recording début in a band led by Eddie CONDON in 1927. After moving to New York he played with the bands of, among others, Glenn MILLER and Benny GOODMAN, attracting attention for his flamboyant playing and becoming one of the stars of Goodman's famous BIG BAND in the mid-1930s.

Goodman and Krupa split up after a quarrel on stage in 1938, and Krupa formed his first SWING band, which enjoyed widespread success before being broken up in 1943 when he was imprisoned (probably unfairly) for drug offences. He reunited with Goodman and then worked for Tommy DORSEY before establishing another band of his own and switching to a BOP style. He worked mainly with small groups after 1951, except for regular reunions with Goodman and others in the 1960s and 1970s. His compositions included the 1929 number 'One Hour', co-written with Red McKenzie (1899–1948), and 'Drum-boogie' (1940).

Kubelik, (Jeronym) Rafael (1914–   ) Swiss conductor and composer, born in Czechoslovakia, who has done much to promote the interests of contemporary Czech music. The son of the famous violinist and composer Jan Kubelik (1880–1940), Rafael Kubelik studied at the Prague Conservatory and made his first appearance as a conductor in 1934. Two years later he was appointed conductor of the Czech Philharmonic Orchestra, with which he visited the UK to considerable acclaim in 1938. Later posts included director of the Brno Opera, another period with the Czech Philharmonic, and – after relocation in the UK and then Switzerland after the Second World War – appointments with the CHICAGO SYMPHONY ORCHESTRA (1950–53), the COVENT GARDEN Opera (1955–58), the Bavarian Radio Symphony Orchestra (1961–79) and the METROPOLITAN OPERA, New York (1972–74). Throughout his career he has continued to champion music written by leading Czech composers, notably Leoš JANÁČEK, although also distinguishing himself as a conductor of Beethoven, Gustav MAHLER and Benjamin BRITTEN. As a composer himself, he has written a number of symphonies as well as concertos, requiems, chamber music and five operas.

Kulturbolschewismus Derogatory term (in English, cultural bolshevism), which was used by the Nazis in denigrating the music of Igor STRAVINSKY, Arnold SCHOENBERG and other non-Aryans. In common with other totalitarian regimes, the Nazis held that artistic radicalism acted as a spur to, or was the expression of, revolutionary politics. So that such dangerous individualism could be more easily controlled, Goebbels arranged for all music, art and literature to be nationalized by the mid-1930s under the Reichskulturkammer. Membership of the organization was mandatory for all artists, and those who dissented from Nazi aesthetics or objected to the racialist ideology (all Jews and Jewish music were excluded) were threatened with internment. Among those to flee rather than submit to the Nazis were Fritz Busch (1890–1951) and Carl Ebert (1887–1980), who crossed the Channel in 1933 and collaborated with John Christie in the foundation of GLYNDEBOURNE.

Another notable figure affected by the ruling was the conductor Arturo TOSCANINI, who was the first foreign conductor to be invited to appear at the Bayreuth Festival. Hitler signed a special exemption to allow him to stay on – but Toscanini withdrew voluntarily in protest against the Nazi victimization. Among other victims of Nazi suppression was Paul HINDEMITH.

> National Socialism puts the personality of a creative artist before his work. The fact that before the new regime Hindemith showed signs of an unGerman attitude disqualifies him from taking part in the movement's cultural reclamation work.
> BERNHARD RUST, Nazi spokesman, 1934

Künneke, Eduard (1885–1953) German composer and conductor, who emerged as one of the leading European composers of the operetta in the 1920s. Having started out as a serious opera composer, he switched to operetta in the early 1920s after the success of *Der Vetter aus Dingsda* (1921). Several of his works were influenced by his interest in JAZZ; they included *Casino Girls* (1923), *Die singende Venus* (1928) and *Traumland* (1941) among numerous others.

Kunz, Charlie (1896–1958) US pianist and bandleader, who led one of the most popular bands of the 1920s and 1930s. He formed his first band at the age of 16 and then moved to London, where his band built up a large following. He also made many recordings of popular hits and was in great demand as soloist on the piano. His most famous number was his signature tune, 'Clap Hands, Here Comes Charlie', which became a national catchphrase. The tune was originally written by Billy Rose (1899–1966), Ballard MacDonald (1882–1935) and Joseph Meyer (1894–1988), who recorded it in 1925. Legend has it that the 'Charlie' referred to was a promiscuous female singer named 'Charline' who was reputed to have passed on gonorrhea – nicknamed the clap – to a number of fellow-musicians. The phrase was adopted by RAF pilots during the Second World War to describe a dramatic manoeuvre in which it seemed the aircraft's wings would touch over the plane.

Kuti, Fela Anipulapo (1938–97) Nigerian singer and saxophonist, who emerged as one of the leading African musicians of modern times in the 1980s. He began his career playing saxophone in a JAZZ band and attracted attention with his outspoken political views. A period in the UK exposed him to a range of musical influences, including SKA and SOUL, and he returned to Nigeria to concentrate on using his music to attack the government. Imprisoned for his views, but released in 1986 after an international campaign, he reclaimed his status as one of the leaders of Third World music and the founder of the AFRO-ROCK style. His many recordings include the albums *Fela Anipulapo Kuti* and *Black Man's Cry*.

kwela Genre of home-grown South African POP music, which developed across southern Africa in the 1940s as an African equivalent of British SKIFFLE, using home-made instruments and characterized by a generally cheerful uptempo sound. Kwela gatherings were often a device used to pursue street gambling and other prohibited activities. As the years passed and the style incorporated a diverse range of European and African influences, the name 'kwela' came to be applied to virtually any music emanating from Black townships.

L

La Scala Italian opera house, which remains one of the most prestigious of all opera venues anywhere in the world. Opened in Milan on the site of the church of Sta Maria della Scala in 1778, La Scala witnessed many classic productions at the turn of the current century, when Arturo TOSCANINI added works by Wagner and Richard STRAUSS among others to what had previously been a largely Italian-dominated repertoire. After being badly damaged by bombs during the Second World War, it was re-opened in 1948 and has since played host to such distinguished conductors as Claudio ABBADO.

Ladnier, Tommy (1900–39) US JAZZ trumpeter, who won acclaim as one of the most accomplished jazzmen of the 1920s and 1930s. Ladnier, who played in a direct BLUES-oriented style, featured with a number of celebrated bands, notably those of Fate Marable (1890–1947), King OLIVER and Fletcher HENDERSON, and also made many appearances with several European stars. He led his own band for a time in the 1930s and collaborated with Sidney BECHET in co-founding the New Orleans Feet-warmers (they were co-owners of a New York tailor's shop) before his early death as the result of a heart attack.

Lady Day *See* Billie HOLIDAY.

Lai, Francis (1932–) French composer and conductor, who won particular acclaim for his film music. Having established his international reputation with his OSCAR-winning music for *Un homme et une femme* (1966), which included the hit 'Today It's You', he went on to write for a long series of British, French and US movies. The most successful of these was his score for the sentimental *Love Story* (1970), for which he wrote 'Where Do I Begin' among other numbers and for which he was rewarded with a second Academy Award. His other credits include *Mayerling* (1968), *Emmanuelle* (1975) and *International Velvet* (1978).

Laine, Cleo (Clementina Dinah Campbell; 1928–) British JAZZ singer, of Anglo-West Indian descent, who is blessed with a rich, wide-ranging voice and who became one of the most familiar faces in contemporary jazz after teaming up with John DANKWORTH in 1952. She and Dankworth were married in 1958 and have since made many recordings, broadcasts and live appearances together. Highlights of her career have included concerts at Carnegie Hall in 1973 and 1983. She is famous for the diversity of her material, from jazz to Arnold SCHOENBERG, Sir William WALTON, Kurt WEILL and Stephen SONDHEIM.

Laine, Frankie (Francis Paul LoVecchio; 1913–) US singer-songwriter and actor, of Sicilian descent, who enjoyed extraordinary chart success in the mid-1950s. Laine first captured the headlines in 1932, when he set a dance marathon record of 145 days (3,501 hours). He was 'discovered' as a singing star of some potential by Hoagy CARMICHAEL in 1946 and went to make many hit recordings, including 13 million-selling discs.

In 1953, with his hit 'I Believe', he achieved the remarkable feat of reaching Number One in the British charts on three separate occasions, topping the charts for 18 weeks in all (for many years the record for any British Number One). Its successors, 'Hey Joe' and 'Answer Me', also got to Number One, giving Laine no fewer than 27 weeks as the Number One artist in a single year (even though 'Answer Me' was banned by the BBC for its semi-religious lyrics). He had a fourth Number One in 1956 with 'A Woman in Love'.

Laine starred at the London Palladium among other popular venues through the 1950s and enjoyed a long career in CABARET and as a television actor. Among his own songs were 'What Could be Sweeter' (1946) and 'Deuces Wild' (1961).

> The virility of a hairy goat and the delicacy of a white flower petal.
> Unidentified US disc jockey

Lamb, Joseph (Francis) (1887–1960) US composer, who wrote some of the most popular RAGTIME tunes. He emerged as one of the leading White ragtime composers, much acclaimed for such hits as 'Sensation' (1908), 'Ethiopia Rag' (1909), 'Cleopatra Rag' (1910) and 'Top Liner Rag' (1916).

Lambert, Constant (1905–51) British composer and conductor, who was particularly acclaimed for his ballet music. The son of a celebrated artist, Lambert studied under Ralph VAUGHAN WILLIAMS at the Royal College of Music in London and was recruited to write music for Diaghilev's Ballets Russes before he had even finished his training. His ballet *Romeo and Juliet* (1926), combining elements of JAZZ and classical music, was a great success when staged in Monte Carlo, after which he appeared as reciter in Sir William WALTON's *Façade* (which was dedicated to him) and collaborated with Dame Edith Sitwell on the ballet *Pomona* (1926).

As well as composing such ballets as *Horoscope* (1937) and *Tiresias* (1950), many of them in his capacity as conductor of the Camargo Society (which eventually became the Sadler's Wells Ballet), Lambert also wrote a wide range of other works, from the jazz-influenced *Elegiac Blues* (1927) and *Rio Grande* (1927), which was based on a poem by Sacheverell Sitwell, to the choral pieces *Summer's Last Will and Testament* (1932–35) and *Dirge* (1940). Also notable were his sonata for piano (1928–29), concerto for piano and nine instruments (1930–31) and the *Aubade héroïque* (1942), which was inspired by the Sadler's Wells Ballet's narrow escape from the Nazis during the invasion of Holland in 1940. His publications on music included the lighthearted *Music Ho!* (1934).

> The appalling popularity of music.
> CONSTANT LAMBERT, chapter title, *Music Ho!*, 1934

Landowska, Wanda (1877–1959) Polish-born pianist and harpsichordist, who did much to revive interest in baroque and classical harpsichord music. A graduate of the Warsaw Conservatory, Landowska studied in Berlin and then settled in Paris, where she continued to pursue her interest in baroque music with her husband. She switched from the piano to the long-neglected harpsichord in the early 1900s, when she had a harpsichord specially made for her, and attracted much attention to the instrument with performances before and after during the First World War (during which she was detained in Berlin). Several notable composers, including Manuel de FALLA and Francis POULENC wrote works specifically for her, and she was invited to perform before many distinguished audiences, including the French sculptor Rodin and (after a sleigh ride through the snow, complete with harpsichord) the Russian novelist Tolstoy.

Landowska founded the École de Musique Ancienne to promote baroque music in 1925, but was forced to flee to the USA when the Germans invaded in the Second World War. Her many recordings included Bach's *Well-tempered Clavier* (1951).

> You play Bach your way and I'll play him *his* way.
> WANDA LANDOWSKA (attributed)

Lane, Burton (1912–) US composer, who won acclaim as a prolific writer for the Broadway stage. He had his first hits in the early 1930s and went on to consolidate his reputation with music contributed to such shows as *Earl Carroll's Vanities* (1931), *Americana* (1932), *Finian's Rainbow* (1947), from which came such hits as 'How are Things in Glocca Morra?', and *On a Clear Day You Can See Forever* (1965). Among his most successful complete scores were *Strictly Dynamite* (1934), *Kid Millions* (1934), *Some Like It Hot* (1939), *Babes on Broadway* (1941) and *Royal Wedding* (1951). His many hit songs included 'Swing It, Sister', 'Your Head on My Shoulder', 'You Took the Words Right Out of My Mouth', 'The Lady's in Love With You', 'You're All the World to Me' and 'Applause, Applause'.

Lang, Eddie (Salvatore Massaro; 1902–33) US JAZZ guitarist, who is acknowledged to have been the first jazz guitarist of major importance. Lang began his career playing with his old friend Joe VENUTI and subsequently worked with, among others, Paul WHITEMAN, King OLIVER and Bing CROSBY (whose contract demanded that Lang participated on any recordings) as well as with BLUES guitarist Lonnie Johnson (1899–1970). Lang's performances demonstrated that the guitar had more potential in jazz than as a simple rhythm instrument, but his career was brought to an abrupt end when he died after being operated on for tonsilitis.

Langford, Frances (Frances Newbern; 1913–) US singer, who enjoyed wide popularity in the 1930s and 1940s through her many broadcasts. Having had to relinquish hopes of a career in classical music after throat problems, Langford became a popular singing star through her regular appearances on Rudy VALLEE's radio programme, and she also sang in the radio shows of Dick Powell and Bob HOPE as well as in a number of movies and with bandleader Spike JONES. Her many hits included 'I'm in the Mood for Love', which she sang in the 1935 film *Every Night at Eight*. She also co-hosted a popular television show in the early 1950s.

Lanza, Mario (Alfredo Arnold Cocozza; 1921–59) US tenor and film actor, of Italian descent, who enjoyed star status with an adoring public during the 1950s. One of the most celebrated tenors of the twentieth century, Lanza reached a huge international audience through such films as *The Great Caruso* (1951), which was based on the life of the great tenor on whom Lanza had modelled his own career; he also sang the music used in the film *The Student Prince* (1954) and had hits with recordings of such songs as 'Be My Love', which reached Number One in 1950, 'The Loveliest Night of the Year' and 'Because You're Mine'.

Lanza was also famous for his reckless life-style, which eventually destroyed him. He was noted particularly for his gluttony – he would eat a huge meal, make himself sick and then start all over again. He was often violent through drink and proved a trial to his agents as he toured Europe and the USA to appear before packed houses, where the audiences often included crowned heads and other dignitaries. His early death, at the age of only 38, was a direct result of his unruly, self-destructive behaviour.

Larrocha (y de la Calle), Alicia de (1923–) Spanish pianist, who emerged as one of the leading figures in Spanish music after the Second World War. Having made her professional début at the age of 12, she won particular acclaim for her

interpretations of the music of Isaac Albéniz (1860–1909) and Enrique GRA-NADOS and went on to collaborate with Sir Georg SOLTI on the music of Mozart. She was appointed director of the Marshall Academy in Barcelona in 1959.

Larynx, the *See* Frank SINATRA.

Last, James (Hans Last; 1929–) German conductor, composer and arranger, who has enjoyed considerable commercial success producing EASY LISTENING versions of rock and pop standards. Last began his career playing double bass in JAZZ bands and went on to play in a number of dance orchestras before establishing his reputation as an arranger and, in the 1960s, developing his own 'non-stop dancing' style, in which sequences of different tunes were linked without breaks for the convenience of dancers. At one point, in 1967, he had no fewer than four albums in the British charts at the same time. He also wrote a number of MIDDLE-OF-THE-ROAD hits of his own, among them 'Games That Lovers Play'. He has toured widely with his own orchestra since 1969.

Last Night of the Proms, the *See* the PROMS.

Last of the Red Hot Mammas, the *See* Sophie TUCKER.

Last Rock 'n' Roll Star, the *See* Freddy CANNON.

Lauder, Sir Harry (MacLennan) (1870–1950) Scottish comedian and singer-songwriter, who had huge success as a star of the Edwardian MUSIC HALL. The son of a potter, Lauder gave up his coal-mining job to concentrate on his stage career, and he went on to portray the archetypal Scotsman (complete with glengarry, kilt and crooked stick) to massive acclaim on both sides of the Atlantic, making his London début in 1900. Among his most popular songs – most of which he wrote himself – were 'Stop Yer Tickling, Jock' (1904), 'I Love a Lassie' (1905), 'Roamin' in the Gloamin'' (1911) and 'Keep Right on to the End of the Road', which became a favourite of troops during the First World War (during which Lauder lost his only son).

Lawrence, Gertrude (Gertrud Alexandra Dagmar Lawrence-Klasen; 1898–1952) British actress, singer and dancer, who became the most popular British actress to appear on Broadway. Famed for her long collaboration with Noël COWARD in a series of plays and MUSICALS, she sang many hit songs in the course of her celebrated career. Among her most popular numbers were 'Limehouse Blues', which she first sang in 1921 in *From A to Z*, 'Poor Little Rich Girl' and 'Someone to Watch Over Me'. She also starred in such musicals as *Nymph Errant* (1933), *Tonight at 8.30* (1936), *Lady in the Dark* (1941) and *The King and I* (1951). Her life story was retold in the film *Star!* (1968).

Lawrence, Jack (1912–) US composer, singer, conductor and author, who wrote numerous hit songs for Hollywood. His most popular numbers included 'All or Nothing at All' (1939), 'If I Didn't Care' (1940), 'Sleepy Lagoon' (1940), 'A Handful of Stars' (1944), 'Linda' (1946) and 'Hold My Hand' (1954). He was also author of 'Heave Ho, My Lads, Heave Ho', the official song of the US Merchant Marine, with which he served.

Lawrence, Syd (1923–) British bandleader, who enjoyed wide success after forming his own band playing in the Glenn MILLER tradition in the late 1960s. Lawrence played in a range of bands, including those of GERALDO and Sidney Lipton (1906–), before branching out on his own and attracting a large audience with a Miller-based repertoire.

Layton and Johnstone Popular US close-harmony singing duo, who enjoyed particular success with British audiences in the 1920s and 1930s. Composer, singer and pianist Turner Layton (1894–1978) and singer Clarence 'Tandy' Johnstone (d. 1953) teamed up in 1922 and numbered among their best-selling hits 'After You've Gone', 'It Ain't Gonna Rain No More', 'River, Stay Away from my Door' and 'Bye, Bye, Blackbird'. Johnstone retired in 1935, when he was implicated in a scandalous divorce case involving a White couple, and died in obscurity, but Layton carried on as a solo performer.

Leadbelly (Huddie William Ledbetter; 1889–1949) Black US BLUES and FOLK singer-songwriter and guitarist, who was among the giants of early twentieth-century blues. A degree of uncertainty

surrounds the origins of Ledbetter's famous stagename. It was arrived at either as a simple play on his real surname, or else in reference to his considerable physical strength, to his dangerous temper or to the 'lead' he carried around in his stomach as a result of an old buckshot wound.

Leadbelly, who was brought up in dire poverty in the best blues tradition, was 'discovered' in 1933 while serving a 30-year sentence at the Louisiana State Prison Farm for murdering another man in a brawl (he was gaoled no fewer than four times for various crimes of violence). A biography brought him fame and subsequently – after his release in 1934 – he made numerous records (often playing a 12-string guitar) of such classics as 'Midnight Special' and 'Rock Island Line', which may or may not have been written by the singer himself. With John Lomax he also wrote the celebrated 'Goodnight, Irene'. Together with 'Blind Lemon' JEFFERSON, with whom he teamed up for a while, he was the leading bluesman of the 1930s and 1940s and his 'Goodnight Irene' reached Number One shortly after he died.

> The blues is a feeling and when it hits you, it's the real news.
> LEADBELLY

> Huddie Ledbetter, frequently known as Leadbelly, had a fairly murky past. I can think of several crimes he committed, including murder twice and influencing Lonnie Donegan.
> GEORGE MELLY, on *Jazz Score*

Leader, the *See* Frank SINATRA.

Lean Lark, the *See* Frank SINATRA.

Leather Lungs *See* Elaine PAIGE.

Lecuona, Ernesto (1896–1963) Cuban composer and pianist, who enjoyed commercial success in the 1930s and 1940s with a wide range of works, from cantatas and operettas to MUSICALS and film music. A child prodigy, who gave piano recitals at the age of five, Lecuona led his own DANCE BAND and toured throughout Europe and the Americas in the 1920s before concentrating on composition. His best-known works included the orchestral *Suite espagnol* (1928) and the hit songs 'Jungle Drums' (1930), 'Andaluzia' (1930), 'Maria, My Own' (1931), 'Siboney' (1931) and 'Dust on the Moon' (1934).

Led Zeppelin British rock band, which emerged as the world's leading HARD ROCK group in the 1970s. The band, initially called the New Yardbirds, assembled around YARDBIRDS guitarist Jimmy Page (1944–) in 1968 and adopted its permanent name on the suggestion of rival drummer Keith Moon (*see* the WHO), who thought the band would 'go down like a lead balloon'. The line-up was completed with bassist John Paul Jones (John Baldwin; 1946–), lead singer Robert Plant (1947–) and drummer John Bonham (1947–80).

The band's hugely influential releases included *Led Zeppelin II* (1969), *Led Zeppelin IV* (1971), from which came the rock classic 'Stairway to Heaven', *Physical Graffiti* (1975) and *The Song Remains the Same* (1976). Among the most acclaimed tracks were 'Whole Lotta Love' (1970), 'Immigrant Song' (1971) and 'Black Dog' (1972).

The group's history was marred by a series of tragedies, which some said were the consequence of Page's interest in black magic (he bought Boleskine House, the reputedly haunted home of self-proclaimed satanist Aleister Crowley). Plant and his family suffered multiple injuries in a car accident in 1975; a caretaker at Page's home committed suicide while his replacement went mad; a rare respiratory problem claimed the life of Page's five-year-old son, Karac; and it was at Page's house in Windsor that John Bonham died of asphyxiation in 1980 after years of addiction to heroin and alcohol. This last disaster precipitated the disbanding of the group, although it re-formed for LIVE AID in 1985 and again in 1988.

Only on one occasion in its 11-year history did the band play under any other name than Led Zeppelin – in 1974 it appeared as Nobs in Copenhagen after Baron von Zeppelin threatened to sue if the band played on Danish soil under his family name.

Lee, Bert (1881–1946) British songwriter, who wrote several of the most celebrated hits to emerge from the late MUSIC HALL tradition. Among the most celebrated of his many hits were such classics as 'Joshuah' (1910), 'Hello, Hello, Who's Your Lady Friend?' (1913) and 'Good-by-ee' (1917).

Lee, Brenda (Brenda Mae Tarpley; 1944–) US ROCK 'N' ROLL singer, nicknamed Little Miss Dynamite in reference both to her hit single 'Dynamite' (1957) and to the 'explosively' powerful voice that issued from her petite frame, who emerged as a leading star in the early 1960s while still a teenager. Lee first attracted attention singing such COUNTRY style standards as 'Jambalaya' (1957), but she then adopted a raunchier, rock 'n' roll approach. Among her many hits were 'Sweet Nothin's' (1959), 'I'm Sorry' (1960), which reached Number One and 'Rockin' around the Christmas Tree' (1960). Under 5 feet tall, she stunned audiences with her powerful voice and mature performances, and some critics refused to believe she could be so young; on one occasion during a tour of France the newspaper *Le Figaro* announced on its front page that she was in reality a 32-year-old midget. She retired in 1967 but made a come-back in 1971, after which she adopted a more conventional country style.

> Arguably the finest White female singer in pop during pre-Beatle years.
> HARDY AND LAING

Lee, Peggy (Norma Delores Egstrom; 1920–) US singer, actress, composer and author, who first emerged as a leading star in the 1940s. After a hard childhood and several false starts, her singing career took off in the early 1940s after she was recruited by Benny GOODMAN, and she went on to enjoy commercial success with such hits as 'Somebody Else is Taking My Place' (1942) and 'Why Don't You Do Right?' (1943). She then went solo and made many more successful recordings, among them 'Waitin' for the Train to Come In' (1945) and 'Fever' (1958), as well as appearing in films and building a reputation as a songwriter with her husband Dave Barbour (1912–65). Her compositions included contributions to the scores for the films *Lady and the Tramp* (1952) and *Tom Thumb* (1958).

Leeds Piano Competition Prestigious triennial piano competition, which has been part of the Leeds Festival of Music (founded in 1858) since 1963. Founded by local music teacher Fanny Waterman (1920–), the competition has witnessed many fine performances and produced many stars, notably Murray Perahia (1947–), who won it in 1972.

Legrand, Michel (1932–) French composer, arranger, conductor, pianist and singer, who has built up a strong reputation as one of the most successful composers for the cinema. He was the son of the celebrated composer and conductor Raymond Legrand (1908–74), who led a popular dance orchestra and who accompanied such stars as Maurice CHEVALIER and Edith PIAF as well as composing for films, including *Mademoiselle Swing* (1942). Having studied under Nadia BOULANGER in Paris, Michel Legrand emerged as a leading film composer in the 1960s with the scores for such movies as *Lola* (1961), *Les Parapluies de Cherbourg* (1964) and *The Thomas Crown Affair* (1968), from which came the Academy Award-winning 'Windmills of Your Mind'. Subsequent film scores have included *The Go-Between* (1970), *Summer of '42* (1971), *Wuthering Heights* (1972) and *Yentl* (1983).

Lehár, Franz (Ferencz Lehár; 1870–1948) Austrian composer, of Hungarian descent, who was acknowledged to be the last great composer of Viennese operettas. A student of the Prague Conservatory, he worked as a military bandmaster (the youngest ever appointed in the Austrian army) before establishing a reputation as a popular composer with such pieces as the waltz 'Gold and Silver' (1902) and his first operettas, getting encouragement from Dvořák and Brahms. *Die lustige Witwe* (*The Merry Widow*; 1905) proved to be his greatest success and made him internationally famous. This and such operettas as *Der Graf von Luxembourg* (*The Count of Luxembourg*; 1909) and *Eva* (1911) did much to popularize the Viennese operetta overseas and greatly influenced the development of the musical comedy in the USA.

After the First World War, Lehár wrote further operettas for the tenor Richard TAUBER and had renewed success with such works as *Der Zarevich* (1927), *Das Land des Lächelns* (*The Land of Smiles*; 1929) and *Giuditta* (1934), which reflected the influence of the composer's friend Giacomo PUCCINI. He also contributed a number of film scores. His last years were disrupted by the Nazi occupation and also by an extended legal wrangle with a woman who claimed authorship of the libretto on which *Giuditta* had been based (as well as by various blackmail plots arising from his interest in the opposite sex).

Lehmann, Lotte (1888–1976) US singer, born in Germany, who was acclaimed as one of the most accomplished operatic sopranos of the interwar years. Born into a musical family, she studied music in Berlin and made her first professional appearance in 1910. She sang under Sir Thomas BEECHAM in London and won particular praise for her mastery of the works of Richard STRAUSS (who wrote *Arabella* and other pieces with her in mind) and a number of Wagnerian roles. The Nazis made her leave Vienna in 1938, and she settled in the USA, where she gave her final performance in 1946.

Lehrer, Tom (Thomas Andrew Lehrer; 1928–) US songwriter, pianist and humorist, who attracted a huge cult audience in the 1950s and 1960s with his sharply satirical repertoire of songs. Although he was a university teacher of mathematics, he released a number of popular albums lampooning a variety of targets, ranging from the arms race to the problems presented by large numbers of pigeons in public places. His songs provided the basis of the 1960 REVUE *Tomfoolery*.

> Life is like a sewer. What you get out of it depends on what you put into it.
> TOM LEHRER, 'We Will All Go Together When We Go'

Lehrstück A musical play with a moral or educational purpose. The term was adopted by a number of German composers and playwrights in the 1920s, when Bertolt Brecht (1898–1955) and others used drama as a vehicle for political expression until the Nazis imposed severe restrictions on it. Kurt WEILL and Paul HINDEMITH were the most important composers associated with such productions.

Leiber & Stoller US songwriting partnership, who produced numerous hits for Elvis PRESLEY and other stars in the 1950s and 1960s. Jerry Leiber (1933–) and Mike Stoller (1933–) came together as students in 1949 and made their name writing rock songs with a marked blues influence. Among the most successful songs to emerge from the Leiber & Stoller stable were 'Hound Dog', recorded by both 'Big Mama' THORNTON and by Presley, Presley's 'Jailhouse Rock', 'Riot in Cell Block Number Nine', the COASTERS hits 'Poison Ivy', 'Charlie Brown' and 'Along Came Jones', Peggy LEE's 'Is That All There Is?', 'There Goes My Baby', which was written for the DRIFTERS, and other numbers recorded by such stars as LaVern BAKER, Elkie BROOKS, the ISLEY BROTHERS, PROCUL HARUM and Joe TURNER. They concentrated on music for the theatre and the big screen from the 1970s.

Leigh, Carolyn (1926–   ) US lyricist and author, who collaborated on numerous popular songs and musical shows of the 1950s and 1960s. As well as contributing to such stage MUSICALS as *Peter Pan* (1954), *Ziegfeld Follies* (1957) and *Little Me* (1962), she also provided the lyrics for several hits, including 'Witchcraft' (1957), 'You Fascinate Me So' (1958) and 'Pass Me By' (1962).

Leigh, Mitch (Irwin Mitchnick; 1928–   ) US composer and arranger, who established his reputation as a writer for the musical stage with the hit Broadway show *Man of La Mancha* (1965). His other compositions have included JAZZ pieces, advertising JINGLES and the somewhat less successful MUSICALS *Cry For Us All* (1970) and *Home Sweet Homer* (1975).

Leigh, Walter (1905–42) British composer, who enjoyed success with his light operas and a range of other light classical music before his premature death. He studied under Paul HINDEMITH in Berlin and won particular acclaim for the light opera *Jolly Roger* (1933); his other works included a concertino for harpsichord and strings (1936) and numerous other orchestral pieces and songs. He died in action at Tobruk during the Second World War.

Lennon, John (Winston) (1940–80) British singer-songwriter and guitarist, who became a pop legend as a leading member of the BEATLES and one half of the hugely successful LENNON AND McCARTNEY songwriting team. Lennon formed his first group – a SKIFFLE outfit called the Quarrymen – while at the local Quarry Bank Grammar School and it was this band that was to provide the nucleus of the Beatles themselves. While Paul McCARTNEY provided much of the melodic content, it was Lennon – irreverent and always eager to explore new experiences and philosophies – who preserved the ROCK roots of the band and constantly pressed his colleagues to break new territory in terms of recording techniques and subject matter.

Lennon eventually wearied of the commercial and artistic pressures of being a Beatle and decided to leave in 1969 to concentrate on new projects – including the Plastic Ono Band – with his Japanese second wife, artist Yoko ONO. Their 'bed-ins' – in which the press were invited to interview Lennon and Ono in bed – made headline news, although subsequent album releases proved uneven in quality. *Imagine* (1971), the title track of which equalled the best of his Beatles material, was hailed as Lennon at his best; more mixed were the receptions that greeted such LPs as *Some Time In New York City* (1971) and *Rock 'n' Roll* (1975). Hit singles included the anthemic 'Give Peace a Chance' (1969) and 'Happy Christmas War is Over' (1972).

Resident in the USA from 1975, Lennon disappeared from the music scene for a lengthy period to bring up his son Sean (he made his last live appearance during an Elton JOHN concert in 1974). Just as he was about to make a long-awaited come-back with the hit album *Double Fantasy* (1980) he was shot dead outside his Manhattan apartment by a deranged fan, Mark Chapman.

Tributes to Lennon after his death included George HARRISON's 'All Those Years Ago' (1981), which featured STARR on drums and McCartney singing backing vocals. His son Julian Lennon (1963–   ) has also developed something of a career as a rock star in recent years, his releases including the album *Mr Jordan* (1989).

> Will people in the cheaper seats clap your hands? All the rest of you, if you'll just rattle your jewellery . . .
>
> JOHN LENNON, during a Royal Command performance, 1963

> If I was a Jewish girl in Hitler's day, I would approach him and become his girlfriend. After ten days in bed, he would come to my way of thinking. This world needs communication. And making love is a great way of communicating.
>
> YOKO ONO, explaining the idea behind the 'bed-ins'

Lennon and McCartney The celebrated songwriting partnership of the 1960s, which produced the great majority of the hit songs recorded by the BEATLES. The partnership began in 1957, while John LENNON and Paul McCARTNEY were both still at school and members of the teenage ROCK 'N' ROLL group the Quarrymen. By the time the Quarrymen had evolved into the

Beatles and recorded their first album, *Please Please Me* (1963), they had already written more than 80 songs.

Although remaining prolific and hugely successful across the decade, the partnership had begun to disintegrate long before it was officially wound up by the High Court in 1971 (Lennon's subsequent track 'How Do You Sleep' was interpreted as a veiled attack on his former colleague). The beginning of the end can perhaps be traced to 'Yesterday' (1965), which was credited to Lennon and McCartney, even though McCartney woke up one morning with the song already formed in his head (although under the surprisingly unromantic title of 'Scrambled Eggs').

By the time of the album *Sergeant Pepper's Lonely Hearts Club Band* (1967), it appears that the majority of the songs were being written independently, as reflected in the single released in the same year with Lennon's 'Strawberry Fields Forever' on one side and McCartney's 'Penny Lane' on the other.

The original handwritten lyrics to songs by Lennon and McCartney were sold by auction in 1992. McCartney's handwritten 'She's Leaving Home' (1967) went for an astonishing £41,000, while Lennon's 'A Day in the Life' (1967) lyric broke all records by selling for £44,000, the proceeds of the sale being presented to a children's home.

In all Lennon and McCartney co-wrote 23 US Number Ones and 25 British chart-toppers, a record for any songwriting partnership.

> There are two things John and I always do when we're going to sit down and write a song. First of all we sit down. Then we think about writing a song.
>
> PAUL McCARTNEY

> We both had our fingers in each other's pies.
>
> JOHN LENNON

Lenoir, Jean (Jean Neuberger; 1891–1976) French songwriter and author, who enjoyed massive commercial success as a writer of romantic love songs. His best-known composition was the classic 'Parlez-moi d'amour' (1930), which Lucienne BOYER turned into a huge hit.

Lenya, Lotte (Karoline Blamauer; 1898–1981) US singer and actress, born in Austria, who is remembered for her involvement in the epoch-making MUSICAL THEATRE

of Bertolt Brecht (1898–1955) and Kurt WEILL in the 1920s and 1930s. She married Weill in 1926 and created several of the roles he wrote with Brecht, achieving particular distinction as Jenny in *The Threepenny Opera* (1928), before emigrating to the USA in the 1930s on the rise of the Nazis. Singing in her own unique, almost out-of-tune way, she included 'Alabama Song' among her most distinctive numbers. Much later in her career she played a small part in *Cabaret* (1966) and a cameo role as a murderous villainess in the James Bond movie *From Russia With Love* (1963).

Leonard, Eddie (Lemuel Gordon Tooney; 1875–1941) US singer-songwriter, actor and author, who had considerable success singing his own compositions in the minstrel style subsequently perfected by Al JOLSON. A soldier in the Spanish-American War of the 1890s, he introduced his own songs as a member of a popular minstrel show and established his reputation with such hits as 'Ida, Sweet As Apple Cider' (1903), 'Roll Dem Roly Boly Eyes' (1912) and 'Oh, Didn't It Rain' (1923). After years as a top entertainer, he lost his audience in the early 1940s. In the hope that he would improve his fortune by reviving old habits, he checked into his old room at New York's Imperial Hotel, only for his lifeless body to be discovered the next morning.

Lerner, Alan Jay (1918–86) US librettist and lyricist, who became famous for his highly successful collaboration with Frederick LOEWE on a series of classic MUSICALS. After teaming up with Loewe in 1942, Lerner provided the lyrics for such hits as *Brigadoon* (1947), *Paint Your Wagon* (1951), *My Fair Lady* (1956), *Gigi* (1958) and *Camelot* (1960), as well as working with a range of other composers, including Kurt WEILL, André PREVIN and Leonard BERNSTEIN. As a writer for MGM, he contributed lyrics to such films as *Royal Wedding* (1951), *An American in Paris* (1951) and *Gigi* (1973). He teamed up briefly with Loewe once more to work on the film *The Little Prince* (1974).

Considered the most accomplished of the heirs of Oscar HAMMERSTEIN II, Lerner was also renowned for his hectic private life, which saw him marry eight times.

> We are not an aria country. We are a song country.
>
> ALAN JAY LERNER

Leslie, Lew (Lewis Lessinsky; 1886–1963) US producer and actor, who had huge success with his all-Black revues of the 1920s and 1930s. A former vaudeville performer, he was particularly celebrated for the acclaimed *Blackbirds* REVUES, which ran in New York and London through the late 1920s and early 1930s and did much to help popularize JAZZ.

Levant, Oscar (1906–72) US pianist, composer, actor, author and conductor, who was particularly associated with the music of George GERSHWIN. Levant started out as a DANCE BAND pianist and even studied under Arnold SCHOENBERG before entering into a close relationship with Gershwin and presenting the premieres of several of his works, including *Rhapsody in Blue* in 1932. He also made many film appearances and wrote such hit songs as 'If You Want the Rainbow (You Must Have the Rain)' (1929) and 'Blame It on My Youth' (1934) before his retirement through ill-health in the early 1950s.

Levant was one of the great wits of his day, and numerous tales were told of his repartee. When a telephone was heard ringing off-stage while he was giving a challenging public piano recital he called out 'If that's for me, tell them I'm busy,' and carried on playing without so much as a pause. When a lady came in late during one of his concerts he started playing in time to her steps, slowing when she did and going faster when she started to hurry, reducing the audience to helpless laughter.

Level 42 British pop group of the 1980s, which established a big following playing in a broad JAZZ-FUNK style. Guitarist Boon Gould (1955–), his brother drummer Phil Gould (1957–), who was eventually succeeded by Neil Conti, bassist and vocalist Mark King (1958–) and keyboard player Mike Lindup (1959–) came together in 1980 and attracted attention with the début album *Level 42. The Early Tapes* and *The Pursuit of Accidents* (both 1982), followed by *World Machine* (1985) confirmed the group as a top SOUL act, and such singles as 'The Sun Goes Down' reached the Top 10. The band adopted a more commercial pop sound later in the decade with such albums as *Running in the Family* (1986) and *Staring at the Sun* (1988). Recent releases include *Guaranteed* (1991) and *Forever Now* (1994).

Levine, James (1943–) US conductor, who won recognition as one of the most respected conductors of recent years. He trained as a pianist before studying conducting at the Juilliard School, New York, and subsequently serving as assistant conductor of the CLEVELAND ORCHESTRA under Georg SZELL. He was appointed music director of the METROPOLITAN OPERA in 1975.

Lewis, George (George Lewis Francis Zeno; 1900–68) US JAZZ clarinettist, who was among the most celebrated exponents of traditional NEW ORLEANS style jazz. Lewis played with several legendary New Orleans bands and subsequently disappeared from view during the 1930s before being rediscovered during the TRAD jazz revival of the 1940s. His most important recordings included several made with Bunk JOHNSON in the mid-1940s, after which he toured widely with his own bands and made many more albums. Ill-health forced his virtual retirement in the late 1950s.

Lewis, Jerry Lee (1935–) US ROCK 'N' ROLL singer and pianist, nicknamed the Killer, who was one the figureheads of the rock 'n' roll era of the 1950s. Lewis began his career playing piano in the brothels of Louisiana and established himself as a star after entering a studio for the first time in 1955. Famed for his furious delivery of such classics as 'Great Balls of Fire' (during which he once set fire to his piano at the climax of his performance, thus eclipsing Chuck BERRY, who was about to come on), he created a wholly new sound, mixing elements of both Black and White music. Other hits included 'Whole Lotta Shakin' Goin' On', 'Breathless', 'High School Confidential', 'Mean Woman Blues' and 'Fools Like Me'.

Lewis's songs and exuberant live shows, which were in marked contrast to his natural shyness, outraged the older generation, who recoiled at the sight of the star pounding the keyboard with his feet and screaming into the microphone. His tendency to smash up hotel rooms only served to increase the furore, but it was his (third) marriage to his 13-year-old cousin Myra Gale Brown in 1958 that eventually caused him the most damage. News of the marriage (fuelled by doubts whether he had divorced his previous wife) broke during a tour of the UK and led to an early flight home. His popular standing was never fully restored in the wake of the scandal, although he continued to tour for many years after and enjoyed something of a come-back in the mid-1960s after the BEATLES listed him among their idols. His later hits, in a broad COUNTRY style, included 'What'd I Say' (1961) and 'What Made Milwaukee Famous (has Made a Loser out of Me)' (1963). He and Myra divorced in 1970; two later wives died in tragic circumstances.

Lee's private life was further blighted in 1962 and again in 1973 with the accidental deaths of his two sons. He has also suffered from alcohol and drug problems and nearly died in 1982 with a perforated ulcer. His life story was told in the film *Great Balls of Fire* (1988).

> Either be hot or cold. If you are lukewarm, the Lord will spew you forth from His mouth.
>
> JERRY LEE LEWIS

Lewis, John (Aaron) (1920–) US JAZZ pianist, arranger and composer, who won acclaim for his work with the likes of Dizzy GILLESPIE and Miles DAVIS among other top names. Lewis joined the Davis band in 1945 and established himself as a brilliant arranger for both Davis and Gillespie before forming a successful partnership with Lester YOUNG in the 1950s. He formed the MODERN JAZZ QUARTET with Milt JACKSON in 1952 and remained its leader until 1974, playing COOL and THIRD STREAM jazz and winning equal acclaim from the jazz and classical camps. In the 1980s he presided over reunions of the MJQ, led his own sextet and worked as musical director of the American Jazz Orchestra. He has also written a number of film scores.

Lewis, Richard (Thomas Thomas; 1914–90) British tenor, who won particular acclaim in a range of modern operatic roles. He first attracted attention singing at GLYNDEBOURNE in 1947 and went on to win praise in operas by such contemporary composers as Benjamin BRITTEN, Arnold SCHOENBERG and Sir William WALTON.

Lewis, Sam M. (1885–1959) US lyricist, who provided the lyrics for many hit songs of the 1920s and 1930s. Lewis gave up a career as a broker to work as a café singer and went on to collaborate as a lyricist with several composers, of whom his most regular partner was Joe YOUNG. His prolific output yielded such hits as 'That Mellow Melody' (1912), 'How Ya Gonna Keep 'em Down on the Farm?' (1919), 'Dinah' (1925), 'Five Foot Two, Eyes of Blue' (1925), 'I'm Sitting on Top of the World' (1925) and 'Now or Never' (1936).

Lewis, Ted (Theodore Leopold Friedman; 1892–1971) US bandleader, clarinettist, singer and composer, nicknamed the High-hat Tragedian of Song, who became popular leading his own quintet in a style much influenced by his own easy-going good humour. Having begun in vaudeville, Lewis, whose trademark was the crushed top hat he always wore, formed his quintet after the First World War and quickly established it as a popular live act. He also made a number of film appearances. His catchphrase 'Is everybody happy?' became widely known, and his most popular numbers came to include his signature tune, 'When My Baby Smiles at Me' and 'Me and My Shadow'. Jimmy DORSEY and 'Muggsy' Spanier (1906–67) were among the distinguished jazzmen to serve in his band at various times.

> Ted Lewis perpetrated one of the greatest frauds of all time on a record. When Benny Goodman was making a record with his band he arranged for all the musicians to shout out 'Play it, Ted' while Goodman was in the middle of a marvellous solo.
>
> BENNY GREEN, on BBC radio's *Jazz Score*

Lewis, Vic (1919–) British bandleader, who emerged as one of the foremost British jazzmen in the 1940s. Lewis gained experience in the late 1930s, when he led bands on both sides of the Atlantic, and he went on to become a well-known figure in the BIG BAND world, playing in both DIXIELAND and more modern styles. At various times he worked alongside many JAZZ greats, including Django REINHARDT, Stéphane GRAPPELLI, Buddy RICH, Tommy DORSEY, Louis ARMSTRONG and Stan KENTON. He concentrated on working as an agent and manager in the 1960s and 1970s, when his confederates ranged from Count BASIE to the BEATLES and Elton JOHN. He returned to BIG BAND jazz in the 1980s.

Liberace (Wladziu Valentino Liberace; 1919–87) US pianist and entertainer, who was renowned for his flamboyance and extravagant showmanship. Having won a place at the Wisconsin College of Music at the age of seven, Liberace appeared as a pianist with the CHICAGO SYMPHONY ORCHESTRA just two years later. He later developed a highly individual act as a solo performer, dressing in dazzling, bejewelled costumes and playing popular standards on his candelabra-adorned, glass grand piano. His playing style was similarly ornamental, and, as he readily admitted, it was calculated to mollify rather than to challenge the ear of his public: 'If I play Tchaikovsky I play his melodies and skip his spiritual struggles ... if there's any time left over I fill in with a lot of runs up and down the keyboard.'

At the height of his career Liberace, whose private life was as colourful as his stage act, was the highest-paid performer in the world, earning $138,000 for a single performance at Madison Square Garden in 1954. He also hosted his own television shows and appeared before capacity audiences on both sides of the Atlantic. Such success made attacks from the critics easier to bear, as he once memorably explained: 'What you said hurt me very much. I cried all the way to the bank.'

He opened a museum celebrating his career in Las Vegas in 1979 and even after his death, from a kidney complaint arising from Aids, was said to be still in contact with the world of music – Michael JACKSON reputedly communicating with him on a regular basis during seances held in a secret room in his mansion home.

lick In ROCK music, a rapid series of notes played between vocal lines (usually on the electric guitar). The term was first heard in the 1920s when it was adopted by JAZZ musicians ('lick' being an alternative for 'try'). *See also* RIFF.

Ligeti, György Sándor (1923–   ) Hungarian composer, born in Romania, who emerged as a leading AVANT-GARDE composer after defecting to the West in 1956. A student of the Budapest Academy of Music, he pursued his radical approach to composition in private, for fear of official disapproval, while working as a teacher. In 1956 he escaped first to Cologne, then settled in Vienna, where he came into contact with such composers as Karlheinz STOCKHAUSEN and Pierre BOULEZ.

Innovative, complex polyphonic compositions, including *Apparitions* (1956–59),

Atmosphères (1961) and *Aventures* (1962), which made music from the patterns of human speech through the central concept of speaking clocks, consolidated his reputation. Among the most influential works that have followed have been the choral *Requiem* (1963–65) and *Lux aeterna* (1966), *Trois Bagatelles* (1961), in which he lampooned the music of John CAGE and several others, a cello concerto (1966), string quartets, *Melodien* (1971), in which he made increased use of harmony and rhythm, the modernistic opera *Le Grand Macabre* (1974–77) and a piano concerto (1986).

The use of his music in Stanley Kubrick's epic film *2001, A Space Odyssey* (1969) brought him a huge international audience. Noted for his humour, Ligeti explained the title of his *Grand Symphonie Militaire Op. 69* thus: 'Oh that was a joke. The Opus number refers, of course, to the sexual position'.

> It is precisely a dread of deep significance and ideology that makes any kind of engaged art out of the question for me.
> GYÖRGY LIGETI

Lightfoot, Gordon (1938–   ) Canadian singer-songwriter, who enjoyed considerable commercial success in the 1970s and 1980s. Under the influence of Pete SEEGER and other contemporary FOLK musicians, Lightfoot wrote several hits for artists such as PETER, PAUL AND MARY before emerging as a performer of his own material with such albums as *Lightfoot* (1965), *The Way I Feel* (1967) and *If You Could Read My Mind* (1970). The title track of *Sundown* (1974) sold over a million copies and remains his biggest hit. He continued to enjoy consistent success with fairly MIDDLE-OF-THE-ROAD, folk-based material over the next 20 years, many of his compositions being COVERED by other artists.

Lill, John (1944–   ) British pianist, who first came to notice after sharing victory in the prestigious Tchaikovsky Piano Competition in 1970. He made his first professional appearance in 1963 and subsequently won praise for his interpretations of the music of Beethoven, recording all his concertos and sonatas, Chopin, Liszt and Sergei RACHMANINOV.

Lincoln Center for the Performing Arts Important arts complex, which was opened in New York in the 1960s. The complex is home to the celebrated Juillard School, the

NEW YORK PHILHARMONIC and the METRO-POLITAN OPERA and incorporates a range of concert halls and theatres.

Lindisfarne British FOLK-ROCK group, which enjoyed considerable commercial acclaim in the early 1970s. Singer, guitarist and pianist Alan Hull (1945–), guitarist Simon Cowe (1948–), harmonica and mandolin player Ray Jackson (1948–), bassist and violinist Rod Clements (1947–) and drummer Ray Laidlaw (1948–) first performed together in New-castle in 1968, as Downtown Faction. Under the permanent name, the group topped the album charts a year later with *Fog on the Tyne*, from which came the hit single 'Meet Me on the Corner'. *Nicely Out of Tune* had similar success shortly afterwards, producing the single 'Lady Eleanor', but the band then went into decline and eventually broke up in 1974, although it staged suc-cessful annual reunions in north-east England from 1976 and went on to release further occasional albums and compilations through the late 1970s and 1980s.

Lindsay, Howard (1889–1968) US librettist, playwright and director, who won acclaim for his contributions to several highly suc-cessful musical shows. Having rejected a career in the church, Lindsay worked in vaudeville and the cinema and, after service in the First World War, teamed up with Rus-sell CROUSE to create librettos for such hits as *Anything Goes* (1934) and *Red, Hot and Blue* (1936), both of which featured the music of Cole PORTER, and *Hooray for What?* (1937). Other fruits of their collaboration included a number of straight plays, including *State of the Union* (1945), which won a Pulitzer Prize. Lindsay also worked on several musi-cal films and numbered among his later lib-rettos those for Irving BERLIN's *Call Me Madam* (1950) and for Richard RODGERS's *The Sound of Music* (1959).

Lipatti, Dinu (Constantin) (1917–50) Romanian pianist and composer, who was widely considered one of the most intelligent and technically accomplished musicians of his day. A pupil of Alfred CORTOT and Nadia BOULANGER in Paris, he toured Germany and Italy with success but was forced to flee to Switzerland when the Second World War broke out. Lipatti's failure to win the 1934 Vienna International Competition caused a major scandal, which climaxed in Cortot

resigning as one of the judges. Lipatti him-self died from leukaemia when he was only 33 years old. His compositions included a concertino for piano and orchestra.

Little Glinka, the *See* Alexander GLAZUNOV.

Little Hammer *See* M.C. HAMMER.

Little Jazz *See* Roy ELDRIDGE.

Little Miss Dynamite *See* Brenda LEE.

Little Miss Sharecropper *See* LaVern BAKER.

Little Richard (Richard Wayne Penniman; 1935–) Black US ROCK 'N' ROLL star, self-styled King of Rock 'n' Roll, who was among the most famous idols of the rock 'n' roll era of the 1950s. The future star, who was born with a slightly shortened arm and leg, washed dishes at a bus station in Macon, Georgia, and toured in vaudeville before winning his first recording contract. He achieved overnight fame in 1956 with 'Tutti Frutti', which was adapted from an obscene song he had been heard humming and was recorded at his first studio session. Wearing make-up, extravagantly dressed and flamboyant in performance, Little Richard produced an enormously suc-cessful series of lively hits, starting with 'Tutti Frutti' and going on to include 'Long Tall Sally' (1956), 'Rip It Up' (1956), 'The Girl Can't Help It' (1956), 'Lucille' (1957) and 'Good Golly Miss Molly' (1957). Audi-ences thrilled to the exuberance of his live act as he hammered out piano notes with his heels and screamed out such nonsensi-cal vocal lines as 'A-wop-bopaloo-bop-a-wop-bam-boom'. His rebellious and extro-vert image, together with his unconcealed homosexuality, did much to create the rock star stereotype of ensuing decades.

It all came to an abrupt end in 1957, when the aircraft in which Little Richard was travelling while on tour in Australia got into trouble after a fire broke out. The star prayed for his survival and when the aircraft landed safely he renounced his past life and pledged himself to God, throwing his famous rings into Sydney harbour. Richard returned to the music business after a number of years as an evangelist, during which he had condemned rock 'n' roll as the DEVIL'S MUSIC, but times had changed and he never quite reclaimed his former status, although his music had influenced a whole generation. Later albums ranged from GOSPEL music to SOUL and revivals of his old hits. He survived a bad car crash in 1985.

> I came from a family where people didn't like rhythm and blues. Bing Crosby, 'Pennies from Heaven', Ella Fitzgerald was all I heard. And I knew there was something that could be louder than that, but I didn't know where to find it. And I found it was me.
> LITTLE RICHARD

Live Aid The mammoth rock concerts that were staged on both sides of the Atlantic on 13 July 1985 as part of the international charity effort in aid of famine relief in Africa. Many of the most famous names in contemporary rock and pop turned out (without payment) to entertain a global audience of some 1.5 billion people from the stages at the Wembley Stadium in London and the JFK Stadium in Philadelphia – among them David BOWIE, Mick JAGGER, Elton JOHN, Paul MCCARTNEY, MADONNA, U2 and Bob GELDOF, who had instigated the whole enterprise. The WHO, STATUS QUO, LED ZEPPELIN and BLACK SABBATH were among the groups to re-form specially for the event, each outfit playing a set of 17 minutes each. In all, the effort raised some £50 million. See also BAND AID.

> It would have been kind of difficult not to get together again for this day.
> PETE TOWNSHEND

Livingston, Jay (Harold Livingston; 1915–) US composer, who wrote many hit songs and film scores in collaboration with Ray Evans (1915–). Having teamed up as musicians on a liner, Livingston and Evans were recruited by Hollywood in 1944 and went on to write such classics as 'Buttons and Bows', from *The Paleface* (1948), 'Mona Lisa', from *Captain Carey USA* (1949), 'My Love Loves Me', from *The Heiress* (1949), 'Home Cookin'', from *Fancy Pants* (1950), and 'Que será, será', from *The Man Who Knew Too Much* (1956).

Livingston, Jerry (1909–) US songwriter and pianist, who wrote many hits for the stage in the 1930s and 1940s. Among his most successful compositions were 'It's the Talk of the Town' (1933), 'Mairzy Doats – and Dozy Doats' (1943) and 'Blue and Sentimental' (1947).

Lizard King, the See Jim MORRISON.

Lloyd, Marie (Matilda Alice Victoria Wood; 1870–1922) British singer and comedienne, nicknamed Our Marie and the Queen of the Halls, who became one of the legends of the late Victorian and Edwardian music hall. Lloyd made her début in the music hall in 1885 (taking her stagename from Lloyd's Weekly News), and she became a star with the hit 'The Boy I Love is up in the Gallery', the success of which effectively destroyed the career of Nelly Power (1853–87), whose signature tune it had been.

She was a top MUSIC HALL performer by the early 1890s and was in great demand for her cocky delivery of such saucy classics as 'Johnny Jones' and 'Oh, Mister Porter'. She also starred in pantomime and on tours to the USA.

Her reputation remained undiminished through the Edwardian era and the First World War, during which she entertained the troops and did much charity work. Among her later hits were 'A Little of What You Fancy' and 'Don't Dilly Dally'. She died shortly after a last performance in Edmonton.

> Every performance of Marie Lloyd is a performance by command of the British Public.
> MARIE LLOYD

Lloyd Webber, Sir Andrew (1948–) British composer, whose MUSICALS enjoyed huge success both in London and on Broadway through the 1970s and 1980s. The son of a composer and himself a student at the Royal College of Music, Lloyd Webber formed a rewarding partnership with lyricist Tim RICE in 1965 and established his reputation with the pop musical *Joseph and his Amazing Technicolour Dreamcoat* (1968), which was originally intended for production in schools. Their subsequent collaboration, the ROCK OPERA *Jesus Christ Superstar*, proved hugely successful as a recording (1970), a stage show (1971) and a film (1973), after which Lloyd Webber worked with playwright Alan Ayckbourn on *Jeeves* (1975) and again with Rice on *Evita* (1978), a romanticized account of the Argentinian political idol Eva Perón, which proved another enormous international success.

Cats (1982), based on T.S. Eliot's *Old Possum's Book of Practical Cats*, continued in the vein of unlikely triumphs, while *Starlight Express* (1984), which had the cast careering around the theatre on roller skates and cost more to stage than any other show in the history of the musical, added another substantial hit to the growing list. *Phantom of the Opera* (1986), *Chess* (1986) and *Aspects of Love* (1989) played to equal acclaim and confirmed Lloyd Webber as one of the most popular composers ever to write for the musical theatre, although critics have ventured to suggest that in pandering to the public taste for strong melodies and visual spectacle more subtle artistic considerations were too often sacrificed.

Lloyd Webber's other compositions include a number of film scores and a *Requiem Mass* (1985), dedicated to his father. He also founded his own Really Useful Theatre Company. He was married for several years to singer Sarah Brightman. His brother, Julian Lloyd Webber (1951–   ) has built up a strong reputation as cellist and composer, and it was for him that Andrew Lloyd Webber composed his 'Variations for Cello' on a theme of Paganini (1986).

Loesser, Frank (1910–69) US composer, who wrote numerous hit songs for stage and screen in the 1940s and 1950s. Having started as a lyricist, he established his reputation as a songwriter and writer of complete shows during the Second World War and subsequently joined the ranks of the most successful Broadway composers with such shows as *Where's Charley?* (1948), the classic *Guys and Dolls* (1950), *The Most Happy Fella* (1956) and *How to Succeed in Business Without Really Trying* (1961). He also enjoyed success with his contributions to many Hollywood movies, his hits including 'How Sweet You Are', from *Thank Your Lucky Stars* (1943), 'Spring will be a Little Late This Year', from *Christmas Holiday* (1944), and 'Ugly Duckling', from *Hans Christian Andersen* (1951). His composition 'Praise the Lord and Pass the Ammunition' was a huge hit during the Second World War. He died prematurely of cancer.

> Frank Loesser . . . one of the unsung heroes of popular music.
> DAVID JACOBS

Loewe, Frederick (1901–88) US songwriter, born in Austria, who wrote some of the most popular MUSICALS of the century in partnership with lyricist Alan Jay LERNER. Loewe

trained as a concert pianist and settled in the USA in 1924, having established his reputation as a songwriter while still a teenager with such hits as 'Katrina', which sold a million copies. His greatest successes came, however, after he teamed up with Lerner in 1942. The couple subsequently won acclaim for their polished musicals *Brigadoon* (1947), *Paint Your Wagon* (1951), *My Fair Lady* (1956), which won a Pulitzer Prize, *Gigi* (1958) and *Camelot* (1960).

> I don't like my music, but what is my opinion against that of millions of others?
> FREDERICK LOEWE (attributed)

loft jazz JAZZ music that is played at an informal venue, such as someone's loft. More often than not such music is of a radical, experimental nature, thus debarring it from some of the more usual commercial venues. *See also* GARAGE ROCK.

Logan, Joshua (Lockwood) (1908–88) US librettist, director and producer, who did much to recreate the modern MUSICAL through his insistence on greater realism. He first ventured into the world of the contemporary musical in 1938 and went on to produce a number of successful shows before ushering in a more gritty and realistic style of musical with *Annie Get Your Gun* (1946). He subsequently played a crucial role in the outstanding *South Pacific* (1949) and also had somewhat more modest success with *Wish You Were Here* (1952), *Fanny* (1954) and so forth. He also directed the film versions of *South Pacific* (1958) and *Camelot* (1967).

Among his many other productions was an adaptation (1950) of Chekhov's *The Cherry Orchard* set in the southern USA and retitled *The Wisteria Trees*; wags quickly dubbed it 'Southern Fried Chekhov'.

Lomax, Alan (1915–   ) US folk-song collector, who, with his father John Avery Lomax (1875–1948), gathered the largest and most influential archive of recorded US FOLK MUSIC. As well as publishing many books on the subject, they promoted the careers of such leading performers as LEADBELLY, Jelly Roll MORTON, Woody GUTHRIE and Muddy WATERS. Later in his career Alan Lomax made similar studies of traditional music in several other countries.

Lombardo, Guy (1902–77) Canadian bandleader, of Italian descent, who led the popular Royal Canadians band from 1917 until his death 60 years later. Having moved to the USA in 1924, the band made many best-selling records, and its best-known hits, made in a distinctive 'sweet' style, included its signature tune 'Auld Lang Syne', 'Sweethearts on Parade', 'Charmaine', 'Boo Hoo', 'You're Driving Me Crazy', 'Red Sails in the Sunset', 'A Sailboat in the Moonlight' and 'Seems Like Old Times'. The band even hosted its own television show in the 1950s and made several film appearances. Admirers included Louis ARMSTRONG, who rated Lombardo's band above all others. When not engaged in leading his band, Lombardo indulged his love of speedboat racing and captured many trophies.

London, Julie (Julie Peck; 1926–   ) US singer and actress, who enjoyed a number of hits in the 1950s and 1960s. She started out as a film actress but established herself as a singer with the album *Julie is Her Name* (1955) and such hits as 'Cry Me a River' (1956).

London Philharmonic Orchestra Celebrated British orchestra, which was founded in 1932 by Sir Thomas BEECHAM. Notable conductors of the orchestra have included Beecham himself, Sir Adrian BOULT, Bernard HAITINK and Sir Georg SOLTI. Now based at the Royal Festival Hall in London, the orchestra has made annual appearances at GLYNDEBOURNE since 1964.

London Sinfonietta British chamber orchestra, which was founded in London in 1968. The Sinfonietta has specialized in performing works by contemporary composers who might not otherwise succeed in finding orchestras to play their music. The orchestra has given the premières of works by, among others, Luciano BERIO, Harrison BIRTWISTLE, Peter MAXWELL DAVIES, Hans Werner HENZE and Karlheinz STOCKHAUSEN.

London Symphony Orchestra Famous British orchestra, which was established in London in 1904. The orchestra – now based at the BARBICAN – was set up by a group of some 50 musicians who had quarrelled with Sir Henry WOOD over his opposition to the use of deputies and quickly built up a strong reputation. Its conductors over the years have included Hans RICHTER, Sir Edward ELGAR, André

PREVIN and Claudio ABBADO. Sir Colin DAVIS was appointed principal conductor in 1994.

London Underground, the The alternative and subversive rock culture, which emerged in London in the mid–1960s. Known from its inception as the Underground, the movement was largely 'manufactured' by a small group of like-minded promoters and entrepreneurs; in this it was unlike the hippie movement in the USA, which sprang up more or less spontaneously.

According to Richard Neville, co-editor of the notorious *OZ* magazine, the burgeoning movement was co-ordinated and encouraged by a 'hippie mafia'. This group of 'pirate' DISC JOCKEYS, journalists and club organizers established the first Underground music paper, *International Times*, and created new venues such as the Spontaneous Underground Club, UFO (Unlimited Freak Out) and the Electric Garden. A wide variety of performers found an audience as a result of these initiatives, including the whimsical acoustic duo Tyrannosaurus Rex (later renamed T. Rex; *see* Marc BOLAN), the satirical cult group the BONZO DOG DOODAH BAND and electrified PSYCHEDELIC bands such as PINK FLOYD and the SOFT MACHINE.

Hallmarks of the early Underground scene were cultivated (and often drug-induced) eccentricity, childlike innocence and good humour. The major musical influences included the BEATLES and the more folk-oriented INCREDIBLE STRING BAND. Largely through the success of the Underground, popular music took a more eclectic and cerebral turn before its dissolution into the ultimately vapid flower power movement.

> That was way way back before
> Wild World War Three
> When England went missing
> And we moved to Paraguay
> Way way back in the nineteen sixties.
> ROBIN WILLIAMSON, 'Way Back in the 1960s', 1967

Lone Cat, the *See* Jesse FULLER.

Long Tall Texan, the *See* Jimmy DEAN.

Loose Tubes, the British JAZZ band, which emerged as a leading JAZZ-ROCK outfit in the 1980s. Formed in 1984, the leaderless 21-piece band featured such talents as trombonist Ashley Slater (1961–   ) and keyboard player Django Bates (1960–   ). It devised a unique sound, which was based on elements raided from the length and breadth of jazz history, through the use of such unconventional jazz instruments as the tuba – as played by Dave Powell (1956–   ) – and flute. The band's innovations enjoyed huge success and an early gig at Ronnie SCOTT's in London had the band and audience spilling out of the venue and continuing the performance with abandon into the small hours.

The band was the first jazz outfit to play at the PROMS (1987), but it became somewhat less active in the 1990s after numerous splinter groups were formed.

Lopez, Vincent (1894–1972) US pianist, composer and bandleader, who achieved fame as a regular broadcasting star and as composer of a series of popular hit songs. Lopez rejected his family's plans for him to enter the Church and instead established himself as a radio DANCE BAND leader in the 1920s. His signature tune 'Nola' became widely known, and other hits by his hand included 'Knock, Knock, Who's There?' and 'The World Stands Still'. Among his musicians were Glenn MILLER, Artie SHAW and Xavier CUGAT. He also became one of the first television chat show hosts.

Los Angeles Philharmonic Orchestra Celebrated US orchestra, which was founded in Los Angeles in 1919. Its conductors over the years have included Otto KLEMPERER, Zubin MEHTA and André PREVIN. In addition to Klemperer, other famous names attracted to the city of Los Angeles as long-term residents have been Igor STRAVINSKY and Arnold SCHOENBERG, although curiously these two great composers met there only once, at a funeral.

Loss, Joe (Joshua Alexander Loss; 1909–90) British bandleader, who led one of the best-known British DANCE BANDS for many years. Having started as a violinist, Loss formed his band in 1930 and subsequently made many recordings, his biggest hits including 'Begin the Beguine' (1939), his signature tune 'In the Mood' (1940) and 'A Tree in the Meadow' (1948). His band starred at numerous prestigious ballroom dancing competitions and made many television appearances. Singers with the Loss band included Adelaide HALL and Vera LYNN.

Love US rock group, which had considerable success in the late 1960s playing in an imaginative RHYTHM-AND-BLUES based style. Led by singer-songwriter and guitarist Arthur Lee (1944–   ) and completed by guitarists John Echols (1947–   ) and Brian MacLean (1947–   ), bassist Ken Forssi (1943–   ) and drummer Alan 'Snoopy' Pfisterer (1947–   ), the band emerged as one of the most popular PSYCHEDELIC outfits on the West Coast. Hit albums included *Love* (1966), *Da Capo* (1967) and *Forever Changes* (1968). Guest stars with the band before it broke up in 1974 included Jimi HENDRIX.

Lovin' Spoonful, the US pop group, which ranked among the best-selling bands of the 1960s with a series of cheerful, up-tempo chart hits in a style that came to be labelled 'good-time music'. Songwriter John Sebastian (1944–   ), guitarist Zal Yanofsky (1944–   ), bassist Steve Boone (1943–   ) and drummer Joseph Campbell Butler (1943–   ) came together in 1964, and they went on to establish themselves as a top chart act with such hits as 'Do You Believe in Magic', 'Daydream' and 'Summer in the City', which reached Number One in the USA. The band broke up in 1968 with trouble over drug charges, and an attempted reunion in the 1970s was not a success.

LP Long player. A vinyl plastic gramophone record, which plays for some 25 minutes per side, usually at a speed of 33 rpm. Normally 12in (30cm) in diameter, the LP was introduced by the Columbia Company in 1948, and it soon became the dominant recording format, ousting the old shellac 78s and remaining unchallenged for some 40 years. LPs were often released as double or even triple sets. The popularity of the audio CASSETTE undermined the status of the LP in the 1970s and early 1980s, but it was not until the development of the more resilient and higher quality COMPACT DISC in the 1980s that the days of the LP were finally numbered, although many listeners have determinedly resisted calls to abandon their treasured collections on vinyl. *See also* SINGLE.

Ludwig, Christa (1928–   ) German mezzo-soprano, who became a favourite star at both the Vienna State Opera (from 1955) and the METROPOLITAN OPERA, New York (from 1959). Her greatest successes have included performances of song-cycles by Gustav MAHLER as well as pieces by Brahms, Mozart and Richard STRAUSS.

Lulu (Marie McDonald McLaughlin Lawrie; 1948–) Scottish singer, who established herself as a popular star in the 1960s. She was honed as a rival to Cilla BLACK and numbered among her early hits 'Shout' (1964), 'To Sir with Love' (1967), 'The Boat that I Row' (1967) and 'Boom Bang-a-bang', with which she won the EUROVISION SONG CONTEST in 1968. A popular television personality, she also worked in CABARET as well as continuing to release the occasional new record, notably the BOWIE single 'The Man who Sold the World' (1974) and a new version of 'Shout' (1986). She married Maurice Gibb of the BEE GEES in 1968, but they divorced in 1973. In 1993 she released the comeback album *Independence*.

Lunceford, Jimmie (James Melvin Lunceford; 1902–47) US bandleader, composer and saxophonist, who won acclaim in the 1930s leading his own all-Black SWING band. Having gained experience playing in the bands of Wilbur Sweatman (1882–1961) and Fletcher HENDERSON, he formed his band in 1929 and subsequently attracted to it numerous talented players. The band rapidly acquired a reputation for flamboyant showmanship as well as for the quality of the arrangements, especially those by Sy OLIVER, that were to influence Glenn MILLER among other bandleaders. Among the most spectacular tricks was the one executed in unison by the horn section – all the players would throw their horns high in the air and catch them in time to the music. Lunceford's most successful hits included 'Because You're You' (1934), 'Rhythm is Our Business' (1934), 'Like a Ship at Sea' (1937), 'Liza' (1939) and 'Lunceford Special' (1939).

Life was not always smooth in Lunceford's band. His refusal to meet modest pay demands, while he himself spent lavishly on aircraft and other luxuries, precipitated a mass walk-out of the musicians in 1942, and the band never attained its old standard again. Lunceford's early death was attributed by some to poison administered by a racist restaurateur who objected to having to feed his Black musicians.

Lupu, Radu (1945–) Romanian pianist,

resident in the UK, who established an international reputation after winning the LEEDS PIANO COMPETITION in 1969. He has attracted particular praise for his performances of nineteenth-century romantic music.

Lutcher, Nellie (1915–) US singer-songwriter and pianist, who recorded numerous hit songs in the late 1940s. Among her biggest hits were 'Hurry on Down', 'He's a Real Gone Guy', 'Fine Brown Frame' and 'You'd Better Watch Out'. Her career was somewhat eclipsed by changing tastes in the 1950s.

Lutoslawski, Witold (1913–94) Polish composer, who emerged as the leading contemporary Polish composer after more liberal cultural attitudes were adopted in Poland in the late 1950s. Lutoslawski's elegant yet challenging works have brought him recognition far beyond Poland's borders. His compositions include the Concerto for Orchestra (1954), *Funeral Music* (1958), which betrayed the influence of Karol SZYMANOWSKI and Béla BARTÓK, *Venetian Games* (1961), which adapted some of the theories of John CAGE, a string quartet (1964), his Second Symphony (1967), a cello concerto (1970), preludes and fugue (1972), *Novelette* (1980) and numerous songs. *Paroles Tissées* (1965) was written for Peter PEARS and first performed at the ALDEBURGH FESTIVAL.

Lutyens, Elisabeth (1906–83) British composer and teacher, daughter of the celebrated architect Sir Edwin Lutyens (1869–1944), who was one of the first English composers to adopt a SERIALIST approach. Her chamber concerto for nine instruments (1939) was profoundly influenced by Arnold SCHOENBERG and Anton WEBERN. Subsequent works ranged from music for small ensembles to full-scale operas, among them *Isis and Osiris* (1969–70) and *Time Off? – Not a Ghost of a Chance* (1968–71).

Luxon, Benjamin (1937–) British baritone, who has established a reputation singing leading roles in operas by largely contemporary composers. His greatest successes – in company with the ENGLISH NATIONAL OPERA and at GLYNDEBOURNE – have included works by Benjamin BRITTEN and Peter MAXWELL DAVIES. He has also made many notable recordings of Victorian songs.

Lynn, Loretta (Loretta Webb; 1935–   ) US COUNTRY singer, the older sister of Crystal GAYLE, who emerged as a top star in the mid–1960s. Such hits as 'Don't Come Home a-'Drinkin' (With Lovin' on Your Mind)' and 'First City' established her reputation, and she subsequently made many television appearances. Among her most popular releases since the 1960s have been the album *Coalminer's Daughter* (1970), which elaborated Lynn's own experiences of life in the coalmining town Butcher Hollow and which was hailed as one of the best country records ever made, and collaborations with Conway TWITTY.

Lynn, Dame Vera (Vera Margaret Welch; 1917–   ) British singer, nicknamed the Forces' Sweetheart, who became a national favourite during the Second World War. A Londoner by birth, Lynn sang with Joe LOSS, Charlie KUNZ and AMBROSE before going solo. She reached a huge wartime audience through her radio programme *Sincerely Yours*, and she and her voice became uniquely identified with the country's dogged resistance to the Nazi threat. Singing songs that appealed to the nation's patriotism and also bolstered the morale of troops far from home, she was unrivalled as the darling of the forces, a fact that was reputed to have caused Gracie FIELDS, whom she displaced as top female singer of her day, considerable annoyance.

She toured widely, entertaining Allied troops with ENSA and winning fans throughout Europe and the USA with such classic recordings as 'Yours', 'We'll Meet Again' and 'The White Cliffs of Dover'. Her hits after the war included the transatlantic chart-topper 'Auf Wiedersehn Sweetheart' (1952) and 'My Son My Son', which reached Number One in the UK in 1954. She also hosted her own television shows.

Lynyrd Skynyrd US rock band, which pioneered SOUTHERN ROCK in the 1970s. The band was named after a professor called Leonard Skinner, who had been instrumental in having group leader Ronnie Van Zant (1949–77) thrown out of college. Playing BLUES-influenced HARD ROCK, the band built up a huge following in the southern USA, its songs reflecting the patriotism and bigoted attitudes long associated with the old Confederacy. Less adventurous than its British counterparts, Lynyrd Skynyrd still made a number of classic recordings, among them 'Sweethome Alabama' and 'Freebird'. Best-selling albums included *Second Helping* (1975), *Gimme Back My Bullets* (1976) and *Street Survivors* (1977). The band suffered a body blow in 1977 when singer Van Zant and guitarist Steve Gaines died in an air-crash; Van Zant was subsequently buried with his favourite fishing rod. The remnants of the group reunited under various names with some success through the 1980s.

Lyttelton, Humphrey (1921–   ) British JAZZ bandleader, trumpeter, broadcaster and author, nicknamed Humph, who first emerged as one of the best-known faces in revivalist British jazz in the 1950s. Lyttelton, who was educated at Eton, formed his first jazz band in 1948, and he subsequently became a hugely popular performer of both TRAD and more experimental MAIN-STREAM jazz over the course of the next four decades, appearing on both sides of the Atlantic. He also guested with Duke ELLINGTON and Eddie CONDON, among other notable jazzmen. His own hit compositions have included 'Bad Penny Blues' (1956), which was, so Paul MCCARTNEY explained, the starting point for the BEATLES hit 'Lady Madonna' (1968). He has also written and broadcast extensively on the subject of jazz and collaborated on the popular Trog newspaper cartoon strip.

> Celebrating 40 years as a bandleader – Humphrey Lyttelton and his Band – a special threat for all jazz fans.
> *Evening Argus*, Brighton 1988

M

Ma, Yo-Yo (1955–) French cellist, of Chinese descent, who has established a reputation as one of the most distinguished cellists of his generation. A child prodigy, he gave his first public performance at the age of five and has since won acclaim playing a wide range of works, notably the cello suites of Bach.

Maazel, Lorin (1930–) US conductor and violinist, born in France, who is considered one of the most distinguished contemporary conductors. Maazel was a child prodigy, conducting at the New York World Fair and at the HOLLYWOOD BOWL in 1939 when he was only nine years old. Subsequently he became a violinist with the Pittsburgh Symphony Orchestra before accepting the post of chief conductor of the Berlin Radio Orchestra (1965–75) and then that of music director of the CLEVELAND ORCHESTRA (1972–82); he was also the first US conductor to appear at Bayreuth (1960). In 1984 he resigned as director of the Vienna State Opera after two years amid some acrimony and returned to the Pittsburgh Symphony Orchestra as music director in 1986.

McCartney, Sir (James) Paul (1942–) British singer-songwriter, bassist and pianist, who became one of the legends of pop music in the 1960s as one of the BEATLES. McCartney began his hugely successful career in the late 1950s, when he formed the skiffle group the Quarrymen with fellow-Liverpudlian John LENNON with whom he established an unsurpassed songwriting partnership (*see* LENNON AND MCCARTNEY). While Lennon stayed faithful to his love of ROCK 'N' ROLL and provided the cutting edge of their subsequent compositions, it was McCartney who was largely responsible for their lyrical and poetic qualities.

After the break-up of the Beatles in 1970, McCartney founded his own group, Wings, and continued in much the same vein, although the lack of a Lennon-figure in the new line-up meant that many critics found subsequent material lacked the incisiveness of earlier releases. Nonetheless, such albums as *Band on the Run* (1973) were best-sellers on both sides of the Atlantic, and McCartney kept the band together until 1981, when he ran into problems over drug charges in Japan and embarked on new musical projects, often in collaboration with his wife Linda (Linda Eastman; 1942–). The single 'Mull of Kintyre' (1977) proved his biggest solo success, selling more copies than any other British record previously released. Among his most successful releases since 1981 have been *Pipes of Peace* (1983), *Give My Regards To Broad Street* (1984), the score of the cartoon *Rupert and the Frog Song* (1984), duets with Stevie WONDER, Michael JACKSON and Elvis COSTELLO, and the classical *Liverpool Oratorio* (1991), on which he worked with Carl DAVIS.

McCartney has used some of the huge wealth he has amassed from his music – he has had more Number Ones than any other artist – to acquire the rights to many classic songs, and he now owns the copyright to most of Buddy HOLLY's great hits. In 1979 his unsurpassed success was acknowledged by the music industry in tangible form when he was awarded a unique rhodium disc to mark 200 million album sales.

MacColl, Ewan (James Miller; 1915–89) Scottish folk singer-songwriter and playwright, who was a leading figure in the FOLK revival of the 1950s. MacColl established his reputation when he co-founded Joan Littlewood's Theatre Workshop, collaborating on such highly acclaimed and politically charged entertainments as *Oh What a Lovely War!* He concentrated on developing his interest in folk music after 1950, founding his own clubs and working with, among others, Alan LOMAX and his second wife Peggy SEEGER. Always stressing that folk music should maintain its traditional relevance to the lives of the working people, MacColl wrote several classics himself, among them 'The Manchester Rambler' (1933), 'Dirty Old Town' (1946), about the town of Salford where spent his childhood, 'Ballad of Springhill' (1958), the pop hit 'The First Time Ever I Saw Your Face' (1958) and 'The Shoals of Herring' (1961). He made numerous recordings of traditional music and broadcast regularly on the radio in the late 1950s and early 1960s, exerting a profound influence over his contemporaries. His legacy includes the stereotype of the folk-singer performing with one hand over his ear – a stance he always adopted when singing unaccompanied ballads.

His daughter, Kirsty MacColl (1959–   ), carved out a career in her own right as a singer-songwriter with considerable success, mixing folk with pop on such acclaimed hits as 'There's a Boy Works Down the Chip Shop Swears He's Elvis' (1981).

McCormack, John (1884–1945) Irish tenor, a US citizen from 1917, who enjoyed worldwide fame through his many recordings of both classical music and traditional Irish ballads. He attracted attention after winning a gold medal at the National Irish Festival in 1902, and he subsequently studied in Italy, making his operatic début at Savona in 1906. He appeared regularly at COVENT GARDEN, London, between 1907 and 1914, opposite such singers as Nellie MELBA, and at the METROPOLITAN OPERA, New York, between 1910 and 1918, but he then concentrated on concert work and recording after conceding that he was a better singer than actor. His most popular records ranged from songs by Handel and Mozart to familiar Irish tunes and drawing-room songs, among them such classics as 'I Hear You Calling Me', 'The Irish Immigrant' and 'It's a Long Way to Tipperary'. He never gave up touring and participated in concerts in support of the Red Cross during the Second World War. Honours heaped on him included the rank of papal count (1928).

MacDonald, Jeanette (1903–65) US singer, nicknamed the Iron Butterfly, who was a top film actress of the 1930s and 1940s, when she appeared regularly in now dated and even ridiculed musical films opposite Maurice CHEVALIER and, most famously, Nelson EDDY. Starring in such films as *The Vagabond King* (1930), *The Cat and the Fiddle* (1934), *Naughty Marietta*

(1935), *Rose Marie* (1935), *Sweethearts* (1938) and *Bitter Sweet* (1940), she sang many hits, among them 'Indian Love Call', which was the first song from the shows to sell a million copies. 'Would You' and 'A Heart That's Free'. Her ambition to develop a career in opera in the 1940s was never realized.

McHugh, Jimmy (1894–1969) US composer and pianist, who became one of the most respected Hollywood composers of the 1930s and 1940s. McHugh established his reputation writing revues for the COTTON CLUB, and subsequently contributed such hits as 'Diga Diga Doo', 'I Can't Give You Anything but Love' and 'On the Sunny Side of the Street' to various stage shows in the late 1920s. Recruited by Hollywood in 1930, he wrote the scores for countless movies, of which the most successful included *Singing the Blues* (1931), *Cuban Love Song* (1931), *Dinner at Eight* (1933), *Have a Heart* (1934), *Every Night at Eight* (1935), *Roberta* (1935), *That Certain Age* (1938), *Happy Go Lucky* (1943) and *Calendar Girl* (1947). Among his best-known compositions and collaborations were 'I'm in the Mood for Love', 'Lovely to Look At', 'I Feel a Song Coming On', 'It's a Most Unusual Day' and 'Coming in on a Wing and a Prayer'.

McKellar, Kenneth (1927–   ) Scottish tenor, who is best known for his many recordings of traditional Scottish airs and other light music since the 1950s. He began his career as a star of opera with the Carl Rosa Company in 1953, but he later traded on his Scottish identity with great success, making many recordings and appearances on television.

Mackerras, Sir Charles (1925–   ) Australian conductor, born in the USA, who is particularly associated with the works of Leoš JANÁČEK, which he helped to popularize in the UK. He was employed initially as an oboist with the Sydney Symphony Orchestra (1943–46) but subsequently became a champion of Janáček while studying in Prague and conducted the British premières of such works as *The Makropoulos Affair* (1964). He served as conductor of the Hamburg State Opera (1965–69), of the Sadler's Wells Opera (1970–77) and of the Sydney Symphony Orchestra (1982–85) before taking up the post of music director of the WELSH NATIONAL OPERA (1986–92). In addition to works by Janáček, he has won acclaim for interpretations of Gluck, Handel and Mozart as well as with his own ballet scores *Pineapple Poll* (1951), which was based on the music of Sir Arthur Sullivan, and *The Lady and the Fool*, inspired by Verdi.

McLaughlin, John (1942–) British RHYTHM-AND-BLUES guitarist, who emerged as a leading figure in the JAZZ-ROCK movement of the 1960s and 1970s and worked with many of the leading FUSION pioneers. In the 1950s McLaughlin taught himself to play the BLUES, which he did with extreme dexterity, and he went on to collaborate with such artists as Georgie FAME and Miles DAVIS, playing on the latter's highly influential albums *In a Silent Way* (1969) and *Bitches' Brew* (1970). In 1971 he founded the Mahavishnu Orchestra to explore the possibilities of jazz-rock with a strong Indian influence and subsequently established a loyal cult following with such albums as *The Inner Mounting Flame* (1972) and *Birds of Fire* (1973). He disbanded the Mahavishnu Orchestra in 1976 and worked with his own Shakti acoustic quartet before moving to Paris to form a partnership with pianist Katia Labeque. More recently he has formed a new acoustic jazz trio and has worked with a revived Mahavishnu Orchestra.

McLean, Don (1945–) US singer-songwriter, whose FOLK-influenced songs won a huge audience on both sides of the Atlantic in the 1970s. His classic hit 'American Pie' (1972), a lament about the death of Buddy HOLLY, established McLean as a star, and it was followed by the equally admired 'Vincent', an elegy to Vincent van Gogh, which reached Number One in the UK in the same year (when it also was played on a daily basis at the Van Gogh Museum in Amsterdam). He also wrote hits for other artists, among them 'And I Love You So' for Perry COMO and 'Wonderful Baby' for Fred ASTAIRE, while he himself was the subject of Roberta FLACK's 'Killing Me Softly with his Song'. McLean topped the pop charts once more in 1980 with a cover version of 'Crying', but he has since concentrated on COUNTRY music.

McLean was turned down by 38 record companies before getting a contract. 'American Pie', at 8 minutes 22 seconds, is the longest single ever to reach Number One in the charts (the second longest being the BEATLES classic 'Hey Jude' at just over 7 minutes).

Macon, Uncle Dave (1870–1952) US COUNTRY singer and banjo player, nicknamed the Dixie Dew-drop, who became the first star of the GRAND OLE OPRY. A former vaudeville performer and farmer, he made his first appearance on the show in 1925 and continued his association with it until his death. He made many recordings of traditional rural music, often in collaboration with fiddler Sid Harkreader (d. 1988).

Maconchy, Dame Elizabeth (1907–94) British composer, of Irish descent, who established her reputation in the 1930s with a wide range of compositions that combined traditional forms with more contemporary musical idioms and reflected the influence of Béla BARTÓK. A pupil at the Royal College of Music, where she studied under Ralph VAUGHAN WILLIAMS, and subsequently a music student in Prague, she composed operas, orchestral pieces, ballets, concertos, string quartets and other chamber music.

McTell, Ralph (Ralph May; 1944–) British singer-songwriter and guitarist, who built up a strong reputation on the FOLK circuit in the late 1960s and then had a huge and unlooked-for success in the pop market with the classic ballad 'Streets of London' (1974). This gentle elegy to the homeless has become a standard number in the repertoire of countless buskers and amateur singers, but it remains McTell's only significant foray into the world of pop. More comfortable writing for the likes of FAIRPORT CONVENTION and playing small folk clubs, he has released many respected folk recordings, among them the albums *Spiral Staircase* (1969) and *Bridge of Sighs* (1987). In the 1980s he also wrote music for various children's television programmes.

Mad Fiddler from Philly, the *See* Joe VENUTI.

Maddox, Rose (Roseea Arbana Brogdon; 1925–) US COUNTRY singer, who was one of the first female vocalists to win a significant following among country fans. She began her career as one of the Maddox family group in the late 1930s and won a reputation as a HILLBILLY style singer before striking out on her own in 1959. With such hits as 'Down, Down, Down', 'We're the Talk of the Town' and 'Loose Talk', she did much to break new ground for a whole generation of female singers.

Maderna, Bruno (1920–73) Italian composer, conductor and violinist, who was one of the celebrated progressive composers of the immediate postwar period. A child prodigy, he went on to experiment with SERIALISM as a codirector of the Milan Radio Electronic Studio alongside Luciano BERIO, and he collaborated with such composers as Luigi NONO and Karlheinz STOCKHAUSEN at the summer school at Darmstadt, which he made his home. His works, in which he eventually came to reject serialist techniques, included *Musica du due Dimensioni* (1952), which was the first composition to combine live musicians with recorded sounds, *Continuo* (1958), the stage work *Hyperion* (1965) and the opera *Satyricon* (1973) as well as further electronic pieces.

Madness British pop group, which enjoyed huge commercial success in the late 1970s and early 1980s. Singers Graham 'Suggs' McPherson (1961–) and Chas Smash (Carl Smyth; 1959–), keyboard player Mike Barson (1958–), guitarist Chris Foreman (1958–), saxophonist Lee Thompson (1961–), bassist Mark Bedford (1961–) and drummer Daniel 'Woody' Woodgate (1960–) came together as Madness in 1978 and soon established a reputation as a leading White SKA outfit. Such hits as 'My Girl', 'Baggy Trousers', 'Embarrassment', 'Our House' and 'It Must be Love', accompanied by zany videos, trod a distinctive path somewhere between REGGAE and straight pop and proved popular with dance audiences. 'House of Fun' reached Number One in 1982, and such albums as *One Step Beyond* (1980) and *Complete Madness* (1982) also did well until the group toned down the humour and, in consequence, lost many fans in the mid-1980s. The band split up in 1986 but re-formed briefly in 1988, to release another LP and the single 'I Pronounce You', and again in 1992.

Madonna (Madonna Louise Veronica Ciccone; 1958–) US pop singer and actress, of Italian descent, who became, in the 1980s, the best-selling female singer in music history. After being educated at a convent school and having worked as a waitress, she embarked on a career as a pop singer, drummer and dancer in the late 1970s, first entering a recording studio in 1982. A year later she had her first hit with 'Holiday', and, after chart success with 'Lucky Star' (1984) and critical acclaim in the film *Desperately Seeking Susan* (1984), she triumphed around the world with the album – and Number One single – *Like A Virgin* (1984), which encapsulated her image of the 'knowing innocent', sexually alluring but at the same time aggressively independent.

Videos accompanying Madonna's hits capitalized on her visual appeal and promoted her secondary career in films, although her performances in such movies as *Shanghai Surprise* (1986) and *Dick Tracy* (1990) attracted mixed reviews. As a singer, she consolidated her status as the world's top female star with hugely successful international tours and with further hit releases in a ROCK-CUM ELECTRO-FUNK style, among them *Like a Virgin* (1985), *True Blue* (1986), which sold over 11 million copies and got to Number One in 28 countries, and *Like A Prayer* (1989), and the singles 'Into the Groove' (1985), 'Papa Don't Preach' (1986), which raised hackles by discussing teenage pregnancy, 'True Blue' (1986), 'La Isla Bonita' (1987), 'Who's That Girl' (1987), 'Vogue' (1990), which was her seventh Number One single, 'Justify My Love' (1991) and 'Erotica' (1992).

Madonna has never been afraid of courting controversy. Massive media hype has surrounded every new project, new heights being reached with the home-movie style film *In Bed With Madonna* (1990) and with her publication of a daring volume of photographs wrapped in aluminium foil and simply entitled *Sex* in 1992. Through the ubiquitous use of her image on posters, calendars etc., she remains the most widely recognized sex symbol of her generation. Her marriage (1985) to actor Sean Penn ended in divorce in 1989. In 1997 she won acclaim as singer and actress in the film musical *Evita*.

Mahler, Gustav (1860–1911) Austrian composer, whose revered Romantic compositions bridged the gap between nineteenth-century classicism and twentieth-century progressivism. Born into a Bohemian peasant community, the young Mahler first attracted attention when he delivered a masterly piano recital at the age of 10, and he won a place at the Vienna Conservatory in 1875, eventually embarking on a career as a conductor and pursuing his ambitions as a composer in his spare time. Inspired by his perception that human existence depended on the interplay of beauty and suffering (reflecting in part the troubled relationship of his parents), he created searingly passionate and atmospheric music that ranged from songs and operas to the 10 symphonies, on which his lasting fame chiefly rests.

Mahler developed his symphonic language in the orchestral songs of the cantata *Das Klagende Lied* (*The Song of Sorrow*; 1878–80) and *Des Knaben Wunderhorn* (*The Youth's Magic Horn*; 1888–99) before embarking on his First Symphony while working as a conductor in Leipzig. He accepted posts at the Royal Hungarian Opera in Budapest and in Hamburg but emerged in his full glory only after the death in 1894 of his rival Hans von Bülow, who had observed of Mahler's Second Symphony (1894): 'If that was music, I no longer understand anything about the subject.'

Mahler's Third Symphony (1896) marked the full flowering of his genius, and a year later he was installed as artistic director of the Vienna Court Opera (and subsequently of the VIENNA PHILHARMONIC), with which – in the course of a golden age of Viennese opera – he revolutionized contemporary opera production. Following Mahler's marriage to Alma Schindler in 1902, the Fifth, Sixth and Seventh Symphonies formed a triptych that is regarded as the summit of the composer's achievement, probing the essence of human existence and at the same time reflecting the composer's own experiences. Other works from this period included the song-cycle *Kindertotenlieder* (*Songs of the Death of Children*; 1904).

Mahler left Vienna in 1907. In the same year he suffered the loss of his four-year-old elder daughter and discovered he had a heart condition. His subsequent works, the Eighth Symphony (1907), otherwise known as the *Symphony of a Thousand* because of the large chorus and orchestral forces required in its performance, *Das Lied von der Erde* (*The Song of the Earth*; 1908), which was based on settings of Chinese poems, and the Ninth Symphony (1910)

were the ultimate expressions of his musical philosophy and for many ushered in a new age; his Tenth Symphony remained unfinished until 1964, when it was 'completed' by the British musicologist Deryck Cooke (1919–76).

Mahler died of heart disease at the age of 51 in the wake of a visit to the USA, but the music he left behind – particularly his innovative approach to tonality and harmony – exercised a profound influence on the development of such heirs as Arnold SCHOENBERG, Anton WEBERN and Dmitri SHOSTAKOVICH.

> Don't bother looking at the view. I have already composed it.
> GUSTAV MAHLER, to a guest at his country retreat

> Fortissimo at last!
> GUSTAV MAHLER, on seeing Niagara Falls, 1907

> Mozart.
> GUSTAV MAHLER, last words

> A tolerable imitation of a composer.
> RALPH VAUGHAN WILLIAMS

It is thought that Mahler provided the model for the character Gustav von Aschenbach, in Thomas Mann's novel *Death in Venice* (1911), which was later adapted as an opera by Benjamin BRITTEN (1973) and as a film (with a SOUNDTRACK based on the Fifth Symphony) by Luchino Visconti (1970). The opera concerns the passion that dying novelist Gustav von Aschenbach (a tenor role) conceives for a young boy, Tadzio (played by a dancer), and ends in the writer's death after he decides to stay in disease-stricken Venice where he can be close to the object of his desire. Mann was eventually obliged to acknowledge that Mahler, whom he had met in Munich some time before the composer's death, had been in his mind when he created Aschenbach:

> I not only gave him the great musician's Christian name, but also in describing his appearance conferred Mahler's mask upon him. I felt quite sure that given so loose and hidden a connection there could be no question of recognition by readers.
> THOMAS MANN

mainstream Loose generic term, which is used to describe JAZZ music that bridged the traditional DIXIELAND style and the more complex modernist styles that emerged after the Second World War. The term was later also applied to the rock music purveyed by leading SUPERGROUPS such as the ROLLING STONES and FLEETWOOD MAC in the 1970s, particularly to distinguish their music from the newer forms adopted by various PUNK ROCK and NEW WAVE bands towards the end of the decade.

Malipiero, Gian Francesco (1882–1973) Italian composer, who achieved fame with a number of works combining contemporary musical ideas with the traditions of Renaissance and medieval music. Descended from one of Venice's oldest aristocratic families and the grandson of a noted composer, Malipiero studied at the Vienna Conservatory and later back in Venice, where he wrote his first compositions under the influence of Wagner and Italian Renaissance music, and in Paris. His presence at the notorious first performance of Igor STRAVINSKY's *Rite of Spring* in 1913 prompted him to take in contemporary influences and, after recovering from the trauma of the First World War, he realized one of his most important works, *Setti Canzoni* (*Seven Songs*; 1918–19), which provided musical settings of seven scenes performed in mime. Other works included 11 symphonies, the ballet *Pantea* (1917–19), a musical version of Pirandello's *Favola del Figlio Cambiato* (which was subsequently banned by Mussolini), and operas based on Shakespeare's *Julius Caesar* (1934–35) and *Antony and Cleopatra* (1937). He also produced a complete edition of the works of Monteverdi.

Malvern Festival Annual music and drama festival, which was first held at Malvern, Hereford and Worcester, in 1929. The festival, established by Sir Barry Jackson (1879–1961), was originally dedicated to theatrical performances, and the first performances of many of George Bernard Shaw's most celebrated plays were staged there. The outbreak of war in 1939 curtailed the tradition and, with the single exception of 1949, it was not revived until 1977, when it was reinstituted as a festival of both drama and music. Particular emphasis is laid on the works of Shaw and of Sir Edward ELGAR, who lived nearby and is actually buried in Malvern.

Mamas and the Papas, the US FOLK-ROCK vocal group, which was one of the most popular Californian acts of the 1960s. The group consisted of 'Mama' Cass Elliott

(Ellen Naomi Cohen; 1943–74), John Phillips (1935–), Phillips's wife Michelle Gilliam (1944–) and Denny Doherty (1941–), and it was closely associated with the burgeoning hippy movement. The Mamas and the Papas came together in 1964 and lasted just four years before disbanding, largely because of Phillips's drug addiction and the breakdown of his marriage. In that time, the group established itself as a major attraction with stirring live performances and such hit singles as 'California Dreamin'' (1966), 'Monday, Monday' (1966), 'Dedicated to the One I Love' (1967). Phillips, who also wrote the hippy anthem 'San Francisco' (1967), was the mastermind behind the celebrated MONTEREY POP FESTIVAL of 1967, which marked the high point of flower power. The three remaining members of the group reunited in 1986, with McKenzie Phillips (daughter of John Phillips and Gilliam) and Spanky McFarlane sharing 'Mama' Cass's role and Scott McKenzie (1944–) subsequently replacing Doherty.

mambo Genre of JAZZ music of the 1940s and 1950s in which the rhythms of Cuban FOLK MUSIC were combined with modern jazz elements to produce a more earthy version of the rumba. Among the leading exponents were the bands of Anselmo Sacasas, Julio Gutierrez, Tito Rodriguez and Perez PRADO and such progressive jazz stars as Dizzy GILLESPIE and Charlie PARKER.

Man in Black, the *See* Johnny CASH.

Man with the Golden Flute, the *See* James GALWAY.

Man with the Orchid-lined Voice, the *See* Enrico CARUSO.

Manchester Group, the Loose association of several promising young English composers, who came together while students at the Royal Manchester College of Music in the 1950s. Dedicated to exploring the new ideas that proliferated throughout European classical music after the Second World War, they included such prestigious names as Harrison BIRTWISTLE, Peter MAXWELL DAVIES, Alexander GOEHR and John OGDON.

Manchester's Beatles *See* the HOLLIES.

Manchester's Brenda Lee *See* Elkie BROOKS.

Mancini, Henry (1924–94) US composer,

conductor, arranger and pianist, who emerged as one of the most respected writers of film scores in the early 1960s. Mancini studied at the Julliard School and was pianist with the Glenn MILLER orchestra before establishing himself as a composer for the cinema and television. His most successful scores include those for *Touch of Evil* (1958), *The Pink Panther* (1963), *Breakfast at Tiffany's* (1961), which won an Academy Award for best score and included the OSCAR-winning 'Moon River', Zeffirelli's *Romeo and Juliet* (1969) and *Victor/Victoria* (1982), for which he received another Academy Award. His music for television's *Peter Gunn* series (1958) earned him one of some 20 GRAMMIES he collected in all. Besides his screen music, he also composed the concert suite *Beaver Valley* (1937).

Manfred Mann British pop group, which established an international reputation during the 1960s. Singer Paul Jones (Paul Pond; 1942–), guitarist Mike Vickers (1941–), later replaced by Jack Bruce (*see* CREAM) and Klaus Voorman (1942–), South African-born keyboard player Manfred Mann (Michael Lubowitz; 1940–), bassist Dave Richmond (1942–), who was later replaced by Tom McGuinness (1941–) and drummer Mike Hugg (1942–) came together in 1962 and had their first big hit with '54321', the signature tune of the television pop show *Ready, Steady, Go*, in 1964. Among the most successful releases that followed were several COVER versions of DYLAN classics – notably 'If You Gotta Go, Go Now' (1965), 'Just Like a Woman' (1966) and 'Mighty Quinn' (1968) – and their own 'Do Wah Diddy Diddy' (1964) and 'Pretty Flamingo' (1966). Mike d'Abo (1944–) replaced Jones in 1966, and the hits continued until 1969 when the group split up to pursue new projects. A later reincarnation of the group – Manfred Mann's Earth Band – had a US Number One in the 1970s with 'Blinded by the Light'. The band was re-formed in 1994.

The group's tour of the Soviet Union in 1965 marked the first time a band from the West had been allowed to perform behind the Iron Curtain.

Manhattan Transfer US vocal group, which enjoyed transatlantic success in the 1970s recording in a nostalgic DOO-WOP style. First formed in 1969, the group, which by 1972 consisted of founder-member Tim Hauser

(1942–), Janis Siegel (1953–), Alan Paul (1949–) and Laurel Masse (1954–), later to be replaced by Cheryl Bentyne, had big hits with such singles as 'Operator' (1975), 'Chanson d'Amour' (1977), 'Boy from New York City' (1980) and 'Spice of Life' (1984).

Manilow, Barry (Barry Alan Pinkus; 1946–) US pop singer and pianist, sometimes nicknamed the Nose, who became an international superstar in the 1970s on the strength of a series of million-selling releases in the EASY LISTENING category. Having worked as a musician for CBS television, Manilow was recruited as arranger and pianist for Bette MIDLER before emerging as a solo star in his own right in 1973. 'Mandy' reached Number One in the UK in 1975; among the numerous hits that followed were 'I Write the Songs' (1976), 'Looks Like We Made It' (1977) and 'Copacabana' (1978), and a series of advertising JINGLES and well-received albums ranging from JAZZ to bland pop ballads. Despite the critics, who found his singing unimpressive, he also established himself as a popular live performer and built up a huge following of devoted (largely female) fans, who treated him as a heart-throb despite his famously large nose. Every one of his first 17 singles reached the Top 40 in the USA, and in 1978 he broke all records when he had three triple PLATINUM albums in just 18 months. Recent releases include *Showstoppers* (1991) and *Hidden Treasures* (1993).

Mann, Barry (1939–) US songwriter, who wrote many hits of the 1960s in collaboration with his wife Cynthia Weil (1942–) as one of the teams recruited by the BRILL BUILDING organization. Among their most successful compositions were 'Uptown', recorded by the CRYSTALS in 1962, 'On Broadway', recorded by the DRIFTERS in 1963, 'We Gotta Get Out of This Place', recorded by the ANIMALS in 1965, 'You've Lost That Lovin' Feelin'', recorded by the RIGHTEOUS BROTHERS in 1965, 'Walking in the Rain', recorded by Jay and the Americans in 1969, 'I Just Can't Help Believing', recorded by B.J. Thomas in 1970, and 'Here You Come Again', recorded by Dolly PARTON in 1977.

Mantovani, Annunzio Paolo (1905–80) Italian-born violinist and conductor, resident in the UK, whose orchestra enjoyed huge success with its carefully created, lush 'cascading strings' sound. Such hits as 'Charmaine' (1951), on which the famous echoed strings effect was introduced, and the British Number One 'Moulin Rouge' (1953) established the Mantovani Orchestra as a great recording favourite; further hits came as the ensemble provided backing for singer David WHITFIELD. Mantovani himself was the first man to sell a million stereo albums, and in 1966 his record company presented him with a diamond-studded baton to mark the sale of 50 million records featuring his orchestra. His own compositions included 'Toyshop Ballet' and 'Serenata d'Amore'.

Mark Twain of Pop, the *See* Randy NEWMAN.

Marks, Johnny (1903–85) US songwriter and radio producer, who is usually remembered for the favourite children's song 'Rudolph the Red-nosed Reindeer' (1949), which sold some 150 million copies. Marks subsequently wrote several other popular Christmas songs, including Brenda LEE's 'Rockin' Around the Christmas Tree' (1960).

Marley, Bob (Nesta Robert Marley; 1945–81) Jamaican REGGAE singer-songwriter and guitarist, nicknamed the Poor Man's Pope, who achieved superstar status in the 1970s and remains the biggest star to emerge from the reggae tradition. Of mixed Anglo-Jamaican descent, Marley had a deprived childhood in the slums of Trench Town, Kingston, and from his early years he interested himself in the radical politics of the Black Power movement, which were to inform much of his most celebrated music. A committed Rastafarian, he championed the rights of the underprivileged both inside and outside music with his band, the Wailers, from the early 1960s when they emerged as a popular SKA outfit. The band eventually adopted the electronic instruments of conventional rock and pioneered the reggae style under the aegis of producer Chris Blackwell (*see* ISLAND RECORDS), who took the group on in 1971.

The albums *Catch a Fire* (1973), *Burnin'* (1973), *Babylon By Bus* (1978), *Exodus* (1977) and *Uprising* (1980), together with massively acclaimed tours, made Marley an international idol and influenced countless Black and White musicians, from the POLICE

to UB40. Among the most successful singles were 'Get Up, Stand Up', 'I Shot the Sheriff', 'No Woman, No Cry', 'Jammin'' and 'Is This Love'.

Marley's international status accorded him considerable political influence in his homeland, and he did what he could to reconcile political opponents and defend the oppressed, efforts that led to both him and his wife Rita being shot and seriously injured in 1976. He collapsed during a concert in 1980 and finally died prematurely of lung cancer at the age of 36 in the following year. His son, Ziggy, subsequently emerged as a reggae star in his father's image and did much to keep his message alive.

Marmalade Scottish pop group, which had a series of hits in the 1960s. Singer Dean Ford (Thomas McAleese; 1946–   ), guitarists Junior Campbell (1947–   ) and Pat Fairlie (1946–   ), bassist Graham Knight (1946–   ) and drummer Alan Whitehead (1946–   ) came together in 1966 out of Dean Ford and the Gaylords. The group's hits included a COVER version of the BEATLES' track 'Ob-la-di, Ob-la-da', which reached Number One in 1968, and such lesser efforts as 'Reflections of My Life' and 'Rainbow'. With various changes in personnel, accelerated in the early 1970s when details of the band's sexual liaisons while on tour were unfortunately revealed in the press, the group continued to perform into the 1980s.

Marquee, the Celebrated JAZZ and ROCK club, in Wardour Street, London, from 1964, which was the focus of the British RHYTHM-AND-BLUES movement in the late 1950s and 1960s. The club opened in 1958 and over the years played host to countless influential bands, from such MAINSTREAM jazz stars as Chris BARBER to BLUES INCORPORATED. It is now sited in the Charing Cross Road.

Marriner, Sir Neville (1924–   ) British conductor, who founded the ACADEMY OF ST MARTIN-IN-THE-FIELDS in 1956. He began his career as a violinist with the LONDON SYMPHONY ORCHESTRA but has been appointed to top positions with the Los Angeles Chamber Orchestra (1969–79) and the Minnesota Symphony Orchestra (1979–86) as well as continuing to direct the Academy and making many admired recordings, several with the ENGLISH CHAMBER ORCHESTRA.

Marsalis, Wynton (1961–) Black US trumpeter, who emerged as one of the leading talents of contemporary JAZZ in the 1980s and has enjoyed equal acclaim playing both jazz and classical works at the highest level. He trained at the Berkshire Music Center at Tanglewood and at the Juillard School, New York, before going on to collaborate with such stars as Art BLAKEY and Miles DAVIS. He has also led his own quintet and partnered his brother, the saxophonist Branford Marsalis (1960–). His recordings include such acclaimed jazz albums as *Think of One* (1983) and *Standard Time* (1987) as well as a compilation of nineteenth-century cornet solos. He gave up classical music in order to concentrate on jazz in the late 1980s.

Martha and the Vandellas Black US vocal group, which emerged as one of the top MOTOWN all-girl acts of the 1960s. Martha Reeves (1941–), who swapped her job as a secretary with Motown for a singing career, formed a trio with Rosalind Ashford (1943–) and Annette Sterling (1942–), who was later replaced by Betty Kelly (1944–), and had a string of dance-oriented hits between 1963 and 1972. Among the most successful releases were 'Come and Get These Memories' (1963), 'Heatwave' (1963), 'Quicksand' (1963), 'In My Lonely Room' (1964) and 'Dancing in the Street' (1964). Attempts by Reeves to establish a solo career in the 1970s were not successful.

Martin, Dean (Dino Paul Crocetti; 1917–) US singer, comedian and film actor, who was a pop idol of the late 1940s and 1950s. Having worked as a boxer (as Kid Crochet), steelworker, casino host and fuel pump attendant, Martin took up music in the late 1930s and emerged as a top star after forming a comedy partnership with Jerry Lewis in 1946. As a singer, he had his biggest success with the transatlantic Number One 'Memories are Made of This' (1956); other hits included 'That's Amore' (1953), 'Everybody Loves Somebody' (1964) and 'Gentle on My Mind' (1969). Among his many films are *My Friend Irma* (1949), *Hollywood or Bust* (1956), *Rio Bravo* (1959), *Kiss Me, Stupid* (1964) and *Airport* (1969). He hosted his own television show in the late 1960s and was constantly in the gossip headlines as one of the highliving 'rat-pack' band of stars associated with Frank SINATRA.

> I'd hate to be a teetotaller. Imagine getting up in the morning and knowing that's as good as you're going to feel all day.
> DEAN MARTIN

Martin, Frank (1890–1974) Swiss composer, resident in the Netherlands, who won recognition as one of the leading composers to adapt themselves to the demands of I 2-NOTE composition. He began his career as a teacher at the Jaques-Dalcroze School, Geneva, and established his reputation with such works as the operas *The Tempest* (1956) and *Monsieur Pourceaugnac* (1962), incidental music for a range of classical dramas, the oratorios *In terra pax* (1944) and *Golgatha* (1949), *Le vin herbé* (1941) for 12 voices, strings and piano, and the *Petite symphonie concertante* (1946) for harp, harpsichord, piano and strings.

Martin, Freddy (1906–83) US saxophonist and bandleader, nicknamed Mister Silvertone, whose band enjoyed commercial success performing jazzed-up versions of famous classical pieces. Among the ensemble's biggest hits were 'Tonight We Love' (1941), which was based on Tchaikovsky's B flat Piano Concerto, 'I Look at Heaven' (1942), which was derived from Grieg's piano concerto, 'Bumble Boogie' (1946), which grew out of Rimsky-Korsakov's 'Flight of the Bumble-bee', and 'Sabre Dance Boogie' (1948), derived from Aram KHACHATURIAN. Other best-sellers included 'The Hut-sut Song' (1941), 'Rose O'Day' (1942), 'To Each His Own' (1946) and 'I've Got a Lovely Bunch of Coconuts' (1948).

Martin, George (1926–) British producer, who achieved lasting fame through his enduring association with the BEATLES in the 1960s. Having trained as a classical oboist, he joined EMI in 1950 and became head of the company's Parlophone label. He signed the Beatles in 1962 after being approached by Brian EPSTEIN and worked closely with them throughout their career, having a direct influence on how their greatest songs were recorded and suggesting backings and so on. The group stayed with him even after he left EMI and set up his own company in 1965. The summit of his contribution was marked by *Sergeant Pepper's Lonely Hearts Club Band*, much of the orchestral backing on which was scored by Martin himself. Other stars with whom Martin worked included Sir Thomas BEECHAM, Cleo LAINE, FLANDERS AND SWANN, Peter Sellers, Cilla BLACK, GERRY AND THE PACEMAKERS, Shirley BASSEY and Jeff BECK. *See also* the FIFTH BEATLE.

Martin, Hugh (1914–) US composer and librettist, who formed a hugely successful partnership with lyricist Ralph BLANE and wrote with him and other collaborators a long series of Broadway and Hollywood hits. He worked as arranger on such stage shows as *The Boys from Syracuse* (1938), *DuBarry was A Lady* (1939) and *Louisiana Purchase* (1940), and included among his film credits *Meet Me In St Louis* (1944) and *Ziegfeld Follies* (1944). Among the shows he wrote for the stage were *Best Foot Forward* (1941), *Love from Judy* (1952) and *High Spirits* (1964).

Martin, Mary (Virginia Martin; 1913–90) US actress and singer, who was a leading star of the Broadway stage from the 1940s to the 1960s. She made her stage début in 1938 and appeared in her first film a year later, going on to star in a long series of hit musicals. Among her most acclaimed performances were those in the films *Birth of the Blues* (1941) and *Happy Go Lucky* (1943), but she enjoyed more consistent success in the theatre with such hits as *One Touch of Venus* (1943), *Annie Get Your Gun* (1947), *South Pacific* (1949), *The Sound of Music* (1959) and *Hello, Dolly!* (1965), becoming a Broadway legend. Songs associated with her name included 'My Heart Belongs to Daddy', 'I'm Gonna Wash That Man Right Out of My Hair' and 'My Favourite Things'. Her son Larry Hagman became famous as the dastardly J.R. Ewing in the US soap opera *Dallas*.

> Oh, she's all right. If you like talent.
> ETHEL MERMAN

Martinon, Jean (1910–76) French conductor and composer, who was particularly acclaimed for his association with the works of Claude DEBUSSY and other French composers as well as Béla BARTÓK and Sergei PROKOFIEV. Conductor of the Radio Eireann Orchestra (1948–50), the Concerts Lamoureux (1951–57), the ISRAEL PHILHARMONIC (1958–60), the CHICAGO SYMPHONY (1963–69) and the French Radio Orchestra (1968–75), he also wrote a number of symphonies and concertos as well as the opera *Hecube*.

Martinů, Bohuslav Jan (1890–1959) Czech composer, who won acclaim for his many neoclassical compositions and was hailed the most important of Leoš JANÁČEK's successors. Dividing his career between France, Switzerland and the USA, he wrote 13 operas, among them *Julietta* (1937) and *Comedy on the Bridge* (1937), ballets, six symphonies, tone poems and many other orchestral pieces and chamber works, of which the *Double Concerto* (1938) was considered his masterpiece. His most diverting compositions included *La revue de cuisine* (1927), a JAZZ parody in which kitchen utensils come to life.

> I do not perform any miracles. I am merely exact.
> BOHUSLAV MARTINŮ

Martyn, John (1948–) Scottish singer-songwriter, singer and guitarist, who established himself in the FOLK-ROCK movement of the late 1960s and early 1970s. His début album *London Conversation* (1968), marked Martyn out as a promising singer-songwriter, and was followed by such albums as *The Tumbler* (1968) and *Stormbringer* (1970), which repeated much the same formula. He collaborated with PENTANGLE's Danny Thompson in the early 1970s and subsequently switched to a more ROCK-oriented electric sound on such releases as *Solid Air* (1973), *One World* (1977), *Grace and Danger* (1980), on which he teamed up with Phil COLLINS, *Glorious Fool* (1981), *Foundation* (1987) and *The Apprentice* (1990).

Master, the *See* Sir Noël COWARD.

Mathis, Johnny (1935–) Black US singer, who first emerged as a top international star in the style of a latterday CROONER in the late 1950s and eventually became the USA's first Black millonaire. A talented athlete, who was invited to try for the Olympic Games in 1956, he first reached the charts in 1958 and subsequently enjoyed nine hits over the next two years with such numbers as 'The Twelfth of Never' (1957) and 'Misty' (1959). His hits since then have included several best-selling albums and such singles as 'I'm Stone in Love with You' (1975) and 'When a Child is Born', which got to Number One in the UK at Christmas in 1976. In 1979 he provided the singing voice of Miss Piggy in *The Muppet Movie*.

Matthews, Jessie (Margaret) (1907–81)

British singer, dancer and actress, who emerged as a transatlantic star of film MUSICALS in the 1930s. After an impoverished childhood, she made her first stage appearance in 1919 and subsequently starred in many hit shows in New York and London, after first attracting notice coming on as understudy to Gertrude LAWRENCE in *Charlot's Revue* (1924). Among her films were *The Good Companions* (1933), *Evergreen* (1934), in which she danced on the ceiling, and *Head Over Heels* (1937), although a later generation of British audiences knew her best for her title role in the long-running BBC radio series *Mrs Dale's Diary*. Among the songs associated with her name were 'My Heart Stood Still', 'A Room with a View', 'Dancing on the Ceiling' and 'Over My Shoulder'. She was married to fellow actor and singer Sonnie Hale (1902–59).

Maxwell Davies, Sir Peter (1934–   ) British composer, who emerged as one of the leading contemporary British classical composers in the 1970s. Renowned for his enthusiasm for working with the young, Davies has also interested himself in the folklore of Scotland and Orkney, where he lives, using Orcadian themes in such works as *Fiddlers at the Wedding* (1973–74), the Viking chamber opera *The Martyrdom of St Magnus* (1976) and *An Orkney Wedding, With Sunrise* (1985). Other works, which include four symphonies, religious music, a string quartet and further operas, incorporate parodies of medieval and Renaissance music. Among the most acclaimed have been the opera *Taverner* (1968), *Eight Songs for a Mad King* (1969) and *Vesalii Icones* (1969). Early in his career he was a co-founder of the New Music MANCHESTER GROUP; later he also formed the performance group the FIRES OF LONDON (1970), which specializes in his works and those of other contemporary composers.

Mayall, John (1933–   ) British blues singer, guitarist and harmonica player, son of a jazz guitarist, who emerged as one of the most respected BLUES-ROCK performers in the UK in the 1960s. Through his band, the Bluesbreakers, he did much to promote the early careers of many other future stars, among them Eric CLAPTON, John McVie of FLEETWOOD MAC and Mick Taylor, who joined the ROLLING STONES. His albums include *Bluesbreakers* (1966), *Crusade* (1967), *A Hard Road* (1967), *The Turning Point* (1970),

Notice to Appear (1976), *Last of the British Blues* (1978), *Chicago Lines* (1988) and *Wake up Call* (1993).

Mayer, Sir Robert (1879–1985) British patron of music, born in Germany, who contributed greatly to the presentation of classical music in London over the course of his immensely long life. Something of a child prodigy, he was accepted as a piano student at the Mannheim Conservatory at the age of six and subsequently received encouragement from Brahms; however, he opted instead for a career in business. He arrived in the UK in 1896 and married a singer, but took a more active role in music when, in 1923, he founded the Robert Mayer Concerts for Children, which continued to run for many years. Mayer devoted himself to promoting various musical enterprises from 1929, and in 1932 he was a co-founder, with Sir Thomas BEECHAM, of the LONDON PHILHARMONIC ORCHESTRA. He also established (1954) the Youth and Music concerts for older children.

MCA US record label, which emerged as one of the leading labels in the 1960s. Derived from a booking agency that was founded before the Second World War, MCA added the US arm of DECCA to its stable (which also includes CHESS among other prestigious labels) in the early 1960s but struggled in the 1970s and 1980s, despite having many leading COUNTRY stars on the rosta.

Meat Loaf (Marvin Lee Aday; 1947–   ) US rock singer and guitarist, who emerged as a top HEAVY METAL star in the late-1970s. Nicknamed Meat Loaf by his football coach because of his considerable bulk, he formed his first rock band in 1967, appeared in *Hair* and several other rock musicals, joined Ted NUGENT's band, and subsequently established himself as a solo star with the album *Bat Out of Hell* (1978), which topped the charts in many countries and ultimately sold some 5 million copies. Subsequent releases were reasonably well-received, although none equalled his sensational first release, the highlight of which was 'You Took the Words Right Out of My Mouth'. Recent albums include *Blind Before I Stop* (1986), *Meat Loaf Live* (1987), *Bat Out of Hell II* (1993) and *Welcome to the Neighbourhood* (1995).

Mehta, Zubin (1936–   ) Indian conductor, pianist and violinist player, who has ranked among the most celebrated conductors in the world since the 1960s. The son of the founder of the Bombay Symphony Orchestra, Mehta trained at the Vienna Academy and was subsequently appointed as music director of the MONTREAL SYMPHONY ORCHESTRA (1961–67) and of the LOS ANGELES PHILHARMONIC (1962–77), which prospered under his leadership. He has since served (1978–91) as music director of the NEW YORK PHILHARMONIC ORCHESTRA and is music director for life of the ISRAEL PHILHARMONIC. In 1986 he conducted a free open-air concert by the NEW YORK PHILHARMONIC in Central Park, New York, which attracted 800,000 people, a record for a classical concert.

> What would a devout Muslim answer as to which of his wives he preferred? One can have preferences about details only – a dimple here, an oboe there.
>
> ZUBIN MEHTA, refusing to say which orchestra was his favourite

Melanie (Melanie Safka; 1947–   ) US pop singer, who became one of the most celebrated female vocalists during the hippy era of the late 1960s. The story runs that Melanie became a pop singer by accident, walking into the wrong audition room when she turned up to try for an acting part. She was rapidly adopted as a favourite of the flower power movement with such hits as 'Tuning My Guitar', 'Lay Down (Candles in the Rain)', which reflected the fact that fans at her concerts were the first to hold up lighted candles during performances, and her biggest success 'Ruby Tuesday'; subsequent chart-toppers, which included 'What Have They Done to My Song, Ma' and 'Brand New Key', were more overtly commercial. Among her most acclaimed albums were *Candles in the Rain* (1970) and *Gather Me* (1971).

Melba, Dame Nellie (Helen Porter Mitchell; 1861–1931) Celebrated Australian soprano, who was hailed as one of the leading opera stars of her era. Born in Melbourne, she came late to music, only studying singing seriously in Europe after her marriage in 1882. She made her début, as Gilda in *Rigoletto*, in Brussels in 1886 and decided to adopt the name Melba in homage to her home. Such was her success that she went on to appear to great acclaim in London, Paris, New York and many other centres, at her best in such parts as Violetta

in Verdi's *La Traviata*, as Lucia di Lammermoor, as Rosina in *The Barber of Seville* and as Mimi in PUCCINI's *La Bohème*.

Melba's performances as the doomed Desdemona in Verdi's *Otello* often reduced the audience to tears; it was not unknown for her to respond to rapturous applause during the death scene to revive and deliver an impromptu rendition of 'Home, Sweet Home' on a piano wheeled onto the stage – and then to die once more so the act could continue. She was created a Dame of the British Empire in 1918 and eventually retired after a final performance at COVENT GARDEN in 1926, although she made so many come-backs that Australians still describe an announcement of an impending retirement as 'doing a Melba'.

The great singer's memory is preserved rather unexpectedly in two popular foodstuffs – the ice-cream dish *pêche melba*, which was dedicated to her by the celebrated chef Escoffier, and Melba toast, wafer-thin slices of toast often served as an accompaniment to the first course of a meal. This culinary curiosity had its origins in a visit to London during which Melba stayed at the Savoy Hotel. When the great singer was inadvertently served with toast that had become very fragile after being cooked too long in the oven, the staff hastened to apologize. Dame Nellie, however, insisted that she found the toast delicious, and the newly discovered delicacy was named in her honour.

> The first rule in opera is the first rule in life: see to everything yourself.
>
> DAME NELLIE MELBA, *Melodies and Memories*

Melchior, Lauritz (1890–1973) US tenor, born in Denmark, who was considered one of the greatest of Wagnerian tenors. Having studied music in Copenhagen, Melchior made his operatic début as a baritone in 1913, as Silvio in Leoncavallo's *I Pagliacci*, and did not switch to tenor roles until four years later. His COVENT GARDEN début in 1924, playing Siegmund in the *Ring* cycle, was highly acclaimed and launched him as an enormously popular interpreter of such Wagnerian roles as Lohengrin, Parsifal and Tristan, which he sang over 200 times. He also sang at Bayreuth and subsequently starred regularly at the METROPOLITAN OPERA in New York (1929–50), as well as appearing in a number of films.

Melly, George (1926–   ) British JAZZ

singer, nicknamed Goodtime George in reference to his convivial nature and reputation for high living and to the John Chilton number 'Goodtime George', which Melly often renders. He emerged as one of the UK's best-loved entertainers in the 1950s. He distinguished himself as a singer with the band of Mick Mulligan in the 1950s and went on to become a leading art and music critic and media personality. Since the 1970s he has appeared regularly as singer with John Chilton's Feetwarmers, singing mostly TRAD standards and instantly recognizable in his natty suits and hats.

Menotti, Gian Carlo (1911–) Italian composer, resident in the USA since 1928, who established a reputation for his operas after the Second World War. A student of the Milan Conservatory as a boy, he continued his music studies in the USA from 1928. His first opera, *Amelia Goes To the Ball*, was performed there in 1937. The METROPOLITAN OPERA included the work in its repertoire a year later, and Menotti became famous. Among his operatic works since then have been *The Medium* (1945), *The Telephone* (1946), in which a girl is so obsessed with telephones that she insists that her lover proposes from a telephone box rather than face to face, *The Consul* (1949), which was his greatest success and ran for eight months in New York, *Amahl and the Night Visitors* (1951), which was written for television, *The Saint of Bleeker Street* (1954), *The Most Important Man* (1971), *St Teresa* (1982) and *Goya* (1986). Other compositions include symphonies and choral pieces. He was also founder of the Festival of Two Worlds at Spoleto, which aims to provide a point of contact between the European and American musical traditions.

Menuhin, Yehudi (1916–) US-born violinist and conductor, a British citizen since 1985, who is considered by many the most gifted violinist of modern times. Menuhin, who hailed from a well-known family of musicians, attracted attention at an early age and proved his talent with a performance of the Mendelssohn concerto at his professional début in 1924. After further public appearances he was accepted as a pupil by Georges ENESCU, who did much to perfect his already admired technical skills.

As a teenager, Menuhin demonstrated his mastery of Bach, Beethoven and Mozart.

Particularly significant was a performance of Sir Edward ELGAR's concerto in 1932, for which the 16-year-old violinist received instruction from the composer himself. He has since continued to appear as a soloist with great distinction, as well as forming memorable partnerships with Stéphane GRAPPELLI and sitarist Ravi SHANKAR (as he is a Jew controversy surrounded his appearance with the BERLIN PHILHARMONIC under Wilhelm FURTWÄNGLER after the Second World War). On other occasions he collaborated with his sister, the pianist Hephzibah Menuhin (1920–80). He has also served in several influential administrative roles, including those of director of the BATH, Gstaad and Windsor festivals, and in 1962 he founded his own school near London to cater for the educational needs of promising young musicians. He established his own chamber orchestra in 1958 and since 1988 has also conducted the English String Orchestra. His contributions to British music have been acknowledged with numerous awards, culminating in a life peerage in 1993.

> Music creates order out of chaos; for rhythm imposes unanimity upon the divergent, melody imposes continuity upon the disjointed, and harmony imposes compatibility upon the incongruous.
> YEHUDI MENUHIN

Mercer, Johnny (John Herndon Mercer; 1909–76) US lyricist, composer and singer, who emerged as one of the leading lyricists of his generation in the 1930s. Mercer contributed to over 1,000 hit songs between 1930 and his death, collecting no fewer than four Academy Awards, and he worked with such prominent composers as Harold ARLEN, Hoagy CARMICHAEL, Jerome KERN, Henry MANCINI and André PREVIN on numerous acclaimed films and stage shows. Among his most successful hits were 'What'll They Think of Next?', 'Any Place I Hang My Hat is Home', 'Lazybones', 'Too Marvellous for Words', 'Hooray for Hollywood', 'On the Atchison, Topeka and the Santa Fé', 'You Must Have Been a Beautiful Baby', 'Days of Wine and Roses', 'Ac-cent-tchu-ate the Positive', 'Blues in the Night', 'In the Cool, Cool, Cool of the Evening', 'That Old Black Magic', 'One for My Baby', 'Something's Gotta Give' and 'Moon River'.

Merman, Ethel (Ethel Agnes Zimmerman; 1909–84) US singer, of German-Scottish descent, who became a major Broadway and Hollywood star on the strength of her powerful singing voice, which won her the nickname the Golden Foghorn. She first attracted attention as a CABARET singer and was cast in *Girl Crazy* (1930), in which she sang 'I Got Rhythm' and became an overnight sensation. She consolidated her reputation as one of the most extrovert characters of US show business with typically brash performances in such hits as *George White's Scandals* (1931), *Anything Goes* (1934), *Red, Hot and Blue* (1936), *DuBarry was a Lady* (1939), *Annie Get Your Gun* (1946), *Call Me Madam* (1950), *Gypsy* (1959) and *Hello, Dolly!* (1970).

Her films included *Anything Goes* (1936), *Alexander's Ragtime Band* (1938), *Call Me Madam* (1953) and *Journey Back to Oz* (1972), in which she was the Wicked Witch. Among the songs associated with her name were 'There's No Business Like Show Business', 'Life is Just a Bowl of Cherries', 'Anything You Can Do', 'The Hostess with the Mostess' and 'Everything's Coming up Roses'.

> Can you imagine the name Zimmerman in bright lights? It would burn you to death!
> ETHEL MERMAN, explaining her stagename

> Broadway has been good for me – but I've been good for Broadway.
> ETHEL MERMAN

Merrill, Bob (Henry Robert Merrill Lavan; 1921–) US composer and lyricist, who collaborated on some of the most successful stage MUSICALS of the 1950s and 1960s. He was recruited by MGM in 1954 and went on to write the books or scores for such major hits as *New Girl in Town* (1957), *Carnival* (1961), *Funny Girl* (1964) and *Sugar* (1972). His hit songs include 'If I Knew You Were Coming I'd've Baked a Cake' (1950), 'How Much is That Doggie in the Window' (1950), 'My Truly, Truly Fair' (1951), 'There's a Pawnshop on a Corner in Pittsburgh, Pennsylvania' (1952), 'Love Makes the World Go Round' (1958) and 'Don't Rain on My Parade' (1964).

Mersey beat Genre of 1960s pop music as purveyed by several major groups hailing from Liverpool, notably the BEATLES. Other exponents of such uptempo RHYTHM-AND-BLUES-based pop to emerge between 1962 and 1965 included GERRY AND THE

PACEMAKERS and many other lesser bands, all of which hoped to profit by association with the FAB FOUR. The name was derived from the *Mersey Beat* pop newspaper, which did much to promote local bands (John LENNON was a regular contributor under the pseudonym Beatcomber). *See also* TOTTENHAM SOUND.

> This godforsaken city with not a decent theatre or concert-hall, and a climate so evil that no self-respecting singer would set foot in it! It's a catarrhal place that has been the cause through centuries of the nasal Liverpool accent.
> SIR THOMAS BEECHAM

Messager, André (Charles Prosper) (1853–1929) French composer, conductor and organist, who won acclaim for his operettas at the turn of the century. After such early successes as the ballet *The Two Pigeons* (1886), he made his mark on the world of operettas with *Véronique* (1898) and *Monsieur Beaucaire* (1919). Other compositions included a symphony (1875) and much chamber music. As a conductor of note, who held top posts at COVENT GARDEN and in Paris and was himself a pupil of Camille SAINT-SAËNS, he was particularly admired for performances of Wagner and presented the premiere of Claude DEBUSSY's *Pelléas et Mélisande* (1902), of which he was the dedicatee.

Messiaen, Olivier (Eugène Prosper Charles) (1908–92) French composer, who emerged as one of the most influential composers of the postwar period. Messiaen was a child prodigy, winning a place at the Paris Conservatoire at the age of 11 and capturing numerous prizes before beginning a career as a professional organist (he was organist at the church of the Trinité in Paris for some 40 years). Among his earliest compositions to attract attention was *L'Ascension* (1934), one of many works to reflect the influence of Catholic mysticism. A prominent member of the YOUNG FRANCE group of composers, he spent much of the Second World War in a prison camp, but continued to compose, his *Quartet for the End of Time* actually being performed behind barbed wire in 1941.

After the war Messiaen built up a reputation as a teacher of music theory – his pupils included Pierre BOULEZ – and he consolidated his standing as one of France's most promising composers with such works as the *Turangalîla-symphonie* (1948), which reflected the influence of Indian music, the *Livre d'orgue* (1951), *Reveil des oiseaux* (1953), *Chronocromie* (1960), *Couleurs de la cité céleste* (1963) and *Et exspecto resurrectionem mortuorum* (1964), which was dedicated to the memory of those killed in both world wars. Among his most important later works, which continued to draw inspiration from nature – particularly birdsong – and from medieval music, were such pieces as *La Transfiguration* (1969), *Des Canyons aux étoiles* (1974), the opera *Saint François d'Assise* (1983) and *La Ville d'En-Haut* (1987). Rejecting the doctrines of ATONAL-ITY and NEOCLASSICISM, he developed his own system of modal harmony.

> Fantastic music of the stars.
> KARLHEINZ STOCKHAUSEN

> Little more can be required to write such things than a plentiful supply of ink.
> IGOR STRAVINSKY

Metheny, Pat (1954–) US guitarist, who established a reputation as one of the leading exponents of JAZZ-ROCK FUSION in the 1980s. He made his recording début in 1976 and subsequently formed his own band as well as collaborating with such singers as Joni MITCHELL, Ornette COLEMAN and David BOWIE. His critically acclaimed albums include *American Garage* (1980), *Offramp* (1982), *Song X* (1986), his most daring AVANT-GARDE creation to date, and *Quartet* (1997).

Metropolitan Opera House Opera house in New York, which is the most prestigious venue for opera anywhere in the USA. Home of the celebrated Metropolitan Opera company until it moved to the LINCOLN CENTER in 1966, the Met opened in 1883 and quickly won recognition as a leading international venue. Virtually all the great singers and conductors of the twentieth century have performed there, and many important new works have had their first performance at the house. Conductors at the Met have included such notable musicians as Leopold Damrosch (1832–1885) and his son Walter Damrosch (1862–1950), Gustav MAHLER and Arturo TOSCANINI. James LEVINE was appointed musical director in 1975.

Miami Pop Festival One of the major pop festivals of the hippy era, which was held in Miami in 1968. Some 90,000 people flocked to see such stars as FLEETWOOD MAC, the GRATEFUL DEAD, Marvin GAYE and Chuck BERRY.

Michael, George (Georgios Kyriacos Panayiotou; 1963–) British singer-songwriter, who enjoyed huge commercial success as a heart-throb of the 1980s first as a member of the TEENY-BOP duo Wham! and then on a solo basis. As Wham!, with Andrew Ridgeley (1963–), Michael was regularly in the British Top 10 in the mid-1980s with such dance hits as 'Bad Boys' (1983), 'Wake Me up Before You Go-go', which topped the charts on both sides of the Atlantic in 1984 and 'Last Christmas' (1984). Even while Wham! was still together, Michael had similar success as a solo artist with the Number One single 'Careless Whisper' (1984) and 'A Different Corner' (1986) and, wishing to be taken more seriously as a SOUL artist, he declared Wham! to be defunct in 1986.

The solo album *Faith* (1987) reached Number One in both the USA and the UK and made Michael the first performer to sell a million CDs (he also became the first White artist to top the r 'n' b charts in the USA). *Listen Without Prejudice* also reached Number One in the USA in 1990. Among the singles were 'Faith', 'Father Figure', 'I Knew You Were Waiting (for Me)', on which he duetted with Aretha FRANKLIN, and 'Don't Let the Sun Go Down on Me', which raised money for Aids research. 'I Want Your Sex' (1987) suffered after various radio stations refused to play it. 'Jesus to a Child', 'Fastlove' and the album *Older* (1996) reached Number One in the UK. An attempt to escape a restrictive long-term contract with Sony in 1994 met with widely-publicized failure in the courts.

Much of Michael's success depended on his appeal as a sex symbol; it was reported that he put a shuttlecock down his trousers before making appearances on stage.

middle eight The middle section of any piece of music, whether of eight bars or not.

middle-of-the-road Music that is not radical in terms of delivery or content. The description, often shortened to MOR, is usually applied to the kind of bland POP or SOFT ROCK suitable for family consumption that is peddled by a core of artists featured in the charts. Those to turn such music into a fine art over the years have included such outfits as ABBA and the CARPENTERS and a majority of COUNTRY artists.

Midler, Bette (1945–) US singer and film actress, nicknamed the Divine Miss M., who owes her first name to her parents' admiration of Bette Davis. She began her career as one of the chorus in *Fiddler on the Roof* in New York and rose to the role of leading lady before building a reputation as a somewhat raunchy entertainer and singer of mixed BLUES, ballads and ROCK 'N' ROLL (her early hits being produced in collaboration with accompanist Barry MANILOW). Her film roles have included the OSCAR-nominated lead part in *The Rose* (1979), which was loosely based on the life story of Janis JOPLIN.

Milhaud, Darius (1892–1974) French composer, who, as one of Les SIX, emerged as a leading contemporary composer between the wars, when he explored the concept of polytonality and wrote several influential jazz-tinged works. A student of the Paris Conservatoire, he mixed with the most progressive writers and musicians of his generation, working particularly closely with the writers Francis Jammes, who collaborated with him on his first opera, *La Brebis égarée* (1915); Paul Claudel, who contributed the libretto of *Christophe Colomb* (1928) and invited Milhaud to compose incidental music for three adaptations of Aeschylus – *Agamemnon* (1913), *Les Choëphores* (1915) and *Les Euménides* (1922); and Jean Cocteau.

During the First World War Milhaud travelled to Brazil as Claudel's secretary and was exposed to the rhythms of Latin-American music, as reflected in his dance suite *Saudades de Brazil* (1921), but even more important was his first exposure to JAZZ, which came during a visit to London in 1920 and was consolidated on a trip to New York in 1922. His ballets *Le Boeuf sur le toit* (1919) and *La Création du monde* (1923) were among the first classical compositions to take in the influence of this music and as such exerted a profound influence on other contemporary composers.

Despite a degree of disability due to rheumatoid arthritis, Milhaud continued to compose prolifically through the 1930s and, after leaving France during the Second World War, in the USA. He returned to France in 1947 and added many more acclaimed works to the list – some influenced by Hebrew FOLK MUSIC – as well as undertaking teaching duties on both sides of the Atlantic for many years. His other compositions included further large-scale operas, 12 symphonies, 19 quartets and pieces for the piano.

> I have no aesthetic rules, or philosophy, or theories. I love to write music. I always do it with pleasure, otherwise I just do not write it.
> DARIUS MILHAUD

> Darius Milhaud is the most gifted of us all.
> ARTHUR HONEGGER

> The worst of it is that you get used to them.
> CHARLES-MARIE WIDOR, of Milhaud's dissonances

Miller, (Alton) Glenn (1904–44) US trombonist, bandleader and arranger, who led one of the most acclaimed SWING bands of them all and became one of the legends of twentieth-century music following his tragically early death. Miller joined his first band as a trombonist in the mid-1920s and, after service under jazzmen such as Benny GOODMAN and the DORSEY brothers, formed his own orchestra in 1937. This first ensemble had to be broken up within months for financial reasons, but its successor, formed almost immediately, quickly established itself as one of the top outfits of the era on the strength of such Miller classics as 'Moonlight Serenade' (1939), which he wrote initially as an exercise, 'Little Brown Jug' (1939), 'In the Mood' (1939), 'Pennsylvania 6–5000' (1940), 'Tuxedo Junction' (1940), 'Chattanooga choo-choo' (1941) and 'Kalamazoo' (1942). The band appeared in the films *Sun Valley Serenade* (1941) and *Orchestra Wives* (1942), but further progress was disrupted by the USA's entry into the Second World War. Miller assumed control of an all-star band in the US army air force in 1942, but was presumed dead when the aircraft in which he was travelling from England to France disappeared in fog over the Channel (the wreckage was never found). His band continued in operation for a few years under other leaders.

The story of Miller's brief career at the top was retold in the film *The Glenn Miller Story* (1953), starring James Stewart.

A bandleader I used to work for always

announced any Glenn Miller number by saying, 'You know Glenn Miller, he did the music for World War II'.

ALAN ELSDON, on BBC radio's *Jazz Score*

Glenn Miller who became a legend in his own lifetime due to his early death.

NICHOLAS PARSONS

Miller, Mitch (1911–   ) US conductor and producer, who had huge commercial success in the 1950s with a series of singalong albums in an EASY LISTENING vein. He also backed many of the most popular balladeers of the era. Having trained as an oboist, he was recruited by COLUMBIA Records and released numerous albums of light music in collaboration with such stars as Frankie LAINE, Johnny MATHIS and Johnnie RAY. His orchestral arrangements were typically highly dramatic and made frequent use of various gimmicky sounds, from cracking whips to the calls of geese. Among his biggest hits were 'The Yellow Rose of Texas' (1955) and such best-selling LPs as *Sing Along with Mitch* (1958). His antipathy to ROCK 'N' ROLL resulted in Columbia lagging far behind other companies in signing emerging stars of the 1950s and 1960s, and among those he turned away were Elvis PRESLEY and Buddy HOLLY.

Miller, Roger (1936–92) US COUNTRY singer-songwriter, who had considerable commercial success in the 1960s. Born in Texas, he wrote hits for singers like Andy WILLIAMS and others before establishing himself as a performer of his own material in 1960. He then won a big following with a mixture of comedy songs and ballads, ranging from 'You Can't Roller Skate in a Buffalo Herd' (1966) and 'Chug-a-lug' (1964) to 'Little Green Apples' (1968) and the British Number One hit 'King of the Road' (1965). Among the lesser hits that followed were 'England Swings' (1965). He returned to the limelight in 1985 with the MUSICAL *Big River*, based on Mark Twain's *Huckleberry Finn*, which proved highly successful on Broadway and won a Tony Award for Best Musical of the Year.

Miller, Steve (1943–   ) US rock singer-songwriter and guitarist, nicknamed the Space Cowboy, who emerged as an enduring BLUES-ROCK attraction in the 1970s. Miller first learned to play guitar with college friend Boz SCAGGS (his first instrument a gift from Les PAUL) and subsequently

enjoyed chart success leading the Steve Miller Band on such albums as *Sailor* (1968), *The Joker* (1973), the title track of which got to Number One, *Fly Like An Eagle* (1976), from which came such hit singles as 'Rock 'n' Me' and 'Fly Like an Eagle' and *Abracadabra* (1980), which provided another chart-topper in the shape of the title track. More recent releases include *Living in the 20th Century* (1987) and *Born 2 B Blue* (1988). The band was one of the star attractions at the MONTEREY POP FESTIVAL.

Millinder, Lucky (Lucius Millinder; 1900–66) US bandleader, who was among the most popular bandleaders of the 1930s and 1940s. As leader of the Mills Blue Rhythm Band (1933–38), he emerged as a top exponent of the HOT style and recruited many outstanding musicians, among them Dizzy GILLESPIE and Eddie 'Lockjaw' DAVIS. Subsequently he adopted a BLUES-tinged style and worked with the singers Rosetta THARPE and Wynonie Harris (1915–69). He eventually broke up his BIG BAND in 1952, after which he made the occasional comeback but was otherwise obliged to diversify with radio presenting, salesmanship and fortune-telling.

No musician himself, he could not even read music. Among his band's odder recordings was the less-than-ecstatically received wartime number 'We're Gonna Have to Stop the Dirty Little Jap'.

Million-dollar Session, the Legendary recording session that took place at the celebrated Sun Record Studio in Memphis on 9 December 1956. Present to record a number of songs that included 'Blueberry Hill' and 'Peace in the Valley' were Elvis PRESLEY, Johnny CASH, Carl PERKINS and Jerry Lee LEWIS. The session was duly recorded, although the tapes of this unique occasion have never been officially released. A reunion, with Roy ORBISON taking Presley's place, was staged in 1985.

Mills Brothers, the US vocal group, which enjoyed an enduring reputation as a top act from the 1930s to the 1970s. The brothers John (1911–36), Herbert (1912–89), Harry (1913–82) and Donald (1915–   ) established a local following in Ohio in the 1920s and were given their own radio programme in 1931. Among their biggest hits were 'Tiger Rag' (1930), on which they imitated various instruments, 'Goodbye Blues',

'Glow Worm', 'Diga Diga Doo', 'You Always Hurt the One You Love' and the Number One 'Paper Doll', which sold over 6 million copies in 1942. Several of their hits were recorded with Bing CROSBY and Louis ARMSTRONG. The death of John Mills in 1936 led to his replacement by his father, John (1882–1967).

Mingus, Charles (1922–79) Black US JAZZ bassist, bandleader and composer, of mixed US, Chinese, Swedish and British descent, who emerged as one of the top jazzmen of his generation despite his insecure and often irascible nature. Born on the West Coast, he joined his first band while he was still in his teens, and he subsequently won a reputation as a supremely gifted string bass player, playing for stars like Louis ARMSTRONG, Lionel HAMPTON and Duke ELLINGTON. As a confederate of performers such as Charlie PARKER, Miles DAVIS, Thelonious MONK and Dizzy GILLESPIE, he became one of the pioneers of modern jazz, and he exerted a profound influence by stretching the perceived capabilities of the jazz bass.

Determined to defy racist attitudes towards Black musicians, he founded his own record company in 1952 and a Jazz Musicians Workshop a year later, insisting on choosing the course of his own career himself and also giving opportunities to other promising players. He made many live recordings on both sides of the Atlantic in the 1960s and 1970s and built up a devoted following, although he was often in difficult financial circumstances and always disturbed by his nervy sensitivity to racial injustice and persecution. Among his most acclaimed (and characteristically highly complex) compositions were 'All the Things You C-sharp' (1955), which was derived from Jerome KERN, 'Pithecanthropus Erectus' (1956), 'Better Git It in Your Soul' (1959) and 'Meditations for a Pair of Wirecutters' (1964). He was also author of a remarkable autobiography, *Beneath the Underdog* (1971).

All the good ones are colourless.
CHARLES MINGUS, of his musicians

minimal music Genre of 'modern' classical music of the 1960s, which was a musical equivalent of 'op art'. Minimal music was characterized by endless repetition of a simple, brief musical figure or melody, often with two or more musicians playing deliberately out of phase with each other, thus creating shifting sound patterns. Mind-numbing monotony could be one effect, similar to that evoked by some narcotics-induced African and pop drumming. Although a US invention, it was for a time promoted in the UK by the Marxist composer Cornelius Cardew (1936–81). Among the more successful works that employed the method were *Four Organs* (1969) by Steve REICH and Philip GLASS's *Music in Fifths* (1969).

minipiano Miniature piano of the kind that enjoyed a brief vogue between the wars. The British firm of W.G. Eavestaff first introduced such instruments in the UK in 1932. The Eavestaff model was just 2 feet 9 inches (84cm) high and 'made to harmonize with every type of decoration'.

Minister of Enjoyment, the *See* KING SUNNY ADE.

Minnelli, Liza (1946–   ) US singer and actress, daughter of Judy GARLAND and film director Vincente Minnelli, who emerged as a top star of the film MUSICAL in the 1960s. Having inherited much of her mother's talent and personality, she quickly established herself as a star of almost equal standing through her Oscar-winning performance in the screen version of *Cabaret* (1972), in which she sang such classics as 'Cabaret' and 'Money, Money'. Other hits included the stage shows *Best Foot Forward* (1963) and *Chicago* (1975) and the films *Journey Back to Oz* (1972), *That's Entertainment* (1974) and *New York, New York* (1977). She overcame addiction to tranquillizers in 1984.

Minton's Playhouse US night club, in Harlem, New York, where the BEBOP style had its birthplace. Run by bandleader Teddy Hill (1909–78), the club hosted regular celebrity nights, which fostered collaboration by such emerging talents as Dizzy GILLESPIE, Coleman HAWKINS, Charlie CHRISTIAN, Charlie PARKER and Lester YOUNG, who were otherwise constrained by the demands of the BIG BANDS and other ensembles that provided them employment. The experiments pursued in the course of these celebrity nights in the early 1940s laid the foundation of the progressive style that was to dominate the development of postwar JAZZ.

Miranda, Carmen (Maria do Carmo Miranda Da Cunha; 1909–55) Latin American singer, nicknamed the Brazilian Bombshell, who became an international star through her appearances in numerous Hollywood MUSICAL films of the 1940s. Born in Portugal and raised in Rio de Janeiro, she arrived in the USA in 1939 and became famous for her colourful performances – and for her lavish costumes, especially her fruit-laden hats. Among the carnival-style hits to issue from her films were 'Cuanto le Gusta', 'South American Way', 'Chica Chica Boom Chic' and 'I Yi Yi Yi Yi'. A heart attack ended a second career as a CABARET star.

Miss Rhythm *See* Ruth BROWN.

Mister Country Music *See* 'Tennessee' Ernie FORD.

Mister Dynamite *See* James BROWN.

Mister Excitement *See* Jackie WILSON.

Mister Five-by-Five *See* Jimmy RUSHING.

Mister Perfectionist *See* Marvin GAYE.

Mister Silvertone *See* Freddy MARTIN.

Mister Teardrop *See* Marty ROBBINS.

Mistinguett (Jeanne-Marie Florentine Bourgeois; 1875–1956) French revue artist, singer, dancer and actress, of mixed Franco-Belgian descent, who became one of the top French entertainers of her generation, notably in partnership with Maurice CHEVALIER. Mistinguett began her career in the music hall but went on to appear in a wide range of entertainments, from revues to light comedies. Among her most famous acts was the scandalous 'Apache Dance', a steamy routine in which she was whipped by a male dancer (in her case, Max Dearly) to Offenbach's 'Valse de rayons' from *Le Papillon*. She teamed up with Chevalier in 1912 and regularly topped the bills with him at the *Folies Bergère* and elsewhere over the next few years, winning admiration for her beautiful legs and extravagant costumes as much as for her singing. Among her most popular songs were such hits as 'Mon homme' (1938). She went on tour to the USA in 1911 and 1951 and to London just once, in 1947.

Mitchell, Joni (Roberta Joan Anderson; 1943–) Canadian singer-songwriter, guitarist and artist, who won almost universal recognition as the most important female singer-songwriter of her generation. Mitchell began as a folk-singer in the early 1960s and made her recording début in 1967 with *Song to a Seagull* (1968). Early compositions to win critical acclaim included 'Big Yellow Taxi', 'Both Sides Now' and 'Ladies of the Canyon'. The album *Clouds* (1969), especially the classic single 'Woodstock', confirmed her as a cult star of the late hippy era, a reputation enhanced by *Blue* (1971), *For the Roses* (1972) and *Court and Spark* (1974), but subsequent albums explored more diverse musical inspirations, with African music and JAZZ leading to new departures on such acclaimed LPs as *The Hissing of Summer Lawns* (1975), *Don Juan's Reckless Daughter* (1978) and *Mingus* (1979), *Wild Things Run Fast* (1982) saw Mitchell adopt a more conventional rock styling, while *Dog Eat Dog* (1985) incorporated sophisticated electronic effects. More recently she has released the albums *Night Ride Home* (1991) and *Turbulent Indigo* (1994) as well as developing her second career as an artist.

mobile A form of modern composition first essayed in the 1950s in which segments of music may be arranged in any order the conductor or musician chooses. Examples include works by Pierre BOULEZ, Luciano BERIO and Karlheinz STOCKHAUSEN.

modern jazz Name often applied to JAZZ music of the postwar period, which denotes the styles that developed after the first emergence of BEBOP in the early 1940s. As a genre, its characteristics include more liberated attitudes towards the demands of rhythm and harmony than were usual in the SWING era that preceded it.

Modern Jazz Quartet Influential US JAZZ group, which was at the forefront of contemporary jazz from its foundation as the Milt Jackson Quartet in 1951 until its effective disbandment in 1974. The quartet – pianist John LEWIS, vibes player Milt JACKSON, bassist Percy Heath (1923–) and drummer Kenny CLARKE, who was replaced by Connie Kay (Conrad Henry Kirnon; 1927–) in 1955 – pioneered the development of so-called 'chamber jazz' in the 1950s and 1960s, marrying jazz with classical motifs. Among its most acclaimed recordings were *Django* (1956), *Fontessa* (1956) and the score for Roger Vadim's film *No Sun In Venice* (1957). The quartet re-formed for a tour of Japan in 1981 and have since continued to appear on a fairly regular, though informal, basis.

modernism In the terminology of contemporary classical music, the progressive style that prevailed in European and US music between the 1930s and the 1960s, as exemplified by the works of such composers as George ANTHEIL, Béla BARTÓK, John CAGE, Aaron COPLAND, Arnold SCHOENBERG and Igor STRAVINSKY. Similarly adventurous and innovative composition from the 1960s was often, in consequence, labelled post-modernist. *See also* ALEATORISM; ATONALITY; FUTURISM; 12-NOTE MUSIC.

A century of aeroplanes deserves its own music.
CLAUDE DEBUSSY

I occasionally play works by contemporary composers for two reasons. First, to discourage the composer from writing any more, and secondly to remind myself how much I appreciate Beethoven.
JASCHA HEIFETZ, 1961

What we know as modern music is the noise made by deluded speculators picking through the slagpile.
HENRY PLEASANTS, *The Agony of Modern Music*, 1955

Three farts and a raspberry, orchestrated.
SIR JOHN BARBIROLLI, on modern music

Monaco, James V. (1885–1945) US songwriter, nicknamed Ragtime Jimmy, who was responsible for a number of enduring standards first heard in popular stage shows and movies. Born in Italy, he emigrated to the USA as a child. His first published song was 'Oh, Mr Dream Man' (1911), and among his many hits were such classics as 'Row, Row, Row' (1912), 'You Made Me Love You' (1913), 'What Do You Want to Make Those Eyes at Me For' (1916), 'My Heart is Taking Lessons' (1937), 'I Can't Tell You Why I Love You, but I Do' (1939), 'Too Romantic' (1940) and 'I'm Making Believe' (1944).

Monckton, Lionel (1861–1924) British composer and music critic, who won acclaim for his highly popular MUSICAL comedies at the turn of the century. He had considerable success with the song 'What Will You Have to Drink?' (1891) and consolidated his reputation with such shows as *The Shop Girl* (1894), *The Circus Girl*

(1896), *The Toreador* (1901), *The Arcadians* (1909) and *The Quaker Girl* (1910). His marriage in 1902 to the popular actress and singer Gertie Millar (1879–1952) was less than perfect, and she left him in 1909.

Monk, Thelonious Sphere (Thelious Junior Monk; 1917–82) Black US JAZZ pianist, bandleader and composer, who was one of the most influential figures in jazz after the Second World War and an architect of the BEBOP style. Monk first attracted attention in 1941 after securing the post of pianist at MINTON'S PLAYHOUSE, where his confederates included many up-and-coming talents. He made his recording début with Charles CHRISTIAN and worked with Lucky MILLINDER, Coleman HAWKINS and Dizzy GILLESPIE, before becoming a bandleader in his own right in 1947, the year in which he made some highly influential recordings in company with Art BLAKEY.

He led a range of BIG BANDS and smaller ensembles, of which the most distinguished included the quintet he formed in the late 1950s, when his musicians included John COLTRANE, and the quartet that he led in the 1960s. His career was somewhat disrupted in the early 1950s when he was prevented from performing for several years as a result of (probably false) drug charges. He also toured widely with the Giants of Jazz outfit in the early 1970s and was invited to play at the White House in 1978. His own highly influential compositions included such classics as 'Round Midnight', 'Epistrophy', 'Ruby My Dear', 'In Walked Bud', 'Off Minor', 'Straight No Chaser', 'Misterioso', 'Blue Monk' and 'Well, You Needn't'.

Observers were sometimes inclined to find fault with Monk's technical skills, thrown by the fact that he had developed his own virtually inimitable playing style, breaking conventional rules.

Monkees, the US pop group, which was deliberately created in 1966 as a US response to the BEATLES. The Monkees were brought together for a lively US television series about a fictitious pop group, imitating the zany cheerfulness of the Beatles films. The line-up, selected more for visual appeal than for musical ability, consisted of former US child actor and drummer Mickey Dolenz (1946–), fellow-Americans and guitarists Peter Tork (Peter

Thorkelson; 1945–) and Mike Nesmith (1942–) and another former child star, British singer Davy Jones (1945–). Talented musician Stephen Stills (*see* CROSBY, STILLS, NASH AND YOUNG) was turned down on the grounds that his teeth were not perfect enough. The series was a huge success on both sides of the Atlantic, and several numbers taken from it (written by a team of respected songwriters) became legitimate TEENY-BOP chart hits – among them such classics as 'Last Train to Clarksville', Neil DIAMOND's 'I'm a Believer' and 'Daydream Believer', all of which reached Number One in 1967.

At first, the actors in the series were allowed no input into the music apart from singing the lyrics, but they were determined to prove that they could make the full transition to real pop stars and played the instruments themselves on some of the later releases. Tork and Nesmith nursed bigger musical ambitions and left the group after the Monkees film *Head* flopped in 1969, precipitating its disbanding, although there were popular reunions (without Tork and Nesmith) in 1975, (without Nesmith, now a COUNTRY-ROCK star) in 1986 and (with all four) in 1997.

Monro, Matt (1930–85) British singer, who established himself as a popular balladeer and CABARET star in the late 1950s. He hosted his own radio programme and enjoyed success with several singles produced by George MARTIN, among them 'Portrait of My Love' (1960), 'My Kind of Love' (1961), 'From Russia with Love' (1963), 'Born Free' (1965) and 'Yesterday' (1965).

Monroe, Bill (William Smith; 1911–) US COUNTRY singer-songwriter, guitarist and mandolinist, nicknamed the Father of Bluegrass, who was among the first great stars of the country genre in the 1930s. He made his first recordings in 1936 and formed his own band two years later, after which he became a regular star of the GRAND OLE OPRY. Among the numerous classic recordings that he made were such BLUEGRASS standards as 'Mule Skinner Blues', 'Blue Moon of Kentucky', 'My Little Georgia Rose' and 'Walking in Jerusalem'. He was voted to the COUNTRY MUSIC HALL OF FAME in 1970.

Monroe, Vaughn (1911–73) US bandleader, singer-songwriter and trumpeter,

who proved a popular dance band singer in the 1940s. His baritone voice was unusual in this context and attracted many admirers. Among his hits were 'Let It Snow! Let It Snow! Let It Snow!', which reached Number One in 1945, 'Ballerina' (1947), which also got to Number One, and the 1949 charttopper 'Riders in the Sky'. He also sang in a number of cowboy MUSICAL films, often performing songs he had written himself.

Monsieur 100,000 Volts *See* Gilbert BÉCAUD.

Monsters of Rock British one-day rock festival, which is a showplace for the best in HEAVY METAL, attracting crowds of anything up to the maximum permitted limit of 72,500 fans. Founded in 1980, the festival takes place at Castle Donington racetrack in Leicestershire every summer. To date, 1989 has been the only year in which it has not been held, a result of the only tragedy to mar the history of the event – the deaths of two fans during a performance by GUNS N' ROSES the year before in the panic that ensued after some scaffolding collapsed during high winds. Stars to perform at the festival have included such heavy metal legends as AC/DC, IRON MAIDEN and WHITESNAKE.

Montand, Yves (Yvo Levi; 1921–91) French-Italian singer, dancer and entertainer, who became a hugely popular international star somewhat in the style of Fred ASTAIRE. Having moved to France from Italy with his family as a child, he established his reputation first as a singer with such hits as 'Dans les plaines du Far-West'. Other songs associated with his name include 'C'est à l'aube' and 'Les feuilles mortes'. He worked in CABARET with Edith PIAF during the war years and made his film début in 1946. Among the many movies that followed were *Les Portes de la nuit* (1946), *The Wages of Fear* (1953), *Let's Make Love* (1960), *Aimez-vous Brahms?* (1961), *Grand Prix* (1967) and *Le Sauvage* (1976). He was married to actress Simone Signoret.

Monterey Pop Festival Major US rock festival that took place in Monterey, California over a weekend in June 1967. Among the stars to perform before a huge crowd of 50,000 spectators were Jimi HENDRIX, the undoubted star of the whole thing, the WHO, Otis REDDING, Janis JOPLIN, the BYRDS, JEFFERSON AIRPLANE and the MAMAS AND THE PAPAS, whose John Phillips was one of the key figures in the organization of the event.

The success of the festival, which marked the full bloom of the hippy movement, effectively inaugurated the era of the great pop gatherings that culminated in WOOD-STOCK in 1969.

Monteux, Pierre (1875–1964) French conductor, a US citizen from 1942, who presided over the first performances of many classics of twentieth-century music in the early years of the century and went on to consolidate his status as one of the most distinguished conductors of his generation. Having trained as a violinist, Monteux played the viola before turning to conducting in the 1890s, and he was appointed conductor of the Ballets Russes in 1911. In collaboration with Serge Diaghilev (1872–1929), he conducted the first performances of works by Maurice RAVEL, Claude DEBUSSY and Igor STRAVINSKY – including the sensational première of *The Rite of Spring*, which caused a furore in 1913.

After the First World War Monteux accepted conducting posts at the METRO-POLITAN in New York (1917–19), the BOSTON SYMPHONY ORCHESTRA (1919–24), the CONCERTGEBOUW Orchestra in Amsterdam (1925–29), the Paris Symphony Orchestra (1929–38), the San Francisco Symphony Orchestra (1936–52) and from 1961 (at the age of 86) the LONDON SYM-PHONY ORCHESTRA. He was particularly respected for his consistent championship of works by contemporary composers, and among his pupils was André PREVIN.

Many years after the première of *The Rite of Spring*, Monteux returned to conduct the same work in Paris. This time the audience was unanimous in its applause, provoking Monteux to remark: 'There was just as much noise as last time, but the tonality was different.' He did, however, admit on another occasion: 'I did not like *Le Sacré* then. I have conducted it fifty times since. I do not like it now.'

Montgomery, Wes (John Leslie Montgomery; 1923–68) US JAZZ guitarist, who was considered the most accomplished of Charlie CHRISTIAN's heirs. A self-taught guitarist, he worked for Lionel HAMPTON in the late 1940s and with various trios and quartets, which included his brothers, the bass player Monk Montgomery (1921–82) and vibra-harpist Charles Montgomery (1930–). Other collaborators included

John COLTRANE. His most admired jazz recordings were made in the 1960s.

Montreal Symphony Orchestra Canadian orchestra, which was founded in Montreal in 1954 and has since established a strong international reputation. Conductors of the orchestra have included such distinguished names as Otto KLEMPERER, Zubin MEHTA and Charles Dutoit (1936–).

Moody Blues, the British pop group, which pioneered the development of ART ROCK back in the 1960s. The initial line-up assembled in 1964, was singer and guitarist Denny Laine (1944–), keyboard player and singer Mike Pinder (1942–), succeeded by Patrick Moraz in 1978, flautist and singer Ray Thomas (1942–), bassist Clint Warwick (1949–), eventually replaced by David Lodge (1943–), and drummer Graeme Edge (1942–); Justin Hayward (1946–) joined after Laine left in 1967. Influenced by RHYTHM-AND-BLUES and increasingly in the possibilities being offered by new electronic instruments, the band made the first steps in what was to become the space age music of such PROGRESSIVE ROCK bands as PINK FLOYD in the 1970s. Its most influential album in this regard was the CONCEPT ALBUM *Days of Future Passed* (1967), and later albums such as *Every Good Boy Deserves Favour* (1971) and *Seventh Sojourn* (1972) continued in much the same vein of sometimes pretentious but still best-selling orchestral rock. Among the hit singles were 'Go Now' (1965) and 'Nights in White Satin' (1967). The band continued to record occasionally in the 1970s and 1980s. Hayward's solo albums include *Classic Blue* (1989) and *A View from the Hill* (1997).

Moog Moog SYNTHESIZER, tradename for a brand of synthesizer, which was one of the first effective versions of the instrument, being operated by a relatively conventional keyboard, although initially only one note could be played at a time. Its inventor, the US electronics engineer Robert Moog (1934–), patented his instrument in 1964.

Moore, Gerald (1899–1987) British pianist, who had a long and hugely celebrated career (1925–67) as the world's most admired accompanist. He won massive respect for his collaboration with such stars as Pablo CASALS, Victoria DE LOS ANGELES, Dietrich FISCHER-DISKAU and Elisabeth SCHWARZKOPF.

> Am I too loud?
> GERALD MOORE, title of autobiography, 1962

Moptops, the *See* the BEATLES.

MOR *See* MIDDLE-OF-THE-ROAD.

Moreschi, Alessandro (1858–1922) Italian singer, who was the last genuine castrato. Castrati singers were once commonplace in the musical circles of Italy and other countries, but their role in twentieth-century music has been largely taken by the counter-tenor. Pope Pius X abolished the operation to produce castrato singers in 1903.

Morgan, Helen (1900–1941) US singer and actress, who established a reputation as one of the great torch singers of her generation before her early death. After experience in night clubs and in vaudeville, she won acclaim in such stage shows as *George White's Scandals* (1925 and 1936), *Show Boat* (1927), in which she created the central role of Julie, *Sweet Adeline* (1929) and *Ziegfeld Follies* (1931) as well as in a handful of films. The first torch singer to make a practice of delivering her songs while sitting on the piano, she eventually fell victim to the alcoholism that increasingly disrupted the latter stages of her career.

Mormon Tabernacle Choir US choir, which established a reputation as one of the world's great choirs, famed for its renditions of largely religious works. It was founded by the Mormons in Salt Lake City and is named after the vast Mormon Tabernacle, built in 1867.

Morricone, Ennio (1928–) Italian composer, who has won international recognition for the SOUNDTRACKS he has contributed to numerous films since the 1960s. His arresting scores for such 'spaghetti westerns' as Sergio Leone's *For a Few Dollars More* (1964) and *The Good the Bad and the Ugly* (1966) had a profound impact on other composers for the big screen and established his reputation. Among the most notable of the scores that followed were those for *Exorcist II* (1977) and *The Mission* (1985), which earned him an OSCAR.

Morrison, Jim (James Douglas Morrison; 1943–71) US rock singer, nicknamed the Lizard King, who became a pop legend as lead singer of the DOORS. The son of a rear-admiral, Morrison was the moving force behind the band's colossal success, his messianic good looks and wild behaviour quickly elevating him to cult status and making him a model for all future rock stars.

The notoriety surrounding Morrison's name reached a climax during a concert in Miami in 1969, when he was led off the stage in handcuffs. He was later found guilty of indecency and profanity and threatened with eight years' hard labour. By now the pressures of fame had taken their toll on the charismatic lead singer, and in 1971 Morrison quit the band and moved to Paris, where he hoped to develop a new career as a poet (his idols included the radical and ill-fated French poets Baudelaire, Rimbaud and Verlaine).

In July 1971, a month after the release of *LA Woman*, Morrison reportedly died of a heart attack in his bath after taking a cocktail of drugs and alcohol, one of rock music's most regretted casualties. Rumour had it that his death was faked and he was in hiding – a view seemingly strengthened by the lack of any living witnesses who saw his body. An album of Morrison's poetry was released in 1978 and he became the object of a thriving cult industry.

> I've read a lot and heard a lot about Morrison, but I don't know much about him.
> JOE ELLIOTT

Morrison, Van (George Ivan Morrison; 1945–) Northern-Ireland-born singer-songwriter and saxophonist, nicknamed the Belfast Cowboy, who has enjoyed a lasting reputation as one of the most respected performers to emerge in the late 1960s, although appealing to a cult following rather than to a mass audience. Morrison first attracted attention as a member of Them in the mid-1960s and launched a solo career in 1966. 'Brown Eyed Girl', a hit in 1967, was followed by the album *Astral Weeks* (1968). Among the varied follow-ups, which combined elements of the BLUES, FOLK, SOUL, ROCK and JAZZ, were *Moondance* (1970), *St Dominic's Preview* (1972), *Hard Nose the Highway* (1973), *It's Too Late To Stop Now* (1974), *Into the Music* (1979), *Beautiful Vision*

(1982), *Avalon Sunset* (1989), *Enlightenment* (1990), *Hymns to the Silence* (1991), *Days Like This* (1995) and *The Healing Game* (1997).

Perhaps Morrison's most unexpected outing was the 1989 duet 'Whenever God Shines His Light', on which he collaborated with Cliff RICHARD.

> I know of no music that is more lewd, feelable, hearable, seeable, touchable, that you can experience more intensely than this.
>
> WIM WENDERS, of Van Morrison's music

Morton, Jelly Roll (Ferdinand Joseph Lamott, Lemott or La Menthe; 1890–1941) Black US JAZZ pianist, bandleader and composer, who was one of the most important early jazz pioneers. A native of New Orleans, he played piano for the clients of the city's brothels (also working as a pimp and a boxing and gambling promoter) before moving to Chicago in 1923 and making numerous recordings of his own songs with his own band, the Red Hot Peppers. Although he was never as commercially successful as his rival Louis ARMSTRONG, Morton had a profound influence on jazz of the period and made many innovative and much-copied arrangements (he is often described as the first important jazz arranger). His biggest hits included 'Jelly Roll Blues' (1905), 'King Porter Stomp' (1906), 'Grandpa's Spells' (1923), 'Black Bottom Stomp' (1925) and 'Cannonball Blues' (1926).

Morton was an incorrigible conversationalist and made many recordings (many at the behest of Alan LOMAX) of reminiscences of New Orleans and his musical beginnings. Among his most outrageous claims was that jazz was his invention and that everyone else was stealing it from him. The development of BIG BAND jazz left him behind, and he died in relative obscurity, although he made a number of fairly unexceptional recordings in the early 1940s.

> Jazz is to be played, sweet, soft, plenty rhythm.
>
> JELLY ROLL MORTON

Most, Mickie (1938–   ) British record producer, who won acclaim for his work with numerous top artists of the late 1960s and 1970s. He played a crucial role in the success achieved by such leading stars as the ANIMALS, Jeff BECK, DONOVAN, HOT CHOCOLATE, Suzi QUATRO, MUD and Kim Wilde, many of whom he recorded on the RAK label he founded in 1969.

Mother Church, the *See* APOLLO THEATRE.

Mother of Soul, the *See* BIG MAYBELLE.

Mother of the Blues, the *See* Ma RAINEY.

Motor City Madman, the *See* Ted NUGENT.

Motörhead British rock band, which emerged as one of the top HEAVY METAL bands of the late 1970s and 1980s. Bassist and singer Lemmy (Ian Kilminster; 1945–   ), a one-time roadie for Jimi HENDRIX and former star of HAWKWIND, guitarist Eddie 'Fast Fingers' Clarke, later replaced by Brian Robertson (1956–   ) and drummer Phil Taylor (1954–   ) came together in 1975 – adopting the name Motörhead after the title of the last track Lemmy wrote for Hawkwind – and rapidly established a reputation as one of the hardest (and loudest) rock groups then active. The band's hit albums included *Overkill* (1979), *Ace of Spades* (1980) and *No Sleep Til Hammersmith* (1981). Celebrating the stereotyped life-style of the dedicated rocker, from alcohol and drugs to sexual aggression, the band repulsed many but retained a large, loyal following well into the 1990s, and Lemmy was one of the most striking frontmen of heavy metal. More recent releases include *No Sleep At All* (1988), *1916* (1991) and *March or Die* (1992). The most recent in a long list of line-ups consisted of Lemmy and Taylor with guitarists Phil Campbell (1961–   ) and Wurzel (Michael Burston; 1949–   ).

Motown Celebrated and highly influential US record company, which was founded by Berry GORDY on a borrowed $800 in 1959 and came to dominate Black music in the 1960s. Based in the car town of Detroit (nicknamed 'Motor City' – hence 'Motown'), Motown prospered through the careful (and secretive) management of the careers of a stable of emerging stars, among whom were Stevie WONDER, the SUPREMES, Smokey ROBINSON, Gladys KNIGHT, Marvin GAYE and the JACKSON FIVE. Motor Town Revue tours (1962–65) helped to subsidize the company and to build up an audience as well as providing the artists with an opportunity to hone their live acts.

Gordy always fostered a 'happy family' image, paying his stars salaries until they established themselves. The reality, however, was often quite different, and many top names eventually quarrelled with their boss over his interference with every aspect of their lives and his reluctance to let them control their own destinies and incomes. The company relocated to Los Angeles in 1971.

Mott the Hoople British rock group, which had considerable success in the early 1970s largely as a result of its association with David BOWIE. Formed in 1969, the group initially consisted of singer and pianist Ian Hunter (1946–   ), keyboard player Verden Allen (1944–   ), guitarist Mick Ralphs (1944–   ), bassist Pete 'Overend' Watts (1947–   ) and drummer Dale 'Buffin' Griffin (1948–   ), who called themselves Mott the Hoople after a character in a novel by Willard Manus. The breakthrough came in 1972 with the epic 'All the Young Dudes' single, written and produced by Bowie, which paved the way for a series of hit albums and lesser singles. Line-up changes were frequent, with Morgan Fisher replacing Allen in 1972, Ariel Bender (Luther Grosvenor; 1949–   ) succeeding Ralphs in 1973, and guitarist Mick Ronson (1945–93) being recruited in 1974, shortly before the band split for good. A derivative called Mott failed to have much impact.

mouldy fig In the terminology of JAZZ, a fan or musician who expresses a preference for TRAD jazz music as opposed to more progressive modern styles.

Mountain US rock band, which was among the leading HARD ROCK acts of the early 1970s. Founded in 1969 by bassist Felix Pappalardi (1939–83) and guitarist Leslie West (Leslie Weinstein; 1945–   ), Mountain established its reputation after appearing at WOODSTOCK and with such well-received albums as *Mountain Climbing* (1970) and *Nantucket Sleighride* (1971), which won comparisons with CREAM. The band broke up in 1972 but re-formed briefly two years later. Its last albums were *Live and Kickin'* (1974) and *Avalanche* (1974). West ran into drug and financial problems, and Pappalardi was murdered by his wife, songwriter Gail Collins.

Mouskouri, Nana (1936–   ) Greek singer, famous for her horn-rimmed spectacles, who established a lasting international reputation in the early 1960s. She trained as a classical musician, but success came after the popular songwriter Manos Hadjidakis started writing songs for her, and she quickly emerged as a star after making her first record in 1959. As well as recording in Greek, she also released singles in various other European languages, winning many awards. Her biggest hits include 'The White Rose of Athens' (1962), 'Guantanamera' (1967) and 'Only Love' (1986). Her long list of hit albums in a pan-European market elevate her to the ranks of the BEATLES and Elvis PRESLEY as one of the best-selling artists of the century.

Move, the British pop group, which had a number of hits in the late 1960s and early 1970s. The Move was formed by bassist and singer Carl Wayne (1944–   ), singer-songwriter and guitarist Roy Wood (1948–   ), guitarist Trevor Burton (1949–   ), bassist Chris 'Ace' Kefford (1946–   ), who left in 1968, and drummer Bev Bevan (1944–   ), who came together in Birmingham in 1966. The group soon established itself as a top PSYCHEDELIC pop act with such hits as 'Night of Fear' (1967). Later hits included 'I Can Hear the Grass Grow' (1967), 'Flowers in the Rain' (1967), 'Fire Brigade' (1967) and 'Blackberry Way' (1968), which was the band's only single to reach Number One in the UK. As a live act, the Move was renowned for both the volume of the music and for a tendency to destroy equipment at the end of the show. Further controversy surrounded the use of a picture of then prime minister, Harold Wilson, in his bath as part of a promotional campaign (the group ended up facing court injunctions). Jeff Lynne replaced Wayne in 1970 and the group folded in 1972 when Wood formed the ELECTRIC LIGHT ORCHESTRA.

'Flowers in the Rain' was the first record played on fledgling BBC Radio One.

Moyet, Alison (Genevieve Alison-Jane Moyet; 1961–   ) British rock singer, nicknamed Alf, who launched a successful solo career in the 1980s after initial success in partnership with Vince Clarke (1961–   ) as Yazoo. After splitting with Clarke in 1983, she enjoyed success with the solo album *Alf*; hits since then have included the JAZZ-influenced 'That Ole Devil Called Love' (1985), 'Weak in the Presence of Beauty' (1987) and *Raindancing* (1987), *Hoodoo* (1991) and *Essex* (1994).

Mud British pop group, which had considerable, if short-lived, chart success in the mid-1970s playing a mixture of GLAM ROCK and up-dated ROCK 'N' ROLL. Founded in 1966, the band consisted of singer Les Gray, guitarist Rob David, bassist Ray Stiles and drummer Dave Mount. The rise of glam rock in the early 1970s enabled the group to make a breakthrough in 1973 with such chart hits as 'Crazy', 'Hypnosis' and 'Dyan-mite'. Among the hits that followed were the Number One singles 'Tiger Feet' (1974), 'Lonely This Christmas' (1974) and 'Oh Boy' (1975), all of which were the work of the CHINN AND CHAPMAN songwriting team. The group returned to the pub circuits where it had begun and remained active into the 1990s, generally trading on the old hits.

Mulligan, Gerry (Gerald Joseph Mulligan; 1927–96) US JAZZ saxophonist, arranger and bandleader, who led many acclaimed bands of various sizes and was one of the pioneers of the COOL style in the late 1940s. His career started when he wrote arrangements for radio, and he went on to play in the bands of Gene KRUPA and others before collaborating with Miles DAVIS on the highly acclaimed recordings eventually collected as *The Birth of the Cool*, his contributions including the songs 'Jeru', 'Boplicity', 'Venus de Milo' and 'Godchild'. He also provided arrangements for the band of Stan KENTON. He later led an admired pianoless quartet, completed by Chet BAKER, drummer Chico Hamilton and bassist Bob Whitlock, and developed a unique baritone saxophone style. Subsequently he led several big bands and also worked with Dave BRUBECK.

> You feel as if you're listening to the past, present and future of jazz all at one time.
> DAVE BRUBECK, of Gerry Mulligan

Munch, Charles (1891–1968) French violinist and conductor, from Alsace, who won acclaim for his work with the finest orchestras on both sides of the Atlantic. Having trained as a violinist in Strasbourg, Berlin and Paris, Munch served in the German army during the First World War and was appointed to a teaching post in

Strasbourg before taking up the leadership of Leipzig's Gewandhaus Orchestra under Wilhelm FURTWÄNGLER (1926–33). He established his reputation as a conductor in Paris, where he was admired for his work with the Société des Concerts du Conservatoire (1938–45). He made his first appearance in the USA in 1946 and two years later was appointed as Serge KOUSSEVITSKY's successor as chief conductor of the BOSTON SYMPHONY ORCHESTRA, where he remained until 1962, championing such French composers as Berlioz and many contemporary works. A founder of the Orchestre de Paris in 1967, he died during a US tour.

Mungo Jerry British pop group, which established a big following in the early 1970s. The group, formed by singer, guitarist and laboratory researcher Ray Dorset (1946–), keyboard player Colin Earl (1942–), guitarist and banjo player Paul King (1948–) and bassist Mike Cole, was originally called the Good Earth, but it was renamed after one of the cats in the poems of T.S. Eliot's *Old Possum's Book of Practical Cats*. The group played SKIFFLE and ROCK 'N' ROLL before enjoying its first chart success with the Number One single 'In the Summertime' (1970). Among the hits that followed were 'Baby Jump' (1971), which also reached Number One, 'Alright Alright Alright' (1973) and 'Longlegged Woman Dressed in Black' (1974). Dorset eventually attempted a solo career but had little success, and the band returned to the pubs and clubs where it had begun. Dorset has since written television theme tunes, minor hits for other artists and club songs for the Wigan football and rugby sides.

Munrow, David (John) (1942–76) British recorder player, who emerged as one of the leading figures in the authentic music revival of the 1960s and 1970s. Founder of the EARLY MUSIC CONSORT OF LONDON in 1967, he did much to promote the performance of early music on authentic instruments and broadcast regularly on the subject before his untimely death. Other projects included providing original music for a number of historical films.

Murder Incorporated *See* NEW YORK PHILHARMONIC ORCHESTRA.

Murphy, C.W. (1875–1913) British songwriter, who contributed many of the classic songs of the Edwardian MUSIC HALL. Among his biggest hits were 'Oh, Oh, Antonio' (1908), 'Has Anybody Here Seen Kelly?' (1909) and 'Hold Your Hand Out, Naughty Boy' (1913).

Murphy, Turk (Melvin E. Murphy; 1915–87) US JAZZ trombonist and composer, who was one of the most prominent figures in the jazz revival of the 1940s. He was a star member of the Lu WATTERS Yerba Buena Jazz Band (1940–50) and led his own group, performing much TRAD material, including the songs of Jelly Roll MORTON, and also writing extensively on the subject.

Musgrave, Thea (1928–   ) Scottish composer, who came to be acknowledged one of the most important AVANT-GARDE composers of her generation. A graduate of Edinburgh University, she studied under Nadia BOULANGER in Paris and went on to establish a reputation in the 1950s for her diatonic compositions with strong Scottish themes, among them *The Suite o' Bairnsangs*, *Cantata for a Summer's Day*, the ballet *A Tale for Thieves* (1953) and the chamber opera *The Abbot of Drimock* (1955).

Musgrave confirmed her standing as a leading contemporary composer after adopting SERIALISM in 1960, and she applied its principles to her trio for flute, oboe and piano (1960) and the opera *The Decision* (1967), which dramatized events surrounding a Scottish mining disaster. She developed her own style, making use of non-synchronized instrumental parts in such abstract theatrical works as the opera *The Voice of Ariadne* (1974), which was inspired by a story by Henry James. Her other works include a viola concerto (1973), the operas *Mary, Queen of Scots* (1977), *A Christmas Carol* (1979) and *Harriet, the Woman Called Moses* (1985), the choral work *Black Tambourine* (1985) and the orchestral composition *The Seasons* (1988).

Her clarinet concerto is unusual in that it dictates that the soloist should roam the playing area, forming musical liaisons with various sections of the orchestra and performing outside the control of the conductor. *See also* AMBULATORY MUSIC.

Music Director of Europe, the *See* Herbert von KARAJAN.

music hall A form of varied musical entertainment, which enjoyed huge popularity throughout the UK at the turn of the century. The music hall tradition had its roots in the 'song-and-supper' rooms and taproom concert halls that were first seen in the early nineteenth century. A series of acts, some musical and others offering knockabout comedy or various speciality turns such as dancing, juggling or acrobatics, were strung together with links provided by a jovial master of ceremonies. Until a change in the law in 1914, audiences were allowed to drink and smoke during performances and were often rowdy to the point of rioting, but the 'halls' were soon established as one of the favourite pastimes of all classes.

Among the most celebrated venues in London were the Canterbury Music Hall, which was established in 1852, the Holborn Empire, which was opened in 1857, and the London Pavilion, which was founded in 1861. Among the great stars were such comics and singers as Dan Leno (1860–1904), Marie LLOYD, Albert CHEVALIER, George ROBEY, Harry LAUDER, Nellie WALLACE, George FORMBY and Gracie FIELDS. Items on the bill ranged from sentimental love ballads to vulgar drinking songs calculated to appeal to even the basest natures. Classic hits to emanate from the halls included such standards as 'The Boy in the Gallery', 'Champagne Charlie' and 'Down at the Old Bull and Bush'.

The heyday of the halls lasted from 1880 to the First World War, after which they went into decline when faced with the rival attractions of the cinema and radio. Such entertainments still attract large audiences to this day, however, and the BBC television series *The Good Old Days*, which recreated the atmosphere and star turns of Victorian and Edwardian times, enjoyed a huge audience. A similar tradition flourished in France at much the same time, while US audiences flocked to vaudeville shows.

music theatre A broad term covering theatrical works that have a strong musical content but that do not fall easily into the categories of opera or musical comedy. Anticipated by the revolutionary dramatic entertainments conceived by Bertolt Brecht and Kurt WEILL in the late 1920s and 1930s, the development of music theatre as a distinct genre really belongs to the 1960s, when such composers as Alexander GOEHR, Peter MAXWELL DAVIES, Harrison BIRTWISTLE and Hans Werner HENZE wrote many such entertainments.

musical The musical comedy, a twentieth-century art form, which developed from the nineteenth-century operetta, fusing spoken dialogue with music. The musical comedy grew out of the cheerful turn-of-the-century operettas of such composers as Franz LEHÁR and Sigmund ROMBERG although the first steps in its emergence can tentatively be traced back to the British impresario George Edwardes (1855–1915), who presented such embryonic musicals as *In Town* (1892) and *A Gaiety Girl* (1893) at the Prince of Wales Theatre in London. These jolly entertainments caught on elsewhere, and audiences in both London and New York flocked to see such music-and-dance spectaculars as *Floradora* (1899) and *The Arcadians* (1909).

Lehár's operetta *The Merry Widow* (1907) was very influential and had a profound impact on such hits as *Chu Chin Chow* (1916). The featherweight musicals of the 1920s and 1930s, such as *No, No Nanette*, *Rose-Marie* (both 1924) and *The Desert Song* (1926), threw up countless classic popular songs thanks to the involvement of such composers as Jerome KERN, Ivor NOVELLO and George GERSHWIN.

The golden age of the musical, as seen on stage and screen, opened during the Second World War, when the genre was transformed in the USA by RODGERS and HAMMERSTEIN's *Oklahoma!* (1943), which built on the success of *Show Boat* (1927) by ushering in a more realistic and dramatically relevant entertainment in which as much attention was given to characterization and plot as to music and spectacle. Rodgers and Hammerstein tightened their stranglehold on the transatlantic musical with such shows as *Carousel* (1945), *South Pacific* (1949), *The King and I* (1951) and *The Sound of Music* (1959). Among the other box offices smashes were Irving

BERLIN's *Annie Get Your Gun* (1946), Cole PORTER's *Kiss Me Kate* (1948), Frederick LOEWE's *My Fair Lady* (1956) and Leonard BERNSTEIN's *West Side Story* (1957).

The 1960s witnessed the rise of a new sub-genre, the ROCK musical, which spawned such fashionable successes as Galt MacDermot's *Hair* (1967), *Tommy* (1975), *Grease* (1978) and Andrew LLOYD WEBBER's *Jesus Christ Superstar* (1970), the first in a long series of classic Lloyd Webber hits – among them *Evita* (1978), *Cats* (1981), which became the longest-running musical ever staged in London's West End, and *Phantom of the Opera* (1986) – that enjoyed equal acclaim in London and on Broadway and challenged the previous US domination of the musical since the war. Other leading writers of the modern musical include Lionel BART, Marvin HAMLISCH and Stephen SONDHEIM.

> Gaily irrational to the point of lunacy.
> NOËL COWARD, of the musical

musique concrète *See* CONCRETE MUSIC.

Muti, Riccardo (1941–) Italian conductor, who ranks among the most respected conductors of his generation. He was principal conductor of the PHILHARMONIA ORCHESTRA (1973–82) and of the PHILADELPHIA ORCHESTRA (1980–92) before assuming the role of musical director at LA SCALA, Milan, in 1993.

Muzak Tradename relating to the CANNED MUSIC that is often heard in shopping centres and other public places. The name was modelled on the tradename Kodak, which is considered one of the most effective of all advertising tags.

> Music is art. Muzak the science.
> Muzak Corporation slogan

> Sound you inhale.
> ERIK SATIE

N

Nabob of Sob, the *See* Johnnie RAY.

Nash, Heddle (1894–1961) British tenor, who made his début singing Count Almaviva in *The Barber of Seville* at Milan in 1924 and became a long-standing favourite at COVENT GARDEN (1925–47). He was particularly acclaimed for his performances in Sir Edward ELGAR's *Dream of Gerontius* and in Handel's *Messiah*.

Nash, Johnny (1940–) Black US singer-songwriter, who established a reputation as a teen-idol in the late 1950s and subsequently emerged as a SOUL and REGGAE star in the 1970s. Among his best-selling singles were 'A Very Special Love' (1957), 'The Teen Commandments' (1958), which he recorded with Paul ANKA and George HAMILTON IV, 'Let's Move and Groove Together' (1965), 'Hold Me Tight' (1968), which marked his conversion to reggae, 'I Can See Clearly Now' (1972), which reached Number One in the USA, and 'Tears on My Pillow' (1975), which got to the top of the British charts. His COVER versions of songs by Bob MARLEY did much to promote the latter's career.

Nashville The traditional home of US COUNTRY music. Nashville, the capital of the State of Tennessee, established its claim as the heartland of country music in 1925, when the GRAND OLE OPRY radio programme, first called *WSM Barn Dance*, was broadcast from the city. The success of the programme lured many country musicians to Nashville, and fans began to talk of the 'Nashville sound', which was characterized by slick vocal backing and the use of violins. The programme also promoted the establishment of recording studios and various music publishing companies specializing in such music. Rival claims from other cities boasting a healthy country sub-culture evaporated in the 1950s under pressure from the growing popularity of ROCK 'N' ROLL, but Nashville has remained synonymous with the genre. By the 1960s half of all the records made by US artists were being made in Nashville, although a tendency towards the over-production of many country records led such artists as Willie NELSON to break away from Nashville and to create a more raw 'outlaw' sound in the 1970s.

Nashville Storyteller, the *See* Tom T. HALL.

National Youth Orchestra British orchestra for young musicians, which was founded in London in 1947 by Dame Ruth Railton (1915–). The orchestra provides an opportunity for 150 promising young musicians to rehearse together and to perform in public under distinguished teachers and conductors. The highlight of most years is the National Youth Orchestra's traditional appearance at the PROMS.

Nazareth Scottish rock group, which was among the leading HARD ROCK acts of the 1970s. Lead singer Dan McCafferty, guitarist Manny Charlton, bassist Pete Agnew and drummer Darryl Sweet began performing as the Shadettes, but they established their reputation after changing their name with their first album *Nazareth* (1971). Roger Glover, of DEEP PURPLE, produced such Nazareth albums as *Razamanaz* (1973), *Loud 'n' Proud* (1973) and *Hair of the Dog* (1975), while subsequent hit singles included 'Broken Down Angel', 'Bad Bad Boy', 'This Flight Tonight', one of several songs by non-rock artists that the band COVERED, 'My White Bicycle' and 'Hot Tracks'. The band subsequently went into decline, although remaining active into the 1990s.

Nelson, Rick (Eric Hilliard Nelson; 1940–85) US pop singer and guitarist, who became a ROCK 'N' ROLL teen-idol of the 1950s and early 1960s. Nelson began his career as a child, performing on his parents' radio and television comedy shows, and he had his first US Number One when he was only 16 years old with a COVER version of

Fats DOMINO's 'Teenager's Romance/I'm Walkin'' (1957). Subsequent hits – when he was known as Ricky Nelson – included 'Be Bop Baby' (1957), 'Stood Up' (1957), 'Poor Little Fool' (1958), 'Travellin' Man' (1960) and 'Hello Mary Lou' (1961). With the decline of rock 'n' roll he switched to a COUNTRY-ROCK style and established a major new following before his premature death in an aircraft crash during a US tour. The biggest of his later hits was the 1972 classic 'Garden Party', which was written in response to his poor reception at a concert in Madison Square Garden (possibly provoked by the fact that he mixed new songs with his old standards or by an inadequate sound system). His film credits included a supporting role in the Western *Rio Bravo* (1958).

> I don't mess around, boy.
> RICK NELSON, catchphrase on his parents' shows

Nelson, Willie (1933–) US singer-songwriter, nicknamed the Red-headed Stranger after one of his albums, who became one of the legends of COUNTRY music as an 'outlaw' pop star in the 1970s. *Red-headed Stranger* (1975), which was the first country album to go PLATINUM, appealing as it did to both country and pop audiences, encapsulated his rebellious attitude to the slickness of conventional country music of the time. Subsequent hit albums – among them the joint classic *Wanted: The Outlaws* (1976) and *Stardust* (1978) – consolidated his standing as a successful CROSSOVER star and included acclaimed collaborations with Waylon JENNINGS, which reflected their reputation as the top-selling live country partnership of the decade, and further duets with such artists as Kris KRISTOFFERSON and Roger MILLER. His most recent releases include *Always on My Mind* (1982), which yielded a hit single in the title track, *City of New Orleans* (1984), *A Horse Called Music* (1989), *Across the Borderline* (1993) and *Spirit* (1996).

Earlier in his career, Nelson sold the rights to his song 'Night Life' for just $150 to raise money to buy a car in which to get to NASHVILLE (the song provided Rusty Draper with a Number One in 1963). He later left Nashville in the early 1970s, somewhat symbolically, when his house burned down. Other hits in the long list of Nelson classics have included 'Crazy'

(1961), 'Hello Walls' (1961), 'The Party's Over' (1967), 'Little Things' (1968), 'If You've Got the Money, I've Got the Time' (1976), 'Good Hearted Woman' (1976), 'Georgia on My Mind' (1978), 'On the Road Again' (1980) and 'Poncho and Lefty' (1983).

neoclassicism School of modern classical music, which flourished between the wars. It maintained that contemporary music should return to the values of clarity of texture, of balance and of restraint associated with classical composition of previous centuries, particularly as embodied in the music of Bach (hence the repeated 'Back to Bach' plea of its defenders). A reaction against the excesses of late romanticism, the neoclassical school placed a new emphasis on tonal harmony and promoted efforts by living composers to address their work to the long-standing musical tradition. Among those who adopted a neoclassical stance, for a time at least, were Paul HINDEMITH, Sergei PROKOFIEV and Igor STRAVINSKY, whose most obviously neoclassical compositions included the opera *The Rake's Progress* (1948–51).

> The 12-tone school tried to revive the spirit of the old forms, while neoclassicism presented replicas of their façades with interesting cracks added.
> ERNST KŘENEK, *Horizons Circled*, 1974

neoromanticism School of modern classical music, which advocates the emotionalism and chromatic exoticism of the romantic movement, as opposed to the more cerebral preoccupations of NEOCLASSICISM. Adherents of the neoromantic school have included Arnold SCHOENBERG, who adopted the ideals of such late romantics as Gustav MAHLER, Jean SIBELIUS and Sir Edward ELGAR.

Netherlands Chamber Orchestra Prestigious Dutch orchestra, which was founded in 1955. The orchestra is especially respected for performances of Bach.

New Age music Genre of atmospheric, instrumental POP music, which is claimed to have beneficial therapeutic properties and which attracted numerous devotees in the early 1980s, when many sought a refuge from a world felt to be over-materialistic and threatened by various man-made ecological disasters. The slowly evolving sound changes of such mood

music, intended to aid meditation and promote a sense of inner well-being, were
condemned by critics as 'yuppie MUZAK'.

New Kids On the Block US pop group,
which enjoyed a brief but highly successful
career in the late 1980s and early 1990s.
Singers Donnie Wahlberg, Jon Knight,
Jordan Knight, Joe McIntyre and Danny
Woods came together in Boston in 1984,
originally calling themselves Nynuk before
renaming themselves after one of their first
recordings. The group had a commercial
breakthrough with the hits 'Please Don't
Go' (1988) and 'You Got It (the Right
Stuff)' (1989) and quickly established a
huge international reputation as the top
TEENY-BOP act. Several more hits followed,
including the chart-toppers 'Hangin'
Tough', 'I'll be Loving You (Forever)' and
'Step by Step', before the bubble burst. The
group launched a come-back in 1994.

New Orleans jazz Traditional JAZZ style,
which dates to the early years of the century when the jazz movement had its
beginnings in the STORYVILLE district of
New Orleans. This earliest expression of
the form put the emphasis on collective
improvisation rather than on virtuoso solo
passages, and it drew on such diverse
sources as the BLUES, RAGTIME and the
songs of TIN PAN ALLEY. Typical bands
consisted a trumpeter, clarinettist, trombonist, bassist, pianist, guitarist or banjo-
player and drummer. Some have credited
the proliferation of such bands in the New
Orleans area to the large numbers of martial instruments that were discarded in the
southern States after the Spanish-
American War.

Early stars of New Orleans jazz included
Jelly Roll MORTON, who claimed to have
invented it, and Buddy BOLDEN. The style,
as adapted by New Orleans-born Louis
ARMSTRONG, the ORIGINAL DIXIELAND JAZZ
BAND and King OLIVER among others, was
eventually transplanted to Chicago and
ultimately evolved into SWING in the late
1920s, but it continues to boast legions of
devotees and practitioners on both sides of
the Atlantic. See also DIXIELAND; TRAD.

New Philharmonia Orchestra See PHIL-
HARMONIA ORCHESTRA.

New Romantics POP genre of the early
1980s, which married SYNTHESIZER pop
with highly fashionable visual imagery.

The genre first gathered pace in London's
clubland and threw up such stars as ADAM
AND THE ANTS, BOY GEORGE, SOFT CELL and
SPANDAU BALLET, all of whom adopted
flamboyant, often historically inspired, costumes and make-up as part of an attempt
to create a new pop élite far removed from
the earthiness of the punks who had preceded them. Reflecting the optimism of the
early 1980s, before economic recession
really took hold, the movement celebrated
the virtues of consumerism and extrava-
gance, but was in decline by 1982.

New Seekers, the See the SEEKERS.

New Wave POP music genre of the late
1970s and early 1980s, that evolved out of
more elemental PUNK ROCK. Loosely speaking, bands belonging to the New Wave
were more imaginative than their punk
predecessors and created music mixing
punk with elements of ART ROCK and PRO-
GRESSIVE ROCK. New Wave stars were
noticeably less radical in outlook and
appearance than the punks, rejecting the
nihilism and violence implicit in the former
movement and aiming at a more sophisticated, commercially acceptable sound.
Leading exponents included BLONDIE, Elvis
COSTELLO, the CURE, DEXY'S MIDNIGHT RUN-
NERS, Joe JACKSON, ORCHESTRAL MANOEUVRES
IN THE DARK, the POLICE, the SIMPLE MINDS
and TALKING HEADS. See also NEW ROMAN-
TICS.

New Wave of British Heavy Metal The
second generation of British HEAVY METAL
artists who emerged in the late 1970s and
1980s, aping such models as DEEP PURPLE,
LED ZEPPELIN and BLACK SABBATH. By the
late 1970s heavy metal was looking like a
spent force with many legendary line-ups
having broken up, but the formation of
such outfits as IRON MAIDEN and DEF LEP-
PARD reversed the trend and soon such
bands were playing to larger heavy metal
audiences than ever before, even without
making significant stylistic advances. The
movement has spawned numerous sub-
genres attempting new things, among
them DEATH METAL, GRINDCORE and
THRASH.

New York Dolls, the US rock band, which
established a transatlantic reputation as
one of the leading HARD ROCK outfits of the
1970s and, in the eyes of many critics,
anticipated the PUNK ROCK explosion of the

late 1970s. Formed in 1972, the New York Dolls consisted of lead singer David Johansen (1950–), guitarist Johnny Thunders (John Genzale; d. 1991), bassist Arthur Harold Kane, guitarist and keyboard player Sylvain Sylvain and drummer Jerry Nolan (d. 1992), who replaced former drummer Billy Murcia (1951–72) on his drug-related death. The band quickly acquired notoriety for excess, fostered by cross-dressing and constant reference to sex and drugs in their live act. An appearance on the relatively sedate British rock programme the OLD GREY WHISTLE TEST, delivering such inflammatory tracks as 'Vietnamese Baby', caused a sensation, but it was only after the band had broken up that its influence as one of the most radical of all GLAM ROCK outfits was fully realized. (The group was managed for a time by British rock impresario Malcolm McLaren, who went on to manage the SEX PISTOLS.) The New York Dolls released just two original albums, *New York Dolls* (1973) and *Too Much Too Soon* (1974).

New York Philharmonic Orchestra US orchestra, founded in 1842, which is the oldest symphony orchestra based in the USA. Celebrated conductors recruited to the NYPO over the years have included Gustav MAHLER, Arturo TOSCANINI, Leopold STOKOWSKI, Sir John BARBIROLLI, Leonard BERNSTEIN, Pierre BOULEZ and Zubin MEHTA. The orchestra's nickname, Murder Incorporated, arose because it is notorious for its tendency to make life as difficult as possible for its conductors. Typical of the orchestra's refusal to bow to even the most distinguished guest conductors was the reply Polish-born conductor Artur Rodzinski (1892–1958) got when he asked if anyone had any suggestions how they might improve their performance of a Mahler symphony: 'Yep. Send for Bruno Walter.'

> It took us five years to have him realize there was nothing he could teach us.
> Unidentified NYP player, of Bruno Walter

Newley, Anthony (1931–) British actor and director, who developed a second career as a pop singer in the early 1960s. Having appeared in such films as *Oliver Twist*, in which he played the Artful Dodger, and *Idle on Parade*, in which he played a character based on British ROCK 'N' ROLL star Terry Dene, he made his recording début in 1959 and had hits with

such singles as 'I've Waited So Long' (1959) and the Number Ones 'Why' (1960) and 'Do You Mind' (1960). He subsequently pursued a theatrical career as writer and star of the MUSICAL *Stop the World – I Want To Get Off* (1961), from which came the single 'What Kind of Fool am I?', among other shows on which he frequently collaborated with Leslie BRICUSSE (1931–). His more successful shows have included *Doctor Doolittle* (1967) and *Willy Wonka and the Chocolate Factory* (1971). *Can Heironymus Merkin Ever Forget Mercy Humpe and Find True Happiness?* (1969) was one of the flops. He was married to actress Joan Collins.

Newman, Alfred (1900–70) US composer, pianist and conductor, who is remembered for his many acclaimed movie SOUNDTRACKS. Newman was a child prodigy, playing the piano in public at the age of eight and subsequently starring in vaudeville as the 'Marvelous Boy Pianist' as well as performing with several major US orchestras. He conducted several popular revues in the 1920s and was eventually recruited by Hollywood in 1930, going on to serve as musical director for Samuel Goldwyn and then for Twentieth Century Fox and contributing scores to over 230 films.

Newman's most celebrated scores included those for *Arrowsmith* (1931), *The Bowery* (1933), *Dead End* (1937), *Alexander's Ragtime Band* (1938), for which he won an Oscar, *Gunga Din* (1939), *Tin Pan Alley* (1940), which brought him a second Academy Award, *The Grapes of Wrath* (1940) and the further OSCAR-winning classics *The Song of Bernadette* (1943), *Mother Wore Tights* (1947), *With a Song in My Heart* (1952), *Call Me Madam* (1953), *Love is a Many-Splendored Thing* (1955), *The King and I* (1956) and *Camelot* (1967).

Newman, Randy (Gary Newman; 1944–) US singer-songwriter and pianist, nicknamed the Mark Twain of Rock, who established a transatlantic reputation for his witty, ironic songs tackling pressing social and moral issues of the day. Newman worked initially as a songwriter for other artists, penning such hits as 'Simon Smith and his Amazing Dancing Bear' for Alan PRICE and others for singers including Gene PITNEY and Judy COLLINS, who won acclaim for her version of his 'I

Think It's Gonna Rain Today' (1966). The group THREE DOG NIGHT subsequently got to Number One in 1970 with his 'Mama Told Me Not to Come', and NILSSON recorded a whole album of Newman songs under the title *Nilsson Sings Newman* (1970).

Newman proved himself a performer in his own right with the album *12 Songs* (1970), and he went on to record such contentious albums as *Good Old Boys* (1974), which challenged the tradition of racism and bigotry in the southern USA. Other targets of his music included slavery ('Sail Away'), Communist paranoia ('Political Science'), religion ('God's Song') and environmental pollution ('Burn On'); 'Short People' (1978) lampooned prejudice of all kinds (although it was taken seriously by some slow-witted listeners who assumed he really had something against the 'vertically challenged'). More recent projects have included the albums *Born Again* (1979), *Trouble in Paradise* (1983), music for such films as *The Natural* (1984), and the JAZZ and RAP-influenced *Land of Dreams* (1988).

Newport Festival US pop festival that took place at Northbridge in 1969 and attracted some 150,000 fans to see such artists as the BYRDS, Joe COCKER, CREEDENCE CLEARWATER REVIVAL and Jimi HENDRIX. Apart from clashes with the police, the Newport Festival is remembered chiefly for the controversy that surrounded Bob DYLAN's performance, which marked his conversion to the electric guitar. Fans of his acoustic classics jeered when he appeared with an electric guitar, but Dylan stuck to his guns and kept playing the electric introduction to his first number over and over for 20 minutes until the noise subsided and he could set about winning the crowd over to his new style.

Newton-John, Olivia (1948–) British pop singer and film actress, who had numerous successes in a range of pop and COUNTRY styles through the 1970s and early 1980s. Grand-daughter of the Nobel Prize-winning physicist Max Born, she was brought up in Australia before making her recording début in 1971 with 'If Not for You' and going on to have minor hits with such singles as 'Take Me Home, Country Roads' (1973) and 'Let Me be There' (1973), although she failed to win the EUROVISION SONG CONTEST with 'Long Live

Love'. Country fans warmed to her, and 'I Honestly Love You' (1974) and 'Have You Ever been Mellow' (1975) both made Number One in the USA, where she was now based. Her performance in the hit MUSICAL *Grease* (1978) broadened her appeal to a wider pop audience, and the duets with John Travolta (1954–) 'You're the One that I Want' and 'Summer Nights' shot to the top of the charts. Further hit singles came from the albums *Totally Hot* (1978) and *Physical* (1980).

The single 'Xanadu' (1980), from the slated movie of the same name starring Newton-John and Gene Kelly, provided her (in collaboration with the ELECTRIC LIGHT ORCHESTRA) with her third British Number One. In 1985 she moved further away from her original sugary image by posing half-naked for the sleeve of her hit album *Soul Kiss*.

Nicholls, Horatio (Lawrence Wright; 1888–1964) British songwriter, arranger and music publisher, nicknamed the Edgar Wallace of Songwriters, who was one of the most prolific and succesful songwriters of his generation. One of the first of the TIN PAN ALLEY songwriters in London and the founder of the celebrated music newspaper *Melody Maker* (1926), he wrote numerous popular hits under a long list of pseudonyms. Among his most celebrated creations were 'Are We Downhearted – No' (1917), 'Wyoming' (1919) and 'Babette' (1925).

Nichols, Red (Ernest Loring Nichols; 1905–65) US JAZZ cornettist and bandleader, who led a series of highly acclaimed bands in the late 1920s and 1930s. His Five Pennies band, which varied considerably in size, recorded much DIXIELAND-based material and numbered among its biggest hits 'Ida, Sweet as Apple Cider' (1927). Members recruited to the band's ranks included trombonist Miff Mole (Irving Milfred Mole; 1898–1961), the DORSEY brothers, Glenn MILLER, Benny GOODMAN and Gene KRUPA among other notable White jazzmen. Nichols went on to lead a number of theatre bands, and he also directed the music on Bob HOPE's radio shows. He re-formed the Five Pennies after the Second World War and was impersonated by Danny Kaye in the biopic *The Five Pennies* (1959).

nickelodeon Automatic piano, of the type

that was installed in bars and HONKY-TONKS throughout the USA in the years before the introduction of the JUKE BOX. Such pianos operated by means of rolls of paper, which worked after insertion of a 5-cent piece.

Nielsen, Carl August (1865–1931) Danish composer and conductor, who, with Jean SIBELIUS, is regarded as the most important Scandinavian composer of modern times. Born in impoverished circumstances, the son of a peasant labourer, Nielsen taught himself to play the violin and cornet and had his first formal musical training after joining a military band in 1879, when he was 14 yers old. He studied at the Copenhagen Conservatory and attracted attention as a composer with his *Little Suite* (1888). He was appointed second violinist in the orchestra of the Chapel Royal a year later and remained in the post for another 16 years before a state pension enabled him to concentrate on his work as a composer.

Memories of his rural upbringing on the island of Fyn remained an influence throughout his life as a composer, and his music is often described as unmistakably Danish in character. The six symphonies Nielsen wrote between 1894 and 1925 – notably the Fourth, 'The Inextinguishable' (1915–16) and the Fifth (1921–22), which is famous for the deafening side-drum solo inserted into an otherwise pastoral passage – were his main achievement. These marked his gradual change from an essentially classical style to one that embodied his concept of 'progressive tonality' – that is, starting a piece in one key and ending it in another – and his First Symphony (1891–92) is one of the earliest examples of the technique.

Among his other works were such orchestral pieces as *Pan and Syrinx: a nature-scene* (1918), the *Helios* overture (1903), the operas *Saul and David* (1902) and *Maskerade* (1905), songs, a piano suite, the *Commotio* (1931) for organ, and a series of concertos for flute, violin and clarinet. He conducted the Royal Theatre Orchestra (1908–14) and the Music Society of Copenhagen (1915–27) and was appointed director of the Copenhagen Conservatory shortly before his death, by which time he was a national hero. His reputation outside his native country grew, somewhat belatedly, after the Second World War.

I think through the instruments them-

selves, almost as if I had crept inside them.
CARL NIELSEN, *Politiken*, 1925

Music is life, and, like it, inextinguishable.
CARL NIELSEN, from his Fourth Symphony, 1916

Nikisch, Artur (1855–1922) Hungarian conductor and violinist, who was among the most revered conductors of his generation. He was appointed conductor of the Leipzig Opera in 1882, of the BOSTON SYMPHONY ORCHESTRA in 1889, of the BERLIN PHILHARMONIC ORCHESTRA and of the Leipzig Gewandhaus Orchestra in 1895, and he toured the USA with the LONDON SYMPHONY ORCHESTRA in 1912. Particularly admired for his performances of Brahms, Bruckner and Tchaikovsky, he never used a score when conducting.

His virtuosity seems to make him forget the claims of good taste.
CLAUDE DEBUSSY

I once mentioned Nikisch in one of our conversations and the maestro immediately said, 'Well, his technique is immense, but here,' and he indicated his heart, 'nothing'.
NIKOLAI MALKO, recalling the words of Felix Mottl, *A Certain Art*, 1966

Nilsson, (Märta) Birgit (1918–   ) Swedish soprano, who was particularly admired for her performances in the operas of Wagner and Richard STRAUSS. A student of the Royal Academy of Music in Stockholm, she made her first professional appearance in 1946 and subsequently established an international reputation, making her US début in 1956. Her best-known roles included Strauss's Electra and Salome, Wagner's Isolde and Brünnhilde, Puccini's Turandot and Leonora in Beethoven's *Fidelio*. Asked what was the secret of singing Isolde so brilliantly, she replied 'Comfortable shoes'. She retired in 1986.

Nilsson, Harry (Harry Edward Nelson; 1941–94) US singer-songwriter, who wrote and recorded numerous hit songs in the late 1960s and 1970s. Ironically, he was best known for two songs that were written by others – 'Everybody's Talking', which was used on the SOUNDTRACK of the film *Midnight Cowboy* (1969), and the Number One hit 'Without You' (1972), which was originally the work of BADFINGER's Pete Ham and Tom Evans. The huge success of 'Without You' ensured that the accompanying album *Nilsson Schmilsson* also did well in the charts. Other albums included *A Little Touch of Schmilsson in the Night* (1973) and *Pussy Cats* (1974), on which he worked with his close friend John LENNON.

> He is the something the Beatles are.
> DEREK TAYLOR, music journalist

Nirvana US rock band, who shot to fame in the early 1990s as the leading exponents of GRUNGE. Based in Seattle and consisting of lead singer and guitarist Kurt Cobain (1967–94), bassist Chris Novoselic, who replaced the first bassist after he lost his fingers in a logging accident, and drummer Dave Grohl, Nirvana made a breakthrough with its second album, *Nevermind* (1991), which encapsulated a fusion of PUNK ROCK with HEAVY METAL. The band's hit singles include 'Smells Like Teen Spirit', 'Come as You Are', 'Lithium' and 'In Bloom'. It consolidated its reputation as one of the foremost bands of the early 1990s with *Incesticide* (1992).

Nirvana was not always so popular: early in the band's career it was booked to play a gig in Seattle, but no one bothered to turn up. Much later, the media lavished eager attention on the band and on the private life of Kurt Cobain in particular, gleefully reporting that his marriage to fellow-singer Courtney Love, of Hole, had begun with the proposal 'I'm worth $6 million. Will you marry me, bitch?' The future of the band was put in jeopardy when Cobain, receiving treatment for drug problems, committed suicide in 1994.

Another band of the same name flourished in the UK in the late 1960s and recorded such popular numbers as 'Rainbow Chase' (1968).

Nitty Gritty Dirt Band, the US rock band, which won acclaim in the late 1960s and early 1970s as one of the most interesting COUNTRY-ROCK outfits. Originally called the Illegitimate Jug Band, the group has had many line-ups since its formation in 1965. Among the key members have been Jeff Hanna (1947–), Bruce Kunkel (1948–), Jimmie Fadden (1948–), John McEuen (1945–), Jim Ibbotson (1947–) and, at an early stage, Jackson BROWNE. The single 'Bojangles', from *Uncle Charlie and His Dog Teddy* (1970), was the band's first significant hit, and it was followed by the much-admired country-rock album *All the Good Times* (1972). The triple album *Will the Circle Be Unbroken* (1973) included appearances by several top country artists. More recent albums, some issued under the shortened name the Dirt Band, have included *An American Dream* (1980), which featured Linda RONSTADT, *Plain Dirt Fashion* (1984) and *Partners, Brothers and Friends* (1985). The band was the first rock group to tour the Soviet Union.

Noble, Ray (1903–78) British bandleader, composer and arranger, who led popular BIG BANDS on both sides of the Atlantic in the 1920s and 1930s and enjoyed particular success backing singer Al BOWLLY. Noble led his first orchestra in 1929 and recruited Bowlly a year later. 'Goodnight, Sweetheart' (1931) provided him with his first big hit and a signature tune; among the many hits that followed – some written for films – were such classics as 'Love is the Sweetest Thing' (1932), 'The Very Thought of You' (1934) and 'Cherokee' (1938), which was taken up by Charlie PARKER. Noble went to the USA in 1934 and led a hugely acclaimed orchestra assembled by Glenn MILLER, establishing himself as a top radio act and backing Fred ASTAIRE on such classics as 'By the Light of the Silvery Moon', as well as making several film appearances playing dotty English gentlemen. He led further bands back in the UK in the late 1930s and early 1940s and eventually retired in the mid-1950s. Among his last big hits were 'Linda' and 'I'll Dance at your Wedding' (both 1947).

Nono, Luigi (1924–) Italian composer, who emerged in the 1950s as one of the most influential politically committed AVANT-GARDE composers of the postwar era. A pupil of Bruno MADERNA, Gian Francesco MALIPIERO and the Swiss composer Tona Scherchen (1938–), he composed his first works in the early 1950s in a strictly SERIALIST style. Later works, mostly written for electronic instruments, moved away from serialism and attempted to defend the political role of contemporary music. His works include the opera *Intolleranza 1960* (1961), which combined live and recorded performances, *Epitaph for Federico Garcia Lorca* (1953), *Incontri* (1955), the cantata *Sul ponte di Hiroshima* (1962) and two piano concertos. He married Arnold SCHOENBERG's daughter Nuria in 1955.

Norman, Jessye (1945–   ) US soprano, who emerged as a leading star of both opera and concert recitals in the early 1970s. Having studied music in Washington and at the University of Michigan, Norman made her opera début in Berlin in 1969, as Elisabeth in Wagner's *Tannhäuser*. Her success led to an invitation to join the Berlin Opera, while further appearances at COVENT GARDEN, London, and LA SCALA, Milan, in 1972 confirmed her standing as one of the foremost sopranos of the day. She has won particular acclaim for her performances of works by Berlioz, Gustav MAHLER, Schubert and Wagner.

Norrington, Roger (1934–   ) British conductor, who has established a reputation as one of the most influential figures in the authentic music movement of recent decades. Having started in his musical career as a professional tenor, he won acclaim for his work with Kent Opera (1966–84), with which he revived important early works by such composers as Monteverdi. He has been musical director of the Schütz Choir of London, the London String Players and the London Baroque Ensemble (1978).

North, Alex (1910–   ) US composer and conductor, who has won wide acclaim for his many film SOUNDTRACKS. Having studied at the Juilliard School, New York, in the early 1930s, he established his reputation with scores for films, ballets, radio, television and the stage. His film credits include *A Streetcar Named Desire* (1951), *The Sound and the Fury* (1959), *Spartacus* (1960) and *Who's Afraid of Virginia Woolf?* (1966).

Northern Sinfonia Orchestra British orchestra, which was founded in Newcastle-on-Tyne by Michael Hall in 1958. It concentrates its activities on northeast England and has won praise for commissioning many new works by promising new composers.

Norvo, Red (Kenneth Norville; 1908–94) US JAZZ xylophonist, vibraphonist and bandleader, who led a series of acclaimed bands in the 1930s and 1940s. Self-taught on the piano and xylophone, he appeared in vaudeville and played for Paul WHITEMAN before forming his first band in 1928. He married the singer Mildred BAILEY, who often worked with him in the 1930s, and they shared the title Mr and Mrs Swing.

After breaking up his own band in 1939, he collaborated with such jazzmen as Benny GOODMAN, Woody HERMAN, Dizzy GILLESPIE and Charlie PARKER. In the 1950s he adopted a more progressive, modern style, partnering Charles MINGUS among others, and continued to attract praise with regular tours until he retired in the mid-1970s. He resumed his career in the 1980s.

Norworth, Jack (John Knauff; 1879–1959) US actor, singer-songwriter, dancer and lyricist, who wrote and performed several classic hit songs of the First World War era. Among his most famous hits were 'Honey Boy' (1907), 'Shine On, Harvest Moon' (1908), which he wrote in collaboration with his second wife Nora BAYES, and 'Take Me out to the Ball Game' (1908).

Nose, the *See* Barry MANILOW; Barbra STREISAND.

novachord Type of ELECTRONIC ORGAN, which was patented by Lawrence Hammond in 1939. Operated from a six-octave keyboard, it worked by means of thermionic-valve oscillators and had the advantage of being able to play whole chords.

Novello, Ivor (David Ivor Davies; 1893–1951) Welsh songwriter, playwright and actor, who became one of the legends of twentieth-century popular music through his many hit MUSICALS and songs. Born in Cardiff, Novello had his first songs published while he was still in his teens as a chorister in Oxford. His first outstanding hit was 'Till the Boys Come Home' (1914), which, under the more familiar title 'Keep the Home Fires Burning', became one of the great songs of the First World War.

After war service Novello developed a career as an actor-manager in London before consolidating his reputation with a series of classic musicals in the 1930s and 1940s, which incorporated many of his most celebrated songs. Among the most successful shows were *Glamorous Night* (1935), *Careless Rapture* (1936), *Crest of a Wave* (1937), *The Dancing Years* (1939), *Arc de Triomphe* (1943), *Perchance to Dream* (1945), *King's Rhapsody* (1949) and *Gay's the Word* (1951), in which he sent up his own style. Among the most enduring songs were such classics as 'And Her Mother Came Too', which was written for the revue *A–Z* (1921), 'Rose of England', from *Crest of a Wave*, and 'We'll Gather Lilacs', which was revived for *Perchance to Dream*. He was also the author of several straight plays, and he collaborated on film adaptations of some of his most acclaimed stage shows. As an actor he was a top matinée idol of the 1920s and 1930s, with a particularly famous profile. *See also* IVOR NOVELLO AWARDS.

novelty record A record that depends heavily on a gimmick – whether technical, musical or lyrical – for its appeal. Novelty records have been an accepted marketing ploy since the earliest days of the recording industry, when every record was itself, of course, something of a novelty. Innumerable artists, from the unknowns to the greatest stars, have profited by adopting some peculiar vocal hiccough or other attention-seeking device or by striking on odd song titles and so forth. No lesser a singer than Elvis PRESLEY released an album – *Elvis Country* (1971) – on which he sang snatches of 'I'm 10,000 Years Old' between tracks. Ray Stevens sang about his camel on 'Ahab the Arab' (1962), and Chuck BERRY resorted to schoolboy innuendo for his 1972 chart-topper 'My Ding-a-ling'.

Other examples have ranged from Randy NEWMAN's 'Short People' (1977), a tongue-in-cheek attack on those of below-average height, which provoked the lofty Tim Conway and Steve Lawrence into answering back with 'Tall People', to singles performed by schoolchildren, dogs, cartoon characters, centenarian Japanese twins and monks.

Among the many instances of records that have provided hits for artists better known for their achievements in other fields are 'If', a COVER version by actor Telly Savalas that went all the way to Number One in 1975; 'Grandad', which did the same for *Dad's Army* star Clive Dunn in 1971; and 'Back Home', which got the England World Cup squad to the top of the charts in 1970.

One of the more successful exponents of the novelty record was Lonnie DONEGAN, whose classic 'Rock Island Line' (1955) was issued by his record company just for its gimmick value. It was the first British pop record to get into the USA Top 10 and effectively launched the SKIFFLE boom of the mid–1950s. Among the 'novelties' he followed it up with were 'My Old Man's a Dustman', which was the first single to go straight into the British charts at Number One, and 'Does Your Chewing-gum Lose Its Flavour on the Bedpost Overnight'.

Other varieties of novelty records include those with unusual sleeve arrangements and picture discs.

Nugent, Ted (1949–) US rock guitarist, variously nicknamed the Detroit Wildman and the Motor City Madman, whose band became one of the most successful HARD ROCK outfits of the 1970s. Nugent formed his first band in Chicago in 1964 and gradually built up a reputation as a leading rock musician, winning particular praise for his live performances (during which he sometimes appeared wearing only a loin-cloth and headband, claiming he hunted his own food). Among the most popular albums were *Ted Nugent* (1975), *Free For All* (1976), *Cat Scratch Fever* (1977) and *Double Live Gonzo* (1978). Later releases failed to offer anything significantly new, and in 1988 he was recruited to join the supergroup Damn Yankees. A new solo album, *Spirit of the World*, appeared in 1995.

Nugent's enthusiasm for promoting himself as a modern savage – further evidenced by such album titles as *Survival of the Fittest* and *Tooth, Fang, and Claw* – has not always worked to his advantage: the SPCA (an animal welfare organization), for instance, took exception when it emerged that he had shot squirrels with a bow and arrow during an archery competition.

> If it's too loud, you're too old.
> TED NUGENT

Numan, Gary (Gary Webb: 1958–) British singer and SYNTHESIZER player, who was one of the pioneers of synthesizer pop in the late 1970s. Having started out as a PUNK ROCK guitarist, he formed Tubeway Army and established himself as a top star with the futuristic 'Are "Friends" electric?' (1979). Similar follow-ups under his own name trod the same ELECTRONIC-ROCK path, the most notable including the Number One single 'Cars' (1979), which he claimed to have written in the space of just a few minutes and which returned to the Top 20 in a remixed version in 1987. Among his albums were *Replicas* (1979), *The Pleasure Principle* (1979), *Telekon* (1980), *Berserker* (1984) and *Outland* (1991). *Living Ornaments 1979–80* (1980) was guaranteed a high listing in the charts when it was made available for just one month and then withdrawn from sale. His love of classic aircraft has resulted in highly publicized life-threatening accidents.

Nyro, Laura (1947–   ) US singer-songwriter and pianist, who wrote numerous hits in the late 1960s. Several tracks from an album she recorded in 1966 became hits for other stars, among them THREE DOG NIGHT, which got to Number One, along with her 'Eli's Coming', and Barbra STREISAND, who recorded her 'Stoney End'. Her other albums include *Gonna Take A Miracle* (1971) and *Mother's Spiritual* (1984), one of her later GOSPEL-influenced releases.

O

Oasis British rock group, which became the leading rock outfit of the mid-1990s. Formed in Manchester in 1991 by brothers Noel (1967–) and Liam (1972–) Gallagher, together with guitarist Paul 'Bonehead' Arthurs, bassist Paul 'Guigs' McGuigan and drummer Tony McCarroll, Oasis grabbed the headlines as much for the incendiary relationship of the Gallagher brothers as for the sensational debut album *Definitely Maybe* (1994). Hailed as successors to the BEATLES, Oasis quickly overwhelmed their rivals BLUR as the top new band in British rock and subsequently topped the album charts again with *(What's the Story) Morning Glory?* (1995), from which came the anthemic 'Wonderwall'. Drummer McCarroll was replaced by Alan White in 1995.

Ocean, Billy (Leslie Sebastian Charles; 1950–) British singer-songwriter, born in Trinidad, who released a series of DISCO and SOUL hits in the 1970s and 1980s. Having trained as a tailor, he established his reputation as a favourite with disco audiences with 'Love Really Hurts Without You' (1975); among the follow-ups were 'Red Light Spells Danger' (1977), the US Number One 'Caribbean Queen' (1984), UK Number One 'When the Going Gets Tough, the Tough Get Going' (1986) and the US chart-topper 'Get Outta My Dreams' (1987). 'When the Going Gets Tough' was included in the SOUNDTRACK of the film *The Jewel of the Nile*, and filmstar Michael Douglas himself sang backing vocals on the record. The catchphrase title of the song was, so legend has it, first uttered by John F. Kennedy's father. Ocean's best-selling albums include *Suddenly* (1984), *Love Zone* (1986) and *Tear Down These Walls* (1988).

Ochs, Phil (1940–76) US singer-songwriter, who was among the first wave of influential FOLK artists to issue from Greenwich Village in the early 1960s. Ochs acquired a large cult following with such PROTEST SONGS as 'Love Me, I'm a Liberal', 'Draft-dodger Rag', 'Here's to the State of Mississippi', 'I Ain't Marchin' Anymore' and 'There but for Fortune'. Like Dylan, he switched to electric guitar and produced some of his best music on *Pleasures Of The Habor* (1967) and *Rehearsals For Retirement* (1969). Quarrels with Dylan, combined with depression, increasing dependence on alcohol and damage to his voice as a result of a mugging while in Africa led Ochs to commit suicide by hanging in 1976.

O'Connor, Des (1932–) British singer and comedian, who established a reputation as a singer of ballads and love songs in an EASY LISTENING vein in the 1960s.

O'Connor, Sinead (1967–) Irish rock singer, who emerged as one of the most original – and controversial – stars of the early 1990s. A naturally contrary nature has got O'Connor into trouble on more than one occasion. Attempts to persuade her to adopt a more feminine image only resulted in her changing to her now famous cropped hairstyle to the initial horror of her record company, and ripping up a picture of the Pope served only to alienate audiences in her native country (one Irish pantomime dame retaliated by tearing up her picture on stage). A characteristic decision not to sing any DYLAN songs during a Dylan festival predictably caused an uproar in 1992. Nonetheless, O'Connor established herself as a singer of passionate integrity with such albums as *The Lion and the Cobra* (1989), *I Do Not Want What I Haven't Got* (1990), *Am I Not Your Girl* (1992) and *Universal Mother* (1994).

Her version of PRINCE's 'Nothing Compares to U' (1990) was, rumour has it, addressed to a pack of cigarettes.

O'Day, Anita (Anita Colton; 1919–) US JAZZ singer, who won acclaim singing with the bands of Gene KRUPA, Stan KENTON, Norman Granz and Benny GOODMAN among others. She established her reputation with Krupa in the early 1940s and sang on such hits as 'Let Me Off Uptown', 'Alreet', 'Kick It' and 'Bolero at the Savoy'. After joining Kenton she had further success with such standards as 'And Her Tears Flowed Like Wine' and 'The Lady in Red', but she returned to Krupa for a second stint in 1945 before going solo from 1946. She starred at the Newport Jazz Festival in 1958, but progress over the next few years was hampered by problems with drug addiction and alcoholism. She recovered after the 1960s and resumed worldwide tours, adding more admirers to her already large audience.

Ogdon, John (Andrew Howard) (1937–89) British pianist and composer, who established a reputation as one of the finest pianists despite the affliction of debilitating mental illness. Having made his London début at the PROMS in 1958, he proved his excellence in 1962, when he shared victory in the prestigious Tchaikovsky Competition in Moscow with Vladimir ASHKENAZY. Subsequently he won acclaim all around the world, particularly for his performances of contemporary works (among them Ferruccio BUSONI's piano concerto), before the onset of mental illness in 1970 prevented him making further appearances for a number of years. A return to the top level in the 1980s was ultimately cut short by his premature death. His compositions included a piano concerto, a sonata and a number of preludes for piano.

Ohio Players, the US pop group, which had considerable commercial success playing disco-funk in the mid-1970s. The group, founded in 1959, consisted of trumpeters Marvin Pierce and Ralph 'Pee Wee' Middlebrooks, saxophonist Clarence 'Satch' Satchell, bassist Marshall 'Rock' Jones, keyboard player Billy Beck, singer and guitarist Leroy 'Sayer' Bonner and drummer Jimmey 'Diamond' Williams. It switched from RHYTHM-AND-BLUES to a DISCO style and had big hits with such albums as *Pain* (1971), *Pleasure* (1973) and *Skin Tight* (1974). Among the singles were the Number Ones 'Fire' (1974) and 'Love Rollercoaster' (1975). The band disappeared from sight with the decline of disco towards the end of the decade.

oi music Reactionary HARD ROCK music of the 1990s, which counters the leftist leanings of many successful contemporary stars. In direct opposition to the liberal and often socialist views of such famous names as Billy BRAGG and Elvis COSTELLO, so-called 'oi music' incorporates the sloganizing anthems of skinheads and various neo-Nazi organizations, which often sponsor their own bands (*see* BLOOD AND HONOUR). Leading exponents of oi music include Skrewdriver and No Remorse.

Oistrakh, David Fyodorovich (1908–74) Russian violinist, who was acknowledged one of the finest violinists of his day. He began his musical training as a young child and attended the Odessa Conservatory. He established his reputation touring the Soviet Union in the 1920s and 1930s, when he won numerous prestigious prizes. Appointed to a teaching post at the Moscow Conservatory in 1934, he proved himself a world-class performer when he won the International Violin Competition in Brussels in 1937. In the following decades he consolidated his international reputation with tours on both sides of the Iron Curtain, forming acclaimed partnerships with Yehudi MENUHIN and other leading figures in the 1950s and 1960s and also making recordings with his son, the violinist Igor Oistrakh (1931–   ). He was particularly admired for his performances of works by Brahms and Tchaikovsky, but he also played many challenging new works by contemporary composers; Sergei PROKOFIEV, Dmitri SHOSTAKOVICH and Aram KHACHATURIAN all dedicated works to him.

O'Jays, the US all-male vocal group, which enjoyed strings of hits in both the 1960s and the 1970s. The O'Jays, which consisted of Eddie Levert (1942–   ), Walter Williams (1942–   ), Bobby Massey, William Powell (1941–77) and Bill Isles, evolved from the 1950s band the Triumphs, and the group recorded its first hit, 'The Lonely Drifter', in 1963. It went on to release a series of modest RHYTHM-AND-BLUES hits but then fell from favour. Isles and Massey left, but the rest of the line-up went on to enjoy their biggest hit of all with the album – and single – *Backstabbers* (1972). Among the hits that followed were 'Love Train' (1972), 'For the Love of Money' (1974), 'Used to be My Girl' (1978) and 'Lovin You' (1987).

The O'Jays started out as the Mascots but changed the name in order to acknowledge the role that US disc jockey Eddie

O'Jay played in promoting them at the outset of the group's career.

Old Dutch *See* Albert CHEVALIER.

Old Grey Whistle Test, the Celebrated British television music programme, which featured leading British and US rock acts through the 1970s. Founded in 1969, it witnessed the great years of the spectacular PROGRESSIVE ROCK bands and – restyled the *Whistle Test* – the birth of PUNK ROCK and the NEW WAVE in the late 1970s. Presenters included Anne Nightingale and Bob Harris. The name of the programme related to the tradition that the 'old greys' – the doorkeepers and other menials working in TIN PAN ALLEY – could be relied on to predict the potential of a new song: if they were still whistling a new tune a week after first hearing it, it was likely to prove a hit.

Old Groaner, the *See* Bing CROSBY.

Old Maestro, the *See* Ben BERNIE.

Old Man, the *See* Arturo TOSCANINI. In fact, Toscanini was only one of a group of celebrated twentieth-century conductors who were exceptionally long-lived. Leopold STOKOWSKI was 95 when he died in 1977, Sir Thomas BEECHAM reached the age of 84 and Pierre MONTEUX lived until he was 88 (just three years before his death he signed a contract to continue conducting the LSO for another 20 years). Sir Malcolm SARGENT (who died at a comparatively early age, in his seventies) credited the long life expectancy of conductors to the rigours of their work, advising one less fit colleague: 'You should do more conducting, old fellow, you should do more conducting.' Stokowski for one took care of his health and trained for his work in the manner of an athlete, taking regular hot and cold needle showers as well as engaging the services of a masseur both before and after concerts. Certainly it seems it pays for a conductor to be in good trim. A possibly apocryphal story has it that a conductor once handed his featherweight baton (weighing half an ounce) to a heavyweight boxer and challenged him to see for how long he could move it about; the boxer quickly gave it up.

I spend up to six hours a day waving my arms about, and if everyone else did the same they would stay much healthier. When I am not working, I put up my feet and relax.
SIR MALCOLM SARGENT

Oldfield, Mike (1953–) British rock guitarist, who had colossal commercial success in 1973 with the classic instrumental album *Tubular Bells*, which became one of the best-selling PROGRESSIVE ROCK albums ever released. The somewhat retiring Oldfield shot to overnight stardom with the issue of the album, on which he played all the instruments; it remained in the UK charts for an incredible five years and ensured the success of the Virgin record label as its very first release (it was also adapted for use in the SOUNDTRACK of the horror film *The Exorcist*). Before then, Oldfield had played mostly in a FOLK-ROCK vein with his sister Sally Oldfield and with Kevin Ayers.

Various follow-up albums – among them *Hergest Ridge* (1974), *Ommadawn* (1975) and *Incantations* (1978) – fared reasonably well but none came close to equalling Oldfield's first success, and he returned to it in 1992 with *Tubular Bells II*, a completely re-recorded version that also got to Number One in the charts. Another album, *The Songs of Distant Earth*, was released in 1994.

Ole Blue Eyes *See* Frank SINATRA.

Oliver, Joe 'King' (1885–1938) US JAZZ cornettist, composer and bandleader, who was among the first great masters of jazz trumpet and who exercised considerable influence over the young Louis ARMSTRONG in the 1920s. Brought up in New Orleans, Oliver did much to spread the popularity of NEW ORLEANS JAZZ throughout the USA. Armstrong was among the many talented recruits to his Creole Jazz Band (founded in 1922) with whom he made classic recordings. The partnership he formed with Armstrong (1922–24) was profoundly important in the development of a new jazz style, and such Oliver compositions as 'Dippermouth Blues' (1923), 'Doctor Jazz' (1927) and 'Slow and Steady' (1928) provided standards for a new generation of jazzmen. It is said that Kid ORY, who enlisted Oliver earlier in his career, bestowed the title 'King' on him, and Armstrong readily admitted that Oliver had influenced him more than any other musician. Oliver himself failed to adapt to changing tastes, however, and problems with his teeth as a result of gum disease marred his playing in his last years. He spent much of the 1930s languishing in obscurity, leading a touring band and finally working as the janitor of a poolroom.

Oliver, Sy (Melvin James Oliver; 1910–88) US composer, arranger, singer and trumpeter, who contributed a number of standards in the SWING style of the 1930s and early 1940s. Taught to play the trumpet by his father, he was recruited as an arranger and trumpeter by Jimmie LUNCEFORD in 1933. He established his reputation with classic arrangements for such hits as 'T'ain't Whatcha Do' and 'Stomp It Off'. Oliver went on to write further acclaimed arrangements for Tommy DORSEY – among them 'Swing High', 'Well, Git It', 'Opus Number One' and 'On the Sunny Side of the Street' – and he led his own band after the Second World War before winning posts as musical director for several record companies, in which capacity he worked with such artists as Billie HOLIDAY, Frank SINATRA and Louis ARMSTRONG. The band he formed in the 1950s enjoyed consistent success until his retirement in 1984, by which time he was universally acknowledged to have been one of the chief architects of MAINSTREAM big band jazz.

Olsen, George (1893–1971) US bandleader, who led one of the most popular dance bands of the 1920s and 1930s. Olsen established his own band after the First World War and contributed to various Broadway shows as well as making a number of film appearances. Among the band's biggest hits was its version of Jerome KERN's 'Who?' (1926) and its signature tune 'Beyond the Blue Horizon'. Olsen led further bands in the late 1930s and during the Second World War, eventually retiring from the music business in 1951.

ondes martenot Influential early electronic instrument, otherwise known as the *ondes musicales*, which was invented in the 1920s by Maurice Martenot (1898–1980) and first demonstrated by him in 1928. Martenot's device attracted the interest of such respected composers as Pierre BOULEZ, Arthur HONEGGER, Olivier MESSIAEN and Edgar VARÈSE, who wrote works for it – notably Honegger's *Joan of Arc at the Stake*

(1935) and Messiaen's *Turangalîla-symphonie* (1948). Operated from a six-octave keyboard, the ondes martenot employs thermionic valve oscillators to produce a sonorous and variable electronic sound. It was rendered obsolete – except for revivals of works specifically demanding its use – by the development of more sophisticated SYNTHESIZERS after the Second World War.

one-hit wonder An artist or group, who releases a best-selling hit but then fails to make much impression with any follow-up release. The catalogue of one-hit wonders in the history of pop is surprisingly long. Among the most notable must be included Jane Birkin and Serge Gainsbourg, who rocketed to Number One in the UK in 1969 with the infamous 'Je t'aime', recreating the sound of love-making; Ricky Valance, who went all the way to Number One with 'Tell Laura I Love Her' in 1960; the SINGING NUN, with 'Dominique' (1963); Zager and Evans, whose single big hit was 'In the year 2525' (1970); and Terry Jacks, who had his one outstanding success with 'Seasons in the Sun' (1974). Norman Greenbaum, whose 'Spirit in the Sky' got to Number One in 1970, saw his only big hit returned to the charts in a version by Doctor and the Medics in 1986 – by which time he had been thrown out of the family home by his wife and was reduced to sleeping in a chicken coop.

> This is their first single, and their most successful so far.
> MARK CURRY

One-string *See* Carl PERKINS.

Ono, Yoko (1933–   ) Japanese AVANT-GARDE artist and singer, who became world-famous through her close personal partnership with John LENNON, whom she married in 1969. Yoko Ono's liaison with Lennon was one of the factors blamed by the media for the breakup of the BEATLES at the end of the 1960s, although her presence was probably only one of several reasons for the group's demise. As a singer, Yoko Ono, whose name means 'Ocean Child', participated in recordings made by the Plastic Ono Band and has released such solo albums as *Approximately Infinite Universe* (1973), *Seasons of Glass* (1981) and *Every Man Has A Woman* (1984) as well as helping to organize posthumous releases of unheard Lennon material. In 1996 she appeared live with Lennon's son Sean.

open form A piece of music that is written so that it can be started and ended at any point at the whim of the conductor or the performers. Examples of such pieces include Karlheinz STOCKHAUSEN'S *Zyklus* (1959) and Pierre BOULEZ'S Third Piano Sonata, the five movements of which may be played in any order, provided that the third movement is always central.

opera's not over till the fat lady sings, the *See under* FAT.

Orbison, Roy (Kelton) (1936–88) US pop star of the early 1960s, nicknamed the Big O, who recorded a number of classic ROCK ballads before falling out of fashion and ultimately making a minor come-back shortly before his death from a heart attack. Orbison started out singing COUNTRY-AND-WESTERN songs, but only established himself as a star after adopting a pop-oriented style. Always performing in a pair of sunglasses (which he used for all his concerts after the British media identified them as his trademark), Orbison enjoyed chart success with such singles as 'Only the Lonely' (1960), 'Blue Angel' (1960), 'Runnin' Scared' (1961), 'Crying' (1961), 'In Dreams' (1963), 'It's Over' (1964) and 'Oh, Pretty Woman' (1964), which reached Number One on both sides of the Atlantic. Ironically, the shy Orbison decided to record 'Only the Lonely' himself only after it had been turned down by both Elvis PRESLEY and the EVERLY BROTHERS.

The only performer to tour with both Presley and the BEATLES early in their careers (as well as with the EAGLES and the BEACH BOYS), Orbison had an unhappy private life. His wife, for whom he wrote the Everly Brothers hit 'Claudette', died in a motorcycle crash in 1966, and two of his sons perished in a fire at his Nashville home in 1968. His last months witnessed the release of the album *Mystery Girl* (1988) and participation in the super-group the Travelling Wilburys, alongside Bob DYLAN and George HARRISON.

> In '75 I went into the studio to make *Born To Run* ... and most of all I wanted to sing like Roy Orbison. Now everybody knows nobody sings like Roy Orbison.
> BRUCE SPRINGSTEEN

Orchestral Manoeuvres in the Dark British NEW WAVE band, which established a reputation for highly polished SYNTHESIZER pop in the late 1970s and early 1980s. Led by singer and bassist Andy McCluskey (1960–) and singer and synthesizer player Paul Humphreys (1961–). OMD came together in 1978 and attracted immediate attention with the début single 'Electricity' and the eponymous first album (both 1980). Subsequent hits included the singles 'Enola Gay' (1980) and the album *Architecture and Morality* (1981), from which came 'Souvenir' and 'Joan of Arc'. *Dazzle Ships* (1983) and other sequels were less well received, and Humphreys left in 1988. McCluskey managed to revive his own fortunes in 1991, however, when the album *Sugar Tax*, with the singles 'Sailing the Seven Seas' and 'Pandora's Box', climbed all the way back to the Top 10. *Liberator* followed in 1993.

Orff, Carl (1895–1982) German composer, who is usually remembered for the much-revived cantata *Carmina Burana* (1937). After music studies in his native Munich, Orff established a reputation as an innovative musical theorist and teacher, co-founding a music school in Munich in 1924 and pursuing his own method, which he claimed made music accessible to children and amateurs alike. His ideas on the teaching of music, which provided the basis of a long-running children's radio series after the war, were laid out in the best-selling *Schulwerk* (1930) and *Music for Children* (1954).

Carmina Burana, which Orff considered his first mature work, used texts of profane medieval Latin poems and drinking songs from a thirteenth-century manuscript found in the Benedictine monastery of Beuron in Bavaria in 1803. It proved to be one of the most influential and widely heard works of the century, despite its initial appropriation by the Nazis, who claimed it as an Aryan masterpiece. Excerpts from it have since been used in all kinds of contexts, including television advertisements, its driving rhythms and climactic phrases making it ideal for evoking a passionate response.

Among Orff's other compositions were numerous songs and a number of rarely performed operas and other choral and dramatic works, among them *Der Mond* (1938), *Die Kluge* (1942), *Antigone* (1949),

Oedipus der Tyrann (1959) and *Prometheus* (1968).

> In all my work, my final concern is not with musical but with spiritual exposition.
>
> CARL ORFF

organist's trousers The shine on the seat of the trousers, which is an occupational hazard of the organist as a result of constantly moving about on the organ bench while pedalling with the feet. In compensation for this, professional organists are entitled to claim income tax allowance for frequent trouser replacement.

organized sound The term preferred by such AVANT-GARDE composers as Edgar VARÈSE to describe their music. Established conventions about what constitutes legitimate music have changed enormously since 1900. A turning point was Arnold SCHOENBERG's piece *Verklärte Nacht* (*Transfigured Night*; 1899), which was turned down by the musical establishment of Vienna because it contained an 'improper chord'. With hindsight, this may be seen as the last gasp of the conservatives who still held true to the Renaissance concept that music should express emotion and give moral or spiritual lift. Igor STRAVINSKY's *Le Sacré du printemps* (*The Rite of Spring*; 1913) challenged further old concepts of what music is or should be, and by 1937 John CAGE was claiming that for him at least no sound was out of bounds.

> Tradition is really just complacency and slackness.
>
> GUSTAV MAHLER

Original Dixieland Jazz Band, the White US JAZZ band, which pioneered NEW ORLEANS JAZZ in New York in the First World War era and made the very first jazz recordings. The ODJB came together in New Orleans around 1905. It subsequently played in Chicago before reaching New York, there winning fame – as the Famous Original Dixieland Jazz Band – through its long residence at the 400 Room at Reisenweber's restaurant. Among the most admired members of the band were its leader, cornettist Nick La Rocca (Dominic James La Rocca; 1889–1961), clarinettist Larry Shields (1893–1953), trombonists Eddie Edwards (1891–1963) and Emile Christian (1895–1973), pianists Henry Ragas (1890–1919) and J. Russell Robinson (1982–1963), and drummer Tony Sbarbaro (1897–1969). The band's biggest hits included such classics as 'Tiger Rag' (1912), 'Livery Stable Blues' (1912), 'Original Dixieland Onestep' (1912), 'Reisenweber Rag' (1917) and 'Ramblin' Blues' (1920). Having taken its pioneering brand of jazz overseas, notably to London after the First World War, the band broke up in 1925, re-forming briefly in 1936.

Orlando, Tony (Michael Anthony Orlando Cassavitis; 1944–) US SOUL singer, of Graeco-Spanish descent, who had a number of transatlantic MIDDLE-OF-THE-ROAD hits in the 1960s and 1970s. Having started as a singer in the DOO-WOP tradition, he scored his first big hit with 'Halfway to Paradise' (1961) and consolidated a reputation as a TEENY-BOP idol with such follow-ups as 'Bless You' and 'Happy Times are Here to Stay'. After something of a lull, he returned to the charts in the 1970s as lead singer of Dawn, enjoying transatlantic Number Ones with 'Knock Three Times' (1971) and 'Tie a Yellow Ribbon Round the Old Oak Tree' (1973). Such was the success of this latter release, describing how a woman ties yellow ribbons around an oak tree to indicate to her lover who is returning from prison that she still loves him, that US hostages being repatriated from Iran in 1981 were greeted by the sight of trees thus festooned throughout the USA. Later hits included 'Say Has Anybody Seen My Sweet Gypsy Rose' (1973) and 'He Don't Love You (Like I Love You)' (1975). He also starred in the Broadway MUSICAL *Barnum* (1980).

Ormandy, Eugene (Eugene Blau; 1899–1985) US conductor and violinist, born in Hungary, who won huge acclaim for his work with the PHILADELPHIA ORCHESTRA over a period of some 50 years. A child prodigy, the five-year-old Ormandy won a place as a violin student at the Budapest Royal Academy and subsequently toured Hungary with great success. He emigrated to the USA in 1920 and worked with New York's Capitol Theater Orchestra, playing the accompaniments to the silent movies and later serving as the ensemble's conductor, before moving to the Minneapolis Orchestra as leader in 1931.

Ormandy began his celebrated association with the Philadelphia Orchestra in 1936, when he was appointed associate conductor, and he inherited Leopold STOKOWSKI's place as music director and conductor in 1938. Under his leadership the orchestra consolidated its international reputation through numerous tours and many recordings. Ormandy, who finally stepped down in 1980, never used a score while conducting.

Ory, Kid (Edward Ory; 1886–1973) US JAZZ trombonist and bandleader, who was one of the pioneering jazz legends of the 1920s and went on to enjoy a long career playing with many of his fellow greats. Ory led a band in New Orleans from around 1911 and attracted to it such emerging talents as Louis ARMSTRONG and Sidney BECHET before uprooting to the West Coast in 1919 and making the first jazz records by any Black jazz band (1922). He did much of his best work immediately after moving to Chicago in 1925, making hugely influential records with Armstrong, Jelly Roll MORTON and King OLIVER among others. He retired from the music business in 1933 to take up work as a chicken farmer and railroad clerk, but he returned to bandleading in 1942 and was one of the foremost figures associated with the TRAD jazz revival then taking place. Composer of such jazz standards as 'Muskrat Ramble', he retired for good in 1966.

> Never play the trombone for nothing.
> KID ORY, on being asked for tips by a young trombonist

Osborne Brothers, the US BLUEGRASS duo, who were among the leading performers in the bluegrass revival of the 1950s. Singer and mandolin-player Bobby Osborne (1931–) and singer and banjoist Sonny Osborne (1937–) starred on numerous radio broadcasts of such music and included among their most popular songs such hits as 'Up This Hill and Down' (1966) and 'Georgia Pinewoods' (1971). Their adoption of electric instruments in the early 1960s surprised many fans but promoted their careers in the long run.

Oscar One of a series of annual awards bestowed by the Academy of Motion Picture Arts and Sciences to reward outstanding achievements in various aspects of film-making – including the composition of SOUNDTRACKS. The goldplated statuettes that are presented to the winners were nicknamed 'Oscars' after a secretary with

the organization observed a striking similarity between the figures and her own uncle Oscar. The first winners of the Best Film Song Award were Con Conrad and Herb Magidson for 'The Continental' from *The Gay Divorce* in 1929. A Best Film Score award was added in 1934 (when it went to Louis Silver for *One Night of Love*) and this was split into Best Film Score and Best Musical Film Score in 1938, when Irving BERLIN was one of the winners (with *Alexander's Ragtime Band*).

Osibisa African rock group of the 1970s, based in the UK, which was among the most successful bands to fuse African and western rock traditions. Led by Ghanaian singer and saxophonist Teddy Osei, who had played in a number of British bands since 1962, Osibisa came together in London in the mid-1960s and released several albums that got into the higher reaches of the British charts. They continued to record through the 1970s and 1980s, their later albums including *Mystic Nights* (1981) and *Live at the Marquee* (1983).

Osmonds, the US family pop group, which was a TEENY-BOP sensation of the mid-1970s. The five Osmond brothers, Alan (1949–), Wayne (1951–), Merrill (1953–), Jay (1955–) and Donny (Donald Clark Osmond; 1957–), had their first musical experiences singing in the Mormon church in Utah to which they belonged, and they established a wider following after appearing at Disneyland and on television. The eponymous first album proved a huge hit, as did the single 'One Bad Apple' (1971), and Donny Osmond doubled up with chart-topping success as a solo singer with such singles as 'Go Away Little Girl' (1971), 'Puppy Love' (1972), 'The Twelfth of Never' (1973) and 'Young Love' (1973). Younger sister Marie Osmond (1959–) meanwhile climbed the charts with 'Paper Roses', and youngest brother Jimmy Osmond (1963–) got to Number One in the UK when he was just nine years old with 'Long-haired Lover from Liverpool' in 1972 (Jimmy went on to work as an adviser to superstar Michael JACKSON, who began as a child star at much the same time). The Osmonds continued to appear in the charts on both sides of the Atlantic until 1978, after which they pursued careers in television and in COUNTRY music with mixed results. A come-back by Donny Osmond in the late 1980s resulted in the single 'Soldier of Love' reaching Number Two in the US charts in 1989. In 1992 he spent a year starring in *Joseph and the Amazing Technicolor Dreamcoat*.

Legend has it that film star Orson Welles observed of Donny Osmond 'He has Van Gogh's ear for music'. In fact, it was the film director Billy Wilder who said it, and he was referring to the US comedy actor Cliff Osmond, who appeared in several of Wilder's films.

O'Sullivan, Gilbert (Ray O'Sullivan; 1946–) Irish singer-songwriter, who enjoyed a brief but spectacular career at the top in the early 1970s. O'Sullivan made his first impression on the charts in 1970 with 'Nothing Rhymed' and subsequently got to Number One in the UK with the mawkish 'Clair' (1972), from the Number One album *Back to Front*, and 'Get Down' (1973) – the former single was addressed to small, giggly girl and the latter one to a dog. O'Sullivan's fall from favour was swift and was followed by acrimonious legal wrangles over his earnings. He returned to the charts, however, in 1980 with 'What's in a Kiss'.

Otis, Johnny (John Veliotes; 1921–) US bandleader, singer, drummer and producer, of Greek descent, who established himself as a star after switching from BIG BAND JAZZ to RHYTHM-AND-BLUES in the late 1940s. His band was among the first to adopt the r 'n' b line-up of three horns and rhythm section and enjoyed a string of hits with such releases as 'Double Crossing Blues' (1949), 'Rockin' Blues' (1951), 'Ma, He's Making Eyes at Me' (1957) and 'Willie and the Hand Jive' (1958). He also worked with Etta JAMES, Nat 'King' COLE, the INK SPOTS and Big Mama THORNTON. Subsequently he became a minister and was prominent in the civil rights campaigns of the 1960s, but he has continued to tour widely with a revived version of his old band, members of which included his guitarist son, Shuggie.

Otway, John (1952–) British singer-songwriter, who established himself as an enduringly popular cult favourite with an eccentric sense of humour. He teamed up with the guitarist Wild Willy Barrett during the PUNK ROCK era and worked as a dustman until emerging as a star with such hits as '(Cor Baby That's) Really Free' (1977), 'Beware of the Flowers (Cos I Think They're Gonna Get You, Yeah)' (1978) and 'DK 50/80' (1980). After parting company with Barrett, he continued to release the occasional new record and to undertake live appearances.

Our Gracie *See* Gracie FIELDS.

Our Marie *See* Marie LLOYD.

Owens, Buck (Alvis Roger Owens; 1929–) US COUNTRY singer, guitarist and bandleader, who emerged as a top country star in the early 1960s. A former truck driver, he worked as a session guitarist before recording his first hit 'Second Fiddle' in 1959. Numerous up-tempo country classics followed over the years, and he had no fewer that 19 Number Ones in the US country charts in the 1960s, among them 'Act Naturally' (1963) and 'I've Got a Tiger by the Tail' (1965). Leading his band the Buckaroos and based in Bakersfield, California, he created what became known as the 'West Coast' country sound and remained an enduring favourite even though the hits petered out in the 1970s and 1980s. He made something of a return to form in the late 1980s with such albums as *Hot Dog!* (1988).

Ozawa, Seiji (1935–) Japanese conductor, who has won international acclaim leading several major orchestras. Ozawa switched from an intended career as a pianist to conducting after breaking two fingers playing rugby and subsequently won a prestigious conducting competition in France (1959). He studied under Herbert VON KARAJAN before taking up appointments as conductor with the Toronto Symphony Orchestra (1965–69), the San Francisco Symphony Orchestra (1970–76) and the BOSTON SYMPHONY ORCHESTRA (1973–).

P

Paderewski, Ignacy Jan (1860–1941) Polish pianist, composer and statesman, who combined a highly acclaimed career in music with public service at the highest level, fulfilling the post of prime minister of Poland for a brief time after the First World War. Having studied at the Warsaw Conservatory, Paderewski embarked on a career as a professional pianist in the late 1880s and was quickly hailed the most distinguished pianist of his generation. He settled in Switzerland in 1889 and subsequently performed in public all over the world before returning to the Warsaw Conservatory as director in 1909. He was an active fundraiser for war victims during the First World War and was appointed Poland's representative to the USA in 1918. A year later he was made Poland's prime minister and minister for foreign affairs, remaining in the posts for just 10 months before returning to his music. He was reinstated as prime minister for a short time when a Polish government-in-exile was established during the Second World War.

Paderewski's compositions included the opera *Manru* (1901), the *Six Humoresques de Concert*, which is famous for its Minuet in G, and a piano concerto.

Paderewski's dual career made him unique among musicians of his generation and guaranteed him a place in history. It also made him very rich, and he became the highest-paid classical concert pianist ever, amassing a fortune of some $5 million in all.

> Piano-playing is more difficult than statesmanship. It is harder to wake emotions in ivory keys than it is in human beings.
> IGNACY JAN PADEREWSKI

> While his competitors were counting his wrong notes, he was counting his dollars.
> HAROLD SCHONBERG, *The Great Pianists*, 1963

Paganini of the Banjo, the *See* Earl SCRUGGS.

Page, Patti (Clara Ann Fowler; 1927–) US JAZZ and COUNTRY singer, nicknamed the Singing Rage, who enjoyed numerous hits in the 1950s. Having made her radio début in 1947, she went on to release a total of 78 chart hits. Among the best-known singles were 'Confess' (1948), 'Tennessee Waltz' (1951), 'I Went to Your Wedding' (1952) and 'Doggie in the Window' (1953). She presented her own television show in the 1950s, switching to country in the 1970s.

Paige, Elaine (Elaine Bickerstaff; 1951–) British singer and actress, nicknamed Leather Lungs because of her considerable vocal power, who won acclaim for her performances in a series of highly successful British MUSICALS in the 1970s and 1980s. She appeared in such shows as *Hair* (1968), *Jesus Christ Superstar* (1972) and *Grease* (1973) before crowning her career with the starring part in Tim RICE and Andrew LLOYD WEBBER's *Evita* (1978) and subsequently appearing in *Cats* (1982), from which came the hit single 'Memory'. In 1985 she teamed up with Barbara Dickson and reached Number One with the duet 'I Know Him So Well' from the musical *Chess*, written by Tim Rice and the male members of ABBA, in which she also starred.

Palmer, Robert (1949–) British SOUL singer, who established an enduring reputation as a top star with an ice-cool image in the 1970s. Palmer has explored a wide range of music since launching his career in the 1960s, beginning with JAZZ-ROCK as lead singer of the Alan Bown Set and of Vinegar Joe, when he partnered Elkie BROOKS, before establishing himself on a solo basis as a RHYTHM-AND-BLUES artist in the mid-1970s. Such albums as *Sneakin' Sally through the Alley* (1974) and *Pressure Drop* (1975) were well received, and he went on to enjoy major success in the singles charts with the likes of 'Every Kinda People' (1978), 'A Bad Case of Lovin' You' (1979), 'Some Guys Have All the Luck' (1982) and 'Addicted to Love' (1985), which was accompanied by a striking video. More recent hits have included the albums *Don't Explain* (1988), *Ridin' High* (1992) and *Honey* (1994).

pantonality Term adopted by Arnold SCHOENBERG in preference to ATONALITY.

Panufnik, Andrzej (1914–91) Polish composer and conductor, of Anglo-Polish descent and resident in the UK from 1954, who established his reputation after the Second World War. Having studied at the Warsaw Conservatory, he survived the Nazi occupation of the city, although all his early compositions were destroyed, and was appointed conductor of the Krakow Philharmonic and of the Warsaw Philharmonic before deserting his native land for the UK for political reasons. He served as conductor of the City of BIRMINGHAM SYMPHONY ORCHESTRA for several years and attracted praise for such sober orchestral compositions as *Sinfonia rustica* (1948) and *Sinfonia sacra* (1963).

Paramor, Norrie (1914–79) British conductor, composer, arranger and producer, who provided backing music for many leading postwar stars. He worked as accompanist for Gracie FIELDS and subsequently collaborated with several popular dance bands and stage shows as well as touring with Bing CROSBY. As a producer for EMI, he recorded with such singers as Cliff RICHARD and Frank IFIELD. He was also the composer of the theme tune for BBC television's *Z Cars* among other contributions to TV and cinema.

Parker, Charlie (Charles Christopher Parker; 1920–55) Black US JAZZ saxophonist, who became – with Dizzy GILLESPIE – the chief architect of modern jazz before his premature death at the age of just 34. The nickname Bird, shortened from 'Yardbird', derived from his liking for fried chicken; Birdland, a jazz club on Broadway, New York, was named in Parker's honour after it opened in 1948. Parker was self-taught and became a professional musician at the age of 14. Early performances were so ill-received that he gave up playing for three months but subsequently redeveloped his playing technique and became a huge favourite, capable of astonishingly fast runs of notes and of infinite improvisation. He appeared in a number of prominent bands and then

played a key role in the birth of BEBOP in partnership with Gillespie and Thelonius MONK at MINTON'S PLAYHOUSE and elsewhere in 1944–5. His COOL style and highly accomplished technique had a profound impact on the contemporary jazz scene, his innovations including fragmented rhythms and complex harmonies. Among his most popular pieces were 'Ornithology', 'Now's the Time' and 'Yardbird Suite'.

Bird formed his own band in 1945 and continued to appear with a variety of other groups, notably the quintet he formed with Miles DAVIS, Duke Jordan, Tommy Potter and Max ROACH in 1947, although his addiction to heroin and weakness for alcohol caused frequent interruptions in his career in his last years. In 1946, after a recording session, he set his hotel room on fire and was subsequently sent to the psychiatric wing of the local gaol and thence to a rehabilitation centre. He continued to play at his best through the 1950s, although attempts to use an orchestral background were not judged an outstanding success.

Bird made his last public appearance at Birdland, the club named in his honour, and got involved in a full-scale row with the pianist; he died eight days later in the hotel suite of the Baroness Pannonica de Koenigswarter, who was a great fan of his. The doctor who examined his drug-ravaged body guessed his age to be around 53.

Critics observed that it was not until the 1960s that jazz music as a whole caught up with Parker and learned to absorb his brilliant contribution. Miles Davis is often quoted as the most important of his stylistic heirs.

> Music is your own experience, your thoughts, your wisdom. If you don't live it, it won't come out of your horn.
> CHARLIE PARKER

> Bird lives.
> Graffito seen in New York on Parker's death, 1955

Parsons, Alan (1949–   ) British producer and engineer, who masterminded a series of influential CONCEPT ALBUMS in the 1970s using established session musicians. A producer at ABBEY ROAD, Parsons contributed to records by groups such as the BEATLES and PINK FLOYD before embarking on 'Alan Parsons Project' albums like *Tales of Mystery* *and Imagination* (1976), which was based on the horror stories of Edgar Allan Poe, *I Robot* (1977), *The Turn of a Friendly Card* (1980), *Gaudi* (1987), which described the construction of the extraordinary modernist cathedral in Barcelona, and *Try Anything Once* (1993). He also worked on the stage show *Freudiana*, which was based on the life of Sigmund Freud.

Parsons, Gram (Cecil Ingram Connor; 1946–73) US COUNTRY-ROCK singer-songwriter and guitarist, who established a strong following before his early drug-related death. A former theology student, Parsons formed the International Submarine Band – acclaimed for the album *Safe At Last* – in 1967. He subsequently wrote for the BYRDS and founded the Flying Burrito Brothers, who won wide acclaim with the album *The Gilded Palace of Sin* (1969). He embarked on a solo career in 1970, releasing the album *GP* (1973) before his death and also collaborating with the ROLLING STONES. *The Return of the Grievous Angel* was issued posthumously in 1974. Among those who admitted to being influenced by Parsons were Emmylou HARRIS, Tom PETTY and Elvis COSTELLO.

Parton, Dolly (Rebecca Parton; 1946–) US COUNTRY singer-songwriter and actress, who emerged as one of the most popular of all country entertainers in the 1970s. Famous for her full-breasted figure and bubbly character, Parton rose to the top of the country charts on the strength of her many acclaimed albums and such hits as 'Dumb Blonde' (1967), 'Joshua' (1971), 'Jolene' (1974), 'Love is Like a Butterfly' (1974), 'Here You Come Again' (1978), 'Two Doors Down' (1978), 'Baby, I'm Burning' (1978), 'Nine to Five' (1980) and 'Islands in the Stream' (1984), several of which also did well in the pop charts. She launched a successful second career as a film actress in 1980 with *Nine to Five*, and the follow-ups included *The Best Little Whorehouse in Texas* (1982).

The success of *Here You Come Again* (1978) with pop audiences made Parton the first female country artist to receive a PLATINUM record award.

Patton, Charley (1887–1934) US BLUES singer-songwriter and guitarist, who was among the legendary bluesmen whose music has influenced succeeding generations of BLUES and ROCK performers. Among

his classic songs, a number of which he recorded in his last years, were 'Pony Blues', 'Frankie and Albert', 'Mississippi Bo Weevil Blues', 'Rattlesnake Blues', 'Love My Stuff', 'Revenue Blues Man' and 'Poor Me'.

Paul, Billy (Paul Williams; 1934–) US SOUL singer, who joined the first rank of soul stars with a series of hits in the 1970s. He made his recording début in 1955, at which time he was working chiefly in a JAZZ style, and went on to join Harold Melvin and the Blue Notes before establishing a reputation as a solo artist. He enjoyed success on both sides of the Atlantic with such hits as 'Me and Mrs Jones' (1972), 'Thanks for Saving My Life' (1974) and 'Only the Strong Survive' (1977). His albums include *360 Degrees of Billy Paul* (1972) and *Wide Open* (1988).

Paul, Les (Lester Polfus; 1915–) US guitarist and guitar designer, nicknamed the Waukesha Wizard after his birthplace, who profoundly influenced the history of rock and pop music when he introduced the first solid-body electric guitars in the late 1940s. Paul broadcast regularly as a COUNTRY guitarist in the 1930s and later led his own jazz-influenced trio, recording with such artists as Bing CROSBY and the ANDREWS SISTERS. The GIBSON Company took up his solid-body electric guitar after initial reluctance in 1947 but sold it under Paul's name with huge and lasting success. In fact, Paul had put together his very first solid-body electric guitar in 1940, when he attached strings to a section of railway sleeper, which he dubbed the 'Log'.

Paul's own hits included such multi-tracked instrumentals as 'Nola', 'Lady of Spain' and 'Brazil' and – with his wife singer Mary Ford (Colleen Summers; 1924–77) – 'How High the Moon' and 'Vaya con Dios'. He reverted to a country style in the 1970s with considerable success, but owes his fame primarily to his classic guitars.

Pavarotti, Luciano (1935–) Italian tenor, who first established a reputation as a superstar of contemporary opera in the 1960s. Pavarotti, the son of a baker in the city of Modena, made his professional début as an operatic tenor in 1961, playing Rodolfo in PUCCINI's *La Bohème* at

Reggio Emilia. He went on to win acclaim at leading opera houses throughout the world in such parts as Idamante in Mozart's *Idomeneo* and the Duke of Mantua in Verdi's *Rigoletto* and in works by Bellini. His performance as Nemorino in Donizetti's *L'Elisir d'amore* was another great favourite and earned him an all-time record of 165 curtain-calls when he sang the part at the Deutsche Opera in Berlin in 1988.

Pavorotti became the best-known opera star in the world through his many recordings and televised concerts. His generous girth and flamboyant manner (he often sings holding a large white handkerchief) make him instantly familiar to millions. Among his best-selling records have been a version of Donizetti's *Lucia di Lammermoor*, which he made with Dame Joan SUTHERLAND, and the phenomenally successful 'Nessun dorma', which rose to the top of pop charts in many countries in 1990, the year in which he teamed up with José CARRERAS and Placido DOMINGO to sing as part of the celebrations marking football's World Cup; the resulting album became the best-selling classical release of all time.

Pavarotti's great talent has nearly been lost to the world on two occasions: in 1947 a blood infection nearly killed him, and in 1975 he survived an aircrash in Milan, which ironically restored to him a passionate love of life. A universally lauded star, he protests that concerts still make him nervous, and he has been known to refuse to go on stage until he has found a bent nail on the floor to bring him luck.

Patzak, Julius (1898–1974) Austrian tenor, who established himself as one of the most admired tenors of the interwar era. Self-taught, he made his opera début in 1923 in Verdi's *Aida* and went on to become a star with the Munich Opera (1928–45) and with the Vienna State Opera (1945–60), excelling in Mozart and as Florestan in *Fidelio*.

Paxton, Tom (1937–) US FOLK singer-songwriter, who was one of the most popular singer-songwriters to emerge from Greenwich Village in the 1960s. Paxton established himself as a leader in the folk revival with such folk classics as 'The Last Thing on My Mind' and 'Ramblin' Boy', the children's song 'Goin' to the Zoo' and such PROTEST SONGS as 'Talking Vietnam Pot Luck Blues' and 'Forest Lawn'. Subsequent

recordings have included the albums *The Complete Tom Paxton* (1971), *New Songs for Old Friends* (1973), which he made in the UK with Ralph MCTELL, *New Songs from the Briar Patch* (1977) and *One Million Lawyers . . . and other Disasters* (1986).

Payne, Jack (John Wesley Vivian Payne; 1899–1969) British bandleader, who led some of the most popular DANCE BANDS of the 1920s and 1930s. Payne led his first band while with the Royal Flying Corps in the First World War, and in 1928 he rose to the post of Director of Dance Music for the BBC, where he led the BBC Dance Orchestra until 1932. He went on to appear in several musical films and worked as a theatrical agent after the Second World War.

payola scandal Corruption scandal, which rocked the world of popular music in the early 1960s. By the end of the 1950s the success of any pop single was closely linked to its rating in the national charts on both sides of the Atlantic, supposedly reflecting its sales with accuracy and impartiality. However, sales in the shops were profoundly influenced by the amount of airplay a record was given on the radio, and when it was revealed that DISC JOCKEYS throughout the USA were accepting gifts and other rewards for pushing certain releases, the whole ethos of the charts was brought into question. An official senate investigation into such practices damaged the careers of several top radio presenters, notably that of the World's Oldest Teenager, Dick CLARK. His colleague Alan FREED was fined and given a suspended prison sentence for his involvement (he died in hospital in 1965 at the age of 43 while facing further charges of income tax evasion).

One side-effect of the scandal was the blackening of the already dubious public image of ROCK 'N' ROLL and a tendency by record companies to promote 'safer' and less aggressive songs and performers in an attempt to regain lost ground.

The word 'payola' was arrived at by combining 'pay' with the Spanish 'ola', used of anything outrageous or on a large scale.

Pearl *See* Janis JOPLIN.

Pears, Sir Peter (Neville Luard) (1910–86) British tenor, who won acclaim through his long association with the works of Benjamin BRITTEN. Having trained at the Royal College of Music, London, Pears toured with the BBC

Singers and was recruited to sing at GLYN-DEBOURNE in 1938. He formed a close partnership with Britten in the USA in 1939 and subsequently, as a member of the Sadler's Wells company, appeared in many of Britten's most acclaimed works after returning to the UK with him in 1943. Among other roles, he created leading parts in *Peter Grimes* (1945), *The Rape of Lucretia* (1946), *Billy Budd* (1951), *Gloriana* (1953), *The Turn of the Screw* (1954), *A Midsummer Night's Dream* (1960) and *Death in Venice* (1973). He also excelled in the works of Bach and recorded songs by Schumann and Schubert as well as Elizabethan lute songs with Julian BREAM. He was co-founder, with Britten, of the ALDEBURGH FESTIVAL in 1948.

pecking JAZZ style of the 1950s, in which short notes were played in bewilderingly rapid succession. Among the leading exponents of the technique was Art TATUM.

Penderecki, Krzysztof (1933–) Polish composer, who emerged as one of Poland's leading musical figures in the 1960s. Influenced by the pointillist techniques of György LIGETI, Penderecki established his reputation with such works as *Anaklasis* (1960), *Threnody for the Victims of Hiroshima* (1960), the *St Luke Passion* (1966), the opera *The Devils of Loudun* (1968–69) and the *Utrenja* (1971), which explored the dramatic potential of such devices as note CLUSTERS and new string and percussion effects. He adopted a more restrained romantic style for such noteworthy compositions as the *Magnificat* (1974), the violin concerto (1976), the opera *Paradise Lost* (1976–78) and the choral *Polish Requiem* (1983).

The *Threnody for the Victims of Hiroshima* is unusual in that it directs string players to play notes on both sides of the bridge of their instruments.

Pendergrass, Teddy (1950–) US RHYTHM-AND-BLUES singer, nicknamed Teddy Bear, who became a big favourite with SOUL fans in the 1970s, when he enjoyed something of a reputation as a sex symbol. A former member of Harold Melvin's Blue Notes, he embarked on a solo career in 1976 and had big hits with such albums as *Teddy Pendergrass* (1977), *Life is a Song Worth Singing* (1978) and *This One's For You* (1982). Hit singles included 'Never knew love like this' (1980) and the duet 'Two Hearts' (1981), with Stephanie Mills. Pendergrass's career

suffered a major setback in 1982 when he was paralyzed as a result of injuries he received when his Rolls Royce crashed into a tree, but he has since returned to the recording studios with such albums are *Heaven Only Knows* (1984), *Love Language* (1984), *Joy* (1988); and *Truly Blessed* (1991).

Pentangle British FOLK-ROCK group, which established a large following in the late 1960s. Led by the acclaimed folk guitarists John Renbourn and Bert Jansch (1943–), backed by bassist Danny Thompson (1939–) and drummer Terry Cox, with vocals supplied by Jacqui McShee, Pentangle came together in 1967 and immediately established itself as a top folk-rock act with such albums as *Pentangle* (1967), *Sweet Child* (1968) and *Basket of Light* (1969). The group split after the acclaimed *Solomon's Seal* (1972), Renbourn and Jansch pursuing successful solo careers, while Thompson joined John MARTYN before embarking on his own solo albums. A brief reunion in the early 1980s culminated in the modestly successful *Open the Door* (1982), and the group reunited again in 1994 for a new LP and tour.

Pepper, Art (Arthur Edward Pepper; 1925–82) US JAZZ saxophonist, of German and Italian descent, who was a key figure in the development of West Coast jazz in the USA. After the Second World War, Pepper played in the band of Stan KENTON (1946–52) and with Buddy RICH (1968–69) as well as leading his own bands and establishing a worldwide reputation in the course of numerous tours. His career was much disrupted by his drug addiction and he spent some time in gaol in the 1950s and 1960s.

Perahia, Murray (1947–) US pianist, who first came to public attention after winning the LEEDS PIANO COMPETITION in 1972. His many acclaimed recordings include all Mozart's concertos, which he often conducts from the keyboard.

Performing Rights Society British organization, based in London, which was established in 1914 to raise moneys due by copyright law to composers, authors and publishers of musical works. With a membership of over 23,000, it represents virtually all published composers in the UK and Ireland, and it is affiliated with similar societies worldwide. A non-profit making body, the PRS uses a small part of the collected revenue 'for any purpose conducive to the improvement or advancement of the composition, teaching, or performance of music', and some provision is also made for the maintenance of a members' hardship fund.

Perkins, Carl (Carl Lee Perkings; 1932–) US singer-songwriter and guitarist, nicknamed One-string in reference to his innovative use of carefully plucked single notes rather than clusters of sounds, who was one of the first great ROCK 'N' ROLL stars of the 1950s. Adopting a ROCKABILLY style, similar to that of the emerging Elvis PRESLEY, Perkins was particularly admired for his innovative guitar style, which was to prove as influential as that of Chuck BERRY and Presley guitarist Scotty Moore. He enjoyed huge success with the rock 'n' roll anthem 'Blue Suede Shoes' (1956) and with such follow-ups as 'Honey Don't', but he missed out on consolidating his reputation when he was forced to recuperate from his injuries after a car crash near Dover, Delaware, in March 1957 in which his brother Jay was killed; as a result Presley rather than Perkins became one of the first rock 'n' roll stars to appear on national television. By the time Perkins had recovered, the moment had passed and he had to be content with a supporting role in most rock 'n' roll histories. He released a number of further classic rock 'n' roll hits, including 'Match Box', after his return, and he subsequently ventured into COUNTRY music, backing Johnny CASH as well as reviving his old standards on a regular basis.

> I've never felt bitter, always felt lucky being in the music business at all. Most kids from my background never drive a new car.
> CARL PERKINS

Perlman, Itzhak (1945–) Israeli violinist, who has won worldwide fame as one of the most distinguished of all contemporary violinists. Despite being confined to a wheelchair as a result of childhood polio, Perlman made his professional début in 1963 and has established a reputation for excellence, playing a wide range of material, from chamber music, which he often plays with Daniel BARENBOIM, Pinchas ZUKERMAN and Vladimir ASHKENAZY, to RAGTIME.

> You see, our fingers are circumcised, which gives it a very good dexterity, you know, particularly in the pinky.
> ITZHAK PERLMAN, when asked why so many famous violinists were Jewish

Persimfans Abbreviation of Pervyi Simfonichesky Ansambl, the name of a Soviet experiment of the 1920s in which the principles of socialist equality were applied to musical performance. It was decided that the symphony orchestra was a reactionary, bourgeois assembly imported from the West in which comrade-workers were subjugated as the hireling lackeys of a single capitalist, imperialist hyena, known as the conductor. The conductor was accordingly dispensed with and the orchestra run on a collective basis. Rehearsals resembled committee meetings, each player being permitted an equal say, with the result that they took five times as long as they had done before and cost a great deal more money. It soon became apparent that an orchestra with 75 conductors was less efficient than an orchestra with a single conductor, and the experiment was quietly abandoned.

Personality Girl, the *See* Annette HANSHAW.

Pet Shop Boys, the British pop duo, who emerged as a top-selling chart act of the 1980s. Singer Neil Tennant (1954–) and keyboard player Chris Lowe (1959–) came together in 1981 and had their first hit in 1985 with 'West End Girls'. They claimed that there was no particular reason they chose the name Pet Shop Boys – they just knew someone who worked in one. Subsequent chart successes included two more Number Ones, 'It's a Sin' (1987) and 'Always on My Mind' (1987); the albums *Please* (1986), *Actually* (1987), *Introspective* (1988), *Behaviour* (1990), *Very* (1993) and *Alternative* (1995) also did well. Other projects have included collaborations with Dusty SPRINGFIELD and Liza MINNELLI.

Peter, Paul and Mary US vocal pop group, which had several FOLK hits in the 1960s, COVERING classic songs by Bob DYLAN. The success Peter Yarrow (1938–), Paul Stookey (Noel Stookey; 1937–) and Mary Allin Travers (1937–) had with such singles as 'Blowin' in the Wind' and 'The Times They are A-Changin'' did much to establish Dylan as a leading singer-songwriter of the period. The group's other hits included versions of 'If I had a Hammer' and 'This Land is Your Land' as well as 'Puff the Magic Dragon', 'Leaving on a Jet Plane' and 'I Dig Rock 'n' Roll Music'. 'Puff the Magic Dragon' was intended as a song for children, but some confused fans assumed other motives and treated it as a hymn to the use of hallucinogenic drugs. Having starred at the NEW-PORT FESTIVAL, Peter, Paul and Mary broke up in 1971. Yarrow was subsequently sentenced for child molesting (he was eventually pardoned by President Carter), and the group was re-formed in 1978, since when it has continued to tour although all three members have also released various solo albums.

Peterson, Oscar (Emmanuel) (1925–) Black Canadian JAZZ pianist, bandleader, singer and composer, who established himself as one of the most popular and commercially successful jazzmen of the postwar era. Peterson's talent was recognized when he was recruited to play in the JAZZ AT THE PHILHARMONIC concerts in the 1950s, and he subsequently toured widely, leading his own trio but also making solo appearances. He collaborated with Ella FITZGERALD in the 1960s and built a reputation as a competent MAINSTREAM jazz composer with such works as *Canadiana Suite* (1965). His most popular recordings have included *Affinity* (1963) and *My Favourite Instrument* (1973), and he has reached a huge television audience through his various lighthearted but erudite television series since the 1970s.

Peterson, Ray (1939–) US pop singer, who established a big following in the late 1950s singing tear-jerking ballads. Peterson, who had overcome polio as a child, emerged as a top star with such hits as 'Tell Laura I Love Her' (1960), which told of a lover's death in a stock car race, and 'Corinna Corinna' (1960). He then tried to switch to COUNTRY music but eventually retired from music in the late 1960s.

Petty, Tom (1952–) US rock singer-songwriter and guitarist, who emerged as a leading successor to such rock heroes of the 1960s as the BAND and the ROLLING STONES. Tom Petty and his band, the Heart-breakers, established a large following in the 1980s in both the USA and Australia,

and even worked as a backing group for Bob DYLAN on world tours. Petty joined George HARRISON, Dylan and Roy ORBISON in the Traveling Wilburys in 1988. His finest albums include *Damn the Torpedoes* (1979), *Pack up the Plantation* (1985), *Full Moon Fever* (1989) and *Into the Great Wide Open* (1991).

Peyer, Gervase (Alan) de (1926–) British clarinettist and conductor, who is considered among the finest clarinettists of modern times. For many years (1955–71) de Peyer was principal clarinettist with the LONDON SYMPHONY ORCHESTRA; he was also a co-founder of the Melos Ensemble and has served as associate conductor of the Haydn Orchestra.

Pfitzner, Hans Erich (1869–1949) German composer, conductor and teacher, who established a reputation in his homeland as the most distinguished of the successors of Richard STRAUSS. Following in the Germanic romantic tradition and resisting the MODERNISM of Arnold SCHOENBERG and his disciples, he won particular praise for such operas as *Palestrina* (1917). Other works included chamber and orchestral music and many songs as well as the cantata *Von deutscher Seele* (1922). Despite his high standing at the start of his career, he spent the war years in poverty and obscurity, but ended his life as a pensioner of the VIENNA PHILHARMONIC ORCHESTRA.

Philadelphia Orchestra US orchestra, which has built up a strong international reputation since its foundation in 1900. Conductors of the Philadelphia Orchestra, which has presented premières of important works by such composers as Gustav MAHLER, Igor STRAVINSKY and Arnold SCHOENBERG, have included Leopold STOKOWSKI, Eugene ORMANDY and Riccardo MUTI.

Philharmonia Orchestra British orchestra, which has made many acclaimed recordings since its foundation by Walter Legge in 1945. Conductors of the Philharmonia, refounded as the New Philharmonia in 1964 (when it became self-governing) but known simply as the Philharmonia since 1977, have included Herbert von KARAJAN, Otto KLEMPERER, Carlo Maria GIULINI, Richard STRAUSS and Arturo TOSCANINI. Lorin MAAZEL was associate principal conductor in 1971–73; Riccardo MUTI was principal conductor in 1973–82.

Phillips, Esther (Esther Mae Jones; 1935–84) US BLUES, JAZZ and pop singer, who had a number of hits in various styles in the 1950s and 1960s. Phillips, who changed her name from Jones after passing an advertisement for Phillips Gasoline, worked as a backing singer for Johnny OTIS when she was 13 years old, but went on to establish herself as a top RHYTHM-AND-BLUES star with such hits as 'Double Crossing Blues' (1950), 'Cupid's Boogie' (1950) and 'Mistrusting Blues' (1950). She returned to the charts in a big way in 1963 with 'Release Me' and went on to star at jazz festivals into the 1970s. Her last major hits before her death, which was hastened by her long-standing drug problems, was 'What a Difference a Day Makes' (1975).

Piaf, Edith (Edith Giovanna Gassion; 1915–63) French CABARET singer-songwriter, nicknamed the Little Sparrow in reference both to her tiny frame and to her stagename 'Piaf' (French slang for sparrow), who became a legend of French popular music after the Second World War. The daughter of a café singer and a circus acrobat, Piaf rose from the most modest of backgrounds and made her first steps in a musical career by working as a street singer in Paris, where she mixed with prostitutes and other outcasts of society. Vulgar, indomitable and neurotic, she attracted attention through her uniquely emotional singing voice, and in time she became one of the best-loved of all French stars. Her radio début in 1936 was followed by numerous recordings, stage appearances and films. Among her hits, several of which she rendered with equal success in both English and French, were such classics as 'La vie en rose' (which she wrote herself), 'Je m'en fou pas mal' and 'Je ne regrette rien', which encapsulated her irrepressible spirit in the face of the harshest difficulties.

Piaf's private life was always chaotic, with failed marriages and an increasing dependence on alcohol and heroin that eventually destroyed her frail health. Millions turned out for her funeral in Paris, and news of her death at the age of 48 was said to have caused the writer and philosopher Jean Cocteau to suffer his fatal heart attack. A street in Paris was renamed in her memory in 1981.

Piano Man, the See Billy JOEL.

pianola An automatically operating piano, specifically one made by the Aeolian Corporation, although the term is now used of such instruments in general. A machine with keys operated by air instead of finger pressure was actually made in France in the 1860s, although a patent was not granted until 1897, when one was awarded to the American E.S. Voley. Known in the USA as a 'player-piano', the pianola was an immediate success, and by 1919 more pianolas were being sold to US buyers than pianos. The machine was almost equally popular in Europe, enjoying its heyday in the years following the First World War. It was available in both grand and upright versions, with Steinway producing its own model, called the 'Steinway-Duo-Art'. All the better-made models are now collectors' pieces.

The mechanism worked by means of a roll of strong paper with perforations punched in it, which passed over a row of air jets, one jet for each note on the piano. Each perforation also represented a note, so that, as a perforation passed over a jet (several doing so at the same time to make a chord), the released air pressure activated the hammer for that particular note. In the early days, an attendant had to work the machine by pumping in air with a pedal, but in time an electrically operated pump was incorporated, and the operator used various levers to control the speed and dynamics of the playing. In the more advanced models quite subtle variations were possible, thus imparting 'feel' to the music as if someone were really playing it by hand.

With a slight alteration to the mechanism it also became possible to record actual performances for later reproduction, the movements of the players' fingers causing the roll to be marked for subsequent perforation. Artur RUBINSTEIN was among the great pianists to perform for such 'Reproducing Pianos', and several composers made piano rolls of their own works. Other composers, including Igor STRAVINSKY, who was impressed by its 'non-interpretative' sound, saw in the pianola a chance to escape the irritating excesses of romantically inclined pianists, and they composed for the instrument. Stravinsky even scored his cantata *The Wedding* with a pianola accompaniment.

The fashion for the pianola was, however, short-lived, and by the end of the

1920s it was obsolete, largely a consequence of the advent of the gramophone and the wireless. One man who stayed loyal to his old pianola was Professor Joad of the BBC Brains Trust, who boasted that he used to 'play' Bach every morning on his machine. This was not, he explained, because he was particularly fond of Bach fugues, but because pedalling was good for his constipation.

Piatigorsky, Gregor (1903–76) Russian cellist and composer, resident in the USA from 1921, who was considered the finest cellist of his generation. Having served as principal cellist of the Bolshoi Theatre Orchestra from 1919, he won acclaim for his collaborations with Vladimir HOROWITZ and Nathan Milstein (1904–), and with Jascha HEIFETZ and Artur RUBINSTEIN.

Picasso of the Piano, the See Erroll GARNER.

Piccaver, Alfred (Alfred Peckover; 1884–1958) British tenor, who became a huge star at the Vienna State Opera. Piccaver's career at the top level began after he auditioned for the Prague Opera in 1907 (as a joke, according to legend) and was taken on. He went on to triumph during his long association with the Vienna State Opera (1910–37).

Pickett, Wilson (1941–) US SOUL singer, nicknamed the Wicked Pickett on account of his lively temper, who established a reputation in the 1960s with a series of hits that made the most of his unique GOSPEL-inspired vocal style. He sang on the Falcons hit 'I Found a Love' (1962) and then launched himself on a solo career with such hits as 'In the Midnight Hour' (1965), 'Don't Fight It' (1965), 'Mustang Sally' (1966), 'Funky Broadway' (1967), 'Hey Jude' (1968) and 'Don't Let the Green Grass Fool You' (1971). In 1994 he served a year in gaol after being found guilty of drink-drive offences.

Pink Floyd British PROGRESSIVE ROCK band, which became one of the most popular of all rock outfits. Founded in 1966 by bassist Roger Waters (1944–) and guitarist Syd Barrett (1946–), the group was originally called the Pink Floyd Sound after the names of two celebrated BLUES singers from Georgia, Pink Anderson and Floyd Council. Synthesizer player Rick Wright (1945–) and drummer Nick Mason (1945–)

joined a little later, and the quartet acquired a reputation as leading exponents of PSYCHEDELIC ROCK, with a dazzling live act – Pink Floyd was the first band to use a light show as an integral part of the performance. Founder-member Barrett dropped out of the band in 1967 and two years later he was committed to a mental asylum as a profound schizophrenic; his place in the line-up went to singer and guitarist Dave Gilmour (1944–); the LP *Wish You Were Here* was later recorded in tribute to Barrett.

Such surreal albums as *The Piper at the Gates of Dawn* (1967), *Ummagumma* (1969), *Atom Heart Mother* (1970) and *Meddle* (1971) were but precursors to the masterpiece, *The Dark Side of the Moon* (1973), which marked the high point of the progressive rock genre and confirmed the band as the equal of any in the world in both commercial and artistic terms. The album remains the best-selling rock album of all time and by 1987 had enjoyed a record 700 weeks in the BILLBOARD charts; it also soared back into the upper reaches of the British charts when it was re-released in 1993.

Wish You Were Here (1975), *Animals* (1977) and *The Wall* (1979) followed with almost equal success before the neurosis-ridden Waters, from whose paranoia *The Wall* had been born, left in the mid-1980s. The band regrouped behind Gilmour and Mason for *A Momentary Lapse of Reason* (1987), *The Division Bell* (1994) and *Pulse* (1995).

In 1990 Roger Waters staged the most spectacular rock concert ever seen when he performed *The Wall* in Berlin: no fewer than 600 people took part in the performance, and another 200,000 helped to build up and then break down a facsimile of the Berlin Wall.

Pinnock, Trevor (David) (1946–) British harpsichordist and conductor, who has won acclaim for his efforts to promote the performance of early music on authentic instruments. Founder of the English Concert in 1972, he has made many notable recordings, including the entire repertoire of the keyboard compositions of Rameau.

Pinza, Ezio (1892–1957) Italian bass singer, who became one of the leading stars at the METROPOLITAN OPERA in New York after his début there in 1926. He remained at the Met until 1948 and subsequently added to his great reputation for masterly performances in such operas as Mozart's *Don Giovanni* and acclaimed appearances in various films and stage MUSICALS, notably *South Pacific* (1949) and *Fanny* (1954). He was noted for his huge appetite and regularly ate 12-course dinners – when one waitress looked shocked at his order when he was appearing in *South Pacific* he snapped 'What's the matter with you? I may be singing musical comedy these days – but I still *eat* grand opera!'

Piston, Walter (1894–1976) US composer, who won acclaim for his many JAZZ-influenced compositions. A student of Nadia BOULANGER, he wrote eight symphonies, a number of concertos for various instruments, the ballet *The Incredible Flutist* (1938), chamber music and string quartets.

Pitney, Gene (1941–) US pop singer-songwriter, nicknamed the Rockville Rocket, who became a top international star with numerous hits in the 1960s. Specializing in epic ballads, he got to the top of the charts with such numbers as 'Town Without Pity' (1961), 'The Man Who Shot Liberty Valance' (1962), '24 Hours from Tulsa' (1963) and 'Something's Gotten Hold of My Heart' (1967). In all, 23 songs by Pitney reached the Top 20 in the UK between 1961 and 1969. He also wrote hits for other artists, among them 'Hello, Mary Lou', which was recorded with huge success by Ricky NELSON, and 'Rubber Ball', which was taken up by Bobby VEE. He also guested as pianist on the ROLLING STONES hit 'Little by Little' (1964). He retired from music to concentrate on his business interests.

platinum disc A single that has sold 2 million copies, or an album that has achieved a million sales. The very first record to 'go platinum' was Johnnie Taylor's 1976 DISCO hit 'Disco Lady'. The first platinum-selling album was the EAGLES' greatest hits LP in 1976. With a total of 17, CHICAGO has amassed more platinum albums than any other group, while Paul MCCARTNEY has won 12 and Barbra STREISAND has earned no fewer than 19.

Platters, the US close-harmony vocal group,

which was among the most popular exponents of DOO-WOP in the 1950s. The original members of the group were Zola Taylor (1934–), Herb Reed (1931–), Alex Hodge, who was replaced by Paul Robi (1931–89), tenor David Lynch (1929–81) and lead singer Tony Williams (1928–92). Using songs mostly written by manager Buck Ram (1907–91), the group made its first forays into the charts in 1953 and was subsequently established as a top commercial act with such hits as 'Only You' (1955), which went straight to Number One on the US RHYTHM-AND-BLUES chart, 'The Great Pretender' (1955), 'My Prayer' (1956), 'Twilight Time' (1958) and 'Smoke Gets in Your Eyes' (1958), all of which got to Number One in various charts. The close-harmony vocal style, derived from that of traditional GOSPEL singers, had a profound influence on numerous other groups, notably the BEACH BOYS and the BEATLES, while the Platters' success in the record shops challenged the existing domination of the charts by White groups covering Black material. The group went into decline in the wake of various changes in the line-up and eventually split amid legal wrangles. Among its latter hits were 'I Love You 1,000 Times' (1966) and 'With This Ring' (1977).

Unusual venues played by the Platters included the submerged nuclear submarine USS *John Adams*, on which they once gave a performance.

player-piano *See* PIANOLA.

Plowright, Rosalind (1949–) British soprano, who was recognized as a highly gifted singer in the 1970s. Victory in the Sofia International Competition in 1979 launched her on an acclaimed singing career, in the course of which she has distinguished herself as a performer of works by Richard STRAUSS and Verdi in particular.

Poet of Nashville, the *See* Tom T. HALL.

Poet of the Organ, the *See* Jesse CRAWFORD.

Poet Princess of Rock, the *See* Patti SMITH.

Pointer Sisters, the Black US all-girl vocal group, which enjoyed a series of hit singles in the 1970s and early 1980s. Sisters Anita (1948–), Bonnie (1950–), June (1954–) and Ruth (1946–) Pointer originally sang in church, but then worked as backing singers for a range of stars before emerging as artists in their own right with such DISCO hits as 'Yes We Can Can' (1973) and the COUNTRY-oriented Number One 'Fairy Tale' (1974). The sisters eventually switched to a rock-pop CROSSOVER style, working as a trio after Bonnie left. The single 'Fire' (1979) reached Number Two in the USA, and the sisters consolidated their status as a top transatlantic act with such hit singles as 'He's So Shy' (1980), 'Automatic' (1984), 'Jump (for My Love)' (1984), 'I'm So Excited' (1984) and 'Dare Me' (1985).

Police, the British rock band, which established a strong commercial following in the early 1980s as one of the leading NEW WAVE acts that succeeded PUNK ROCK. Lead singer and bassist Sting (Gordon Sumner; 1951–   ), US drummer Stewart Copeland (1952–   ) and guitarist Andy Summers (1942–   ), who replaced Henri Padovani, came together in 1977 and rapidly perfected a unique style, mixing punk influences with those of REGGAE, JAZZ and conventional pop. Audiences initially took them to be a punk outfit because of their bleached hair, although this look was actually the legacy of their appearance as three blonds in a chewing-gum advertisement.

The singles 'I Can't Stand Losing You' (1978) and 'Roxanne' (1978), hits on both sides of the Atlantic, were followed by the highly acclaimed album *Regatta de Blanc* (1979), from which came the UK Number Ones 'Message in a Bottle' and 'Walking on the Moon'. World tours consolidated the group's reputation, and it maintained its status as one of the top bands of the early 1980s with such releases as *Zenyatta Mondatta* (1980), *Ghost In the Machine* (1981) and *Synchronicity* (1983), from which came the chart-topping singles 'Don't Stand So Close to Me' (1980), 'Every Little Thing She Does is Magic' (1981) and 'Every Breath You Take' (1983).

The trio went on to develop solo careers, Sting adopting a JAZZ style for *Dream of the Blue Turtles* (1985) and winning praise for his contributions to the big charity events of the mid-1980s; he has also established a reputation as a film actor and has done much work on behalf of the Amazonian Indians.

Pollack, Ben (1903–71) US bandleader and drummer, nicknamed the Father of Swing,

who led one of the most popular DANCE BANDS of the late 1920s and 1930s. He took over his first band in the mid-1920s and attracted to it such star soloists as Glenn MILLER and Benny GOODMAN. He lost most of his musicians to Bob CROSBY in 1934 but set up a new band and continued to enjoy wide popularity until retiring from music in the 1940s. He subsequently staged a come-back, but got into severe financial trouble and ultimately hanged himself.

Pollack, Lew (1896–1946) US songwriter and pianist, who wrote numerous hits of the 1920s and 1930s. Classics by his hand included 'My Yiddishe Momme' (1925), on which he collaborated with Jack Yellen (1892–1958), 'Charmaine' (1926), 'Miss Annabelle Lee' (1927) and 'At the Codfish Ball' (1936).

Pollini, Maurizio (1942–   ) Italian pianist and conductor, who has won particular acclaim for his interpretations of the music of Chopin and of Arnold SCHOENBERG. He established his international reputation in 1960, when he won the Warsaw Chopin Competition at the age of 18.

PolyGram Dutch record company, which is part of the huge Philips Gloeilampenfabrieken organization. Descended from the German branch of HIS MASTER'S VOICE, the PolyGram name was introduced in 1972, when the division's pop groups were issued under Polydor (and subsequently Mercury) and classical music under DGG (Deutsche Grammophon). Among the major names signed by PolyGram since then have been the BEE GEES, SLADE, DEXY'S MIDNIGHT RUNNERS and DEF LEPPARD. More stars were added when PolyGram acquired DECCA in 1980. The Philips company itself was at the forefront during the development of the COMPACT DISC in the 1980s.

pomp rock Sub-genre of rock music, which caters specifically for those bands that adopt a more sophisticated style with emphasis on a high standard of musicianship and individual excellence. Examples of the genre have included QUEEN and JOURNEY among many others.

Pomus and Shuman US songwriting team, which was responsible for a string of classic RHYTHM-AND-BLUES and pop hits in the 1950s and 1960s. Writing for such artists as the DRIFTERS and Elvis PRESLEY, Doc

Pomus (Jerome Pomus; 1925–91) and Mort Shuman (1936–91) came up with hits including 'A Teenager in Love', 'Save the Last Dance for Me', 'Surrender' and 'I Count the Tears'. On his own, Pomus wrote such hits as 'Young Blood', recorded by the COASTERS in 1957, while Shuman created 'Here I Go Again' for the HOLLIES and 'Little Children' for Billy J. Kramer (1943–).

Pons, Lily (Alice Joséphine Pons; 1898–1976) US soprano, born in France, who became one of the legendary stars of the METROPOLITAN OPERA in New York. She made her professional début in *Lakmé* by Delibes in 1928 and subsequently enjoyed a lengthy and hugely successful association (1931–59) with the Met. Her recordings included the much-acclaimed 'Bell Song' from *Lakmé*. She married the conductor André KOSTELANETZ in 1938.

Poor Man's Pope, the *See* Bob MARLEY.

pop Popular music, usually taken to refer to the commercially oriented music peddled by pop stars of all descriptions since the ROCK 'N' ROLL revolution of the 1950s. This all-embracing term has long attracted more than its fair share of venom, and many JAZZ, rock and classical musicians have long fought shy of the label, with its connotations of money-grabbing, fashion-dominated, mindless, teenage dance music. At its best, however, pop has risen up on the talents of such hugely successful artists as the BEATLES, ABBA, Elvis PRESLEY, MADONNA and Michael JACKSON as the voice of a whole generation and an expression of youthful exuberance. On occasion, too, it still attempts something of greater depth for the discerning, mature listener. *See* ACID HOUSE; BUBBLEGUM; DISCO; ELECTRO-FUNK; GLAM ROCK; RAP; REGGAE; ROCKABILLY; SKIFFLE; SOUL; SYNTHESIZER POP; TEENY-BOP.

Pop music is the classical music of now.
PAUL McCARTNEY

I think popular music in this country is one of the few things in the twentieth century that have made giant strides in reverse.
BING CROSBY

Life would be awful if we were trapped in genius all the time. But pop music is the hamburger of every day ... if you go for a quick lunch, you don't have pheasant and wine of 1935.
PIERRE BOULEZ

I've always said that pop music is disposable ... if it wasn't disposable, it'd be a pain in the fuckin' arse.
ELTON JOHN

Listen kid, take my advice, never hate a song that has sold half a million copies.
IRVING BERLIN, to Cole Porter

Pope, the *See* Frank SINATRA.

Popp, Lucia (1939–93) Austrian soprano, born in Czechoslovakia, who established an international reputation singing the great roles of Mozart and Wagner. A popular star of the Vienna State Opera, she made her début in 1963 and subsequently won acclaim at leading opera venues around the world.

Pops *See* Louis ARMSTRONG.

pork chop Early JAZZ style, which enjoyed some popularity in the 1900s. Its characteristic feature was that it was played rather more slowly than the up-tempo jazz played by most pioneering jazz bands of the era.

pornophony Derogatory term that was used by a number of Soviet critics to attack Dmitri SHOSTAKOVICH's opera *Lady Macbeth of the Mtsensk District* (1936) and other 'formalist' works (*see* FORMALISM). The strength of the opposition to the work was much fuelled by the uncompromising plot of the opera, which revolved around a multiple murderess and included gang rape among other extreme scenes.

Porter, Cole (1891–1964) US songwriter, who, as the author of numerous witty classics for stage and screen, won a reputation as perhaps the greatest songwriter of the century. Born into an affluent family in Peru, Indiana, Porter wrote his first songs while studying law, and he served in the French Foreign Legion during the First World War after his first comic opera *See America First* (1916) failed to make an impression. Subsequently he contributed a number of songs to revues, starting with *Hitchy-Koo of 1919*, and by the end of the 1920s was acknowledged as one of the most promising songwriters of his generation.

Porter came into his own as a writer of lively and tuneful musical shows for stage and screen in the 1930s, and he went on to contribute a long series of box office smashes. Hit songs from his stage shows included 'Let's Do It', from *Paris* (1928); 'What is This Thing Called Love?', from *Wake Up and Dream* (1929); 'Love for Sale', from *The New Yorkers* (1930); 'Night and Day', which was written expressly for Fred ASTAIRE in the musical comedy *Gay Divorce* (1932); 'I Get a Kick Out of You', 'Anything Goes' and 'You're the Top', all from *Anything Goes* (1934); 'Miss Otis Regrets' (1934), 'Begin the Beguine' and 'Just One of Those Things', from *Jubilee* (1935); 'It's De-lovely', which was inspired by a sunset in Rio and was a highlight of *Red, Hot and Blue* (1936); 'My Heart Belongs to Daddy', from *Leave it to me!* (1938); 'Too Darn Hot', from *Kiss Me, Kate* (1948); 'I love Paris', from *Can-Can* (1953); and 'All of You', from *Silk Stockings* (1955).

Among his most popular films were *Born to Dance* (1936), *Rosalie* (1937), *Hollywood Canteen* (1944), from which came the classic cowboy song 'Don't Fence Me In', and *High Society* (1956), for which he wrote 'True Love', 'Well, Did You Evah' and 'Who Wants to be a Millionaire'.

A riding accident suffered by Porter in 1937 left a legacy of pain (one leg was eventually amputated after many operations), and after the death of his wife in 1956 the celebrated songwriter spent his final years in seclusion. His life story was told in the film *Night and Day* (1946), with Cary Grant as Porter himself.

> All the inspiration I ever needed was a phonecall from a producer.
> COLE PORTER

> The Adlai Stevenson of songwriters ... he was an aristocrat in everything he did and everything he wrote. Everything had class.
> LARRY ADLER

Poulenc, Francis Jean Marcel (1899–1963) French composer and pianist, who emerged as a leading contemporary composer between the wars with works whose attractively frivolous character often concealed an underlying seriousness. Having learned to play the piano, Poulenc, the son of a wealthy pharmaceutist, established his reputation with the JAZZ-influenced *African Rhapsody* (1917) and *Trois mouvements perpetuels* (1918) for piano and became one of the celebrated group of French composers dubbed Les SIX, despite lacking formal Conservatory-style training. Having completed army service (1918–21), he enjoyed

another big success in 1923 with the deliberately playful and (then) somewhat daring ballet *Les Biches*, which was written for Diaghilev's Ballets Russes. Subsequent compositions ranged from the *Concerto champêtre* (1928) for harpsichord and orchestra, written for Wanda LANDOWSKA, and operas, to sonatas for piano and various wind instruments and settings of poems by such surrealist and symbolist writers as Louis Aragon, Guillaume Apollinaire, Jean Cocteau, Paul Éluard, Max Jacob and de Vilmorin. Many of his songs were composed specifically for the tenor Pierre Bernac (1899–1979), for whom Poulenc often worked as accompanist on both sides of the Atlantic. Other compositions reflected his sincere Roman Catholicism, notably his *Litanies à la Vierge Noire de Rocamadour* (1936), which consisted of a series of sacred choral passages, and the *Quatre Motets pour un temps de pénitence* (1939).

The emotional national turmoil brought about by the outbreak of war in 1939 inspired such compositions as *La Figure humaine* (1943), which celebrated the indomitable spirit of the oppressed, and the song 'C' (1943), which was based on lines by Aragon about the Nazi crossing of a bridge in the French village of Cé, although the war period also saw the composition of a witty setting of the children's story *Babar the Elephant*, written for young relatives of his.

From the end of the war, Poulenc continued to consolidate his reputation with such works as the extraordinary surrealist and witty opera *Les Mamelles de Tirésias* (1947), which has the heroine Thérèse changing sex in order to liberate herself, *La Voix humaine* (1948), which was based on lines by Cocteau, a setting of the *Stabat Mater* (1951), the notably sombre large-scale opera *Les Dialogues des Carmélites* (1956), which traced the fate of some Carmelite nuns who were guillotined in the French Revolution, *Le Travail du peintre* (1956), which returned to the writings of the poet Éluard, and the *Gloria* (1959). He also wrote sonatas in memory of Sergei PROKOFIEV and Arthur HONEGGER.

> My music is my portrait.
> FRANCIS POULENC

> Above all do not analyse my music – love it!
> FRANCIS POULENC

Pousseur, Henri (1929–) Belgian composer, who joined the ranks of the most influential AVANT-GARDE composers of the 1960s and 1970s. A pupil of Pierre BOULEZ's, he began in a strictly serial style but later concentrated more on the social implications of his work. Often using electronic instruments, he has explored various harmonic styles in such pieces as the opera *Votre Faust* (1961–67), in which the audience is invited to make decisions affecting the action, *Couleurs croisées* (1968), which incorporated an instrumental version of the classic protest song 'We Shall Overcome', *L'Invitation à l'Utopie* (1971) and *Songs and Tales from the Bible of Death* (1979).

Powell, Bud (Earl Powell; 1924–66) US JAZZ pianist, who became one of the leading BEBOP stylists of the 1940s. Having played for the band of Cootie Williams (1908–85) in the early 1940s, Powell collaborated with such jazzmen as Dizzy GILLESPIE at MINTON'S PLAYHOUSE and went on to make a number of highly acclaimed recordings, usually as part of a trio or quintet (other members of which included Charles MINGUS, Max ROACH and Charlie PARKER). His career was much disrupted by mental problems (possibly the result of a police beating) and drug addiction.

power metal Sub-genre of HEAVY METAL, in which bands employ sophisticated electronic effects to achieve a stunning range of sounds at maximum volume. Advantages of the use of such equipment include the need for only a small line-up of two or three players, because the equipment does the rest.

Prado, Perez (Damaso) (1916–89) Cuban bandleader, pianist, organist, composer and arranger, who had considerable success playing in the MAMBO style, mixing Mexican and Cuban music with SWING. He established his reputation with such music in the mid-1940s and toured widely through the Americas with the band he founded in 1948 as well as making many recordings. Among his most popular mambo compositions were 'Mambo Jambo' (1950), 'Cherry Pink and Apple Blossom White' (1955) and 'Patricia' (1958).

prepared piano A specially altered piano, which is used in the 'indeterminate' music of such composers as John CAGE. The prepared piano is a conventional piano with objects inserted between some of the strings – for example, a screw and a piece of cardboard in Cage's *Second Construction* (1940) or a small bolt, a screw with nuts, and 11 pieces of fibrous weather stripping in his *Bacchanale* of the same year. Later works not only introduced more objects but also gave precise instructions about where they should be placed. The idea was to develop the capacity of the piano as a percussive instrument and thus to experiment with new sounds.

Such 'brutal' interference with the piano has long since been superseded by the use of electronic instruments, although a number of composers, including Olivier MESSIAEN, Pierre BOULEZ and Karlheinz STOCKHAUSEN, have further explored the concept of the piano as a percussion instrument.

Presley, Elvis (Aaron) (1935–77) US singer and guitarist, nicknamed the King, the King of Rock 'n' Roll, Elvis the Pelvis (*see below*) and, early in his career, the Hillbilly Cat, who became one of the great legends of twentieth-century POP music as the biggest star to emerge from the ROCK 'N' ROLL era of the 1950s. The son of a farmhand, Presley hailed from Tupelo, Mississippi, and made his first recording (in 1953) as a present for his mother when he was 18 years old and working as a truck driver. Producer Sam Phillips was impressed by his voice and got him back to his SUN RECORDS studios in Memphis where, in July 1954, they recorded his first single, 'That's All Right, Mama' (written originally by bluesman Arthur CRUDUP). He quickly established a following with COUNTRY audiences and was snapped up by RCA, which saw him emerge as a pop phenomenon with the release of his first US Number One, 'Heartbreak Hotel' (1956), which stormed to the top of the charts in the COUNTRY, pop and RHYTHM-AND-BLUES categories.

Presley's fusion of the Black and White musical traditions, combining the BLUES, country and ROCKABILLY, coupled with his sensual, hip-gyrating live performances, caused a sensation, and he became a massive star almost overnight after appearing on national television. Teenagers went wild at gigs featuring 'Elvis the Pelvis' and bought such follow-ups as 'Hound Dog' (1956), 'Blue Suede Shoes' (1956), 'Don't be Cruel' (1956), 'Jailhouse Rock' (1957),

'All Shook Up' (1957) and 'Love Me Tender' (1958) in unprecedented numbers.

Elvis's career was temporarily interrupted in 1958 when he began two years' army service, and when he returned he exchanged his old rock 'n' roll rebel image with that of a cleaned-up, all-American boy, which was calculated to have a broader appeal. His music also changed, and in the place of the rather 'dangerous' rock 'n' roll of the pre-army days he soared to the top of the charts on both sides of the Atlantic with lush pop ballads and GOSPEL-inspired numbers, among them 'It's Now or Never' (1960), 'Are You Lonesome Tonight?' (1961), 'Surrender' (1961) and 'Return to Sender' (1962).

The unparalleled success of the early years laid the foundations of a legend, but further artistic progress in the 1960s was hindered while Presley concentrated on developing a second career as a filmstar, appearing in some 30 films in all. Most of these were less than impressive and spawned few hits (he only appeared in films with happy endings after his mother Grace said she had been upset when he 'died' in *Loving You*).

Presley finally staged a come-back in the late 1960s, when he returned to live performances and added to his long list of hits such new releases as 'In the Ghetto' and 'Suspicious Minds'. It soon became evident, however, that he was in gradual decline, suffering from weight and drug problems and appearing almost a travesty of his old self in ludicrous sequined costumes loaded with jewellery.

By now his long-standing success and the astute management of 'Colonel' Tom Parker (1909–97) – a former sideshow salesman who was said to have painted sparrows yellow and sold them as canaries – had made Presley immensely wealthy and he retreated with a small circle of sycophants, which were known as the 'Memphis Mafia', into the self-contained world he had created behind the walls of his palatial mansion GRACELAND. Presley's young wife Priscilla Beaulieu, whom he had married in 1968, divorced him in 1973, and he eventually succumbed to the pressures of obesity and drug problems, his lifeless body being found in his bathroom by a girlfriend.

The superstar's death, apparently the result of an accidental overdose of prescribed drugs, traumatized the world of pop music. Several fans committed suicide,

while Graceland and his grave became places of pilgrimage for millions of the faithful. Many believed that he had not died at all and that he was really in hiding somewhere else in the world; to this day the tabloid press devotes space to stories alleging that Presley has been spotted working as a garage mechanic, in a supermarket and in other humble surroundings as far away as Australia. None of these reports has been verified. Within years of Presley's demise anything labelled 'Elvis' was deemed to be dead or out of date.

Presley's impact upon the history of rock and pop is undisputed, and he remains the quintessential pop star. He was also the best-selling solo artist of all time, with sales of some 150 million records in all, including over 94 gold singles and some 40 gold albums.

The nickname Elvis the Pelvis derived from his notoriously suggestive hip-waggling performing style, which he had copied from Black performers he had seen. Parents throughout the USA were scandalized when they saw Presley gyrating his hips on television, and Ed Sullivan for one swore that he would not allow Presley on his show (he quickly relented, however, when it became clear how big a star Presley was becoming – on condition that the camera showed the singer from the waist up only). Teenagers screamed their approval of his 'sexy' dancing and it remained a feature of his live act throughout his career:

> This cat came out in red pants and a green coat and a pink shirt and socks, and he had this sneer on his face and he stood behind the mike for five minutes, I'll bet, before he made a move. Then he hit his guitar a lick, and he broke two strings. I'd been playing ten years, and I hadn't broken a *total* of two strings. So there he was, these two strings dangling, and he hadn't done anything yet, and these high school girls were screaming and fainting and running up to the stage, and then he started to move his hips real slow like he had a thing for his guitar ... he made chills run up my back, man, like when your hair starts grabbing at your collar.
> BOB LUMAN

> I was very lucky. The people were looking for something different and I came along just in time.
> ELVIS PRESLEY

> Is it a sausage? It is certainly smooth and

damp-looking, but whoever heard of a 172lb sausage six feet tall?

Time magazine review of film *Love Me Tender*, 1956

I don't know anything about music – in my line I don't have to.

ELVIS PRESLEY

A weapon of the American psychological war aimed at infecting a part of the population with a new philosophical outlook of inhumanity ... to destroy anything that is beautiful, in order to prepare for war.

Review of Elvis Presley in East German newspaper, *c*.1958

Nothing really affected me until Elvis. If there hadn't been Elvis, there would not have been the Beatles.

JOHN LENNON

Elvis was as big as the whole country itself, as big as the whole dream. He just embodied the essence of it and he was in mortal combat with the thing. It was horrible and at the same time, it was fantastic. Nothing will ever take the place of that guy.

BRUCE SPRINGSTEEN

Preston, Billy (1946–   ) Black US keyboard player and singer, who won acclaim both for his work with the BEATLES in the 1960s and for his solo hits of the 1970s. Preston began his career as a backing musician, playing for singers such as LITTLE RICHARD and Sam COOKE before meeting up with the BEATLES and becoming the first outside musician to participate on their recordings (starting with 'Get Back'). As a result of this he became one of those identified as the FIFTH BEATLE. He also developed a career as a solo star, releasing such hit singles as 'That's the Way God Planned It' (1969), 'Outa Space' (1972), 'Will It Go Round in Circles' (1973), 'Nothing from Nothing' (1974) and, with Stevie WONDER's ex-wife Syreeta, 'With You I'm Born Again' (1980). He continued to work as a backing musician, contributing to records by the ROLLING STONES and Ringo STARR.

Pretenders, the Anglo-American rock group, which was among the most commercially successful rock acts of the early 1980s. Led by US rock singer Chrissie Hynde (1951–   ), the Pretenders made an immediate impact with 'Stop Your Sobbing' and with the chart-topping eponymous début album (1979), from which

came the Number One hit single 'Brass in Pocket'. The group had further chart hits with songs such as 'Talk of the Town' (1981), 'Message of Love' (1981), 'Back on the Chain Gang' (1982), '2000 Miles' (1983) and 'I Got You Babe' (1985). The band was substantially re-formed after the departure (and subsequent drug-related death) of bassist Pete Farndon (1953–83), who was replaced by Malcolm Foster, and the death (also drug-related) of guitarist James Honeyman-Scott (1957–82), who was succeeded by Robbie McIntosh. Hynde broke up the band in 1985 but was back a year later with a totally new line-up. Recent releases include *Last of the Independents* (1994) and *The Isle of View* (1995).

Hynde's name has been romantically linked with those of Ray Davies of the KINKS and Jim Kerr of the SIMPLE MINDS, to whom she was briefly married; she baulked, however, at a proposal of marriage from Sid Vicious of the SEX PISTOLS, suggested as a means to enable her to stay longer in the UK.

Pretty Things, the British rock band, which was among the most admired and uncompromising RHYTHM-AND-BLUES outfits of the 1960s. The name was taken from one of Bo DIDDLEY's hits. Lead singer Phil May (1944–   ), guitarists Dick Taylor (1943–   ) and Brian Pendleton, who was later replaced by keyboard player John Povey (1944–   ), bassist John Stax (1944–   ) and drummer Viv Prince (1944–   ) came together in 1963 and were soon established as stars in the mould of the ROLLING STONES. Among the group's hits was the single 'Honey I Need You' (1965) and such LPs as *Emotions* (1967), the ROCK OPERA *SF Sorrow* (1968) and *Freeway Madness* (1972). The band finally split up in the mid-1970s after numerous line-up changes but reunited for new albums in 1980 and 1984.

Previn, André (Andreas Ludwig Priwin; 1929–   ) US conductor, pianist and composer, born in Germany of Russian descent, who has established a reputation as one of the most widely known figures in modern classical and JAZZ music through his many recordings and broadcasts. Having moved to Hollywood with his family before the outbreak of the Second World War, Previn began as a jazz pianist and wrote and arranged music for Hollywood, winning OSCARS with his contributions to *Gigi*

(1958), *Porgy and Bess* (1959), *Irma la Douce* (1963) and *My Fair Lady* (1964). He went on to study under Pierre MONTEUX and then established a reputation as a concert pianist and conductor. He followed Sir John BARBIROLLI as conductor of the Houston Symphony (1967–70) and subsequently conducted the LONDON SYMPHONY ORCHESTRA (1968–79) and the Pittsburgh Symphony Orchestra (1976–).

Previn's most notable recordings include all the piano concertos of Mozart; others have ranged from COVER versions of songs by Fats WALLER to selections of his film music and admired interpretations of Ralph VAUGHAN WILLIAMS, Sir William WALTON and Dmitri SHOSTAKOVICH. Among his compositions are concertos for guitar and sitar and a suite of piano preludes as well as the musicals *Coco* (1969) and *The Good Companions* (1974), and the musical play *Every Good Boy Deserves Favour* (1977), on which he collaborated with playwright Tom Stoppard.

> The basic difference between classical music and jazz is that in the former music is always greater than its performance – whereas the way jazz is performed is always more important than what is being played.
> ANDRÉ PREVIN, *The Times*, 1967

Prey, Hermann (1929–) German baritone, who has achieved international acclaim as an opera and concert singer. Having made his début at Wiesbaden in 1952, he went on to star at Salzburg and COVENT GARDEN among other leading venues around the world, winning great respect for his performances of Mozart, Rossini and Wagner. His singing of Lieder is highly regarded.

Prez *See* Lester YOUNG.

Price, Alan (1942–) British singer and keyboard player, who recorded a number of hits in the 1960s and 1970s. Price established his reputation as a founder-member of the ANIMALS but went solo in 1965, going on to release such hit singles as 'I Put a Spell on You', 'Simon Smith and his Amazing Dancing Bear' and 'Jarrow Song'. He also made some popular recordings with Georgie FAME and wrote scores for such films as *O Lucky Man* (1973) and *Alfie Darling* (1974) as well as the musical *Andy Capp* (1982).

Price, Leontyne (1927–) Black US soprano, who became one of the most distinguished Black performers to grace the contemporary opera stage. Having studied at the Juillard School, New York, she established her reputation singing Bess in *Porgy and Bess* by George GERSHWIN in the early 1950s and went on to win respect in a range of roles, notably in the operas of Verdi.

Price, Dame Margaret (1941–) Welsh soprano, who has established an international reputation for her performances in the operas of Mozart and Verdi and her interpretation of Lieder. She began her career with the WELSH NATIONAL OPERA, making her début with the company in 1962 in *The Marriage of Figaro*.

Pride, Charley (1938–) Black US COUNTRY singer and guitarist, who established a popular following after becoming the first Black singer to star on the GRAND OLE OPRY. He learned to play the guitar on the cotton plantation where he was born and, after abandoning a promising career in baseball because of injury, went on to enjoy equal success with country and pop audiences with such hits as 'All I Have to Offer You is Me' (1969), 'Kiss an Angel Good Morning' (1971) and 'She's Too Good to be True' (1972). Later hits, such as 'You Win Again' (1980) and 'Night Games' (1983), were confined to country circles.

Prima, Louis (1911–78) US trumpeter, bandleader, singer and composer, who led popular JAZZ and SWING bands through the 1930s and 1940s. Influenced by King OLIVER and Louis ARMSTRONG, he played for Red NICHOLS before forming Prima's New Orleans Gang, for which he recruited a number of highly talented musicians. Among his biggest hits were 'Sing, Sing, Sing' (1936), 'Bell Bottom Trousers' (1945), 'Oh Babe' (1950) and 'Yeah, Yeah, Yeah' (1950). He later became a popular CABARET star, noted for his novelty nonsense vocals, and worked on the soundtracks of a number of films, including Walt Disney's *The Jungle Book* (1969).

Prince (Prince Rogers Nelson; 1958–) Black US pop singer-songwriter and guitarist, who emerged as a top ELECTRO-FUNK performer in the 1980s. The son of a JAZZ bandleader, Prince learned to play a variety of instruments and proved his talent when he played everything on his début album *For You* (1978). Right from the start of his career he presented an eye-catching, provocative image, appearing virtually naked for some live shows and emphasizing the erotic content of his music through daring sleeve illustrations and a scandalous stage act (one group of Christian extremists claimed that secret messages in his songs advocated devil worship). He was a major star by the early 1980s, being considered a more elemental version of Michael JACK-SON, but went on to win acclaim with albums pushing forwards the development of funk by absorbing the influences of jazz, DISCO and RHYTHM-AND-BLUES. His best-selling releases have included the singles 'I Wanna be Your Lover' (1979), 'Little Red Corvette' (1983), 'When Doves Cry' (1984), 'Kiss' (1986) and 'Batdance' (1989) as well as such albums as *Dirty Mind* (1980), *1999* (1982), *Purple Rain* (1984), *Sign o' the Times* (1987), *LoveSexy* (1988), *Diamonds and Pearls* (1991), *Come* (1994), *The Black Album* (1994) and *The Gold Experience* (1995).

Prince is renowned for his unpredictable character. When many record shops refused to stock his *Black Album* he responded by having all copies of it destroyed. His record company forgave him his excesses, however, and a contract he signed for some $100 million was at the time the most lucrative deal ever made in the pop business. In 1993 he announced that he was rejecting the name Prince and was to be called the Artist Formerly Known as Prince.

> A toothpick in a purple doily.
> British press review

Prince of Wails, the *See* Johnnie RAY.

Prince Roving Hand *See* Joe WALSH.

Printemps, Yvonne (Yvonne Wignolle; 1895–1977) French actress and singer, who first emerged as a major star of stage revue in the First World War era. She made her professional début in 1908 and quickly established herself as a favourite at the *Folies Bergère*, subsequently diversifying into straight drama and starring in comedies by her husband Sacha Guitry. Her most popular songs included Sir Noël COWARD's 'I'll Follow My Heart'.

Proby, P.J. (James Marcus Smith; 1938–) US singer, who had a brief but highly successful career in the 1960s. Proby became an overnight star after appearing on British television, and he enjoyed chart success

with such singles as 'Hold Me' (1964) and singles taken from the MUSICAL *West Side Story*, which capitalized on his unusually wide vocal range. It all came to an end for the pony-tailed star in somewhat ludicrous circumstances when the press turned against him, getting good copy out of his notorious unpredictability and ridiculing his infamous stage act during which his tight velvet trousers were apt to split. Various attempts at a come-back were doomed to failure.

Procul Harum British rock group, who recorded one of the classic pop hits of the late 1960s – 'A Whiter Shade of Pale' (1967). Procul Harum (a Latin tag meaning 'beyond these things') consisted of lead singer and pianist Gary Brooker (1945–), keyboard player Matthew Fisher (1946–), guitarist Ray Royer (1945–), bassist Dave Knights (1945–) and drummer Bobby Harrison (1943–), although there were many changes in line-up over the years. The group came together in 1967 on the break-up of the Paramounts, performing material written by Brooker and lyricist Keith Reid (1946–). 'A Whiter Shade of Pale' (based on a theme from Bach) was the group's first single and stormed to Number One; it remains one of the great pop hits. Subsequent releases – for which guitarist Robin Trower (1945–), bassist Chris Copping (1945–) and drummer B.J. Wilson (1947–) were among those to be recruited – included the albums *A Salty Dog* (1969), *Home* (1970) and *Grand Hotel* (1971), and the final single 'Pandora's box' (1974). The group split up in the late 1970s but re-formed in 1991 for the album *The Prodigal Stranger*.

progressive rock Genre of British rock music of the 1970s, which was championed by such bands as KING CRIMSON, YES, PINK FLOYD, GENESIS and EMERSON, LAKE AND PALMER. The music favoured a break with the conventional pattern of short verse and chorus on readily accessible themes and offered instead works of considerable length with many sections and often obscure lyrics. Consequently most progressive rock was ill-suited to the singles market, although it did help to stimulate interest in the album charts.

With album sleeves designed by such pop artists as Roger Dean (who worked for such bands as Yes and URIAH HEEP), as well as highly imaginative stage sets and costumes and concept-based lyrics, progressive rock was readily identified as the next step forward in the ART ROCK tradition and dominated the LP market until the mid-1970s. Record labels associated with the genre included ISLAND RECORDS, Charisma and EMI. The genre eventually lost its way and suffered a loss of credibility as tastes changed, the advent of less sophisticated PUNK ROCK and the NEW WAVE making most established stars look boring, pretentious and irrelevant.

Among the classic albums to issue from the heyday of progressive rock in the early 1970s was the Pink Floyd classic *The Dark Side of the Moon* (1973), which remains the best-selling LP ever released.

Prokofiev, Sergei Sergeievich (1891–1953) Ukrainian-born composer and pianist, whose enduringly popular melodic masterpieces written in a modern idiom have placed him among the most respected of all twentieth-century composers. Prokofiev showed a flair for writing music as a child of five and had already composed a symphony, four operas, two sonatas and a number of piano works by the time he was admitted to the St Petersburg Conservatory at the age of 13. There, under Nikolai Rimsky-Korsakov (1844–1908) and others, he proved himself a gifted pianist and won a prestigious prize with his first piano concerto (1911), establishing himself as a leading modernist composer whose works were transfigured by his understanding of multi-tonal harmony and his incorporation of propulsive 'motor' rhythms.

Prokofiev's *Classical Symphony* (1917), which was written in a broadly neoclassical style, was well received on its first performance in 1918, following which he settled in the USA. There, he won great acclaim as a pianist although failing to overcome the controversy that surrounded his modernist style of composition. The opera *The Love of Three Oranges* (1919) provoked mixed reactions when it was staged in Chicago in 1921, and his third piano concerto (1921) did little better. A year later Prokofiev emigrated to France, where he wrote the avant-garde ballet *Le Pas d'acier* (*The Age of Steel*; 1925) for Serge Diaghilev and such subsequent masterpieces as *The Fiery Angel* (1926), which took witchcraft as its subject, the ballet *The*

Prodigal Son (1928), the Third (1928) and Fourth (1930) Symphonies and the Fourth (1931) and Fifth (1932) Piano Concertos.

Prokofiev returned to the Soviet Union in the mid-1930s, braving state accusations of FORMALISM, and continued to compose in an increasingly lyrical style. Among the finest compositions from the last great phase in his career were such works as the film scores *Lieutenant Kijé* (1934), *Alexander Nevsky* (1939) and *Ivan the Terrible* (1945), the acclaimed ballets *Romeo and Juliet* (1936) and *Cinderella* (1944), another five symphonies, the classic *Peter and the Wolf* (1936), which introduces children to the instruments of the orchestra while telling an exciting story, the opera *War and Peace* (1943) and further sonatas and string quartets.

Prokofiev wrote little more after attracting renewed state criticism in 1948, although he was restored to favour with the award of the Stalin Prize in 1951. His death came on the same day as that of Stalin himself.

> It is the duty of the composer, like the poet, the sculptor or the painter, to serve his fellow men, to beautify human life and point the way to a radiant future. Such is the immutable code of art as I see it.
> SERGEI PROKOFIEV

> It is obviously a work of major importance, but I was rather alarmed to find how easy and agreeable it seemed to me at first hearing.
> SIR ADRIAN BOULT, of Prokofiev's Fifth Symphony, *My Own Trumpet*, 1973

Proms, the The hugely popular annual classical promenade concert festival, which is staged every summer under the auspices of the BBC at London's Albert Hall. The Proms were founded in 1895 by Sir Henry WOOD and were held for some 50 years under his control, first at the Queen's Hall in London, then transferring to the Albert Hall when the Queen's Hall was destroyed by bombs in 1941. The BBC became involved in their organization in 1927 and now present live radio and television broadcasts of the event, in which the emphasis tends to be put on major British works from all periods, although recent years have seen the premieres of specially commissioned works and more experimental programmes. Opera was first included in 1961.

The Last Night of the Proms, which is dedicated to a programme of British music, has long been a focus for rather over-blown patriotic sentiment. Audiences at the Last Night are much more raucous than audiences at most other concerts, and they include large numbers of relatively young music lovers, who bring along Union Jack flags and all manner of patriotic paraphernalia to celebrate this uniquely British event. Typical of the jests popular with Last Night promenaders is the singing of incorrect 'A' notes in an attempt to mislead the orchestra when it is tuning up. A number of other time-honoured traditions have grown up with the Proms. One of the most cherished is the singing of ELGAR's 'Land of Hope and Glory', with which each annual gathering ends (it was first presented at the Proms in 1901). Attempts to drop this ritual by conductor Mark Elder in 1990, when the Gulf War was in the news, met with vociferous protests, and Elder was replaced by Andrew Davis, who was careful not to make the same mistake. Other traditional items include Henry Wood's *Fantasia on British Sea Songs*, first performed in 1905 on the centenary of Trafalgar and the hymn 'Jerusalem'.

Popular conductors associated with the Proms have included Wood himself, who appeared regularly until 1942, Sir Adrian BOULT, Constant LAMBERT and Sir Malcolm SARGENT.

Prophet of Love, the *See* Barry WHITE.

protest song A song with lyrics that purport to air some social injustice. The great era of the protest song was the 1960s, when many left-wing singer-songwriters rebelled against the vacuity of the lyrics of much popular music of the previous decades and cast themselves in the role of mouthpieces for the social conscience. Among their targets were racism, US involvement in Vietnam and political oppression of all kinds. Masters of the protest song included Bob DYLAN (treading in the footsteps of Woody GUTHRIE), Pete SEEGER, Tom PAXTON, Phil OCHS, Joni MITCHELL and Joan BAEZ.

> Erotic politicians, that's what we are. We're interested in everything about revolt, disorder and all activity that appears to have no meaning.
> JIM MORRISON

PRS *See* PERFORMING RIGHTS SOCIETY.

psychedelic rock *See* ACID ROCK.

pub rock Movement in British rock music in the mid-1970s, which anticipated the development of PUNK ROCK. Many bands felt uneasy with the stereotype of the big, commercially oriented, rock SUPERGROUPS fostered by the major record companies, and they opted instead to pursue their music in the more intimate surroundings of clubs and backrooms of pubs, where they established loyal cult followings while retaining their 'street credibility'. Among the few to build major careers from such modest beginnings were Elvis COSTELLO and Ian DURY.

Puccini, Giacomo (1858–1924) Italian composer, who was acknowledged the leading Italian opera composer of modern times long before his death. Born into a musical family in Lucca, Puccini received musical training as a child and became a church organist at the age of 14. He studied at the Milan Conservatory in the early 1880s, by which time he had already conceived a love of opera, and produced evidence of his burgeoning talent for strong melody and orchestration with the orchestral piece *Capriccio sinfonico*. His first opera, *Le Villi* (1884) was well enough received to encourage him to persevere, although his second effort, *Edgar* (1889) was not a success and is now lost. At much the same time he provoked a scandal by embarking on an affair with the married Elvira Gemignani; she bore him a son, and the couple set up home in the Tuscan village of Torre del Lago, where he was to write most of his best work. They were finally able to marry in 1904.

The opera *Manon Lescaut* (1893) proved a huge success and established Puccini's reputation as a national hero. It was quickly followed by the equally acclaimed *La Bohème* (1896), *Tosca* (1900) and *Madama Butterfly* (1904), all of which have remained enduring opera favourites ever since. A public scandal in 1909, triggered by the suicide of a maid in the Puccini household after she was (falsely) accused by Elvira of having an affair with the composer, caused Puccini considerable distress and disrupted his work for some years to come. Of the works he did subsequently complete the most important were *The Girl of the Golden West* (1910), in which Enrico CARUSO starred when the work was given its premiere in New York and – perhaps his most impressive achievement –

the fantastical *Turandot*, which was left unfinished at the composer's death but was completed by other hands and first performed in 1926.

> I have heard the composer Puccini well spoken of ... He follows modern trends, which is natural, but remains attached to melody, which is above passing fashions.
>
> GIUSEPPE VERDI, letter, 1884

> I act as executioner to these poor frail creatures. The Neronian instinct manifests and fulfils itself.
>
> PUCCINI, of his heroines

Puente, Tito (Ernesto Antonio Puente; 1920–) US bandleader, pianist, composer, saxophonist and percussionist, nicknamed the King, who established a popular following performing in the MAMBO and CHA-CHA-CHA styles. Puente formed his first band in 1947, enjoyed a series of mambo hits in the 1950s and then helped to popularize the cha-cha-cha. Subsequent recordings in a Latin-jazz CROSSOVER style included *My Fair Lady Goes Latin* and *Puente in Percussion*.

Pulp British rock group, which emerged as one of the leading bands of the mid-1990s. The group was formed, as Arabacus Pulp, in Sheffield in 1979 by singer Jarvis Cocker but only attracted significant interest from 1993, with a line-up of Cocker, guitarist Russell Senior, keyboard player Candida Doyle, bassist Steve Mackey and drummer Nick Banks. *Pulpintro – The Gift Recordings* (1993) did well and was followed by the hit albums *His 'N' Hers* (1994), *Different Class* (1995) and *Countdown 1992–1983* (1996). The hit singles included 'Common People' (1995).

Cocker won notoriety in 1996 after he interrupted a performance by Michael JACKSON during the Brit Awards in London in protest at Jackson's 'Messiah-like' image.

punk rock Genre of unsophisticated HARD ROCK, which utterly transformed the development of conventional rock and pop when it exploded on the scene in 1976. At a time when rock and pop were languishing under the twin evils of DISCO and various PROGRESSIVE ROCK outfits past their sell-by date, punk represented a return to rock roots and a new realignment behind the nihilist angst of a generation traumatized by economic recession and political indifference. The punk movement first sparked to life in London's urban subculture and quickly created heroes quite unlike those of conventional rock and pop – uncompromising, anarchic and often deliberately unappealing in visual terms. Exponents and fans alike adopted torn black leathers, radical, spiky haircuts and skin-piercing safety-pins in a brash rejection of accepted fashion, and gathered together in down-at-heel venues to overdose on high-volume, unpolished, repetitive and distorted guitar rock attacking Establishment values with a minimum of musical pretension.

Among the most celebrated – and notorious – punk outfits were the SEX PISTOLS, who were masterminded by impresario Malcolm McLaren (former manager of the embryonic punk band the NEW YORK DOLLS) and released the first major punk hit in the form of the much-banned 'God Save the Queen' (1977). Others included TELEVISION, the CLASH, the DAMNED, the JAM, Joy Division, SIOUXSIE AND THE BANSHEES and the STRANGLERS.

The movement, which lacked any coherent philosophy beyond its instinctive nihilism, came to a climax very quickly and had disintegrated, like the majority of the bands it fostered, by the end of the decade, though its legacy was preserved in the music of a whole generation of NEW WAVE bands and had an influence across virtually the whole range of contemporary rock and pop (though less so in the USA, where 'punk' was first used to describe a genre of GARAGE BAND rock back in the 1960s).

> Punk has the life expectancy of a scab.
>
> *Time Out*

Q

quadraphonic Sound system in which music is reproduced through four speakers instead of the conventional two used in stereo. Such systems were strenuously marketed after their introduction in the early 1970s, and a quadrophonic system was first used in live performance back in 1972, when PINK FLOYD performed in quadrophonic at the Rainbow in London.

Quatro, Suzi (1950–   ) US rock singer and bass guitarist, who had a series of GLAM ROCK hits in the 1970s. The daughter of a jazz bandleader, she set up her first all-girl group as a teenager and subsequently attracted the attention of producer Mickie MOST, who brought her to the UK. The raunchy hit single 'Can the Can', written by CHINN AND CHAPMAN, reached the top of the British charts in 1973 and was followed by the equally aggressive '48 Crash', 'Daytona Demon', 'Devil Gate Drive', which in 1974 became her second Number One, 'Too Big' and 'The Wild One', before Quatro adopted a mellower style in the late 1970s for numbers such as 'If You Can't Give Me Love' and 'She's in Love with You'. She completed the transformation from leather-clad teen rebel by appearing in the stage MUSICAL *Annie Get Your Gun*.

Queen British rock group, which established a reputation for musical flamboyance over the course of one of the most commercially successful careers in contemporary music. Charismatic lead singer Freddie Mercury (Frederick Bulsara; 1946–91), who was born in Zanzibar, gifted guitarist Brian May (1947–   ), bassist John Deacon (1951–   ) and drummer Roger Taylor (1949–   ) came together in 1972 as successors to May and Taylor's band Smile. Mercury had also released such early efforts as 'I Can Hear Music' under the pseudonym Larry Lurex. Launched in 1972, Queen immediately earned a name for its energetic, large-scale live act, based initially on relatively conventional HARD ROCK. The album *Queen* (1973) failed to make much impression, but the band got into the charts for the first time in 1974 with the single 'Killer Queen' and followed this initial success up with *Queen II*, *Sheer Heart Attack* (1974) and the chart-topping album *A Night at the Opera* (1975), from which came the epic 6-minute 'Bohemian Rhapsody'.

'Bohemian Rhapsody' (1975), which took three weeks to make and mixed opera with rock, stormed to Number One in the UK and remained there for nine weeks, confirming Queen as a top chart act. By virtue of the adventurous promotional film that accompanied the single, it also ushered in the age of the pop video, in which almost as much attention was paid to the visual impact of a new release as to the music itself.

Numerous singles in a variety of rock and pop styles followed, among them the anthemic 'We are the Champions', 'Somebody to Love', 'Another One Bites the Dust', 'Crazy Little Thing Called Love', 'Under Pressure', on which Queen collaborated with David BOWIE, and 'Radio Ga-Ga'. The group's best-selling albums included *A Day at the Races* (1976), the SOUNDTRACK for the film *Flash Gordon* (1980), *The Miracle* (1989) and *Innuendo* (1991). An appearance at the LIVE AID event in 1985 stole the show; Bob GELDOF himself commented on the act: 'It was the perfect stage for Freddie – he could ponce about in front of the whole world.'

The death of the flamboyant Mercury in 1991 as a result of Aids was much lamented in the pop press and prompted fellow-members of the band to acknowledge that he was irreplaceable. 'Bohemian Rhapsody' went straight back to Number One for five weeks on a wave of public mourning; a host of stars joined together for a concert at Wembley a year later in his memory.

Queen of Country Music, the *See* Emmylou HARRIS; Kitty WELLS; Tammy WYNETTE. Maybelle Addington Carter was also sometimes given this sobriquet; *see* the CARTER FAMILY.

Queen of Soul, the *See* Aretha FRANKLIN.

Queen of the Blues, the *See* Dinah WASHING-
TON.

Queen of the Halls, the *See* Marie LLOYD.

Queen of the Teen Weepers, the *See* Lesley
GORE.

Quilter, Roger (1877–1953) British composer, who established a reputation with his
popular settings of works by great English
poets among other compositions. Having
completed his musical training in Frankfurt,
he won acclaim with elegant settings of
songs by Shakespeare and poems by Herrick
and Tennyson as well as the *Children's Over-*
ture (1914), which was based on well-
known nursery rhymes. He also wrote the
music for the children's play *Where the Rain-*
bow Ends and pieces for orchestra and piano.

Quintette du Hot Club de France Legendary French JAZZ group of the 1930s, which
brought together the outstanding talents of
Stéphane GRAPPELLI and Django REINHARDT.
Founded in 1932, the group was the first
non-US outfit to have a major influence on
the development of jazz. The quintet
recorded dozens of records during the 1930s
and 1940s, only ceasing operations with
Reinhardt's death in 1953. Grappelli re-
formed the Hot Club format in the 1960s
and 1970s.

R

r 'n' b *See* RHYTHM-AND-BLUES.

Rabbit *See* Johnny HODGES.

race music Term formerly used in the USA to describe music identified with the Black population, especially the BLUES. Echoing the segregation imposed on US Blacks in everyday life, the record industry effectively 'ghettoized' Black music by issuing such music on separate labels from the early 1920s and subsequently compiling specialist charts. Many were uneasy with the term (adopted by record companies in preference to 'Negro music'), and it was eventually replaced after the Second World War by the more acceptable RHYTHM-AND-BLUES.

Rachmaninov, Sergei (Vassilyevich) (1873–1943) Russian composer, pianist and conductor, who is admired for his numerous romantic works for the piano. Rachmaninov, the fifth of six children, came from a relatively comfortable family background but saw his parents split up as their fortunes declined, like those of many other landed families. Somewhat ironically, this apparent misfortune freed him from the expectations demanded of a young aristocrat and allowed him to become a student at the St Petersburg Conservatory and then, with the support of the elderly Tchaikovsky, in Moscow, where he won a Gold Medal for composition in 1892 on the strength of a symphony, a one-act opera and some songs.

Recognized as one of the most accomplished of contemporary pianists, Rachmaninov rapidly consolidated his reputation as a composer with such works as the First Piano Concerto (1891; revised 1917), the celebrated Prelude in C sharp (1892), *Polichinelle* (1892) and the opera *Aleko* (1893). Tchaikovsky's death in 1893 inspired him to write his First Suite for Two Pianos and an *Elegiac Trio* in his memory, but he suffered a temporary setback when his First Symphony was attacked for its MODERNISM on its premiere in 1897 (a reception possibly exacerbated by the fact that the conductor was said to have been drunk). The work's reception led the composer to destroy the score and abandon composition for a time. (The symphony was later resurrected with some success after his death.)

A gradual return to composition in 1898 (partly the work of a hypnotist who assured the unconscious composer he would be successful) was followed by invitations to visit London as composer, pianist and conductor for the Philharmonic Society and the start of a long and happy marriage to Natalya Satin. He proved his talent beyond doubt with the enduringly popular Second Piano Concerto (1901), which was later used as the SOUNDTRACK for the film *Brief Encounter*, but was unable to write much over the ensuing years because of his commitments as a pianist and conductor.

A move to Dresden in 1906 brought some respite, and he added to his compositions the Second Symphony, the First Piano Sonata and the tone poem *The Isle of the Dead*. He wrote a Third Piano Concerto for a tour of the USA in 1909 and subsequently combined work with the Imperial Music Society and as conductor of the Moscow Philharmonic Concerts with the composition of the choral symphony *The Bells* (1913) and further piano music and songs.

Rachmaninov fled from Russia during the Revolution in 1917 and divided his remaining years between Switzerland and the USA, where he died of cancer. He wrote little more in the years immediately after the Revolution, protesting 'How can I compose without melody?', but resumed activity in 1926. Among his last compositions were the Fourth Piano Concerto (1927) and the *Rhapsody on a Theme of Paganini* (1934), in which he employed the simple ruse of turning a theme by Paganini's upside down.

When not writing music, conducting or playing the piano, his greatest pleasure came from driving fast cars and cruising in his speedboat on Lake Lucerne.

My dear hands. Farewell, my poor hands.
SERGEI RACHMANINOV, on learning he had
cancer

Even an ordinary broken chord is made to
disclose rare beauties; we are reminded of
the fairies' hazelnuts in which diamonds
were concealed but you could break the
shell only if your hands were blessed.
NEVILLE CARDUS, review of Rachmaninov
concert, the *Manchester Guardian*, 1939

. . . the only pianist I have ever seen who did
not grimace. That is a great deal.
IGOR STRAVINSKY

The prospect of having to sit through one of
his extended symphonies or piano concertos tends, quite frankly, to depress me.
All those notes, and to what end?
AARON COPLAND

Radio Caroline British offshore 'pirate' radio
station, which attracted a large audience in
the 1960s and proved a spur to the establishment of a mainstream pop station under
the aegis of the BBC. Radio Caroline started
operations in March 1964, based on the
former Danish passenger ferry *Frederica*,
which was moored off Frinton-on-Sea and
was thus outside the jurisdiction of the
authorities, which had imposed a ban on
commercial radio networks. The venture
proved a huge success, and numerous similar stations were set up before changes in the
law in 1967 – the year in which the BBC's
Radio One pop station was founded – made
all such enterprises illegal. Several top Radio
One DISC JOCKEYS, including Tony Blackburn
and Johnny Walker, started out with Radio
Caroline.

ragtime Lively syncopated piano music, of the
type that came into vogue in the USA at the
turn of the century and remained popular
until around 1915, when it was eclipsed by
JAZZ. First explored by Black musicians, the
genre, called ragtime because of the 'ragged'
rhythms employed (possibly inspired by
banjo strumming), rapidly caught on, with
many White performers adopting the style.
Scott JOPLIN emerged as the most significant
of all the ragtime composers, writing such
classics as 'Maple Leaf Rag' (1899).
Although he failed to prove the style could
sustain a longer work, specifically an opera,
Joplin's music was revived with huge success many years later as the SOUNDTRACK for
the film *The Sting* (1973), which made his
tune 'The Entertainer' a big hit. Other ragtime writers included May AUFDERHEIDE.

Ultimately, the ragtime style was
hijacked by Irving BERLIN and other TIN
PAN ALLEY songwriters and contributed to
the birth of the charleston; it also had some
influence on many leading jazz composers
of the 1920s. Classical composers to tinker
with the form included Charles IVES and
Igor STRAVINSKY, who composed *Ragtime
for Eleven Instruments* (1918) and *Piano-rag
Music* (1920).

White music – played black.
JOACHIM BERENDT, *The Jazz Book*, 1976

A wave of vulgar, filthy and suggestive
music has inundated the land. The pabu-
lum of theatre and summer hotel orchestras is coon music. Nothing but ragtime
prevails and the cake-walk with its
obscene posturings, its lewd gestures. It is
artistically and morally depressing and
should be suppressed by press and pulpit.
The Musical Courier, 1899

'The Real American Folk Song is a Rag.'
IRA GERSHWIN, song title

You know, I never did find out what
ragtime was.
IRVING BERLIN, composer of 'Alexander's
Ragtime Band'

Ragtime Jimmy *See* James V. MONACO.

Raimondi, Ruggero (1941–) Italian
bass, who has attracted widespread praise
for his interpretations of nineteenth-
century Italian operas since making his
début in 1964. His successful appearances
have also included those in the title roles of
Mozart's *Don Giovanni* and of Mussorgsky's
Boris Godunov.

Rainey, Ma (Gertrude Pridgett; 1886–
1939) Black US BLUES singer-songwriter,
nicknamed the Mother of the Blues, who
pioneered the classic blues style in the
early years of the twentieth century.
Having begun her career in minstrel shows
as a teenager, she married fellow-singer
William 'Pa' Rainey in 1904 and became
the first stage performer of the blues. She
made several records in the 1920s, including some with Louis ARMSTRONG, and
appeared in vaudeville in the 1930s with
her own Georgia Band, earning a reputation as an unsurpassed live performer of
the blues. Her most celebrated recording
was a version of 'See See Rider'. She was
also active as a teacher of blues technique,
her pupils including Bessie SMITH.

Raitt, Bonnie (1949–) US BLUES and folk singer-songwriter and guitarist. After moderate success with *Give It Up* (1972), *Takin' My Time* (1973), on which she adopted the electric guitar, and *Home Plate* (1975), she attracted a big audience with *Sweet Forgiveness* (1977), from which came 'Runaway'. She returned to the upper reaches of the album charts with *Nick of Time* (1989) and also won acclaim for her work with John Lee HOOKER. Recent releases include *Luck of the Draw* (1991) and *Longing in their Hearts* (1994).

Bonnie's father, John (Emmett) Raitt (1917–), starred in the Broadway musical *Carousel* and in the 1957 film *The Pajama Game*.

Ramones, the US rock band, which established themselves as one of the top US PUNK ROCK acts of the late 1970s. Guitarist Johnny (John Cummings; 1952–), bassist Dee-Dee (Douglas Colvin; 1952–), lead singer Joey (Jeffrey Hyman; 1952–) and (until 1977) drummer Tommy (Tom Erdelyi; 1952–) all adopted the surname Ramone, and the group came together in 1974, although the eponymous début album, notable for such hard-hitting and concise 2-minute tracks as 'Now I Wanna Sniff Some Glue' and 'Beat on the Brat', was not released for a further two years. Subsequent releases included the albums *Ramones Leave Home* (1976) and *Rocket to Russia* (1977), from which came the single 'Sheena is a Punk Rocker'. Phil SPECTOR produced *End of the Century* (1980), which included a hit COVER version of 'Baby I Love You', but subsequent hits were few and far between, even though they enjoyed something of a return to form with *Too Tough To Die* (1985).

Rampal, Jean-Pierre (1922–) French flautist, who is widely regarded as the leading postwar exponent of the flute. He has won acclaim playing a wide range of works, from chamber music to compositions from the eighteenth century and modern works. He is particularly respected for his insistence on playing early music on authentic instruments and has made many celebrated recordings. Several prominent composers, including André JOLIVET and Francis POULENC, have written works for him.

rap POP genre, which emerged as the dominant pop dance music of the late 1980s. Rap music, a descendant of REGGAE, is characterized by rapidly chanted, rhyming vocal lines and a hypnotic, repetitive beat. It originated among young Blacks in Harlem and the Bronx in the early 1980s and subsequently attracted numerous fans on both sides of the Atlantic, proving a ready vehicle for expression of political and personal frustration. At first it was a tool in the armoury of night club DISC JOCKEYS, who were exploring the possibilities of adding their own vocals to FUNK backings, embellished with various sound effects and SCRATCHING; ultimately rap produced its own stars, some of whom were simply disc jockeys who had stepped adroitly into the spotlight. Among the most popular rappers were Grandmaster Flash, the Sugar Hill Gang, whose 'Rapper's Delight' (1979) was the first big rap hit, NWA (Niggaz With Attitude), Vanilla Ice, M.C. HAMMER and Public Enemy. In 1991 Daddy Freddy established his claim as the fastest rapper in the world when he uttered 528 syllables in just a minute.

Rap acquired the usual trappings of any pop music genre, with its own dress code (baseball caps, bright sweatshirts and baseball boots or rollerskates) and sub-culture, with fans playing their music on portable 'ghettoblasters' and writing their adopted nicknames on walls and bus shelters with spray paint. *See also* HOUSE MUSIC.

Raspberries, the US pop group, which had some success in the early 1970s with music aimed at a mainly teenage audience. Led by classically trained singer, keyboard player and guitarist Eric Carmen (1949–) and completed with guitarist Wally Bryson (1949–), bassist Dave Smalley (1949–) and drummer Jim Bonfanti (1948–), the Raspberries came together in 1970. The group's first big hit was 'Go All the Way' (1972). After changes in the line-up, the group returned to the upper reaches of the charts with 'Overnite Sensation', from the album *Starting Over* (1974), before splitting up a year later. Carmen subsequently established himself as a successful solo artist, his hits including 'All by Myself' (1976), which was derived from a theme by Sergei RACHMANINOV, and 'Hungry Eyes' (1987).

Rattle, Simon (1955–) British conductor, who won recognition as one of the foremost conductors of his generation in the course of his lengthy association with the City of BIRMINGHAM SYMPHONY ORCHESTRA. Born in Liverpool, Rattle assembled his first orchestra at the age of 15 and went on to study at the Royal Academy of Music in 1971. He won a prestigious conducting competition in 1974 and was appointed conductor of the Bournemouth Symphony Orchestra and Sinfonietta for two years. Subsequently he conducted the Royal Liverpool Philharmonic Orchestra (1977–80) and the London Choral Society (1979–84) before arriving in Birmingham in 1980; since then he has worked to make the CBSO the equal of the best in the world, overseeing their move to a new hall in 1991. He has also appeared as a guest conductor with the BERLIN PHILHARMONIC ORCHESTRA, the LONDON SINFONIETTA and elsewhere.

Rattle is particularly noted for his interpretations of the music of Gustav MAHLER and other early twentieth-century composers, and he has won equal acclaim for his presentation of such operas as *Porgy and Bess* at GLYNDEBOURNE. Modern works associated with his name have included Peter MAXWELL DAVIES's First Symphony, which he premièred in 1978. In 1990 he embarked on an ambitious 10-year project, performing a sequence of concerts celebrating the music of successive decades of the twentieth century.

Ravel, (Joseph) Maurice (1875–1937) French composer, of mixed Swiss-Basque descent, who established a reputation as one of the leading composers of his time with much highly popular and richly orchestrated music. Ravel showed a talent for music at an early age, but found piano practice irksome and had to be bribed with small financial rewards for every half hour spent at the keyboard. A student of the Paris Conservatoire, he was much influenced by Claude DEBUSSY and by his teacher Gabriel FAURÉ, and won immediate recognition as a composer of promise with such works as the *Jeux d'eau* for piano, a much-revived string quartet, *Pavane pour une infante défunte* (1899 and 1910) and the orchestral song cycle *Shéhérazade* (1903), although some found him too innovative for comfort.

Ravel's failure to secure victory in the Prix de Rome in 1905 caused a major row within the music establishment and culminated in the resignation of the head of the Conservatoire, a trauma which left a lasting mark on the young composer, who nonetheless contrived (typically) to keep his feelings to himself. He went on to consolidate his reputation with such celebrated compositions as the *Sonatine* (1905), for piano, the *Histoires naturelles* (1906), for voice and piano, the orchestral *Rapsodie espagnole* (*Spanish Rhapsody*; 1908), the piano suites *Gaspard de la nuit* (1908) and *Ma mère d'oye* (*Mother Goose*; 1908), which he subsequently orchestrated, the opera *L'Heure espagnole* (*The Spanish Hour*; 1909) and the *Valses nobles et sentimentales* (1911). The ballet *Daphnis et Chloë* (1912) was commissioned by Diaghilev, through whom Ravel met and befriended Igor STRAVINSKY.

After the First World War, during which he served as a driver before being invalided out with dysentery, Ravel was further traumatized by the loss of his mother (1917), but he continued to compose without pause, his sources ranging from JAZZ to oriental music, and he toured widely to universal acclaim. Important works from the last phase of his career included the suite *Le Tombeau de Couperin* (1917), for piano, the opera *L'Enfant et les sortilèges* (*The Child and the Spells*; 1925), the *Chansons madécasses* (1926), for voice and chamber ensemble, the wildly successful ballet *Boléro* (1928), which enjoyed a new lease of life in the 1980s after it was used as the backing music for Jayne Torvill and Christopher Dean's gold medal-winning ice-dancing performance in the 1984 Olympic Games, and the song-cycle *Don Quichotte à Dulcinée* (1933). He also conceived a brilliant orchestration of Mussorgsky's *Pictures from an Exhibition* (1922).

Throughout his life, Ravel retained a love of childhood and got great pleasure from his collection of automated toys, which he proudly showed to any visitors to his home.

> I've still so much music in my head. I have said nothing. I have so much more to say.
> MAURICE RAVEL, shortly before his death

> A piece for orchestra without music.
> MAURICE RAVEL, of *Boléro*

> All music, after his, seems imperfect.
> ROMAIN ROLLAND

> The most perfect of Swiss clockmakers.
> IGOR STRAVINSKY

> There is a definite limit to the length of time a composer can go on writing in one

dance rhythm. This limit is obviously reached by Ravel toward the end of *La Valse* and toward the beginning of *Boléro*.
CONSTANT LAMBERT, *Music Ho!*, 1934

Rawsthorne, Alan (1905–71) British composer, who established a reputation with his many scores for stage and screen as well as with admired symphonies, concertos and other works in a smooth, abstract style. Rawsthorne abandoned studies in dentistry to enrol as a student at the Royal Manchester College of Music and went on to develop his own style of composition, exploring SERIALISM without sacrificing tonality. His *Theme and Variations* (1937), for two violins, established him as a composer of great promise, and this was followed by such acclaimed works as the *Symphonic Studies* (1938) and two piano concertos (1939 and 1951). Among other creations were three symphonies, the *Street Corner* overture (1944), a quintet for piano and wind (1963), and chamber and instrumental music. His film SOUNDTRACKS included those for the films *Burma Victory* (1945) and *Uncle Silas* (1947).

Ray, Johnnie (John Alvin; 1927–90) US pop singer-songwriter and pianist, nicknamed the Cry Guy, who was a popular heart-throb of the early 1950s. Ray's speciality was his performance of such emotional numbers as 'Cry' (1951), which he delivered on his knees with tears rolling down his cheeks. The more Ray wept, the more his largely teenaged audience went wild in a manner that foreshadowed BEAT-LEMANIA a decade or more later. Otherwise known as the Prince of Wails and the Nabob of Sob, Ray (who was of part Blackfoot-Indian descent) was half-deaf as the result of a childhood accident, but he made no attempt to hide his hearing-aid, to the further delight of thousands of sympathetic fans.

Ray enjoyed cult status for several years before his music was eclipsed by the arrival of ROCK 'N' ROLL (the young Elvis PRESLEY was frequently compared with him when he first attracted public attention). His other hits included 'The Little White Cloud That Cried' (1951), 'Such a Night' (1954), 'Just Walkin' in the Rain' (1956), 'Yes Tonight Josephine' (1957) and 'I'll Never Fall in Love Again' (1958). In retrospect, he was one of the first pop singers to capitalize on open emotional displays and

the first to succeed as much through the strength of his popular image as on the appeal of his music alone.

> I've got no talent, still sing flat as a table. I'm a sort of human spaniel. People come to see what I'm like. I make them feel, I exhaust them, I destroy them.
> JOHNNIE RAY

RCA Radio Corporation of America. An international record label, which has long been one of the giants of the recording industry. RCA acquired the Victor recording company in 1929, thus handling records by such legends of classical music as Arturo TOSCANINI and Enrico CARUSO as well as issuing releases by emerging JAZZ stars, who came to include Charlie BARNET, Duke ELLINGTON, Benny GOODMAN and Glenn MILLER among many others. Stars recruited to RCA after the Second World War ranged from Dizzy GILLESPIE and Mario LANZA to Jim REEVES, Elvis PRESLEY, David BOWIE and Dolly PARTON. The German Bertelsmann organization acquired control of RCA in the 1980s.

Missed opportunities included letting both the CARPENTERS and Herb ALPERT go when it was concluded that neither would ever produce any hits – both made a fortune for A & M, which Alpert founded.

Rea, Chris (1951–) British singer-songwriter and guitarist, of Irish-Italian descent, who had considerable commercial success playing rock-based pop in the late 1970s and 1980s. Having started out with a band called Magdalene (subsequently renamed Beautiful Losers) in 1975, Rea established himself as a solo artist in 1976 with the album *Whatever Happened to Benny Santini?*, which included the hit single 'Fool If You Think It's Over'. He consolidated his reputation with a series of albums, of which both *Road to Hell* (1989) and *Auberge* (1990) got to Number One in the UK. More recent releases include *God's Great Banana Skin* (1992) and *Espresso Logic* (1993).

Red-headed Music Maker, the *See* Wendell Woods HALL.

Red-headed Stranger, the *See* Willie NELSON.

Redding, Otis (1941–67) US RHYTHM-AND-BLUES and SOUL star, nicknamed the Crown Prince of Soul, who enjoyed huge success in the mid-1960s with such songs as 'Pain in My Heart', 'Respect', 'I've been Loving You Too Long', 'My Girl', 'Shake' and 'Try a Little Tenderness', which attracted both Black and White audiences. The son of a Baptist preacher, Redding sang GOSPEL as a child and his first hit 'These Arms of Mine' (1963). He went on to establish himself as one of the giants of soul, who was particularly admired for his powerful live performances of slow, passionate ballads.

Redding's career as a soul legend ended abruptly with his death shortly after a celebrated appearance at the 1967 MONTEREY POP FESTIVAL when the aircraft he was piloting crashed into Lake Monona, Wisconsin. That same year he replaced Elvis PRESLEY as top male vocalist in the lists published by the UK's *Melody Maker*. In the wake of Redding's death, his single '(Sittin' on the) Dock of the Bay' stormed to the top of the charts on both sides of the Atlantic.

Reddy, Helen (1942–) Australian singer, who established herself as a favourite with fairly conventional MIDDLE-OF-THE-ROAD pop in the 1970s. Among her hits were 'I am Woman' (1972), which got to Number One and was taken up as an anthem by women's rights organizations, 'Delta Dawn' (1973) and 'Angie Baby' (1974).

Redman, Don (1900–64) US JAZZ composer, arranger, bandleader, singer and saxophonist, who led a highly popular BIG BAND in the 1930s and collaborated with many of the leading jazzmen of the SWING era. He began as a saxophonist under Fletcher HENDERSON in the mid-1920s and went on to work with the likes of Louis ARMSTRONG and Paul WHITEMAN before founding his own band in 1931. Among his biggest hits, which had a profound influence on other arrangers of the burgeoning swing style of which Redman was one of the chief architects, were 'Save It, Pretty Mama' (1929), 'Chant of the Weed' (1931), 'Hot and Anxious' (1932), 'If It Ain't Love' (1934) and 'Flight of the Jitterbugs' (1939). He may also have had a hand in writing the classic Hoagy CARMICHAEL hit 'Stardust'. He continued to work as a bandleader and arranger during and after the Second World War as well as working as music director for Pearl BAILEY.

Reed, Jerry (Jerry Hubbard; 1937–) US COUNTRY singer-songwriter and guitarist, nicknamed the Guitar Man. Best known for 'Guitar Man', which was also recorded by Elvis PRESLEY with Reed on guitar, his other hits of the late 1960s and early 1970s included 'US Male', 'Amos Moses', 'Georgia Sunshine', 'Alabama Wild Man' and 'When You're Hot, You're Hot'. He has also acted in a number of films, often alongside Burt Reynolds.

Reed, Jimmy (1925–76) Black US BLUES singer, guitarist and harmonica player, who was one of the most popular and influential Chicago bluesmen of the 1950s and 1960s. Born on a Mississippi cotton plantation, Reed achieved fame with such much-covered blues classics as 'Honest I Do' (1957), 'Baby, What Do You Want Me To Do?' (1960), 'Big Boss Man' (1961) and 'Bright Lights, Big City' (1961), which he delivered in his distinctive drawling voice. Reed was illiterate, a problem that was overcome by his wife Mary Lee 'Mama' Reed, who could read, whispering the lyrics to him as he was recording (her voice is sometimes overheard on the finished results). Among those to take up Reed's songs in homage to him were the ROLLING STONES and the YARDBIRDS. He was one of the first musicians to use a harness so that he could play guitar and harmonica at the same time, an innovation that was widely copied in the 1960s. Despite his success, Reed died in poverty, an alcoholic.

Reed, Lou (1942–) US rock singer-songwriter and guitarist, who became a rock superstar, first as a founder of the VELVET UNDERGROUND and, later, as a solo artist. Reed's credentials as a leading performer of AVANT-GARDE rock were firmly established with the Velvet Underground in the late 1960s, when he was one of the coterie associated with New York pop art guru Andy Warhol. His charismatic style was further developed after the band split up, when he teamed up with David BOWIE in the early 1970s, and it was fully realized on the classic album *Transformer* (1972), which included the celebrated 'Walk on the Wild Side'. *Berlin* (1973) was intense and equally poetic and included the memorable 'Caroline Says', while *Metal Machine Music* (1975) was more experimental, consisting of feedback and assorted electronic noises. Hailed as an idol by PUNK fans in the late 1970s, Reed returned to the limelight in 1989 with the acclaimed *New York*, which included the hits 'Dirty Boulevard' and 'Romeo had Juliette'. Also acclaimed were *Songs for Drella* (1990), which recalled the Warhol years, *Magic and Loss* (1992) and *Set the Twilight Reeling* (1996).

'Walk on the Wild Side' was inspired by the various exotic characters Reed met through Warhol, chiefly the transvestites 'Holly' Woodlawn, who really did 'hitchhike her way cross the USA', Jackie Curtiss, who claimed to be possessed by the spirit of James Dean, and Candy Darling (James Lawrence Slattery), together with street hustler 'Little Joe' Dallesandro – all of whom had starred in various Warhol movies. Almost constantly under the influence of hard drugs provided by the 'Sugarplum Fairy' mentioned in the song, Warhol's 'stars' mostly met sad fates in later years; Candy died of cancer of the blood in 1974 after taking pills to develop the breasts, while Jackie died of a drug overdose in 1985.

> The music is all. People should die for it. People are dying for everything else, so why not the music?
> LOU REED

Reese, Della (Dellareese Taliaferro; 1931–) Black US GOSPEL and pop singer, who had a series of big hits in the late 1950s and early 1960s. Having toured with such artists as Mahalia JACKSON in the 1940s, she established a reputation in the pop world with such hits as 'And That Reminds Me' (1957), 'Don't You Know' (1959), 'Not One Minute More' (1959), 'The Most Beautiful Words' (1961) and 'Bill Bailey' (1961).

The original 'Bill Bailey, Won't You Please Come Home' was written by Hughie Cannon (1877–1912) in 1902, and the song was a big favourite with MUSIC HALL audiences. Many years later, it was revealed that it had been inspired by a conversation Cannon had once had with a late-drinker of that name: the resulting publicity of the man's domestic problems resulted in the real Bill Bailey being divorced by his wife. Cannon himself took to drink and drugs and died in the workhouse.

Reeves, Jim (James Travis Reeves; 1924–64) Celebrated US COUNTRY singer, nicknamed Gentleman Jim because of his unruffled, gentlemanly demeanour, who became a cult figure after his early death. Reeves had a career as a professional baseball player and radio presenter, but he launched himself as a country singer and guitarist after filling in for Hank WILLIAMS when he did not turn up for a broadcast. Reeves established his reputation as one of the most popular country stars with such hits as 'Four Walls' (1957), 'He'll Have to Go' (1960), 'I Love You Because' (1964), 'I Won't Forget You' (1964) and 'Distant Drums' (1966), and he was almost constantly at the top of the charts in the late 1950s and early 1960s. It all came to an end when the aircraft in which he was travelling crashed in Tennessee during a storm. He was elected to the COUNTRY MUSIC HALL OF FAME in 1967.

Most macabre of all was an album of 'duets' that was released in 1981, on which Reeves's voice was matched with that of Patsy CLINE, who also died in an aircrash.

Reger, (Johann Baptist Joseph) Max(imilian) (1873–1916) German composer, pianist, organist, conductor and teacher, who established a reputation as one of the most innovative composers active at the turn of the century. Director of music at Leipzig University (1907–11) and of the celebrated Meiningen Orchestra (1911–13), he developed his own system of chromatic harmony while professing loyalty to the music of Bach, thereby arousing controversy among conservatives and modernists alike. His many works for orchestra and keyboard instruments include variations based on Bach (1904), Mozart (1914) and Telemann (1914) as well as a piano concerto (1910), a clarinet quintet (1915) and over 250 songs. His admirers included Sergei PROKOFIEV.

> The American music critic Irving Kolodin ... pointed out that Reger's name is the same either forward or backward, and that his music displays the same characteristic.
> GERVASE HUGHES, *Sidelights on a Century of Music*, 1969

> I am sitting in the smallest room of my house. I have your review before me. In a moment it will be behind me.
> MAX REGER, in answer to one of his critics

reggae Popular music genre, which

developed in Jamaica and subsequently exerted a powerful influence on pop music in the UK. With the emphasis placed on the second and fourth beats of each 4/4 bar, reggae has a bouncy, cheerful rhythm, which proved immediately accessible to a wide audience when it was first heard in the 1950s (when it was often labelled bluebeat or SKA). Another feature was 'toasting', the addition of lines of street poetry chanted by disc jockeys over a reggae backing, which anticipated the development of RAP years later.

After pioneering work by such performers as Desmond DEKKER and Jimmy CLIFF, reggae was imported to the UK on a major scale in the 1970s, when it was enthusiastically adopted by both Black and some White bands (the most successful of which included the POLICE and UB40). The lyrics of most reggae songs reflect the preoccupations of a young, often socially disadvantaged audience, although some artists – notably the Rastafarian hero Bob MARLEY, the biggest reggae star of them all – used it to apply pressure for political change, arguing in favour of reconciliation and freedom from oppression.

Reggae faded from the British scene in the 1980s, but made a minor come-back in the 1990s in the form of 'ragga', which combined reggae with RAP.

The word reggae itself is thought to have been derived from the Jamaican *rage-rage* (an argument) or *streggae* (rudeness), although an alternative theory has it as slang for 'regular people' (meaning the masses in general).

> Don't just move to the music, listen to what I'm saying.
> BOB MARLEY

> Reggae means comin' from the people, y'know? Like a everyday thing. Like from the ghetto. From *majority*. Everyday thing that people use like food, we just put music to it and make a dance out of it. Reggae mean *regular* people who are suffering, and don't have what they want.
> TOOTS HIBBERT

Reich, Steve (1936–) US composer, who established a reputation as one of the leading figures in the MINIMALIST style in the 1960s. His works, reflecting his interest in oriental music and in the concept of phaseshifting and the slow evolution of musical patterns, have included such pieces as *Drumming* (1971), *Music for Pieces of Wood* (1973), *Music for 18 Music-* ians (1976), *Variations* (1978), and *The Desert Music* (1984). He has led his own ensemble of percussionists since the early 1970s.

Reinhardt, Django (Jean Baptiste Reinhardt; 1910–53) Belgian-born gypsy guitarist, who became one of the few non-American musicians to win recognition as a JAZZ legend. Wandering Europe and North Africa, Reinhardt, who could not read, taught himself to play the guitar, the banjo and the violin. Further progress was threatened in 1928, when the 18-year-old musician suffered severe damage to his left hand in a caravan fire, but he adapted his fingering technique and established himself as one of the most innovative and gifted guitarists in the world. In 1934 he formed an unlikely alliance in Paris with the brilliant violinist Stéphane GRAPPELLI and went on to record numerous highly acclaimed albums with the QUINTETTE DU HOT CLUB DE FRANCE. Among Reinhardt's own compositions was the highly popular 'Nuages'.

Reinhardt switched to electric guitar after the Second World War and collaborated with such jazzmen as Dizzy GILLESPIE and Duke ELLINGTON before his premature death. British guitarist Diz Disley, who was much influenced by Reinhardt, took his place when the quintet was re-formed by Grappelli in the 1960s. Remembered now for his music, Reinhardt was once equally renowned for his flamboyant, gypsy character, which expressed itself not only through his guitar but in his unpredictability (he often failed to turn up for bookings) and love of excitement (he was an inveterate gambler).

R.E.M. US rock band, which established a huge international following from the mid-1980s. Comprising singer Michael Stipe (1960–), guitarist Peter Buck (1956–), bassist Mike Mills (1956–) and drummer Bill Berry (1958–), R.E.M. – short for Rapid Eye Movement – came together in 1980 and achieved cult status with such albums as *Murmur* (1983), *Reckoning* (1984), *Life's Rich Talent* (1986), *Document* (1987), *Out of Time* (1991), *Automatic For the People* (1992) and *Monster* (1994).

Remedios, Alberto (1935–) British tenor, who has established himself as one of the leading Wagnerian tenors of his generation. He won particular acclaim with the ENGLISH NATIONAL OPERA in the 1970s, when his roles included Siegmund and Siegfried in *The Ring*.

REO Speedwagon US rock band, which became established as one of the most enduring international rock acts to emerge from the 1970s. The band, which consisted of pianist Neil Doughty (1946–), drummer Alan Gratzer (1948–), singer and guitarist Kevin Cronin (1951–), bassist Bruce Hall (1953–) and guitarist Gary Richrath (1949–), was named after an early fire-engine designed by Ransom E. Olds. It came together in Illinois in 1970 and quickly established a reputation as an exciting live act. A string of moderately successful early albums was followed by the platinum-selling *You Get What You Play For* (1977) and *You Can Tune a Piano, But You Can't Tuna Fish* (1978). Subsequent hits included the albums *Hi Infidelity* (1980), from which came such singles as 'Keep on Lovin' You', which got to Number One in the USA, and 'Take It on the Run', *Wheels Are Turning* (1984), which produced a second US Number One single in 'Can't Fight This Feeling', and *Life As We Know It* (1987). The band has gone into a decline in the wake of the departures of Richrath and Gratzer.

Respighi, Ottorino (1879–1936) Italian composer, who is remembered chiefly for his tone poems echoing the influence of his teacher Nikolai Rimsky-Korsakov (1844–1908). Born in Bologna, Respighi trained as a violinist and viola player before joining the St Petersburg Opera Orchestra in 1900 and receiving early training as a composer under Rimsky-Korsakov and, in Berlin, under Max Bruch (1838–1920). When he returned to Italy, where he was eventually appointed director of the St Cecilia Conservatory in Rome, he established his reputation with a series of nine operas – of which the most successful was *La Fiamma* (1934). More influential, however, were the brilliantly orchestrated, romantic-impressionist tone poems, including his masterpiece *The Fountains of Rome* (1917), *The Pines of Rome* (1924), *Church Windows* (1927), *Three Botticelli Pictures* (1927) and *Roman Festivals* (1929). Among other works of note were his series of *Ancient Airs and Dances* (1917–32), which were inspired by Italian music of past eras, as was the suite *The Birds* (1927) and the ballet *La Boutique fantasque* (*The Fantastic Toyshop*; 1919), which was commissioned by Diaghilev and which evoked the music of Rossini, culminating in the celebrated 'Can-can'.

retro-rock ROCK genre of the late 1980s and 1990s, in which the styles of bands of the 1960s and 1970s are recreated with the benefit of modern electronic instuments. Among the favourite models are the ROLLING STONES and the KINKS.

Revel, Harry (1905–58) British composer and pianist, who wrote numerous hits for vaudeville and the cinema. He played throughout Europe in a Hawaiian band and with a larger dance orchestra, before winning acclaim with his writing for the *Ziegfeld Follies* and other prominent revues, which led to his being recruited by Hollywood in 1932. His hits for the big screen – mostly in collaboration with the lyricist Mack GORDON – included the scores for *The Gay Divorce* (1934), *Poor Little Rich Girl* (1936), *Head Over Heels* (1936) and *My Lucky Star* (1938). Among the most popular Gordon–Revel compositions were 'Stay as Sweet as You are' (1934), 'Paris in the Spring' (1935) and 'Goodnight My Love' (1936).

Revere, Paul, and the Raiders US pop group of the 1960s, which enjoyed considerable commercial success with largely teenage audiences in the USA while never making a breakthrough in the UK. Led by pianist Paul Revere (Paul Revere Dick; 1942–) and singer Mark Lindsay (1942–), the group made its recording début with such instrumentals as 'Beatnik Sticks' (1960) and 'Like Long Hair' (1961). The group called itself the Downbeats, Paul Revere and the Nightriders before settling on the permanent name, under which, dressed in costumes based on uniforms of the Revolutionary period, it enjoyed no fewer than 24 hits in the US charts, among them 'Steppin' Out' (1965), 'Hungry' (1966) and (without Revere) 'Indian Reservation' (1971).

revue Form of musical entertainment, in which a series of songs, sketches and other items, often matters of topical interest, are strung together, although not necessarily linked. The revue had its roots in France in the mid-nineteenth century, when such shows became the staple entertainment at the *Folies Bergère* and elsewhere. The first English revue was Seymour Hicks' *Under the Clock* in 1893, and the first on Broadway was *The Passing Show* of 1894.

The revue entered its golden age between the wars when top names associated with it included such stars as Josephine BAKER, Irving BERLIN, Jack BUCHANAN, C.B. COCHRAN, André CHARLOT, Noël COWARD, George GERSHWIN and Ivor NOVELLO. In the USA, revue reached new heights of spectacle under the control of Florenz ZIEGFELD (whose shows ran from 1907 to 1957) and became a byword for theatrical glamour.

The heyday of the revue passed with the advent of cinema and television and the rise of the MUSICAL, but the form enjoyed a fresh lease of life in the 1950s and 1960s when a new generation of British comedians and singers appeared in *Beyond the Fringe* (1961) and other sharply satirical, more intimate shows. Other postwar stars included comedienne Joyce Grenfell (1910–79) and singers FLANDERS AND SWANN. Revues of the 1960s were more risqué, even resorting to displays of nudity in an attempt to lure back audiences.

Reynolds, Debbie (1932–) US film actress, singer and dancer, who starred in numerous hit film MUSICALS of the 1950s. After huge success in *Singin' in the Rain* (1952), she went on to appear in such movies as *Tammy and the Bachelor* (1957), in which she sang the hit song 'Tammy', *The Unsinkable Molly Brown* (1964) and *What's the Matter with Helen?* (1971) among many more. Her hit records included 'Aba Daba Honeymoon' (1950). She was married to fellow-singer Eddie FISHER.

rhythm-and-blues Term popularized by the US *Billboard* magazine in 1949 to describe what had previously been called RACE MUSIC until it was realized that the phrase was causing offence in some quarters. A combination of various BLUES and White pop elements, r 'n' b was characteristically energetic, sophisticated and aggressively 'streetwise', tackling issues relevant to modern urban society. Performers of the music, who in the early days at least were mostly Black, adopted electrically amplified instruments and the saxophone, and many became stars, the first generation of rhythm-and-blues kings including Chuck BERRY, Ray CHARLES, Sam COOKE, Bo DIDDLEY, Fats DOMINO, Elmore JAMES, B.B. KING, LITTLE RICHARD, the PLATTERS and Muddy WATERS, who enjoyed equal popularity with Black and White audiences. The genre continued to develop through the 1940s and early 1950s, ultimately giving birth to ROCK 'N' ROLL.

Among the many celebrated artists happy to don the mantle of r 'n' b since then have been the DRIFTERS, the ROLLING STONES and the JACKSON FIVE. Others who in the 1960s preferred to use the terms SOUL and FUNK while remaining essentially r 'n' b stars included Otis REDDING and James BROWN.

Jerry Wexler, of ATLANTIC RECORDS, is credited as the man who invented the term rhythm-and-blues, although he himself admitted: 'The music was not particularly rhythmic, and it was almost never blues.'

> It's not a music. It's a disease.
> MITCH MILLER, of rhythm-and-blues, 1969

rhythmicon Early electrical keyboard instrument, which was invented by Russian physicist Lev Theremin (1896–) in collaboration with the US composer Henry COWELL. It was used primarily as a percussion instrument, producing complex cross-rhythms.

Rice, Tim (Timothy Miles Bindon Rice; 1944–) British lyricist, who formed a highly successful collaboration with Andrew LLOYD WEBBER in the late 1960s. Their MUSICAL *Joseph and the Amazing Technicolor Dreamcoat* (1968) was followed by the startling *Jesus Christ Superstar* (1973), which marked the beginning of Lloyd Webber's reign as the top composer for the musical stage of his generation. This success was repeated in 1978 when the pair teamed up once more for the equally acclaimed *Evita*, after which Rice collaborated with other composers for the musicals *Blondel* (1983) and *Chess* (1988).

Rich, Buddy (Bernard Rich; 1917–87) US JAZZ drummer and bandleader, who was among the most acclaimed jazz drummers of his generation. Rich made his stage début with his parents when he was just a child, appearing on Broadway at the age of four, already an accomplished drummer. He formed his own band when he was 11 years old, and he went on to play the drums for such leading figures as Artie SHAW and Tommy DORSEY before forming his first BIG BAND in 1946 in collaboration with Frank SINATRA. Always flamboyant, he was at his best leading a big orchestra, although he also led smaller ensembles.

Rich, Charlie (1932–95) US COUNTRY singer, nicknamed the Silver Fox in reference to his silver hair, who had transatlantic success with both country and pop audiences in the late 1960s and early 1970s. Initially planning to be a saxophonist, Rich started in JAZZ, but he moved to Memphis and established a reputation as a country star with MIDDLE-OF-THE-ROAD pop appeal with such hits as 'Mohair Sam' (1965), 'Behind Closed Doors' (1973), 'The Most Beautiful Girl' (1973) and 'Every Time You Touch Her' (1975).

Richard, Sir Cliff (Harry Roger Webb; 1940–   ) British pop singer, born in India, who has enjoyed one of the longest and most successful careers in the history of British pop. He came to the UK when he was seven years old, eventually finding employment as a factory clerk. The young Harry Webb made his first appearances as a singer with an amateur SKIFFLE group called the Drifters, with which he won a booking for a Butlin's summer season in Clacton. When he was 17 he made his recording début as a budding ROCK 'N' ROLL star in the mould of Elvis PRESLEY with 'Move It' (1958). This was an immediate hit and made Richard and his backing band, later renamed the SHADOWS, an overnight sensation (although some people expressed outrage at the 'scandalous' sexual innuendo of Richard's hip-gyrating live act).

'Livin' Doll', which went all the way to Number One a year later, was distinctly mellower in tone and widened Richard's appeal, anticipating his development as a favourite with MIDDLE-OF-THE-ROAD audiences. Again following the example set by Elvis, Richard and the Shadows developed a second career in television and films, starring in a series of light-hearted MUSICAL romps, including *The Young Ones* (1961) and *Summer Holiday* (1963). The hits continued into the 1960s with such chart-toppers as 'Travellin' Light' (1959), 'Please

Don't Tease' (1960), 'I Love You' (1960), 'The Young Ones' (1962), 'The Next Time/Bachelor Boy' (1963), 'Summer Holiday' (1963) and 'The Minute You're Gone' (1965).

Richard and the Shadows had parted company by 1968, the year that Richard represented the UK in the EUROVISION SONG CONTEST with 'Congratulations' (he finished runner-up). Subsequently he announced his conversion as a born-again Christian, for a time combining his activities in music with spreading the gospel (and a love of tennis). He went on to star in the stage musical *Time* (1986) and subsequently in *Heathcliff* (1996) while still continuing to make regular appearances in the charts with new singles.

Among his many hits since the 1960s have been 'Power to All Our Friends' (1973), 'Miss You Nights' (1976), 'Devil Woman', which was – surprisingly – his first US Top 10 hit, 'We Don't Talk Anymore', which got to Number One in 1979, 'Mistletoe and Wine' (1988) and 'The Best of Me' (1989), which brought his tally of singles to 100.

Richie, Lionel (Brockman) (1949–   ) Black US singer-songwriter, who established himself as a SOUL superstar in the early 1980s. As lead singer of the COMMODORES, Richie was already famous before starting out on a solo career in 1982 (he had also had a Number One hit singing the duet 'Endless Love' with Diana ROSS in 1981). *Lionel Richie* (1982) was followed by the best-selling *Can't Slow Down* (1984), from which came the hit single 'Hello', which got to Number One in the UK. Other hits have included 'All Night Long' (1983) and 'Say You, Say Me' (1985), which won an Oscar. He was one of the organizers behind the USA for Africa charity effort in the mid-1980s, co-writing 'We Are the World' with Michael JACKSON. Recent releases have included *Back to Front* (1992) and *Louder than Words* (1996).

Richman, Jonathan (1951–   ) US rock singer and guitarist, who established a loyal cult following in the late 1970s leading his band the Modern Lovers. Influenced by the VELVET UNDERGROUND, Richman developed a studiedly bizarre style, which attracted considerable attention in the PUNK ROCK era of the late 1970s. While the Modern Lovers line-up was in a state of constant flux, Richman released a series of critically if not commercially acclaimed albums as well as the occasional hit single, notably 'Road Runner' (1977) and 'Egyptian Reggae' (1977).

Richter, Sviatoslav (Teofilovich) (1915–) Russian pianist, who established an international reputation as an interpreter of works ranging from Bach to Beethoven and Benjamin BRITTEN. A student at the Moscow Conservatory, Richter enjoyed a particularly close association with Sergei PROKOFIEV, presenting the premières of three of his piano sonatas and helping to conduct the first performance of the second cello concerto; the composer dedicated his ninth piano sonata to Richter. He has also won acclaim as an accompanist and for his collaborations with the cellist Mstislav ROSTROPOVICH, although he has also acquired a reputation for disappointing audiences by cancelling appearances at the last moment when finding his performance did not meet his own high standards.

Riddle, Nelson (1921–85) US conductor, composer, arranger and trombonist, who collaborated with many of the most acclaimed singers of his era as well as leading a popular BIG BAND. Riddle worked with artists like Tommy DORSEY and Bob CROSBY in the 1940s and subsequently joined CAPITOL Records, where he provided backing for such stars as Nat 'King' COLE, Frank SINATRA, Judy GARLAND and Ella FITZGERALD. Leading his own band, he recorded numerous popular SWING albums and also worked on a host of film SOUNDTRACKS, the most celebrated including *St Louis Blues* (1958), *Lolita* (1962), *How To Succeed In Business Without Really Trying* (1966), *Paint Your Wagon* (1969) and *The Great Gatsby* (1974), for which he was awarded an OSCAR. Among his compositions for television was the music for *Batman* (1967).

riff Jazz term, which refers to a particular musical phrase that is repeated at regular intervals during a piece. SWING bands of the 1920s and 1930s often employed riffs played either by a soloist or by a section playing in harmony and made great use of it in improvisation. The excitement generated could be almost overwhelming and created a sense of great exhilaration in audiences. The concept of the riff goes back, in fact, to Negro ring shouts and hollers, the BLUES and spirituals, and before that to West African music, in which much use was made of repetitive phrases. The term, possibly a shortening of 'refrain', has since been adopted in rock music, where it is usually applied to fast guitar LICKS.

Right Said Fred British pop trio, who had considerable chart success in the early 1990s. The trio, which consisted of the shaven-headed, fitness-enthusiast brothers Fred and Richard Fairbrass with guitarist Rob Manzoli, was named after a 1960s NOVELTY hit by actor Bernard Cribbins. The trio came together in 1990 and captured a big audience with the self-mocking 'I'm Too Sexy'. Follow-ups included 'Don't Talk, Just Kiss' and 'Deeply Dippy', which got to Number One in 1992. Cribbins himself made an appearance on one of their videos.

Righteous Brothers, the US pop duo, nicknamed the Blue-eyed Soul Brothers, who had huge commercial success in the 1960s. Singers Bill Medley (1940–) and Bobby Hatfield (1940–) were not brothers at all but found that their contrasting voices suited each other perfectly as part of the group the Paramours and later as the Righteous Brothers. Their biggest hit by far was the classic 'You've Lost that Lovin' Feeling' (1965), produced by Phil SPECTOR, which topped the charts on both sides of the Atlantic and featured once more when re-released in 1969 and again in 1977. Lesser follow-ups included 'Just Once in My Life', 'Unchained Melody', which topped the charts on re-release in 1990, 'Ebb Tide' and '(You're my) Soul and Inspiration', which got to Number One in the USA in 1966. Medley and Hatfield fell out in the late 1960s and pursued solo careers, ultimately reuniting in 1974 with a new hit, 'Rock 'n' Roll Heaven', and then splitting once more. In 1987 Medley teamed up with Jennifer Warnes for the hit '(I've had) The Time of My Life'.

ring modulator Electronic musical instrument, which was adopted by various AVANT-GARDE composers in the 1950s. Capable of producing complex electronic effects, it was employed with some success, notably by Karlheinz STOCKHAUSEN, in such works as *Mixtur* (1964), in which he used a ring modulator to modify the sounds made by conventional orchestral instruments, and *Mantra* (1970), which was for two ring-modulated pianos.

Ritter, Tex (Woodward Maurice Ritter; 1905–74) US COUNTRY singer-songwriter and film actor, who became a top star singing in the COUNTRY-AND-WESTERN tradition. Having been brought up on a Texas ranch and working as a cowboy in reality, he was able to back up his claims as the genuine article (unlike some other Hollywood cowboys), and he eventually won the role of the Lone Ranger on the radio. He also appeared in a number of MUSICAL Westerns from the 1930s onwards, his biggest hits including the title song of the classic *High Noon* (1952).

Roach, Max (1925–) Black US JAZZ drummer and bandleader, who emerged as one of the most influential drummers in the developing BEBOP style in the 1940s. Playing with jazzmen like Charlie PARKER and Dizzy GILLESPIE in the mid-1940s, he went on to lead his own band as well as guesting with Miles DAVIS, Lester YOUNG and with JAZZ AT THE PHILHARMONIC in the 1950s. Highlights of his live performances have included a 10-minute solo played on just one high-hat cymbal.

roadie A member of the support crew, which travels with a particular star or band on tour, erecting and dismantling the arrays of equipment used in concerts. Bob Adams, who worked for the BEATLES, Cliff RICHARD and the EVERLY BROTHERS, is sometimes credited as having been the first professional roadie.

Robbins, Marty (Martin Robertson; 1925–82) US COUNTRY singer-songwriter, nicknamed Mister Teardrop, who established a reputation as one of the most popular of all country balladeers in the 1950s. Among his hits, many of which were in a COUNTRY-AND-WESTERN style, were 'Singin' the Blues' (1954), 'A White Sport Coat (and a Pink Carnation)' (1956), 'El Paso' (1960) and 'I Walk Alone' (1968). When not playing country, he was to be found stock car racing. He died shortly after being elected to the COUNTRY MUSIC HALL OF FAME.

Robeson, Paul (1898–1976) Black US singer and actor, who achieved superstar status on the strength of his rich bass-baritone voice and acting ability. The son of a preacher, Robeson studied law and distinguished himself as an athlete before taking up an acting career and winning acclaim in such stage classics as *All God's Chillun Got Wings* (1924) and *The Emperor Jones* (1925). He repeated some of his stage roles to renewed acclaim in films and added to his credits the starring role in *Othello*, in which he toured in the 1940s and – after a number of years in disgrace following criticisms by the notorious Un-American Activities Committee – also appeared during a British tour in 1958. He is probably best remembered, however, for his singing of Negro spirituals and especially for his rendition of 'Ol' Man River' in Jerome KERN's *Showboat*, a performance preserved in the film made in 1936.

> The best musical instrument wrought by nature in our time.
> ALEXANDER WOOLLCOTT, of Robeson's voice

Robespierre *See* Gabriel Urbain FAURÉ.

Robinson, Smokey (William Robinson; 1940–) Black US SOUL singer-songwriter, who became one of the top MOTOWN stars of the 1960s and 1970s. Robinson began his career singing with the Matadors, later renamed the Miracles, and they were among the first groups signed by Berry GORDY (1958). Robinson quickly established a reputation as a leading singer-songwriter and in time rose to the post of vice-president of Tamla MOTOWN in recognition of his not inconsiderable achievements. Among his hits with the Miracles were 'Shop Around' (1960), 'You Really Got a Hold of Me' (1962), 'Tracks of My Tears' (1965) and 'Tears of a Clown' (1967), which was co-written by Stevie WONDER and became a transatlantic chart-topper. Robinson, who masterminded the rise of another Motown vocal group, the TEMPTATIONS, parted company with the Miracles in 1972 and subsequently returned to the Number One spot with 'Being With You' (1981). Further progress in the 1980s was disrupted by drug addiction.

> America's greatest living poet.
> BOB DYLAN

Robinson, Tom (1950–) British singer-songwriter, who enjoyed star status for his witty songs celebrating homosexuality and dwelling on a range of politically relevant issues in the PUNK ROCK era of the late 1970s. Having worked for a time with the KINKS, Robinson formed his own band and had chart success with the anthemic 'Glad to be Gay' and such ebullient follow-ups as '2–4–6–8 Motorway'. He then got into debt, formed a new band under the title Sector 21 and had renewed success with the single 'War Baby' (1983). He continued to work as a songwriter, sometimes in collaboration with Elton JOHN and Peter GABRIEL, and re-formed his old band in 1989.

Robison, Carson J. (1890–1957) US singer-songwriter and guitarist, who wrote some classic COUNTRY hits of the 1920s. A popular radio broadcaster, Robison penned such enduring favourites as 'The Runaway Train' (1925), 'I Got a Gal in Kansas' (1930), 'Home, Sweet Home, on the Prairie' (1935) and 'Life Gets Tee-jus, Don't It' (1948).

rock Broad spectrum of contemporary POP music, which takes in everything from dance music with some serious lyrical intent to RHYTHM-AND-BLUES and HEAVY METAL. A dividing line between straightforward pop and rock was first suggested in the 1960s, when it became desirable to distance more ambitious artists from those whose only aim was to satisfy a mass appetite for sentiment and up-tempo dance music. The term rock came to be applied particularly to high-volume, amplified guitar music as purveyed by numerous bands in the late 1960s and early 1970s, although the almost immediate emergence of such sub-genres as ART ROCK, FOLK-ROCK and PROGRESSIVE ROCK and the introduction of the terms HARD ROCK and soft rock underlined the multifaceted nature of the field. Perhaps the closest anyone came to pinpointing the difference between rock and pop was the general recognition that of the two top bands of the 1960s, the BEATLES belonged primarily to pop, while the ROLLING STONES were more accurately described as a rock outfit.

The issue of what was rock and what was pop was debated at length in the House of Lords in 1990 in relation to the licensing of new radio stations; they concluded in the end that it was impossible to draw a clear line between the two (and by

extension that the difference did not really exist). *See also* ACID ROCK; PUNK ROCK; ROCK OPERA.

> Rock music must give birth to orgasm and revolution.
> JERRY RUBIN, *Do It!*, 1970

> Good rock stars take drugs, put their penises in plaster of Paris, collectivize their sex, molest policemen, promote self-curiosity, unlock myriad spirits, epitomize fun, freedom and bullshit. Can the busiest anarchist on your block match THAT?
> RICHARD NEVILLE, *Playpower*, 1970

rock 'n' roll POP music genre of the 1950s that transformed the history of popular music of the twentieth century, giving birth to the modern ROCK and POP traditions. Rock 'n' roll emerged as a distinct musical form in the mid-1950s when White US musicians first adopted the RHYTHM-AND-BLUES and BOOGIE-WOOGIE styles that had hitherto been associated chiefly with their Black counterparts. With the emphasis on simple driving rhythms and repeating three-chord patterns, the new style quickly caught on in the dance halls, where it inspired a frenetic version of the jive, and became the voice of teenage rebellion, personified visually in the high fashion style of the teddy boys. Queen Elizabeth II herself cancelled a royal showing of a new Humphrey Bogart film in order to see the rock 'n' roll movie *Rock Around the Clock*, which introduced thousands of youngsters to the genre in 1956.

Among the pioneers were Bill HALEY, who triumphed with the rock 'n' roll anthems 'Rock Around the Clock' (1955) and 'Shake, Rattle, and Roll' and Carl PERKINS, whose classic 'Blue Suede Shoes' provided Elvis PRESLEY with one of his earliest rock 'n' roll hits, LITTLE RICHARD, Buddy HOLLY, Jerry Lee LEWIS, Gene VINCENT and, in the UK, such paler imitations as Billy FURY, Cliff RICHARD and Tommy STEELE.

The heyday of rock 'n' roll was relatively short-lived. The disappearance of Presley from the scene on his enlistment in the army in 1958, together with the untimely deaths of Holly and Eddie COCHRAN and the disgracing of Berry and Lewis meant that the rock 'n' roll era was effectively over by 1960, when the final nail was put in the coffin by the PAYOLA SCANDAL.

The term 'rock 'n' roll' was popularized by the US radio disc jockey Alan FREED, who was one of the first presenters to promote such music, playing Black r 'n' b material to a largely White audience. A song entitled 'Rock and Roll' had, however, been recorded – by the BOSWELL SISTERS – as early as 1934. In Black slang, both 'rock' and 'roll' are synonyms for sexual intercourse.

> The effect of rock 'n' roll on young people is to turn them into devilworshippers; to stimulate self-expression through sex; to provoke lawlessness, impair nervous stability, and destroy the sanctity of marriage.
> REV ALBERT CARTER, 1956

> Rock 'n' roll is an asylum for emotional imbeciles.
> RICHARD NEVILLE

> Rock and roll is phoney and false, and sung, written and played for the most part by cretinous goons.
> FRANK SINATRA, 1957

> It makes me feel big and great, like I've won a football pool or something.
> Unidentified rock 'n' roller, London, 1956

rock opera Genre of MUSICAL THEATRE, in which drama is mixed with ROCK. The golden age of the rock opera was the late 1960s and early 1970s, when such box office hits as *Hair* (1969), *Tommy* (1969) and *Jesus Christ Superstar* (1970) were among the most talked-about shows on either side of the Atlantic. *See also* CONCEPT ALBUM.

rock steady Embryonic form of REGGAE.

rockabilly Embryonic rock style of the 1950s, in which the ROCK 'N' ROLL and HILLBILLY genres were fused. Rockabilly was born in the southern USA and represented the first White rock 'n' roll. Among the biggest names associated with the genre, which flourished between 1956 and 1959, were Elvis PRESLEY, Carl PERKINS, Rick NELSON, Roy ORBISON and the EVERLY BROTHERS. Years later, such bands as the Stray Cats enjoyed chart success playing in a revived rockabilly style.

Rockin' Chair Lady, the *See* Mildred BAILEY.

Rockville Rocket, the *See* Gene PITNEY.

Rod the Mod *See* Rod STEWART.

Rodgers, Jimmie (James Charles Rodgers; 1897–1933) US singer and guitarist, nicknamed the Father of Country Music and the Singing Brakeman in reference to his previous employment as a brakeman on the railroads in Mississippi, who was the first great star of COUNTRY music. Rodgers sold some 20 million records between 1928 and 1933 and had such huge hits as 'The Soldier's Sweetheart', 'Blue Yodel', 'In the Jailhouse Now' and others reflecting his past employment on the railroads. He appeared in the film *The Singing Brakeman* in 1931 but died two years later from tuberculosis.

Rodgers's music absorbed the influence of contemporary BLUES and in turn exerted a profound effect on a whole generation of country stars, of whom the most prominent included Hank WILLIAMS. In 1961 he became the first star to be elected to the Country Music Hall of Fame; a US postage stamp was issued in his memory in 1977.

Rodgers, Richard (Charles) (1902–79) US composer, who became one of the legends of US MUSICAL THEATRE through his acclaimed collaborations with the lyricists Lorenz HART and Oscar HAMMERSTEIN II. Rodgers teamed up with Hart in 1919 while they were still students at Columbia University and went on to enjoy a long series of hit Broadway MUSICALS between 1926 and 1930, presenting shows that had real impact as dramatic stories. Among the most popular of their early shows were *The Girl Friend* (1926), *One Dam Thing After Another* (1927), *A Connecticut Yankee* (1927) and *Ever Green* (1930).

Rodgers and Hart were recruited by Hollywood in 1930 but resumed their Broadway careers four years later. *On Your Toes* (1936) included the celebrated 'Slaughter on Tenth Avenue' sequence as well as the hit song 'There's a Small Hotel', while *Babes in Arms* (1937) triumphed with such hits as 'My Funny Valentine' and 'The Lady is a Tramp'. After further success with such shows as *The Boys from Syracuse* (1938), they had a rare flop with *Pal Joey* (1940), which included 'Bewitched, Bothered, and Bewildered', although the show was later revived with greater success in 1952.

Hart died in 1943, by which time Rodgers had already formed a new partnership with Hammerstein, which was to surpass all his previous triumphs (to Hart's chagrin). *Oklahoma!* (1943) ushered in a new age in the history of the musical with its realistic plot and fully integrated songs including 'You'll Never Walk Alone'. German film director Ernst Lubitsch (1892–1947) was one of the many who recognized the show as a distinct improvement on previous musicals, observing: 'this was the first musical I ever saw on the stage where the people were not complete idiots.' It was followed by such enduring classics as *Carousel* (1945), *South Pacific* (1949), *The King and I* (1951), *Flower Drum Song* (1958) and *The Sound of Music* (1959).

Hammerstein's death in 1960 effectively brought Rodgers' career to a close, although he formed further collaborations with Stephen SONDHEIM among others in his last years.

> Imagine it taking two people to write one song.
>
> COLE PORTER, of 'Some Enchanted Evening'

Rodrigo, Joaquín (1901–) Spanish composer, who is usually remembered for his celebrated guitar concerto, which, like much of his other music, evoked Spanish musical tradition. Blind from the age of three, Rodrigo demonstrated an early talent for music, and he studied under Paul DUKAS in Paris, where he formed a friendship with Manuel de FALLA. Having returned to Spain after the Civil War, his *Concierto de Aranjuez* (1939) for guitar and orchestra proved a huge success and was followed by numerous other compositions in a similar style for such instruments as the harp, the violin and the piano. Works from later in his career included the *Fantasia for a Gentleman* (1954), which was composed expressly for Andrés SEGOVIA, and the *Concierto Pastorale* (1978) for flute and orchestra, which was written at the request of Irish flautist James GALWAY.

Rogers, Kenny (Kenneth Donald Rogers; 1938–) US COUNTRY singer, who had considerable success in both the country and pop charts in the 1960s and 1970s. His hits included 'Ruby Don't Take Your Love to Town' (1969), a song about a maimed Vietnam veteran, which he recorded with the First Edition, with which he was lead singer until their split in the mid-1970s. He emerged as a popular solo star, getting to Number One in the UK with 'Lucille' (1977), a lacrimose ballad about a woman deserting her husband and four children. Other hits included 'Coward of

the County', which returned him to the top of the British charts in 1980, Lionel RICHIE's 'Lady' (1980), the duet 'We've Got Tonight' (1983), which he made with Sheena Easton, and others with Dolly PARTON, notably 'Islands in the Stream' (1983).

Rogers, Roy (1911–) US COUNTRY-AND-WESTERN singer and cowboy actor, nicknamed the King of the Cowboys and the Singing Cowboy, who starred in numerous musical Westerns of the 1940s, usually in company with his horse Trigger (1932–65) and heroine Dale Evans (1912–), whom he married in 1947. A former truck driver and fruit-picker, he starred in his first Western in 1938. Among the hits to emerge from his popular matinée movies were the likes of 'Hi-yo, Silver' (1938) and his theme tune 'Happy Trails to You'. After Trigger died, Rogers had the horse stuffed and installed in a place of honour in his home.

Rolling Stone US rock music paper, which was founded in San Francisco in 1967 by the music journalist Jann Wenner as the mouthpiece of PROGRESSIVE ROCK. The title of the paper was inspired by the song 'Rolling Stone' recorded by bluesman Muddy WATERS, which also provided the name of the British rock band the ROLLING STONES and which was revived in 1965 with enormous success by Bob DYLAN, as 'Like a Rolling Stone'. The rolling stone image provided a powerful and lasting motif for the combination of youthful vigour and adolescent alienation on which music of the 1960s thrived.

Rolling Stones, the Celebrated British rock group, which established itself one of the legends of British RHYTHM-AND-BLUES and rock in the 1960s. The Stones came together in 1962 following (so legend has it) a chance meeting on a train between Mick JAGGER, destined to become the band's charismatic lead singer, and guitarist Keith Richard(s) (1943–), with whom Jagger was to write many of the group's classic songs. They quickly realized their shared interest in r 'n' b and went on to found their own group – named in reference to a song by bluesman Muddy WATERS – in collaboration with guitarist and singer Brian Jones (Lewis Brian Hopkin-Jones; 1942–69), subsequently enlisting bassist Bill Wyman (1936–   ), pianist (and later road manager) Ian Stewart (1938–86) and drummer -Charlie Watts (1941–   ).

Playing COVER versions of r 'n' b songs, the group quickly won a following and, with the support of George HARRISON, made its recording début in 1963. The first hit was with the LENNON and MCCARTNEY 'I Wanna be Your Man' and by 1964 – on the strength of such hits as 'Not Fade Away', 'It's All Over Now' and 'Little Red Rooster' – the Rolling Stones ranked alongside the BEATLES as the top group in contemporary ROCK and pop. One critic later observed that 'the Beatles became the kids who charmed a nation. The Stones were the louts who kicked it in the bollocks'.

Concentrating on material written by Jagger and Richard (sometimes credited under the pseudonyms Nanker and Phelge) from 1965, the Stones conquered the world with the classic single 'Satisfaction'. They quickly established themselves as the quintessential ROCK 'N' ROLL rebels, constantly in the headlines with tales of excess involving women (some very young), alcohol and drugs (there were several arrests on drug charges and Jagger only escaped a prison sentence after appeals in the press). Their music, in the form of such timeless classics as 'Get off of My Cloud' (1965), 'Paint It Black' (1966), 'Let's Spend the Night Together' (1968), 'Honky Tonk Woman' (1969), 'Jumping Jack Flash' (1969) and 'Brown Sugar' (1971), reflected their rebellious persona. Among the hit albums were *Their Satanic Majesties' Request* (1967), *Beggars' Banquet* (1968), *Through the Past Darkly* (1969), *Let It Bleed* (1969), *Sticky Fingers* (1971), *Exile On Main Street* (1972) and *Goat's Head Soup* (1973).

Controversy surrounding the group reached new heights in 1969, when a Black fan waving a gun was knifed to death by the Hell's Angels policing the Altamont Festival during a free performance. The death of the drug-addicted Jones, who had led the band in the early years but ended up dreaming of joining the BEATLES and drowned in his swimming-pool shortly after leaving the group, was another blow. Mick Taylor (1948–   ) took Jones's place and was in turn succeeded in 1974 by Ronnie Wood (1947–   ).

The band continued to trade on its standing as one of the top acts of the 1960s for many years afterwards, although it was generally agreed that later work, which explored such unlively territories as FUNK and even DISCO, lacked the fire and originality of the early years, and the Stones were identified by some under the heading DINOSAUR ROCK. However, they continued to win acclaim for their lively stage act in the course of spectacular world tours. Among later releases were *Some Girls* (1978), *Tattoo You* (1980), *Dirty Work* (1986), followed by individual members' own projects, *Steel Wheels* (1989) and *Voodoo Lounge* (1994). Bill Wyman retired in 1993.

> I knew what I was looking at. It was sex. And I was just ahead of the pack.
> ANDREW OLDHAM, Stones manager

> They look like boys whom any self-respecting mum would lock in the bathroom.
> *The Daily Express*, 1964

Rollins, Sonny (1929–   ) US JAZZ saxophonist, who was hailed as one of the most influential tenor-sax players of the postwar era. He won acclaim for his work with the likes of Bud POWELL, Miles DAVIS, Charlie PARKER and Thelonious MONK and has since consolidated a reputation as one of the most accomplished of all jazz soloists. His hit compositions included 'Oleo', 'Airegin' and 'Alfie's Theme', from the film *Alfie* (1966).

Romberg, Sigmund (1887–1951) US composer, born in Hungary, who wrote some of the most celebrated operettas of the 1920s. Having trained as an engineer, Romberg emigrated to the USA in 1909 and there established a reputation in the musical theatre with such operettas as *Blossom Time* (1921), the US version of *Das Dreimäderlhaus*, which was based on the music of Schubert, and the enduring classics *The Student Prince* (1924) and *The Desert Song* (1926). Hit songs included 'When Hearts are Young', 'Lover, Come Back to Me' and 'Close as Pages in a Book'. He also worked on other projects in collaboration with others, including George GERSHWIN and Oscar HAMMERSTEIN II.

> It's the kind of music you go into the theatre whistling.
> GEORGE GERSHWIN

Ronettes, the US all-girl vocal group, which was among the most successful acts discovered by producer Phil SPECTOR in the

1960s. Sisters Ronnie (Veronica; 1943–)
and Estelle (1944–) Bennett, and Nedra
Talley (1946–) teamed up with Spector in
1963 and had transatlantic chart success
with such hits as 'Be My Baby' (1963),
'Baby I Love You' (1963), 'Best Part of
Breaking Up' (1964) and 'Do I Love You'
(1964). Ronnie Bennett eventually became
Spector's wife (they subsequently divorced),
and the Ronettes disbanded in 1966.

Ronstadt, Linda (Marie) (1946–) US pop
and COUNTRY singer, who had a series of hits
in the 1970s. Among her most successful
releases were the singles 'Different Drum'
(1967), 'You're no Good' (1974) and 'When
Will I be Loved' (1974) as well as a long
series of hit albums. Revelations about her
relationship with Californian governor
Jerry Brown were much in the news in the
early 1980s.

Rose, David (1910–90) US composer, born
in the UK, who wrote several popular instrumental hits of the 1940s and 1950s. He
worked with such band leaders as Benny
GOODMAN and Jack HYLTON and went on to
enjoy success with many of his compositions, including 'Holiday for Strings'
(1943), 'Lovers' Serenade' (1949) and 'The
Stripper' (1961), which became the one
tune associated with strip acts above all
others. He was married briefly (1941–43) to
Judy GARLAND.

Rose, Fred (1897–1954) US singer-
songwriter and pianist, who wrote a
number of early COUNTRY classics, often in
collaboration with such great stars as Gene
AUTRY, Sophie TUCKER, Roy ACUFF and Hank
WILLIAMS. His most celebrated hits included
'Be Honest with Me' (1941) and 'Tears on
My Pillow' (1941).

Ross, Diana (1944–) Black US singer, who
established herself as an enduring favourite
with both SOUL and pop audiences in the
1960s. As one of the SUPREMES, Ross gradually established herself as the leader of the
trio by 1965 and eventually embarked on a
highly successful solo career in 1970.
Among her many chart hits have been
'Ain't No Mountain High Enough' (1970),
'Remember Me' (1970), 'I'm Still Waiting'
(1971), 'Touch Me in the Morning' (1973),
'Do You Know Where You're Going To?'
(1973), 'Love Hangover' (1976), 'Upside
Down' (1980) and (with Lionel RICHIE)

'Endless Love' (1981). 'I'm Still Waiting'
was released in the UK, where it got to
Number One, only after Radio One disc
jockey Tony Blackburn badgered Tamla
MOTOWN; Ross herself was startled when
British fans went wild when she sang it,
because the single had fared much less well
in the USA.

Having left the Motown label in 1981,
Ross returned to the top of the British charts
in 1986, with 'Chain Reaction'. She did her
best in the role of Billie HOLIDAY in the 1972
film *Lady Sings the Blues* and won acclaim for
the music for the film, if not for her acting.
An appearance in *The Wiz* (1978), a bizarre
all-Black version of *The Wizard of Oz*, met
with an even cooler response.

Rostropovich, Mstislav Leopoldovich
(1927–) Russian cellist, pianist and conductor. Having been taught to play the cello
by his parents, Rostropovich studied at the
Moscow Conservatory, where he later
taught, under Dmitri SHOSTAKOVICH and
went on to victory in a series of prestigious
musical competitions. Tours to the West in
the 1950s consolidated his international
reputation as a uniquely gifted cellist, and
he mixed with many of the leading figures in
contemporary classical music, striking up
particularly friendly relations with Benjamin BRITTEN, who dedicated several works
to him, as did Aram KHACHATURIAN, Sergei
PROKOFIEV and Shostakovich among others.

Rostropovich made his first appearance
as a conductor in 1968 and has subsequently established a second career as a respected
conductor of orchestras all over the world.
He also played the piano for his wife, the
soprano Galina Vishnevskaya (1926–).
Criticism by the Soviet regime persuaded
him to emigrate in 1975 and to accept the
post of conductor with the National Symphony Orchestra of Washington, but he
returned to his homeland in the wake of the
political changes of the late 1980s.

> The magnificent cellist Rostropovich, look-
> ing very much like a bank clerk but playing
> like an angel.
> JACK BRYMER, *From Where I Sit*, 1979

Rota, Nino (1911–79) Italian composer,
who is usually remembered for his film
music. Among his most celebrated scores
were those for Fellini's *La dolce vita* (1959),
Roma (1971) and *Casanova* (1977), and
scores for Zeffirelli as well as music for the
first two films in the *Godfather* trilogy.

Roussel, Albert (1869–1937) French composer, who developed his own musical style from the late Romantic music of César Franck (1822–90) and Vincent D'INDY, under whom he studied early in his career. Surviving naval service in Indo-China in the early 1880s and with the Red Cross during the First World War, Roussel drew on his experiences of the Far East for such early compositions as the orchestral *Evocations* (1911) and the opera-ballet *Padmavati* (1918), which incorporated Indian musical scales. Among his later works, some of which fell into the impressionist and later the neoclassical category, were four symphonies, operas, ballets, chambers pieces, piano music and songs. His most celebrated compositions include the *Eighteenth Psalm* for chorus and orchestra (1928) and the Third Symphony (1930). Among his pupils at the Schola Cantorum were Erik SATIE and Edgar VARÈSE.

> Roussel is a sort of Debussy trained in counterpoint.
> PAUL LANDORMY

Roxy Music British pop group, which had considerable chart success during the GLAM ROCK era of the early 1970s. Fronted by singer Bryan FERRY and completed by keyboard player Brian ENO, guitarist Phil Manzanera (1951–   ), drummer Paul Thompson (1951–   ) and saxophonist Andy Mackay (1946–   ) together with a succession of bassists, Roxy Music came together in the late 1960s. The group was among the pioneers of the glam rock movement, adopting dazzling costumes and an extravagant but elegant musical style. The albums *Roxy Music* (1972) and *For Your Pleasure* (1973) were bestsellers, and the band was regularly in the upper reaches of the singles charts with such hits as 'Virginia Plain' (1972), 'Street Life' (1973) and 'Love is a Drug' (1975).

Eno left in the wake of disagreements over future plans, and Ferry divided his time between developing his solo career and maintaining Roxy Music's progress with such further releases as *Stranded* (1973) and the relatively unsuccessful *Siren* (1975). *Manifesto* (1979) saw something of a return to form, and the group's version of John LENNON's 'Jealous Guy' (1980), intended as a tribute to the murdered star, became its first British

Number One. The band split up after issuing a live album in 1983.

Roy, Harry (1900–71) British bandleader and singer, nicknamed the King of the Hot-Cha, who led one of the earliest JAZZ orchestras to earn a reputation in the UK. Roy formed the Original Chrichton Lyricals after the First World War and went on to establish an international following, the band eventually evolving into Harry Roy and his RKOlians. Among the most popular HOT numbers associated with the band were 'Tiger Rag' and 'Bugle Call Rag'. He made a come-back as a leader of BIG BANDS and other TRAD groups in the 1960s before committing suicide to escape his debts.

Royal Festival Hall British concert hall, on London's South Bank, which was opened in 1951 as one of the capital's most prestigious venues for classical music. Designed by Sir Leslie Martin and Sir Robert Matthew for the Festival of Britain in what was then a daringly innovative, modernist style, the building did indeed attract many top names, although its design (at least before subsequent modification in 1964) came in for a good deal of criticism. Sir Thomas BEECHAM hated it, comparing it to a 'disused mining shack in Nevada – frivolous and acoustically imperfect' and on another occasion dismissing it as 'an inflated chicken coop'. It is now home to the LONDON PHILHARMONIC ORCHESTRA.

Royal Philharmonic Orchestra British orchestra, which was founded by Sir Thomas BEECHAM in 1946 and has gone on to win acclaim as one of the finest ensembles in the world. It has been self-governing since 1961 and has attracted such prestigious conductors as Wilhelm KEMPE, Antal DORATI, André PREVIN and Vladimir ASHKENAZY.

Rózsa, Miklós (1907–   ) US composer, born in Hungary, who wrote several ballets before establishing a second career as a celebrated writer of SOUNDTRACKS for Hollywood. He wrote his first film music for Alexander Korda in the UK in the late 1930s and finally arrived in Hollywood in 1940. Among his many film credits were those for *The Four Feathers* (1939), *Five Graves to Cairo* (1943), *Spellbound* (1945), for which he won an Oscar, *A Double Life*

(1947), which brought him a second Academy Award, *Quo Vadis* (1951), *Bhowani Junction* (1956), *Ben Hur* (1959), which brought his tally of Oscars to three, *El Cid* (1961) and *The Green Berets* (1968).

Rubbra, (Charles) Edmund (1901–86) British composer, who won acclaim for his accomplished orchestral and choral music drawing on both religious and poetical inspiration. Hailing from a somewhat impoverished background, Rubbra attracted the attention of the music establishment when he staged a concert dedicated to the works of the British composer Cyril Scott (1879–1970) in 1917, and he was subsequently invited to study music seriously at Reading University and under Gustav HOLST and Ralph VAUGHAN WILLIAMS at the Royal College of Music. Among his compositions were 11 symphonies, of which the most often revived is the Fifth (1948), three concertos, chamber music and two masses.

Rubinstein, Artur (1887–1982) US pianist, born in Poland, who maintained his standing as one of the most gifted musicians of his generation over the course of an immensely long career. Rubinstein proved to be a child prodigy, mastering Mozart's A major Piano Concerto when he was 12 years old and studying under such luminaries as Max Bruch (1838–1920) and Ignacy PADEREWSKI. International tours, in the course of which he collaborated with artists such as Pablo CASALS, consolidated his reputation as a great pianist and made him rich (he received 70 per cent of the gross takings of each concert). The fact that he always got top billing when appearing in a trio with the great violinist Jascha HEIFETZ and cellist Gregor Piatigorsky (1903–76) once led Heifetz to complain: 'If the Almighty himself played the violin, the credits would still read 'Rubinstein, God and Piatigorsky', in that order.' He was not arrogant about his success, however, and was not riled when a doorman attempted to stop him entering a hall where he was due to perform because all the seats were taken, mildly inquiring instead 'May I be seated at the piano?'

Rubinstein continued to appear into his late eighties and made many classic recordings, including the entire works of Chopin and Beethoven's concertos as well as music by Brahms, Schubert and Schumann.

> Sometimes I think, not so much am I a pianist, but a vampire. All my life I have lived off the blood of Chopin.
> ARTUR RUBINSTEIN

rumba Dance music rhythm, which came into vogue in the 1930s and had a profound influence on the history of BIG BAND and SWING music. An importation from Cuba, the rumba is characterized by its ornate, seductive, syncopated rhythms, and it proved highly popular with ballroom dancers on both sides of the Atlantic.

Rundgren, Todd (1948–   ) US rock singer-songwriter and guitarist, nicknamed Runt, who emerged as a top rock attraction of the 1970s. His biggest hits included 'Hello It's Me', which he recorded with his band the Nazz in 1969 and again in 1973 as a solo artist, 'I Saw the Light' (1972) and 'Can We Still be Friends' (1978). He formed a new group, Utopia, in 1974 but concentrated on work as a producer in the 1980s.

Runt *See* Todd RUNDGREN.

Rush Canadian rock band, which established itself as the leading Canadian HEAVY METAL outfit in the 1970s. Singer and bassist Geddy Lee (1953–   ), guitarist Alex Lifeson (1953–   ) and drummer John Rutsey, later replaced by Neil Peart (1952–   ), came together in 1969, and the group established itself with the eponymous début album (1974). The band's gutsy guitar sound and sci-fi inspired lyrics won a huge following, and such albums as *A Farewell to Kings* (1977), *Permanent Waves* (1980), *Grace Under Pressure* (1984), *Hold Your Fire* (1987), *Roll the Bones* (1991) and *Counterparts* (1993) were big chart successes. The Canadian government awarded the band the title Ambassadors of Music in 1979.

Rushing, Jimmy (James Andrew Rushing; 1902–72) US JAZZ and BLUES singer, nicknamed Mister Five-by-Five in reference to his full frame (he was 20 stone in weight, if not quite 5 feet square) and to a 1942 song with that title, who won fame singing with the bands of Count BASIE and other leading jazzmen. Among the songs he both wrote and sang with Basie, Benny GOODMAN and

Buck CLAYTON and others were 'Sent for You Yesterday', 'Evil Blues' and 'I'm Gonna Move to the Outskirts of Town'.

Russell, Leon (1941–) US singer-songwriter, guitarist and pianist, who joined the ranks of the most respected rock musicians in the 1970s. Having worked extensively as a session musician, he enjoyed critical acclaim with the album *Look Inside the Asylum Choir* (1968), which he made with guitarist Marc Benno (1947–) and subsequently with such releases as *Leon Russell* (1970), *Leon Russell and the Shelter People* (1971), *Stop All That Jazz* (1974) and, with his wife Mary McCreary, *Wedding Album* (1976). Recent albums include *Anything Can Happen* (1992). He also collaborated with such performers as Eric CLAPTON, Joe COCKER, Rita COOLIDGE, George HARRISON and the ROLLING STONES.

Russian Association for Proletarian Music Soviet state organization that replaced the more liberal ASSOCIATION FOR CONTEMPORARY MUSIC in 1931. The RAPM took exception to the FORMALIST works of such composers as Dmitri SHOSTAKOVICH and Sergei PROKOFIEV, obliging them to withdraw works or reframe them in a manner that would make them comprehensible to everyone (one of the ideals of SOCIALIST REALISM). Composers who prospered under the RAPM included Alexander Borodin (1833–87), whose works were felt to have relevance to the Soviet socialist society while not threatening any subversion of officially approved moral values.

Russian Mendelssohn, the *See* Alexander GLAZUNOV.

Ryder, Mitch (William Levise; 1945–) US RHYTHM-AND-BLUES singer, who won fame leading Mitch Ryder and the Detroit Wheels in the late 1960s. Acclaimed for his energetic live performances, Ryder had big hits with 'Jenny Take a Ride' (1966) and 'Devil with a Blue Dress On/Good Golly Miss Molly' (1966). He went solo in 1967 and enjoyed something of a come-back as a performer in the early 1980s, when his album *Never Kick a Sleeping Dog* (1983) reached the US charts. Recent releases include *Rite of Passage* (1994).

S

Sade (Helen Folasade Adu; 1959–) British SOUL singer, of Nigerian-British descent, who enjoyed considerable commercial success in the 1980s with hits combining soul with JAZZ and ROCK influences. Her most successful albums have included *Diamond Life* (1984), *Promise* (1985), *Stronger Than Pride* (1988) and *Love Deluxe* (1992). Her biggest hit singles included 'Your Love is King' (1983), 'Smooth Operator' (1983) and 'Paradise' (1988).

Saint-Saëns, (Charles) Camille (1835–1921) French composer, organist and pianist, who exerted a profound influence over the development of French classical music over the course of his immensely long career and was the dominant figure in Parisian musical life at the turn of the century. Saint-Saëns was a child prodigy, performing the piano music of Beethoven and Mozart in public from the age of 10, and he went on to win recognition from no less a figure than Franz Liszt – who befriended him in 1852 – as the 'world's greatest organist'. As a performer he championed works by leading German composers and reawakened interest in works dating from the Baroque period, but he also did much to promote the efforts of his contemporaries, founding the Société Nationale de Musique to encourage young composers such as Gabriel FAURÉ – although he did express antipathy towards the music of such forward-looking composers as Claude DEBUSSY and Igor STRAVINSKY.

Saint-Saëns wrote a wide range of works, but is usually remembered for his Third Symphony (1886), written for the Philharmonic Society in London, and the lively *Carnival of the Animals* (1886), a fantasy for two pianos and orchestra, which he considered one of his less important pieces and refused to have performed while he was alive. Among other compositions – the majority of which have been judged by history to be elegant but superficial – were the oratorio *The Promised Land* (1913), the opera *Samson and Delilah* (1877), the *Danse Macabre* (1874) and a series of celebrated concertos, notably the G minor Piano Concerto (1868).

> It is possible to be as much of a musician as Saint-Saëns; it is impossible to be more of one!
> FRANZ LISZT

> Saint-Saëns has informed a delighted public that since the war began he has composed music for the stage, melodies, an elegy and a piece for the trombone. If he'd been making shell-cases instead it might have been all the better for music.
> MAURICE RAVEL, letter, 1916

Sainte-Marie, Buffy (1941–) Canadian singer-songwriter and guitarist, of Red Indian descent, who emerged as one of the most popular stars of the PROTEST SONG genre of the 1960s. Having established a reputation as one of the leading performers in Greenwich Village, Saint-Marie had huge hits with such singles as 'Codine' (1964) and 'Universal Soldier' (1964), which was later recorded by DONOVAN. Others, such as 'My Country 'tis of Thy People You're Dying' and 'Bury My Heart at Wounded Knee', reflected her Red Indian ancestry. 'Soldier Blue' (1970) was used in the Mike Nichols film of the same title, while subsequent releases were written in a COUNTRY vein. Her albums included *It's My Way* (1964) and *Illuminations* (1969), on which she experimented with electric instruments. Subsequently she retired from music and collaborated on the children's television series *Sesame Street*. Her song 'Up Where We Belong', used in the film *An Officer and a Gentleman* (1982), earned her an OSCAR. She returned to the studios in 1992 with *Coincidence and Unlikely Stories*.

salsa Genre of Latin-American BIG BAND dance music, which enjoyed a vogue in the 1970s. Characteristics of the salsa (the Spanish word for 'sauce' or 'spice') include a range of RUMBA rhythms and a strong brass sound.

Sam and Dave US SOUL vocal duo, who were

among the most respected soul acts of the 1960s. Samuel Moore (1935–) and Dave Prater (1937–88) began as GOSPEL singers, but, after being 'discovered' by Otis REDDING, they proved to have beautifully matching voices on such soul classics as 'Hold On, I'm Comin'' (1966) and 'Soul Man' (1967). They split in 1968 but re-formed briefly in 1979.

samba Variety of Latin-American dance music, which caught on outside Brazil in the 1940s. Its lively, syncopated rhythms quickly established it as a favourite with ballroom dancers. It also provided the starting-point for the BOSSA NOVA.

sampling The use of brief extracts from other records, speeches and so forth in a new recording, which is practised extensively in the 1980s by various RAP and other artists. The increasing tendency of producers to help themselves to entire backing tracks from already-issued hits caused much debate and legal arguments, as well as indicating the sterility of much pop music in the wake of PUNK ROCK and NEW WAVE. *See also* HOUSE MUSIC.

Santana, Carlos (1947–) Mexican rock guitarist, who established a reputation as an extremely versatile electric guitarist in the late 1960s. He built up a large following in the hippy era and consolidated his international standing with an acclaimed appearance at WOODSTOCK. His most celebrated albums include *Santana* (1969), *Abraxas* (1970) and *Amigos* (1976) as well as ventures into FOLK-ROCK and JAZZ-ROCK. Among the hit singles were cover versions of 'Black Magic Woman' (1970) and 'She's Not There' (1977).

Sargent, Sir (Harold) Malcolm (Watts) (1895–1967) British conductor, who became one of the legends of modern British music. A protégé of Sir Henry WOOD, he won a teaching post at the Royal College of Music in 1924 and went on to win huge acclaim with the HALLÉ (1939–42) and Liverpool Philharmonic (1942–47) orchestras, particularly for his concerts during the war years. He served as conductor of the BBC SYMPHONY ORCHESTRA (1950–57) and led the Royal Choral Society (1928–67) and the HUDDERSFIELD CHORAL SOCIETY as well as presiding over the PROMS from 1948 until his death.

Sargent was famed for his sartorial elegance but he was by no means of a frivolous nature; musicians who offended him would be rewarded with a black look that could last as long as 15 seconds or was even saved up till the next movement if the player concerned attempted to avoid eye contact.

Sargent's stern views on how the members of his orchestras should be treated also caused offence from time to time. In particular, he was resented for claiming (in an interview for the *Daily Telegraph* in 1936) that no musician was worth more than 15/- a week (the same earned by a plumber's mate) and for opposing pension schemes for musicians:

> As soon as a man thinks he is in his orchestral job for life, with a pension waiting for him at the end of it, he loses something of his supreme fire. He ought to give his life's blood with every bar he plays. It sounds cruel, but it is for the good of the orchestra.

His remarks went down very badly in view of the fact that he had only just returned from a cure in Switzerland that had been funded by members of his own orchestra.

Sargent was a consummate showman, who liked to be seen in beautifully tailored suits that contrasted with the often shabby tails of his musicians – he was nicknamed Flash Harry. His dapper appearance once caused a particular stir when he was conducting in Sydney, Australia: unused to seeing their conductor arrive for rehearsals in a suit and wearing a red carnation in his buttonhole, members of the orchestra slipped out of the hall and returned with toffee apples in their own lapels (to the amusement of the great man himself). The sobriquet Flash Harry arose from a radio announcer's link after a broadcast of the BBC's *Brains Trust*, in which Sargent had participated, saying that the programme would now go 'like a flash' over to a Sargent concert.

> Ah – Flash in Japan.
> SIR THOMAS BEECHAM, on hearing that Sargent was to tour Japan

> Just a little more reverence, please, and not so much astonishment.
> SIR MALCOLM SARGENT, to the singers of Handel's 'For Unto Us a Child is Born'

Sarony, Leslie (1897–1985) British singer-songwriter and entertainer, who was one of the most popular variety and radio stars before and after the Second World War. He was particularly celebrated for his comic songs, which included the likes of 'Jake the Peg' and – by his own hand – 'I Lift up My Finger and I Say "Tweet-tweet"'' (1929) and 'Ain't It Grand to be Bloomin' Well Dead' (1932).

satanic metal Synonym for BLACK METAL.

Satchmo *See* Louis ARMSTRONG.

Satie, Erik (Alfred Leslie) (1866–1925) French composer, of Franco-Scottish descent, who exerted a profound influence as one of the most innovative – and controversial – composers of the early part of the century. A student of the Paris Conservatoire, Satie left after just a year and worked as a café pianist while writing such early pieces as *Trois Sarabandes* (1887), *Trois Gymnopédies* (1888) and *Trois Gnossiennes* (1890), in which he began to explore the possibilities of dissonance. Influenced in the meantime by medieval plainsong and further by the Rosicrucians, he embarked on a course of further study under Vincent D'INDY in 1905 in the hope of improving his technical skills, and he won champions in Claude DEBUSSY, Maurice RAVEL and Jean Cocteau, who collaborated with him on the Dadaist ballet *Parade* (1917) (as did Picasso and Diaghilev). Considered by many his masterpiece, *Parade* stayed faithful to absurdist principles, with parts incorporated for typewriter and siren. At much the same time, he also laid down the principles of what was to emerge as FURNITURE MUSIC. Among his last works were *Socrates* (1918), for chorus and orchestra, and the ballets *Mercure* (1924) and *Relâche* (1924), which included a film sequence by René Clair.

Satie's music attracted many admirers, and he was a figurehead of the group of important young composers who became identified as Les SIX, and later also of the less well-known School d'Arceuil. Many of his compositions bore evidence of his ironic, ready wit and of his desire to puncture the pretentiousness surrounding much classical music, not least in their sometimes eccentric titles, which included the piano duet *Three Pearshaped Pieces* (written in reply to criticism that his music lacked shape) and *Limp Preludes for a Dog*. Another composition, *Vexations* (1893), was a musical joke – it consists of just a few bars of music with the instruction that they be played 840 times.

> Before I compose a piece, I walk round it several times, accompanied by myself.
> ERIK SATIE

> To be played with both hands in the pocket.
> ERIK SATIE, instruction on a piano piece

Sayer, Leo (Gerard Hugh Sayer; 1948–) British pop singer-songwriter, who had several chart hits in the 1970s. A protégé of Adam FAITH, Sayer had his first big hit in 1973 with the single 'The Show Must Go On', for which he dressed as the archetypal crying clown. Among the string of hits that followed were 'One Man Band', 'Long Tall Glasses', 'Moonlighting', 'You Make Me Feel Like Dancing', 'When I Need You', which got to the top of the British charts and also topped the US charts in 1977, and 'More Than I Can Say'. His hit albums included *Silver Bird* (1974), *Endless Flight* (1976) and *Cool Touch* (1993).

Scaggs, Boz (William Royce Scaggs; 1944–) US rock musician, who became one of the most popular rock stars of the 1970s. Scaggs began his career as guitarist (1967–68) with the Steve MILLER Band (he and Miller went to the same school in Dallas), but he went on to establish himself as a solo artist with such SOUL-influenced albums as *Slow Dancer* (1974), *Silk Degrees* (1976) and *Middle Man* (1980). He disappeared from music for a while in the 1980s, returning in 1988 with *Other Roads*.

scat Style of improvised JAZZ singing, in which the singer strings together all manner of nonsense sounds, as though the voice is simply another instrument in the band. Scat singing was probably first developed by Louis ARMSTRONG (although Jelly Roll MORTON also claimed the honour), out of necessity when he forgot the words, but the technique quickly caught on, and many performers – especially Ella FITZGERALD – were particularly admired for their mastery of the style, including, in recent times, stars like Cleo LAINE.

Schertzinger, Victor (1880–1941) US composer, conductor, violinist and film director, who was particularly celebrated for his many movie SOUNDTRACKS. His numerous credits as film composer included *The Love Parade* (1929), *One Night of Love* (1934), which was one of several MUSICALS he directed, *The Music Goes Round* (1936), *Road to Singapore* (1940), *Kiss the Boys Goodbye* (1941) and *The Fleet's In* (1941).

Schifrin, Lalo (Boris Schifrin; 1932–) US composer and conductor, who collaborated with many of the best-known names in contemporary JAZZ but is usually remembered for his numerous film scores. Having worked as arranger for jazzmen such as Dizzy GILLESPIE and Count BASIE, he contributed the SOUNDTRACKS for such films as *The Cincinnati Kid* (1965), *Bullitt* (1968) and *Dirty Harry* (1971), as well as the theme tunes for television's *Mission Impossible* and *The Virginians*.

Schnabel, Artur (1882–1951) US pianist and composer, born in Austria, who is ranked among the most acclaimed of all concert pianists. Schnabel began his professional career in 1890, when he was eight years old, and he went on to establish a reputation as an unsurpassed performer of the works of Beethoven and Schubert among other composers, making numerous admired recordings. Married to the noted contralto Therese Behr, he lived in Germany for many years but left for the USA with the rise of the Nazis. Somewhat curiously, although he rarely performed contemporary works, he composed in a markedly modern I 2-NOTE style, his compositions including three symphonies, five quartets, songs and much piano music.

When asked to reveal the secret of great piano playing, he replied: 'I always make sure that the lid over the keyboard is open before I start to play.'

> When a piece gets difficult make faces.
> ARTUR SCHNABEL, advice to Vladimir Horowitz

> I know two kinds of audience only – one coughing and one not coughing.
> ARTUR SCHNABEL, *My Life and Music*, 1961

Schnittke, Alfred (1934–) Russian composer, whose compositions in contemporary musical idioms have ranged from experiments with SERIALISM to ELECTRONIC MUSIC. He trained in Vienna and Moscow and was one of the first Russians to come to grips with contemporary western classical music in the 1960s. His works include symphonies, concertos for violin and for piano, the oratorio *Nagasaki* (1958), the

orchestral ... *pianissimo* ... (1969), a requiem (1975), *Passacaglia* (1980) and chamber music.

Schnozzle or Schnozzola *See* Jimmy DURANTE.

Schoenberg, Arnold Franz Walter (1874–1951) US composer, born in Austria, who exercised a profound influence over the development of contemporary classical music through his invention of SERIALISM. Schoenberg, a native of Vienna, taught himself to play a variety of instruments as a child and had scant musical training beyond advice from his brother-in-law, the composer Alexander von ZEMLINSKY. His early compositions were written in a relatively conventional style, developed from Wagner, and included such pieces as a string quartet (1898), *Verklärte Nacht* (1899) for string sextet, which was initially refused performance because it incorporated an 'inadmissible' chord, and the tone poem *Pelleas und Melisande* (1903). Among those to recognize his promise was Richard STRAUSS, who secured a scholarship for him and thus enabled him to spend more time on composition.

In the wake of a scandal involving the suicide of a young painter, who had had a brief affair with his wife, Schoenberg turned his back on tonality in the hugely influential second string quartet (1908) and in the song-cycle *The Book of the Hanging Gardens* on which he was then working. Subsequently, in *Three Piano Pieces* (1909), the monodrama *Erwartung* (1909) and *Pierrot Lunaire* (1912), he made further steps into uncharted territory by challenging accepted notions of melody and dissonance.

The choral *Gurrelieder* (1911) proved a popular success, but further progress was interrupted by war service. After the war, Schoenberg continued to develop the theory of serialism or I 2-NOTE MUSIC, in which composition was dictated – or in Schoenberg's terms liberated – by giving all 12 notes of the chromatic scale equal emphasis. In practical terms, he illustrated the use of serialism in such works as the suite for piano (1923), *Serenade* (1923), a wind quintet (1924), the third string quartet (1927) and *Variations for Orchestra* (1928).

Having been appointed to an academic teaching post at the Vienna Academy in 1910 and there communicating his revolutionary concepts to such pupils as Alban

BERG and Anton WEBERN, Schoenberg fled from Austria in 1933 and eventually settled in the USA, where he accepted a teaching post at the University of California. Among his last works – some of which embraced tonality while others continued to move away from it – were the fourth string quartet (1936), a violin concerto (1936), *A Survivor From Warsaw* (1947), for chorus and orchestra, and the epic opera *Moses und Aron*, which remained unfinished at his death.

One of the most controversial composers of the century, Arnold Schoenberg was belatedly recognized as an innovator of major significance in the years following his death.

Moses und Aron is often nicknamed the Chuck Steak Opera. First performed at COVENT GARDEN in 1956, it necessitates the delivery of plentiful supplies of chuck steak for use in the sacrificial scene in Act II – 'Dance Round the Golden Calf' – in which 'human' flesh is thrown around on stage.

> He is young and perhaps he is right. Maybe my ear is not sensitive enough.
> GUSTAV MAHLER, of Schoenberg

> Harmony! Harmony!
> ARNOLD SCHOENBERG, last words

Schreier, Peter (1935–) German tenor and conductor, who has won equal praise for his singing of Lieder and for his performances in Mozart operas. He made his professional début with the Berlin State Opera in 1961 in Beethoven's *Fidelio*.

Schuman, William (Howard) (1910–92) US composer, who emerged as one of the most influential figures in contemporary classical music in the USA on the strength of both his compositions and his contributions as head (1945–62) of the celebrated Juillard School of Music, New York. Having trained at Columbia University, in Salzburg and under Roy Harris (1898–1979), Schuman proved a prolific composer, his works including symphonies, the overtures *American Festival* and *William Billings*, the *New England Triptych* (1956), the ballet *Undertow* (1945), the opera *The Mighty Casey* (1953), which took baseball as its subject, and concertos for piano and violin.

Schumann, Elisabeth (1885–1952) US soprano, born in Germany, who won fame for her performances of works by Mozart

and Richard STRAUSS. After extensive formal musical training, Schumann embarked on a professional career in 1909, appearing in Wagner's *Tannhäuser*. Subsequently she joined Richard Strauss at the Vienna State Opera and went on to develop a reputation as one of the finest exponents of his music, touring the USA with him in the 1920s. She was driven out of Austria by the Nazis in 1938 and settled in the USA.

Schwartz, Arthur (1900–84) US composer, who wrote numerous hits for the Broadway stage in the 1930s and 1940s. Among his most popular songs were 'I Guess I'll Have to Change My Plan' (1929), 'Something to Remember You By', from *Three's A Crowd* (1930), 'Dancing in the Dark', from *The Band Wagon* (1931), 'Louisiana Hayride', from *Flying Colors* (1932), 'You and the Night and the Music', from *Revenge With Music* (1934), and 'Look Who's Dancing', from *A Tree Grows In Brooklyn* (1951). He also wrote extensively for Hollywood.

Schwarzkopf, (Olga Maria) Elisabeth (Friederike) (1915–) German soprano, who was widely admired for her singing of both opera and Lieder. Having made her professional début in Berlin in 1942, Schwarzkopf moved to the Vienna State Opera in 1943 and subsequently emerged as a favourite star at COVENT GARDEN, where she made many appearances in a range of German and Italian works. She attracted particular praise for her interpretations of Mozart, Wagner, PUCCINI and Richard STRAUSS, particularly in Strauss's *Der Rosenkavalier*, and made many celebrated recordings. She retired in 1972.

Scott, Ronnie (Ronald Schatt; 1927–96) British JAZZ saxophonist and bandleader, who became one of the best-known faces in British jazz at his celebrated jazz club in Gerrard Street, later relocated to Frith Street, London. Scott worked for band leaders like Ted HEATH, before establishing his own first band in 1953 and opening his famous club in 1959. Subsequently he won acclaim leading a range of small ensembles. Among his most celebrated albums are *Battle Royal* (1952) and *Serious Gold* (1977).

Scottish Opera Scottish opera company, which has established an international reputation since its foundation in 1962.

Created by Sir Alexander GIBSON, the company has been based at the Theatre Royal, Glasgow, since 1975 and has conducted numerous tours of Scotland and northern England.

Scotto, Renata (1934–   ) Italian soprano, who has won particular praise for her performances in the operas of Puccini and Verdi. Having trained in Milan, she made her début in 1953 in *La Traviata*.

Scratch Orchestra, the A group of crypto-musicians, assembled in 1969 by the AVANT-GARDE composer Cornelius Cardew (1936–81), which believed in Marxist 'free' expression. It was made clear that no experience or even instrument was necessary, but simply an enjoyment of participating en masse in 'events'. A representative sample from Cardew's book *Scratch Music* (1972) was the 'String Piece':

> A piece of string is stretched from one side of the room to the other. Audience are on one side, players on the other. To play, a person must cross from the audience side to the playing side and vice versa. Players read the score from one side to the other. Embellishments can be attached to the string . . . if the string breaks, or is cut, the piece ends.

Cardew was an articulate exponent of the art of musical INDETERMINACY and was elected a fellow of the Royal Academy of Music; he recanted, however in the mid-1970s to return to more accessible types of music (his subsequent works including revolutionary Maoist songs).

scratching The practice of manipulating a record on the turntable to produce a controlled scratching noise. DISC JOCKEYS in various night clubs and DISCOS developed the technique in the early 1980s and it became a characteristic of RAP music.

screamer donna Slang term for a stand-in who is brought in to produce highpitched screams on behalf of a prima donna, thus preserving the soprano's singing voice.

Scriabin, Alexander Nikolayevitch (1872–1915) Russian composer and pianist, who won acclaim for the innovative piano pieces he composed in the early years of the century. Born into a noble Russian family, Scriabin attended the Moscow Conservatory and subsequently established an international reputation as a pianist, usually playing his own works, which, in the

early years, were imitative of Chopin. He was appointed to a teaching post at the Conservatory in 1898 and henceforth devoted himself to composition. Scriabin's third symphony, *The Divine Poem* (1903), was inspired by his interest in theosophic mysticism, as were *The Poem of Ecstasy* (1908) and *Prometheus: The Poem of Fire* (1910), which remains a leading example of so-called COLOUR MUSIC.

Scriabin's unconventional mystical beliefs centred around a vision of Armageddon in which he played a Messiah-like role by achieving a moment of perfect artistic ecstasy (hence his interest in multi-media creations). He wrote five symphonies in all, as well as 10 piano sonatas, and many other piano pieces before his death from septicaemia.

> I was once a Chopinist, then a Wagnerist, now I am only a Scriabinist.
> ALEXANDER SCRIABIN, 1903

> A musical traveller without a passport.
> IGOR STRAVINSKY

> Scriabin's music sounds like I think – sometimes. Has that far off cosmic itch. Divinely fouled up. All fire and air . . . it was like a bath of ice, cocaine and rainbows.
> HENRY MILLER, *Nexus*, 1945

Scruggs, Earl (1924–   ) US COUNTRY banjo player, nicknamed the Paganini of the Banjo, who formed a celebrated partnership with Lester FLATT as the Foggy Mountain Boys. Scruggs established himself as one of the great banjo players in the BLUEGRASS tradition and became, with Flatt, one of the big stars of the GRAND OLE OPRY in the late 1950s. They split in 1969, and Scruggs went on to lead the Earl Scruggs Revue, which incorporated the use of electric instruments.

Searchers, the British pop group, which was among the leading MERSEY BEAT bands to emerge in the wake of the BEATLES. The group, which consisted of lead singer and guitarist Mike Pender (Mike Prendergast; 1942–   ), guitarist John McNally (1941–   ), bassist Frank Allen, who replaced Tony Jackson (1940–   ) and drummer Chris Curtis (Christopher Crummey; 1941–   ), had chart success between 1963 and 1965 with such hits as 'Sweets for My Sweet', 'Sugar and Spice', 'Needles and Pins', 'Don't Throw Your Love Away', 'Someday We're Gonna Love Again' and

'When You Walk in the Room'. Derivatives of the original band continued to perform for many years afterwards.

Sedaka, Neil (1939–   ) US singer-songwriter, who combined a reputation as one of the most successful pop songwriters to work for the BRILL BUILDING team with numerous chart hits as a performer of his own material. Having trained as a classical pianist (Artur RUBINSTEIN himself once selected him as the best classical pianist in New York), Sedaka established himself as a songwriter in collaboration with lyricist Howard Greenfield, penning such hits as 'Stupid Cupid' (1958). He also proved to be one of the most prolific songwriters then active, once writing a song a day every day for a year. 'I Go Ape', one of his own songs, provided him with his first big success as a performer and was followed by the likes of 'Oh Carol' (1959), which was dedicated to Carole KING – who responded with 'Oh! Neil' – 'Calendar Girl' (1960), 'Happy Birthday Sweet Sixteen' (1961), 'Breaking Up is Hard to Do' (1962) and 'Laughter in the Rain' (1974). His hits for other artists included 'Puppet Man', recorded by Tom JONES, 'Is This the Way to Amarillo?', which Tony Christie took up, 'Solitaire', which was covered by Elvis PRESLEY and Andy WILLIAMS among others, and 'Love Will Keep Us Together', which the Captain and Tennille took to Number One in the USA in 1975.

Seeger, Pete (1919–   ) US singer-songwriter, nicknamed America's Tuningfork, who was one of the most acclaimed pioneers of the postwar FOLK revival. Seeger, one of the founders of the celebrated Almanac Singers in 1940, went on to further success with the Weavers and – while facing persecution as a suspected Communist in the McCarthy era – embarked on a solo career. Among his most celebrated songs were 'If I Had a Hammer' (1949), 'Where Have All the Flowers Gone?' (1956) and 'Turn! Turn! Turn!' (1962). Unlike DYLAN and others, he refused to 'commercialize' his sound by going electric in the mid-1960s. His half-sister Peggy Seeger (Margaret Seeger; 1935–   ) married Ewan MACCOLL and released numerous folk albums, while half-brother Mike Seeger (1933–   ) also established a reputation as a folk-singer and instrumentalist. *See also* HOOTENANNY.

Seekers, the Australian vocal group, which became a top pop act of the 1960s. Judith Durham (1943–   ), Keith Potger (1941–   ), Bruce Woodley (1942–   ) and Athol Guy (1940–   ) came together as the Seekers in Melbourne and arrived in the UK in 1964. The group's biggest hits included 'I'll Never Find Another You' And 'The Carnival is Over', both of which reached Number One in 1965. The group broke up after a number of lesser hits, and Potger established a new line-up under the name the New Seekers. This reincarnation of the group had a transatlantic hit with 'I'd Like to Teach the World to Sing' (1972), from the tune used in a Coca-Cola advertisement, and subsequently recorded 'Beg, Steal or Borrow' for the EUROVISION SONG CONTEST that year. Other hits included 'You Won't Find Another Fool Like Me' (1974). The other members of the New Seekers were Eve Graham (1943–   ), Lyn Paul (1949–   ), Peter Doyle (1949–   ), Marty Kristian (1947–   ) and Paul Layton (1947–   ).

Seger, Bob (1945–   ) US singer-songwriter, who led the popular ADULT-ORIENTED ROCK Silver Bullet Band in the 1970s and 1980s. The melodic *Live Bullet* proved a best-seller in 1976 with its mix of HARD ROCK and White SOUL and established Seger as a substantial rock star with appeal to a mass audience. Other releases include the albums *Night Moves* (1976), *Stranger in Town* (1978), *Against the Wind* (1980), *The Distance* (1983), *Like a Rock* (1986), *The Fire Inside* (1991), and *It's a Mystery* (1995).

Segovia, Andrés (1893–1987) Spanish guitarist, who became one of the most admired masters of classical guitar. Segovia was self-taught and embarked on a career as a professional guitarist while he was still in his teens. He won immediate acclaim and went on to appear all around the world, doing much to spark a renaissance in classical guitar music. He also widened the guitar repertoire, adapting music by Bach, Handel and Mozart among others for the instrument as well as commissioning new works from such composers as Joaquín RODRIGO and Manuel de FALLA.

semitone up In POP music, a substitute for modulation. Pop songs do not usually modulate (change key) as classical music often does, but instead consist of a MIDDLE EIGHT between repeated passages. The semitone up is introduced to liven up the melody on the second or third repetition, the whole line shifting up by half a tone without warning or preparatory harmonies. It is the modern equivalent of the *Schusterflech* – the repetition of a passage at different degrees of the scale (normally higher) sometimes called a 'sequence' (as employed in Handel's *Messiah*, for instance).

Sentimental Gentleman of Swing, the *See* Tommy DORSEY.

serialism The study and practice of 12-NOTE MUSIC, in which composition is governed by certain structural devices, usually a given series of pitch classes or set of notes. Some commentators have drawn a distinction between serialism and 12-note music but most consider them one and the same thing. Critics of serialism labelled it KNITTING-PATTERN MUSIC and many traditionalists have poured scorn on such formulae for writing music since the 1920s, when the concept was first advanced by Arnold SCHOENBERG and others. When Richard STRAUSS was told by a serial composer that he had spent five years sweating over a single work, Strauss replied: 'If you find composition so difficult, why do you bother?'

> With it, music moved out of the world of Newton and into the world of Einstein. The tonal idea was based on a universe defined by gravity and attraction. The serial idea is based on a universe that finds itself in perpetual motion.
> PIERRE BOULEZ

> How can inspired form in music be scientifically differentiated from empty form?
> EDUARD HANSLICK, in *Johannes Brahms*, 1961

> The fact is, there are no rules and there never were any rules, and there never will be any rules of musical composition except rules of thumb; and thumbs vary in length, like ears.
> GEORGE BERNARD SHAW, *Music in London, 1890–1894*, 1931

Serkin, Rudolph (1903–91) US pianist, born in Austria of Russian descent, who established an international reputation for his performances of chamber music. Among his most admired recordings have been collaborations with violinist Adolf Busch (1891–1952) and idiosyncratic interpretations of the music of Bach, Beethoven, Brahms, Mozart and Schubert.

session man A musician hired to play for recording sessions, who is usually well known for his technical proficiency and ability to switch between styles. King of the British session-men is guitarist Jimmy Page (*see* LED ZEPPELIN), who is said to have played on between a third and a half of all rock and pop releases between 1963 and 1967.

Sessions, Roger (Huntington) (1896–1985) US composer, who emerged as one of the most respected figures in contemporary classical music through his many compositions, which explored both neoclassicist and serialist styles, and his extensive theoretical writings. Sessions was a child prodigy, winning a place at Harvard University when he was only 14 years old, and going on to complete his musical training with such respected musicians as Ernest BLOCH. His early neoclassical compositions reflected the influence of Igor STRAVINSKY, but subsequently he explored the possibilities of ATONALITY and SERIALISM, being particularly influenced by the music of Arnold SCHOENBERG. The violin concerto of 1953 was his first foray into fully fledged 12-NOTE MUSIC. Other works from his prolific output included nine symphonies, two concertos, three string quartets, the opera *Montezuma* (1964) and piano music besides much else.

Sessions held a number of prestigious teaching posts and wrote many books on modern music.

78 A record disc, which revolves at 78 rpm – once the format in which vitually all recorded music was available – which was accepted as the usual turntable speed for new recordings by about 1918 and remained the rule until after the Second World War when the LP was first developed. Most record companies stopped issuing 78s in 1958, switching to discs running at 33 rpm and 45 rpm; Buster Brown's single 'Fannie Mae' (1960), which was released at both 78 and 45 rpm is said to have been the last 78 of all. Rare revivals of the 78 format have included a gimmick track designed to run at that speed on the album *Wow*, which was released by the US rock band Moby Grape in 1968, when most record-players still allowed a 78 rpm option. *See also* EP; SINGLE.

Sex Pistols, the British PUNK ROCK group,

which was the most notorious of all the bands to pioneer the punk movement in the late 1970s. Bassist Sid Vicious (John Simon Ritchie; 1957–79), whose frenetic performances became a byword for punk excess, singer Johnny Rotten (John Lydon; 1956–), guitarist Steve Jones (1955–) and drummer Paul Cook (1956–) were managed by the independently minded Malcolm McLaren, who was one of the gurus of the punk explosion and had previously managed the NEW YORK DOLLS and went on to guide ADAM ANT.

The band won a contract with EMI, but this was abruptly terminated after the release of 'Anarchy in the UK' (1976) and threats of a walkout by EMI staff. There was a furore over the group's abusive behaviour during an infamous television interview, and the irreverent 'God Save the Queen' (1977) – in the year of the Queen's Silver Jubilee – lost the subsequent contract with A & M RECORDS, which took exception to the band's conduct during a wild party at its offices. By this time, however, on the strength of the singles and the album *Never Mind the Bollocks* (1977), the Sex Pistols had become heroes to an entire generation of disillusioned youth, and the group prospered on the Virgin label, consolidating its reputation as the most celebrated – and loathed – band to emerge in the punk era.

The band appeared in a carefully engineered biopic, *The Great Rock 'n' Roll Swindle* (1978), which attacked the whole rock establishment, but the group quickly disintegrated with Rotten's departure, alienated by Vicious's antics. Vicious – whose pseudonym was bestowed by Rotten, who had a hamster of that name – took over on vocals but eventually moved to the USA and died of a drug overdose awaiting trial for the murder of his girlfriend Nancy Spungen. Lydon formed the more musically adept Public Image Limited and the Sex Pistols were laid to rest until revival under Lydon in 1996.

> Burning down concert halls and destroying record companies is more creative than being successful.
> MALCOLM MCLAREN, 1978

> You just pick a chord, go twang and you've got music.
> SID VICIOUS

Shadows, the British pop group, which shot to fame as the backing band for Cliff

RICHARD, although the members established themselves as stars in their own right. Led by guitarist Hank Marvin (Brian Rankin; 1941–) and completed by guitarist Bruce Welch (Bruce Cripps; 1941–), bassist Jet Harris (1939–) and drummer Tony Meehan (1943–), the Shadows – who began under the name the Drifters until the more famous US group of the same title took legal action – began to carve out a niche independent of Richard in 1960 and had immediate successes (1960–63) with such instrumentals as 'Apache', 'FBI', 'Kon-Tiki', 'Wonderful Land', 'Dance On', 'Foot Tapper' and 'Guitar Tango', all of which featured Marvin's distinctive FENDER Stratocaster guitar sound. The group continued to make reappearances – with various changes in the line-up – in the charts through the 1960s and 1970s and represented the UK in the 1975 EUROVISION SONG CONTEST with 'Let Me be the One'. Live performances always included the so-called 'Shadow step', a somewhat modest routine in which the three guitarists stepped to and fro in unison.

Sham 69 British rock group, which enjoyed a brief career at the top during the PUNK ROCK era of the late 1970s. Consisting of lead singer Jimmy Pursey (1955–), guitarist Dave Parsons, bassist Albie Slider and drummer Mark Cain, Sham 69 established a huge following with such anthemic singles as 'If the Kids are United' (1978) and 'Hersham Boys' (1979), and the group came to be identified with the frustrations and aggressiveness of the oppressed. Violence at Sham 69 gigs prompted Pursey to break up the group in 1979; attempts to re-form it with a new line-up aroused little interest.

Shangri-Las, the US vocal group, which was among the most popular all-girl acts of the 1960s. Sisters Mary and Betty Weiss together with Mary Ann and Margie Ganser had their first success with 'What's Wrong with Ringo?' (1964) and consolidated their reputation with the classic 'Remember (Walking in the Sand)' (1964). The melodramatic 'Leader of the Pack', about the death of a teenage biker, got to Number One in the USA in 1965, and it was followed by numerous lesser singles – among them 'Give Us Your Blessings' and 'Dressed in Black' – before the run of hits ended and they were obliged to eke out a living trading on their old standards.

Shankar, Ravi (1920–   ) Indian sitar-player and composer, who established an international reputation in the 1950s and 1960s championing Indian music throughout the West. Shankar built up a large following in his native India in the 1940s and later toured widely through Europe and the USA, where he formed influential partnerships with a wide range of musicians, from Yehudi MENUHIN to the BEATLES. He founded a school for the study of Indian music in Los Angeles and also wrote extensively for the sitar and other instruments, his compositions including two concertos and music for *Gandhi* among other films. His unique contribution to Indian cultural life was reflected in his election to the Indian parliament in 1986.

Shannon, Del (Charles Weedon Westover; 1939–90) US singer-songwriter, who has been described as 'the last great rock 'n' roll star'. Among his most successful releases were 'Runaway', which reached Number One on both sides of the Atlantic in 1961, 'Hats Off to Larry' (1961) and 'Keep Searchin' (We'll Follow the Sun)' (1964). 'Runaway' was, incidentally, the first major pop hit on which an electric organ was used – anticipating its extensive use throughout pop towards the end of the decade. His version of 'From Me to You' (1963) made him the first US singer to COVER a song by the BEATLES. Shannon made a come-back in the 1980s with the album *Drop Down and Get Me* (1983) and further releases reprising is old hits, but he died in somewhat mysterious circumstances, being found dead of gunshot wounds, probably suicide.

Shapiro, Helen (1946–   ) British pop singer and actress, who established herself as a top star while still at school. Her second release, 'You Don't Know', soared to the top of the British charts in 1961, when she was just 14 years old. She topped the charts just once more, also in 1961, with the follow-up 'Walkin' Back to Happiness' but her musical career foundered somewhat after touring in 1963, when she was overshadowed by the success of her support group, the BEATLES. She developed a second career as a stage actress in the late 1970s, when she won particular

acclaim in *Oliver!* and other shows, while continuing to record old favourites and other songs in a light JAZZ style.

Sharkey, Feargal (1958–   ) Northern Ireland-born rock singer, who established a big following as lead singer with the Undertones before pursuing a successful solo career. The Undertones prospered in the late 1970s and had chart hits with such singles as 'My Perfect Cousin' (1980), while well-received albums included *The Undertones* (1979), *Hypnotized* (1980) and *Positive Touch* (1981). The group split up in 1983, and Sharkey had his biggest success yet with an eponymous solo album (1985). He also collaborated with people like Vince Clarke and Dave Stewart (*see* EURYTHMICS).

Sharp, Cecil (James) (1859–1924) British musicologist, who did much to lay the foundation for the revival in FOLK MUSIC in the early years of the century. The founder of the English Folk Dance Society (later renamed the ENGLISH FOLK DANCE AND SONG SOCIETY) in 1911, he toured widely through the UK and also in the USA, collecting and subsequently publishing numerous songs that might otherwise have disappeared. His publications had a profound influence on many leading composers, not least Ralph VAUGHAN WILLIAMS and Gustav HOLST.

shave-and-a-haircut two bits *See* Bo DIDDLEY.

Shaw, Artie (Arthur Jacob Arshawsky; 1910–   ) US JAZZ clarinettist, composer and bandleader, who was one of the most celebrated bandleaders of the SWING era of the 1930s and 1940s. Although he nursed ambitions of writing more serious music, Shaw established himself as a popular favourite in 1937, when 'Begin the Beguine' was a massive international hit. His band, which was one of the first to include both Black and White musicians and did much to popularize the use of strings in swing music, went on to win acclaim from all quarters, consolidating its standing with such further hits as 'Frenesi' (1940), 'Stardust' (1941) and 'Dancing in the Dark' (1941). Shaw also worked with smaller ensembles, notably the Gramercy Five, with which he recorded such classics as 'Summit Ridge Drive' (1941). His band's theme tune was his own composition 'Nightmare', and other compositions included a jazz concerto (1941). His clarinet playing was at its best on the celebrated 'Gloomy Sunday', one of the most moving – and melancholy – of all jazz classics (many suicides were blamed on it). He retired from bandleading in 1955. He was married eight times, his wives including Lana Turner and Ava Gardner.

> I'd like to tell a funny story about Artie Shaw, but there aren't any.
>
> AL COHN

Shaw, Sandie (Sandra Goodrich; 1947–) British pop singer, who had considerable chart success in the 1960s. A protégée of Adam FAITH, she made her recording début when she was 17 years old and working in a car factory. She got to Number One in the UK in 1964 with '(There's) Always Something There to Remind Me'. Subsequent chart hits included 'Long Live Love', which topped the charts in 1965, and 'Puppet on a String', with which she won the EUROVISION SONG CONTEST in 1967, and she became the first British female soloist to have three Number One singles. Shaw was particularly known for her gimmick of never wearing shoes when performing on stage. She married designer Jeff Banks, but they were later divorced, and she enjoyed something of a come-back in the 1980s when she was invited to sing with several bands re-creating classic pop singles from the 1960s. Her backing band, the Paramounts, eventually re-formed as PROCUL HARUM.

Shearing, George Albert (1919–) US JAZZ pianist and composer, born in the UK, who established a reputation as a world-renowned pianist despite being blind from birth. He made his first visit to the USA in 1946 and subsequently moved there permanently, winning acclaim for his mastery of the BOP style. Among his many hit records have been 'September in the Rain' (1949) and 'Lullaby of Birdland' (1952). One famous story has Shearing being asked to show another sightless man across a busy road – and duly complying, fortunately without mishap.

> Not yet.
>
> GEORGE SHEARING, when asked if he had been blind all his life

Shelton, Anne (1927–94) British singer, who established a large following during the Second World War. Her biggest wartime hits came with such numbers as 'Lili Marlene', 'I'll be Seeing You', 'Galway Bay' and 'Arrivederci Darling'. She also starred with the Glenn MILLER band, Bing CROSBY and, after the war, alongside Sophie TUCKER.

Shirelles, the US all-girl vocal group, which had a series of hits in the early 1960s. Addie Harris (1940–82), Shirley Owens (1941–), Beverly Lee (1941–) and Doris Kenner (1941–) came together in 1958 and established their reputation with 'I Met Him on a Sunday' that same year. Follow-ups included 'Will You Still Love Me Tomorrow' (1961) and 'Soldier Boy' (1962). With various changes in the line-up the Shirelles – later retitled Shirley and the Shirelles – continued in business until 1982.

Shirley and Lee US vocal duo, nicknamed the Sweethearts of the Blues, who had several RHYTHM-AND-BLUES hits in the mid–1950s. Shirley Pixley Goodman (1937–) and Leonard Lee (1935–) started early: Shirley was just nine years old when they made their recording début in 1949. Among their biggest hits were 'I Feel Good' (1956) and 'Let the Good Times Roll' (1956). Never the sweethearts they pretended to be, they split up in 1963.

Shirley-Quirk, John (1931–) British baritone, who won particular acclaim in the operas of Benjamin BRITTEN as well as appearing in concerts around the world. A former member of the St Paul's Cathedral choir, he created major roles in several of Britten's greatest works, including *Death in Venice* (1973), as well as being an admired Eugene Onegin.

shock rock Genre of HARD ROCK, in which much emphasis is put on strong theatrical imagery designed to jolt audiences. The form was pioneered in the early 1970s by the likes of Alice COOPER, famous for his snakes and electric chairs.

Shore, Dinah (Frances Rose Shore; 1917–94) US singer and actress, who became one of the most popular radio singers of the early 1940s. Having appeared with the band of Xavier CUGAT and on the Eddie CANTOR show, she consolidated her reputation with such hits as 'Yes, My Darling Daughter' (1940), 'Blues in the Night' (1942) and 'I'll Walk Alone'

(1944) as well as hosting her own television show and appearing in a number of films.

Shostakovich, Dmitri Dmitriievich

(1906–75) Russian composer, who established himself as one of the most important (and prolific) composers of his generation, despite living under the restrictive Soviet regime imposed by Stalin. Shostakovich undertook early musical studies at the St Petersburg Conservatory and had composed the first of his 15 symphonies before he left in 1923. The symphony won many admirers and was performed elsewhere in Europe and in the USA, while the composer himself was accorded additional praise as a pianist in top international competition.

Shostakovich went on to write extensively both for the concert hall and for the stage and the cinema. Among his many influential works were 15 string quartets, two operas, six concertos, an operetta and much piano and vocal music. Although acknowledged as one of the Soviet Union's leading composers, Shostakovich did experience some difficulty with the ruling powers in the 1930s, when all artists were expected to conform to the dictates of the state and his exploratory style was attacked as decadently MODERNIST. After an adaptation of Gogol's story The Nose (1929), the opera Lady Macbeth of the Mtsensk District (1934) – a sympathetic portrayal of a woman who murders her husband and father-in-law – was singled out for particular criticism, being condemned by Pravda and dismissed as 'a leftist bedlam instead of music' and 'petty-bourgeois clowning'. Pravda continued: 'The composer apparently does not set himself the task of listening to the desires and expectations of the Soviet public. He scrambles sounds to make them interesting to formalist elements who have lost all taste.'

Shostakovich hastily admitted his mistakes, withdrew his Fourth Symphony, which was then in rehearsal, and revised the opera under the title Katerina Ismailova, while his Fifth Symphony (1937) was introduced as 'the creative reply of a Soviet artist to just criticism'.

Less controversial was the so-called 'Leningrad Symphony', the Seventh, which was written in praise of the Soviet army's heroic defence (1941–44) of Leningrad against the invading Nazis during the Second World War (the composer himself served as a firefighter in the stricken city). Shostakovich was able to pursue adventurous modernist lines more openly after Stalin's death, although his Thirteenth Symphony (1962) again fell foul of the authorities after expressing sympathy with the victims of anti-Jewish bigotry. Some of the more intimate chamber music of his last years bore witness to the loneliness and melancholy into which he fell before his death.

When not occupied with his music, few activities brought Shostakovich greater pleasure than going to watch a football match.

The last great symphonist.
The Times, obituary

Showaddywaddy

British pop group, which had some success in the pop charts in the 1970s. Formed by the merger of the Hammers and the Choice and consisting of singers Dave Bartram and Buddy Gask, drummers Romeo Challenger and Malcolm Allured, guitarists Trevor Oakes and Russ Field and bassists Rod Deas and Al James, Showaddywaddy triumphed on television's New Faces talent programme and subsequently specialized in pop versions of ROCK 'N' ROLL classics. The group had hits with the likes of 'Hey Rock and Roll' (1974), 'Three Steps to Heaven' (1975), 'Under the Moon of Love', which reached Number One in 1976, and 'Pretty Little Angel Eyes' (1978).

Sibelius, Jean Julius Christian

(1865–1957) Finnish composer, who ranks alongside Gustav MAHLER as the most celebrated symphonist of the early twentieth century. Sibelius, who originally thought of becoming a violinist, took up music after giving up plans to go into the law, and he studied in Berlin and in Vienna. He remained faithful, however, to his Scandinavian roots, returning to Finland in 1891 and drawing much inspiration from both the northern landscape and from the legends told in the epic Kalevala. On the strength of such early works as the Kullervo symphony (1892) and the tone poems En Saga (1892), the Lemminkäinen Suite (1895) and the patriotic Finlandia (1899), Sibelius rapidly established a reputation as Finland's leading composer. He also attracted interest in Britain, where his champions included Sir Henry WOOD, although he rarely left his native country to undertake foreign tours.

Sibelius's highly original style, which marked him apart from virtually all contemporaries, was best realized in his great symphonies, written between 1899 and 1924. The early symphonies were relatively conventional, but later compositions became steadily more individualistic. The Third Symphony (1907) adopted a neo-classical form, while the Fourth Symphony (1911), which stretches the limits of tonality, has been called his most significant work.

Other compositions included a violin concerto (1903), the string quartet *Voces intimae* (1909) and the tone poems *Pohjola's Daughter* (1906) and *Tapiola* (1925) as well as many songs. Strangely, he wrote virtually nothing more after 1925, remaining largely silent for the last 30 years of his life, although he actually wrote the bulk of an Eighth Symphony but later destroyed the score.

> Sibelius justified the austerity of his old age by saying that while other composers were engaged in manufacturing cocktails he offered the public pure cold water.
> NEVILLE CARDUS, the *Manchester Guardian*, 1958

> Ah, Sibelius! Poor, poor Sibelius! A tragic case!
> NADIA BOULANGER

silence The absence of sound, the role of which has been fundamentally reassessed in music in the course of the twentieth century. Perhaps the most controversial and well-known expression of this new analysis of the nature of silence in music was John CAGE's *4' 33"*, which is four and a half minutes of silence broken only by applause at the end. Each member of the orchestra has a part in front of him, with time signatures and key given, but no notes marked, simply rests.

> The material of music is sound and silence. Integrating these is composing.
> JOHN CAGE, *Silence*, 1961

Composers and performers before Cage had commented on the possibilities of silence and its potential as something more than a mere disappearance of sound:

> The tense silence between two movements – in itself music in this environment – leaves wider scope for divination than the more determinate, but therefore less elastic, sound.
> FERRUCIO BUSONI, *Sketch for a new aesthetic of music*, 1907

Others also recognized silence as a positive element of music. In his Second Symphony Gustav MAHLER indicated the exact lengths of silence between movements, and the Hungarian composer György LIGETI often prescribed the length of silence to be maintained at the end of his works, allowing time for the 'unheard melodies' provoked by the heard ones.

> After silence, that which comes nearest to expressing the inexpressible is music.
> ALDOUS HUXLEY

Sills, Beverley (1929–) US soprano, nicknamed Bubbles, who established a reputation as one of the leading coloratura sopranos of the postwar era. She won particular acclaim in roles by Donizetti and Bellini while with the New York City Opera, which she joined in 1955 and eventually headed as director (1979–89).

Silver Fox, the *See* Charlie RICH.

Silvester, Victor (Marlborough) (1900–78) British ballroom dancer and bandleader, who established his reputation as a top dance bandleader in the 1930s. As an admired professional dancer, Sylvester came to realize that there was a shortage of good, new, strict-tempo dance records, and so he formed his own DANCE BAND, releasing such hits as 'You're Dancing on My Heart' (1935), which became his signature tune. He also broadcast regularly on the BBC for many years.

Simon, Carly (1945–) US singer-songwriter and guitarist, who had several transatlantic hits in the 1970s. Promoted at first as a female Bob DYLAN, she had hit singles with such folky, SOFT ROCK ballads as 'You're So Vain' (1972), which was alleged to have been addressed to James TAYLOR or to Mick JAGGER, 'Mockingbird' (1974) and 'Nobody Does It Better' (1977), which was used as the SOUNDTRACK of a James Bond movie. Among the albums were *Anticipation* (1971), *No Secrets* (1972) and *Hotcakes* (1974). She divorced husband James Taylor in the 1980s and returned to the spotlight with the hits 'Why' (1982), 'Coming Around Again' (1987) and 'Let the River Run' (1988).

Simon and Garfunkel US close-harmony duo, who had worldwide commercial success in the 1960s and early 1970s and ultimately went on to substantial solo careers. Schoolfriends Paul Simon (1941–) and Art Garfunkel (1942–), who started out as Tom and Jerry, became established as stars with both FOLK-ROCK and pop audiences through such early hits as 'The Sound of Silence' (1965), which reached Number One in the USA, and the SOUNDTRACK for the classic movie *The Graduate* (1968). Their smooth, emotive style guaranteed the success of such enduring singles as 'Scarborough Fair' (1966), 'Mrs Robinson' (1968) and 'Bridge Over Troubled Water' (1970), while such albums as *Parsley, Sage, Rosemary and Thyme* (1966) and *Bridge Over Troubled Water* (1970) rapidly attained the status of pop classics.

After the two stars went their separate ways in the early 1970s, Paul Simon eventually emphatically confirmed his standing as an international superstar by drawing inspiration from the music of the Third World. *Graceland* (1986) somewhat controversially featured the musical traditions of South Africa, while *Rhythm of the Saints* (1990) incorporated music from South America. Garfunkel meanwhile had success as an actor and enjoyed two Number Ones in the UK with 'I Only Have Eyes for You' (1975) and 'Bright Eyes' (1979), which was used in the epic cartoon *Watership Down*. They reformed briefly for an acclaimed free concert in 1981.

> I had an uncle who had a lot of bad luck as a composer. Actually, he had a lot of near misses like 'Seventy-four Trombones' and then he almost had a hit with 'Trouble Over Bridgwater'.
>
> ACKER BILK

Simone, Nina (Eunice Waymon; 1933–) Black US JAZZ singer and pianist, who established a reputation as a top jazz singer capable of considerable emotional intensity in the late 1950s. Her most successful recordings include 'I Loves You Porgy' (1959), 'To be Young, Gifted and Black' (1969) and 'My Baby Just Cares for Me', which was a big chart hit in 1987 after being used in a perfume advert. Her albums include *It is Finished* (1972) and *Baltimore* (1978). She has built up a particularly strong following in Europe, while enjoying less success in her native USA, where she was a prominent figure in the civil rights campaigns of the 1960s.

Simple Minds, the Scottish rock band,

which was one of the most successful groups to emerge from the NEW WAVE in the early 1980s. Lead singer Jim Kerr (1959–), guitarist Charlie Burchill (1959–), bassist Derek Forbes, keyboard player Mike MacNeil (1958–) and drummer Brian McGee came together initially as a PUNK outfit under the name Johnny and the Self Abusers, but only established a reputation after changing their name and issuing such albums as *Once Upon a Time* (1985), *New Gold Dream* (1983), *Sparkle in the Rain* (1984), *Live in the City of Light* (1987) and *StreetFighting Years* (1989). Hit singles have included 'Promised You a Miracle' (1982), 'Don't You Forget About Me' (1985), which topped the US charts, and the EP 'Belfast Child' (1989). There have been numerous changes to the original line-up, and eventually only Kerr and Burchill remained of the founder-members. The album *Good News from the Next World* appeared in 1995.

Simply Red British pop group, which rose to star status in the late 1980s as one of the leading British White SOUL outfits. Led by gifted red-haired singer Mick Hucknall (1960–), Simply Red came together in Manchester in 1982 and had huge hits with such singles as 'Holding Back the Years' (1986), which reached Number One in the USA, 'Ev'ry Time You Go Away' (1987) and 'If You Don't Know Me by Now' (1989), which came from the highly acclaimed album *A New Flame* (1989). *Stars* topped the album charts in 1991, as did *Life* in 1995 and *Greatest Hits* in 1996.

Sims, Zoot (John Haley Sims; 1925–85) US JAZZ saxophonist, who played with many of the great jazzman of his generation. Influenced by Lester YOUNG, Sims won acclaim for his economic style in the BIG BANDS of Benny GOODMAN, Woody HERMAN, Stan GETZ, Stan KENTON and Gerry MULLIGAN among others, and he was also particularly admired for his collaborations with Al Cohn (1925–).

simultaneity Alternative term for a chord, which was adopted by some composers of 12-NOTE MUSIC. The advantage of the term in their eyes was that it avoided the implication that such a grouping of notes had a diatonic function.

Sinatra, Frank (Francis Albert Sinatra;

1915–) Celebrated US singer and film actor, of Italian descent, who established himself as a heart-throb with an international reputation in the 1950s. He is known by such nicknames as Bones (sometimes the Bony Baritone, on account of his spare frame), the Chairman of the Board, the Croon Prince of Swoon, the Dago (on account of his Italian ancestry), Frankie Boy, the Gov'nor, Groovey Galahad, the King of the Rat Pack, the Leader, the Lean Lark (despite the fact that at birth he weighed a full 13 pounds), the Larynx, the Pope, Prince Charming of the Juke Boxes, the Svengali of Swing, the Swooner and, most often, Old Blue Eyes. Sinatra made his radio début in 1938 and subsequently sang with the bands of Tommy DORSEY and other popular bandleaders, attracting the adulation of a largely teenaged audience. Among his early hits, many of which were orchestrated by Nelson RIDDLE, were such numbers as 'I'll Never Smile Again' (1940), 'All or Nothing at All' (1943), 'Goodnight Irene' (1950), 'Three Coins in a Fountain' (1954), 'Love and Marriage' (1956) and 'Witchcraft' (1958).

Sinatra surprised many pundits when he demonstrated his abilities as a straight actor, appearing in numerous successful films and becoming a major Hollywood star. His performance in *From Here To Eternity* (1953) won him an Academy Award; other films included *High Society* (1956), *Pal Joey* (1957) and *The Manchurian Candidate* (1962). Among the most famous of his subsequent hits were 'Strangers in the Night' (1966) and 'Something Stupid' (1967), which he sang as a duet with his daughter Nancy Sinatra (1940–), as well as collaborations with such stars as Count BASIE and Duke ELLINGTON. 'My Way' (1969), another huge hit, gave rise in the 1980s to the term 'The Sinatra Doctrine', which in political jargon referred to the change in Soviet policy, allowing other socialist states to progress 'their way' without interference.

Sinatra was constantly in the gossip columns in the 1950s and 1960s both for his stormy marriages and as head of the 'ratpack' of famous stars, who liked a good time. More sinister were his alleged links with the criminal underworld.

> It was my idea to make my voice work in the same way as a trombone or violin – not sounding like them, but 'playing' the

voice like those instruments.
FRANK SINATRA

> Sinatra's idea of Paradise is a place where there are plenty of women and no newspapermen. He doesn't know it, but he'd be better off if it was the other way round.
HUMPHREY BOGART

> He's the kind of guy that, when he dies, he's going up to heaven and give God a bad time for making him bald.
MARLON BRANDO

Singer's Singer, the *See* Mel TORMÉ.

Singing Barber, the *See* Perry COMO.

Singing Brakeman, the *See* Jimmie RODGERS.

Singing Capon, the *See* Nelson EDDY.

Singing Composer, the *See* Sammy FAIN.

Singing Cowboy, the *See* Gene AUTRY; Roy ROGERS.

Singing Cowboy from Brooklyn, the *See* Ramblin' Jack ELLIOTT.

Singing Nun, the Stagename of the Belgian nun Sister Luc-Gabrielle (Jeanne Deckers; 1933–85), who had unexpected success in the pop charts in 1963 with the Number One hit single 'Dominique', which told the story of St Dominique (founder of the Dominican order). Dubbed Soeur Sourire (the Smiling Nun) in France, she recorded the song in aid of her convent and became an overnight sensation; the song itself stayed at Number One in the USA for 4 weeks, displacing Elvis PRESLEY.

Fame proved a mixed blessing, however, and the Singing Nun eventually left the convent to live a reclusive existence with another former nun, Annie Pecher (1944–85). Attempts at consolidating her reputation in music with such follow-ups as 'The Smiling Nun is Dead' and 'The Golden Pill', which supported artificial birth control, were doomed to failure, and a revamped DISCO version of her original hit fared no better in 1981. In severe financial difficulties and addicted to tranquillizers, she finally killed herself in a suicide pact with Pecher. The story of her rise to fame was romanticized in the film *The Singing Nun* (1966), starring Debbie Reynolds.

The success of the Singing Nun inspired several imitations, among them one Father

Duval and Sister Janet Mead, who enjoyed a Number Four hit with 'The Lord's Prayer' (1974). In 1994 a group of monks from Spain trod the same path when their recording of an ancient religious air got into the charts in several European countries. The SUPREMES, meanwhile, are one of the few groups to have appeared in nuns' habits (in a 1968 episode of *Tarzan*).

> Being called the Smiling Nun is not easy when you have no reason to smile.
> JEANNE DECKERS

Singing Rage, the See Patti PAGE.

Singing Ranger, the See Hank SNOW.

Singing Sheriff, the See Faron YOUNG.

single A smaller version of the LP, which rotates at a speed of 45 rpm and usually has space for one song on each side. The single was pioneered by the RCA Victor record company in 1948, who used the codename Madame X in the planning stages for the sake of security, and in time it revolutionized the pop market, replacing the more cumbersome 78. See also EP.

Siouxsie and the Banshees British rock band, which established a strong following in the PUNK ROCK era of the late 1970s but outlived most other contemporary line-ups. Led by singer and guitarist Siouxsie Sioux (Susan Janet Dallion; 1957–), who began as a fan of the SEX PISTOLS and recruited Sid Vicious himself as drummer before he went on to join McLaren's infamous creation, the Banshees came together in 1975 and triumphed initially on Siouxsie's striking visual image. However, the group quickly proved to have genuine musical capabilities, and such albums as *The Scream* (1978), *Kaleidoscope* (1980), from which came the singles 'Christine' and 'Happy House', and *Tinderbox* (1986) were among the most accomplished and musical of punk recordings, incorporating the influence of AFRO-ROCK among other features. The group split in 1996 after their last album, *The Rapture* (1995).

Sister Sledge US all-vocal group, which was among the top DISCO SOUL acts of the 1970s and early 1980s. Debbie (1955–), Jonie (1957–), Kim (1958–) and Kathy (1959–) Sledge made their début as Sister Sledge in the early 1970s but established their presence firmly in the charts recording songs for Nile Rodgers and Bernard Edwards (see CHIC) from 1979. Among the group's hits were 'We Are Family' (1979), 'All American Girls' (1981), 'Sister Sledge' (1981) and 'Frankie' (1985).

Six, Les Group of six French composers who joined forces in Paris in 1918 under the influence of Jean Cocteau and Erik SATIE. The six members of the group, who were first described as 'Les Six' by music journalist Henri Collet in 1920, were Georges AURIC, Louis DUREY, Arthur HONEGGER, Darius MILHAUD, Francis POULENC and Germaine TAILLEFERRE. In so far as they had a shared philosophy, they were committed to opposing the romantic and impressionist traditions in French music. They had ceased to act as a group by 1925.

> Their work was momentarily amusing; but as far as exploration and discovery are concerned, it had about as little to do with pioneering as an expensive and over-heated journey in a 'Blue Train', and its ideal (if it had one) was a commonplace 'Madonna of the Sleeping-Cars'.
> J.B. TREND, *Manuel de Falla*, 1929

Six-Five Special British television programme, which became a leading forum for ROCK 'N' ROLL in the late 1950s. The programme was launched in early 1959 and thrived on its innovative mix of music and comedy. The brainchild of BBC producer Jack Good, the show had a cheerful, spontaneous appeal and attracted a mass audience in its brief run of roughly a year.

> There was chaos. The band was blaring. The kids were jiving, and I was shouting at the top of my voice for more noise, more action. Then the chief walked in. He gazed dumbfounded at what was happening to his programme. Silence descended on the studio. I broke into a sweat. 'Carry on,' he said, then beat a hasty retreat.
> JACK GOOD

ska Jamaican POP music of the 1960s, which was closely related to REGGAE. As well as reggae, ska combined elements of CALYPSO, JAZZ, BEBOP and RHYTHM-AND-BLUES, typically incorporating a number of brass instruments. Stars associated with such music included Desmond DEKKER and Jimmy CLIFF. The genre experienced a revival in the late 1970s, when such multi-racial British bands as the BEAT and UB40 launched the TWO-TONE movement.

Skaggs, Ricky (1954–) US COUNTRY singer, who emerged as one of the leading stars of a new generation of country performers in the 1980s. His many hit singles have included 'Crying My Heart out over You' (1981), 'I Wouldn't Change You if I Could' (1982), 'Uncle Pen' (1984) and 'You Make Me Feel Like a Man' (1985).

skiffle British POP music style of the 1950s, which bore a close resemblance to ROCK 'N' ROLL. Fast, fun and unsophisticated, skiffle had its origins in the improvised music that was played by impoverished Blacks in Chicago in the 1920s, enthusiasts knocking out tunes on homemade instruments in an attempt to raise money to pay their rents. Equipped with all manner of instruments, from paper-and-comb to banjo and jug, the best of these bands actually made it to the recording studio, variously identifying themselves as JUG, SPASM or WASHBOARD bands. The style itself combined elements of FOLK MUSIC, the BLUES and COUNTRY.

The first noteworthy player of British skiffle in the 1950s was jazzman Ken COLYER, whose band included Chris BARBER and Lonnie DONEGAN, who was to emerge as the most popular of all the skiffle stars. Audiences responded to the simplicity and vitality of the genre, which drew its material from folk music and the blues, and numerous amateur bands sprung up, typically equipped with guitars, drums, kazoos, washboards and other cheap or homemade instruments (one favourite being a bass constructed from a tea-chest and broom handle). Classic skiffle hits included Colyer's 'Take This Hammer' and Donegan's 'Rock Island Line'. Many former skiffle players eventually graduated as straight rock 'n' rollers (among them John LENNON).

> I picked songs that were, for example, Leadbelly songs, but also songs that could be understood not just by some old spade in the cotton-fields sixty years ago, but also by the tram-driver in East Ham High Street.
> LONNIE DONEGAN

Skydog See Gregg ALLMAN.

Slade British pop group, which was one of the most successful of the GLAM ROCK bands of the early 1970s. Top-hatted lead singer Noddy Holder (1950–), high-heeled guitarist Dave Hill (1952–), bassist Dave Lea (1952–) and drummer Don Powell (1950–) came together in 1966 and operated under a variety of different names before achieving fame as Slade with their brand of cocky, basic, heavy rock. Slade remains the only British band to enjoy three consecutive Number Ones immediately following their release – 'Cum On Feel the Noize' (1973), 'Skweeze Me Pleeze Me' (1973) and 'Merry Xmas Everybody' (1973). In all, the group had six Number One hits in the UK (though none in the USA), the others being 'Coz I Luv You' (1971), 'Take Me Back 'Ome' (1972) and 'Mama Weer All Crazee Now' (1972). The band stayed together long after the glam rock era had ended and staged a series of come-backs through the 1980s and 1990s playing its old songs.

Slade, Julian (1930–) British composer, who established a reputation as a leading writer for the musical stage in the 1950s. His best-known creations include the hit MUSICAL *Salad Days* (1954) and such lesser follow-ups as *Free As Air* (1957), *Hooray for Daisy* (1959), *Vanity Fair* (1962) and *Out of Bounds* (1973).

sleaze-rock Genre of HARD ROCK, representing a radical version of the GLAM ROCK style of the 1970s. Celebrating heavy drinking, sexual excess and other forms of debauchery, sleaze-rock has produced its own stars on both sides of the Atlantic, notably the US bands the NEW YORK DOLLS and GUNS N' ROSES.

sleeve The outer covering, usually made of card, in which an LP is packaged. Record sleeves became an art form in their own right in the 1960s, when, for the first time, the visual image of POP and ROCK stars became almost as important as the music they made.

Perhaps the most celebrated – or infamous – of all record sleeves was that designed in 1969 for the BEATLES' *Abbey Road* album (although another contender for the honour is their *Sergeant Pepper's Lonely Hearts Club Band* LP with its collage of famous faces). The *Abbey Road* cover fuelled bizarre speculation concerning the group, fans reading deep significance into the tiniest details of the photograph of the Fab Four walking on a zebra crossing. In particular, attention was drawn to Paul McCartney's bare feet and to the registration plate (LMW 28IF) of a Volkswagen Beetle parked nearby (attempts to have the car towed away before the photograph was taken had not been completed). These were, it was claimed, coded messages to the effect that McCartney had died (rumour had it that he had been decapitated in a car crash) and a lookalike had been used for the sleeve). Bare feet, it was revealed, were a sign of mourning in Sicily, while the registration plate referred to the fact that McCartney would have been '28 if' he had lived (the luckless owner had his number plates stolen many times in later years).

As 'proof' of the theory that a stand-in had been used for McCartney, fans pointed to the fact that he was out of step with the other three and was holding a cigarette in his right hand (whereas the real McCartney was known to be left-handed).

The hysteria died down only after it became evident that the lookalike not only looked like McCartney, but also played, spoke and indeed *was* McCartney:

> I just turned up at the photo session. It was a really hot day and I think I wore sandals. I only had to walk around the corner to the crossing because I lived pretty nearby. I had me sandals off and on for the session. Of course, when it comes out people start looking at it and they say, 'Why has he got no shoes on? He's never done that before' ... turns out to be some old Mafia sign of death or something.
>
> PAUL McCARTNEY

Novelty sleeves since the 1960s have included that for MADONNA's 'Material Girl' 12-inch single, which was liberally doused with perfume.

Slezak, Leo (1873–1946) Austro-Czech tenor, who was among the great dramatic tenors of the early twentieth century. Slezak's name is usually associated now with one of the legendary mishaps to befall a performance of *Lohengrin* (in May 1900). The mobile swan that was due to transport Slezak across the stage in one of the climactic moments of Wagner's opera set off without him when (one version has it) he was momentarily distracted by a hubbub in the audience at the news that Mafeking had been relieved. Apparently unconcerned at the obvious error, Slezak is reputed to have pulled out his watch and

inquired 'Wann geht der nächste?' ('What time is the next one?').

slide guitar *See* BOTTLENECK.

Slowhand *See* Eric CLAPTON.

Smack *See* Fletcher HENDERSON.

Small Faces, the British pop group, which enjoyed a string of hits in the late 1960s and early 1970s and became idols for 'mods' everywhere. The band, formed in 1965, consisted of bassist Ronnie Lane (1946–97), singer Steve Marriott (1947–91), keyboard player Jimmy Winston and drummer Kenny Jones (1948–), and it released such hit singles as 'Whatcha Gonna Do about It' (1965), 'Sha-la-la-la-lee' (1966), 'All or Nothing', which got to Number One in 1966, 'Itchy-coo Park' (1967) and 'Lazy Sunday Afternoon' (1967). Marriott then left, and the band, renamed the Faces, was re-formed with the addition of keyboard player Ian McLagan (1945–), who replaced Winston, and singer Rod STEWART and guitarist Ron Wood, who had been part of Jeff BECK's group. The new line-up prospered through the association with Stewart, who was emerging as a major solo star, but the group eventually split up in 1975, Stewart pursuing his solo career while Wood joined the ROLLING STONES and Jones went on to join the WHO. Ronnie Lane was forced to retire, suffering from multiple sclerosis.

Oddities released by the group included a single extravagantly titled 'You Can Make Me Dance, Sing or Anything (Even Take the Dog for a Walk, Mend a Fuse, Fold away the Ironing Board, or Any Other Domestic Short Comings)'.

Smith, Bessie (Elizabeth Smith; 1894–1937) Black US singer-songwriter, nicknamed the Empress of the Blues, who became one of the legends of BLUES music between the wars. The emotional intensity of Smith's performances won her a huge Black and White audience as well as a massive income by the standards of the times. Having trained under Ma RAINEY, she went on to make many famous records with Fletcher HENDERSON and Louis ARMSTRONG and to star in the classic movie *St Louis Blues* (1929). Among her most celebrated songs, usually on themes of loneliness and despair, were 'Downhearted

Blues' (1923), 'St Louis Blues' (1924), 'Young Woman's Blues' (1926) and 'Backwater Blues' (1927).

With her career in decline, Smith died in traumatic circumstance following a car accident near Clarkesdale on her way to an engagement in Mississippi; because she was Black she was refused admission at the nearest Whites-only hospital and died of loss of blood when she was finally admitted to the nearest mixed-race hospital (events traced in Edward Albee's play *The Death of Bessie Smith*, although recent research suggests the story is a myth). Among those who claimed to have been influenced by her were Billie HOLIDAY and Janis JOPLIN.

> She once said to me ... 'You're gonna sing "Blacksnake Blues" for me real good tonight or I'm gonna break you neck'. She was a wonderful woman.
>
> VICTORIA SPIVEY

Smith, Huey (1934–) US RHYTHM-AND-BLUES pianist, nicknamed Huey 'Piano' Smith, who enjoyed several hits in the late 1950s with the Clowns. Their most successful recordings included 'Rocking Pneumonia and the Boogie Woogie Flu' (1957), 'High Blood Pressure' (1958) and 'Don't You Just Know It' (1958). Smith regularly backed LITTLE RICHARD among other stars of the era, but he had less success in ensuing decades and eventually retired from music to work as a gardener.

Smith, Kate (1907–86) US singer, nicknamed the Songbird of the South, whose name is uniquely associated with Irving BERLIN's 'God Bless America', which in Smith's capable hands became the USA's unofficial national anthem. Berlin gave the song to Smith after deciding it was too florid for his stage shows, and she turned it into a classic, singing it regularly at big public gatherings. Among her other hits were 'When the Moon Comes Over the Mountain' (1931) and 'River, Stay 'Way from My Door' (1932).

Smith, Patti (1946–) US singer-songwriter, nicknamed the Poet Princess of Rock, who emerged as an acclaimed cult star in the 1970s. Influenced by the VELVET UNDERGROUND, she first won acclaim for her poetry, being awarded an honorary degree by the college from which she had been ignominiously expelled some years earlier. The HARD ROCK backing underlying such albums as *Horses* (1975) and *Easter* (1978) had a powerful influence on the development of PUNK ROCK. 'Because the Night', written for *Easter* in collaboration with Bruce SPRINGSTEEN, provided her with a rare hit single; she also collaborated for a time with Bob DYLAN. Smith's career nearly came to a premature end in 1977 when she broke her neck in a 15-foot fall from the stage during a concert in Florida; she eventually retired to raise a family, making a come-back in 1988 with *Dream of Life*.

Smiths, the British rock band, which was among the most successful outfits to hail from Manchester in the 1980s. Singer (Stephen) Morrissey (1959–), guitarist Johnny Marr (John Maher; 1963–), bassist Andy Rourke and drummer Mike Joyce (1963–) came together in 1982 and had their first hit with 'This Charming Man' (1983). Among the hit albums that followed were *The Smiths* (1984), *Hatful of Hollow* (1984), *Meat is Murder* (1985), the acclaimed *The Queen is Dead* (1986) and *Strangeways, Here We Come* (1987). The Smiths split up in 1987, and Morrissey embarked on a solo career with the Number One album *Viva Hate* (1988).

Smyth, Dame Ethel (Mary) (1858–1944) British composer, who won particular acclaim for her operas. She had studied in Germany and developed a distinctive style combining German and English elements. Among her admired operas are *Fantasio* (1898), *The Wood* (1902), *The Wreckers* (1909), *The Boatswain's Mate* (1916), *Fête galante* (1923) and *Entente cordiale* (1926). She was also committed to women's suffrage and was imprisoned for her views in 1911.

> The legend relates that one afternoon while Adam was asleep, Eve, anticipating the Great God Pan, bored some holes in a hollow reed and began to do what is called 'pick out a tune'. Thereupon Adam spoke: 'Stop that horrible noise,' he roared, adding, after a pause, 'besides which, if anyone's going to make it, it's not you but me!'
>
> DAME ETHEL SMYTH, *Female Pipings in Eden*, 1933

snap, crackle and pop Derogatory nickname for 12-NOTE MUSIC, referring to the serial ('cereal') nature of such compositions ('snap, crackle and pop' being an advertising slogan for a well-known breakfast cereal).

Snow, Hank (Clarence Eugene Snow; 1914–) Canadian COUNTRY singer, nicknamed the Singing Ranger, who first attracted attention touring Canada and the USA in the 1930s. He became a naturalized US citizen and appeared regularly on the GRAND OLE OPRY and also in Europe. Among his hits were 'I'm Movin' On' (1950), 'Golden Rocket' (1950), 'I Don't Hurt Anymore' (1954) and 'I've Been Everywhere' (1962). He was voted to the COUNTRY MUSIC HALL OF FAME in 1979.

socialist realism The officially sanctioned doctrine of the Soviet regime in Stalinist Russia, which dictated that all the arts, including music, should dedicate themselves to the glorification of the Soviet political vision. Developed in the 1930s, the doctrine of socialist realism threatened the well-being of art of all kinds for the next 30 or more years. In musical terms, such important composers as Dmitri SHOSTAKOVICH and Sergei PROKOFIEV were obliged to disguise any 'anti-social' themes in their work and at least to appear willing admirers of the Soviet system. A number of composers of previous centuries also suffered from such attentions: the sombre penultimate movement of Tchaikovsky's Sixth Symphony, for instance, had to be played at an earlier point in the work at the orders of the Soviet authorities, who felt that its despairing atmosphere was inimical to the ideals of social optimism and so was best tucked away within the work rather than left to the very end. *See also* FORMALISM; RUSSIAN ASSOCIATION FOR PROLETARIAN MUSIC.

> I can't listen to music too often . . . it affects my nerves.
> LENIN

sock rhythm The heavy beat that was adopted by HONKY-TONK bands in the early 1950s as a precursor of ROCK 'N' ROLL. Playing in BARRELHOUSES and JUKE-JOINTS across the USA, more and more bands employed a heavier beat in an attempt to make themselves heard above the noise of the juke boxes, slapping the strings of the double bass and guitars to create a fuller percussive sound (hence the phrase 'sock it to me').

Söderström, Elisabeth (1927–) Swedish soprano, who emerged as one of the leading

sopranos of the 1950s. She has won particular acclaim at GLYNDEBOURNE and with the Swedish Opera singing the music of Leoš JANÁČEK, Monteverdi, Mozart, Richard STRAUSS and Tchaikovsky.

Soft Cell *See* ALMOND, MARC.

Soft Machine, the British rock group, which was among the most celebrated PROGRESSIVE ROCK outfits of the late 1960s. Despite almost constant changes in personnel, the Soft Machine proved itself one of the most creative underground bands of the period, ranking among the most admired PSYCHEDELIC groups and at the same time taking in such diverse influences as JAZZ. Prominent members of the band included singer and drummer Robert WYATT, guitarist and singer Kevin Ayers (1945–) and keyboard player Mike Ratledge (1943–). Notable albums included the début *Soft Machine* (1968), which was characterized by its eccentric humour. The Soft Machine was one of the progressive rock bands to build up a major following in other European countries, especially in France.

soft rock *See* ROCK.

Solomon (Solomon Cutner; 1902–88) British pianist, who was one of the most admired exponents of chamber music. Solomon was a child prodigy, playing Tchaikovsky's first concerto in public when he was eight years old. He gave the first performance of Arthur BLISS's piano concerto (1939) among other works. Paralysis forced him to retire in 1965.

Solti, Sir Georg (1912–97) British conductor and pianist, born in Hungary, who established a reputation as one of the leading European conductors after the Second World War. Having studied music in Budapest, where his teachers included Béla BARTÓK, Ernö DOHNÁNYI and Zoltán KODÁLY, he accepted a post at the Budapest Opera but subsequently fled to Switzerland on the outbreak of war. He won a prestigious piano competition in Geneva in 1942 and after the war was appointed music director of the Bavarian State Opera (1946–52). He went on to conduct with the Frankfurt Opera (1952–61), at COVENT GARDEN (1961–71), the Orchestre de Paris (1972–75) and the LONDON PHILHARMONIC ORCHESTRA (1979–83), and he was music director of the CHICAGO SYMPHONY ORCHESTRA (1969–91).

He won particular acclaim for his interpretations of the music of Richard STRAUSS, Mahler, Beethoven, Verdi and Wagner and has made many admired recordings, including the first entire *Ring* cycle (1966). He has amassed an unsurpassed total of some 30 GRAMMIES during his recording career.

Sondheim, Stephen Joshua (1930–) US composer and lyricist, who first emerged as a leading writer for the musical stage in the 1950s. He studied under Milton BABBITT before, with the encouragement of Oscar HAMMERSTEIN, establishing himself as a gifted lyricist and composer through his collaboration on such hit MUSICALS as *West Side Story* (1957), *Gypsy* (1959) and *Do I Hear a Waltz?* (1965). *A Funny Thing Happened on the Way to the Forum* (1962), which was entirely his own work, consolidated his reputation with a Tony Award. Hit shows by his pen since then have included *Anyone Can Whistle* (1964), *Company* (1970), *Follies* (1971), *A Little Night Music* (1973), from which came the hit single 'Send in the Clowns', *Sweeney Todd* (1979), the Pulitzer Prize-winning *Sunday in the Park with George* (1983), *Into the Woods* (1987) and *Assassins* (1990). *Side by Side by Sondheim* (1976) was a popular compilation of some of his best songs. Other projects have included scores for such films as *Reds* (1981).

Song Painter, the *See* Mac DAVIS.

Songbird of the South, the *See* Kate SMITH.

Sonny and Cher *See* CHER.

Sons of the Pioneers US vocal group, which became one of the first legends of the COUNTRY-AND-WESTERN style. The group was formed by Roy Rogers (1911–), Bob Nolan (1908–80), Tim Spencer (1908–74), Hugh Farr (1903–80) and Karl Farr (1909–61), although there were subsequently many changes in personnel, and had huge hits with the likes of 'Tumbling Tumbleweeds' (1927), 'Cigareetes and Whusky and Wild, Wild Women' (1947), 'Careless Kisses' (1949) and 'Roomful of Roses' (1949). The Sons of the Pioneers also made many film appearances.

Sophie Tuckshop *See* Sophie TUCKER.

soul Genre of pop music, which emerged from RHYTHM-AND-BLUES in the 1960s and became one of the dominant musical forms, in time attracting both Black and White audiences. Soul developed with growing Black self-awareness in the 1960s and became a means of expression of Black pride and determination to win equal rights. The first star to be labelled a soul artist rather than simply an r 'n' b man, although the distinction between the two genres is vague in the extreme, was the legendary Ray CHARLES, who not only sang of the trials and tribulations of the ordinary Black American but, by implication, also called for political change. Among the countless stars recruited by companies such as MOTOWN and STAX RECORDS to follow in his wake were Sam COOKE, Aretha FRANKLIN, Marvin GAYE, Otis REDDING, James BROWN, the SUPREMES, Lionel RICHIE and Stevie WONDER. So-called 'blue-eyed soul' or 'White soul', in which White artists imitated the Black style, emerged in the 1970s; leading exponents have included HALL AND OATES and SIMPLY RED.

> Soul music is when you take a song and you make it a part of yourself, a part that is so real and so true that people think it's really happened to you.
>
> RAY CHARLES

Soul Brother Number One *See* James BROWN.

soundtrack Music accompanying a film, which is usually for atmospheric effect. In the early years of the twentieth century, when films were silent, the pianist or a small orchestra generally chose the accompanying music themselves or else improvised as the film was projected. Typical pieces included popular light classics and the stereotypical 'helterskelter' music used for chase sequences. Sometimes a musical score was distributed with the film and rehearsed for the short run, so that the musicians would be able to keep up with the action. Some of these were specially commissioned – Camille SAINT-SAËNS's score for *L'assassinat du Duc de Guise* (1908) being the very first.

The advent of sound in the late 1920s required that new conventions were established, and most feature films required music for title sequences as well as incidental accompaniment to heighten emotional effects of various kinds. By and large, these criteria have remained unchanged for many years, with most film music falling within the stylistic ambit of late Romanticism (whether for Robin Hood or for intergalactic warfare). Notable scores, some original and others making use of well-known classics, have included the following:

> Battleship Potemkin (Edmund Meisel; 1925)
>
> The New Babylon (Dmitri Shostakovich; 1929)
>
> King Kong (Max Steiner; 1933)
>
> Lieutenant Kijé (Sergei Prokofiev; 1934)
>
> Things To Come (Arthur Bliss; 1936)
>
> Of Mice and Men (Aaron Copland; 1939)
>
> Dangerous Moonlight (Richard Addinsell; 1941)
>
> Henry V (William Walton; 1944)
>
> Brief Encounter (Sergei Rachmaninov; 1945)
>
> Beauty and the Beast (Georges Auric; 1946)
>
> The Killers (Miklós Rózsa; 1946)
>
> The Third Man (Anton Karas; 1949)
>
> The Bridge on the River Kwai (Malcolm Arnold; 1957)
>
> Psycho (Bernard Herrmann; 1959)
>
> The Guns of Navarone (Dimitri Tiomkin; 1961)
>
> Dr Zhivago (Maurice Jarre; 1965)
>
> Elvira Madigan (Mozart; 1967)
>
> 2001: A Space Odyssey (Richard Strauss; 1968)
>
> Death in Venice (Gustav Mahler; 1971)
>
> Deliverance (Arthur 'Guitar Boogie' Smith; 1972)
>
> Star Wars (John Williams; 1977)
>
> Chariots of Fire (Vangelis; 1981)
>
> Paris, Texas (Ry Cooder; 1984)
>
> The Mission (Ennio Morricone; 1985)

Ralph VAUGHAN WILLIAMS wrote the score for Scott of the Antarctic (1948) and enlarged upon it for his Sinfonia Antarctica, his Seventh Symphony. Of writing for films, he warned: 'You must not be horrified if you find that a passage which you intended to portray the villain's mad revenge has been used by the musical director to illustrate cats being driven out of the dairy. The truth is that within limits any music can be made to fit any situation.'

Adolf Deutsch summed up the role of the film composer thus: 'A [film] musician is like a mortician. He can't bring a body back to life, but he can make it look better.' Arthur BLISS insisted that any worthy piece of film music should be judged solely for its musical worth, but other composers averred that music has a particular but subservient role in the cinema, which places it in a unique category of its own.

The soundtrack for Saturday Night Fever stands as the best-selling soundtrack ever made, with sales of over 26 million copies.

> Film music is like a small lamp that you place below the screen to warm it.
> AARON COPLAND

southern rock Rock genre associated with bands from the southern USA. Singing of such traditional subjects as drink and women, the genre has at times been criticized for links with White racist attitudes. Leading exponents of southern rock have included the ALLMAN BROTHERS, LYNYRD SKYNYRD and latterly the Georgia Satellites and the Black Crows.

Space Cowboy, the See Steve MILLER.

Spandau Ballet British NEW ROMANTIC band, which enjoyed considerable chart success in the early 1980s. Singer Tony Hadley (1960–), guitarist Gary Kemp (1959–), bassist Martin Kemp (1962–), drummer John Keeble (1959–) and saxophonist Steve Norman (1960–) came together as Spandau Ballet in the late 1970s and established themselves as fashion trendsetters with such hits as 'True', which got to Number One in the UK in 1983 and 'Gold'. The album Parade (1984) was well received but it was not until 1986 that the follow-up Through the Barricades, on the contentious subject of Northern Ireland, appeared. Failure to repeat earlier successes led the band to break up.

Spanish Gershwin, the See Manuel de FALLA.

Spanish Sinatra, the See Julio IGLESIAS.

Sparks, the US pop duo, based in the UK, who had a string of big chart hits in the 1970s. The brothers Ron (1948–) and Russell (1953–) Mael made their recording début in the late 1960s and went on to enjoy some nine British chart hits. Among their greatest successes were 'This Town Ain't Big Enough for the Both of Us' (1974), 'Amateur Hour' (1974) and 'Never Turn Your Back on Mother Earth' (1975). Having started out as a GLAM ROCK outfit, the brothers had further success playing in a DISCO style with such singles as 'Beat the Clock'. They remained active through the 1980s, based first in Germany and later back in the USA.

spasm band The name by which the small JAZZ bands formed by impecunious Blacks in the cities of Chicago and New Orleans and elsewhere in the early years of the century were often known. Spasm bands consisted of amateur musicians playing homemade instruments such as the WASH-BOARD and the JUG in a bid to raise enough money to pay their rents. The music they played was fast, cheerful and spontaneous and was sometimes identified as SKIFFLE.

Specials, the British pop group, among the pioneers of the TWO-TONE genre of the late 1970s. The group, consisting of keyboard player Jerry Dammers (Gerald Dankin; 1954–), singers Terry Hall (1959–) and Neville Staples, guitarists Lynval Golding (1951–) and Roddy Byers, bassist Horace Panter and drummer John Bradbury, came together in 1977 and quickly established a reputation with SKA fans with such singles as 'A Message to You Rudy' (1979) and 'Ghost Town' (1981), which got to Number One and which became identified with the riots that erupted in several British cities at the same time. The group split in 1982, with Hall, Staples and Golding having further success as the Fun Boy Three and issuing such singles as 'It Ain't What You Do It's the Way That You Do It', which they made with BANANARAMA in 1983. A new line-up in 1984, under the title Special AKA, lasted only a short time. The band reunited in 1996 for *Today's Specials*.

Spector, Phil (Philip Harvey Spector; 1940–)US record producer, nicknamed the First Tycoon of Teen, who created the famous 'wall of sound'. Spector's first hit was his own 'To Know Him is to Love Him' (1958), which he wrote in memory of his father; subsequent hits ranged from songs by leading Black artists to classics by the BEATLES. His wall of sound style, which depended on the use of extensive multi-dubbing, had a fundamental effect on the development of pop music in the 1960s (despite detractors), and he was a millionaire by the time he was 21. He became disillusioned with the business in the late 1960s, but returned to work with such stars as John LENNON and Leonard COHEN.

speed metal Genre of HEAVY METAL in which conventional guitar rock is delivered at breakneck speed, often by line-ups centred on two lead guitarists. *See also* THRASH.

Spice Girls British pop group, notable for their 'girl-power' attitude. Geri Halliwell, Emma Bunton, Victoria Adams, Melanie Brown and Melanie Chisolm came together in 1994, after an advertisement was placed in *The Stage*. Their first single 'Wannabe' was Number One in the UK for 7 weeks in 1996, swiftly becoming Number One in 36 countries, including the USA. Geri, Emma, Victoria, Mel B and Mel C followed with the UK Number One 'Say You'll Be There', the UK Christmas Number One 'Two Become One' and their debut album *Spice*.

Spinners, the British FOLK group, which became established as an enduring favourite in the 1960s. The group, Tony Davis (1930–), Mike Groves (1936–), Hugh Jones (1936–) and Cliff Hall (1925–), was founded in 1958 and went on to appear regularly on television.

Spirit US rock band, which built up a cult ACID ROCK following on the West Coast in the late 1960s. Guitarist and singer Randy California (Randy Wolfe; 1951–), singer Jay Ferguson (John Ferguson; 1947–), bassist Mark Andes (1948–), keyboard player John Locke (1953–) and drummer Ed Cassidy (1931–) released such best-selling albums as *Spirit* (1967), *The Family That Plays Together* (1968) and *The 12 Dreams of Dr Sardonicus* (1970). Changes in the line-up led to a decline in the group's fortunes, although new albums continued to appear through the 1970s and 1980s.

Spivey, Victoria (Regina) (1906–76) Black US singer, who emerged as one of the outstanding BLUES singers of her generation. 'Black Snake Blues' (1926) made her famous, and she went on to appear in several films as well as with the bands of such jazz legends as Louis ARMSTRONG. Among her other hits were 'Toothache Blues' (1928) and 'Moaning the Blues' (1929).

Springfield, Dusty (Mary O'Brien; 1939–) British pop singer, who enjoyed considerable commercial success in the 1960s. She started out with her brothers Tom and Tim as the Springfields but established herself as a solo star with such hits as 'I Only Want to be With You' (1963), 'You Don't Have to Say You Love Me', which got to Number One in the UK in 1966, and 'Son of a Preacher Man', from the hit album *Dusty in Memphis* (1968). She made something of a comeback in 1987 singing with the PET SHOP BOYS on 'What Have I Done to Deserve This' although new solo releases received a mixed response.

Springsteen, Bruce (Frederick Joseph) (1949–) US singer-songwriter and guitarist, who has been given the nickname the Boss as a reflection of his sustained popularity over a period of some 20 years; the nickname was being widely used in the media by the mid-1980s. He emerged as a rock superstar of the 1970s and 1980s with his brash, though often introspective, version of BLUE COLLAR rock. He first attracted interest in the late 1960s when he was described by some as the 'New Dylan', and such early releases as *Greetings from Asbury Park* (1973) and *The Wild, the Innocent and the E-Street Shuffle* (1974) were well-received. *Born to Run* (1975) was hailed as one of the most original rock albums of the decade, but contractual problems disrupted further progress and he concentrated on touring for the next few years, consolidating his reputation as a rock star in close touch with the urban middle-America of which he sang. He became a particular favourite in the car city Detroit, and legend has it that he signed his first contract appropriately enough on the bonnet of a car between sets.

Darkness on the Edge of Town (1978) and *The River* (1981) continued to explore the romance and bitterness of life for the average US worker but, after the classic *Nebraska* (1982), it was *Born in the USA* (1987) that was to win him unchallenged recognition as possibly the greatest rock star of his generation and earned him the nickname the Future of Rock 'n' Roll. More recent releases have included the more intimate *Tunnel of Love* (1988), which went straight into both the US and British charts at Number One, and the twin releases *Lucky Town* and *Human Touch* (both· 1992) and *The Ghost of Tom Joad* (1995). He broke up E. Street Band, formed in 1973, in 1989.

Squatty Roo *See* Johnny HODGES.

Squeeze British pop group, which enjoyed success in the late 1970s and early 1980s playing in an appealing light rock style. The group, consisting of singers and guitarists Chris Difford (1954–) and Glenn Tilbrook (1957–), keyboard player Julian 'Jools' Holland (1958–), bassist John Bentley (1951–) and drummer Gilson Lavis (1951–), came together in 1974

and had hits with such singles as 'Take Me I'm Yours' (1978), 'Cool for Cats' (1979), 'Up the Junction' (1979) and 'Labelled with Love' (1981). Without Holland, Squeeze had further success with the album *East Side Story* (1981) and *Sweets from a Stranger* (1982) but then broke up. The group soon reformed to release such new LPs as *Cosi Fan Tutti Frutti* (1985), *Babylon And On* (1987), *Play* (1991), *Some Fantastic Place* (1993) and *Ridiculous* (1995).

Stafford, Jo (1920–) US singer, who sang with popular dance bands of the 1940s and became a well-known radio performer. Leading the vocal group the Pied Pipers, she sang with bands such as that of Tommy DORSEY before developing a career as a radio star alongside Bing CROSBY and Frank SINATRA and others. Her hits included 'Dream' (1945), 'You Belong to Me' (1951) and 'Make Love to Me!' (1954).

Staple Singers, the US vocal group, which emerged as a highly popular GOSPEL act. Founded by Roebuck 'Pops' Staples (1915–), with his four children Cleotha, Pervis, Yvonne and Mavis, the Staple Singers had such hits as 'Uncloudy Day' (1955), 'Why (am I Treated So Bad?)' (1967), 'I'll Take You There' (1972), which reached Number One, 'If You're Ready (Come Go With Me)' (1972) and 'Let's Do It Again' (1975). 'Pops' Staples staged a comeback in 1993 with the album *The Neighbourhood*.

Starr, Ringo (Richard Starkey; 1940–) British drummer, singer and actor, who achieved superstar status as drummer with the BEATLES. Called Ringo because of the rings he always wore and Starr after he used the name during a summer season at a Butlin's holiday camp, he left Rory Storm and the Hurricanes and joined the Beatles in 1963, replacing Pete Best and remaining in the drummer's seat until the band broke up in 1970. As an occasional singer with the group, his credits included 'Act Naturally', 'With a Little Help from My Friends' and 'Yellow Submarine'. His subsequent solo career was less distinguished, although he had some success with the albums *Ringo* (1973) and *Goodnight Vienna* (1974) and made a number of film appearances. Other projects included providing the voice-over for the children's television series *Thomas the Tank Engine* and leading the All-Starr Band in the late 1980s and once more in 1992 (members including Dave EDMUNDS, Todd RUNDGREN and Joe WALSH).

Ringo's contribution to the Beatles was less crucial than that of the other three perhaps, but nonetheless significant. It was, for instance, Ringo who came up with the phrase 'hard day's night', subsequently used for the celebrated single, album and film – as Paul MCCARTNEY recalled:

> He would say to us, 'God, it's been a hard day's night'. We'd say, 'Say that again'. 'Tomorrow Never Knows' is also one of his. Ringo talked in titles. We had to follow him around with a notebook and pencil. You never knew what he would say next.

(It has been suggested, however, that Starr was merely quoting the phrase from John LENNON's book *In His Own Write*.)

Status Quo British rock and pop group, who became enduring favourites of the 1970s and 1980s. Lead singer and guitarist Francis Rossi (1949–), bassist Alan Lancaster (1949–), keyboard player Roy Lynes and drummer John Coghlan (1946–) started out in 1962 as the Spectres, but became famous after changing their name and adding singer and guitarist Rick Parfitt (Rick Harrison; 1948–) in 1967. The psychedelic single 'Pictures of Matchstick Men' provided the group with its first hit but a golden era beckoned with the departure of Lynes and the adoption of a harder, yet still optimistic and good-humoured, BOOGIE rock sound in the early 1970s. Among the classic singles that followed were 'Paper Plane' (1972), 'Caroline' (1973), 'Down Down' (1974), 'Rockin' All Over the World' (1977), 'Whatever You Want' (1979), 'What You're Proposing' (1980) and 'You're in the Army Now' (1986). Personnel changes disrupted progress in the early 1980s, but the band, now a legend to a generation of rockers, continued to issue hit singles and albums as well as making celebrated live appearances. In 1996 the band protested strongly when Radio 1 refused to play records by Quo and other 'old' rock groups.

Stax Records US record company, based in Memphis, which played a prominent role in the development of SOUL in the 1960s. Stax was named after founders Jim Stewart and his sister Estelle Axton, who recruited such stars as BOOKER T. AND THE M.G.S, the

STAPLE SINGERS, SAM AND DAVE, Isaac HAYES and Otis REDDING before folding in the early 1970s.

Steele, Tommy (Thomas Hicks; 1936–) British singer and guitarist, nicknamed the British Elvis Presley when he emerged as the leading UK challenger to PRESLEY. He became the UK's top ROCK 'N' ROLL star in the mid-1950s, when he and his Steelmen were a hugely popular chart act. Steele was a merchant seaman with the Cunard Line when he attracted attention playing with SKIFFLE groups while on leave in London in 1956. His first record, 'Rock with the Caveman' (1956), was followed by such hits as 'Singing the Blues' (1956) and 'The Little White Bull' (1959) but he quickly deserted rock 'n' roll for a career as a stage and film entertainer, subsequently appearing in such shows as *Half a Sixpence* (1963), *Finian's Rainbow* (1968) and *Singin' in the Rain* (1983), which he also directed.

> I was fortunate enough to see Tommy Steele at the Sunderland Empire last week. He's terrific. The Pelvis hasn't got a look in. From now on it's Tommy, not Elvis, for me!
>
> *New Musical Express*, letter, 1956

Steeleye Span British FOLK-ROCK band, which built up a huge following in the early 1970s. Steeleye Span was formed by singer and guitarist Tim Hart, singers Maddy Prior and Gay Woods, guitarist Terry Woods and bassist Ashley Hutchings, who came together in 1969, and – although the line-up kept changing – the group quickly established itself as a favourite with folk-rock audiences. Among the hit albums were *Now We are Six* (1974), *Commoner's Crown* (1975) and *All around My Hat* (1975). Having attracted contributions from such revered musicians as Martin CARTHY, the group continued in operation through the 1980s and into the 1990s, but subsequent releases failed to excite equal interest in a fast-changing musical climate.

The name Steeleye Span was inspired by that of an eponymous character in the traditional song 'Horkston Grange'.

Steely Dan US rock band, which established an international reputation in the 1970s. Led by bassist Walter Becker (1950–) and singer and keyboard player Donald

Fagen (1948–   ), Steely Dan – a name purloined from the William Burroughs novel *The Naked Lunch* – was launched in 1972 with *Can't Buy a Thrill*, from which came the singles 'Do it Again' and 'Reeling in the Years'. The band consolidated its reputation with such releases as *Countdown to Ecstasy* (1973), *Pretzel Logic* (1974), which spawned the hit single 'Rikki Don't Lose That Number', *Katy Lied* (1975), *The Royal Scam* (1976), which included 'Haitian Divorce', *Aja* (1977) and *Gaucho* (1980). The band broke up a year later after Becker sustained severe injuries in a car accident, only to reunite in 1993.

Steiner, Max (Maximilian Raoul Steiner; 1888–1971) US composer, born in Austria, who established a reputation as one of the great Hollywood composers with the scores for some 300 movies. He studied music under, among others, Gustav MAHLER, arrived in the USA in 1914 and worked with such composers as George GERSHWIN and Jerome KERN before being recruited by Hollywood in 1929. Among his many film scores were those for *Rio Rita* (1929), *King Kong* (1933), *Flying Down To Rio* (1933), *The Informer* (1935), which brought him his first OSCAR, *Top Hat* (1935), *A Star Is Born* (1937), *Gone With the Wind* (1939), *Now Voyager* (1942), for which he earned a second Academy Award, *Casablanca* (1943), *Since You Went Away* (1944), for which he received his third Oscar, *The Big Sleep* (1946), *The Treasure of the Sierra Madre* (1948), *The Jazz Singer* (1953), *The Searchers* (1956) and *A Summer Place* (1959).

Steppenwolf Canadian rock band, which was among the hardest rock acts to achieve major commercial success in the late 1960s. Led by lead singer John Kay (Joachim F. Krauledat; 1944–   ), Steppenwolf – named after the title of the novel by Herman Hesse – was completed by guitarist Michael Monarch (1950–   ), keyboard player Goldy McJohn (1945–   ), bassist John Morgan, who replaced Rushton Moreve, and drummer Jerry Edmonton (1946–93). The band's first hit, 'Born to be Wild' (1968), became an anthem for rebellious bikers everywhere. Subsequent releases included the single 'Magic Carpet Ride' (1968) and the albums *At Your Birthday Party* (1968) and *Monster* (1969), which heralded a mammoth tour to around 1,000 venues. The band, which went through various line-up changes, broke up in 1974, reforming in 1980 and again in 1990 for *Rise and Shine*.

Stern, Isaac (1920–   ) US violinist, born in the Soviet Union, who emerged as one of the world's leading violinists in the late 1930s. Having emigrated to the USA as a child, Stern showed early promise as a violinist and made his professional début in San Francisco in 1936. He consolidated his growing reputation with acclaimed tours of Europe and went on to collaborate with pianist Eugene ISTOMIN and cellist Leonard Rose (1918–84), winning particular praise for his performances of Beethoven and Brahms. He was appointed chairman of the American-Israel Cultural Foundation in 1964. In 1981 he won an Oscar for his part in the film *Mao to Mozart: Isaac Stern in China*.

Stevens, Cat (Steven Giorgiou; 1947–   ) British singer-songwriter, who had huge success in the late 1960s and early 1970s with a series of folk-tinged pop singles. Usually remembered for the hit single 'Morning has Broken', he also visited the upper reaches of the charts with the likes of 'Matthew and Son', 'I'm Gonna Get Me a Gun', 'The First Cut is the Deepest', 'Moonshadow' and 'Can't Keep It In'. Albums included *Teaser and the Firecat* (1971), *Catch Bull at Four* (1972), *Foreigner* (1973) and *Buddha and the Chocolate Box* (1974). Subsequently he retreated from the public eye and attempted to live down his old life on becoming a convert to Islam, changing his name to Yusuf Islam. He attracted controversy in 1989 when he expressed sympathy with the death sentence passed by Ayatollah Khomeini on the novelist Salman Rushdie.

Stevens, Shakin' (Michael Barratt; 1948–   ) Welsh singer, who enjoyed a string of hits in the 1980s singing in a ROCK 'N' ROLL revival style. He began his career as a latterday rock 'n' roller in the late 1960s and enjoyed a reputation as a live performer for a number of years before making his first big hit, 'Hot Dog', in 1980 in the wake of starring in the MUSICAL *Elvis*. Among the hits that followed were COVERS of such rock 'n' roll standards as 'This Ole House' (1981) and 'Green Door' (1982) as well as the occasional new song.

My second hit was a flop.
SHAKIN' STEVENS

Stewart, Rod (Roderick David Stewart; 1945–) British pop singer, nicknamed Rod the Mod, who achieved superstar status in the 1970s. Having toyed with professional football, he instead learned to play guitar but subsequently made a mark as a vocalist with his raw, gravelly voice. He collaborated with Jeff BECK before taking over as lead singer with the FACES in 1969 and went on to establish himself as a solo star in the GLAM ROCK era of the early 1970s, finally leaving the band in 1975. 'Maggie May' reached Number One on both sides of the Atlantic in 1971, and he subsequently added to his list of hits such classics as 'Sailing' (1975), 'Tonight's the Night' (1976), 'I Don't Want to Talk About It' (1977), 'Hot Legs' (1977), 'Do Ya Think I'm Sexy' (1978) and 'Downtown Train' (1990). His albums have included *Every Picture Tells a Story* (1971), *Never a Dull Moment* (1972), *Atlantic Crossing* (1975), *Blonds Have More Fun* (1978), *Tonight I'm Yours* (1981), *Body Wishes* (1983), *Every Beat of My Heart* (1986), *Vagabond Heart* (1991) and *A Spanner in the Works* (1995).

Rod Stewart was not always the confident performer familiar to millions of fans: at one early Beck concert he decided to sing the first two songs from behind the set after stage-fright prevented him going on.

Sting *See* POLICE, the.

Stockhausen, Karlheinz (1928–) German composer, who emerged as the leading figure in AVANT-GARDE music during the postwar era. As a young man Stockhausen combined musical studies under Frank MARTIN and Olivier MESSIAEN with physics, although he wrote such early pieces as *Kreuzspiel* (1951) and *Kontrapunkte* (1952) not for electronic devices but for conventional instruments. He immersed himself in the science of SERIALISM and other related avant-garde techniques and began to explore the possibilities of electronically generated music after co-founding West German Radio's electronic music studio in 1953. He was particularly attracted by the prospect of devising a music that could be entirely controlled and kept free of interference from the performers.

Gesang der Jünglinge (1956), for human voice and electronics, *Klavierstücke* (1957) and *Gruppen* (1957), for three orchestras,

indicated the development of a more radical, spatially aware form of new music, and he continued to pursue these trains of thought into the 1960s with such works as *Kontakte* (1960) and *Momente* (1962), pioneering live performances of electronic music. Elements of INDETERMINACY were introduced in such works as *Zyklus* (1959), which allowed a single percussionist to start and end where he liked, *Stimmung* (1968) and *Mantra* (1970), with the musicians being invited to influence the course of the music by improvisation. He also experimented with new forms of notation to free written music from any preconceived prejudices on the part of performers. Extreme examples of this approach included one passage from *Aus den sieben Tagen* (1968), in which the players were requested to go without food for four days while living in seclusion and then to come together late at night to play whatever music spontaneously suggested itself.

More recent compositions, which have aimed to create a mesmeric state in which performers and audience are free to 'communicate' with complete freedom, have included the linked series *Donnerstag* (1980), *Samstag* (1984) and *Montag* (1988).

> Look, down there you can see the ocean of light that is Vienna. In a few years' time I will have progressed so far that, with a single electronic bang, I'll be able to blow the whole city sky-high!
> KARLHEINZ STOCKHAUSEN, *Music and Politics*, 1982

> 'Have you heard any Stockhausen?' Sir Thomas Beecham was asked. 'No,' he replied, 'but I believe I have trodden in some.'
> Attributed

> More boring than the most boring of eighteenth-century music.
> IGOR STRAVINSKY

Stokowski, Leopold (Anthony) (Antoni Stanislaw Boleslawowich; 1882–1977) US conductor, born in the UK of Irish-Polish descent, who became one of the most celebrated conductors of his day. Stokowski trained at London's Royal College of Music, where he was the youngest student ever, and went on to win huge acclaim conducting the Cincinnati Orchestra (1909–12) and the PHILADELPHIA ORCHESTRA

(1912–38). Highlights of his career included his collaboration with Walt Disney on the score for the epic cartoon *Fantasia* (1940). He was also founder of the HOLLYWOOD BOWL Orchestra (1945) and of the American Symphony Orchestra (1961).

Stokowski's technique as a conductor was unusually strenuous, and his vigorous use of the baton gave him neuritis in the right shoulder, with the result that he had to use his left hand and eventually stopped using a baton altogether. He was also a great self-publicist and was regularly interviewed and photographed during and after his training sessions (which he followed as religiously as a prize-fighter). He was renowned for his firm ideas about music and how it should be played, and critics observed that he 'Stokowskized each composer whom he took into his dictatonic hands'. His gift for presentation (he once had his hands lit by a spotlight so that they cast huge shadows on the ceiling) offended many purists. Jean SIBELIUS said of him: 'He is a very fine man I am sure, and interested in many things – but not, I think, in music.'

Stokowski knew how to defend himself, however, and he was notorious for the methods he used to punish musicians who had offended him. It was not unheard of for him to invite a musician's family to rehearsal and then to single the luckless individual out for merciless criticism. On another occasion he rounded on some women in the audience and berated them for knitting during the music. At no less a venue than Carnegie Hall, he once warned listeners: 'Musicians paint their pictures on silence – we provide the music, and you provide the silence.'

Stokowski's career was one of the longest in twentieth-century music but evidently not long enough for the man himself: in the year of his death, at the age of 95, he signed a contract that would have kept him on the podium for another decade.

Stolz, Robert (1880–1975) Austrian conductor and composer, who is remembered for his popular operettas. As well as such operettas as *Whirled into Happiness* (1921) and *Wild Violets* (1932), he also wrote music for the cinema and various songs and marches. He became chief conductor at the Theatre an der Wien in Vienna in 1905.

stomp *See* BOOGIE-WOOGIE.

Stone, Lew (Louis Steinberg; 1898–1969) British bandleader, pianist and composer, who led a popular dance orchestra in the 1930s and 1940s. Having started out as a pianist for AMBROSE and Jack PAYNE among others, he took up bandleading in 1929 and went on to make many hit recordings as well as to work on various film scores and in the MUSICAL THEATRE. Singers with his celebrated Monseigneur band included Al BOWLLY.

Stone, Sly (Sylvester Stewart; 1944–) Black US singer-songwriter and keyboard player, who pioneered psychedelic SOUL with the Family Stone in the late 1960s. Backed by guitarist Freddie Stone (1946–), bassist Larry Graham (1946–), pianist Rosie Stone (1945–), trumpeter Cynthia Robinson (1946–), saxophonist Jerry Martini (1943–) and drummer Greg Errico (1946–), Stone, who started out as a disc jockey, launched Sly and the Family Stone in 1967 and had his first big hit a year later with 'Dance to the Music'. The group was hailed for its performance at WOODSTOCK in 1969, and it went on to release such acclaimed albums as *Stand!* (1969) and *There's a Riot Goin' On* (1971), which is thought to have been the first recording ever made with the use of drum machine. The band broke up in the mid-1970s when Stone's drug addiction became worse (he was gaoled for drug offences in 1987).

Stone Roses British pop group, which established a large cult following in the 1980s. Hailing from Manchester and consisting of singer Ian Brown, guitarists John Squire and Andy Couzens, who was replaced by Gary 'Manny' Mountfield in 1987, bassist Peter Garner and drummer Alan 'Reni' Wren. Stone Roses came together in 1985 and built up a reputation for such dance-oriented pop hits as 'Made of Stone', 'She Bangs the Drums', 'Fool's Gold' and 'One Love'. The group attracted a certain notoriety for its outlandish behaviour during interviews and for deliberately provocative lyrics. Squire and Wren left in 1996.

Storyville The redlight district of New Orleans, which was the birthplace of JAZZ in the early years of the twentieth century. Black musicians, who were otherwise rarely paid for their music, were able to make a relatively good living playing for the clients of the many brothels in the area, which was called Storyville – or the District – after alderman Joseph Story, who had attempted to gather all the city's brothels and gambling dens in the one place. Efforts to drive the brothels out of the area during the First World War resulted in the heartland of contemporary jazz being relocated further north, in Chicago.

> In the brothels, music had the same function as wine, spirits and striptease; it helped prepare clients for the main event upstairs.
>
> TONY PALMER, *All You Need Is Love*, 1976

Strait, George (1952–) US COUNTRY singer, who emerged as one of the top country stars of the 1980s. While continuing to work as a farmer when not performing, he topped the country charts on a regular basis with such HONKY-TONK style hits as 'Unwound' (1981), 'Does Fort Worth Ever Cross Your Mind?' (1984) and 'The Chair' (1986) as well as establishing a strong reputation as a live act.

Stranglers, the British rock band, which emerged as just about the only major PUNK ROCK outfit with real musical ability in the late 1970s. Lead singer and guitarist Hugh Cornwell (1949–), drummer Jet Black (Brian Duffy; 1938–), bassist Jean-Jacques Burnel (1952–) and keyboard player Dave Greenfield came together in 1974. Such albums as *Rattus Norvegicus* (1977) and *No More Heroes* (1977) together with such singles as 'Peaches' and 'No More Heroes' established the group's credentials as a punk band with real musicality, and it gradually won acceptance with a wider NEW WAVE audience. Later releases adopted a rather more moderate stance and included such commercial hits as 'Golden Brown' (about heroin), which did well in the charts in 1982, although the group retained the all-black outfits that dated from the punk era. Other albums included *The Raven* (1979), *Feline* (1982), *Aural Sculpture* (1984), *Dreamtime* (1986) and *10* (1990), following which Cornwell (who was gaoled for drug offences in 1980) left. *Stranglers in the Night* appeared in 1992, *About Time* in 1995 and *Written in Red* in 1997.

Strauss, Richard (1864–1949) German composer and conductor, who was hailed for his tone poems, operas and songs in the romantic tradition of Mozart and Wagner. Born in Munich, where his father was a composer and horn player, Strauss showed early promise, publishing his first compositions while he was still in his teens. He went on to establish a reputation with a series of brilliantly realized tone poems, beginning with *Aus Italien* (1886), *Macbeth* (1887) and *Tod und Verklärung* (1889) and continuing with *Till Eulenspiegels lustige Streiche* (1895), *Also sprach Zarathustra* (1896), *Don Quixote* (1897) and *Ein Heldenleben* (1898), which took as its subject matter Strauss's struggles with hostile critics.

As a composer of opera, Strauss followed the ill-received *Guntram* (1893) and the sensational *Salome* (1905), which was condemned as blasphemous and obscene, with the highly praised *Elektra* (1908), which stretched the concept of tonality to its limits and remains the crowning point of his early experimental years. It also marked the beginning of a fruitful partnership with librettist Hugo von Hofmannsthal (1874–1929), with whom Strauss worked on the enduring (if musically less adventurous) *Der Rosenkavalier* (1910) and on *Ariadne auf Naxos* (1912, revised 1916), *Die Frau ohne Schatten* (1917), *Die Aegyptische Helena* (1927) and *Arabella* (1932).

Other works by Strauss included the *Symphonia Domestica* (1903), the late opera *Capriccio* (1942), a highly regarded body of Lieder, which he often performed at the piano to the singing of Elisabeth SCHUMANN, and *Metamorphosen* (1945), for string ensemble. Also acclaimed as a conductor with the Vienna Opera and elsewhere, he accepted high posts under the Nazis but later stepped down and was excused his apparent collaboration after the Second World War on the grounds that he was trying to protect his Jewish daughter-in-law.

> The last great event in European music.
>
> ROMAIN ROLLAND, of Strauss's music

> From time to time the cruellest discords are succeeded by exquisite suavities that caress the ear with delight. While listening to it all I thought of those lovely princesses in Sacher Masoch who lavished on young men the most voluptuous kisses while drawing red-hot irons over their lovers' ribs.
>
> CAMILLE SAINT-SAËNS

His absurd cacophony will not be music even in the thirtieth century.

CÉSAR CUI, letter, 1904

Stravinsky, Igor Feodorovich (1882–1971) Russian composer, whose often controversial, innovative ballets and other works won him a lasting reputation as one of the most important figures in twentieth-century music. Raised in St Petersburg by musical parents, the young Stravinsky read law before meeting Nikolai Rimsky-Korsakov (1844–1908) and deciding on a career in music instead. He studied under Rimsky-Korsakov for three years and was subsequently commissioned by the impressario Serge Diaghilev (1872–1929) to write a ballet for the Ballets Russes. The colourfully orchestrated *The Firebird* (1910), based on a traditional Russian fairytale, was the result. It was enthusiastically received and brought him immediate fame, which was consolidated by the equally successful although more challenging *Petrushka* (1911).

Quite different, though, was the reception of what was ultimately to be recognized as a masterpiece – *The Rite of Spring* (1913) – which explored entirely new modernist territory and evoked a savage, dangerous world where conventional and civilized values had little meaning. Uproar greeted the first performance at the Théâtre des Champs-Elysées in Paris under conductor Pierre MONTEUX, when the innovative nature of the work (strong, irregular rhythms and harsh dissonances) provoked a violent reaction in the customarily well-behaved audience. The ballet was hardly under way when members of the audience began to voice their protests against this 'new music' and soon the auditorium was filled with the sounds of heated argument and insults. Only the determination of Monteux and the leadership of Nijinsky on the stage kept the performance going. Even after the ballet was over the furore continued in the press, one critic changing the French title *Le Sacré du Printemps* to *Massacre du Printemps*. The Comtesse de Pourtalès, who had been in the audience, was heard to observe: 'This is the first time in 60 years anyone has dared insult me!'

Stravinsky emigrated to Switzerland during the First World War but moved to France in 1920. After *The Soldier's Tale* (1918) and the ballet *The Wedding* (1920),

he adopted a broadly neoclassical style for such works as *Pulcinella* (1919), *Symphonies of Wind Instruments* (1920), which was written in memory of Claude DEBUSSY, and the ballets *Apollo Musagetes* (1928) and *Persephone* (1933). Other compositions of this period included pieces that reflected the influence of JAZZ and RAGTIME, notably *Ragtime for Eleven Instruments* (1918) and *Piano-rag Music* (1919), as well as various instrumental pieces experimenting with different tonal effects – among them *Oedipus Rex* (1927), which utilized a text by Jean Cocteau. *The Symphony of Psalms* (1930) was less abstract in style but retained the distinctly Russian air of most of his work.

Having emigrated to the USA in 1939, Stravinsky became an American citizen in 1945 and went on to embrace SERIALIST techniques. Alongside such collaborators as George Balanchine (1904–83), he returned to the ballet with such new works as *Agon* (1957). Other late compositions included the *Mass* (1948), the neoclassical opera *The Rake's Progress* (1951), *In Memoriam Dylan Thomas* (1954), *Threni* (1958), *Movements for piano and orchestra* (1959), *The Flood* (1962), *Abraham and Isaac* (1963) and the *Requiem Canticles* (1966). He was buried in Venice.

First listen! Then boo.

GABRIEL ASTRUC, to hecklers at the first performance of *The Rite of Spring*, 1913

The twentieth century's Ninth Symphony.

SERGE DIAGHILEV, of *The Rite of Spring*

New music? Hell, there's been no new music since Stravinsky.

DUKE ELLINGTON

Bach on the wrong notes.

SERGEI PROKOFIEV

Stravinsky looks like a man who was potty-trained too early and that music proves it as far as I'm concerned.

RUSSELL HOBAN, *Turtle Diary*, 1975

My music is best understood by children and animals.

IGOR STRAVINSKY, the *Observer*, 1961

street corner sound *See* DOO-WOP.

Streisand, Barbra (Joan) (1942–) US singer and actress, nicknamed the Nose, who established herself as a top star of stage and screen MUSICALS in the 1960s and 1970s. Streisand started her career as a night club singer in Greenwich Village in the early 1960s and went on to win overnight stardom with her Broadway début in *I Can Get It for You Wholesale* (1962). She confirmed her status as a top musical star as lead in the stage and screen versions of *Funny Girl*, which brought her an OSCAR in 1968, in *Hello, Dolly!* (1969) and in *On A Clear Day You Can See Forever* (1970). She concentrated on her film career in the 1970s, starring in such films as *The Owl and the Pussycat* (1970), *What's Up, Doc?* (1972) and *A Star is Born* (1976), for which she won a second Academy Award. The ambitious *Yentl* (1983) saw her combine the roles of star, director and producer. More recent films include *Nuts* (1987). Among her hits have been 'The Way We Were' (1974), 'You Don't Bring Me Flowers' (1978), with Neil DIAMOND, and 'No More Tears' (1979), with Donna SUMMER.

stride piano Piano-playing technique, in which the left hand ranges over extended chords in a steady walking rhythm. The style caught on in the 1930s, exponents included Fats WALLER and Duke ELLINGTON.

Stupenda, La *See* Dame Joan SUTHERLAND.

Stylistics, the US vocal group, which enjoyed numerous SOUL hits in the early 1970s. Russell Thompkins, Airron Love, James Smith, James Dunn and Herbie Murrell formed the Stylistics in 1968 and had such hits as 'You're a Big Girl Now' (1971), 'You are Everything' (1971), 'I'm Stone in Love with You' (1972), 'Betcha by Golly, Wow' (1972) and 'You Make Me Feel Brand New' (1974). The Stylistics continued to tour after the hits came to an end, reduced to a trio.

Styne, Jule (Julius Kerwin Stein; 1905–81) US composer, who was one of the leading composers for the stage and screen in the late 1930s. Having trained at the Chicago College of Music, he played piano with the CHICAGO SYMPHONY ORCHESTRA before concentrating on composition. His numerous hit shows have included *Gentlemen Prefer Blondes* (1949), *Peter Pan* (1954), *Bells are Ringing* (1956), *Gypsy* (1959), *Funny Girl* (1964) and *Sugar* (1972). Among the many hit songs he wrote (often in collaboration with Sammy CAHN) for the screen were 'There Goes That Song Again', 'Diamonds are a Girl's Best Friend', 'Everything's Coming up Roses', 'It's Magic' and 'Three Coins in the Fountain'.

Styx US rock band, which became one of the most popular ADULT-ORIENTED ROCK outfits of the 1970s with a brand of POMP ROCK. The band, formed by singer and keyboard player Dennis de Young (1947–), singer and guitarist James Young (1948–), bassist Chuck Panozzo, guitarist John Curulewski, who was later replaced by Tommy Shaw (1954–) and drummer John Panozzo (1947–96), came together in 1972 and gradually established a reputation with such hit albums as *Styx II* (1973), *The Grand Illusion* (1977), *Pieces of Eight* (1978) and *Cornerstone* (1979). The band's live act, featuring lasers and other theatrical effects, attracted more fans, and it continued to prosper with such new releases as *Paradise Theater* (1980) and *Kilroy was Here* (1983) before disbanding in 1984. The members reunited in 1990, with Glenn Burtnick replacing Shaw, and released *Edge of the Century*.

Suede British rock band, which enjoyed chart success in the mid-1990s. Comprising singer Brett Anderson (1967–), guitarist Bernard Butler (1970–), bassist Mat Osman (1967–) and drummer Simon Gilbert (1965–), Suede formed in 1990 and won a large following with the albums *Suede* (1993), *Dog Man Star* (1994) and *Coming Up* (1996). Singles have included 'Animal Nitrate' (1993) and 'Stay Together' (1994).

Summer, Donna (Ladonna Adrian Gaines; 1948–) Black US DISCO singer-songwriter, nicknamed the Disco Queen, who enjoyed enormous popularity in the 1970s. Summer began her career as one of the cast of a German production of the rock MUSICAL *Hair* and subsequently, in collaboration with disco producer Giorgio Moroder, established herself as one of the most popular disco singers with such overtly sexual numbers as 'Love to Love You Baby' (1975), 'I Feel Love' (1977) and 'MacArthur Park' (1978). She then underwent a complete change of image, singing duets with Barbra STREISAND and aiming at a new career as a committed Christian SOUL singer, in which guise her hits included 'State of Independence' (1982).

Sun Ra (Herman 'Sonny' Blount: 1914–93) US JAZZ composer, pianist and bandleader, who established a reputation as one of the most colourful and eclectic jazz personalities of his generation. He began as a pianist for most colourful and eclectic jazz personalities of his generation. He began as a pianist for Fletcher HENDERSON in the late 1940s and formed his own Arkestra band in the 1950s, going on to explore a range of styles, from hard bop to Afro-Latin and TRAD; inspiration came from sources as varied as science-fiction and the mythology of ancient Egypt. He was one of the first to embrace a FREE JAZZ style, when he met with incomprehension from many quarters until fashions caught up with him. Admirers within music have included John COLTRANE, who is said to have kicked drugs through his friendship with Sun Ra, and Karlheinz STOCKHAUSEN.

Typical stunts pulled by Sun Ra included attempts to conceal his birth date, on the grounds of its astrological importance for the world, and claims that he arrived on the planet from Saturn.

Sun Records US record label, which played a crucial role in the birth of ROCK 'N' ROLL in the mid-1950s. Founded in Memphis in 1950 by Sam Phillips (1923–), the label became one of the most significant in pop history after Phillips recruited the young Elvis PRESLEY in 1954. With the money earned from the deal under which Presley moved to RCA in 1955, Phillips was able to recruit a whole stable of burgeoning talents, who included Carl PERKINS, Johnny CASH, Roy ORBISON and Jerry Lee LEWIS. Phillips subsequently diversified into other business interests and sold Sun Records in 1969.

supergroup A POP group, which stands apart from the ordinary run of bands in having an outstanding line-up of already-established talent. The supergroup was a creation of the late 1960s, when various agglomerations of talent were formed and re-formed as established stars moved from one group to another. Among the most celebrated were CROSBY, STILLS, NASH AND YOUNG, Blind Faith, EMERSON, LAKE AND PALMER and – from a later era – the Travelling Wilburys. Perhaps the most remarkable of them all, however, was the short-lived BAND AID enterprise of the mid-1980s. The term is also sometimes used of long-established bands whose commercial success has elevated them above all but a handful of other contemporaries – examples including the ROLLING STONES, LED ZEPPELIN, GENESIS and ABBA.

Supertramp Anglo-US rock group, based in Germany, which enjoyed considerable commercial success in the 1970s. Led by singer and keyboard player Rick Davies (1944–) and multi-instrumentalist Roger Hodgson (1950–), Supertramp began as a PROGRESSIVE ROCK outfit but gradually adopted a more accessible pop-oriented sound that brought mass appeal. The group's best-selling releases have included the albums *Crime of the Century* (1974), *Crisis? What Crisis?* (1975) and *Breakfast in America* (1979). Hodgson left in 1983.

Supremes, the Black US vocal group, which was one of the most successful all-girl line-ups of the 1960s. Founded in the late 1950s as the Primettes, the Supremes – Florence Ballard (1943–76), Mary Wilson (1944–), and, following the departure of Betty Travis, Diana ROSS – were signed by MOTOWN in 1961 and enjoyed huge success with such SOUL classics as 'Where Did Our Love Go' (1964), 'Baby Love' (1964), 'Come See About Me' (1964), 'Stop! In the Name of Love' (1965), 'Back in My Arms Again' (1965) and 'I Hear a Symphony' (1965), all of which reached Number One (including an unprecedented five consecutive US chart-toppers). The hits, mostly the work of the HOLLAND, DOZIER AND HOLLAND songwriting team, continued with the likes of 'You Can't Hurry Love' (1966), 'You Keep Me Hanging On' (1966), 'Love is Here and Now You're Gone' (1967) and 'The Happening' (1967).

Ballard, who had begun as the lead singer of the trio but had gradually been ousted by Ross, left the group, feeling aggrieved, and was replaced by Cindy Birdsong (1939–) in 1967. Subsequent hits, such as 'Love Child' (1968) and 'I'm Gonna Make You Love Me' (1968), were released under the name Diana Ross and the Supremes, but the group went into decline after Ross went solo in 1970.

The luckless Ballard fell on hard times after leaving the group and died in poverty.

> With lacquered wigs and blasted smiles, they ensured ... that the emasculation of Black music would be finally completed.
> TONY PALMER, *All You Need Is Love*, 1976

Sutherland, Dame Joan (1926–) Australian singer, nicknamed La Stupenda, who was one of the great coloratura sopranos. Having made her professional début in Sydney in 1951, Sutherland completed her training at the Royal College of Music in London and went on to win acclaim at COVENT GARDEN in Mozart's *The Magic Flute* (1952). Of her many greatly admired operatic roles, the most famous include that of Lucia in Donizetti's *Lucia di Lammermoor*. She retired in 1990.

On one occasion, in Naples in 1961, she won even greater applause than usual when she carried on regardless after her petticoat came unpinned and descended gracefully to the floor, from where the tenor Renato Cioni rescued it with a triumphant flourish.

Svengali of Swing, the *See* Frank SINATRA.

Sweet, the British pop group, which had a string of hits during the GLAM ROCK era of the early 1970s. Lead singer Brian Connolly (Brian McManus; 1948–97), guitarist Frank Torpy, who was replaced by Andy Scott (1949–) in 1971, bassist Steve Priest (1950–) and drummer Mick Tucker (1948–) came together in 1968 and, after teaming up with CHINN AND CHAPMAN, enjoyed their first hit with 'Co-Co' (1971). Among the various hits that followed were 'Wig Wam Bam' (1972), 'Blockbuster' (1973) and 'Teenage Rampage' (1973). The group split up in 1981, re-forming in 1985 but failing to recapture past success.

Sweet Mama Stringbean *See* Ethel WATERS.

Sweethearts of the Blues, the *See* SHIRLEY AND LEE.

swing Genre of JAZZ dance music that swept the USA and the UK in the 1930s and early 1940s (a period now dubbed the Swing Era). Virtually synonymous with BIG BAND jazz, swing depended technically on the rolling, suggestive off-the-beat rhythms that were perfected by such jazzmen as Benny GOODMAN and Duke ELLINGTON – although there was little room for the free improvisation that was associated with other jazz forms (including BEBOP, which succeeded it in the 1940s).

> It's jam, but arranged.
> EDWARD FARLEY, 1936

Swooner, the *See* Frank SINATRA.

synthesizer An electronic musical instrument, which is capable of producing a fan-tastically varied range of sounds. First developed in the 1920s (*see* ONDES MARTENOT), the modern synthesizer has been revolutionized by the incorporation of complex microchip technology, and the operator of such a system can now imitate virtually any real instrument with a high degree of authenticity as well as producing many new sounds. *See also* MOOG.

> The synthesizer world opens the door to musical infinity.
> JOHN MCLAUGHLIN, 1975

> Not many composers have ideas. Far more of them know how to use strange instruments which do not require ideas.
> GEORGE GERSHWIN, *The Composer in the Machine Age*, 1930

Szell, Georg (1897–1970) US conductor, born in Hungary, who is usually remembered for his long association (1946–70) with the celebrated CLEVELAND ORCHESTRA. A protégé of Richard STRAUSS at the Berlin State Opera, he also worked briefly as conductor of the (Royal) Scottish Opera (1937–39) and of the METROPOLITAN OPERA, New York (1942–46) as well as in Strasbourg, Prague, Darmstadt, Düsseldorf and The Hague.

> Ladies and gentlemen, I want you to know that during my stay in London your orchestras have been most generous to me. When tuning, all I asked for was one pitch. You have invariably given me two or three at least!
> GEORG SZELL, speech from the podium.

Szymanowski, Karol (1882–1937) Polish composer and pianist, born in the Ukraine, who emerged as the leading Polish composer of his age. Born of musical parents, Szymanowksi composed his first pieces as a child and went on to win encouragement from the pianist Artur RUBINSTEIN. He studied music in Warsaw and established his reputation with his compositions for the piano, which reflected the influence of Chopin, for whom he had a lifelong admiration. Later works were influenced by Richard STRAUSS, and he won praise for his Second Symphony (1910). He responded to the innovations of Igor STRAVINSKY in his choral Third Symphony (1916) and began to explore the concepts of tonality and chromaticism while keeping within a broadly impressionist style. The opera *King Roger* (1925) reflected his respect for ancient cultures, while other works included the ballet *Harnasie* (1932), the second violin concerto (1932), and the choral *Stabat Mater* (1926). Afforded official recognition with important posts towards the end of his life, Szymanowski is now considered the most important Polish composer since Chopin and before Krzysztof PENDERECKI.

T

T. Rex *See* Marc BOLAN.

Tailleferre, Germaine (1892–1983) French composer and pianist, resident in the USA from 1942, who was one of the group of composers known as Les SIX. Influenced by Gabriel FAURÉ and her teacher Maurice RAVEL, she wrote such works as the ballets *Marchand d'oiseaux* (1923) and *Parisiana* (1955) as well as operas, operettas, the orchestral *Pastorale*, concertos, chamber music and songs.

Take That British pop group, which emerged as the latest in a series of teen-idols in the early 1990s. Mark Owen, Gary Barlow, Jason Orange, Howard Donald and Robbie Williams, who took the name Take That from a newspaper caption for a picture of MADONNA, came together in Manchester in 1990. The group's hits included the singles 'It Only Takes a Minute', 'Could It be Magic', 'A Million Love Songs', 'Why Can't I Wake Up with You?', 'Relight My Fire', 'Babe', 'Everything Changes', 'Sure', 'Back for Good' and 'How Deep is your Love'. The band split in 1996.

talking box Electronic device by means of which an electric guitarist 'talks' through his instrument. A voice tube connects the mouth with the guitar, which is in turn connected to a SYNTHESIZER. The device was the invention of rock guitarist Jeff BECK.

Talking Heads US rock group, which emerged as one of the most influential NEW WAVE bands of the early 1980s. Led by former design students Scottish singer David Byrne (1952–) and bassist Tina Weymouth (1950–), backed by guitarist Jerry Harrison (1949–) and drummer Chris Frantz (1951–), Talking Heads came together in 1974 and established a large following with the album *Talking Heads* (1977). Other band names considered were the Vague Dots and the Portable Crushers. Heavily influenced by Lou REED and the VELVET UNDERGROUND, the group consolidated its reputation for skilful, synthesized rock with

an eccentric experimental edge in such releases as *Fear of Music* (1979), on which the group collaborated with Brian ENO, *Remain in Light* (1980), which produced the hit single 'Once in a Lifetime', *The Name of the Band Is Talking Heads* (1981), which incorporated African musical motifs, *Little Creatures* (1985) and *Naked* (1988). The group split up in the late 1980s to pursue individual projects. Weymouth and Frantz married in 1977 and formed the funk outfit Tom Tom Club in 1981, while Harrison founded Casual Gods and Byrne went solo.

Tamla Motown US record label, which was founded by Berry Gordy in 1959 as part of his MOTOWN organization. Berry had wanted to call it 'Tammy', after a hit by Debbie REYNOLDS, but was prevented from doing so by copyright. Many of the great Motown hits – including those made by the TEMPTATIONS – appeared on the label. Years later, Motown star Smokey ROBINSON paid tribute to Gordy by naming his daughter Tamla.

Tangerine Dream German rock group, which was among the top synthesizer rock outfits of the early 1970s. Led by keyboard player Edgar Froese (1944–), who started out with fellow-keyboardist Klaus Schultze and flautist Conrad Schnitzler but has since worked with differing line-ups, Tangerine Dream came into being in 1968 and pioneered ELECTRONIC ROCK with such cult albums as *Electronic Meditation* (1970), *Phaedra* (1974), *Stratosfear* (1976) and *Force Majeure* (1979). Subsequent releases, among them *Le Parc* (1985), ventured even further into the technology of contemporary rock with the increased use of SAMPLING and computers but lacked the radicalism of earlier works.

Tatum, Art(hur) (1909–56) Black US JAZZ pianist, who established a reputation as the greatest pianist in jazz history – despite being almost blind. Tatum made his professional début in the 1920s and broadcast regularly on the radio, before touring widely with his own trio and quartet, astonishing colleagues and fans alike with his virtuosity. He made many classic recordings in the 1950s, both with his groups and on a solo basis, his albums including the highly regarded *God is In the House* (1973), so titled in reference to a compliment paid by Fats WALLER when he realized Tatum was present in the audience at one of his gigs. Among his many admirers was the classical pianist Vladimir HOROWITZ. His early death was the result of uraemia.

Tauber, Richard (Ernst Seiffert; 1892–1948) Austrian tenor, later a British subject, who became one of the most celebrated singers of the century. Having trained as a singer in Germany, he made his professional début as Tamino in *The Magic Flute* in 1913 and went on to establish a reputation at the Vienna State Opera and elsewhere as an unsurpassed performer of Mozart and Franz LEHÁR, who wrote several of his most famous operettas specifically for Tauber's remarkable voice – notably *The Land of Smiles* (1929), which brought the singer his biggest hit in the form of the song 'You are My Heart's Delight'. He took British citizenship in 1940 and consolidated his fame as a star performer of operetta in London as well as appearing as a conductor; among the operettas actually penned by his hand was *Old Chelsea* (1943). His film credits included *Blossom Time* (1934), *Heart's Desire* (1935) and *Waltz Time* (1946).

Tavener, John Kenneth (1944–   ) British composer, who emerged as one of the leading musical figures of his generation. While completing studies at the Royal Academy of Music in the early 1960s under Sir Lennox BERKELEY, Tavener attracted attention with his prize-winning cantata *Cain and Abel* (1965), which was the first of many works to treat religious themes. The cantata *The Whale* (1968), based on the story of Jonah, consolidated his reputation and was followed by such further compositions as *In alium* (1968), for voice, orchestra and recorded sounds, the *Celtic Requiem* (1969), *Ultimos ritos* (1972), *Little Requiem for Father Malachy Lynch* (1972), the opera *Thérèse* (1976), which dramatized the life of St Thérèse of Lisieux, *The Last Prayer of Mary Queen of Scots* (1977) and *The Immurement of Antigone* (1979). Other works, such as *Akhmatova* (1980) and *The*

Protecting Veil (1987) reflected his conversion to the Russian Orthodox Church; other influences have included the music of Olivier MESSIAEN and Igor STRAVINSKY. His most recent compositions include the orchestral *Dance Lament of the Repentant Thief* (1991).

Taylor, James (1948–   ) US rock singer-songwriter, who established himself as one of the top rock stars of the 1970s. Taylor was signed by APPLE in the UK in 1968 and profited through his early association with the BEATLES before returning to the USA a year later. There he achieved immediate recognition with the album *Sweet Baby James* (1970), from which came the single 'Fire and Rain' and *Mud Slide Slim* (1971), which spawned the Number One single 'You've Got a Friend'. Subsequent releases have included duets with his then-wife Carly SIMON and songs on environmental issues.

Taylor's career has been blighted by mental illness and drug problems. His experiences of life inside mental institutions were relayed in his 1971 composition 'Knockin' around the Zoo'.

TB *See* Sir Thomas BEECHAM.

Te Kanawa, Dame Kiri (Janette) (1944–   ) New Zealand-born soprano, of mixed European-Maori descent, who established a reputation as one of the most popular operatic stars of her time. Having won praise for her singing throughout Australasia, she moved to the UK to complete her studies and went on to win acclaim in her COVENT GARDEN début in 1970 in Wagner's *Parsifal* under Sir Colin DAVIS. Since then she has appeared on both sides of the Atlantic in a wide range of roles, winning particular admiration for her performances in the operas of Mozart and Verdi and making many recordings; her performance at the wedding service of the Prince of Wales to Lady Diana Spencer in 1981 confirmed her as an international star. She also ventured into the lighter side of classical music and pop (she provided 'World in Union' for the World Rugby Cup) and has also recorded native Maori music.

A viable alternative to valium.
IRA SIFF. *Independent.* 1990

Teagarden, Jack (Weldon Leo Teagarden; 1905–64) US JAZZ trombonist and singer, of Red Indian descent, who earned a reputation as the oustanding trombonist of his generation. Teagarden was among the most celebrated jazzmen of the 1930s, when he collaborated with the likes of Paul WHITEMAN and also led his own bands. He also sang with the band of Louis ARMSTRONG in the late 1940s before forming new bands in the 1950s and partnering such fellow-stars as Earl HINES. His mastery of the trombone as a jazz instrument is sometimes compared with that of Louis ARMSTRONG with the trumpet and John COLTRANE with the saxophone. Numbers particularly associated with his name included 'I'm Coming Virginia', 'Stars Fell on Alabama' and 'Basin Street Blues'. His death was hastened by ceaseless touring and his heavy drinking.

Tear, Robert (1939–) Welsh tenor, who won particular acclaim through his long association with the English Opera Group. A former choirboy at St Paul's Cathedral, he established himself as a leading performer in the operas of Benjamin BRITTEN, his voice resembling that of Peter PEARS, and he has also sung Verdi and Mozart with SCOTTISH OPERA.

Tears for Fears British rock group, which came to be regarded as one of the top SYNTHESIZER pop outfits of the 1980s. Singer and bassist Curt Smith (1961–) and singer, guitarist and keyboard player Roland Orzabal (1961–) came together after the SKA group Graduate folded and, with the addition of keyboard player Ian Stanley and drummer Manny Elias, had early hits with 'Mad World' and the album *The Hurting* (1983). Later releases included the albums *Songs from the Big Chair* (1985), from which came 'Shout' and 'Everybody Wants to Rule the World' and *Seeds of Love* (1989) before the band split.

Tebaldi, Renata (1922–) Italian soprano, who was considered the only serious rival to Maria CALLAS as the leading lyric soprano of her era. Having survived polio as an infant, she became one of the favourites at LA SCALA, Milan, where she appeared under Arturo TOSCANINI, and at the METROPOLITAN OPERA in New York. Her most celebrated roles included leading parts in the operas of Verdi and Puccini, as well as the title role in Francesco CILÈA's *Adriana Lecouvreur*.

techno POP music genre, which emerged

from ACID HOUSE in the early 1990s. The techno style, in which the SYNTHESIZER rock of such European bands as TANGERINE DREAM was grafted onto HOUSE DANCE music, was first perfected in Detroit and subsequently swept clubs and discos on both sides of the Atlantic, replete with accompanying visual motifs based on the PSYCHEDELIC era of the late 1960s.

Teddy Bear *See* Teddy PENDERGRASS.

teeny-bop POP music that is aimed specifically at teenagers or at even younger age groups. Although the teenage market was a key influence on the development of ROCK 'N' ROLL in the 1950s, it was not until the 1950s that the record companies made concerted efforts to exploit the newly recognized buying potential of the young. Several groups, such as the MONKEES and the ARCHIES, were specifically created to appeal to younger pop fans (*see* BUBBLEGUM) and particular attention has been paid to satisfying the younger buying market ever since. In the early 1970s there was a rash of teeny-bop releases by the likes of David CASSIDY, the OSMONDS and the BAY CITY ROLLERS, and the charts were regularly dominated by such teen-idols. More recent examples have included the anodyne pop peddled by Australians Jason Donovan and Kylie Minogue, who enjoyed considerable pop success in the late 1980s after leaving the cast of the television soap opera *Neighbours*, and the 1990s 'sensations' NEW KIDS ON THE BLOCK and TAKE THAT. *See also* WEENY-BOP.

Television US rock group, nicknamed the Ice Kings of Rock, which established a cult following during a brief career in the PUNK ROCK era of the late 1970s. Singer and guitarist Tom Verlaine (Tom Miller; 1949–), guitarist Richard Lloyd, bassist Richard Hell (Richard Myers; 1949–), who soon left, and drummer Billy Ficca came together in New York in 1974. Influenced by groups like the VELVET UNDERGROUND, the band released the critically acclaimed album *Marquee Moon* (1977) and the less successful *Adventure* (1978) before breaking up (the live *Blow-Up* following shortly after). The group re-formed, however, in 1991 and re-launched a joint career with the highly praised album *Television*.

telharmonium Electrically powered instrument, which is acknowledged by most music historians to have been the very first electronic instrument. The telharmonium, which weighed 200 tons, was invented by Thadeus Cahill in the USA in 1906 for the express purpose of transmitting music over the telephone lines to the hotels and restaurants of New York.

Temple, Shirley (1928–   ) US film actress and singer, who became the quintessential Hollywood child star in the 1930s. The curly haired Temple was first seen on the big screen when she was four years old, and she had her first big movie hit with *Stand Up and Cheer* in 1934, in which year she won a special Academy Award. Films such as *Little Miss Marker* (1934), *Curly Top* (1935) and *Heidi* (1937) were designed as vehicles for her undoubted talent as dancer and singer. Among her most popular songs were 'On the Good Ship Lollipop', 'Animal Crackers in My Soup' and 'At the Codfish Ball'.

Temple's film career tailed off as she grew older and she retired from the cinema in the 1950s. Following her marriage to Charles Black in 1950 she built a second career in politics, becoming US ambassador to several countries.

Temptations, the Black US all-male vocal group, which was among the top SOUL acts fostered by the MOTOWN organization. Eddie Kendricks (1939–92), David Ruffin (1941–91), Otis Williams (Otis Miles; 1941–   ), Paul Williams (1939–73) and Melvyn Franklin (David English; 1942–95) had huge success with such dance-oriented classics as 'My Girl', one of several of the hits provided for them by Smokey ROBINSON, 'Since I Lost My Baby', 'Cloud Nine', 'You're My Everything', 'Just My Imagination', 'I Can't Get Next to You' and the 1971 chart-topper 'Papa was a Rolling Stone', by which time both Ruffin and Kendricks had left. Albums included *Together* (1970), which the Temptations made in collaboration with the SUPREMES.

10cc British pop group, originally called Hotlegs, which enjoyed massive commercial success in the 1970s. Singers and guitarists Eric Stewart (1945–   ) and Lol Creme (1947–   ), singer and bassist Graham Gouldman (1946–   ) and drummer Kevin Godley (1945–   ) enjoyed a Number Two hit as Hotlegs with 'Neanderthal Man' (1970) before being re-named by producer Jonathan KING (10cc being the amount of semen ejaculated by the human male in sexual intercourse). Among the hit singles that followed were 'Donna' (1972), 'Rubber Bullets' (1973), 'Wall Street Shuffle' (1974), the classic 'I'm Not in Love' (1975), which reached Number One in the UK, and 'Art for Art's Sake' (1975). Godley and Creme then left, going on to build a reputation for video production work and designing a guitar synthesizer dubbed the 'Gizmo', and, after a further Number One in 1978 with 'Dreadlock Holiday', the band finally broke up in 1983, reuniting in 1992.

Ten Years After British BLUES-ROCK group, which enjoyed a brief career at the top in the late 1960s. Led by widely admired singer and guitarist Alvin Lee (Graham Barnes; 1944–   ) and completed by bassist Leo Lyons (1943–   ), keyboard player Chick Churchill (1946–   ) and drummer Ric Lee (1945–   ), the band shot to fame after appearing at WOODSTOCK in 1969. It had big hits with the such singles as 'I'm Going Home'. Among the albums were *Ssssh ...* (1969), *Stonedhenge* (1969) and *Rock and Roll Music to the World* (1972). After a break in 1975, the band re-formed in 1977 as Ten Years Later and released two further albums, and then came together once more in 1989 for *About Time*. Lee's guitar work, highlights of which included rubbing his guitar against the foot of the microphone stand, had a profound effect on the style of numerous AXE heroes in later years.

Tennessee Plowboy, the *See* Eddy ARNOLD.

Tennstedt, Klaus (1926–   ) Highly regarded German conductor, who won particular acclaim for his interpretations of the music of Gustav MAHLER. He was appointed conductor of the LONDON PHILHARMONIC ORCHESTRA in 1983 but his recent career has been much disrupted by ill-health.

Tetrazzini, Luisa (1871–1940) Italian soprano, who became one of the most celebrated opera stars of her generation. Although she rarely attempted much as an actress, Tetrazzini won huge acclaim because of her vocal dexterity. A large woman, she was also famous for her prodigious appetite, and the dish chicken Tetrazzini was named in her honour. On one occasion co-star John MCCORMACK had such difficulty raising her from the floor in the death scene of *La Traviata* that both performers eventually collapsed in a state of helpless laughter.

Tex, Joe (Joseph Arrington; 1933–82) US singer-songwriter, who emerged as one of the first major SOUL stars and who has since been credited as pop music's first RAP artist. Having made his recording début in the late 1950s, Tex had his first hit with 'Baby You're Right' (1961). Among the hits that followed were 'Hold What You Got' (1965), 'You Got What It Takes' (1965), 'The Love You Save' (1965), 'The Letter Song' (1966), 'I Gotcha' (1972), and 'Ain't Gonna Bump No More (With No Big Fatwoman)' (1977). He died after a heart attack.

Texas Troubadour, the See Ernest TUBB.

Teyte, Dame Maggie (Margaret Tate; 1888–1976) British soprano, who was among the most admired singers of her generation. Having trained at the Royal College of Music in London, she completed her studies in Paris, where she attracted the attention of Claude DEBUSSY, who coached her in the role of Mélisande in his opera *Pelléas et Mélisande* and also played piano for her when she was performing his own songs. Equally acclaimed in opera, operetta and musical comedy, her recordings included a highly influential album of Debussy songs made with pianist Alfred CORTOT in 1937. Other highlights of her career included the first performance of *The Perfect Fool* (1923) by Gustav HOLST. She retired in 1955.

> I've never had a gramophone; I never had a picture of myself in my life.
> MAGGIE TEYTE, 1959

Tharpe, Sister Rosetta (Rosetta Nubin; 1915–73) Black US GOSPEL and BLUES singer and guitarist, who became one of the great stars of the modern gospel tradition. Recording with such artists as Cab CALLOWAY and Lucky MILLINDER, she had hits with 'Pickin' the Cabbage', 'Rock Me', 'Shout, Sister, Shout' and 'Up above My Head'. She continued to perform to great acclaim even after having a leg amputated not long before her death.

Theodorakis, Mikis (1925–) Greek composer, who was at the forefront of a revival of Greek FOLK MUSIC in the 1960s. After studying music in Athens and seeing service in the Second World War, Theodorakis continued his musical training under Olivier MESSIAEN in Paris after being deported from Greece and went on to establish a reputation as a composer with such compositions as his First Symphony (1950) and *Five Cretan Songs* (1950). He later wrote several chamber pieces and music for the theatre as well as the ballet *Antigone* (1958). Most popular of all, though, was his score for the film *Zorba the Greek* (1965), which was rapidly taken up as an anthem by those opposing the dictatorial military government in Greece. Other compositions have included the pop oratorio *Axion Esti* (1966), a further three symphonies and the opera *Kostas Kariotakis* (1985).

Theodorakis himself was elected to the Greek government in 1964 and was subsequently imprisoned (1967) for his outspoken views, only being released three years later after international protests. He returned to parliament in 1976, again as a Communist, but resigned in 1986, disillusioned by political progress.

theremin Early electronic instrument, invented in the 1920s by the Russian physicist Lev Theremin, in which the 'note' – or rather the frequency of an oscillating current – was controlled by the movements of the performer's hand close to an antenna. Several composers wrote music especially for the instrument, taking advantage of its ethereal, glissando effects.

Thibaud, Jacques (1880–1953) French violinist, who was among the most acclaimed violinists of his generation. 'Discovered' while playing the violin in the Café Rouge in Paris, he is usually remembered for his part in the celebrated trio he formed with Alfred CORTOT and Pablo CASALS. The fact that he indulged freely in wine, women and gourmet food meant that he had little time to practise his art and consequently his repertoire was unusually small. He died in an air crash in the Alps, but his name is preserved in the Long-Thibaud Competition that he co-founded in 1943.

Thin Lizzy British rock group, which enjoyed considerable commercial success in the 1970s. Led by Irish-born singer and bassist Phil Lynott (1951–86) and completed at its peak by guitarists Brian Robertson (1956–) and Scott Gorham (1951–) together with drummer Brian Downey (1951–), Thin Lizzy enjoyed its first hit with a rock interpretation of the traditional 'Whiskey in the Jar'. Among the hits that followed were the singles 'The Boys are Back in Town' (1976) and 'Dancin' in the

Moonlight' (1977) and the albums *Jail-break* (1976), *Johnny the Fox* (1976), *Bad Reputation* (1977) and *Black Rose* (1979).

Lynott eventually went solo on the group's demise in 1983 and remained in the headlines for his unruly private life. He married the daughter of television celebrity Leslie Crowther in 1980 and had success in the charts with the likes of 'Dear Miss Lonely Hearts' and 'Yellow Peril', but eventually succumbed to his drug addiction after an overdose. Thin Lizzy was revived for a charity concert in 1986, with Bob GELDOF taking Lynott's role.

Thin White Duke, the *See* David BOWIE.

third stream CROSSOVER style in which a marriage of JAZZ and classical music is attempted. Classical musicians of the calibre of Igor STRAVINSKY, Paul HINDEMITH and Aaron COPLAND had incorporated jazz elements in their works since the 1920s, but it was only in the 1960s that 'third stream' began to be discussed as a distinct genre. The US composer Gunther Schuller (1925–) introduced the term in 1959. Overcoming the reluctance of classical musicians to improvise and the fact that few jazzmen could read music well, such composers as Dave BRUBECK had some success with the concept, although it has remained of interest to a largely cult audience.

Thompson, Richard (1949–) British singer-songwriter and guitarist, who emerged as one of the most respected figures on the British FOLK-ROCK scene in the late 1960s. Thompson established his reputation while with FAIRPORT CONVENTION (1967–71), for which he wrote such classics as 'Crazy Man Michael' and 'Farewell, Farewell'. He embarked on a successful solo career with the acclaimed *Henry the Human Fly* (1972) and followed it with *I Want to see the Bright Lights Tonight* (1974), on which he collaborated with his wife Linda. A series of lesser albums culminated in the pair splitting up, personally and professionally, before the time of *Time of Kindness* (1983). Subsequently, however, Thompson staged something of a renaissance and enlarged his audience with a number of highly crafted albums mixing folk, rock, BLUES and JAZZ styles, ultimately winning recognition as a folk-rock figurehead. Recent releases have

included *Amnesia* (1988), *Rumour and Sigh* (1991), *Mirror Blue* (1994) and *You? Me? Us?* (1996).

> I don't play them much. Every couple of years. If a new one comes out, it's nice to play it for a while. But then you start to realize it's just a record like all the others. It's fallible. It's got mistakes in it.
> RICHARD THOMPSON, of his LPs, in *Q* magazine, 1974

Thompson Twins, the British pop group, exponents of SYNTHESIZER pop in the early 1980s. Originally a line-up of seven, which was later reduced to singer and bassist Tom Bailey (1957–), congas and synthesizer player Joe Leeway (1957–) and percussionist Anna Currie (1959–), the Thompson Twins, named after the comic detectives in *Tin Tin*, came together in 1977 and finally achieved fame in 1982 with the single 'Lies'. Among the hits that followed were *Quick Step and Side Kick* (1983) and the singles 'Hold Me Now' (1983), 'Doctor Doctor' (1984), 'Lay Your Hands on Me' (1985) and 'Get That Love' (1986). Leeway left in 1986.

Thomson, Virgil (1896–1989) US composer, whose music combined his US musical heritage and the influence of contemporary French composers. Thomson completed his musical studies under Nadia BOULANGER in Paris, where he came into contact with Erik SATIE and Les SIX, whose influence was to have a profound effect on his later career. His early works included the operas *Four Saints in Three Acts* (1928) and *The Mother of Us All* (1947), on both of which he collaborated with Gertrude Stein, but he established his reputation initially as a music critic, being appointed to the staff of the New York *Herald Tribune* on returning to the USA in 1940. Among the works that followed were several film scores, including that for Robert Flaherty's *Louisiana Story* (1948), the opera *Lord Byron* (1968), ballets, three symphonies and other orchestral and choral pieces as well as a series of musical portraits of various friends.

> The way to write American music is simple. All you have to do is be an American and then write any kind of music you wish.
> VIRGIL THOMSON

> In Thomson ... it is at times hard to decide whether one is dealing with ironically

masked significance or with kindergarten stuff.

ERNST KŘENEK, *Musik im goldenen Westen*, 1949

Thornhill, Claude (1909–65) US bandleader, pianist, composer and arranger, who won many admirers for his arrangements in the 1930s and 1940s. Thornhill started his career as a bandleader remarkably early, forming his first group at the age of six. Subsequently he worked on a riverboat and with such talents as Bunny BERIGAN, Paul WHITEMAN, Benny GOODMAN, Billie HOLIDAY and Ray NOBLE in New York before being recruited by Hollywood. He went on to establish a popular BIG BAND in 1939 and led a series of smaller groups after the Second World War, often using arrangements by Gil EVANS. His most celebrated arrangements included 'Loch Lomond', 'Annie Laurie', 'O sole mio' and 'Hungarian dance'.

Thornton, Big Mama (Willie Mae Thornton; 1926–84) Black US BLUES singer, who ranked among the most respected blues stars of the 1950s and 1960s. Her biggest hits included the original versions of 'Hound Dog' (1953) and 'Ball and Chain' (1969).

Big Mama was present when fellow-blues musician Johnny Ace (pianist to B.B. KING) accidentally killed himself backstage at the Houston Auditorium on Christmas Eve 1954: Ace put a gun to his head and pulled the trigger either thinking it was unloaded or else as part of a game of Russian roulette.

thrash Genre of HEAVY METAL, in which the emphasis is on HARDCORE rock played at high speed and maximum volume. Thrash emerged as a distinct sub-genre in New York in the early 1980s under the influence of PUNK ROCK and has produced such cult star line-ups as Anthrax and Metallica. *See also* SPEED METAL.

Three Degrees, the Black US vocal group, which was the most successful all-girl group of their generation. Fayette Pickney, Linda Turner and Shirley Porter had their first hit back in 1965 but only established themselves as a top chart act in the early 1970s after Turner and Porter were replaced by Sheila Ferguson and Valerie Thompson. Among their biggest hits were 'When Will I See You Again' (1974) and 'My Simple Heart' (1979). No harm was done to the group's popularity when it was disclosed that they were the Prince of Wales's favourite group.

Three Dog Night US pop group, which enjoyed considerable transatlantic success in the early 1970s. The group was formed from singers Danny Hutton (1946–), Chuck Negron (1942–) and Cory Wells (1942–), together with guitarist Mike Allsup (1947–), keyboard player Jimmy Greenspoon (1948–), bassist Joe Schermie (1948–) and drummer Floyd Sneed (1943–), who came together in 1968 and quickly established a following among R 'N' B fans. Hit releases – mostly COVERS – included the singles 'One' (1969), 'Mama Told Me Not to Come' (1970) and 'Joy to the World' (1971) and the albums *Captured Live at the Forum* (1969) and *Golden Biscuits* (1971). The band gradually disintegrated in the late 1970s.

The name Three Dog Night was apparently a reference to an Aboriginal phrase describing a very cold night (during which the freezing aborigines curled up with their dogs for warmth). Danny Hutton enjoyed a second career providing voices for Hanna-Barbera cartoons.

Thrush and the Blue Voice, the *See* Carlos GARDEL.

Tiger, the *See* FABIAN.

Timber *See* Sir Henry WOOD.

timps The kettledrums, otherwise the timpani (*timpano* being Italian for a drum). The term timpani has substantially replaced the old 'kettledrum' since 1900. The traditional kettledrum had taps all the way round the rim and these had to be carefully adjusted in order to change the pitch; the introduction of pedal timpani around the turn of the century made this much easier and also allowed the execution of glissandi, an effect used, for example, in Carl NIELSEN's Fourth Symphony and on more than one occasion by Béla BARTÓK.

Tin Pan Alley The mythical place where popular music is composed, packaged and published – and by extension, popular music itself. The term dates from the early 1920s and is derived from the phrase 'tin-pan shower', a rural Americanism for a noisy serenade or any discordant racket.

Another explanation of the term is that it refers to the noise raised by rival musicians when one of their number auditioned for too long or too loudly. In so far as Tin Pan Alley can be given a geographical location, it lies in the region of West 28th Street, New York, in the USA and in Denmark Street, London in the UK – although the once-resident music publishers have long since departed for larger premises elsewhere. *See also* BRILL BUILDING.

Tiomkin, Dimitri (1894–1979) US composer, conductor and pianist, born in Russia, who is usually remembered for his many classic film scores. Having studied music at the St Petersburg Conservatory, where his teacher was Alexander GLAZUNOV, he arrived in the USA in 1925. Winner of several Academy Awards, he wrote the music for such films as *Lost Horizon* (1937), *The Moon and Sixpence* (1942), *Portrait of Jennie* (1948), *High Noon* (1952), *The High and the Mighty* (1954), *Giant* (1956), *Gunfight at the OK Corral* (1957), *The Old Man and the Sea* (1958), *The Alamo* (1960) and *The Guns of Navarone* (1961).

Tippett, Sir Michael Kemp (1905–   ) British composer, who has been described as the most important British composer since Benjamin BRITTEN. A graduate of the Royal College of Music where his teachers included Sir Adrian BOULT and Sir Malcolm SARGENT, Tippett was politically active in the 1930s, identifying with the plight of the unemployed during the Depression and conducting an orchestra of out-of-work musicians in London. He was gaoled as a conscientious objector during the Second World War but was already being hailed as a major musical talent on the strength of such early works as the first sonata for piano (1937), a concerto for double string orchestra (1939) and the much admired oratorio *A Child of Our Time* (1944), which concerned the real-life murder of a Nazi official by a young Jewish boy.

After the war Tippett won praise for a series of operas, which were both technically advanced and committed to his humanist philosophy. As well as the operas *The Midsummer Marriage* (1955), which took seven years to finish, the dissonant *King Priam* (1962), *The Knot Garden* (1970), which revolves around the passions of seven people meeting in a garden, *The Ice Break* (1977) and *New Year* (1989),

he has written four symphonies, four string quartets, four piano sonatas, song cycles and the oratorio *The Mask of Time* (1983). Influences on his work have ranged from Beethoven to the BLUES. He taught at London's Morley College in the 1940s and was appointed president of the London College of Music in 1983.

> If, in the music I write, I can create a world of sound wherein some, at least, of my generation can find refreshment for the inner life, then I am doing my work properly.
> MICHAEL TIPPETT, *Moving into Aquarius*, 1959

toasting In REGGAE, the tradition of chanting improvised lyrics live over a pre-recorded backing. The idea reached its apotheosis some years later in RAP.

Top of the Pops Celebrated BBC television music programme, based on the pop charts, which has run without a break since 1964. Providing pop fans with a weekly glimpse of current chart heroes, the programme has become an institution, in spite of the carpings of its many critics, who have condemned its superficiality and commercial bias. The fact that artists frequently mime to their records has also proved a bone of contention, even with the artists themselves – Wizzard's Roy Wood (*see* the MOVE), for instance, got into trouble for making little or no pretence that he was actually singing. The programme remains important for the influence it has over the buying public, although the emergence of rival programmes adopting a more in-depth approach in the 1980s obliged the BBC to restyle some aspects of the programme's presentation.

Artists screened on the very first edition, on New Year's Day 1964, were the DAVE CLARK FIVE, the ROLLING STONES, the HOLLIES, Dusty SPRINGFIELD and the Swinging Blue Jeans. Famous mishaps since then have included an embarrassing moment when Jimi HENDRIX found himself miming to a single by Alan PRICE ('I like the voice, man, but I don't know the words') and an introduction by disc jockey Alan Freeman, who garbled the title 'Cast Your Fate to the Winds' as 'Cast Your Wind to the Fate'. For many years, highlights of the programme included the dancing of Pan's People, a troupe of girl dancers who attracted the outrage of many viewers scandalized by their short skirts.

Tormé, Mel(vin Howard) (1925–   ) US
JAZZ singer, actor, songwriter, pianist and
drummer, nicknamed the Singer's Singer
and the Velvet Fog, who was a popular star
of the 1940s. He made his début as a
singer on the radio when he was only four
years old, and he subsequently sang with
several leading bands and in a number of
musical films. With his group the Mel-
tones, he recorded the hit 'What is This
Thing Called Love?' with Artie SHAW in
1944 and went solo soon after; other hits
included 'The Christmas Song' (1946),
'County Fair' (1948), 'Careless Hands'
(1949), 'California Suite' (1949) and
'Mountain Greenery' (1954).

Tornados, the British pop group, which was
the first British act to top the US singles
charts. Guitarists Alan Caddy (1940–   )
and George Bellamy (1941–   ), keyboard
player Roger Lavern (Roger Jackson;
1938–   ), bassist Heinz Burt (1942–   )
and drummer Clem Cattini (1939–   )
came together in 1961 and – after working
as backing musicians for Billy FURY – established themselves as one of the great
instrumental groups with such hits as 'Telstar' (1962), which became a transatlantic
Number One (Telstar was the name of a US
communications satellite that had been
recently launched). The Tornados then
went into a gradual decline, finally breaking up in 1965, but reuniting briefly in the
mid-1970s and again in 1989.

Tortelier, Paul (1914–90) French cellist,
composer and conductor, who was one of
the most accomplished cellists of his generation. A graduate of the Paris Conservatoire, Tortelier was recruited by the BOSTON
SYMPHONY ORCHESTRA (1937–40) and went
on to win acclaim throughout the USA and
Europe both as a soloist and in concert
with other gifted members of his family. A
distinguished teacher at the Paris Conservatoire, where his pupils included Jacqueline DU PRÉ, he also wrote a number of
pieces, including the *Israel Symphony*
(1956), and wrote extensively about
music. His son Yan Pascal Tortelier
(1947–   ) became principal conductor of
the BBC Philharmonic in 1992, while his
daughter Maria de la Pau (1950–   ) won
acclaim as a pianist.

Toscanini, Arturo (1867–1957) Italian
conductor, nicknamed the Old Man because
he continued working into his nineties, who
became one of the legends of twentieth-
century classical music. Having shown
early promise as a musician, the young
Toscanini was enrolled as a student at the
Parma Conservatory at the age of nine, and
he later embarked on a career as a professional cellist, performing in the premiere of
Verdi's *Otello* in 1887. He made his début as
a conductor when he was 19 years old,
quickly establishing himself as one of the
most able conductors of his generation and
appearing at virtually all the leading opera
houses, where he won particular praise for
his interpretations of Verdi, PUCCINI,
Wagner and Richard STRAUSS.

Famous for often conducting entirely
from memory, he also became renowned for
his bad temper, being nicknamed 'Tosca-
nono' because of his frequent shouts of 'No,
no, no, NO!' at players under his baton. His
rages were legendary. He would hurl scores
at players, bellowing 'I understand you
make the mistake once, yes, but I do not
understand you make it a second time,' and
he was generally unforgiving towards
musicians who offended him.

Toscanini was three times appointed to
top posts at LA SCALA (1898–1903,
1906–08 and 1920–29), but the managing directors were not heartbroken when he
left. He once rehearsed Mozart's *Don Giovanni* for three months, only to drop it after
the dress rehearsal, saying 'it can't be done'.
Other appointments included conductor at
the METROPOLITAN OPERA, New York
(1908–21).

When Toscanini was appointed to conduct the re-formed Philharmonic Orchestra
(1929–36) in New York, players there
expected the worst and were not disappointed. Everything they had heard about
the great man breaking more batons than
any other conductor and being able to spot
an incorrect bow movement at 10 yards
was quite true. When one trumpeter fell foul
of his new master, the condemnation was
damning: 'God tells one how the music
should sound, but you stand in the way.'
During another difficult rehearsal he told his
orchestra: 'After I die I am coming back to
earth as the doorkeeper of a bordello. And I
won't let a one of you in.' Some of the musicians even kept pictures of a scowling
Toscanini to show to their children, warning them that he would pay them a visit if
they misbehaved.

Refusing to conduct under the Fascists in Germany and Italy, Toscanini ended his career with the National Broadcasting Company Symphony Orchestra (1937–53), which was created specifically for him. He gave his last performance in 1954, at the age of 87.

> I am a pig.
>
> ARTURO TOSCANINI, to Sir John Barbirolli, 1940

Tosh, Peter (Winston MacIntosh; 1944–87) Jamaican singer-songwriter, who became one of the top REGGAE stars of the 1970s and 1980s. Tosh, who had started out as one of Bob MARLEY's backing band the Wailers, embarked on a solo career in 1973, earning a reputation for his songs on issues of social concern. Among his albums were *Legalize It* (1976), which pressed for the decriminalization of marijuana, *Equal Rights* (1977), *Bush Doctor* (1978), on which he sang with Mick JAGGER, *Mama Africa* (1983) and *No Nuclear War* (1987). He consolidated his large following in the 1980s, but his career was tragically cut short when he was shot dead by extortionists at his house in Kingston.

Toto US rock band, which became established as a top ADULT-ORIENTED ROCK act in the late 1970s. The group, which consisted of former SESSION musicians singer Bobby Kimball (Robert Toteaux; 1967–), who was later replaced by Dennis 'Fergie' Fredericksen (1951–) and then Joseph Williams, guitarist Steve Lukather (1957–), keyboard players Steve Porcaro (1957–) and David Paich (1954–), bassist David Hungate and Jeff Porcaro (1954–92), came together in 1978 and won immediate acclaim with its technically polished, eponymous début album (1978). Among the most successful of the band's releases since then have been *Toto IV* (1982), from which came the hit single 'Africa', *Fahrenheit* (1986), *The Seventh One* (1988) and *Kingdom of Desire* (1992). Toto also provided the soundtrack for the disastrous science-fiction movie *Dune* (1984).

Tottenham Sound, the The pop music of the London-based group the DAVE CLARK FIVE, which enjoyed a vogue in the mid-1960s. A rival to the MERSEY BEAT of the BEATLES, the Tottenham Sound was the only serious challenge to the LENNON AND MCCARTNEY regime around 1964–65.

Toussaint, Allen (1938–) US composer, singer and pianist, who wrote numerous RHYTHM-AND-BLUES classics in the 1960s. Having started out as a pianist, he wrote such hits as 'Java', 'Ride Your Pony', 'Working in a Coalmine', 'Mother-in-Law' and 'Holy Cow', in addition to making records himself and running his own studio in New Orleans. He has since worked with such artists as Joe COCKER and Paul SIMON.

Townshend, Pete *See* the WHO.

Toxic Twins, the *See* AEROSMITH.

Toyah (Toyah Ann Willcox; 1958–) British pop singer and actress, born in Birmingham, who emerged as a top NEW WAVE artist in the early 1980s. Having appeared as a punk in Derek Jarman's film *Jubilee*, she established herself in the charts on the strength of her image as a colourful young punk rebel. 'It's a Mystery' (1981), her first big hit, was followed by such singles as 'I Want to be Free' (1981). At the same time she continued to consolidate her reputation as a film actress, appearing in further Jarman movies and on stage in *Trafford Tanzi*. She eventually married former KING CRIMSON star Robert FRIPP, but her chart successes petered out with a series of less accessible and more challenging releases in the late 1980s.

trad Traditional JAZZ, as played by numerous jazz revivalists yearning for the good old days before the development of SWING and BEBOP and other modern styles. Generally playing the good-time music associated with the original DIXIELAND bands of the early part of the century, such musicians are often dubbed 'mouldy figs' by their detractors, who argue that jazz by its very nature must be innovative and constantly changing. Trad as a genre established itself in the 1940s, when exponents of COOL jazz threatened to take their music further still from its cherished roots. Beneficial side-effects of the revival included the tracing and recording of many of the early jazz pioneers, whose music would otherwise have been lost to future generations.

Traffic British rock group, which, during a brief but highly celebrated career in the late 1960s, pioneered the PROGRESSIVE ROCK style. Lead singer, keyboard player and guitarist Steve Winwood (1948–), guitarist Dave Mason (1947–), woodwind player Chris Wood (1944–83) and drummer Jim

Capaldi (1944–) came together in 1967 and had immediate success with such PSY-CHEDELIC singles as 'Paper Sun' and 'Hole in My Shoe' as well as with the album *Mr Fantasy*. *Traffic* followed in 1968, but clashes between Mason and Winwood led to the band breaking up that year. Capaldi, Wood and Winwood reunited for *John Barleycorn Must Die* (1969) and they had another big success with *Low Spark of High-Heeled Boys* (1971) before their joint career went into decline, although *Where the Eagle Flies* (1974) marked a return to form. They reunited in 1994 for *Far From Home*.

Travis, Merle (1917–83) US COUNTRY singer-songwriter and guitarist, who had numerous hits after the Second World War. A former US marine, he established himself as a country legend with such songs as 'Old Mountain Dew', 'Dark as a Dungeon' and 'Sixteen Tons' and made several film appearances. It was at Travis's suggestion that the first solid-body electric guitars were built.

Tremeloes, the British pop group, which had a string of hit singles in the mid-1960s. The group consisted of lead singer and guitarist Brian Poole (1941–), guitarist Graham Scott, who was soon replaced by Rick West (Richard Westwood; 1943–), saxophonist (and subsequently bassist) Ken Howard (1942–) and drummer Alan Blakely (1942–), who switched to guitar and keyboards with the addition of drummer Dave Munden (1943–). The Tremeloes came together in 1959 and won their first recording contract (with Decca) in 1962, in competition with the BEATLES. They had big hits with singles like 'Twist and Shout' and 'Do you Love Me', which topped the charts in the UK in 1963, and then Poole went solo, eventually retiring from the limelight to run the family butcher shop. He was succeeded by Len 'Chip' Hawkes (1946–), with whom the group returned to the top of the charts with such hits as 'Here Comes My Baby' and 'Silence is Golden' (1967), the group's second British Number One. Attempts to adopt a stronger ROCK sound failed in the early 1970s, and the Tremeloes ended up on the CABARET circuit. Hawkes's son Chesney Hawkes became a teen-idol in the early 1990s.

tribute band A POP group that seeks to imitate one of the classic bands of the past, copying the appearance, mannerisms and speech of the stars as well as seeking to reproduce their music as faithfully as possible. Most successful of the tribute bands that enjoyed a vogue in the early 1990s was the Australian group Bjorn Again, which was based on the Swedish pop group ABBA, although others included mimics of the ROLLING STONES. The BEATLES have spawned more tribute bands than most. The most remarkable of them was undoubtedly the Bumblers, who were formed in the USA to send up the Fab Four in 1964; the Bumblers were Bing CROSBY, Sammy DAVIS JNR, Dean MARTIN and Frank SINATRA.

Troggs, the British pop group, which enjoyed huge transatlantic success in the mid-1960s. At its peak, the group consisted of lead singer Reg Presley (Reg Ball; 1943–), guitarist Chris Britton (1945–), bassist Peter Staples (1944–) and drummer Ronnie Bond (Ronnie Bullins; 1943–92), and it had massive hits with such classics as 'Wild Thing' (1966), 'With a Girl Like You' (1966), which got to Number One in the UK, 'I Can't Control Myself' (1966), 'Give It to Me' (1967) and 'Love is All Around' (1967). The group was subsequently rocked by line-up changes but stayed in business with the occasional new release, notably the single 'Feels Like a Woman' (1972) and the album *Athens to Andover* (1991), on which it collaborated with rock group REM.

truth JAZZ slang for a piece of music that is so perfect that it communicates something about the essential nature of its subject, be it love or existence itself. It was first heard among aficionados in the 1940s.

> Jazz has always been a man telling the truth about himself.
> QUINCY JONES

> The jazz band can be used for artificial excitement and aphrodisiac purposes, but not for spreading eternal truths.
> ARTHUR BLISS, 'Music Policy', 1941

Tubb, Ernest (Dale) (1914–84) US COUNTRY singer and guitarist, nicknamed the Texas Troubadour, who became one of the top exponents of the WESTERN SWING style. Influenced by the music of Jimmie RODGERS, he had his first big hit in 1942 with 'I'm Walking the Floor Over You' and went on to star on the GRAND OLE OPRY, pioneering the use of the electric guitar in country circles.

Among the hits that followed were 'Tomorrow Never Comes' and 'Filipino Baby'. His record shop in Nashville became world famous.

> This place sure could hold a lot of hay.
> ERNEST TUBB, on seeing Carnegie Hall for the first time, 1947

Tubes, the US rock band, which established an international reputation with its brand of rock theatre in the 1970s. Bassist Rick Anderson, keyboard players Vince Welnick and Michael Cotten, guitarists Roger Steen and Bill Spooner, singers Fee Waybill and Re Styles and drummer Prairie Prince came together in 1972 and rapidly perfected their colourful and often daring live act. *The Tubes* (1975), which included 'White Punks on Dope' and 'Mondo Bondage', brought immediate acclaim, and it was followed by albums like *Young and Rich* (1976), *Remote Control* (1979), *Outside, Inside* (1983), from which came 'She's a Beauty', and *Love Bomb* (1986), which did less well and marked the band's swansong.

Tucker, Sophie (Sonia Kalish; 1884–1966) US singer and actress, nicknamed the Last of the Red Hot Mommas after the title of her song 'I'm the Last of the Red Hot Mammas', which was written by Jack Yellen. Tucker became a legendary star of CABARET and vaudeville in the 1920s. Born in Russia, she established a reputation as one of the great characters of contemporary entertainment with a particularly brash and often frankly coarse sense of humour. She was recruited as a black-face singer by Florenz ZIEGFELD for the *Follies* in 1909 and included among her biggest hits 'Some of These Days' (1926) and 'My Yiddishe Momme' (1928). She led her own band in the 1930s and made several appearances both on Broadway and in film MUSICALS of the 1930s and 1940s. Her generous size led to her also being dubbed Sophie Tuckshop by her fans.

> Hiya, king!
> SOPHIE TUCKER, to George V, 1934

> From birth to age eighteen, a girl needs good parents. From eighteen to thirty-five, she needs good looks. From thirty-five to fifty-five, she needs a good personality. From fifty-five on, she needs good cash.
> SOPHIE TUCKER (attributed)

Tuckwell, Barry (1931–) Australian horn player and conductor, who has won recognition as the foremost horn player of modern times. Having arrived in the UK in 1950, Tuckwell won acclaim for his work with the LONDON SYMPHONY ORCHESTRA before embarking on a solo career in 1968 and going on to form his own celebrated wind quintet. Several leading contemporary composers, including Thea MUSGRAVE, have written works for him.

Turner, Dame Eva (1892–1990) British soprano, who was hailed as one of the outstanding operatic sopranos to grace the British stage. She won acclaim while with the Carl Rosa Opera company in the 1920s and was subsequently invited to perform at LA SCALA under Arturo TOSCANINI. Her most celebrated role was the title part in PUCCINI's *Turandot*.

Turner, Joe (Joseph Vernon Turner; 1911–85) US BLUES singer-songwriter, nicknamed Big Joe, who emerged as one of the top stars of the RHYTHM-AND-BLUES scene in the 1950s. Turner formed an influential partnership with pianist Pete Johnson in the 1930s and subsequently made many recordings with Art TATUM and others before adapting his blues-shouting style to r 'n' b in the 1950s. Among the biggest hits he subsequently enjoyed were the classics 'Shake, Rattle and Roll', 'Corrine Corrina', 'Lipstick, Powder and Paint' and 'Sweet Sixteen'.

Turner, Tina (Annie Mae Bullock; 1938–) Black US singer and actress, who established herself as a top RHYTHM-AND-BLUES star in the 1960s in company with husband Ike Turner (1931–) and later forged a second career as a solo artist. Trading on her powerful vocal capabilities and visual appeal, she married former blues pianist Ike Turner in 1958 and enjoyed major commercial success with singles produced by Phil SPECTOR. 'It's Gonna Work Out Fine' (1961), 'River Deep, Mountain High' (1966), 'Proud Mary' (1971) and 'Nutbush City Limits' (1973) were among the hits that brought them a huge mixed-race audience. They divorced in 1976, but Tina Turner continued to prosper with her singing, but also acting in the rock opera *Tommy* (1975) and in the film *Mad Max Beyond Thunderdome* (1985). Her solo albums have included *Private Dancer* (1984), *Break Every Rule* (1987), *Live in Europe* (1988), *Foreign Affair* (1989) and *Wildest Dreams* (1996); among the singles have been 'Let's Stay Together' (1983) and 'What's Love Got to Do with It?' (1984).

Turtles, the US pop group, which were regularly in the singles charts on both sides of the Atlantic in the mid-1960s. Singers Howard Kaylan (Howard Kaplan; 1945–) and Mark Volman (1944–), guitarists Al Nichol (1945–) and Jim Tucker, bassist Chuck Portz (1945–), who was later replaced by Jim Pons and drummer Don Murray (1945–), who was succeeded by John Barbata, got together as a surfing band but subsequently established themselves as idols of the protest movement with a cover of DYLAN's 'It Ain't Me Babe' (1966). Among the hits that followed were 'Let Me Be' (1966), 'Happy Together' (1967), 'She'd Rather be with Me' (1967), 'Elenore' (1968) and 'You Showed Me' (1969). The group split up before the end of the decade, Kaylan and Volman going on to work with Frank ZAPPA and as Flo and Eddie.

12-note music Atonal system of composition, which was developed in the 1920s by the Austrian composer Arnold SCHOEN-BERG. Also known as dodecacophony, the system works on the principle that all notes are equal – that is, there is no hegemony of 'superior' notes that are used more often because they happen to fall within the scale of the key in which the work is written. Thus, 12-note music is not written in a particular key but is based on a 12-note sequence decided on by the composer and repeated, played back to front and so forth, with various modulations and other variant factors added.

Not surprisingly, the advent of 12-note music was greeted with fierce controversy. Opposition was particularly strong in Germany and Austria where the Nazis took exception to it, identifying it with the Jews (Schoenberg himself was Jewish) and possibly seeing in its system of equal notes parallels with Communist thinking. Among those to experiment further with the 12-note system in their music were Alban BERG, Anton WEBERN and Igor STRA-VINSKY. *See also* KNITTING-PATTERN MUSIC; SERIALISM.

> From now on music will no longer be what it was, but has become what it will be. This change can be likened to the change from the Euclidean geometry to

the higher mathematics of a Minkowski, an Einstein.
> LOUIS DANZ, 'Schoenberg the Inevitable', in *Schoenberg*, 1937

> There is little probability that the 12-note scale will ever produce anything more than morbid or entirely cerebral growths. It might deal successfully with neuroses of various kinds, but I cannot imagine it associated with any healthy and happy concept such as young love of the coming of Spring.
> ARNOLD BAX, *Music and Letters*, 1951

> I can see it taking no part in the music-lover's music-making.
> BENJAMIN BRITTEN

> No theme but 12 variations on it.
> Anonymous critic of Berg's Twelve Piano Variations (1908)

Twentieth-century Gabriel, the *See* Erskine HAWKINS.

Twitty, Conway (Harold Jenkins; 1933–93) US singer, who became a top COUNTRY star with a record tally of US Number Ones to his credit. Having started out as a country artist, he won a contract with SUN RECORDS and went on to adopt a ROCK 'N' ROLL style. Basing his vocal delivery on that of Elvis PRE-SLEY, he had early hits with such singles as 'It's Only Make Believe' (1958), which reached Number One on both sides of the Atlantic, 'Story of My Love' (1959), 'Lonely Boy Blue (1959) and 'Mona Lisa' (1959). He reverted to a more conventional country style and became a long-standing favourite with country fans, often in partnership with Loretta LYNN. The pseudonym Conway Twitty is said to have come about after the star passed through towns called Conway and Twitty during an early tour; Peter Sellers invented his own parody of Twitty under the name Twit Conway. Twitty's name is preserved in two business enterprises in which he had a hand – on a chain of burger restaurants called Twitty Burgers and the other a theme park in Hendersonville called Twitty City.

two-tone Name given to the SKA revival, which swept British pop music in the late 1970s and early 1980s. Such multi-racial bands as the BEAT and UB40 forged a new marriage between the Black REGGAE tradition and White pop.

Tyler, Bonnie (1953–) Welsh rock singer,

who won acclaim in the late 1970s and 1980s for her distinctive, husky vocal delivery (actually the result of an only partially successful throat operation). After a lengthy period as a club singer, Tyler had a big hit with the single 'Lost in France' (1976) and went on to have renewed success with such releases as 'It's a Heartache' (1978), 'Total Eclipse of the Heart' (1983), 'Rockin' Good Way' (1984), 'Holding Out for a Hero' (1984) and 'Hide Your Heart' (1988); her albums include *Faster than the Speed of Night* (1983), *Sweet Dreams and Forbidden Fire* (1984) and *Bitterblue* (1991).

U–V

U2 Irish NEW WAVE rock band, which conquered the world in the 1980s with a unique brand of guitar rock. Lead singer Bono (Paul Hewson; 1960–), guitarist the Edge (David Evans; 1961–), bassist Adam Clayton (1960–) and drummer Larry Mullen (1961–) came together, under the name Feedback, in 1976 while the various members were still at school in Dublin. The fact that Bono – whose pseudonym was borrowed from one Bono Vox, hearing aid supplier – was the only member who could not play an instrument led to a move, fortunately unsuccessful, to have him replaced.

Following the success of the albums *Boy* (1980), *October* (1981), the chart-topping *War* (1983) and the live set *Under a Blood Red Sky* (1983), U2 consolidated their reputation with *The Unforgettable Fire* (1984), *The Joshua Tree* (1987), *Rattle and Hum* (1988), *Achtung Baby* (1991), *Zooropa* (1993) and *Pop* (1997) and the group appeared live with such stars as Bruce SPRINGSTEEN, Bob DYLAN and B.B. KING. The anthemic 'Sunday, Bloody Sunday' was one of several songs to arouse political controversy, although most have hailed the band for its committed humanitarian stand on contemporary moral issues – it rejected violence of all kinds and took part in various charitable and political events.

> I'm a member of the Frisbeetarian order. I believe that when you die, your soul goes up on a roof and you can't get it down again.
> BONO

UB40 British pop group of the early 1980s, which broke new ground with its multiracial line-up playing White REGGAE. Lead singer Ali Campbell (1959–), guitarist Robin Campbell (1954–), the sons of Scottish-born folksinger Ian Campbell, bassist Earl Falconer (1959–), keyboard player Mickey Virtue (1957–), saxophonist Brian Travers (1959–), drummer Jim Brown (1957–), percussionist Norman Hassan (1958–) and backing singer Terence 'Astro' Wilson (1957–) came together in Birmingham in the late 1970s and quickly established a large and loyal following. The band's political sympathies were underlined by the lyrical content of such singles as 'One in Ten', which related to the current unemployment figures, while the band's name was derived from the UK government form issued to those claiming unemployment benefit. 'Red Red Wine' (written by Neil DIAMOND) reached Number One in 1983 and topped the US charts on its re-release in 1988; the group's COVER of 'I Got You Babe' (1985), with Chrissie Hynde, brought a second British chart-topper. Best-selling albums have included *Signing Off* (1980), *Labour of Love* (1983), *Rat in the Kitchen* (1986) and *Promises and Lies* (1993).

UFO British rock band, which emerged as a popular HEAVY METAL outfit in the 1970s. Lead singer Phil Mogg (1951–), drummer Andy Parker, bassist Pete Way and guitarist Mick Bolton came together in 1969 as Hocus Pocus. As UFO, the band had moderate success with early PSYCHEDELIC space-rock releases and then switched to a HARD ROCK style on the acclaimed *Phenomenon* (1974), with Michael Schenker replacing Bolton. Among the hit albums that followed were *Lights Out* (1977) and the live *Strangers in the Night* (1979). Schenker left in 1978, and the band went into decline with various line-up changes, disbanding in 1983, and attempts at reunions since then have failed to excite much interest.

Ukulele Ike *See* Cliff EDWARDS.

Ultravox British NEW WAVE rock group, which was among the best-selling electropop acts of the early 1980s. Lead singer John Foxx (Dennis Leigh), keyboard player Billy Currie (1952–), bassist Chris Cross (Chris Allen; 1952–), guitarist Steve Shears and drummer Warren Cann (1952–) issued a début album, *Ultravox*, in 1977 but had little success until Robin

Simon replaced Shears and singer and guitarist Midge Ure (James Ure; 1953–   ) took the place of Foxx when he went solo. The LP *Vienna* (1980), incorporating a title track that made a best-selling single, established the band's reputation; among the albums that followed were *Rage in Eden* (1981), *Quartet* (1982), *Monument* (1983) and *Lament* (1984). Ure's solo career took off after he co-wrote the BAND AID single 'Do They Know It's Christmas?' in 1984, and Ultravox broke up after *U-Vox* (1986). Ure himself topped the British charts in 1985 with 'If I was'. A re-formed Ultravox had limited success in 1993 with *Revelation*.

Uncrowned King of Light Music, the *See* Eric COATES.

Uptown Palace, the *See* APOLLO THEATRE.

Uriah Heep British rock band, which was established as one of the most enduring rock institutions in the early 1970s. The group, which consisted of lead singer David Byron (1947–85), guitarist Mick Box (1947–   ), keyboard player Ken Hensley (1945–   ), bassist Paul Newton and drummer Alan Napier, was named after the character in Charles Dickens's *David Copperfield*, and it made its mark as a pioneer of HEAVY METAL with the début album *Very 'Eavy, Very 'Umble* (1970). Other releases included *Look At Yourself* (1971), *Demons and Wizards* (1972), *Return to Fantasy* (1975), *Abominog* (1982) and – after numerous changes in line-up – *Live in Moscow* (1988), which marked the group's concerts as the first heavy metal outfit to play in the Russian capital.

USO United Service Organizations, the US equivalent of the British ENSA unit.

utility music Music that is written with a specific social or political purpose or need in mind. In the early years of the century the possibilities of music for a wider range of purposes than pure enjoyment or spiritual enlightenment were largely unrealized. Elbert Hubbard spoke for many when he observed in 1900: 'Music is the only one of the arts that can not be prostituted to a base use.' Within years, however, Hubbard was to be proved quite wrong.

The term 'utility music' was coined by the German composer Besseler in 1925 (as *Gebrauchsmusik*) to describe the tendency of

contemporary German composers to produce music for mass consumption (something made possible by the development of the media). This included music written for the wireless, the cinema, for performance by amateurs and pieces composed for overtly political purposes.

The Swiss composer Arthur HONEGGER was typical, producing much utility music for films and radio documentaries as well as more 'serious' works. In the UK, meanwhile, Benjamin BRITTEN wrote music for documentaries put out by the General Post Office in the 1930s (it was while working on these that he met the poet W.H. Auden) in the belief that the composer should be of use to society: 'I believe that the artist *should* be part of his community, *should* work for it and be used *by* it. Over the last hundred years this has become rarer and rarer and the artist and community have both suffered as a result.'

Aaron COPLAND, Paul HINDEMITH and Carl ORFF similarly felt an obligation to serve the needs of society as composers, Hindemith writing copiously for amateur musicians, while Sir Edward ELGAR's 'Pomp and Circumstance Marches' were also intended to fulfil a jingoistic public purpose ('Land of Hope and Glory' becoming an unofficial second national anthem).

A more sinister side to utility music was revealed in Soviet Russia under Stalin, however, and many Soviet composers were commissioned to write works that aimed to bolster the image of communist ideology (*see* SOCIALIST REALISM). In Germany the propaganda films of the Third Reich demanded suitable musical accompaniment, which, when not Wagner (Hitler's favourite composer), was composed specifically for the purpose.

> We must cultivate a sense of musical citizenship: why should not the musician be the servant of the State and build national monuments like the painter, the writer or the architect?
> RALPH VAUGHAN WILLIAMS

> Music is essentially useless, as life is: but both lend utility to their conditions.
> GEORGE SANTAYANA, *Little Essays*, 1920

> There is no regular demand for musical material as there is for writing material or boxes of matches; there is only a demand for something which creates its own demand – a good piece of music.
> CONSTANT LAMBERT, *Music Ho!*, 1934

Vagabond Lover, the *See* Rudy VALLEE.

Valens, Ritchie (Richie Valenzuela; 1941–59) US pop singer, of part-Mexican descent, who had a brief career at the top in the late 1950s. Valens owed the recording contract he won in 1958 to his good looks, but he quickly established himself as a popular star with such classic hits as 'Come On Let's Go' (1958), 'Donna' (1958) and 'La Bamba' (1958). His career ended prematurely when he was killed in the same air crash that claimed the lives of the BIG BOPPER and Buddy HOLLY.

The real 'Donna', incidentally, was Donna Fox, a 15-year-old girl with whom Valens once had a date. Later in life she became a mortgage consultant.

Vallee, Rudy (Hubert Prior Vallee; 1901–86) US singer-songwriter, actor, saxophonist and bandleader, who was one of the first CROONERS to establish a following in the 1930s. Vallee led his first professional DANCE BAND in 1927 and showed promise as a singer with such early hits as 'I'm Just a Vagabond Lover', which provided him with his nickname, and 'My Time is Your Time'. Success as a live and radio performer brought Vallee a huge devoted audience, and he was elevated to idol status. He appeared in a number of films and reigned supreme in the early 1930s before the emergence of Bing CROSBY. After service in the Second World War he concentrated on his film career, although he continued to perform such old favourites as 'As Time Goes By', 'Dancing with Tears in My Eyes', 'Life is Just a Bowl of Cherries' and 'Say It Isn't So'.

Van Halen US rockband, which became one of the top HEAVY METAL outfits of the 1980s. Lead singer Dave Lee Roth (1955–), guitarist Eddie Van Halen (1957–), drummer Alex Van Halen (1955–) and bassist Michael Anthony (1955–) came together in 1974 and finally made a commercial breakthrough with a COVER version of 'You Really Got Me', before consolidating their reputation with such albums as *Van Halen* (1978) and *Van Halen II* (1979). Roth emerged as one of the liveliest frontmen in rock, while Eddie Van Halen became something of an 'AXE hero', mixing rock with elements of SOUL and the BLUES. The hit single 'Jump', from *1984*, topped the US

charts in 1984. The band broke up in 1986, but re-formed, with Sammy Hagar (1947–) taking Roth's place, and went on to release three platinum-selling LPs in the shape of *5150* (1986), the title of which referred to a police code for 'criminally insane', *OU812* (1988) and *For Unlawful Carnal Knowledge* (1991), which caused controversy when the title was reduced to the inevitable acronym based on the first letter of each word. *Balance* topped the US charts in 1995 and *The Best of Van Halen* became Number One in the UK in 1996, in which year Hagar was replaced by the returning Roth.

Van Heusen, James (Edward Chester Babcock; 1913–90) US songwriter and pianist, who became one of the most successful of all the TIN PAN ALLEY writers, providing hits for such singers as Bing CROSBY and Frank SINATRA. He teamed up with among others, Jimmy DORSEY, Johnny BURKE and Sammy CAHN on many of his most celebrated hits. Among his best-known compositions were 'It's the Dreamer in Me' (1938), 'Imagination' (1939), 'Birds of a Feather' (1941), 'Moonlight Becomes You' (1942), 'Swinging on a Star' (1944), 'Going My Way' (1944), for which he won an Oscar, 'Nancy (with the Laughing Face)' (1944), 'Personality' (1945), 'Would You' (1945), 'Busy Doing Nothing' (1949), 'Here's That Rainy Day' (1953), 'Love and Marriage' (1955), 'The Tender Trap' (1955), 'Come Fly with Me' (1958), 'High Hopes' (1959), 'Call Me Irresponsible' (1963) and 'Thoroughly Modern Millie' (1967).

Vandross, Luther (1951–) US SOUL singer, who emerged as a top star in the 1980s after years as a backing singer. He established a following in the late 1970s with the DISCO hits 'Searching' and 'The Glow of Love' and developed as a solo artist with the album *Never Too Much* (1981). Releases since then have included *Forever, For Always, For Love* (1982), *Busy Body* (1983), *The Night I Fell in Love* (1985), *Give Me the Reason* (1986), *Any Love* (1988), *Power of Love* (1991) and *Songs* (1994).

Vangelis (Vangelis Odyssey Papathanassiou; 1944–) Greek keyboard player and composer, resident in the UK, who established an international reputation in the 1980s. A child prodigy, who played the piano in public when he was six years old, Vangelis had some success backing Demis

Roussos but only became a top solo star in 1981, with his epic score for the movie *Chariots of Fire*, for which he earned an Oscar. Subsequent projects have included albums and the SOUNDTRACK for the films *Blade Runner* (1982), *The Bounty* (1984) and *1492 – Conquest of Paradise* (1992).

Vanilla Fudge US rock band, which was among the most popular bands of the psychedelic era of the late 1960s and one of the first pioneers of HEAVY METAL. Keyboard player Mark Stein (1947–), guitarist Vince Martell (1945–), bassist Tim Bogert (1944–) and drummer Carmine Appice (1946–) first took the name the Pigeons, but changed their name and had a first success with an extraordinary COVER version of 'You Keep Me Hanging On' (1967), which featured on the acclaimed eponymous début album. Other releases before the band broke up in 1970 included *The Beat Goes On* (1968) and *Near the Beginning* (1969).

Varèse, Edgard (1883–1965) US composer and conductor, born in France, who was one of the first pioneers of electronic music. Having written his first opera when he was 12 years old, Varèse decided against a career as an engineer (defying his parents' wishes) and studied under Vincent D'INDY and others in Paris. He destroyed all his early works (with the exception of the DEBUSSY-influenced *Un grand sommeil*) and came under the influence of Ferrucio BUSONI and Richard STRAUSS in Berlin, where he established the Symphonischer Chor to perform ancient music.

After war service, Varèse settled in the USA in 1916 and there became a co-founder of the International Composers' Guild (1921), set up to promote new music. He also established a controversial reputation as a composer of radical new works in which he explored the possibilities presented by unusual ensembles of instruments. Notable compositions included *Offrandes* (1921), *Hyperprism* (1923), which scandalized audiences on its première under Leopold STOKOWSKI with its repetitions and use of tone CLUSTERS, *Octandre* (1924), *Intégrales* (1925), *Ionisation* (1931), which was written for 41 percussion instruments and two sirens, and *Density 21.5* (1936), which was written for a solitary platinum flute (the density of platinum being 21.5).

Among the compositions Varèse wrote for electronic media after the Second World War were *Desérts* (1954), which mixed live performers with tape-recorded sounds, and *Poème électronique* (1958), which used electronic devices alone. His last work, *Nocturnal*, was finished by other hands after his death.

> Music which should pulsate with life, needs new means of expression, and science alone can infuse it with youthful vigour.
> EDGARD VARÈSE, 1917

Vaughan, Frankie (Francis Abelson; 1928–) British CABARET singer, who had a string of hits in the late 1950s and early 1960s and established himself as an enduring favourite with EASY LISTENING audiences. Having made his début as a singer in 1950, he topped the British charts in 1957 with 'Garden of Eden' and again in 1961 with 'Tower of Strength'. Other standards associated with his name include 'Green Door' and 'Give Me the Moonlight', which he usually delivers complete with top hat and cane. Film appearances have included *Let's Make Love* (1960) with Marilyn Monroe and Yves MONTAND.

Vaughan, Sarah (Lois) (1924–90) Black US singer and pianist, nicknamed the Divine One, who ranked alongside Billie HOLIDAY and Ella FITZGERALD as one of the great female JAZZ vocalists. Having sung gospel as a child, Vaughan won a competition at the APOLLO THEATRE in Harlem in 1942, following which she was recruited to sing with the band of Earl HINES. She quickly established a reputation for her brilliant technique and went on to sing with such jazzmen as Billy ECKSTINE, Dizzy GILLESPIE, John KIRBY and Count BASIE, becoming a pioneer of the COOL style. Hits associated with her name included 'Whatever Lola Wants' (1955), 'Passing Strangers' (1957) and 'Broken-hearted Melody' (1959) as well as many more by Duke ELLINGTON and George GERSHWIN.

Vaughan Williams, Ralph (1872–1958) British composer, nicknamed VW, who did much to free contemporary English classical music from the influence of the German tradition and explored the potential of FOLK MUSIC as a source for new works. After studies under Sir Hubert Parry (1848–1918) and Sir Charles Stanford (1852–1924) at the Royal College of Music, Vaughan Williams – the son of a clergyman and a descendant of Charles Darwin and Josiah Wedgwood through his mother – completed his training with Max Bruch (1838–1920) in Berlin and with Maurice RAVEL in Paris and, with his friend Gustav HOLST, developed his abiding interest in English folk music from 1902. Such early works as the orchestral tone poem *In the Fen Country* (1904), the three *Norfolk Rhapsodies* (1906) and *Fantasia on a Theme by Thomas Tallis* (1910) demonstrated the extent to which he was indebted to the English musical tradition. In a similar way, the four-act opera *The Pilgrim's Progress* (1949) was based on John Bunyan's classic English text, and the ballad-opera *Hugh the Drover* (1914) recreated English village life of a hundred years before.

The symphonic tone poem *London Symphony* (1913) depicted life in the capital before the First World War, while the ballet *Job* (1930) drew inspiration from William Blake's biblical illustrations. His first symphony, *A Sea Symphony* (1909), was inspired by the English coastline, though it also made use of the poetry of Walt Whitman, but it was the Third Symphony, the *Pastoral Symphony* (1922), that was to mark the first expression of his mature style.

Later symphonies sounded a more pessimistic and troubled note, perhaps reflecting the rise of Fascism and the threat it represented to the English way of life; the Sixth Symphony is thought to evoke the horror the composer experienced on the exploding of the first atom bombs at the end of the Second World War (although Vaughan Williams himself did not admit such influences). The Seventh Symphony, the *Sinfonia Antartica* (1952), was derived from the score he wrote for the film *Scott of the Antarctic* (1948); other film music included scores for several war films and that for *The Vision of William Blake* (1957).

Among his other compositions were the opera *Sir John in Love* (1929), the ballet *Old King Cole* (1923), a mass in G minor (1922), the oratorio *Sancta Civitas* (1926), the cantata *Hodie* (1954), chamber music, 'Linden Lea' and other songs, and such celebrated pieces as 'The Lark Ascending', for violin, and *Fantasia on Greensleeves*. He also edited the *English Hymnal* (1906) and taught at the Royal College of Music from 1919.

By the time of Vaughan Williams's death he was universally recognized as the most important English composer since Sir Edward ELGAR. For many years afterwards musicians who had died were said to have 'gone on tour with VW'.

> I don't know whether I like it, but it's what I meant.
> RALPH VAUGHAN WILLIAMS, of his Fourth Symphony

> It's a rum go!
> RALPH VAUGHAN WILLIAMS, on being asked what he thought of music

> ... looks like a farmer ... on his way to judge the shorthorns at an agricultural fair.
> STEPHEN WILLIAMS

> His is the music of a gentleman-farmer, noble in inspiration, but dull.
> AARON COPLAND, 1931

> The Vaughan Williams world of half-lights, of melodies that seem to want to delay the unpleasant moment when they must sound as if they have arrived somewhere.
> COLIN WILSON, *Brandy of the Damned*, 1964

Vee, Bobby (Robert Velline; 1943–) US pop singer, who emerged as a star after filling in at engagements for Buddy HOLLY after the latter's death. Vee had big chart hits with such singles as 'Devil or Angel' (1960), 'Rubber Ball' (1960), 'Take Good Care of My Baby' (1961), 'Run to Him' (1961) and 'The Night Has a Thousand Eyes' (1963). He staged a minor comeback in 1967 with 'Come Back When You Grow Up'.

One musician released from Vee's backing band because (according to Vee) he had no future in the music business was one Robert Zimmermann – later to find fame as Bob DYLAN.

Velvet Fog, the See Mel TORMÉ.

Velvet Underground, the US rock band, which became a cult in the late 1960s. Named after the title of an infamous pornographic book, the Velvet Underground came together in New York originally as the Primitives but changed the group's name on the suggestion of pop-art guru and film-maker Andy Warhol, who became the band's mentor in 1965. Singer-songwriter and guitarist Lou REED, bassist Sterling Morrison (1940–95), drummer Maureen Tucker (1941–) and multi-instrumentalist and songwriter John Cale (1942–   ) firmly established themselves as cult icons with the AVANT-GARDE début album, *The Velvet Underground and Nico* (1967), which featured the extraordinary vocals of former model Nico (Christa Päffgen; 1938–88).

Reed removed the band from the influence of Warhol and Nico and recorded, in just one day, the classic *White Light, White Heat* (1967), which was followed by *The Velvet Underground* (1969) and *Loaded* (1970). The various members of the band eventually moved on to new projects, Reed in particular establishing himself as a solo star, while Cale and Nico did further work together. Morrison became an English teacher and Tucker started a family. The band finally ceased to exist formally in 1973 but was nevertheless proclaimed the godfather of PUNK ROCK towards the end of the decade. Nico died of a brain haemorrhage after falling off her bicycle while on holiday in Ibiza. A reunion was staged in 1990 and a come-back tour in the UK in 1993 met with critical acclaim.

Venuti, Joe (Giuseppe Venuti; 1903–78) US JAZZ violinist and bandleader, nicknamed the Mad Fiddler from Philly, who was one of the first to exploit the violin as a jazz instrument. He established his reputation in the 1920s, playing for, among others, Paul WHITEMAN, Bix BEIDERBECKE, Jimmy DORSEY and Bing CROSBY, and he made many acclaimed recordings. He also formed an admired partnership with the guitarist Eddie LANG, remaining a respected figure in jazz circles until his death, having overcome addiction to alcohol in the 1960s. He was particularly renowned as a practical joker, his tricks including slipping a dead-drunk Beiderbecke into a bath full of purple Jello and pouring flour down a tuba in a rehearsal for the film *King of Jazz* (1930).

vibes JAZZ slang for the vibraphone. The vibraphone is a variety of xylophone with resonating metal tubes and lids that open and close, which is driven by an electric motor (which creates the vibration in the sound). The vibraphone (or vibra-harp), which was invented by Hermann Winterhoff in 1916, has only rarely been used outside jazz, although Alban BERG was one classical composer to make some use of it in his work, notably in his opera *Lulu*. A player of the vibes is termed a vibrist.

Vienna Boys' Choir Austrian choir, which is among the most famous choirs in the world, with countless classic recordings and performances to its credit. The choir was founded in 1498 to serve the Imperial Chapel, where it is based to this day. As well as devotional music, the choir also performs much secular material and has collaborated with the Vienna State Opera.

Vienna Philharmonic Orchestra Austrian Orchestra, founded in 1842, which has long been regarded as one of the finest orchestras in the world. The orchestra presents both opera (with the Vienna State Opera) and concerts (notably the world-famous New Year events from the Golden Hall) and has attracted a long series of highly acclaimed conductors over the years, the most notable including Gustav MAHLER, Wilhelm FURTWÄNGLER, Bruno WALTER, Herbert von KARAJAN and Claudio ABBADO.

Villa-Lobos, Heitor (1887–1959) Brazilian composer and educationalist, who built an international reputation on his many works combining the European and Brazilian musical traditions. Having been taught to play the cello by his father, the young Villa-Lobos, who was from Rio de Janeiro, developed an interest in traditional Brazilian music and toured remote regions of the country, ultimately emerging as the most celebrated Latin-American composer of the century. His Third Symphony, *A guerra* (1922), won wide praise and – through the support of Artur RUBINSTEIN – he completed his studies in Paris in the 1920s, where he came under the influence of Maurice RAVEL's music.

Rudepoema (1926) and other early works consolidated his growing reputation, and he became the most influential figure in Brazilian music on his return to his native country in 1930, when he oversaw the establishment of the Brazilian Academy of Music in 1945 and the founding a symphony orchestra. Among his many compositions, the most important included 14 *Chôros* (1920–29), the nine *Bachianas Brasilieras* (1930–45), which mixed Bach with Latin-American dance rhythms, 12 symphonies, the operas *Izaht* (1914), *Madalena* (1947) and *Yerma* (1955), ballets, 17 string quartets and numerous concertos as well as pieces for the theatre.

A truly creative musician is capable of

producing, from his own imagination, melodies that are more authentic than folklore itself.

HEITOR VILLA-LOBOS (attributed)

Vincent, Gene (Vincent Eugene Craddock; 1935–71) US singer-songwriter and guitarist, who became one of the legends of the ROCK 'N' ROLL era and the archetypal rebellious rock star. Service in the US Navy came to an end when Vincent injured his left leg in a motorbike accident (leaving him with a permanent limp), and he rose to fame as a rock 'n' roller with the Blue Caps, his hits including 'Be-bop-a-lula' (1956), 'Ain't She Sweet' (1956), 'Race with the Devil' (1956), 'Blue Jean Bop' (1956) and 'Lotta Lovin'' (1957). While other rock 'n' rollers toned down their wild images towards the end of the decade, Vincent – kitted out in black leathers after emigrating to the UK in 1959 – remained uncompromisingly rough, and he built up a big working-class following (though he was in reality polite and respectful to interviewers and fellow stars).

Injuries sustained in the car crash that claimed the life of Eddie COCHRAN while the pair were on tour in the UK in 1960 exacerbated Vincent's leg problems, and his career went into a steady decline, to his great disappointment. Though struggling with an alcohol problem, he continued to perform throughout the UK in the early 1960s then attempted to switch to COUNTRY in the USA in 1965. The move met with no success, and he returned to the UK 1969, finally dying from an ulcer at the age of 36.

> Gene Vincent ... sounded like a Southern razor boy who could slit a man from ear to ear without flinching an eyelid or missing a beat of 'Be-bop-alula'.
>
> TONY PALMER, *All You Need Is Love*, 1976

Vinton, Bobby (Stanley Robert Vinton; 1935–) US singer, who recorded several hit ballads in the 1960s. His most successful releases included 'Roses are Red', which topped the US charts in 1962, 'Blue

Velvet' (1963), 'Mr Lonely' (1964) and 'My Melody of Love' (1972).

Vishnevskaya, Galina (1926–) Russian soprano, who has earned a worldwide reputation as one of the finest sopranos on the contemporary stage. Married to the celebrated cellist Mstislav ROSTROPOVICH, she has won particular acclaim for her performances of the operas of Benjamin BRITTEN, and it was expressly for her that Britten wrote the soprano role in his *War Requiem* (1962).

Von Tilzer, Harry (1872–1946) US songwriter, who established himself as one of the leading talents of TIN PAN ALLEY in the early years of the century. Among his most celebrated songs were 'A Bird in a Gilded Cage' (1900), 'Down Where the Wurzburger Flows' (1902), which was rewritten as the music hall classic 'Down at the Old Bull and Bush' and 'What you Goin' to do When the Rent Comes Round' (1905). His brother, Albert Von Tilzer (1878–1956), was also a songwriter, responsible for such hits as 'Take Me Out to the Ball Game' (1908), 'Give Me the Moonlight' (1917) and 'Roll Along, Prairie Moon' (1935).

vout Variety of JIVE talk, which was devised by the eccentric JAZZ entertainer Slim GAILLARD. Gaillard pioneered 'vout' or 'vout oreenie' during the 1930s, when he played alongside such greats as Charlie PARKER ('Yardbird Oreenie') and Dizzy GILLESPIE ('Daz McSkivens Vout Oreenie') and used it on such successful recordings as 'Flat Foot Floogie'. In 1946 he even released a piece of music under the title *Opera in Vout*, although it was not, in act, an opera and furthermore it contained little vout. Gaillard's eccentricity and vout talk did not always work in his favour, however, and at least one of his records, 'Yep Roc Heresy', was banned by a US radio station, which feared that it was in some way subversive (in reality, the lyrics were taken from an Armenian restaurant menu).

W

Waits, Tom (1949–) US singer-songwriter, who won acclaim for his distinctive albums mixing ROCK with JAZZ and BLUES elements. Waits made his recording début in 1973 with *Closing Time* and went on to win a large cult following with his deliberately down-at-heel image and ironic wit. Subsequent releases have included *Nighthawks at the Diner* (1975), *Small Change* (1976), the trilogy *Swordfish Trombones* (1983), *Raindogs* (1985), *Frank's Wild Years* (1987), *Bone Machine* (1992) and *Black Rider* (1993). He has also appeared in a number of films and was nominated for an OSCAR for the SOUNDTRACK of *One From the Heart* (1983).

> I told you I was sick.
>
> TOM WAITS, his suggestion for his epitaph

Wakeman, Rick (1949–) British keyboard player, who after classical training established a highly successful pop career. A student of the Royal College of Music, London, Wakeman won acclaim for his work with the Strawbs, David BOWIE, Cat STEVENS and YES before embarking on a solo career and having big commercial hits with such CONCEPT ALBUMS as *The Six Wives of Henry VIII* (1973), *Journey to the Centre of the Earth* (1974) and *The Myths and Legends of King Arthur and the Knights of the Round Table* (1975). He has since composed several notable film scores.

Walker, Junior (1942–95) US singer and saxophonist, who had a string of hits with his band the All Stars on the MOTOWN label in the 1960s. Walker formed the All Stars in 1964 and had chart successes with such RHYTHM-AND-BLUES singles as 'Shotgun' (1964), 'I'm a Road Runner' (1966), 'How Sweet It Is' (1966), 'What Does It Take to Win Your Love' (1969), 'Walk in the Night' (1973) and 'Take Me Girl I'm Ready' (1973). Walker left Motown in 1978 and embarked on a solo career.

Walker, T-Bone (Aaron Thibeaux Walker; 1910–75) US BLUES singer and guitarist, who was the first bluesman to switch to an electric guitar. Influenced by both the blues and JAZZ traditions, T-Bone Walker took up the electric guitar at much the same time as blues guitarist Lonnie Johnson (1899–1970) and went on to record such classics as 'Call It Stormy Monday'. His music had a profound influence on countless guitarists, his admirers including B.B. KING and Chuck BERRY.

Walker Brothers, the US pop trio, resident in the UK, who had a string of hits in the mid-1960s. Singer and guitarist John Maus (1943–), hearthrob singer and bassist Noel Scott Engel (1944–) and drummer Gary Leeds (1944–), who changed their names to Walker on settling in the UK, had their first big hit with 'Love Her' (1965), which was quickly followed by the chart-topper 'Make It Easy on Yourself' (1966) and 'My Ship is Coming In' (1966) among other singles. 'The Sun Ain't Gonna Shine Anymore' got to Number One in 1966, but the trio fell out and broke up a year later to pursue solo careers, Scott Walker recording several Jacques BREL numbers in the late 1960s. They reunited in 1976 for *Lines*, from which came the hit 'No Regrets'.

wall of sound *See* Phil SPECTOR.

Waller, Fats (Thomas Wright Waller; 1904–43) Black US JAZZ pianist, composer, bandleader and singer, who established himself as the master of the STRIDE piano style in the 1920s. Defying the wishes of his father, a Baptist minister who considered music a tool of the Devil, Waller learned to play the piano as a boy and found work in the cinemas, cafés and theatres of New York, perfecting his inimitable rumbustious and goodhumoured style. He teamed up with lyricist Andy Razaf (1895–1973) in the 1920s and together they wrote such piano-based classics as 'Ain't Misbehavin'' and 'Honeysuckle Rose'; other hits included 'I'm Gonna Sit Right Down and Write Myself a Letter', 'My Very Good

Friend the Milkman', 'Rosetta', 'The Joint is Jumpin'', 'Jitterbug Waltz', 'Two Sleepy People' and 'Your Feet's Too Big'.

Waller made numerous records with his own groups and also won acclaim for his appearances with the bands of Fletcher HENDERSON and Jack TEAGARDEN among others. His influence on countless jazz pianists – notably Art TATUM – was profound. He was also renowned for his enthusiastic life-style: over-indulgence in food and drink, coupled with his exhausting life on the road, contributed to his premature death from pneumonia on a train while travelling between bookings.

> The black Horowitz.
>
> OSCAR LEVANT

Walsh, Joe (1945–) US rock guitarist and singer-songwriter, nicknamed Prince Roving Hand, who has enjoyed a long career both as a star performer with various top bands and on a solo basis. A former member of the James Gang, Barnstorm and the EAGLES, from 1975, he has also had success with such solo albums as *But Seriously, Folks* (1976), *There Goes the Neighborhood* (1981) – an LP originally titled *Days of Lines and Noses – Got Any Gum?* (1987) and *Ordinary Average Guy* (1991).

Walsh was present at Kent State University on 4 May 1970, when clashes between students and the Ohio National Guard left four students dead.

Walter, Bruno (Bruno Walter Schlesinger; 1876–1962) US conductor, born in Germany, who won wide acclaim for his interpretations of the work of Mozart and Gustav MAHLER. Having studied from an early age to be a pianist, Walter made his début as a conductor in 1894 and then worked with the Hamburg Opera, where he met Mahler, who was to become a close friend. Walter was appointed Mahler's assistant at the Vienna State Opera in 1901 and was closely involved in the first performances of several of his great compositions, conducting the premiere of *Das Liede von der Erde* in 1911 and of the Ninth Symphony in 1912. He became director of the Munich Opera (1914–22), of the Berlin State Opera (1925–33), of the Leipzig Gewandhaus Orchestra (1929–33), of the VIENNA PHILHARMONIC (1933–8) and a star conductor at the Salzburg Festival (1925–37) as well as appearing regularly at COVENT GARDEN (1922–31). He emigrated to the USA on the rise of the Nazis, taking US citizenship in 1946, but continued to conduct all over the world, enjoying a fruitful association with the gifted Kathleen FERRIER at the start of her career.

> The end of his baton is like a cradle in which he rocks me.
>
> LOTTE LEHMANN

Walton, Sir William (Turner) (1902–83) British composer, resident in Italy from 1948, who was recognized as one of the most distinguished heirs of Sir Edward ELGAR for his highly original and deeply patriotic works. Of musical parents, Walton studied music at Oxford University where he came under the influence of the celebrated Sitwell family, with whom he lived for many years. His collaboration with poet Edith Sitwell on the extraordinarily colourful and witty *Façade* (1922) made him famous when he was just 20, although the first performance caused something of a scandal with its nonsense lyrics, verbal fireworks and quotations from such popular songs as 'I Do Like to be Beside the Seaside'.

He adopted a romantic neoclassical style for the overture *Portsmouth Point* (1925) and explored a more lyrical mode of expression while still allowing his sense of humour occasional free rein. Influenced by the music of Paul HINDEMITH and Igor STRAVINSKY, he consolidated his reputation as one of the leading English composers of his generation with such compositions as the viola concerto (1929), the oratorio *Belshazzar's Feast* (1931), the violin concerto (1939), the cello concerto (1957), two symphonies (1935 and 1960), the operas *Troilus and Cressida* (1954) and *The Bear* (1967), *Variations on a Theme by Hindemith* (1963), the ballets *The Wise Virgins* (1940) and *The Quest* (1943), and the ceremonial pieces *Crown Imperial* (1937) and *Orb and Sceptre* (1953).

Of particular note was his film music, which included the scores for such classic movies as *Henry V* (1944), *Hamlet* (1947) and *Richard III* (1955), which all starred Laurence Olivier, and *The Battle of Britain* (1969).

> I seriously advise all sensitive composers to die at the age of thirty-seven. I know I've gone through the first halcyon period, and am just about ripe for my critical damnation.
>
> WILLIAM WALTON, letter, 1939

A favourite saying of his was that to compose music was far worse for him than to bear children is for a woman, as it took longer than nine months and was much more painful.

SUSANNA WALTON, *William Walton: Behind the Façade*

War US pop group, which had success with SOUL and FUNK fans in the 1970s. Keyboard player Leroy 'Lonnie' Jordan (1948–), guitarist Howard Scott (1946–), flautist and saxophonist Charles Miller (1939–), bassist Morris 'B B' Dickerson (1949–), drummer Harold Brown (1946–), harmonica-player Lee Oskar (1946–) and percussionist Papa Dee Allen (1931–88) started out as the backing band for Eric Burdon (of ANIMALS fame) before setting out on their own in the early 1970s. The group topped the US charts with such singles as 'The Cisco Kid' (1973), 'Why Can't We be Friends' (1975) and 'Summer' (1976). War went into decline after the disco-oriented *Galaxy* (1978).

Waring, Fred (1900–84) US conductor, composer and bandleader, who became a top radio star of the 1930s. Waring established his reputation leading the popular Pennsylvanians DANCE BAND in the 1920s and hosted his own radio shows, later moving into television. When not playing or promoting his music, he was busy marketing his own inventions, which included a food mixer and a travelling iron.

Warren, Harry (Salvatore Guaragna; 1893–1981) US songwriter, of Italian descent, who became one of the most successful TIN PAN ALLEY composers of his day, writing numerous hits for Hollywood in collaboration with Al DUBIN and others. Having taught himself to play several instruments as a child, Warren worked as a drummer and in the cinema before settling on a career as a songwriter after service in the First World War. Among his most celebrated hits were 'Nagasaki' (1928), 'Shuffle off to Buffalo' and 'Forty-second Street', from *Forty-Second Street* (1933), 'We're in the Money', from *Gold Diggers of 1933*, 'Keep Young and Beautiful', from *Roman Scandals* (1933), 'I'll String Along with You', from *Twenty Million Sweethearts* (1934), 'I Only Have Eyes for You', from *Dames* (1934), 'Lullaby of Broadway', from *Gold Diggers of 1935*,

'About a Quarter to Nine', from *Go Into Your Dance* (1935), 'Sweet and Low', from *Broadway Gondolier* (1935), 'With Plenty of Money and You', from *Gold Diggers of 1937* (1936), 'You Must Have Been a Beautiful Baby', from *Hard To Get* (1938), 'I Yi Yi Yi Yi', from *That Night in Rio* (1941), 'Chattanooga Choo Choo', from *Sun Valley Serenade* (1941), 'I've Got a Gal in Kalamazoo', from *Orchestra Wives* (1942), 'You'll Never Know', from *Hello, Frisco, Hello* (1943), 'The Polka Dot Polka', from *The Gang's All Here* (1943), 'The More I See You', from *Billy Rose's Diamond Horseshoe* (1945), 'On the Atcheson, Topeka and the Santa Fé', from *The Harvey Girls* (1946), and 'You Wonderful You', from *Summer Stock* (1950).

Warwick, Dionne (Marie Dionne Warrick; 1940–) Black US SOUL singer, who had numerous hits in the 1960s and 1970s. Having been reared on GOSPEL, she had big hits with such records as 'I'll Never Love This Way Again', 'Anyone Who Had a Heart', 'Walk On By' and – with the Detroit Spinners – 'Then Came You', which reached Number One in 1974. She made a comeback in the 1980s with *Heartbreaker* (1982), *Friends* (1985) and *Love Songs* (1990), and with the Aids charity single 'That's What Friends are For' (1985).

At one point early in her career she added an additional 'e' to her surname to become Dionne Warwicke after advice from an astrologer to the effect that this would bring her luck; the ruse failed, however, and her career went into decline until she reverted to the original spelling.

washboard Improvised musical instrument, which was often used by impoverished JAZZ and SKIFFLE bands as part of the rhythm section. In the early jazz years SPASM BANDS around the USA frequently employed washboards among other household items, using thimbles to 'play' them. A number of bands made a particular feature of the washboard, the most successful of them including the Washboard Rhythm Kings of the 1920s and 1930s.

Washington, Dinah (Ruth Lee Jones; 1924–63) Black US BLUES singer, nicknamed the Queen of the Blues, who won wide acclaim in the 1940s and 1950s. Having sung in various choirs as a child, she became famous singing with Lionel

HAMPTON's band in Chicago in the mid-1940s, after which she embarked on a solo career. Her greatest hits included 'Blow Top Blues', 'This Bitter Earth', 'Evil Gal Blues' and the classic 'Stormy Weather'. She diversified into RHYTHM-AND-BLUES and pop before her early death as the result of a drug overdose.

Waters, Ethel (1896–1977) Black US singer, nicknamed Sweet Mama Stringbean because she was very slim, who established herself as a top star in the 1930s and went on to enjoy a long career as a popular singer and entertainer. Born after her mother was raped at the age of 12, she prospered in vaudeville in the 1920s and went on to sing with the bands of Benny GOODMAN and the DORSEY brothers, becoming one of the leading acts at the legendary COTTON CLUB. She appeared in numerous films, performed at Carnegie Hall in 1938, hosted her own show on Broadway and participated in the evangelical events staged by Billy Graham. Songs associated with her name included 'I'm Coming, Virginia', 'Stormy Weather', 'Heat Wave' and 'Taking a Chance on Love'.

Religious devotion sometimes threatened to conflict with her career as a singer. Once, when dress rehearsing *Cabin in the Sky* on Broadway in 1940, Waters announced that God had told her that she must resign from the show because 'it has become vulgar' and stormed back to her dressing-room; it was only after it was pointed out by a frantic producer that God would surely not want the cast to lose their jobs that she relented and, after a further audience with the Divine Authority, agreed to continue (the show was a huge hit).

Waters, Muddy (McKinley Morganfield; 1915–83) Black US JAZZ guitarist and singer, nicknamed the King of the Chicago Blues, who became a legend of RHYTHM-AND-BLUES. Waters (whose pseudonym was acquired when he was a boy through his fondness for playing in a muddy creek) was a Mississippi farmhand until he was 'discovered' by folklorist Alan LOMAX in 1941 and went on to make many classic recordings. Waters established his reputation with his first big hit, 'Louisiana Blues' (1951); other classics by his hand included 'I'm a Man', 'I'm Your Hoochie Coochie

Man', 'Honey Bee', 'Got My Mojo Working' and 'Rollin' Stone'. Waters' electric r 'n' b style exerted a major influence on the development of ROCK 'N' ROLL – notably in the UK after a British tour in 1958, which made him an idol of Mick JAGGER and a model for other White bluesmen. The ROLLING STONES named themselves after his classic song and were quick to acknowledge their debt to the great man, who was once moved to remark of Jagger: 'He took my music – but he gave me my name.'

Popularity with the swinging generation of the 1960s led Waters to adapt temporarily to new musical tastes, and he even ventured into psychedelia with such albums as *Electric Mud* (1968) and *After the Rain* (1968). He survived a serious car crash in 1973 and returned to live performing in the famous 'Last Waltz' concert given by the BAND in 1976. He played at the White House for Jimmy Carter in 1978 and continued recording until his death from a heart attack.

> All my life I was having trouble with women ... I've done a lot of writing about women. Then, after I quit having trouble with them, I could feel in my heart that somebody would always have trouble with them, so I kept writing those blues.
> MUDDY WATERS

Watters, Lu (Lucious Watters; 1911–89) US JAZZ trumpeter and bandleader, who became one of the leading stars of the TRAD scene in the 1940s. Watters established his reputation as leader (1939–50) of the celebrated Yerba Buena Jazz Band, which won acclaim all around the world. He gave up music in 1950, studied geology and worked as a chef.

Waukesha Wizard, the *See* Les PAUL.

WEA Warner-Elektra-Atlantic, the third largest record company in the world. Warner Brothers began a music business in the 1930s and attracted many leading stars to the company's labels. Stars connected with the organization in recent decades have included Van MORRISON, Joni MITCHELL, Neil YOUNG, FLEETWOOD MAC, Dwight Yoakam and Emmylou HARRIS.

Weather Report US JAZZ-ROCK group, which established a cult following in the 1970s. Keyboard player Joe Zawinul (1932–), saxophonist Wayne Shorter (1933–), bassist Miroslav Vitous (1947–   ), drummer Alphonse Mouzon (1948–   ) and percussionist Airto Moreira (1941–   ) came together in 1970 and quickly established themselves as leaders in the jazz FUSION style with such albums as *Weather Report* (1970), *Sweetnighter* (1973), *Black Market* (1976), *Heavy Weather* (1977) and *Night Passage* (1980). They broke up after *This Is This* (1986).

Weavers, the US FOLK vocal group, who played a key role in the folk revival of the 1950s. The group, consisting of Pete SEEGER, Lee Hays (1914–81), Ronnie Gilbert and Fred Hellerman (1927–   ), was formed in 1949 and had hits with such numbers as 'Goodnight, Irene', 'If I Had a Hammer' and 'When the Saints Go Marching In', establishing a reputation for left-wing political sympathies. After several line-up changes, the group disbanded in 1963.

Webb, Chick (William Henry Webb; 1909–39) US JAZZ drummer, composer and bandleader, who became one of the most popular figures of the SWING era of the 1930s. A dwarf with a hunched back, Webb led bands at Harlem's Savoy Ballroom in New York and elsewhere in the 1920s and won acclaim as one of the most inventive and forceful of all swing drummers. Among his hits as a composer were 'Jungle Mama' (1929) and 'Strictly Jive' (1937). After his early death, leadership of his band passed to Ella FITZGERALD, who was one of Webb's discoveries as well as his adopted daughter.

Webb, Jimmy (1946–   ) US singer-songwriter, pianist, arranger and producer, who wrote a number of MOTOWN classics and also had some success as a performer in his own right. Among the hits he contributed for other artists were 'By the Time I Get to Phoenix', 'Up Up and Away' and 'Wichita Linesman' for Glen CAMPBELL and the Fifth Dimension, 'MacArthur Park', which he recorded with actor Richard Harris in 1968, and other hits for the SUPREMES. His own albums included *Words and Music* (1970) and *Land's End* (1974).

Webern, Anton (Friedrich Wilhelm von) (1883–1945) Austrian composer and conductor, who was one of the most important exponents of SERIAL music between the

wars. Inspired by Wagner, Webern completed his music training in Vienna, his birthplace, and came under the influence of his teacher Arnold SCHOENBERG. Subsequently he worked as a conductor in Prague and elsewhere, maintaining links with Schoenberg and Alban BERG, who shared his interest in ATONALITY and serialism.

Typical works in the Webern canon are succinct, with many pieces lasting over less than a minute; his total published canon amounts to little over 4 hours' music. The characteristic feature of his work is Webern's own concept of 'sound melody', in which every note is given its own dynamic and melodic identity, and this abandonment of traditional harmony was to have a profound influence on many successors. Among the most important of his works are the *Passacaglia for Orchestra* (1908), the *Five Movements for String Quartet* (1909), *Six Orchestral Pieces* (1910), *Six Bagatelles for String Quartet* (1913), *Five Orchestral Pieces* (1913), *Three Sacred Folk Songs* (1924), written in the year that he adopted Schoenberg's 12-NOTE method with the intention of combining it with classical forms, and *Variations for Orchestra* (1940).

Webern earned a somewhat precarious living drifting from one conducting post to another and suffered from official disapproval after the Nazi Anschluss of 1938, when his music was banned in Germany and Austria. His career ended prematurely when he was shot dead while smoking a cigar in the street by a nervous US soldier after the liberation.

> In fifty years one will find it obvious, children will understand it and sing it.
> ANTON WEBERN, of his music

> Doomed to a total failure in a deaf world of ignorance and indifference, he inexorably kept on cutting out his diamonds, his dazzling diamonds, the mines of which he knew to perfection.
> IGOR STRAVINSKY

Webster, Ben(jamin Francis) (1909–73) US JAZZ saxophonist and arranger, who played with many of the great names in jazz in the 1930s and 1940s. Webster won acclaim for his work with the likes of Fletcher HENDERSON, Cab CALLOWAY, Roy ELDRIDGE and Duke ELLINGTON, with whom he recorded 'Cotton Tail' among other classics, and was considered by many second only to Coleman HAWKINS as the leading tenor saxophonist of his generation.

Weems, Ted (Wilfred Theodore Weymes; 1901–63) US bandleader, who led a popular DANCE BAND between the wars. Among his hits were 'Somebody Stole My Gal' (1923), 'Piccolo Pete' (1929), his theme tune 'Out of the Night' and 'Heartaches' (1933). Singers with his band included Perry COMO.

weeny-bop POP music that is aimed at the very young, usually taken to be the pre-teen age group. *See also* TEENY-BOP.

Weill, Kurt (1900–50) German composer, a US citizen from 1943, who achieved lasting fame in the MUSICAL THEATRE for his collaboration with the playwright Bertolt Brecht (1898–1955) in the 1920s. A pupil of Ferruccio BUSONI, Weill established his credentials as a writer for the satirical AVANT-GARDE theatre of Berlin in the early 1920s with such operas as *The Protagonist* (1926) before finding his ideal partner in Brecht. In partnership with Brecht, Weill devised the music for such socially pertinent dramatic works as *The Rise and Fall of the City of Mahagonny* (1927), which incorporated the classic 'Alabama Song' and caused riots when it was staged in Leipzig three years later, and *The Threepenny Opera* (1928), based on *The Beggar's Opera*, from which came the classic 'Ballad of Mack the Knife'. Other early works included two symphonies, a violin concerto, *The Lindbergh Flight* (1928) and *The Seven Deadly Sins* (1933), on which Weill worked with Brecht in Paris.

With the rise of the Nazis Weill, a Jew, emigrated to the USA with his wife, the singer Lotte LENYA, and there established a successful career on Broadway – often in collaboration with librettist Maxwell Anderson (1888–1959) – with such slick but relatively unadventurous MUSICALS as *Knickerbocker Holiday* (1944), which included the acclaimed 'September Song', *Lady in the Dark* (1941), *One Touch of Venus* (1943), *Street Scene* (1947) and *Lost in the Stars* (1949). His success was curtailed somewhat prematurely by his death from a heart attack.

> I don't give a damn about posterity. I want to write for today!
> KURT WEILL

Wells, Kitty (Muriel Deason; 1918–   ) US COUNTRY singer, nicknamed the Queen of Country Music, who established herself as a top star in the early 1950s. Her husband, country star Johnny Wright (1914–   ), gave her the pseudonym Kitty Wells after a well-known folk-song and accompanied her first on the radio and then on the GRAND OLE OPRY and other top country shows. Her biggest hits included the likes of 'It Wasn't God who Made Honky-tonk Angels' (1952), 'Makin'' Believe' (1955) and 'Jealousy' (1958).

Wells, Mary (1943–92) US singer, who became the first top-selling female artist on the MOTOWN label. Having made a major impact on the charts with the likes of 'The One Who Really Loves You' (1962) and 'You Lost the Sweetest Boy' (1963), Wells got to Number One in 1964 with the classic 'My Guy'. Subsequently she toured to acclaim with the BEATLES and had further lesser hits later in the 1960s. Her career ended prematurely with her death from cancer of the throat.

Welsh National Opera Welsh opera company, founded in Cardiff in 1946, which has established itself as one of the leading British companies. Under the directorship of such distinguished figures as Sir Charles GROVES and Sir Charles MACKERRAS, the company has won particular acclaim for its productions of works by Verdi, Leoš JANÁČEK and Benjamin BRITTEN. It was the first UK company to stage Alban BERG's *Lulu*.

western swing COUNTRY music genre that evolved in the 1930s as traditional HILLBILLY music was mixed with the BLUES and JAZZ to create a new, sophisticated style. To the traditional string instruments of hillbilly were added saxophones, trumpets, clarinets, pianos and amplified steel guitars. Leading exponents included the bands of Bob Wills, Pappy O'Daniel, Spade COOLEY, Hank Thompson and Pee Wee King. The heyday of western swing was in the Depression years of the 1930s, when audiences were often admitted to concerts in exchange for gifts of food.

Weston, R(obert) P(atrick) (1878–1936) British songwriter, who wrote many classics of the post-Edwardian MUSIC HALL. Among his best-known songs were 'I'm Henery the Eighth I am' (1911), 'Sister Susie's Sewing Shirts for Soldiers' (1914), the classic wartime song 'Good-bye-ee'

(1917) and 'When Father Papered the Parlour' (1926). A collaboration with his son Harris Weston produced the classic 'Knees up, Mother Brown'.

Wham! *See* George MICHAEL.

Whispering Bill *See* Bill ANDERSON.

White, Barry (1944–) Black US singer, nicknamed the Prophet of Love, who enjoyed a series of transatlantic hits in the mid-1970s. He established his reputation as writer of the hit 'Walkin' in the Rain with the One You Love' for Love Unlimited in 1972 and then embarked on a solo career. His biggest hits included 'I'm Gonna Love You Just a Little Bit More Baby' (1973), 'You're the First the Last My Everything', which got to Number One on both sides of the Atlantic in 1974, 'Can't Get Enough of Your Love Babe' (1974) and 'You See the Trouble With Me' (1976).

White, Josh(ua Daniel) (1908–69) Black US BLUES singer and guitarist, who was one of the most celebrated bluesmen of the 1940s and 1950s. From an impoverished background, he worked as a guide for blind blues performers, including 'Blind Lemon' JEFFERSON, before establishing his own reputation as a musician. Songs associated with his name included 'Frankie and Johnny', 'The Foggy Foggy Dew' and 'Strange Fruit'.

white metal Genre of HEAVY METAL music, which developed in reaction to the popularity of satanist BLACK METAL in the 1980s. The most successful exponents of such Christian rock have included Stryper.

Whiteman, Paul (1890–1967) US JAZZ bandleader, composer and violinist, nicknamed the King of Jazz, who was among the most celebrated bandleaders of his generation. Having been taught to play the violin by his father, Whiteman played classical music before establishing a reputation leading his own DANCE BANDS in the 1920s. Early hits included 'Whispering' (1920) and 'Three o'Clock in the Morning' (1923), and he went on to form a celebrated relationship with George GERSHWIN, commissioning the classic 'Rhapsody in Blue' (1924) and other examples of 'symphonic jazz'. Among the outstanding musicians in his band were Bix BEIDERBECKE, Benny GOODMAN, Jack TEAGARDEN and Frank Trumbauer (1901–56); singers who began their careers with him included Bing CROSBY.

Whitesnake British HEAVY METAL band, who emerged as a top HARD ROCK act in the 1980s. Formed by ex-DEEP PURPLE singer David Coverdale (1951–), who recruited an ever-changing line-up of SESSION musicians and other former Deep Purple stars, Whitesnake had its origins in his solo albums *Whitesnake* and *Northwinds* in the late 1970s. Notable releases since then have included *Trouble* (1978), *Love Hunter* (1979), *Ready and Willing* (1980), from which came the single 'Fool for Your Loving', *Live in the Heart of the City* (1980) and *Whitesnake 1987*, which spawned the singles 'Is This Love' and 'Here I Go Again'. The band went into temporary retirement in 1992 while Coverdale worked with guitarist Jimmy Page (*see* LED ZEPPELIN).

Whitfield, David (1926–80) British singer, who was the best-selling British vocalist of the 1950s. Having had his first hit with 'Bridge of Sighs' in 1953, he topped the British charts with 'Answer Me' (1953) and 'Cara Mia' (1954), which he made with the orchestra of MANTOVANI and with which he became the first British artist to top the US charts. His pop career went into permanent decline with the advent of ROCK 'N' ROLL and he switched to opera.

Whiting, Richard A. (1891–1938) US songwriter, who was one of the most successful TIN PAN ALLEY composers and subsequently wrote many further classics for Hollywood. Among his many hits were 'It's Tulip Time in Holland' (1915), 'Till We Meet Again' (1918), 'Whispering' (1920), 'Ukelele Lady' (1925), 'Louise', from the film *Innocents of Paris* (1929), 'One Hour With You', from the film of the same name (1932), 'On the Good Ship Lollipop', from *Bright Eyes* (1934), and 'Too Marvelous for Words', from *Ready, Willing and Able* (1937).

Whitman, Slim (Otis Dewey Whitman; 1924–) US COUNTRY singer and left-handed guitarist, who emerged as a top star in the 1950s. Whitman gave up plans to become a baseball professional when his career was interrupted by the Second World War, and he then established a following in country music circles. 'Rose Marie', from the celebrated MUSICAL of the same name, topped the British charts in 1955; two years earlier he topped the US charts with another song from the same show – 'Indian Love Call'. Among subsequent hits on the US country charts were such standards as 'Twelfth of Never' and 'It's All in the Game'. He enjoyed a comeback in the 1970s, when he was particularly warmly received by audiences in the UK.

Whittaker, Roger (1936–   ) British singer-songwriter and guitarist, who established himself as a favourite balladeer in the 1960s. Transatlantic hits have included 'Steel Man', 'I Don't Believe in If Anymore', 'If I were a Rich Man', 'Durham Town', 'The Last Farewell' and 'The Skye Boat Song'.

Who, the British rock group, which was among the leading English bands that dominated transatlantic pop in the 1960s and 1970s. School friends lead singer Roger Daltry (1945–   ), guitarist and songwriter Pete Townshend (1945–   ; nicknamed Birdman in reference to his distinctive profile), and bassist John Entwhistle (1944–   ), who were later joined by drummer Keith Moon (1947–78) got together in 1964 as the Detours and then as the High Numbers, establishing a devoted mod following and attracting some notoriety for destroying their instruments at the end of live appearances (a gimmick they adopted after Townshend broke the neck of his guitar by accident during a concert in Harrow). Renaming themselves the Who because some fans thought their posters were advertising bingo sessions, the band had its first big hit with 'I Can't Explain' (1965), which was followed by such singles as 'Anyway, Anyhow, Anywhere' (1965) and the classic 'My Generation' (1965), which became an anthem for rebellious youths everywhere (the stuttered 'g-g-g-generation' was alleged to evoke the stammer associated with drug users).

Among subsequent hit singles were 'Substitute' (1965), 'I'm a Boy' (1965), 'I Can See for Miles' (1967), 'Pinball Wizard' (1969) and 'Won't Get Fooled Again' (1971), while their acclaimed albums included *My Generation* (1965), the ROCK OPERA *Tommy* (1969), which disc jockey Tony Blackburn dismissed as 'sick', *Who's Next* (1971), *Quadrophenia* (1973), which

– like *Tommy* – was later turned into a successful film, and *Who Are You?* (1978). The band headlined at WOODSTOCK and other major festivals and was constantly in the news with tales of on-stage brawls, drug abuse and the latest escapades of Keith Moon.

Moon was one of the wild men of rock. On stage he destroyed his drumkits; off stage he drove luxury cars into swimming pools (he once accidentally ran over and killed his chauffeur while evading a gang of skinheads), wrecked hotel bedrooms, dropped firecrackers down lavatories, threw television sets out of windows and drank heavily. On one occasion he blew up his drumkit with gunpowder at the end of a performance on US television and managed to blow himself up as well, causing film star Bette Davis, watching in the wings, to collapse in a dead faint. When asked what in life he feared most, he answered 'Having to grow up' – but he never really did. The morning after announcing his engagement to a Swedish model he was found dead from natural causes, having taken drugs prescribed to combat his alcoholism.

In 1979 11 people died in the crush at a Who concert in Cincinatti, and in 1982 the members of the band (who had already pursued solo careers for some years) finally announced that – after 14 Top Ten hits in 18 years – they were breaking up; successful reunions were staged in 1985, 1989 and 1996. The surviving members have since concentrated on solo projects, Townshend going into publishing.

> When I'm 30 I'm going to kill myself, 'cos I don't ever want to get old.
> ROGER DALTRY, 1965

> I smash a guitar because I like them. I usually smash a guitar when it's at its best.
> PETE TOWNSHEND, 1966

> The moon won't rise tonight.
> Banner at Knebworth Festival after Moon's death.
> 1978

Widor, Charles-Marie (Jean Albert) (1844–1937) French composer and organist, who is remembered for his many compositions for the organ. Organist at St Sulpice, Paris (1870–1934), he was widely admired for his interpretations of the music of Bach and was still winning new converts when he was 90 years of age. He wrote 10 organ symphonies, but is, perhaps, best known for the Toccata from the Fifth Symphony; other works included the opera *Les Pêcheurs de Saint-Jean* (1905), a further five symphonies, two piano concertos, a cello concerto, *Une Nuit de Walpurgis* for chorus and orchestra, songs and piano and chamber music.

> To play the organ properly one should have a vision of Eternity.
>
> CHARLES-MARIE WIDOR

Wilde, Marty (Reginald Smith; 1939–   ) British singer, who became one of the top ROCK 'N' ROLL acts of the 1950s. Modelling himself on Elvis PRESLEY, Wilde had his first big hit with 'Endless Sleep' (1958). Among the hits that followed with his backing band the Wildcats were 'Donna', 'Rubber Ball' and 'Bad Boy'. He became a popular television star after the hits fell off, and later his daughter Kim Wilde (1960–   ) established herself as a top chart act in the 1980s with such hits as 'Kids in America' (1981) and 'You Keep Me Hanging On' (1986).

Williams, Andy (Howard Andrew Williams; 1930–   ) US singer, who established himself as a popular light entertainer on both sides of the Atlantic through his long-running television shows. Williams, who sang in church choirs as a boy, made his recording début as one of the Williams Brothers in 1944 with the hit 'Swinging on a Star', on which they sang with Bing CROSBY. Subsequent solo hits included 'Walk Hand in Hand' (1956), 'Butterfly' (1957), which topped the British charts, 'Can't Get Used to Losing You' (1963), 'Where Do I Begin?' (1971) and 'Tell It Like It Is' (1976).

The young Andy Williams is credited as having dubbed in the singing voice of Lauren Bacall in the classic movie *To Have and Have Not* (1945), although the truth of this rumour has never been satisfactorily established.

Williams, Big Joe (1903–82) Black US BLUES singer and guitarist, who won acclaim for his deceptively simple bottleneck guitar technique and unmistakable vocals. A former cotton-picker from the Mississippi Delta, Williams had big hits with the likes of 'Baby, Please Don't Go', 'Rollin' and Tumblin'' and 'Special Rider'.

Williams, Clarence (1898–1965) US composer, bandleader, pianist and guitarist, who is remembered for his association with some the great JAZZ pioneers. Having run

away from home to join a minstrel show, he collaborated with Jelly Roll MORTON in New Orleans and subsequently teamed up as a composer and pianist with the likes of Louis ARMSTRONG, Bessie SMITH and Ethel WATERS. Among his most famous songs were 'I Wish I Could Shimmy Like My Sister Kate' (1919), 'Baby, Won't You Please Come Home' (1920), 'Tain't Nobody's Bizness If I Do' (1922) and 'Organ Grinder Blues' (1928).

Williams, Hank (Hiram Hank Williams; 1923–53) US COUNTRY singer, nicknamed the Father of Country Music, who became one of the great country legends. Born in Alabama, Williams formed his first band when he was 14 years old and arrived in NASHVILLE in 1946. He appeared on the GRAND OLE OPRY in 1949 and enjoyed his first major hit with 'Lovesick Blues' (1949). Numerous hits – mostly by his own hand – followed, many being subsequently covered by other artists and becoming standards. The most successful included 'Hey, Good Lookin'', 'Jambalaya', 'Your Cheatin' Heart' and 'Move It On Over'. The pressures of fame exacted a heavy price, however, and Williams – whose problems were compounded by severe back pain resulting from a birth defect – became an alcoholic, a problem that led to his divorce and his sacking from the Grand Ole Opry. It all came to an end on New Year's Day 1953 while travelling in the back of a car to an engagement when he succumbed to a heart attack brought on by over-indulgence in alcohol, women and drugs. He was just 30 years old. His last hit in his own lifetime was 'I'll Never Get Out of This World Alive'. His son, Hank Williams Jnr (1949–   ), nicknamed Bocephus, subsequently established his own career as a successful country singer-songwriter.

Williams, John (Christopher) (1942–   ) Australian guitarist and composer, who emerged as one of the leading classical guitarists of his generation after studying with the great Andrés SEGOVIA. The son of a respected guitarist, Williams worked with Segovia in the late 1950s and subsequently won acclaim playing a wide range of guitar music, from classical to FOLK and JAZZ. His instrumental pop group Sky had some success with fans of unchallenging melodic pop in the early 1980s and he also gave much-admired performances with fellow-guitarist Julian BREAM.

Williams, John (Towner) (1932–   ) US

composer and conductor, who is celebrated for his many movie SOUNDTRACKS. Among the best-known of his film scores have been those for *Jaws* (1975), which brought him his first OSCAR, *Star Wars* (1977), for which he received his second Academy Award, *The Empire Strikes Back* (1980) and *E.T.* (1982), which brought his tally of Oscars to three. He was appointed conductor of the Boston Pops Orchestra in 1980.

Williams, Mary Lou (Mary Elfrieda Scruggs; 1910–81) US JAZZ pianist and composer, whose hits in the early 1930s anticipated the development of COOL jazz and established her as a leading jazz innovator. Playing for Andy Kirk's Twelve Clouds of Joy band, she had big hits with such numbers as 'Little Joe from Chicago' and 'What's Your Story, Morning Glory?' and went on to win the admiration of Dizzy GILLESPIE and other modernists, with whom she often played in ensuing decades. Influential compositions from the latter part of her career included the 'Zodiac Suite', which was taken up by the NEW YORK PHILHARMONIC, as well as numerous religious works. She remained a revered figure into the 1970s, playing everything from TRAD to AVANT-GARDE.

Williamson, Malcolm (Benjamin Graham) (1931–) Australian composer, pianist and organist, resident in the UK, whose prolific output has brought him recognition as a leading contemporary composer. A student of Eugene GOOSSENS, he settled in the UK in 1950 and gradually earned a reputation as a composer, whose works reflected both his Roman Catholic faith and the influence of the music of Olivier MESSIAEN among others. As well as writing such operas as *Our Man in Havana* (1963) and *The Violins of St Jacques* (1966), symphonies, concertos and chamber music, he has attracted praise for his pieces for children, which have included *The Happy Prince* (1965). He was appointed Master of the Queen's Musick in 1975 and in this role has written music for various royal events, notably *Mass of Christ the King* (1977) on the occasion of the silver jubilee of Elizabeth II and *Songs for a Royal Baby* (1985).

Williamson, Sonny Boy (Aleck Ford; 1899–1965) Black US BLUES singer and harmonica-player, who became one of the legends of the CHICAGO BLUES. Having collaborated with Elmore JAMES on the classic

'Dust My Broom' (1951), he went on to establish himself as a solo artist, appearing with the likes of the YARDBIRDS among other admirers in the UK. His much-covered hits included 'Help Me', 'Don't Start Me Talking' and 'Nine Below Zero'.

Calling himself Rice Miller at the start of his career, he adopted the name Sonny Boy Williamson in an attempt to pass himself off as another respected blues singer of the same name, who had been murdered in a robbery in 1948.

Wilson, Jackie (Jack Leroy Wilson; 1934–84) Black US RHYTHM-AND-BLUES singer, nicknamed Mister Excitement, who was an R 'N' B star of the late 1950s and 1960s. Having decided against a career in boxing after pressure from his family, Wilson became lead singer of the Dominoes in 1959 and had a Number One hit with 'Lonely Teardrops'. Other hits followed, and he built up a reputation as a thrilling live performer. Somewhat unusual were his hits 'Night' and 'Alone at Last', which were based on two classical tunes, 'My Heart at Thy Sweet Voice' by Camille SAINT-SÄENS and Tchaikovsky's first piano concerto respectively. 'Reete Petite' (1957) (the first single bought by the young Elton JOHN) returned to the British charts in 1986, when it went all way to Number One, after being used in a popular television advert.

The excitement unfortunately extended to Wilson's private life, and in 1961 he was lucky to survive after he was shot in the stomach by a jealous female fan. A heart attack during a concert in 1975 left him permanently disabled.

Wilson, Sandy (Alexander Galbraith Wilson; 1924–) British composer, who is usually celebrated for the enduringly popular MUSICAL *The Boy Friend* (1953), a nostalgic evocation of the music of the 1920s. Less successful compositions since then have included *Valmouth* (1958) and contributions to such shows as *Divorce Me, Darling* (1964), *As Dorothy Parker Once Said* (1969) and *Aladdin* (1979).

Wings *See* Paul MCCARTNEY.

Winter, Johnny (1944–) US rock singer and guitarist, who established himself as a top BLUES-ROCK performer in the late 1960s. An albino, Winter developed a strong interest in Black RHYTHM-AND-BLUES and established a reputation as an outstanding blues guitarist in the 1960s while struggling with uncertain health and addiction to drugs. Later in his career he adopted a more conventional HARD ROCK style, and he also worked with such noted bluesmen as Muddy WATERS. His albums include *Johnny Winter* (1969), *Nothing But the Blues* (1977) and *Serious Business* (1987). His younger brother Edgar Winter (1946–), also an albino, released such acclaimed albums as *Entrance* (1970) before establishing his Edgar Winter Group as a popular live act and releasing such further albums as *They Only Come Out At Night* (1972) and *Shock Treatment* (1974). The two brothers united briefly in 1976 for *Together*.

Wishbone Ash British rock band, who built up a large following in the 1970s. Drummer Steve Upton (1946–), singer and bassist Martin Turner (1947–) and lead guitarists Ted Turner (David Alan Turner; 1950–) and Andy Powell (1950–) adopted the name Wishbone Ash in 1970 and established themselves with the hit album *Argus* (1973), on which they incorporated FOLK-ROCK material. There were further albums – among them *Wishbone Four* (1973) and *There's the Rub* (1974) – and line-up changes in the 1970s, and the group had something of a come-back in the 1980s when the original four members returned for *Nouveau Calls* (1987).

Withers, Bill (1938–) US SOUL singer, who established himself in the 1970s. Among his biggest hits were 'Ain't No Sunshine' (1971), 'Lean on Me' (1972) and 'Just the Two of Us' (1981). His albums have included *Just As I Am* (1971), *Live at Carnegie Hall* (1973) and *Watching You, Watching Me* (1985).

Wizard of the Wurlitzer, the *See* Jesse CRAWFORD.

Womack, Bobby (1944–) US SOUL singer-songwriter and guitarist, who established a lasting reputation in the 1960s. Contributing hits for the likes of the ROLLING STONES and other R 'N' B artists, Womack won recognition as a solo star with such releases as 'What is This', 'Looking for Love', 'That's the Way I Feel about Cha' and 'Harry Hippie'. He adopted a COUNTRY style for a while before returning with the acclaimed r 'n' b albums *The Poet* (1981), which spawned

the single 'If You Think You're Lonely Now' and *The Poet II* (1984).

Womack's private life was marred by tragedy when his brother Harry was shot dead by his girlfriend after she found another woman's clothes in his wardrobe (in fact they belonged to Bobby's girlfriend).

Wonder, Stevie (Steveland Morris; 1950–) Black US singer-songwriter, keyboard player, drummer and guitarist, who became one of the legends of Black pop music despite the disadvantage of having been blinded as a baby when given too much oxygen in an incubator. Having started out as a harmonica player, 'Little' Stevie Wonder became a protégé of Ray CHARLES and of Smokey ROBINSON at MOTOWN and enjoyed his first Number One, 'Fingertips' (1963), while still a child. Numerous hits in a light SOUL-pop style followed in the 1960s before he left Motown in 1971 and adopted a more distinctive FUNK approach that allowed him to experiment with JAZZ sounds and to incorporate newly developed SYNTHESIZER technology. Among his biggest hits have been 'Uptight' (1965), 'Yester-me, Yester-you, Yester-day' (1969), 'My Cherie Amour' (1969), 'Superstition' (1973), 'You are the Sunshine of My Life' (1973), 'He's Mista Know It All' (1974),'Living for the City' (1974), 'I wish' (1976), 'Happy Birthday' (1981), 'Ebony and Ivory' (1982), on which he duetted with Paul MCCARTNEY, and the Oscar-winning Number One 'I Just Called to Say I Love You' (1984). His albums have included *Talking Book* (1972), *Innervisions* (1973), *Songs in the Key of Life* (1976), *Hotter than July* (1980), *Characters* (1987) and *Conversation Peace* (1995).

Wood, Sir Henry (1869–1944) British conductor and composer, nicknamed Timber, who was the founder and long-time chief conductor of the PROMS. Trained at the Royal Academy of Music, London, he began his career as a conductor of opera and began his long association with the proms in 1895, going on to champion many new works by contemporary composers. His own *Fantasia on British Sea Songs* became a regular feature of the event after being premiered there in 1905.

Wood was one of the great characters of modern classical music. He had many attributes, but was renowned for his vanity. When he was asked to stand in for Sir Thomas BEECHAM (who was considered little more than a flamboyant upstart by Wood), his postcard in reply was typically curt: 'Very well, I will do it for you, but if you ever want me again during my conducting life, don't forget that I am the doyen of British conductors, and as such I think I ought to be consulted ... before everyone else is.'

Wood was a strict disciplinarian and was merciless to musicians who failed to be punctual for rehearsal, brandishing his watch at any latecomers. Everything had to be prepared to the last detail. Even the patter he delivered from the podium during rehearsal was written down on his score, orchestras being urged to play 'Like a cavalry charge!' at one point in Beethoven's Fifth Symphony or else being given the line 'Onward rushing to its doom!' during Sergei PROKOFIEV's *Romeo and Juliet*. He supervised the tuning of every instrument in the orchestra and was also very particular about his choice of baton, having unusually long white ones made to order and painting them with two coats of matt white paint so that they would still be visible but not reflect the lights.

A garland of flowers is always placed on Wood's bust on the last night of the proms in the Albert Hall. *See also* Paul KLENOVSKY.

Woodstock The most famous of all the rock festivals, which took place in the USA in the 1960s. Woodstock itself is a small town in the foothills of the Catskill Mountains, the range of hills in upstate New York where legend has it Rip van Winkle fell asleep for 20 years and thus missed entirely the events of the American Revolution. The festival took place at Yasgur's Farm on 15–17 August 1969, under the title of the Woodstock Music and Art Fair; the location was chosen because Bob DYLAN had a house nearby – although in the event he disappointed the organizers by refusing to appear.

For many, Woodstock was the highpoint of the cultural revolution of the 1960s, although for others it also marked the passing of the hippie dream and the substitution of the idealism associated with it by cynical commercialism. Surviving film and recordings of the event testify to the fact that, with a few notable exceptions such as

Arlo GUTHRIE singing 'Coming into Los Angeles' and Richie Havens delivering a classic version of 'Freedom', most of the performances were unremarkable (despite the presence of such stars as Jimi HENDRIX, Joan BAEZ, the WHO, the GRATEFUL DEAD and CROSBY, STILLS, NASH AND YOUNG).

Perhaps the most optimistic and lasting recollection of Woodstock was Joni MITCHELL's much-recorded hit 'Woodstock', which made its first appearance later that year on the album *Ladies of the Canyon*. For Mitchell, who was not present, Woodstock signified something more than youthful escapism into a weekend of 'mind-expanding' drugs, free love and mud, being rather a symbol of the possibility of change for the better in the face of such traumas as the Vietnam War, then at its height:

> By the time we got to Woodstock
> We were half a million strong
> And everywhere there was song and
>   celebration
> And I dreamed I saw the bombers
> Riding shotgun in the sky
> And they were turning into butterflies
> Above our nation.

Contrary to the expectations of the authorities, there were few problems with the 450,000-strong crowd. Three people died (one of exhaustion, one of a heart attack and another from a drug overdose) and three women actually gave birth during the course of the festival.

> A generation that believed it was saving the world by wallowing in mud at rock festivals for days on end, dressed in some of the silliest clothes ever seen, stuffed to the eyebrows with hallucinogenics, listening to distant millionaires droning on about togetherness, should feel thoroughly ashamed of itself.
>
> ROBERT ELMS, the *Observer*, 1984

world music Category of contemporary POP and ROCK music, which is taken to include music from artists outside the traditional homes of western pop – that is, the USA and Europe. It applies in particular to those brands of music in which the conventions of rock and pop are grafted on to indigenous musical traditions. Particular attention has been paid in recent years to music from South America, Africa and the Middle East.

World's Greatest Entertainer, the *See* Al JOLSON.

World's Oldest Teenager, the *See* Dick CLARK.

Wurlitzer Tradename for a make of electric organ, which was installed in countless early cinemas and ballrooms throughout Europe and the USA from its first development by German-born Franz Wurlitzer (1831–1914) in 1910. The Mighty Wurlitzer, with its extravagant array of stops and pipes, was credited with a breathtaking choice of sounds, although its capabilities have long since been dwarfed by the modern SYNTHESIZER.

Wyatt, Robert (1945–   ) British singer-songwriter and drummer, who established his reputation while with the SOFT MACHINE in the late 1960s and went on to enjoy a successful solo career. Having been one of the driving forces behind the success of Soft Machine, Wyatt's career was interrupted in 1973 when he broke his back in a fall shortly after issuing his début solo album *The End of an Ear* (1971). He returned to the limelight, however, with such releases as *Rock Bottom* (1974) and *Ruth is Stranger than Richard* (1975) and had a major hit in the singles charts with a COVER version of the Neil DIAMOND classic 'I'm a Believer' (1974). Subsequent releases have reflected his political sympathies and have ranged from the *The Animals Soundtrack* (1982), written for a film about animal abuse, to the single 'Shipbuilding' (1983), made with Elvis COSTELLO, which questioned the validity of the Falklands campaign, and 'The Last Nightingale' (1984), which raised funds for striking miners.

Wynette, Tammy (Virginia Wynette Pugh; 1942–   ) US COUNTRY singer, variously nicknamed the Queen of Country Music and the First Lady of Country Music, who established a large following in both country and pop circles in the 1970s. A former beautician who married for the first time when she was 17 years old and subsequently remarried another four times, she topped the charts with such tales of marital relevance as 'Stand by Your Man', 'D.I.V.O.R.C.E.' and 'I Don't Want to Play House'. She has recorded more country chart-toppers than any other female singer.

X–Z

Xenakis, Yannis (1922–) French composer, born in Romania though brought up in Greece, who emerged as a leading AVANT-GARDE composer. He escaped from Greece after fighting with the Greek resistance against the Nazi invaders, during which time he was wounded and lost the sight in one eye, and settled in France, where he worked as an architectural engineer alongside the great architect Le Corbusier (1887–1965). Acclaimed for his designs for the Brussels Exposition in 1958, he developed a second career as a composer after studying with Paul HINDEMITH, Darius MILHAUD and, later Olivier MESSIAEN. Intrigued by the possibilities presented by the incorporation of chance in music, he developed the so-called 'symbolic music', in which the sequence of the notes is determined on a random mathematical basis with the aid of a computer. Other experiments led to 'stochastic music', in which he assembled 'clouds' or 'masses' of music with the expressed aim of drawing the listener 'toward a total exaltation in which the individual mingles, losing his consciousness in a truth immediate'.

Radical examples of his work have included the *Pithoprakta* (1956), which was derived from calculations based on the Maxwell-Boltzmann law governing the movement of gas molecules, *Duel* (1959), which pitted two conductors against each other, *Terretektorh* (1966), in which the players are scattered around the auditorium, the FOLK-influenced *Cendrées* (1974), the string quartet *Tetras* (1983) and the orchestral *Thallein* (1985).

Yancey, Jimmy (1898–1951) US JAZZ pianist, who established a reputation as one of the most popular exponents of the BOOGIE-WOOGIE style in the late 1930s and early 1940s. Having played the piano in Chicago in the early 1920s and perfected his mastery of piano blues, he gave up music for a time, but then returned with huge success in 1939, going on to make classic recordings of such numbers as 'Yancey Stomp', 'State Street Special' and 'Five o'Clock blues'. He often worked in collaboration with his wife, the blues singer Estella 'Mama' Yancey (1896–1986).

Yardbird *See* Charlie PARKER.

Yardbirds, the British rock band, which was among the most influential exponents of BLUES-ROCK in the UK in the 1960s. Initially consisting of lead singer Keith Relf (1943–76), guitarists Andrew 'Top' Topham (1947–) and Chris Dreja (1946–), bassist Paul Samwell–Smith (1943–) and drummer Jim McCarty (1943–), the group came together in 1963 and prospered after Topham was replaced by Eric CLAPTON, who won fame for his blues-oriented style. The band switched to PSYCHEDELIC ROCK after Clapton was succeeded by Jeff BECK. Hits included 'For Your Love' (1965), 'Heart Full of Soul' (1965) and 'Shapes of Things' (1966). The Yardbirds disbanded in 1968, by which time members of the group included the young Jimmy Page, who re-formed the band as the New Yardbirds (later renamed LED ZEPPELIN). McCarty led his own Box of Frogs band, which included Dreja and Samwell-Smith, and released such albums as *Box of Frogs* (1984) and *Strange Lane* (1986). Relf died in 1976 when he was electrocuted.

Yes British rock group, which was among the leading PROGRESSIVE ROCK outfits of the 1970s. Formed in 1968, Yes went through innumerable changes of personnel but at its height in the early 1970s included lead singer Jon Anderson (1944–), guitarists Pete Banks and Steve Howe (1947–), bassist Chris Squire (1948–), drummers Bill Bruford (1948–) and Alan White (1949–), and keyboard players Tony Kaye, Rick WAKEMAN and Patrick Moraz (1948–). The band's most successful releases included the albums *The Yes Album* (1971), *Fragile* (1971), *Close to the Edge* (1972) and *Tales from Topographic Oceans* (1973). The band was temporarily suspended in the mid-1970s while individual members pursued solo careers, but the members reunited for two further albums. Wakeman and Anderson left in 1980, but the band soldiered on with ex-Buggles Trevor Horn and Geoff Downes. Progress in the 1980s was disrupted by further changes in the line-up, which saw most of the original cast – Anderson, Bruford, Wakeman and Howe – return to the fold (although they were unable to call themselves Yes for a while because of legal difficulties). *Union* proved a big hit in 1991, as did *Talk* in 1994.

Youmans, Vincent (Millie) (1898–1946) US songwriter, who wrote numerous hits for Broadway and Hollywood. Having rejected a career as a hatter, he wrote such hits as 'No, No, Nanette' and 'Tea for Two', from *No, No, Nanette* (1925), 'Sometimes I'm Happy', from *Hit the Deck* (1927), and 'Flying down to Rio', from the film of the same name (1933).

Young, Faron (1932–96) US COUNTRY singer, nicknamed the Singing Sheriff, who emerged as a top star in the 1950s through appearances on the GRAND OLE OPRY and *Louisiana Hayride* programmes. His hits included 'Country Girl' (1959), 'Hello, Walls' (1957) and 'It's Four in the Morning' (1971). He committed suicide in Nashville, with a career total of 42 Top Ten hits.

Young, La Monte (1935–   ) US composer, who established a reputation as an innovative AVANT-GARDE composer in the 1960s. Inspired by the incorporation of random chance in music and by the tutelage of John CAGE and Karlheinz STOCKHAUSEN, he has produced some of the most radical music of recent years under such bizarre titles as *Poem for Chairs, Tables and Benches* (1960) and *The Tortoise Recalling the Drone of the Holy Numbers as They Were Revealed in the Dreams of the Whirlwind and the Obsidian Gong, Illuminated by the Sawmill, the Green Sawtooth Ocelot, and the High-tension Line Stepdown Transformer* (1964). He formed his own Theatre of Eternal Music in 1962.

> Turn a butterfly (or any number of butterflies) loose in the performance area ... the doors and windows may be opened, and the composition finishes when the butterfly flies away.
> LA MONTE YOUNG, instructions for one of his pieces

Young, Lester (Willis) (1909–59) Black US JAZZ saxophonist, nicknamed Prez (short for President) by Billie HOLIDAY, who became one of the great jazz legends of the 1940s when he anticipated the development of the COOL style. As well as working closely with Holiday, Young also won acclaim playing with such stars as Fletcher HENDERSON, Count BASIE and Dizzy GILLESPIE as well as with his own bands. His recruitment for service in the US Army in 1944 was not a success, largely because of a decline in his health associated with his addiction to drugs and alcohol; he was released from the ranks in 1945 after a court martial. Despite his worsening health, he continued to appear with Basie and others in the 1950s, making his last appearance at the Blue Note Club, Paris, in 1959. Among his most admired recordings were 'Shoe Shine Boy', 'Lady be Good' and 'Lester Leaps In'. His technique had a profound influence on many other saxophonists of the period.

> I named him the President, and actually I was the Vice-President ... we were the royal family of Harlem.
> BILLIE HOLIDAY

Young, Neil (1945–   ) US singer-songwriter, born in Canada, who achieved superstar status as part of CROSBY, STILLS, NASH AND YOUNG and subsequently established himself as a widely admired solo artist. After work with the band BUFFALO SPRINGFIELD, Young made his recording début with the albums *Neil Young* (1969) and *Everybody Knows This is Nowhere* (1969), but it was his role in the Crosby, Stills, Nash and Young album *Déjà Vu* (1970), with his classic ballad 'Helpless', that confirmed him as a leading FOLK-ROCK star with an international reputation. Creative tensions within the group soon led to Young concentrating on his solo career; *After the Goldrush* (1970) and *Harvest* (1972) – from which came the celebrated 'Heart of Gold' – were acclaimed as classics with their mix of country ballads, poetic epics and basic rock songs. Subsequent releases have included *On the Beach* (1974), *Comes a Time* (1978), *Rust Never Sleeps* (1979) and the ROCKABILLY-based *Everybody's Rockin'* (1983).

The SOUL-influenced *This Note's For You* (1988) came with its own video parodying the famous Pepsi advertisement made by

Michael JACKSON; the presence of a stand-in Jackson with blazing hair led to the video being banned for a time on US television, but it subsequently won an award for best video of the year. Among recent releases have been *Freedom* (1989), *Ragged Glory* (1990), *Harvest Moon* (1992), *Unplugged* (1993) and *Sleeps With Angels* (1994).

Young, Paul (1956–   ) British pop singer, who became a top star in the 1980s. Having worked as lead singer with various unknown bands, Young shot to fame after going solo. His SOUL-influenced hits included 'Wherever I Lay My Hat (That's My Home)', which reached Number One in the UK in 1983, 'Love of the Common People' (1983), the US chart-topper 'Every Time You Go Away' (1985) and 'Don't Dream It's Over' (1991). His album *No Parlez* (1983) topped the charts, but his career faltered somewhat in the late 1980s after a break caused by throat problems, although *Other Voices* (1990) saw a partial return to form.

Young, Victor (1900–56) US composer, violinist and conductor, who was celebrated for his many movie SOUNDTRACKS. A child prodigy who won acclaim as a violinist at the age of six, he worked as a classical violinist before being recruited by Hollywood in the 1930s. Among his 300 film scores were those for *For Whom the Bell Tolls* (1943), *The Uninvited* (1944), *Samson and Delilah* (1949), *Shane* (1953) and *Around the World in Eighty Days* (1956), for which he won an OSCAR. Among his hit songs were 'Falling in Love with You' (1930) and 'Any Time, Any Day, Anywhere' (1933).

Young France Group of AVANT-GARDE composers who attracted considerable attention in the 1930s. Consisting of Olivier MESSIAEN, Yves Baudrier (1906–   ), André JOLIVET and Daniel Lesur (1908–   ), the group – founded in Paris in 1936 – attempted to emphasize the values of 'sincerity, generosity and artistic good faith' in music and to make it relevant to the listener's personal life. The composers had ceased to operate as a group by the time war broke out in 1939.

Zak, Pyotr Polish AVANT-GARDE composer, who was the subject of a celebrated hoax in the late 1970s. The BBC broadcast what purported to be the latest of Zak's pieces but it was subsequently revealed that the work

– and indeed Zak himself – was the invention of the programme's producers, Keller and Bradshaw, who had put together the piece by random improvisation on a variety of percussion instruments. A number of critics were taken in by the hoax.

Zappa, Frank (1940–93) US ROCK guitarist and singer-songwriter, of Italian and Greek descent, who was a leading figure in AVANT-GARDE rock in the late 1960s and 1970s. Leading his band the Mothers of Invention, Zappa established a reputation as one of the more radical rock figures of the time with such unconventional albums as *Freak Out* (1966), which was one of the first CONCEPT ALBUMS, *We're Only In It For the Money* (1968), which was a satirical send-up of *Sergeant Pepper's Lonely Hearts Club Band*, *Weasels Ripped My Flesh* (1970), *Hot Rats* (1970), *Apostrophe* (1972) and *Jazz From Hell* (1988), mixing rock with jazz, folk, pop, classical and other disparate influences; he also conducted the ROYAL PHILHARMONIC ORCHESTRA on one occasion and worked with Pierre BOULEZ. True to his penchant for the surreal and his parodic convention-defying humour, he named his children Dweezil and Moon Unit (they briefly formed a band called Fred Zeppelin). He died of cancer after a long illness.

Zemlinsky, Alexander von (1871–1942) Austrian conductor and composer, resident in the USA in his last years, who won acclaim for his neoclassical operas, which he often conducted himself on the Vienna stage at the turn of the century. A protégé of Gustav MAHLER (and subsequently the teacher and brother-in-law of Arnold SCHOENBERG), Zemlinsky enjoyed considerable success with such operas as *Sarema* (1897), *Es war einmal* (1900), *Eine florentinische Tragödie* (1917), *Der Zwerg* (1921) and *Der Kreidekeis* (1932), as well as with his three symphonies, his four quartets and various songs and piano pieces. His music was largely neglected until the centenary of his birth, which signalled a reawakening of interest.

Ziegfeld, Florenz (1869–1932) US theatre impresario, whose long-running *Follies* were among the most spectacular musical entertainments ever staged on Broadway. Ziegfeld presented the first edition of the celebrated *Follies* in 1907 and subsequently established himself as a Broadway legend, whose shows were famous for glamour and sophistication. He opened his own Ziegfeld Theatre in 1927 and produced numerous other musical shows, among them *Show Boat* (1927), *Whoopee* (1928) and *Bitter Sweet* (1929). Stars to appear under the Ziegfeld banner included Eddie CANTOR, Maurice CHEVALIER and Fred ASTAIRE.

The chorus line in some of the early editions of the *Follies* amounted to no fewer than 120 dancers, a record that stood until 1983.

Zombies, the British rock group, who were among the leading bands to emerge from the BEAT movement of the early 1960s. Singer-songwriter Colin Blunstone (1945–), guitarist Paul Atkinson (1946–), keyboard player Rod Argent (1945–), bassist Chris White (1943–) and drummer Hugh Grundy (1945–) made their recording début in 1963 and subsequently had big hits with such numbers as 'She's Not There' (1964) and 'Time of the Season' (1969), which was actually released after the group had disbanded. Argent and Blunstone went on to enjoy moderately successful solo careers. The band re-formed in the late 1980s and released *New World* in 1991.

Zukerman, Pinchas (1948–) Israeli violinist, of Polish descent, who emerged as one of the leading contemporary violinists as joint winner of the prestigious Leventritt Prize in 1967. Also admired as a viola player and conductor, he has won particular acclaim playing chamber music. He was appointed director of the St Paul Chamber Orchestra in Minnesota in 1980.

zydeco Genre of Black music from Louisiana and Texas, which emerged as an equivalent of traditional White cajun music in the 1940s. Based on cajun, which evolved in the mid-nineteenth century, and a mixture of French and African-rooted dance music forms and the BLUES, zydeco produced its own stars, among the best known of whom were accordionist Clifton Chenier (1925–87), Rockin' Sidney (Sidney Simien; 1938–), 'Queen' Ida Lewis and Buckwheat Zydeco. Instruments used included the accordion, the saxophone and the washboard, in addition to electric guitars and drums.

The name zydeco came from a dialect pronunciation of the phrase *les haricots sont pas salés* ('the snap beans aren't salted'), the name of a popular one-step.

ZZ Top US rock band, which became established as a top BOOGIE BLUES act in the 1970s. Formed in 1969 by singer and guitarist Billy Gibbons (1949–) and singer and bassist Dusty Hill (Joe Hill; 1949–), the band consolidated its growing reputation by adopting a distinctive visual image – they sported long beards and over-size sunglasses (drummer Frank Beard (1949–), somewhat ironically, confined himself to a moustache). The band's best-selling albums have included *Rio Grande Mud* (1972), *Tres Hombres* (1973), *Fandango!* (1975), *Deguello* (1979), *Eliminator* (1983) and *Recycler* (1990).